425

A HISTORY OF
GREEK PHILOSOPHY

VOLUME III

A HISTORY OF
GREEK PHILOSOPHY

BY

W. K. C. GUTHRIE
F.B.A.

*Master of Downing College and
Laurence Professor of Ancient Philosophy in the
University of Cambridge*

VOLUME III

THE FIFTH-CENTURY
ENLIGHTENMENT

CAMBRIDGE
AT THE UNIVERSITY PRESS
1969

Published by the Syndics of the Cambridge University Press
Bentley House, 200 Euston Road, London N.W. 1
American Branch: 32 East 57th Street, New York, N.Y. 10022

© Cambridge University Press 1969

Library of Congress Catalogue Card Number: 62–52735
Standard Book Number: 521 07566 1

Printed in Great Britain
at the University Printing House, Cambridge
(Brooke Crutchley, University Printer)

To the memory of my daughter Anne
with whom I discussed the
plan of this volume

CONTENTS

vii

Contents

Contents

Contents

PART TWO

SOCRATES

Contents

For the head of Socrates represented on the cover see p. 387, n. 1.

PREFACE

This volume must begin with an apology. I had originally intended it to include Plato, but although he is necessarily invoked for information and comparison, the volume concentrates on the thinkers of the fifth century, including Socrates, and leaves Plato for the next. As a result, the whole work will probably consist of six volumes instead of five. There were external reasons for this, in the time that it has taken me, among my other duties, to write it, and the fact that the more restricted field has proved enough to fill a volume of reasonable length. I hope however that the separation is justified by the consideration, elaborated at the beginning of Part Two (pp. 325 f.), that the Sophists and Socrates belong to the same exuberant world of the Athenian Enlightenment and Plato to a different, more mature and reflective, and in many respects disillusioned, period of thought. Like Burnet, I came as I wrote to see in Socrates a man of the Periclean age, who 'watched the building of the new Parthenon from start to finish', and to feel the need to 'replace him among the surroundings of his own generation'.[1]

A difficult decision was whether to continue the arrangement of the previous two volumes and deal with each thinker separately, or to order the chapters by subjects. In the end it seemed unwise to try to separate the contributions of these more or less contemporary participants in a continuing debate, and the other arrangement promised to offer advantages for students interested in topics which (unlike those typical of Presocratic thought) are under equally lively scrutiny today. I have however tried to get the best of both worlds by subjoining to my examination of these discussions a brief account of each of the principal participants. On this question too I have said a little more in the book itself (pp. 261 f.).

Readers will probably be struck by the more discursive character of the present volume, and the inclusion of a number of figures not usually reckoned as philosophers. I trust that this will not seem

[1] Burnet, *Essays and Addresses*, 131.

inappropriate, considering the topics with which it deals. The philosophy of the time was closely bound up with problems of practical living, with views on morals and politics and the origin and purpose of organized societies, and the biggest difficulty which it presented was that of setting limits to the subject. What an authority on the eighteenth century has said of the *philosophes* of that epoch is equally true of the Sophists, namely that 'while the Enlightenment was a family of philosophes, it was something more as well: it was a cultural climate, a world in which the philosophes acted, from which they noisily rebelled and quietly drew many of their ideas, and on which they attempted to impose their programme'.[1] One cannot isolate the Sophists from their contemporary world, from writers like Thucydides, Euripides, Aristophanes and the orators, while at the same time any tendency to allow the volume to develop into a history of Greek literature had, for obvious reasons, to be resisted.

Another temptation to discursiveness was provided by the analogies, which I found inescapable, between this period of intellectual and moral ferment in Greece and later periods of European thought, including the Renaissance, the Enlightenment of the seventeenth and eighteenth centuries, and not least our own troubled age. This temptation too I have not resisted entirely, while freely acknowledging both my own lack of expertise in these later fields and the danger (which I hope I have not ignored) of making comparisons that are facile and superficial. The title itself is a concession to the comparative viewpoint, and such justification as I can muster for using it will be found on p. 48. To speak of analogies indeed is incorrect. They are rather instances of direct continuity, the fruit of a renewed study and understanding of the thought of the ancient world, and to take some notice of them will, I hope, add to the interest of the work for others just as it has contributed greatly to my own enjoyment in writing it. In any case it was unavoidable, because, as will appear, even modern scholars who have written on the history of fifth-century thought, and whose assistance was indispensable to me, have themselves been drawn into the Sophists' debate and found themselves taking sides. Whatever our

[1] Peter Gay, *The Enlightenment: an Interpretation (the rise of modern paganism)*, London, 1967, p. xii.

claims to be writing objective history, we are all caught up in it and become part of our subject.

A recent writer has remarked on the powerful impact which has always been made by fresh and immediate contact with the great minds of ancient Greece. More than once it has proved an inspiration to struggles for political freedom, so much so that the authorities of Czarist Russia, unable to suppress classical studies entirely, sought to combat their revolutionary effect by confining them to the harmless channel of the textual exegesis of a few selected authors instead of allowing them the more dangerous outlet of education in ancient political theory.[1] Without departing from the limited aims of a historian, I may be allowed to hope that the link uniting Greek political and social ideas to the reconciliation of freedom with order in the modern world may never be broken.

On one point I should like to declare my position now, so that those for whom it is open to criticism may be aware of it from the start. In using Plato as a source, I have paid little attention to an argument often used, that he could not have directed his own attacks against men who were writing up to sixty years before himself, and that therefore his Protagoras is not Protagoras but a disguised Aristippus, his Prodicus a mouthpiece for Antisthenes and so on. Isocrates shows plainly in his *Helen* (§ 2) how lacking in originality were the eristics of his and Plato's time, simply repeating what had been said by Protagoras, Gorgias or Melissus, and Plato was wise enough to go for the great originals rather than their less talented imitators. In any case his procedure needs no special explanation, since it can be paralleled in most ages. Freud, and not only his followers, arouses the liveliest support and antagonism among men whose working life did not begin until after his death, and will, I am sure, continue to do so for many years to come. But in the philosophical world the phenomenon is too common to need illustration. Plato himself could name a contemporary when he wanted to, as witness his patronizing reference to Isocrates in the *Phaedrus*. That some theories which he mentions and attacks without attribution are those of his own generation is perfectly

---

[1] H. G. Graham, 'The Classics in the Soviet Union', *Class. World*, LIV (1960–1), 107.

possible, but the question must be decided in each case on the evidence, not *a priori*.

Books have most frequently been referred to in the text and notes by short titles, and articles by periodical and date only. Full particulars of books, and titles and page-references for articles, will be found in the bibliography. The fragments of the Sophists, and other texts relating to them, are included in the *Fragmente der Vorsokratiker* of Diels and Kranz (abbreviated DK) on the curious principle explained in my second volume, p. 345, n. 1. They are also to be found, with certain additions, Italian translation and commentary, in the four fascicules of Untersteiner's *I Sofisti*. This is referred to here as *Sof.*, followed by the number of the fascicule, whereas *Sophs.* stands for his book on the Sophists in its English translation by K. Freeman. The texts in an 'A' section of DK (*Testimonia*) have their number preceded by this letter, and those in a 'B' section, purporting to be actual quotations from the philosopher in question, are designated 'fr.' (fragment). Treatises in the Hippocratic Corpus have been referred to by book (when in more than one book) and chapter, followed uniformly by the volume and page in Littré's edition. Those who prefer to consult the *Corpus Medicorum Graecorum* (originally edited by Heiberg, Leipzig, 1927) for the particular treatises which it includes will not, I hope, find the passages difficult to locate.

Translations, from both ancient and modern authors, are my own unless otherwise stated.

I should like to express my gratitude to the many scholars who have responded to the request made in my first volume and sent me offprints of articles and even copies of books. Their help has been most valuable and their generosity is greatly appreciated. I should also like to thank Mrs Doris Watson, who has typed the major part of the book, and Mr John Bowman, who compiled the index of passages. For the general index I must take the responsibility as before.

DOWNING COLLEGE, CAMBRIDGE   W.K.C.G.
SEPTEMBER 1968

LIST OF ABBREVIATIONS

Most works cited in abbreviated form in the text will be easily recognizable under the author's or editor's name in the bibliography. It may however be helpful to list the following:

PART ONE

THE WORLD OF THE SOPHISTS

I

INTRODUCTION

'To describe is to select; to select is to evaluate; to evaluate is to criticize.'

Gouldner, *Enter Plato*, 168.

The first two volumes of this history dealt in part with questions which might be said to have been settled long ago, and to possess now an interest which is purely historical. We no longer debate whether the earth is round or flat, and if we want to discover the origin and substance of the stars, we are hardly likely to be helped by the speculations of Xenophanes or Anaxagoras. With the change that came over philosophy in the fifth century, we are plunged into a discussion of questions which are as relevant now as they were when first raised by the Sophists. Whatever we may think of the Sophistic movement, we must all agree that (as Alban Lesky puts it in his history of Greek literature) no intellectual movement can be compared with it in the permanence of its results, and that the questions which the Sophists posed have never been allowed to lapse in the history of Western thought down to our own day.[1] This is obvious from many recent writings on the period, in which the conflict between the Sophistic and Platonic points of view is expounded, even by professional scholars, in tones not so much of dispassionate historical investigation as of vehement partisanship. It is difficult to remain impartial in discussing questions which are of such vital importance to the preservation of civilized values in our own day.

---

[1] Lesky, 341. Many of course have made the same point. One may take at random a German (W. Schmid, *Gesch.* 1.3.1, 216): 'The questions and controversies of that time have lost nothing of their actuality'; or an Italian (Gigante, *Nom. Bas.* 15): 'The theoretical foundation of the general doctrine of law in the twentieth century recapitulates the speculation of fifth-century Greek Sophistic.' Its effect on the Enlightenment of the eighteenth century is vividly portrayed in Ernst Cassirer's *Philosophy of the Enlightenment*, especially ch. 6, where he justifies his statement (p. 285) that 'after more than two thousand years the eighteenth century establishes direct contact with the thinking of antiquity... The two fundamental theses represented in Plato's *Republic* by Socrates and Thrasymachus oppose each other again.' They still stand opposed today.

Introduction

In spite of the shift of interest from natural phenomena to human affairs, there are nevertheless essential connexions between the Presocratic tradition and the new intellectual ferment generated by the Sophists. The preface to the last volume described the Presocratics as preoccupied with the nature of reality and its relation to sensible phenomena. This question of the relation between reality and appearance remains at the root of things, and in one form or another constitutes the fundamental difference between rival philosophies. On the one hand we have a complex of ideas whose basis may be loosely summed up in such terms as empiricism, positivism, phenomenalism, individualism, relativism and humanism. Appearances are constantly shifting, from one moment to the next and between one individual and another, and they themselves constitute the only reality. In morals this leads to a 'situational ethics', an emphasis on the immediately practical and a distrust of general and permanent rules and principles. Such rules or principles could remain valid only if instituted by some divine power, and religious beliefs, along with many other hitherto unquestioned traditions, are challenged on the grounds that they cannot be verified by positive evidence. This outlook in its turn is opposed by the attempt to restore, with philosophical justification, a belief in absolute standards and permanent and unvarying truths existing above, and unaffected by, sensible phenomena and individual actions and events. We may call it (using similarly evocative but as yet undefined terms) absolutism, idealism or transcendentalism. The first view is typified by the sayings of Protagoras, earliest and greatest of the Sophists, that man is the measure of all things and the existence of gods an undemonstrable assumption. The second is rooted in the teaching of Socrates, but culminates later in Plato's ideal theory, according to which such concepts as justice and beauty, as well as identity and equality and many others, have an existence apart from the human mind, as independent and unvarying standards to which human perceptions and human actions can and must be referred. With this goes naturally a view of the world as the product of divine intelligence.

It is remarkable how many arguments that might be thought to be ethical or political, and so to deal with purely practical matters, depend in fact on much deeper philosophical issues. This is none the less true because the men of action who put them into practice may not always be aware of it; and often the connexion is in fact a fully conscious one. Politics and morals, general theories of human nature, metaphysics and epistemology cannot be separated. On the surface we may have political differences about the relative merits of monarchy and republicanism, democracy and totalitarianism, and the general question of where sovereignty should lie, whether in the hands of one man, a select aristocracy or the whole people. We have questions, demanding immediate action, of slavery and its abolition, of colonial rule, or race-relations. Below this is a level of ideas which, while still remaining on the human plane, are more abstract and theoretical, raising fundamental questions of human nature. Are all men naturally equal? Is the existence of rulers and subjects, masters and servants, merely a matter of practical convenience, or is it grounded in ineradicable natural differences? In studying the various answers that have been given to these questions, the historian will often find that their explanation lies at a third, still deeper level. They rest on assumptions about the nature of reality and the workings of the universe, determining man's position within it, on the issues of divine government *versus* chance, a cosmos whose members are all organically related as opposed to a collection of unrelated parts thrown together at random.

An example is furnished by the English civil war of the seventeenth century. On the surface it is a political struggle between two rival factions, King and Parliament, as to which should govern. Beneath this was the question whether men are naturally, or divinely, divided into higher and lower orders; and those who believed that they were based this belief on the existence of a hierarchical dispensation prevailing throughout the whole of nature. At the head is God, the supreme ruler, after him the angels, then man, who in turn is lord over the animals, beneath which come plants and lowest of all the inanimate world. God himself has ordained that there should be higher and lower orders of being, and intended that a similar pattern should be followed in human society. Here, in divine ordinance, lay the ultimate sanction for absolute monarchy. Christian principles, which most of us now believe to teach that all men are equal in God's sight, were then invoked to prove precisely the opposite.[1]

What is invoked here is the analogy between microcosm and macrocosm, the order of human society and the order of nature, involving the conception of the universe as a divinely constructed and close-knit organism, which goes back to Plato and beyond. Equally deeply rooted in Greek thought was the rival philosophy that found its political expression in the idea of a social compact upheld by Locke and others. The relations between a ruler and his subjects are based on acceptance of this compact, which lays obligations on both sides. It is no divine ordinance but a purely human agreement, and a people has the right to depose a ruler who breaks it just as he may punish his subjects if they disobey the laws in which it is embodied. The idea of law as no more than an agreement, instituted by men and alterable by consent, is, as we shall see, basic to the humanism of the Greek Sophists, and is attacked by Plato, for whom justice and law exist in their own right, and all that we can do is to try to reproduce them, so far as possible, in our relations with one another. For a later parallel one might cite Hugo Grotius, in whose work 'the Platonism of modern natural law is most perfectly expressed... In enacting his various positive laws the legislator follows an absolutely universally valid norm which is exemplary for his own as well as for every other will.'[2] The Sophists had held up nature as the antithesis of law, wrongly, said Plato, for nature itself, as the product of rational design, is the supreme embodiment of law and order.

In epistemology the one philosophy, initiated by Parmenides and elaborated by Plato, displays unbounded confidence in the powers of human reason, which for Plato is based on the essential identity of reason in man and God. Parmenides rejected the senses entirely, and

---

[1] Filmer thought it 'a fault scarce pardonable in a Christian' to believe in a community of goods and equality of persons (Greenleaf, *Order, Empiricism and Politics*, 92). For Pusey the mere recognition of rank and station was still 'a fact in God's providence' (Report of the Royal Commission on the Universities 1852, on the wearing of distinctive gowns by noblemen). Cf. Miss M. A. Stodart reviewing *Jane Eyre* in the *Quarterly Review*, 84 (December 1848), 173–4: 'Altogether the auto-biography of Jane Eyre is pre-eminently an anti-Christian composition. There is throughout it a murmuring against the comforts of the rich and against the privations of the poor, which, as far as each individual is concerned, is a murmuring against God's appointment.'

[2] E. Cassirer, *Philosophy of the Enlightenment*, 240.

Plato would allow them no loftier role than as a starting-point which the mind must quickly leave behind. If heeded too much, they could only be a hindrance to the comprehension of reality. Knowledge only deserved the name if it was absolute and universal, and to attain such knowledge it was necessary to transcend experience, penetrating the veil of sense and rousing into consciousness truths that were latent in the mind because that immortal essence had already been vouchsafed a direct vision of them in its disembodied state.

The reappearance of this outlook in later history can be strikingly illustrated by a passage from Dr W. H. Greenleaf's book *Order, Empiricism and Politics* (276 f.) describing rationalism in seventeenth-century England:

The rationalist philosophers of the time . . . shared many features of thought with the empirical tradition but basically their views were contrary to its tenets. While the empiricist acknowledged the importance of the rational faculty and had great faith in its ability to understand the reality of things, he nonetheless placed primary emphasis on the need to base the process of reasoning on a solid foundation of experience. Reliable sense-data were the first requirement of his inductive method. On the other hand, the rationalist tended to stress the unique significance of reason alone and to argue that the other faculties of memory and imagination, far from being of assistance in the comprehension of reality, presented obstacles to its achievement. Information derived from the senses was, therefore, obscure, unreliable and misleading, and it was only by transcending experience to the higher level of reason that indubitable conclusions could be reached. This reason was an innate faculty, an inner light, placed in every individual by God, which guaranteed its compatibility with the reality of his creation. It was self-sufficient in the sense that its intuitions alone provided the clear and precise understanding characteristic of and basic to true knowledge. Like the empirical reason, it analysed and resolved things into basic 'natures'; however, these were not mere names (as they were to the empiricist), but real, absolute ideas.

This account is drawn from contemporary English sources, but its derivation will be obvious to any reader of Plato; and, although the author goes on to name Descartes, with his vision of a 'universal mathematical science', as the prototype of such notions, the seventeenth-century rationalists knew their Plato too, and no doubt looked on him as their first ancestor. The idea of mathematics as a model of exact and rational science is certainly not absent from his works. It is the Platonic philosophy which Macaulay rightly singled out as dominant over men's minds up to the time when Francis Bacon turned them in a new direction.

The empirical outlook holds a much more modest view of the human faculties. Doubts of the adequacy of our equipment to attain truth were first voiced in a religious context in contrast to the clarity of divine vision,[1] but in Ionians like Anaxagoras and Democritus we see rather the modesty of the scientific spirit. For Democritus in his more pessimistic moments, 'we know nothing, for truth is in the depths', and 'either truth does not exist or it is hidden from us'. But he was not a complete sceptic.[2] The senses give a false picture of reality, and for the mind to probe beneath their 'bastard knowledge' is not easy; but at least for him there was a reality behind appearances, whether or not we could grasp it fully. Even this was abandoned by some of the Sophists in favour of an out-and-out phenomenalism. Such radical scepticism as that of Protagoras and Gorgias was hardly helpful to the progress of scientific thought. It was a violent reaction from the extreme rationalism of the Eleatics, but it owed much to the attitude of contemporary Ionian scientists, whose religious agnosticism or disbelief, denial of final causes, and humility before the magnitude of cosmic problems in comparison with the feebleness of human perceptions cleared the way for every variety of free thought. Here too they have their counterparts in other periods, including our own. As to the upsurge of the scientific spirit at the Renaissance, no one can read far in the literature of the time without observing its openly acknowledged connexion with the Greek philosophers. Stimulus to empirical methods and the whole empirical way of thought came from the revival of Greek learning as much as from contemporary advances in knowledge. A founder of experimental science like Francis Bacon knew well that the two competing schools of thought in his own day reflected a similar conflict of ideas in the ancient world. He wrote for instance in *De Augmentis Scientiarum*:

[1] E.g. by Alcmaeon, Xenophanes and Heraclitus. See vol. I, 344, 398.
[2] Fr. 117 and A 112. See vol. II, 461 f.

For this reason the natural philosophy of Democritus and others who have removed God and mind from the fabric of the world, who have attributed the construction of the universe to an infinity of attempts and experiments on the part of nature (which they called by the single name of chance or fate) and assigned the causes of particular things to necessity, without admixture of final causes, seems to me (so far as one may conjecture from the fragmentary remains of their philosophy) to be, so far as physical causes are concerned, on a much firmer basis, and to have penetrated more deeply into nature, than the philosophy of Plato and Aristotle; and this solely for the one reason, that they wasted no thought on final causes, whereas Plato and Aristotle forced them in at every turn.[1]

Kathleen Nott was hardly fair to Bacon in giving Lord Russell the credit for pointing out that there are two main lines of development through European thought in so far as it stems from the Greeks, the idealist and the empirical, one beginning with Plato and the other with Democritus. Like most people since Bacon she is a partisan: 'On the whole, the humane developments have sprung from the empirical approach, while those which are anti-human can be linked with various forms of philosophical idealism.'[2]

The opposition between Platonic idealism and the empiricism and scepticism of the Sophists will form the main theme of the present volume and its successor.[3] This immediately presents a problem for the study of Sophistic thought. With the Sophists we are in the same situation as with the Presocratics, of reconstructing the ideas of men whose own writings are for the most part no longer available, and our richest source of information is Plato himself, their philosophical opponent. At the same time the dramatic skill with which he presents their personalities and conversation, and the sheer charm of his literary productions (seldom if ever equalled by any other philosopher),

---

[1] *De Augm. Sc.* bk. 3, ch. 4. I have translated the Latin, which will be found in vol. 1 of the Ellis and Spedding edition, 569f. Their own translation is in vol. IV, 363f.

[2] 'German Influence on Modern French Thought', *The Listener*, 13 January 1955.

[3] Two points should be noted here. (1) At a later stage it will be necessary to determine more precisely who the Sophists were, and what is the meaning of the word. At present I am allowing myself to use it in a broad sense to stand for certain trends of thought which the men called Sophists certainly represented, even if not exclusively. (2) It is usual to couple Socrates with Plato in this connexion, because it is through the mouth of Socrates that Plato delivers most of his attacks on the Sophists in his dialogues. The position of Socrates, however, is more complex, and for the present it will be preferable to speak of Plato alone as at the opposite pole from Sophistic thought.

make an almost indelible impression on our minds. The present century has seen a particularly violent controversy over the fairness or otherwise of Plato's account and the relative merits of the two ways of looking at the world.

Until comparatively recently the prevailing view, the view in which a scholar of my own generation was brought up, was that in his quarrel with the Sophists Plato was right. He was what he claimed to be, the real philosopher or lover of wisdom, and the Sophists were superficial, destructive, and at worst deliberate deceivers, purveyors of sophistry in the modern sense of that term. Since the 1930s, however, we have seen a strong movement to reinstate the Sophists and their kin as champions of progress and enlightenment, and a revulsion from Plato as a bigoted reactionary and authoritarian who by blackening their reputation has ensured the suppression of their writings. Sir Karl Popper has christened them 'the Great Generation', and it is they who are primarily referred to in the title of Professor Havelock's book *The Liberal Temper in Greek Politics*. To him they represent the spearhead of liberal and democratic thinking in Greece, which was overwhelmed by the big battalions represented by Plato and Aristotle.[1] In 1953 the American scholar R. B. Levinson could say, sadly, that 'today friendship for Plato is to be found chiefly among those scholars (and their friends and disciples) whose vision of him antedated the rise of Nazism'. It is true that a powerful impetus to this movement was given by the rise of totalitarian governments in Europe and the second world war, and it was indeed disturbing to learn that the aim of the German Nazi party, as described in its official programme, was the production of 'guardians in the highest Platonic sense'. Another form of attack was the psychoanalytical, which saw Plato as a guilt-ridden homosexualist with an irresistible urge to dominate.[2]

[1] For an interesting critique of Havelock's book see L. Strauss, 'The Liberalism of Classical Political Philosophy', in *J. of Metaph.* 1959. I would commend in particular his final paragraph, in which he speaks of 'the danger that stems from the inspiration of scholarship by what is called a philosophy', and of the alleged tolerance which 'turns into violent hatred of those who have stated most clearly and most forcibly that there are unchangeable standards founded in the nature of man and the nature of things'.

[2] The fullest and most influential attack on Plato and eulogy of the empiricists is Sir Karl Popper's *The Open Society and its Enemies* (1945, 5th ed. 1966). The attack in its modern form began with W. Fite's *The Platonic Legend* (1934), and has grown into a considerable literature,

However, as I have tried to show, such a dispute goes deeper than contemporary events or fashionable theories, and in fact disagreement over Plato's presentation of the Sophists is older than some of the disputants on either side seem to remember. From the middle of the nineteenth century the question was vigorously and ably debated. Zeller's *History* in its first edition (1844–52) was probably the last to uphold unchallenged the view that the teaching of even the best of the Sophists was bound in the end to reduce everything to a matter of individual preference and prejudice, and turn philosophy from the search for truth into a means of satisfying the demands of selfishness and vanity; and that the only way out was that of Socrates, who sought to win back by reason a deeper, surer foundation for both knowledge and morality (ZN, 1439). This view had been particularly strongly held in Germany, and was opposed by Grote in the powerful ch. lxvii of his *History of Greece*. The German historians of philosophy, he complained, 'dress up a fiend called "Die Sophistik", whom they assert to have poisoned and demoralised by corrupt teaching the Athenian moral character'. Grote was a utilitarian and a democrat, at a period when, in describing the rise of Athenian democracy, he was constrained to remark that 'democracy happens to be unpalatable to most modern readers'.[1] His vindication of the Sophists was hailed as a 'historical discovery of the highest order' by Henry Sidgwick in 1872, who summarized the current opinion of the Sophists thus:

They were a set of charlatans who appeared in Greece in the fifth century, and earned an ample livelihood by imposing on public credulity: professing to teach virtue, they really taught the art of fallacious discourse, and meanwhile propagated immoral practical doctrines. Gravitating to Athens as the Prytaneion of Greece, they were there met and overthrown by Socrates,

from which the following is a selection: R. H. S. Crossman, *Plato Today* (1937, 2nd ed. 1959); A. Winspear and T. Silverberg, *Who Was Socrates?* (1939, written from a Marxist standpoint); O. Neurath and J. A. Lauwerys, *Plato's Republic and German Education*, and the controversy which followed it (including contributions from G. C. Field and C. E. M. Joad), in the *Journal of Education* for 1945; E. A. Havelock, *The Liberal Temper in Greek Politics* (1957); *Plato, Totalitarian or Democrat?*, essays ed. by T. L. Thorson (1963); *Plato, Popper and Politics*, ed. Bambrough (1967). The best and fullest justification of Plato against his attackers is Levinson's *In Defense of Plato*, with a full bibliography up to its date of publication (1953). For the psychoanalytical approach of H. Kelsen see Levinson, pp. 100ff.

[1] Grote, *History* (6th ed. 1888), vii, 52, and iv, 106. The first edition of this work was almost exactly contemporary with Zeller's.

who exposed the hollowness of their rhetoric, turned their quibbles inside-out, and triumphantly defended sound ethical principles against their pernicious sophistries.

Yet he did not go all the way with Grote. To Grote's statement that few characters in history have been so hardly dealt with as these so-called Sophists, he retorted: 'They had in their lifetime more success than they deserved, and many better men have been worse handled by posterity.' Sidgwick's main criticism was that in his anxiety to do justice to the Sophists Grote had exaggerated the partisanship of Plato. For Grote, Plato

not only stole the name out of general circulation in order to fasten it specially upon his opponents the paid teachers, but also connected it with express discreditable attributes, which formed no part of its primitive and recognised meaning, and were altogether distinct from, though grafted upon, the vague sentiment of dislike associated with it.

The reaction against commentators like Stallbaum, said Sidgwick, who 'treat their author as if he were a short-hand reporter of actual dialogues', was necessary and right, but nevertheless 'one always feels that the satirical humour of Plato was balanced by the astonishing versatility of his intellectual sympathy'.[1] Jowett also published a judicious criticism of Grote in the introduction to his translation of Plato's *Sophist* (1871), in which he argued that the principal Sophists may well have been good and honourable men, but that their bad reputation at Athens was something already current for a variety of reasons (they were foreigners, made large fortunes, excited youthful minds and so on), and was by no means an invention of Plato.[2] A further appraisal came in a long and well-reasoned essay by Sir Alexander Grant. His conclusions were that Grote had succeeded in disposing of the former sweeping denunciations of the Sophists, but that even so they were not all either morally blameless or philosophically adequate, and that the 'subtle and discriminating pictures drawn by Plato' did not deserve the censure they received at his hands.[3]

Reading these scholars of a past generation tempts one to linger

---

[1] See Sidgwick's two articles in *J. Phil.* 1872 and 1873.
[2] Jowett, *Dialogues of Plato* (4th ed. 1953), III, 325 ff.
[3] Grant, *The Ethics of Aristotle* (4th ed. 1885), I, 104–55.

and quote at length. That would be disproportionate, but at least it is important to show that Plato's portrayal of the Sophists, so hotly debated today, was well and truly put on trial by the great Victorians, many of whom were not only fine scholars but men of affairs with experience in political, educational and other fields.[1] Needless to say, their conclusions, like those of their successors, were not unaffected by their personal political or philosophical beliefs. Karl Joël in 1921 (*Gesch.* 674f.) noted how the positivists rallied in support of the Sophists, especially in England from Grote and Lewes onwards. In Germany Theodor Gomperz (under Grote's influence), Laas and Nietzsche in his positivist period did the same. More surprisingly at first sight, Joël adds on the same side 'Hegelian intellectualism', which hailed them as 'masters in reflective reasoning', and 'out of its philosophy of history understood all and pardoned all'. On the other hand, it was inevitable that, history having taken the course it has, Plato should now be suffering from the lavish praise that was bestowed on him by some English commentators of the late nineteenth and early twentieth century. Staunchly liberal as they might be in their personal beliefs, they could yet, under the influence of what Havelock has called 'the Oxford school of neo-idealism', see him in the image of a Victorian liberal like themselves. There is some substance in Havelock's claim (*Lib. Temper*, 19) that in one at least of these writers 'exposition reads as if it were fervent apology', and 'the naturalists and the materialists, the Sophists and the democrats, are treated only as faint and futile voices protesting off-stage'. A reaction was inevitable in the shocks and disillusion that overwhelmed Europe as our century advanced. In the following pages I hope to set forth the intellectual conflict of the fifth and fourth centuries B.C. as far as possible in the light of contemporary evidence, and see it as arising out of its own crises and its own educational and social needs. We need not fear that either its intrinsic interest or its continuing relevance will thereby be diminished.

[1] Of Grote and Jowett it is unnecessary to speak, and Grant served for eight years in educational posts in India. Havelock's description of the Sophists' methods as essentially those of democratic processes is anticipated by Grote, especially in VII, 39, n. 2 (on p. 40, col. 2).

II

TOPICS OF THE DAY

In the last volume (ch. VI) I briefly sketched the climate of thought in
the fifth century, especially at Athens, and the effect in several different
fields of the substitution of natural for divine causation. The present
chapter will attempt an outline of the main causes and features of this
changing outlook, before we go on to consider the meaning of
Sophistic and investigate each separate topic in detail.

To determine the causes of an intellectual revolution is always a
rash undertaking, and when a great many things are happening
together it is not always easy to distinguish cause from effect; but a
few things may be mentioned as more likely to belong to the former
category. We have already dismissed, on chronological grounds, the
assumption that the 'Presocratics', and in particular the Ionians,
could all have been influential in moulding the thought of the Sophists.
If there is any causal connexion between the ideas of Democritus and
those of Protagoras or Gorgias, it is more likely to have been the other
way round. On the other hand the influence of the Eleatics on Protagoras and Gorgias is undeniable, as is that of Heraclitus on Protagoras,
and Gorgias is said to have been a pupil and follower of Empedocles.[1]
One of the most powerful influences for humanism is to be found in
the theories of the natural origins of life and society which were a
feature of Ionian thought from Anaximander onwards. Life, including
human life, was the product of a kind of fermentation set up by the
action of heat on damp or putrefying matter, and social and political
groups were formed by agreement as man's only effective form of
defence against non-human nature. The cosmogonies themselves
assisted in banishing divine agents from the world, not because they
were evolutionary rather than creative—the idea of divine creation
was never prominent in Greek religion—but because they made more
difficult the Greek habit of seeing divine or semi-divine beings every-

[1] See vol. II, 135.

14

where in nature. It was a blow to religion when even the stars and the sun were asserted to be ignited clouds, or rocks torn from the earth and put into orbit by the cosmic vortex. The Olympians, even if they did not create the world, had at least controlled it, but the theories of the natural philosophers left no part for Zeus to play in the production of rain, thunder or lightning, nor for Poseidon in the terror of earthquakes.[1]

In so far as the new spirit was a reaction from an interest in external nature to a concentration on human affairs, the Presocratics contributed to it by what must have seemed in many eyes their failure. It is, after all, the world of sensible experience and its impact on them with which men have to come to terms if they are to carry on a satisfying and happy life. This is for most of us the 'real world', yet in their different ways philosophers as wide apart as Parmenides and Democritus denied its reality and undermined the evidence of the senses. To the plain man's question: 'I can believe my own eyes, can't I?', their answer was a definite 'No'. Either motion and change were illusion, and 'what is' an immovable plenum, or else the only real things were atoms which were expressly denied to have any sensible qualities at all. Moreover the speculative character of their theories made them highly vulnerable, and the ingenuity of a Gorgias was quite capable of using arguments of the Eleatic type to prove the direct contrary of the Eleatic conclusion: not 'what is, is', but what is is not, and nothing exists (pp. 193 ff. below). Besides their remoteness, the Presocratics were discredited by their mutual contradictions. Each believed himself to be nearest to the truth, but were there any solid grounds for trusting one rather than another? Gorgias attacked on this front too. For him they were simply, like orators, masters of the art of verbal persuasion.[2]

---

[1] It should hardly be necessary to repeat the often-stated truth that the rationalism of any so-called age of enlightenment is by no means universal. The rejection of divine agency is confined to a section of the educated and intellectual. When in Plato's lifetime (373 B.C.) the Achaean city of Helike was overwhelmed by a combined earthquake and tidal wave, opinion was still divided between 'the piously inclined' (including Heraclides of Pontus), who ascribed the disaster to the wrath of Poseidon, and the rationalists who explained it solely by natural causes. See Strabo 8.7.2 and Diodorus 15.48 (Heracl. Pont. fr. 46 Wehrli). Thucydides tells how, during the plague at Athens, many sought aid from religious rites (2.47.4), but he himself obviously attributes it to purely natural causes.

[2] Gorg. *Hel.* 13 (DK, II, 292). See p. 51 below.

Often adduced as a cause of the new humanism is the widening of horizons through increasing contacts with other peoples, in war, travel and the foundation of colonies. These made it increasingly obvious that customs and standards of behaviour which had earlier been accepted as absolute and universal, and of divine institution, were in fact local and relative.[1] Habits that to the Greeks were wicked and disgusting, like marriage between brother and sister, might among the Egyptians or elsewhere be regarded as normal and even enjoined by religion. The history of Herodotus is typical of the mid fifth century in the enthusiasm with which he collects and describes the customs of Scythians, Persians, Lydians, Egyptians and others and points out their divergence from Hellenic usage. If all men, he says, were asked to name the best laws and customs, each would choose his own; and he illustrates this by the story of Darius, who summoned some Greeks and Indians to his court and first asked the Greeks for what consideration they would consent to eat their dead fathers. When they replied that they would not do it for anything, he turned to the Indians (of a tribe who normally ate the bodies of their parents) and asked them if anything could persuade them to burn their fathers (as the Greeks did), whereupon they cried aloud at the mere mention of such impiety.[2] Euripides too noted that incest is practised among non-Greek peoples, 'and no law forbids it' (*Andr.* 173–6), and shocked many by making a character say (again with reference to incest) that no behaviour is shameful if it does not seem so to those who practise it (fr. 19).[3]

[1] It is remarkable how persistently this kind of thing reappears as responsible for a questioning of the moral code. H. L. A. Hart (*Law, Liberty and Morality*, 68) mentions as a cause of division and hesitation over the issues of sexual morality 'in our own time' the free discussion of it 'in the light of the discoveries of anthropology and psychology'. The exceptional freedom of discussion now tolerated must have other roots, for enough anthropology and psychology to show up the relativity of moral codes was known to Herodotus, and again to seventeenth-century Europe (cf. especially Greenleaf, *Order, Empiricism and Politics*, 198), let alone to the Victorians.

[2] Hdt. 3.38; not, incidentally, a very good argument for moral relativity, since it showed both parties agreed on the fundamental moral principle, that parents should be honoured in death as in life: the dispute was only about the means of fulfilling it. Thucydides (2.97.3–4) notes a custom of the Odrysians in Thrace which is the direct opposite of one observed in Persia.

[3] As we shall see (pp. 119 f. below), Socrates did not agree that a law was any the less universal and divine because some people broke it: incest, for instance, brings an unavoidable penalty, for its effects are dysgenic.

Such examples could be multiplied, but it should be remembered that contact between Greeks and barbarians was no new thing. The Ionian Greeks of the Anatolian coastal strip had been in close contact with Orientals for centuries, and their intellectual progress owed much to foreign sources. Trade and colonization took them to the Black Sea and Mesopotamia, and the Milesian colony Naucratis was founded in Egypt in the seventh century.[1] Sojourns among Egyptians and Chaldaeans are recorded of early philosophers and sages like Solon, and are perfectly credible. The same may be said about the effect of the codification of laws. The unquestioning acceptance of law and custom, we are told, was no longer possible in a time of legislative activity. 'A code of laws drawn up by a human lawgiver whose name was known . . . could not be accepted in the old way as part of the everlasting order of things.' So Burnet (*T. to P.* 106), and the work of Protagoras in drawing up the laws for Thurii in 443 is sometimes quoted as a relevant example. But the names which Burnet mentions are Zaleucus, Charondas and Solon, whose activity can hardly be held responsible for the emergence of new theories denying the religious sanction of law in the period following the Persian Wars. The Greeks had seen laws in the making long before that, yet they continued to attribute them to the instructions of Apollo, advising the legislator through his oracle at Delphi.[2] The causes of the reasoned rejection of tradition which marked the middle of the fifth century were exceedingly complex, and, even if the inflammable mixture can be analysed, it may remain difficult to see why the spark was applied to it just when it was.[3]

Undoubtedly the successes of the Greeks against barbarians had given them enormous self-confidence and pride in their achievements; and, although popular opinion was still ready to lend an ear to stories of the personal intervention of gods or heroes at Marathon and elsewhere, the feeling that they had stood alone and overcome was strong, especially among the Athenians. They had been the leaders of Greek

[1] See vol. 1, 29 f., where the mention of the eighth century must be corrected. R. M. Cook in *JHS*, 1937, 227 ff., concludes that Naucratis was founded about 615–610.

[2] For details see my *Greeks and their Gods*, 184–9.

[3] Diels in *Hermes*, 22, noted some signs that the 'enlightenment' of the Sophists had its forerunners as early as the sixth century, particularly among logographers like Hecataeus of Miletus. See on this Dümmler, *Akad.* 250.

resistance and borne the brunt of the Persian attack, and their consciousness of strength developed into an urge to dominate the rest and turn their former allies into subjects. If asked by what right they did this, they would reply as Thucydides shows them doing in the Melian Dialogue that it is a 'law of nature' that the stronger should do what is in their power and the weak give way (pp. 85 f. below).

This consciousness of power was being fostered from another direction by a new emphasis on the triumphs of human invention and technique. It is too easily assumed that the Greeks as a whole believed in an ideal of knowledge for its own sake, divorced from practical aims, and despised the useful arts, and there is some justice in recent claims that this generalization results from the academic habit of relying too heavily on Plato and Aristotle as representative of the Greek mind. In the fifth century the practical achievements of the human race were admired as much as their understanding of the universe. The stages of man's material progress were celebrated, for instance, by all the three great tragedians, as well as by philosophers like Anaxagoras and Democritus and the Sophist Protagoras. They might be associated with the name of Prometheus, patron saint of technology, or an unknown god as in Euripides's *Supplices* (201 f.), but, if so, his first gift to men is sagacity or ingenuity, and the rest follows from that. In the famous chorus of Sophocles's *Antigone* (332 ff.) there is no mention of higher beings: 'man with his skills' (περιφραδὴς ἀνήρ) is the most dread and wonderful thing in the world. The technical triumphs extolled by these writers include speech and writing, hunting and fishing, agriculture, the domestication of animals and their use in transport, building, cookery, mining and metalwork, shipbuilding and navigation, spinning and weaving, pharmacy and medicine, calculation, astronomy and the mantic arts. It is a list entirely in the spirit of Macaulay's catalogue of the fruits of Baconian science, in which his express purpose was to show up by contrast the practical barrenness of Greek thought. A difference is that the Englishman, besides omitting the art of prophecy, includes new weapons of war among the blessings of progress. Perhaps the Greek also showed his wisdom by adding at the end of the list of technical achievements that they may be used for evil ends as well as good. So too Theseus in the *Hippolytus* (Eur.

Hipp. 915 ff.) asks to what purpose it is that men teach ten thousand arts and discover every ingenious device, when their science does not tell them how to put sense into the head of a man who has not got it.

Social and political changes played their part, especially the growth of democracy at Athens. This was a gradual process, begun by Solon (who first introduced the principle of appointing public officials by a combination of election and lot) and continued by Cleisthenes after the Peisistratid tyranny. It was already far advanced by the time of the Persian Wars, and completed by the reforms of Pericles and Ephialtes about 458. These opened the archonship to the lowest classes and introduced pay for the archons, *boulé* and people's courts, thereby making it not only legal but practically possible for the poorer citizens to give up their time to public affairs. At the same time they introduced the lot in its pure form for appointment to many offices, that is, without preliminary election of candidates; and of course any citizen could speak and vote in the Assembly, which passed laws, declared war and concluded treaties. This situation naturally encouraged the belief that one man's opinion was as good as another's, for, as Socrates complained, although in matters considered technical no one would be consulted unless he could give proof of his training and competence, where the art of government was concerned the Athenians would listen to anyone—smith or shoemaker, rich or poor. These anti-democratic sentiments were not lost on his critics (p. 411 below), but the faults of the system (very different from a modern democracy) were glaring, not the least being fickleness. The treatment of Mytilene by the Athenian democracy illustrates its dangers, and perhaps its virtues also. After putting down a revolt there in 428, the Assembly under the influence of Cleon sent a trireme with orders to kill every man in the city and enslave the women and children. Next day they repented of this atrocious cruelty, and after a second debate reversed the decision by a tiny majority and despatched a second trireme post-haste to cancel the order. By eating at their oars and taking it in turns to sleep the rowers managed to arrive before it was put into effect. In this case the weakness of the democracy in the face of mob-oratory was just counterbalanced by its readiness to reconsider and give both sides a fair hearing.[1] The little island of Melos was less fortunate, and its inhabitants suffered the fate originally intended for Mytilene. Their crime was to prefer neutrality to inclusion within the Athenian empire.

While the harsh realities of history, in a period of unscrupulous imperialism and war of Greek with Greek, were encouraging corresponding theories of the right of the powerful to do as they pleased—the kind of theories that are commonly associated with the names of some of the Sophists—the spread of democracy was creating the demand which the Sophists claimed to supply in their capacity of professional educators. The road to political success was open to anyone, provided he had the wit and the training to outdo his competitors. In the absence of universities or colleges of adult education the gap was filled, to their profit, by men like Protagoras, who gloried in the title of Sophist and proudly advertised his ability to teach a young man 'the proper care of his personal affairs, so that he may best manage his own household, and also of the State's affairs, so as to become a real power in the city, both as speaker and man of action'. For this purpose the prime necessity was to master the art of persuasive speaking, and it has even been argued (by Heinrich Gomperz) that the whole teaching of the Sophists is summed up in the art of rhetoric.[2] That is a considerable exaggeration; the *areté* which Protagoras claimed to impart consisted of more than that. But one of them, Gorgias, did indeed laugh at the professed teachers of civic virtue. The art of clever speaking, he said, was all that he taught and all that any ambitious young man need learn. It was the master-art, for the man with the gift of persuasion had all the other experts in his power. (On this, however, see pp. 271f. below.)

I have spoken as if the political circumstances and public actions of the Greek states gave rise to the irreligious and utilitarian moral

---

[1] Thuc. 3.36ff. (The speeches on this occasion are referred to on pp. 86f. below.) The size of modern states would forbid a complete, as opposed to a representative, democracy, even if one were desired, and probably the only places where it can be observed today are the Universities of Oxford and Cambridge, where similar instances of vacillation are not unknown.

[2] At the other extreme Bignone (*Studi*, 32) contrasted the orators, 'living amid the harsh realities of politics', with the Sophists, who led the 'sheltered and segregated lives of paid educators of the public'. I imagine that this is the first and last time that we can expect to see the life of the Sophists described as *ombratile e appartata*!

theories of the thinkers and teachers, but it is more likely that practice and theory acted and reacted mutually on one another. Doubtless the Athenians did not need a Thrasymachus or a Callicles to teach them how to deal with a recalcitrant island, but the speeches which Thucydides puts into the mouths of the Athenian spokesmen, in what he represents as a set debate with the Melian assembly, bear unmistakable marks of Sophistic teaching. Pericles was a friend of Protagoras, and when Gorgias appeared before the Athenians in 427 the novel flowers of oratory with which he pleaded the cause of his Sicilian fatherland aroused their astonished admiration (p. 179, n. 3, below). If the Sophists were a product of their age, they also assisted in their turn in crystallizing its ideas. But at least their teaching fell on well-prepared ground. In Plato's opinion it was not they who should be blamed for infecting the young with pernicious thoughts, for they were doing no more than mirror the lusts and passions of the existing democracy:

Every one of these individual professional teachers, whom the people call Sophists and regard as their rivals in the art of education, in fact teaches nothing but the beliefs of the people expressed by themselves in their assemblies. This is what he claims as his wisdom.[1]

Whether Plato was right we can only say, if at all, at a much later stage of our study.

Turning (so far as the two can be distinguished) from causes to features of the change, the most fundamental is the antithesis between *physis* and *nomos* which was developed at this time among natural and humanistic philosophers alike. Once the view had gained currency that laws, customs and conventions were not part of the immutable order of things, it was possible to adopt very different attitudes towards them. On the one hand Protagoras could argue that accepted canons of good behaviour, including some restraint on selfish appetites and consideration for others, although not an original and essential part of human nature, were necessary for the preservation of society, and life in societies was necessary for actual survival. At the other extreme

---

[1] *Rep.* 493 a. The whole passage 492 a – 493 d is illuminating.

is the rampant individualism of those, like Plato's Callicles, who maintained that ideas of law and justice were merely a device of the majority of weaklings to keep the strong man, who is nature's just man, from his rightful place. *Nomos* and *physis* were enemies, and right was on the side of *physis*. The Sophist Antiphon drew an elaborate contrast between the works of *nomos* and those of *physis*, the former being unnecessary and artificial curbs imposed on nature by human agreement, the latter necessary and of natural origin. In the idea that laws are a matter of human agreement, 'covenants made by the citizens' as Hippias called them (p. 138 below), instead of divinely sanctioned, we have the essence of the theory of the social compact or contract which was developed especially in Europe of the seventeenth and eighteenth centuries. In the eyes of Callicles it condemned them, whereas Critias, through the mouth of Sisyphus in his play of that name, represented the invention of law as an important step on the road from men's originally 'disorderly and brutish' life to civilization. An unequivocal statement of the contractual theory of law is ascribed by Aristotle to Lycophron, a pupil of Gorgias, and in its historical form, as a theory of the origin of law, it is clearly stated by Glaucon in the *Republic* as a current view which he would like to see refuted.

Besides laws in the ordinary sense, contemporary opinion recognized the existence of 'unwritten laws', and the relation between the two illustrates well the transitional nature of this period of thought. For some, the phrase denoted certain eternal moral principles, universally valid and overruling the positive laws of men because their origin was from the gods. This conception is best known from the splendid lines of Sophocles in the *Antigone* (450 ff.), where Antigone defends the burial of her dead brother contrary to the edict of Creon by declaring: 'It was not Zeus or Justice who decreed these *nomoi* among men, nor did I deem your proclamation so mighty that you, a mortal, could overthrow the sure, unwritten laws of the gods.' Later we shall look at other references to these divine laws which have existed for all time, and their superiority to the faulty and changeable decrees of men. However, with the spread of democratic ideas the phrase took on a new and more sinister meaning. The codification of law came to be seen as a necessary protection for the people. Not only

Euripides (*Suppl.* 429 ff.) saw it as a guarantee of equal rights and a bulwark against tyranny, but also in practice the restored democracy at the end of the Peloponnesian War expressly forbade a magistrate to make use of unwritten law (p. 126 below).

Here is another discussion which finds its reflection in the second great period of enlightenment, Europe of the seventeenth and eighteenth centuries A.D. On the one hand we have Rousseau writing:

To these three kinds of law [political, civil, criminal] a fourth should be added, and it is the most important of them all. It is to be found not graven on pillars of marble or plates of bronze but in the heart of the citizens. It is the true foundation on which the State is built, and grows daily in importance . . . I refer to manners, customs, and, above all, opinion.

Then for a different point of view we can turn to Locke:

The law of nature being unwritten, and so nowhere to be found but in the minds of men, they who, through passion or interest, shall miscite or misapply it cannot so easily be convinced of their mistake where there is no established judge; and so it serves not as it ought, to determine the rights and fence the properties of those that live under it, especially where everyone is judge, interpreter, and executioner of it too, and that in his own case; and he that has right on his side, having ordinarily but his own single strength, hath not force enough to defend himself from injuries or to punish delinquents.[1]

The growth of atheism and agnosticism at this time was also connected with the idea of *nomos*. Beside the classic utterance of Protagoras, that he could not say whether gods existed or not, one may set the curious and thought-provoking words of Euripides's Hecuba in her plea for mercy (*Hec.* 799 ff.): the gods, she says, have power, and so has *nomos*, which is master of the gods because it is by *nomos* that we believe in them and live according to standards of right and wrong. For Critias the gods were the invention of an ingenious legislator to prevent men from breaking the laws when not under supervision. Prodicus may, like some nineteenth-century anthropologists, have seen the early stages of religion as two, first the

[1] Rousseau, *Social Contract*, 2.14 (trans. Hopkins); Locke, *Second Treatise on Civil Government*, 2.136. (Both passages may conveniently be found in the World's Classics volume *Social Contract*, ed. Barker, 313 and 115.)

deification of useful natural objects like the sun and rivers, corn and the grape, and later of human discoverers or inventors of such essentials as bread and wine, shelter, and the useful arts in general. This has been called an ancient example of the theory of the advance from fetishism to anthropomorphism.[1]

An attractive aspect of the *nomos–physis* antithesis is that it sponsored the first steps towards cosmopolitanism and the idea of the unity of mankind. Here *nomos* plays the part of *die Mode* in Schiller's hymn, which divides those who are naturally brothers. That is how Hippias sees it in Plato's *Protagoras*, speaking of those who come from different Greek states. Antiphon went further (as Hippias may also have done), and after censuring distinctions based on high or low birth proceeded to declare that there is no difference in nature between barbarians and Greeks. With this disapproval of distinctions based on birth and race, one would have expected him to include a condemnation of slavery, and he may well have done so; but there is no mention of it in the fragments. The only witness in the fifth century to the existence of a belief that slavery is unnatural is Euripides, whose characters utter such sentiments as 'Only the name brings shame to a slave: in all else slave is no worse than free, if he be a good man'. This is not necessarily the dramatist's own opinion, for others in his plays will damn all slaves alike as a worthless and greedy lot. Not many years after him, however, Alcidamas is quoted as having written that God set all men free and nature has made no man a slave; and by Aristotle's time there were certainly some who maintained that slavery was unnatural. (The subject is treated in ch. VI (4) below.)

One of the most important lessons taught in the lectures and handbooks of the Sophists was the art of speaking with equal cogency on both sides of a question. Protagoras started from the axiom that 'there are two arguments on every subject'. We may recognize the virtues of seeing both sides of a question, and the democratic quality of a willingness to give them both a hearing, and yet be alive to the dangers of such doctrine unless it is kept in very scrupulous hands. In fact it was being imparted, for high fees, to headstrong and ambi-

---

[1] The evidence for ascribing the two-stage theory to Prodicus is not absolutely conclusive. It is discussed on pp. 238 ff. below.

tious youth. In the eyes of Gorgias 'the word' was a despot who could do anything, but like a slave of the lamp it would be at the service of those who took his courses. Reading the remains of Gorgias's writings, one is not inclined to accuse Plato of unfairness when he makes him disclaim any responsibility for the use to which his teaching may be put by others. It was subversive stuff, both morally and epistemologically, for the conviction that men could be persuaded of anything went naturally with the relativity of Protagoras's 'man the measure' doctrine and the nihilism of Gorgias's treatise *On Nature or the Non-existent*.

Finally, one of the most hotly debated questions of the day, which because it was taken up by Socrates continued to be discussed by Plato and even Aristotle, sprang directly from the Sophists' appearance in the new role of paid educators. They claimed to teach *areté*, but was this something that could be instilled by teaching? *Areté* when used without qualification denoted those qualities of human excellence which made a man a natural leader in his community, and hitherto it had been believed to depend on certain natural or even divine gifts which were the mark of good birth and breeding. They were definitely a matter of *physis*, cultivated, as a boy grew up, by the experience of living with and following the example of his father and elder relations. Thus they were handed on naturally and scarcely consciously, a prerogative of the class that was born to rule, and the thought that they could be implanted by an outsider, offering schematic instruction in return for payment, was anathema to fathers of the old school. Hence the urgency to a young man like Meno—high-born and wealthy yet a pupil and admirer of Gorgias—of the question which he springs on Socrates at the beginning of the dialogue that bears his name: 'Can you tell me, Socrates, whether *areté* can be taught? Or is it a matter of practice, or natural aptitude, or what?'

The above is a foretaste of some of the topics of burning interest in the lifetime of Socrates which we shall be examining in detail in later chapters: the status of laws and moral principles, the theory of man's progress from savagery to civilization replacing that of degeneration from a past golden age, the idea of the social compact, subjective

25

theories of knowledge, atheism and agnosticism, hedonism and utilitarianism, the unity of mankind, slavery and equality, the nature of *areté*, the importance of rhetoric and the study of language. But first something about the class of men who are usually named as the chief propagators of the new humanism and rationalism. What was a Sophist, and what do we know of the individuals who posed these questions that have exercised thoughtful minds ever since?

III

WHAT IS A SOPHIST?

(1) THE WORD 'SOPHIST'[1]

The Greek words *sophos*, *sophia*, usually translated 'wise' and 'wisdom', were in common use from the earliest times, and, standing as they do for an intellectual or spiritual quality, naturally acquired some delicate shades of meaning which can only be crudely illustrated here. At first they connoted primarily skill in a particular craft. A shipwright in Homer is 'skilled in all *sophia*', a charioteer, a steersman, an augur, a sculptor are *sophoi* each in his occupation, Apollo is *sophos* with the lyre, Thersites a contemptible character but *sophos* with his tongue; there is a law in Hades (for comic purposes) that whoever excels his fellow-craftsmen in 'one of the great and clever arts' shall have special privileges until someone else comes along who is 'more *sophos* in his art'.[2] This sense merges easily into that of generally knowing or prudent, by way of a line like that of Theognis (119 ff.) that it is easy for a *sophos* to detect counterfeit coinage, but much more difficult to unmask a man of spurious character. Here *sophos* might still mean an expert (there are experts in testing coinage, but alas none in testing humanity), though more probably it is going over to the meaning of knowledgeable in general. In a similar doubtful position is Hesiod's description of Linus, the mythical singer and musician, as 'versed in all kinds of *sophia*' (fr. 153 Rzach). In this way it was used of the seven *Sophoi*, Wise Men or Sages, whose wisdom consisted chiefly of practical statesmanship and was enshrined in brief gnomic sayings, or of anyone of good sense (Eur. *I.A.* 749).

---

[1] In what follows, in addition to primary sources I have made especial use of the following, to which a reader may be referred for further information and views: Grote, *History*, VII, 32 ff.; Grant, *Ethics*, I, 106 ff.; ZN, 1335, n. 1; Jowett, *Dialogues of Plato*, III, 326 ff.; Kerferd in *CR*, 1950, 8–10; Morrison in *Durham U.J.* 1949, 55–63.

[2] *Il.* 15. 412; Pind. *Pyth.* 5. 115; Aesch. *Suppl.* 770 and *Sept.* 382; Soph. *O.T.* 484; Eur. fr. 372 and *I.T.* 1238; Soph. *Ph.* 439 f.; Aristoph. *Frogs* 761 ff.

What is a Sophist?

Along with generalization, a term of value like this, implying positive approval, inevitably suffers division into a 'true' and a 'false' meaning according to the user's point of view. The *sophia* of charioteer, shipwright or musician must have been to a large extent acquired by learning, but Pindar no doubt pleased his royal patron when he wrote that he who knows much by nature is wise (*sophos*), in contrast to the chattering crows who have gained their knowledge by learning. Not the man who knows many things is *sophos*, said Aeschylus, but he whose knowledge is useful. At the same time there creeps in an ironic note, a hint that the *sophos* is too clever and may overreach himself. Taxed by the wily Odysseus (whom he has earlier described as a *sophos* wrestler) with acting in a way that is not *sophon*, Neoptolemus replies that what is right and just is better than what is *sophon*. So we get the oxymoron of a chorus in Euripides: when men set themselves up against the gods, their *sophia* is not *sophon*, they are clever but not wise. The verb *sophizesthai*, to practise *sophia*, which Hesiod used of acquiring skill in seamanship and Theognis of himself as a poet, suffered a parallel development until it meant to trick or deceive, or to be over-subtle.[1]

The word *sophistes*, 'sophist', is a noun of the agent derived from the verb.[2] As Diogenes Laertius remarked (1.12) long after it had acquired an uncomplimentary sense, *sophos* and *sophistes* were once synonymous. This appears especially in Herodotus, who applies the name 'sophist' to Pythagoras, Solon and the founders of the Dionysiac cult, and says that all the sophists of Greece visited Croesus's Lydian capital, including Solon. That the Seven Sages were called sophists we know from a fragment of Aristotle and from Isocrates, who says that they were given this name 'which is now held in dishonour among you'. Isocrates dwells on the change which has come over the word, which he equates with his conception of philosophy:

[1] References for this paragraph: Pind. *Ol.* 2.86; Aesch. fr. 390; Soph. *Ph.* 1246 (and cf. the use of σόφισμα and σοφίζεσθαι at 14 and 77); Eur. *Bacch.* 395; for σοφίζεσθαι Hes. *Op.* 649; Theognis 19; Eur. *Bacch.* 200. With Theognis cf. Solon 1.52, where σοφία is used of poetry. When Pericles finds the young Alcibiades's questions are getting awkward, he closes the discussion with 'at your age we too τοιαῦτα ἐσοφιζόμεθα' (Xen. *Mem.* 1.2.46). B. Gladigow in *Hermes*, 1967, has collected examples of the invidious sense of σοφός in Euripides.

[2] Kerferd in *CR*, 1950, 8, gives a classified list, with references, of the earlier uses of the word.

It offends me to see chicanery more highly regarded than philosophy, as the accuser who puts philosophy in the dock. Who of the men of old time would have expected this, among you of all people who pride yourself on your wisdom (*sophia*)? It was not so in our forefathers' time. They admired those who were called sophists and envied their associates ... The best evidence of this is that they chose Solon, the first Athenian citizen who bore that title, to rule the state.[1]

Probably it was assumed that a *sophistes* would be a teacher.[2] This accords with the fact that the name was often applied to poets, for in Greek eyes practical instruction and moral advice constituted the main function of the poet. Solon himself was a poet, and J. S. Morrison has suggested that it was in this capacity that he first attracted attention and came to be entrusted with the preservation of political harmony.[3] Before him Hesiod had written his *Works and Days* both as a manual of instruction for farmers and as a vehicle for ethical precept. Theognis is full of ethical maxims, some of general import and some in support of the threatened supremacy of the upper class. Parmenides and Empedocles were poets, and the great dramatists of the fifth century, both tragic and comic, certainly regarded themselves as having an educational mission. The contest which Aristophanes stages in Hades between Aeschylus and Euripides is fought on moral rather than aesthetic ground, and in the course of it Aeschylus expressly declares that, although the story of Phaedra's guilty love as Euripides told it might be true, a poet should conceal such wickedness rather than present it on the stage, because 'as schoolboys have teachers to show them the way, so poets are teachers of men'. Euripides himself, challenged to state the grounds on which a poet deserves admiration, replies: 'For his wit and good advice, and because he makes men better citizens.' So much is common ground between the disputants,

---

[1] Hdt. 4.95.2, 1.29.1, cf. also 2.49.1; Aristotle fr. 5 Rose, Ross p. 79; Isocr. *Antid.* 235, 312. For Isocrates's use of the word see also Grant, *Ethics* I, 111–13.

[2] In Hdt. 1.29.1, 2.49.1 and 4.95.2, the translator in the Penguin series, Mr de Selincourt, renders the word each time by 'teacher', which besides sounding very natural in its English contexts is probably as accurate as an English equivalent can be.

[3] Morrison in *Durham U.J.* 1949, 59. His article contains much of the evidence that (as Jaeger also maintained in *Paideia* I, 293) the Sophists were the heirs of the educational tradition of the poets. Not that this was their sole inheritance. Nestle was more correct when he called them heirs of the Ionian philosophers as well (*VMzuL*, 252). So also in effect Morrison, *loc. cit.* 56.

and it is exactly what the professed Sophist Protagoras claimed to do.[1]

So we find that at its earliest known occurrence, in an ode of Pindar, the word *sophistes* clearly means poet. With poetry went music, for the lyric poet was his own accompanist. Athenaeus quotes a line of Aeschylus about a *sophistes* playing the lyre to illustrate his statement that 'all who practise the art of *mousiké* used to be called sophists', and the reference to the singer and musician Thamyris as *sophistes* in Euripides's *Rhesus* is quoted as another example. Here however the Muse is speaking of him with hatred and disgust, and the word probably carries something of the unfavourable tone which it acquired early in the fifth century.[2]

It looks however as if in the fifth century the word was beginning to be used of prose-writers in contrast to poets, as the didactic function came to be more and more fulfilled through this medium. Some of the Seven Sages, in their capacity as *sophistai* or teachers, uttered in prose the kind of maxims which Theognis or Simonides uttered in verse, and this may have sown the seeds of the distinction.[3] Xenophon (*Mem.* 4.2.1) says that Euthydemus collected 'many of the written works of the most celebrated poets and sophists'. Among the latter would be a man like Anaxagoras, whose book we know to have been on general sale, and whom Aeschines of Sphettus may have bracketed as a *sophistes* with Prodicus, one of the recognized 'Sophists'.[4]

A *sophistes* writes or teaches because he has a special skill or knowledge to impart. His *sophia* is practical, whether in the fields of conduct and politics or in the technical arts. If anyone could make the products of every separate craft, and in addition all the things in the natural world, he would indeed be a wondrous *sophistes*, says Glaucon in the *Republic* (596d), and a similar phrase, 'a marvellous

[1] Aristoph. *Frogs* 1053–5, 1009f.

[2] Pind. *Isth.* 5.28; Aesch. fr. 314; Eur. *Rhes.* 924.

[3] Schmid, *Gesch. gr. Lit.* 1.3.1, 14.

[4] That Aeschines did this is generally taken as fact (e.g. by Zeller, ZN, 1335, n. 1). This would be good contemporary evidence for the appellation, but the passage in question does not guarantee more than that it was used of the two men by Athenaeus. It runs as follows (Ath. 5.200b, Aesch. fr. 34 Dittmar): ὁ δὲ Καλλίας αὐτοῦ (i.e. Aeschines's dialogue *Callias*) περιέχει τὴν τοῦ Καλλίου ... Προδίκου καὶ Ἀναξαγόρου τῶνσοφισ τῶν διαμώκησιν. Anaxagoras was also called *sophistes* by Diodorus (12.39, DK, 59 A 17). For Anaxagoras's book see vol. II, 269.

(*deinos*) *sophistes*', is uttered in the same tone of incredulity by Hippo-lytus in Euripides (*Hipp.* 921) of a man who could make fools wise. So the noun occurs with an objective genitive meaning a deviser or contriver ('I became a *sophistes* of many calamities', Eur. *Heracl.* 993). Hence the sense of expert, pundit, for instance in mathematics. Socrates in the *Meno* (85 b), having by means of diagrams got Meno's slave to recognize the diagonal of a square, tells him 'the name the *sophistai* give it is "diagonal"', and Xenophon (*Mem.* 1.1.11, perhaps with the Pythagoreans chiefly in mind) speaks of 'what is called the *kosmos* by the *sophistai*'. In the same vein Socrates says of the wise Diotima, with a touch of humour, that she answered his question 'like a real *sophistes*'.[1] Here the translation of Michael Joyce, though lengthy, strikes the right note: 'with an air of authority that was almost pro-fessorial'. When Socrates in the *Lysis* (204a) says of a certain Miccus that he is 'no common man, but a very competent *sophistes*', the compliment to his gifts as a teacher is genuine. An even more striking use of the word in a complimentary sense is in Xenophon (*Cyrop.* 3.1.14 and 38ff.): the Armenian prince Tigranes tells Cyrus of a teacher with whom he was associating, and whom Xenophon calls *sophistes*. His father put the man to death, in the belief that he was corrupting Tigranes, but so noble was his character that before his execution he sent for Tigranes and told him not to hold it against his father, because he had acted out of ignorance. That such a term should be applied to the natural philosophers is only to be expected, and Isocrates includes Alcmaeon, Empedocles, Ion of Chios, Parmenides and Melissus along with Gorgias among 'the *sophistai* of past days' (*Antid.* 268). In the other few instances recorded one seems to detect a hint of that disparaging note of which we shall have to speak next. Diogenes of Apollonia called his predecessors *sophistai* in the course of writing against them (vol. II, 363), and, when the Hippocratic treatise *On Ancient Medicine* (ch. 20) speaks of 'certain doctors and *sophistai*' who claim that one cannot be versed in medicine without understanding the whole nature of man, it is strongly attacking their position.

---

[1] Plato, *Symp.* 208c. The same phrase, τέλεος σοφιστής, is used jokingly of Hades in the *Cratylus*, 403e, with reference to his powers of persuasion.

What is a Sophist?

The Athenians, like other people, tended to be suspicious of intellectuals, pundits, professors and the like. Their qualities were summed up in a word difficult to translate: *deinotes*, with the adjective *deinos*. Derived from a noun meaning 'fear', it stands for anything terrible or dreadful, as for instance in Homer weapons, the glare of a foe, the whirlpool Charybdis, thunder, lions. Of a goddess, it is coupled with 'reverend', and may have conveyed an idea more like 'the fear of the Lord'. This sense of 'awful' persists, often with a suggestion of the strange, incomprehensible, uncanny; and so used the word contributes to some of the most moving, and untranslatable, lines of Greek tragedy. Hephaestus cannot bring himself to chain Prometheus to the rock because 'kinship is something *deinon*'. Clytemnestra hates and fears her son, yet when she hears of his death cannot feel the expected joy and relief because 'to give birth is *deinon*'—the fact of motherhood has a strange power. Degenerating, as words do, in popular use, it became coupled with *sophos* to mean clever or skilful: the Egyptians are *deinoi* (terrible fellows) for devising stratagems, Prometheus is *deinos* at wriggling out of difficulties, a good driver is *deinos* at his art. It also, and particularly, meant clever in speech or argument.[1]

Anyone who had this quality was a natural object of suspicion to his less clever fellows, as Antiphon the orator, says Thucydides (8.68.1), was to the Athenian public 'on account of his reputation for *deinotes*', and later Demosthenes alleges (*De cor.* 276) that Aeschines has called him '*deinos*, sorcerer, sophist and the like'. Here we have *deinos* expressly coupled with *sophistes* as an insult to be resented, and, though Demosthenes is a fourth-century figure, the idea of the *sophistes* as a man who claims superior knowledge, and can have the claim ironically flung back at him, occurs as early as Aeschylus. His Prometheus, the bringer of fire to men, who taught them all crafts and raised them from savagery to civilization, is roughly addressed by Hermes as 'you, the sophist, who have sinned against the gods', and is mocked

[1] Aesch. *P.V.* 39; Soph. *El.* 770; Aesch. fr. 373 and *P.V.* 59. The expression δεινὸς λέγειν is frequent. The degeneration resembles that of the English 'terribly' or 'awfully'. It is amusingly illustrated in Plato, *Prot.* 341a–b, where Socrates tells how the purist Prodicus rebukes him for using *deinos* as a term of praise, calling Protagoras '*deinos* and *sophos*', 'awfully clever'. *Deinos*, said Prodicus, properly applies to evils like disease, war, poverty.

by Kratos as a duller *sophistes* than Zeus.[1] The two criticisms, that a sophist is not so clever as he thinks he is, and that his cleverness is used for wrong purposes, are hinted at again in a fragment of Sophocles (97 Nauck): 'A well-disposed mind, with righteous thoughts, is a better inventor than any *sophistes*.'

Sophocles was an exact contemporary of Protagoras, and in him the word could have been coloured by the appearance on the scene of Sophists as a professional class.[2] Aristophanes too was well aware of their existence when he satirized sophists in the *Clouds*, but still used the word in a more general sense, in which it could include (for those who disapproved of him) Socrates, although he took no fees and is constantly represented by Plato as the Sophists' inveterate opponent. At *v*. 331 the Clouds are said to be the foster-mothers of a crowd of 'sophists', who are itemized as soothsayers from Thurii, quack doctors, lazy long-haired and beringed dandies, dithyrambic poets and bogus astronomers—a pretty comprehensive list. At 360 Socrates and Prodicus are mentioned together as 'meteorosophists' or experts in celestial phenomena. At 1111 Socrates promises that his teaching will turn young Pheidippides into a clever sophist, on which his unwilling pupil comments 'A poor pale-faced devil, you mean', and at 1309 the word as applied to Strepsiades by the chorus means nothing but 'trickster', in allusion to his cheating of his creditors.

The word 'sophist' then had a general sense as well as the special one of which we have yet to speak, and in neither sense was it necessarily a term of opprobrium. (Compare the judgment of Socrates on the professional Miccus.) If we remember the educational vocation of Greek poets, we may say that the word which comes nearest to it in English is teacher or professor. From early in the fifth century it could be pronounced with a depreciatory inflexion, as may the words pundit or intellectual today. In the hands of the conservative Aristophanes it became definitely a term of abuse implying charlatanry and deceit, though still by no means confined to the class of professional Sophists. We cannot therefore agree with Grote in blaming Plato

---

[1] *P.V.* 62. Prometheus would not deny the title. He boasts of his σοφίσματα, and laments that he has no σόφισμα to get him out of his present plight. The word is for him synonymous with μηχάνημα, τέχνη and πόρος. But already it can be thrown back at him with irony.

[2] I am reserving the capital initial for the members of this profession.

33

as solely responsible for casting discredit on the word (p. 12 above). What existed already was more than a 'vague sentiment of dislike', nor is it true that 'what was new was the peculiar use of an old word which Plato took out of its usual meaning, and fastened upon the eminent paid teachers of the Sokratic age'.[1] Apart from the evidence of Xenophon, it would have been quite impossible for Plato to have referred, in the manner and the contexts in which he does so refer, to the paid teachers as Sophists if that had not been their recognized title. A view like Grote's can only be upheld by the uncritical practice (which will not be followed here) of accepting as fact all references to the Sophists in Plato which are either neutral or sympathetic ('Even Plato is forced to admit . . .') and dismissing any less complimentary remarks as due solely to illiberal prejudice. When Protagoras in Plato's *Protagoras* avows himself a Sophist and an educator in spite of the odium which attaches to the term, an odium which he explains as due to the fact that they enter the great cities of Greece as foreigners and attract their most promising young men away from their relations and friends by claiming that their own teaching is better, there is no reason to doubt the reality of the state of affairs which he describes. His boast has an element of bravado: it needs courage to declare oneself a Sophist. Equally true to the character of the Athenians is the remark of Socrates in the *Euthyphro* (3c) that it does not matter if they think somebody *deinos* provided he keeps it to himself, but if he starts imparting his superior cleverness to others by teaching they get angry, whether from jealousy or some other cause. Here Socrates has his own plight in mind, but plainly the observation applies to the professional Sophists too; indeed he shared their reputation, as the *Clouds* makes plain. In the next century Aeschines the orator could refer to him casually as 'Socrates the sophist'.[2]

---

[1] Grote, *History*, VII, 35 and 37. Nor shall we follow Popper (*O.S.* 263, n. 52) in saying that Plato is 'the man who by his attacks on the "Sophists" *created* the bad associations connected with the word'. (My italics.) A fairer statement is Havelock's (*Lib. Temper*, 158): 'The playwrights of Old Comedy played upon the prejudice [against intellectualism], if they indeed did not create it, and when Plato uses the word *sophistes* it has lost its dignity. He cannot forget, perhaps, the burlesques staged in his youth which he had either read or seen.'

[2] *In Timarch.* 173. It was in the same speech that Aeschines called Demosthenes a sophist. Though the lapse of centuries makes it of doubtful relevance to the present discussion, it is interesting that Lucian could refer to Christ as 'that crucified sophist' (*Peregrinus* 13).

(2) THE SOPHISTS

(a) Professionalism

In the lifetime of Socrates the word came to be used, though not solely, of a particular class, namely professional educators who gave instruction to young men, and public displays of eloquence, for fees. They recognized their descent from the earlier tradition of education by the poets; indeed Protagoras, in the somewhat self-satisfied speech which Plato puts into his mouth (*Prot.* 316d), accuses Orpheus and Musaeus, Homer, Hesiod and Simonides of using their poetry as a disguise, through fear of the odium attached to the name descriptive of their real character, which was that of Sophists like himself.[1] (The anachronistic confusion is in keeping with the light-hearted tone which Plato adopts in the dramatic parts of this dialogue, for needless to say no professional stigma attached to the name in earlier days, and in any case, as we have seen, it was in fact applied to the poets.) In the *Meno* (91e–92a) Plato speaks of 'many others' besides Protagoras who have practised the Sophists' profession, 'some before his time and others still alive'. Of professionals before Protagoras we have no record, and indeed Socrates in the *Protagoras* (349a) addresses him as the first to take payment for his teaching. Plato may have been thinking of a man like the Athenian Mnesiphilus, who is mentioned by Herodotus (8.57) as an adviser of Themistocles and of whom Plutarch writes in a passage of some interest for the development of the sophistic profession (*Them.* 2):

[1] The same was said by Plutarch (*Pericles* 4) of Damon, a Sophist who was a pupil of Prodicus and friend of Socrates (Plato, *Laches* 197d). He was chiefly known as an authority on music but, says Plutarch, though a leading Sophist and in fact the mentor of Pericles in politics, he used his musical reputation to hide his δεινότης. This however did not avail him and he was ostracized. His association with Pericles is confirmed by Plato (*Alc. I* 118c) and Isocrates (*Antid.* 235), and his ostracism (already in Arist. *Ath. Pol.* 27.4) by the discovery of an ostracon bearing his name (DK, 1, 382 n.). In the *Republic* (400b, 424c) Plato makes it clear that his interest in musical modes was bound up with wider questions of their moral and social effects. He goes so far as to say that in Damon's view 'the modes of music are never disturbed without unsettling the most fundamental political and social conventions' (trans. Shorey). If more were known of him he might occupy an important place in the history of the sophistic movement, but in our comparative ignorance he can only appear as a footnote to it. Texts are in DK, 1, no. 37, and modern studies include W. D. Anderson, 'The Importance of the Damonian Theory in Plato's Thought' (*TAPA*, 1955; see also his book *Ethos and Education in Greek Music* and its review by Borthwick in *CR*, 1958); ch. 6 of F. Lasserre, *Plut. de la musique*; J. S. Morrison in *CQ*, 1958, 204–6; H. John, 'Das musikerziehende Wirken Pythagoras' und Damons' (*Das Altertum*, 1962).

He was neither an orator nor one of those called philosophers of nature. Rather he made a practice of what was called *sophia* but was in reality political shrewdness (*deinotes*) and practical sagacity, and so perpetuated what one might call a school which had come down in succession from Solon. His successors combined it with the art of forensic eloquence, and, transferring their training from action to speech, were called Sophists.[1]

References to the Sophists as paid for their work are frequent in Plato,[2] and occur also in Xenophon, Isocrates and Aristotle. The character of the Sophists may have changed, but they remained professionals from Protagoras to the time of Isocrates at least. 'Those who sell their wisdom for money to anyone who wants it are called Sophists', says Socrates in Xenophon (*Mem.* 1.6.13), and adds a comment more caustic than anything in Plato. In the *Meno* (91c ff.) it is Anytus, a typical well-bred member of the governing class, who violently abuses them, and Socrates who is their somewhat ironic defender. Isocrates in his old age[3] defended the profession, which he equated with his own philosophical ideal, an ideal much closer to Protagoras than to Plato. The best and greatest reward of a Sophist, he says, is to see some of his pupils become wise and respected citizens. Admittedly there are some bad Sophists, but those who make a right use of philosophy ought not to be blamed for the few black sheep. In conformity with this he defends them from the charge of profiteering. None of them, he says, made a great fortune or lived other than modestly, not even Gorgias who earned more than any other and was a bachelor with no family ties.[4] Plato on the other hand emphasizes their wealth, saying for instance that Protagoras earned more from his *sophia* than Phidias and ten other sculptors put together (*Meno* 91d), and Gorgias and Prodicus more than the practitioners of any other art (*Hipp. Maj.* 282d). Aristotle describes a Sophist as one who makes money out of an apparent but unreal

[1] On Mnesiphilus see further Morrison, *Durham U.J.* 1949, 59, and Kerferd, *CR*, 1950, 9f.
[2] E. L. Harrison in *Phoenix*, 1964, 191, n. 44, has collected thirty-one Platonic references to the Sophists' earnings. What is known about the practice of individuals will be noted below in the sections devoted to them (pp. 262ff.).
[3] He was 82 when he wrote the *Antidosis*; see §9. For the Protagorean standpoint of Isocrates see Morrison's comparison of Platonic and Isocratean *philosophia* in *CQ*, 1958, 216–18.
[4] *Antid.* 155f. Dodds (*Gorg.* 7), in his argument that Gorgias was not a Sophist, tries to explain away this passage, as well as Plato, *Hipp. Maj.* 282b5 and Isocr. *Antid.* 268.

wisdom, and, setting aside the jibe, this and other passages are evidence that paid Sophists still existed in his time.[1]

The professionalism of the Sophists is emphasized by the fact that Protagoras had two classes of pupil: young men of good family who wished to enter politics, and those, like a certain Antimoerus of Mende (not, that is, an Athenian), who was studying 'for professional purposes (ἐπὶ τέχνῃ), to become a Sophist himself'.[2] In the *Protagoras* (313c) Socrates describes a Sophist as 'a seller of the goods by which a soul [or mind] is nourished', and suggests reasons why a young man should hesitate before entrusting himself to such a one: like retailers of bodily foods, they praise their wares indiscriminately without a dietitian's knowledge of their wholesomeness; unlike foods, their products enter the mind directly, and cannot be kept in jars until we find out which to consume and how and in what quantities. By the time Plato wrote the *Sophist* (where Socrates takes no part in the main argument) they had simply become (along with other undesirable characteristics) 'paid hunters of rich young men'. Mistrust of the Sophists was not confined to Plato. The outburst of Anytus must be true to life, as it is also when young Hippocrates, son of a 'great and prosperous house', blushes for shame at the thought of becoming one himself (*Prot.* 312a). In the *Gorgias* (520a) Socrates's most violent opponent, Callicles, dismisses them as 'worthless fellows', and in the *Phaedrus* (257d) Phaedrus asserts that the most powerful and respected politicians are afraid to write speeches and leave works of their own to posterity, for fear of being called Sophists. Plato himself, though he disagreed with the Sophists, was much gentler in his handling of the best of them like Protagoras, Gorgias and Prodicus. A disparaging remark about Sophists, in connexion with Prodicus, is put into the mouth of Laches, not Socrates (*Laches* 179d). Xenophon, in a moral epilogue to his treatise on hunting (ch. 13), castigates them as masters of fraud.[3]

---

[1] *Soph. El.* 165a21; cf. 183b36ff. (where μισθαρνούντων recalls the μισθαρνοῦντες ἰδιῶται of Plato, *Rep.* 493a) and *EN* 1164a30.

[2] *Prot.* 315a. For Sophistic as a τέχνη cf. e.g. τὴν σοφιστικὴν τέχνην 316d, and Protagoras 40 years ἐν τῇ τέχνῃ, *Meno* 91e.

[3] If the *Cynegetica* is by Xenophon, which some have doubted. See Lesky, *Hist. Gr. Lit.* 621f. Others have maintained that the passage is influenced by Plato's *Sophist* (Grant, *Ethics* I, 111) and have pointed out that both were written after the brilliant first generation of Sophists were dead. So, one may presume, were the *Protagoras* and *Meno*, yet it is Protagoras, Gorgias, Hippias and Prodicus who are still for Plato the representative Sophists.

What is a Sophist?

The attitude of the Athenian public was ambivalent, reflecting the transitional situation of Athenian social and intellectual life. The Sophists had no difficulty in finding pupils to pay their high fees, or audiences for their public lectures and displays. Yet some among the older and more conservative[1] strongly disapproved of them. This disapproval was linked, as Plato shows, to their professionalism. Why should this be? We are accustomed to thinking of teaching as a perfectly respectable way of earning a livelihood, and there was no prejudice in Greece against earning a living as such. Socrates was the son of a stonemason and probably followed the same trade, but (unpopular as he was in many quarters) this was never held against him. Poets had been paid for their work, artists and doctors were expected to charge fees both for the practice of their art and for teaching it to others.[2] The trouble seems to have lain first of all in the kind of subjects the Sophists professed to teach, especially *areté*. Protagoras, when asked what Hippocrates will learn from him, replies (*Prot.* 318e): 'The proper care of his personal affairs, so that he may best manage his own household, and also of the State's affairs, so as to become a real power in the city both as speaker and as man of action.' In short, says Socrates, the art of citizenship, and Protagoras emphatically agrees. Though some of them taught many other things as well, all included political advancement in their curriculum, and the key to this, in democratic Athens, was the power of persuasive speech.[3]

[1] This does not necessarily mean aristocratic or oligarchic as opposed to democratic. Anytus was a leading democrat. The division between democrat and anti-democrat cut across that between high-born and plebeian. Pericles, who completed the democratic revolution, was an Alcmaeonid like Cleisthenes who started it. Dr Ehrenberg has called him 'the aristocratic democrat'. Cf. his remarks on p. 65 of his *Soc. and Civ. in Gr. and Rome*: 'The old aristocratic education was out of touch with the realities of contemporary life, but it was largely the same leading class which governed the democratic state.' Cf. also M. A. Levi, *Pol. Power in the Anc. World*, 65, 90.

[2] See e.g. Isocr. *Antid.* 166; Ar. *Rhet.* 1405b24 (poets); Plato, *Prot.* 311c, *Meno* 91d (sculptors); *Prot.* 311b and Hdt. 3.131.2 (doctors). Further references are in Nestle, *VMϟuL*, 259, n. 36. Zeno the philosopher is said by Plato to have exacted the impressive fee of 100 minas for a course (*Alc. I* 119a), though, when late authorities say the same of Protagoras (as indeed they do of Gorgias, Diod. 12.53.2), Zeller dismisses it as highly exaggerated (ZN, 1299, n. 2). Yet Zeno does not seem to have shared the name or the blame of the Sophists.

[3] Similarly in the *Clouds* (v. 432) Socrates, who is there caricatured as among other things a professional Sophist (cf. 98 ἀργύριον ἤν τις διδῷ), assures Strepsiades that through his instruction ἐν τῷ δήμῳ γνώμας οὐδείς νικήσει πλείονας ἤ σύ. At *Gorg.* 520e Socrates suggests a reason why teaching this kind of thing is generally frowned on.

Gorgias indeed concentrated solely on rhetoric and refused to be included among the teachers of *areté*, for he held that rhetoric was the master-art to which all others must defer.[1] Now 'to teach the art of politics and undertake to make men good citizens' (*Prot.* 319a) was just what at Athens was considered the especial province of the amateur and gentleman. Any upper-class Athenian should understand the proper conduct of affairs by a sort of instinct inherited from his ancestors, and be prepared to pass it on to his sons. Even Protagoras admitted this, while claiming that it still left room for his pedagogic art as a supplement.[2] In the *Meno* passage already referred to Socrates innocently suggests to Anytus, a prominent democratic leader who became his chief accuser, that the Sophists are the proper people to instil into a young man the *sophia* which will fit him to manage an estate, govern a city, and in general show the *savoir-faire* proper to a gentleman. When Anytus reviles them as a menace to society, and Socrates asks to whom then, in his opinion, a young man should turn for such training, he replies that there is no need to mention particular individuals, for 'any decent Athenian gentleman whom he happens to meet will make him a better man than the Sophists would'.

The grounds on which Socrates criticized their fee-taking were rather different, and typical of the man. He held (we have this not from Plato but Xenophon) that by accepting money they deprived themselves of their freedom: they were bound to converse with any who could pay their fees, whereas he was free to enjoy the society of anyone he chose (*Mem.* 1.2.6, 1.6.5). He went so far as to call it prostitution, selling one's mind being no better than selling one's body. Wisdom was something that should be freely shared between friends and

---

[1] Pp. 271ff. below. ἀρετῆς διδάσκαλοι was Plato's regular way of referring to the Sophists (Dodds, *Gorgias*, 366). For Gorgias see *Meno* 95c, *Gorg.* 456c–e, especially οὐ γὰρ ἔστιν περὶ ὅτου οὐκ ἂν πιθανώτερον εἴποι ὁ ῥητορικὸς ἢ ἄλλος ὁστισοῦν τῶν δημιουργῶν ἐν πλήθει. Gorgias even admits that his pupils will learn from him the principles of right and wrong 'if they don't happen to know them already' (460a), while at the same time maintaining that the teacher is not responsible for the use made of his teaching. For the correctness of including Gorgias among the Sophists see now E. L. Harrison in *Phoenix*, 1964 (against Raeder and Dodds).

[2] I do not understand how anyone can read the brilliant and sympathetic speech of Protagoras in the *Protagoras* from 323c to 328c and still hold that Plato in his representations of the best of the Sophists was setting out to blacken their memory.

loved ones (1.6.13). This was how philosophy had been regarded hitherto, especially in the Pythagorean school, of which Plato certainly, and Socrates probably, was an admirer. The complex Socratic–Platonic concept of *eros*, a sublimated homosexual love, will also have been at work.

(b) Inter-city status

The Sophists, then, were disliked for different reasons both by philosophers like Socrates and Plato and by leading citizens like Anytus. The odium which they incurred in the eyes of the establishment was not only due to the subjects they professed; their own status was against them. Not only did they claim to give instruction in what at Athens was thought to be for the right people a kind of second nature, but they themselves were not Athenian leaders or even citizens. They were foreigners, provincials whose genius had outgrown the confines of their own minor cities. Some of them first went abroad on official missions, as Gorgias to Athens to plead the cause of Leontini against Syracuse in 427.[1] Both he and Prodicus of Ceos took the opportunity, while presenting their cities' case before the Council, of advancing their own interests by giving classes and demonstrations which brought in considerable sums (*Hipp. Maj.* 282b–c). Hippias, too, boasted of the number of diplomatic missions on which his city employed him (*ibid.* 281a). Leontini, Ceos or Elis afforded inadequate outlet for their talents. At Athens, the centre of Hellenic culture at the height of its fame and power, 'the very headquarters of Greek wisdom' as Plato's Hippias calls it (*Prot.* 337d), they could flourish; but there they had no chance of becoming political figures themselves, so they used their talents to teach others. It was no wonder that, as Protagoras said, the position of such men could easily become precarious. Plato refers to it again more than once, in the *Apology* (19e) and in the *Timaeus* where Socrates says (19e) that the Sophists are very good speechmakers in general, but that 'their habit of wandering from city to city and having no settled home of their own' is a disadvantage when it comes to matters of active statesmanship in

[1] Plato, *Hipp. Maj.* 282b, Diod. 12.53.1–2. Thucydides also tells of the embassy from Leontini (3.86.3), but without mentioning Gorgias.

war or negotiation. This has been cited as an example of Plato's disparagement of the Sophists, but is only a statement of evident fact.[1]

(c) Methods

The Sophists gave their instruction either to small circles or seminars or in public lectures or 'displays' (*epideixeis*).[2] The former might be conducted in the house of a patron like Callias, the richest man in Athens, who was said to have spent more money on the Sophists than anyone else (Plato, *Apol.* 20a). His home is the scene of the gathering in Plato's *Protagoras*, and his hospitality to the Sophists and their admirers seems to have turned it into a rather unhomelike place. Protagoras paces the forecourt attended by a considerable crowd, including both Athenians and the foreigners whom he draws, like a Pied Piper, from every city that he passes through. In the opposite portico Hippias is holding forth to another circle, and Prodicus is occupying a former store-room which Callias has had to convert into a bedroom owing to the large number staying in the house. He too has his own circle of listeners round his bed. Callias's hall porter is understandably sick of the sight of Sophists. When hosts were so complaisant, even public displays could take place in private houses. We hear of Prodicus giving one at Callias's (*Axioch.* 366c),[3] and when Socrates and Chaerephon have missed a display by Gorgias, evidently in some public place, Callicles assures them that Gorgias is staying with him and will put on another performance at home for their benefit. Sometimes the displays would be in a gymnasium or other place of resort. Cleon accuses the Athenian assembly of behaving 'more like the audience at Sophists' displays than a serious deliberative body' (Thuc. 3.38.7). Hippias tells Socrates that in two days' time he will be giving a recital 'in the School of Pheidostratus', and Prodicus did the same in the Lyceum (*Hipp. Maj.* 286b, *Eryxias* 397c). Prices

---

[1] The point about the alien status of the Sophists is made by Joël, *Gesch.* 646f., who remarks, adapting a well-known story of Plato's, that if Themistocles had been a Seriphian he would have become a Sophist! At *Rep.* 493a the Sophists are μισθαρνοῦντες ἰδιῶται, which is also a fair description.

[2] The two methods are mentioned together in connexion with Prodicus at *Hipp. Maj.* 282c: πιδείξεις ποιούμενος καὶ τοῖς νέοις συνών.

[3] Even if our authority is of doubtful reliability for the actual fact, the author probably knew that such occurrences did take place.

of admission are mentioned more than once, as $\frac{1}{2}$, 2 and 4 drachmas for a performance by Prodicus (*Axioch.* 366 c). Socrates laments that his knowledge of correct diction is inadequate because he had only been able to afford the 1 dr. lecture of Prodicus and not the 50 dr. one.[1]

The display might take the form of inviting questions from the audience. This is mentioned as a practice of Gorgias (*Gorg.* 447 c, *Meno* 70 c), and Hippias was bold enough to do the same before the great pan-Hellenic concourse at Olympia (*Hipp. Min.* 363 c–d). Alternatively the Sophist gave a display of continuous eloquence on a prepared theme and from a written text. Such were the Trojan dialogue of Hippias (*Hipp. Maj.* 286 a, described by its author as 'splendidly composed'), and the speeches of Gorgias at Olympia, Delphi and Athens, the last a funeral oration for the dead in battle.[2] These declamations might be simply rhetorical exercises on mythical themes, designed to show how, with skill and effrontery, the most unpromising case could be defended. Of such we still possess two specimens in the *Helena* and *Palamedes* of Gorgias. Besides Gorgias and Hippias, Protagoras also claimed to excel in both genres, long and elaborate speeches and the technique of question and answer (*Prot.* 329 b, 335 a).

The appearance of the Sophists at the great festivals of Olympia and elsewhere had a threefold significance. First, it is further evidence that they considered themselves to be in the tradition of the poets and rhapsodes. Xenophanes and Empedocles had, like other poets, introduced their own work to the public by recitation either in person or through a rhapsode. Poets and rhapsodes wore special clothes, in particular a purple robe.[3] Hippias and Gorgias did the same (DK, 82 A 9), and Hippias made his own finery (*Hipp. Min.* 368 c). It has to be remembered that we are still in an age when it was much more usual to hear a literary work read than to read it to oneself, and

[1] Many think that the 50 dr. must have been for a course, though the expression is πεντηκοντάδραχμος ἐπίδειξις (*Crat.* 384 b). Cf. Ar. *Rhet.* 1415 b 15. Judging by what we know of the Sophists' standards, 50 dr. would have been rather little for a whole course. Euenus (p. 45 below) charged 5 minae, and Isocrates about the year 390 mentions 3–4 minae as the price for which Sophists are prepared to impart their secrets.

[2] See Philostr. *V.S.* 1.9.5 (DK, 82 A 1) and Gorgias frr. 5 a–9.

[3] Empedocles at Olympia, D.L. 8.66; his poems recited there by a rhapsode, *ibid.* 63; Xenophanes αὐτὸς ἐρραψῴδει τὰ ἑαυτοῦ, *idem* 9.18. For the poets' garb see Morrison, *Durham U.J.* 1949, 58, n. 21.

recitation at a pan-Hellenic festival, or in one of the cities,[1] was a way of making a new work known. Formerly the subjects had been poems, especially epic poems, and, although by the fifth century the public reading of prose authors was also common,[2] the elaborate epideictic rhetoric of the Sophists, when performed at the Olympian or Pythian games, aimed at something further. It was (and this is the second point) agonistic, competing for prizes in set contests as did the poets, musicians and athletes. Hippias speaks of 'entering the lists' (ἀγωνί-ζεσθαι) at Olympia and being unbeaten (*Hipp. Min.* 364a). This competitiveness came to be a general characteristic of the Sophists. For Protagoras any discussion is a 'verbal battle', in which one must be victor and the other vanquished (*Prot.* 335a), in contrast to Socrates's expressed ideal of the 'common search', one helping the other that both may come nearer the truth. The contest, said Gorgias, needs both boldness and wit, for the argument, like the herald at Olympia, summons whoever will come, but crowns only those who can succeed.[3] Thucydides is contrasting himself with the Sophists when he says that his own work is not intended as a 'competition-piece for a single occasion' but a possession for all time. As often, Euripides makes his characters speak in true contemporary sophistic style when Creon's herald sings the praises of monarchy as opposed to democracy and Theseus replies (*Suppl.* 427f.): 'Since you yourself have started this competition, listen to me; for it is you who have proposed a battle of words.'[4] Thirdly, the festivals were occasions for

---

[1] Isocrates comments on the fact that the first founders of the great festivals instituted athletic contests only, and praises Athens as a city where one can see 'contests not only of speed and strength but also of speech and wit and other accomplishments, for which prizes of great value are awarded' (*Paneg.* 1ff., 45). Isocrates made this speech at the age of 92, some half-dozen years after the death of Plato, but cf. Cleon's criticism of the Athenians in Thucydides (3.38.4, ἀγωνοθετοῦντες ... θεαταὶ τῶν λόγων).

[2] Plutarch, *Mal. Hdt.* 862, speaks of Herodotus reading his work to the Athenians. Thuc. 1.21.1 and 22.4 compares the effect of *hearing* the work of logographers and hearing his own. (Nestle, *VMzuL*, 260 with n. 41.)

[3] Gorgias fr. 8 DK. DK translate as if ὁ γάρ τοι λόγος καθάπερ τὸ κήρυγμα were simply τὸ γὰρ κήρυγμα. Whether this is due to inadvertence, or they intended to impute the mention of the λόγος to Clement, I do not know (they give no note on the passage), but the elaborate balance of the clauses shows that Clement is giving a verbatim extract from the rhetorician, and I see no reason to suppose that the simile is an importation of his own.

[4] With ἀγώνισμα and ἁμίλλας in these lines cf. D.L. 9.52 of Protagoras καὶ πρῶτος ... λόγων ἀγῶνας ἐποιήσατο, and Plato, *Prot.* 335a, where Protagoras says πολλοῖς ἤδη εἰς ἀγῶνα λόγων ἀφικόμην ἀνθρώποις.

members of all the Greek city-states to meet together and forget their differences, and the public appearance there of the Sophists was symbolic of a pan-Hellenic outlook that went naturally with their habit of staying in different cities in turn. Gorgias was as welcome in Larissa as in Athens, and Hippias (even more remarkably) in Athens as in Sparta. The subject of Gorgias's Olympic oration was *homonoia*, concord, and his advice, which he repeated in his Athenian funeral oration, was that Greek states should turn their arms against the barbarians, not against each other. We have already seen Hippias upholding the brotherhood of all Greeks.[1]

(d) Interests and general outlook

It is an exaggeration to say, as has often been said,[2] that the Sophists had nothing in common save the fact that they were professional teachers, no common ground in the subjects that they taught or the mentality which these produced. One subject at least they all practised and taught in common: rhetoric or the art of the *logos*.[3] In Athens in the mid fifth century to be an effective speaker was the key to power. 'The word is a mighty despot', as Gorgias said in one of his surviving declamations (*Hel.* 8, DK, II, 290); and with the art of *logos* would go all that was necessary for a successful political career. When young Hippocrates is asked what he thinks a Sophist is, he replies: 'A master of the art of making clever speakers' (*Prot.* 312d). The speaker's art they practised themselves, taught personally, and expounded in written handbooks (*technai*) covering both rhetorical argument and the correct use of language in general.[4] All save Gorgias would admit

---

[1] Gorgias A 1 (Philostr. 1.9.5), and fr. 5b. Plato, *Meno* 70b, *Hipp. Maj.* 283b.

[2] E.g. T. Gomperz, *Gr. Th.* 1, 415: 'It is illegitimate, if not absurd, to speak of a sophistic mind, sophistic morality, sophistic scepticism and so forth.' (Even the bare fact of being professional teachers can have an effect: some at least would be prepared to maintain that there is such a thing as a schoolmasterly or donnish mind.) For a similar point of view see H. Gomperz, *Soph. u. Rh.* 39.

[3] See the evidence collected by E. L. Harrison, *Phoenix*, 1964, 190ff., nn. 41 and 42. Schmid's contention (*Gesch. gr. Lit.* 1.3.1,56f.) that rhetoric was unknown among the early Sophists and introduced by Gorgias in the last third of the century is not borne out by the evidence.

[4] For the written *technai* see Plato, *Phaedr.* 271c οἱ νῦν γράφοντες... τέχνας λόγων and cf. 266d. Isocrates, *In Soph.* 19, speaks of 'those of an earlier generation' who wrote τὰς καλουμένας τέχνας. Protagoras's ὀρθοέπεια is mentioned in the same context by Plato (267c; see p. 205, n. 2, below), and the list of his works in D.L. includes τέχνη ἐριστικῶν. According to Plato (*Soph.* 232d) he published sets of arguments to enable a man to hold his own against

to being teachers of *areté* (of which, as understood by them, the art of persuasive speech was a prerequisite), and one may suspect that Gorgias's disclaimer was a little disingenuous (pp. 271 f. below): his teaching of rhetoric was aimed at securing for his pupils the same kind of success in life that Protagoras promised as a teacher of *politiké areté*.[1] In accordance with their claim to be the educational successors of the poets, the Sophists included in their art of *logoi* the exposition and criticism of poetry. This is well attested for Protagoras (pp. 205, 269, below), and another Sophist, Euenus of Paros ('fee 5 minae', Pl. *Apol.* 20b), who was especially interested in knowing why Socrates should have taken to writing poetry in prison (*Phaedo* 60d), also lectured on poetry, as well as writing it himself.[2] It is also recorded of Hippias and Antisthenes (pp. 282, 309 below).

Apart from this one overriding interest, many of them had their own specialities. Hippias prided himself on his polymathy and versatility. He not only taught mathematics, music and astronomy (which Protagoras derided as useless for practical life)[3] and had perfected his own system of memory-training, but claimed mastery over many handicrafts as well.[4] It has been said of the Sophists that they were as much the heirs of the Presocratic philosophers as of the poets. W. Schmid has claimed for Protagoras a debt to Heraclitus, Anaxagoras, the Milesian physicists and Xenophanes, and gives him the credit for making the paradoxical conclusions of Heraclitus and

experts in divers arts and crafts. He also wrote on grammar. For Gorgias see Plato, *Phaedr.* 261b–c. He τέχνας ῥητορικὰς πρῶτος ἐξεῦρε, Diod. 12.53.2 (DK, A 4). D.L. 8.59 speaks of him as ὑπερέχοντα ἐν ῥητορικῇ καὶ τέχνην ἀπολελοιπότα, and Quintil. 3.1.8 (A 14) puts him among the *artium scriptores*. Thrasymachus wrote a rhetorical τέχνη (Suda, A 1) which seems to have been known as the Μεγάλη Τέχνη (B 3). For something of its content see *Phaedr.* 267c with DK, B 6. Prodicus and Hippias are also mentioned in Plato's review of the βιβλία τὰ περὶ λόγων τέχνης γεγραμμένα (*Phaedr.* 266dff.), and Hippias's expertise in the minutiae of speech at *Hipp. Min.* 368d. Prodicus's passion for distinguishing between apparent synonyms is often referred to by Plato, e.g. *Prot.* 337c, *Euthyd.* 277e (περὶ ὀνομάτων ὀρθότητος), *Laches* 197d (ὀνόματα διαιρεῖν). More on this below, pp. 222f.

[1] Cf. E. L. Harrison in *Phoenix*, 1964, 188f. Bluck has pointed out (on *Meno* 73d) that *areté* according to Gorgias is there said to be 'the capacity to govern men', which is precisely what Gorgias himself, in the *Gorgias* (452d), claims to impart through the art of persuasion. See also p. 181, n. 2, below.

[2] See *Phaedr.* 267a. Some fragments of his elegiacs have survived, and will be found in Diehl, *Anth. Lyr.* 1.78ff. Aristotle quotes him a number of times.

[3] For a more definite reason for Protagoras's quarrel with mathematics, based on his general theories of knowledge and reality, see vol. II, 485f.

[4] Plato, *Prot.* 318d–e, *Hipp. Min.* 368b–d; Philostr. *V.S.* 1.11.1 (DK, 86 A 2).

Parmenides generally current in educated circles. (See *Gesch. gr. Lit.* 1.3.1,16 and 38.) On the other hand it has been said that they had no interest in natural philosophy at all. There can be no doubt that they were familiar with the writings of the philosophers and that their general outlook, with its rationalism, rejection of divine causation, and tendency to scepticism, owed much to them. This is not inconsistent with a fundamental difference of aim, and, making allowance for this, there was also a meeting ground in their common interest in anthropology, the evolution of man as a product of nature and the development of human society and civilization. But there is little positive evidence of a serious interest in cosmology or physical questions generally, though this has sometimes been claimed for Protagoras on the basis of a quotation in Eustathius from the comic poet Eupolis (DK A 11), who ridiculed him for 'pretending an interest in the heavens but eating what came out of the ground'. This is slender, and probably comic slander like Aristophanes's jibe against Socrates and Prodicus together as 'meteorosophists'.[1] In Plato's *Protagoras* (318e, a better source), Protagoras disclaims an interest in all such unpractical studies. At the gathering in the house of Callias (*ibid.* 315c), Hippias is shown answering questions about 'natural science and astronomy', and in the *Hippias Major* (285b) Socrates speaks to him of 'the stars and other celestial phenomena, in which you are such an expert'; but his pride was in the astonishing breadth and variety of the topics on which he could discourse. His acquaintance with each must have been extremely superficial, and there is no suggestion that, except possibly in mathematics, he had any original contribution to offer. Galen reports a work of Prodicus (fr. 4) *On the Nature of Man* which repeats the title of a Hippocratic work and shows an interest in physiology. Some fragments of Antiphon (between 22 and 43 in DK) seem to reveal an interest of Presocratic type in questions of cosmology, astronomy, earth and sea. Cicero speaks (*De or.* 3.32.126–8) of Prodicus, Thrasymachus and Protagoras as having spoken and written *etiam de natura rerum*; but he

[1] As Schmid notes (*Gesch.* 1.3.1,36, n. 3), after the trial of Anaxagoras μετεωρολόγος became a general term of abuse. One may compare also Plato, *Apol.* 26d, and, for Anaxagoras as the high priest of μετεωρολογία, *Phaedr.* 270a.

puts this in the right perspective when he connects it with the Sophists' claim to hold forth on any subject whatsoever and answer any question that can be put to them. Among the 'practitioners of every art', with whom Protagoras undertook to enable a pupil to argue on their own ground, would no doubt be the cosmologists and astronomers. The aim was to be a good talker and to make debating points, not to acquire a scientific interest in a subject for its own sake.

One branch of Presocratic philosophy had a profound influence on sophistic as on all other Greek thought: the extreme monism of Parmenides and his followers. Its challenge to the evidence of the senses, and rejection of the whole sensible world as unreal, inspired a violent reaction in the empirical and practical minds of the Sophists, who opposed it in the name of common sense. Protagoras, we are told, took time off from teaching political *areté* to write a work on Being which was directed against 'those who uphold the unity of Being',[1] and Gorgias in his *On Non-Being* showed his mastery of Eleatic argument by turning it against its inventors. Yet the Sophists could not, any more than other pretenders to serious thought, brush aside the Eleatic dilemma, which forced a choice between being and becoming, stability and flux, reality and appearance. Since it was no longer possible to have both, the Sophists abandoned the idea of a permanent reality behind appearances, in favour of an extreme phenomenalism, relativism and subjectivism.

The Sophists were certainly individualists, indeed rivals, competing with each other for public favour. One cannot therefore speak of them as a school. On the other hand to claim that philosophically they had nothing in common is to go too far. They shared the general philosophical outlook described in the introduction under the name of empiricism, and with this went a common scepticism about the possibility of certain knowledge, on the grounds both of the inadequacy and fallibility of our faculties and of the absence of a stable

---

[1] Protag. fr. 2. The informant is Porphyry, who mentions that 'by accident' he has come across this book himself. Some have tried to identify it with other known works of Protagoras. Bernays (*Ges. Abh.* I, 121), followed by T. Gomperz, Nestle and others, said it was only another name for the Καταβάλλοντες or Ἀλήθεια. For Untersteiner, on the other hand (*Sophs.* 11), this is incorrect, and it belongs to the second part of the Ἀντιλογίαι, while von Fritz (*RE*, XL. Halbb. 919f.) thought it might be an independent work. The title does not occur in D.L.'s list of Protagoras's works, which is however defective.

reality to be known. All alike[1] believed in the antithesis between nature and convention. They might differ in their estimate of the relative value of each, but none of them would hold that human laws, customs and religious beliefs were unshakeable because rooted in an unchanging natural order. These beliefs—or lack of beliefs—were shared by others who were not professional Sophists but came under their influence: Thucydides the historian, Euripides the tragic poet, Critias the aristocrat who also wrote dramas but was one of the most violent of the Thirty Tyrants of 404 B.C. In this wider application it is perfectly justifiable to speak of a sophistic mentality or a sophistic movement in thought. The Sophists, with their formal instruction backed by writing and public speaking, were prime movers in what has come to be known as the Age of Enlightenment in Greece. This term, borrowed from the German, may be used without too much misgiving to stand for a necessary transitional stage in the thought of any nation that produces philosophers and philosophies of its own. Thus Zeller wrote (ZN, 1432): 'Just as we Germans could hardly have had a Kant without the Age of Enlightenment, so the Greeks would hardly have had a Socrates and a Socratic philosophy without Sophistic.'[2] That Socrates and Plato could never have existed without the Sophists is repeated by Jaeger (*Paid.* I, 288), and this in itself would make them repay study even if they were not (as some of them are) important figures in their own right.

[1] This is expressly attested for Protagoras, Gorgias, Hippias and Antiphon, and can be confidently asserted of Prodicus, who shared Protagoras's view of the practical aims of his instruction (Plato, *Rep.* 600 c–d). It is traceable in later Sophists like Alcidamas and Lycophron, and it would be difficult to produce a clear counter-instance.

[2] Burnet (*Th. to P.* 109) complains of the influence which this 'superficial analogy' has had over German writers, and claims that if there is any parallel it occurs much earlier, and Xenophanes not Protagoras is its apostle. But Xenophanes was rather the first swallow that does not make a summer; the sophistic Age of Enlightenment means not only Protagoras but Prodicus, Gorgias, Hippias, Antiphon, Critias, Euripides and many others. Burnet's next remark, that 'it is not to religion but to science that Protagoras and Gorgias take up a negative attitude', is a strange one to make of the man who declared that he did not know whether there were gods or not. As a general rule such warnings against facile analogies are salutary, but the resemblances between the Enlightenment and the age of the Sophists are certainly many and striking. The relationship of the *philosophes* and their contemporaries to their predecessors in the ancient world, both Greek and Roman, is discussed by Peter Gay in *The Enlightenment* (1967), 72–126 (chapter entitled 'The First Enlightenment').

(e) Decline or adolescence?

To a hostile contemporary like Aristophanes, sophistic ideas were a symptom of decline. The great days of Greece were those of the Persian Wars, when men were men. Courage and hardiness, simplicity of life, high moral standards were all attributed to this immediately preceding generation. Now, he lamented, all standards are being abandoned and no one can distinguish right from wrong, or, if they do, they blatantly uphold the wrong and despise the right. The young generation are luxury-loving, effeminate, immoral and cowardly. Look at the drama: no longer do playwrights choose high and noble themes as Aeschylus did. Instead we have Euripides with his plays of adultery, incest and deceit, his flaunting of the mean and sordid, his endless quibbling talk. All this, thought Aristophanes, came of following the new atheistical science and the new morality of the Sophists.

This view—that Greece had already passed the peak of her greatness and that the Sophists were a sign of the times and by their own teaching hastened her decline—has tended to reappear in modern histories. On the other hand Karl Joël in the 1920s (*Gesch.* 674f.) was already seeing, in the intellectual ferment of which they were the leaders, not decline but the 'Rausch der Jugend'. Like the young they were ambitious, contentious, breaking out in all directions. In the same strain T. Gomperz (*Gr. Th.* 1.480) perceived in the rhetoric of Gorgias 'the streaming and unbridled vitality of an age in which the young blood leaps with a wayward pulse, and the mind's activity is in excess of the matter at its disposal'. Grant (*Ethics* 1, 76f.) worked out a division of morality into three eras: 'first, the era of popular or unconscious morals; second, the transitional, sceptical or sophistic era; third, the conscious or philosophic era'. (In the third era, of course, the three stages will exist contemporaneously among people of different education and intellectual powers.) He noted a parallel development in the individual:

The simplicity and trust of childhood is succeeded by the unsettled and undirected force of youth, and the wisdom of matured life. First, we believe because others do so; then, in order to obtain personal convictions, we pass through a stage of doubt; then we believe the more deeply but in a somewhat different way from what we did at the outset.

Now if one thinks of the great things that lay ahead—the philosophies of Plato and Aristotle, to be followed by the Stoics, Epicureans and other philosophers of the Hellenistic age—there can be no doubt that, however it may be with Greek history in general, with the Sophists Greek thought entered not on its decline but on its early manhood.[1]

(f) Rhetoric and scepticism

There was, we have seen, one art which all the Sophists taught, namely rhetoric, and one epistemological standpoint which all shared, namely a scepticism according to which knowledge could only be relative to the perceiving subject. The two were more directly connected than one might think. Rhetoric does not play the part in our lives that it did in ancient Greece. Nowadays the words 'success' or 'a successful man' suggest most immediately the world of business, and only secondarily that of politics. In Greece the success that counted was first political and secondly forensic, and its weapon was rhetoric, the art of persuasion. Following the analogy, one might assign to rhetoric the place now occupied by advertising. Certainly the art of persuasion, often by dubious means, was no less powerful then, and, as we have our business schools and schools of advertising, so the Greeks had their teachers of politics and rhetoric: the Sophists. *Peitho*, Persuasion, was for them a powerful goddess; 'the charmer to whom nothing is denied', Aeschylus called her (*Suppl.* 1039 f.), and Isocrates a century later reminded his Athenian audience that it was their custom to offer her an annual sacrifice (*Antid.* 249). Gorgias in his *Encomium of Helen*—a school exercise in rhetoric, sophistic in every sense—names speech and persuasion as the two irresistible forces. 'He who persuaded did wrong by compelling, but she who was persuaded acted under the compulsion of the word and it is vain to upbraid her.' Thus Helen is absolved from blame and depicted as a helpless victim, deserving pity, not hatred or condemnation.[2]

It was part of rhetorical instruction to teach the pupil to argue with

[1] The comparison of the stages of Greek thought to the stages of an individual life is also made by Cornford in *Before and after Socrates*, 38 ff. For further comment on Grant's division see p. 164 below.

[2] In Aeschylus on the other hand it is Paris whose hand is forced by Persuasion, 'the insufferable child of Doom (*Ag.* 385 f.). Pindar speaks of the 'lash of Persuasion' (*Pyth.* 4.219).

equal success on both sides of a question. As Protagoras said, 'On every topic there are two arguments contrary to each other'. He aimed at training his pupils to praise and blame the same things, and in particular to bolster up the weaker argument so that it appeared the stronger.[1] Rhetorical teaching was not confined to form and style, but dealt also with the substance of what was said. How could it fail to inculcate the belief that all truth was relative and no one knew anything for certain? Truth was individual and temporary, not universal and lasting, for the truth for any man was simply what he could be persuaded of, and it was possible to persuade anyone that black was white. There can be belief, but never knowledge.

To prove his point that 'persuasion allied to words can mould men's minds as it wishes', Gorgias adduced three considerations, which illustrate the way in which the Sophists' teaching grew out of the life and philosophy of their times (*Hel.* 13):

1. The theories of the natural scientists, each one thinking that he has the secret of the universe, but in fact only pitting one opinion against another and setting up the incredible and the invisible in the eye of the imagination.

2. The inevitable contests and debates of practical life [as in the law courts or the Assembly], where a single speech can delight and convince the crowd just because it is artistically and cleverly contrived, not because it contains the truth.

3. The disputes of philosophers, which only go to show the rapidity with which thought can demonstrate the mutability of opinions and beliefs.

In such an atmosphere it is not surprising that an epistemology should gain favour according to which 'what appears to me *is* for me, and what appears to you *is* for you', and that no man can be in a position to contradict another.[2]

(g) *Fate of sophistic literature: Plato and Aristotle*

Finally, a word about the loss of the Sophists' writings. Havelock has written of Greek liberalism, which roughly corresponds to what

---

[1] See D.L. 9.51 and Protagoras A21 and C2 in DK.

[2] For such opinions in Protagoras see Plato, *Theaet.* 152a, *Euthyd.* 286c. The subject is resumed in ch. VIII below.

is here called the sophistic outlook, that 'to chart its course with precision is a difficult task, impossible but for the twin guide-posts supplied by the *ipsissima verba* of these two men' (*L.T.* 255). The two in question are Democritus and Antiphon, and since on the same page he has to warn us that 'the chronology of Antiphon's life, nay his very identity, is in doubt'; since moreover the liberal temper is represented for him not only by these two but by Archelaus, Protagoras, Prodicus, Hippias, Gorgias, Thrasymachus, Lycophron and others, this is a somewhat pessimistic view. His suggestion that these are the only two contributors to the school of thought in the classical age who are documented by their own utterances is happily belied by what he says elsewhere.[1] Nevertheless it is true that the fifth-century empiricists are represented for us in the main by meagre fragments, or more or less hostile paraphrases, of the extensive writings which they produced. Hitherto historians had assumed that this, though unfortunate, was accidental: many other works of classical Greece have perished, not surprisingly, in the passage of upwards of 2,400 years. But their modern champions see a more specific reason determining the fate of the Sophists, namely the authority of Plato and Aristotle. Plato's idealism carried the day, and, since he himself would have liked to suppress the teaching of his opponents, his followers duly suppressed it; or at least, as contrary philosophies became entrenched, nobody saw reason to preserve what were generally considered unorthodox and objectionable views. So it has come about, to quote Havelock (*L.T.* 18), that 'the history of Greek political theory, as also of Greek politics, has been written in modern times exactly as Plato and Aristotle would have wished it to be written'.

Here again, like Sidgwick with Grote, one may say that these critics have a real point which others have neglected, but that they probably overstate their case. What they allege may have been part-cause, but other reasons, no less plausible, suggest themselves for the loss. It has been pointed out that in general the Sophists were not scholars writing philosophical and scientific treatises for the future.

[1] On p. 157 he speaks in the same terms of *ipsissima verba* of Thrasymachus, Gorgias and Protagoras. (For T. Gomperz, *Gr. Th.* I, 490, 'the sole surviving literary monument of the movement known as sophistry' was the Hippocratic treatise *On the Art* [of medicine]!)

They were rather teachers, lecturers and public speakers, whose aim was to influence their own age rather than to be read by posterity. Moreover, since much of their work was educational, of the handbook type, it would naturally get incorporated in the handbooks of later teachers, including Aristotle, which would be regarded as superseding it. Aristotle, besides writing his own *Art of Rhetoric*, compiled a summary of the earlier 'Arts', from their originator Tisias onwards, of which Cicero wrote that he not only lucidly explained the precepts of each teacher but so exceeded the originals in brevity and attractiveness of style that no one any longer consulted them, preferring to read Aristotle as a much more convenient exponent of their teaching.[1]

While on the subject of Aristotle it may be as well to issue a caveat against speaking of 'Plato and Aristotle' in one breath,[2] as if their opposition to sophistic empiricism were equal and identical. On the subjects in which the Sophists were primarily interested, Aristotle's standpoint was in many ways closer to theirs than to Plato's. True, he shared Plato's teleological view of the world, and on the question of realism *versus* nominalism he is usually supposed to have been a Platonist. That is to say, though he gave up the transcendence of the Platonic Forms, he continued to believe in the existence of permanent substances or essences corresponding to universal terms—*universalia in rebus* if not *ante res*. In general this may be true,[3] but his position is complex, and it cannot be asserted without qualification when we turn from his metaphysics to his treatment of human action both individual and collective, that is, his ethical, social and political theory. For one thing, he drew an explicit distinction between the aims, and in consequence the methods, of scientific investigation on the one hand and inquiry into the problems of human behaviour and character on the other. In the former, the most exacting standards of accuracy must be demanded, but these would be inappropriate to the study of

---

[1] Cic. *De inv.* 2.2.6. See Jaeger, *Paideia* I, 302 and Untersteiner, *Sophists*, 9. Untersteiner does recognize, as an additional reason for the loss, the different turn taken by the prevailing philosophies in succeeding generations.

[2] As Havelock regularly does, e.g. on pp. 12, 17, 18, 19, 32, 34 (five times) in his *Liberal Temper*.

[3] See however Miss Anscombe in Anscombe and Geach, *Three Philosophers*, 31 f.

human material, which is undertaken not for theoretical but for practical ends. In the *Ethics* he puts the point many times, perhaps most forcibly in the statement that to demand strict logical proof from an orator is no more sensible than allowing a mathematician to use the arts of persuasion.[1] In the ethical field the abandonment of Plato's absolute, self-existent moral norms or patterns had far-reaching effects, for it made possible a divorce of theory from practice, of knowledge from action, which for Plato had been unthinkable. Aristotle can write (1103b27): 'The object of our inquiry is not to know what virtue is, but to become good men', whereas on the Socratic–Platonic view 'to know what virtue is' was an essential prerequisite of becoming good. He openly prefers Gorgias's method of enumerating separate virtues to the Socratic demand for a general definition of virtue, which he calls self-deception (*Pol.* 1260a25), and in the first book of the *Ethics*, which contains one of his most sustained and effective attacks on the Platonic theory of Forms, we find a defence of the relativity and multiplicity of goods which might almost have been written by Protagoras.[2]

[1] 1094b25. See also 1098a26ff. (the carpenter is not looking for the same straightness as the geometer), 1104a3, 1102a23.

[2] The brevity of the above remarks may lay them open to a charge of over-simplification. In so far as Aristotle believed in the relativity of goodness, it was only in the first of the two senses enumerated on p. 166 below, and he was Socratic enough to combine it with a belief in a single function of man as such, resulting from our common human nature and overriding the different subordinate functions of individuals or classes. This and related points are well brought out in Lloyd's article on Aristotle's biological analogies in *Phronesis*, 1968, in which however one is conscious all the time of an influential figure standing in the background though never mentioned: Protagoras.

IV

THE 'NOMOS'-'PHYSIS' ANTITHESIS IN MORALS AND POLITICS

(1) INTRODUCTORY

The two terms *nomos* (pl. *nomoi*) and *physis* are key-words—in the fifth and fourth centuries one might rather say catch-words—of Greek thought. In earlier writers they do not necessarily appear incompatible or antithetical, but in the intellectual climate of the fifth century they came to be commonly regarded as opposed and mutually exclusive: what existed 'by *nomos*' was not 'by *physis*' and *vice versa*. It is with this use of the terms that we shall now be chiefly concerned.

The meaning of *physis* should have emerged clearly enough in previous volumes. It can safely be translated 'nature', though when it occurs in conjunction with *nomos* the word 'reality' will sometimes make the contrast more immediately clear.[1] *Nomos* for the men of classical times is something that *nomizetai*, is believed in, practised or held to be right; originally, something that *nemetai*, is apportioned, distributed or dispensed.[2] That is to say, it presupposes an acting subject—believer, practitioner or apportioner—a mind from which the *nomos* emanates. Naturally therefore different people had different *nomoi*, but, so long as religion remained an effective force, the devising mind could be the god's, and so there could be *nomoi* that were applicable to all mankind. 'Human laws (*nomoi*) are sustained by the one divine law' said Heraclitus (fr. 114, vol. I, 425), and for Hesiod (*Erga* 276, echoed in the myth of Protagoras, Plato, *Prot.* 322d) Zeus has laid down 'a law for all men', that unlike the beasts they should possess justice. This conception persisted in the Sophistic age. Even the rationalist Thucydides can speak of the self-seeking party politicians of his day as partners in crime rather than observers of the divine

---

[1] See vol. I, 82f., vol. II, 351–3 and 353, n. 1.
[2] See Pohlenz in *Philol.* 1948, 137 = *Kl. Schr.* II, 335, and the references in Ehrenberg, *Rechtsidee*, 114, n. 1.

law.[1] It appears also in the 'unwritten laws' of Sophocles's *Antigone*, which are divine and everlasting and which no mortal can successfully defy, as Creon learns too late (*v.* 1113; on 'unwritten laws' see pp. 118ff. below). But when belief in gods is undermined, and they are no longer 'current coin' (*nomisma*),[2] this universal authority for *nomos* no longer exists. Then the phrase 'unwritten law' takes on a new and more sinister meaning, appropriate to the political realism of the age.

The earlier history of the terms *nomos* and *physis* is interesting, but has been told more than once.[3] We have now reached the point where a new generation has divorced *nomos* from *physis*, as what is artificially contrived from what is natural, and sometimes what is false (though commonly believed) from what is true. The latter sense of *nomos* we have met in philosophical contemporaries of the Sophists: Empedocles denying birth and destruction but confessing that he conforms to *nomos* by using the terms, and Democritus declaring that sensible qualities exist only in *nomos*.[4] However, in the Sophists, historians and orators of the day (and in the tragedian Euripides, another spokesman of the new thought) the antithesis was more commonly invoked in the moral and political spheres. Here its more important uses are two: (i) usage or custom based on traditional or conventional beliefs as to what is right or true, (ii) laws formally drawn up and passed, which codify 'right usage' and elevate it into an

---

[1] Thuc. 3.82.6. And even Gorgias, who believed in suiting his rhetoric to the occasion (καιρός), could speak of war-heroes as observing the θειότατον καὶ κοινὸν νόμον (fr. 6).

[2] Aristoph. *Clouds* 248, playing on the two senses of the word. 'Coinage' is the commonest, but for the other see Aesch. *Sept.* 269, Eur. *I.T.* 1471, Pind. fr. 203 Bowra (p. 132 below).

[3] The fullest treatment is F. Heinimann's *Nomos und Physis* of 1945, reprinted 1965. In a notice of the reprint in *L'Ant. Class.* for 1965, E. des Places mentions some works that have appeared on the subject in the interval. Pohlenz's article with the same title in *Hermes*, 1953, is avowedly a critique of Heinimann's work. His article *Nomos* in *Philol.*, 1948, treats briefly the etymology and semantic development of the word. On *nomos* see also Ehrenberg, *Rechtsidee*, 114ff.

[4] Emped. fr. 95 (vol. II, 156); Democr. fr. 9 (vol. II, 440). Reminiscent of Empedocles is Hippocr. *De victu* 1.4 (VI, 476 L.) ὁ νόμος γὰρ τῇ φύσει περὶ τούτων ἐναντίος, where τούτων refers to the identity of becoming and perishing with mingling and separation. Cf. also *Morb. sacr.* 17 (VI, 392 L.): the seat of thought and feeling is the brain; the φρένες (lit. 'diaphragm', but used in ordinary Greek to mean mind or sense) have a name which is owed to chance and *nomos* and does not correspond to reality. In this sense the pair νόμῳ–ἐτεῇ or νόμος–ἐόν (or ἀλήθεια, cf. Soph. fr. 83.3 N.) comes close in sense to the common expression λόγῳ μὲν... ἔργῳ δέ. In Hdt. 4.39.1 λόγῳ could replace νόμῳ without detriment to sense or idiom. (Cf. 4.8.2.)

obligatory norm backed by the authority of the state. The first was the earlier use, but was never lost sight of, so that for the Greeks law, however much it might be formulated in writing and enforced by authority, remained dependent on custom or habit. 'The law', wrote Aristotle (*Pol.* 1269a20), 'has no power to compel obedience beside the force of custom.' To some extent this remains true in any society. As H. L. A. Hart has written (*Law, Liberty and Morality*, 51): 'It is of course clear (and one of the oldest insights of political theory) that society could not exist without a morality which mirrored and supplemented the law's proscription of conduct injurious to others.' In primitive society there is little if any difference between the two, for custom itself has binding force. Codification only becomes necessary at a fairly advanced stage of civilization. Hence, in origin, the oscillation of the word between the two ideas. Since, however, they are already separated for us, and no English word has the same coverage, it will be best to retain the Greek. It will serve to remind us that, since the same word *nomos* expressed both ideas, 'the distinction between what is legally enforceable and what is morally right was much less clear-cut among the Greeks than it is with us'.[1]

It will be convenient to deal under separate headings with topics which are normally regarded as distinct, but an examination of the *nomos–physis* antithesis (the effects of which have been outlined in an introductory way in the previous chapter) must come first, because it will be found to enter into most of the questions of the day. Discussion of religion turned on whether gods existed by *physis*—in reality—or only by *nomos*; of political organization, on whether states arose by divine ordinance, by natural necessity or by *nomos*; of cosmopolitanism, on whether divisions within the human race are natural or only a

[1] Dodds, *Gorgias*, 266. Heinimann (*N. u. Ph.* 78) quotes passages from Hdt. to show that there was no sharp distinction in his time between the two senses, custom and law. The original coincidence of custom and law (noted by Pohlenz in *Hermes*, 1953, 426) has an obvious bearing on the question of 'unwritten laws'. The derivative verb νομίζειν has a similar range, though the sense of law-making is rarer and that of believing much the commonest. The two occur together in Xen. *Rep. Lac.* 2.4: Lycurgus ἐνόμιζεν ἐνὶ ἱματίῳ δι' ἔτους προσεθίζεσθαι, νομίζων οὕτως... ἄμεινον ἂν παρεσκευάσθαι. It means 'to make a practice of' in Hdt. 4.59.2: the Scythians νηοὺς οὐ νομίζουσι ποιεῖν — it is not their *nomos*. In the same chapter it occurs in the sense 'believe in' (gods) and 'believe that' (Ge is the wife of Zeus). That in the indictment of Socrates θεοὺς οὐ νομίζων indicates actual disbelief is shown below, p. 237, n. 2. The sense 'to set up, institute' appears in Thuc. 2.38, and cf. Arist. *Pol.* 1275b7.

matter of *nomos*; of equality, on whether the rule of one man over another (slavery) or one nation over another (empire) is natural and inevitable, or only by *nomos*; and so on. The plan involves a risk of overlapping, which must be kept in check; but a little may even be desirable, to show how the various questions were interlocked in contemporary thought. This chapter will explain the antithesis itself in more detail, and the ways in which, once established, it led to very different estimates of the relative value of *physis* and *nomos* in the moral and political field.

The question who was responsible for the distinction in the first place has often been discussed, but is probably unreal, and at least un-answerable on the evidence we have. Aristotle called it a widespread *topos* recognized by 'all the men of old' as a means of trapping an opponent into paradox (*Soph. El.* 173 a 7). Heinimann cites a passage in the Hippocratic *De aere aquis locis* as the earliest occurrence, but the statement of it attributed to Archelaus (A 1 and 2 DK) is probably earlier, and in any case is the first known mention of it in an ethical context.[1] The slightly comic juxtaposition of physical and ethical in the version of Diogenes Laertius ('He said that living creatures first arose from slime, and that justice and baseness exist not naturally but by convention') is doubtless due to the naivety of the compiler, and we cannot tell in what words Archelaus expressed the thought; but it may legitimately remind us of the historic connexion between evolutionary physical theories and theories of the conventional origin of morality and law. Archelaus was a contemporary of Democritus.

---

[1] Heinimann, *N. u. Ph.* 13 ff. The testimony to the views of Archelaus pretty certainly goes back to Theophrastus's special study of him mentioned by D.L. (5.42). The context in the medical writer is anthropological and ethically neutral: he will describe the differences between different races whether these are due to νόμος or φύσις. As to date, Archelaus must have been older than Socrates, and Hippocrates was probably a few years younger, in spite of the rather loose statement of Aulus Gellius, *N.A.* 7.21 (*RE* VIII, 1803, Jones in Loeb Hippocr. I, xliii). Heinimann dates *De aere, etc.* to shortly before the Peloponnesian War, Pohlenz (who thought it was by Hippocrates himself) after 428, and from the way the distinction is introduced thought it must have been already familiar. He inclined to Archelaus as the originator. See his article in *Hermes*, 1953, and, for Archelaus in general, vol. II, 339 f., Heinimann 111–14. He was an Athenian of the Periclean age, contemporary with the first generation of Sophists. The combination of an interest in the origin of life with that of human society and laws recalls Protagoras, but it is impossible to assign priority between them, beyond saying with some confidence that Protagoras was the older man.

We are entering a world in which not only sweet and bitter, hot and cold, exist merely in belief, or by convention, but also justice and injustice, right and wrong.[1] Doubts about the order and stability of the physical world as a whole, and the dethronement of divinity in favour of chance and natural necessity as causes, were seized upon by upholders of the relativity of ethical conceptions and became part of the basis of their case. To see that this was so, we need only look ahead to the time when Plato took the field against them: to combat their distasteful moral theories he felt compelled to construct a whole cosmogony, in which the first place was given to intellect and conscious design. It is, he says, the idea that the cosmos has come about by chance that has made possible the denial of absolute standards of right and wrong (pp. 115 f. below).

Law, then, and moral standards enforced by public opinion, are not god-given as was formerly believed. They are something imposed by man on his fellows, or at best created by agreement to set a limit on the freedom of each individual. In this way

the use of history and experience helped to evolve a rather different set of standards, not of traditional moral goodness or badness but simply of success or failure, expediency or inexpediency ... None of the rules was absolutely rigid or invariable: they had always to be adapted to changing conditions ... The voyages of discovery ... revealed numerous different systems of morality ... To none of these customs, so infinite in matter and diversity, could 'permanent authoritie' be attributed. The idea of a universal moral law was, therefore, to this extent on the wane, and it became *pari passu* more credible to regard moral rules as merely customary and relative, as having grown up to meet the needs of particular people in given places and times. On this view, 'interest' was what seemed to underlie ethical standards, an attitude which readily lent itself to some sort of hedonistic or utilitarian interpretation.

This passage, which so well describes the changing climate of thought in fifth-century Athens, was in fact written about seventeenth-century England,[2] and could be applied with almost equal propriety

---

[1] This juxtaposition of physical and moral as equally subjective is made in connexion with Protagoras by Plato, *Theaet.* 171e–172a.

[2] Greenleaf, *Order, Empiricism and Politics*, extracts from pp. 197–9.

to the 'situational ethic' of today.[1] As we proceed we shall find plenty of reference to expediency or interest (τὸ συμφέρον) as a standard, especially in Thucydides. In the political sphere Untersteiner quotes a pleasing[2] example from Lysias: 'The first thing to keep in mind is that no man is by nature either an oligarch or a democrat, but each strives to set up the kind of constitution which would be to his own advantage.'

With this denial of the absolute status of law and moral values, or any place for them in the permanent nature of things, the stage is set for a controversy between the two, but admission of the contrast does not of itself decide the outcome. The place to be accorded to law and tradition was, in Greece at least, by no means determined by the initial admission that they are artificial, and men who agreed on that could nevertheless draw different practical conclusions from it. For convenience, three main positions may be distinguished: support of *nomos* against *physis*, support of *physis* against *nomos*, and an attitude of hard-headed realism or fact-facing which without passing judgment declares that the more powerful will always take advantage of the weaker, and will give the name of law and justice to whatever they lay down in their own interests. It will retain the name for as long as they keep their power.

(2) THE UPHOLDERS OF 'NOMOS'

(a) *Anthropological theories of progress*

'What is this pact but the means by which man, as a relatively weak and defenceless creature, is able to maintain a biological status, which otherwise he could never achieve?'

H. G. Baynes, 'Psychological Origins of Divine Kingship', *Folklore*, 1936, 91.

We have already had occasion to refer to theories of human progress which in the fifth century, as a natural corollary of physical theories of the evolution of life from inanimate matter, began to replace the

---

[1] Cf. *Time Magazine* (22 April 1966): 'The traditional values are giving way to "situation ethics"—meaning that nothing is inherently right or wrong, but must be judged in context on the spur of the moment.'

[2] Pleasing in its reminder of Private Willis in *Iolanthe*, with whose faith in nature as the arbiter of party-political allegiance the orator was not in agreement. The quotation is from Lysias, *Apol.* (or. 25), 8 (Untersteiner, *Sof.* IV, 74).

mythical idea of degeneration from a primeval perfection (see vol. II, 473). They can be traced in Democritus, and appear in the most diverse authors, in Aeschylus as well as Euripides, in the Hippocratic Corpus, the Sophist Protagoras, and the aristocrat Critias; and somewhat later in the tragic poet Moschion. Though Sophocles does not picture the original savage state, his praise of man's technical progress in the *Antigone* presupposes the same order of events. Prometheus, 'Forethought' or 'The Forethinker', may be brought in as the teacher, or left out; his presence seems to matter little. In Aeschylus he is there, but only as bestower of intelligence, who taught men to use their own minds. In Euripides the benefactor is unknown ('whichever of the gods it was who first gave us wits'), and in Sophocles it is man himself who by his own achievements has become the marvel of the world. Moschion, though later,[1] reflects an indifference already evident in the fifth century when he writes that the author of the process was time itself, whether aided by Prometheus or necessity or simply by the promptings of experience and nature.

According to these accounts, the first men lived like animals, without clothes or houses, in caves and holes. They had no idea of combining together, but scattered over the countryside feeding on whatever offered itself. Even cannibalism was resorted to. They died in great numbers, from cold, from diseases caused by the crudity of their diet, and from the attacks of wild beasts. At length their hardships impressed on them the necessity of combining for survival, and with the need for rational communication they gradually learned to turn their inarticulate cries into speech. They also proceeded, through a stage of storing wild produce for the winter, to cultivation of the soil and the growing of corn and vines. This marked the beginning of civilized life in communities, recognition of the rights of others and the rudiments of law and order. Demeter giver of grain was also Thesmophoros, Law-bringer. After all, as Rousseau pertinently remarked, who would be so absurd as to take the trouble of cultivating

---

[1] Possibly third century B.C. See Diehl in *RE*, XXXI. Halbb. 345. The author of the Hippocratic *De vet. medicina* (ch. 14; 1, 600 L.) says that although medicine is a purely human art, developed by rational investigation, its inventors thought it worthy of being attributed to a god, as indeed it commonly is (ὡς καὶ νομίζεται); Edelstein's *Idea of Progress*, 54, n. 71, is open to correction on this point.

a field, if the state of society was such that it might be stripped of its crop by anyone who took a liking to it?[1] This comes out particularly in the claim of the Athenians to have been the originators both of corn-growing and of laws and constitutional government.[2] Side by side with these advances we read of the domestication of animals and the acquisition of technical skills. Houses and cities were built, the use of fire made cookery possible and led to the extraction and working of metals, ships were launched and overseas trade developed, and disease was held in check. Greek doctors saw the maintenance of health as very largely a matter of correct diet, and for the fifth-century author of *On Ancient Medicine* (ch. 3; 1, 576–8 L.) the healing art began when cultivated foodstuffs, cooked meals and a balanced diet replaced the 'animal-like' regime of primitive man, a process which in his opinion covered a lengthy period of time, and was brought about [not by Asclepius but] by 'necessity'.

These soberly rationalistic accounts of human development are in strong contrast to the older religious conceptions of degeneration from an age of perfection, the 'golden race' of Hesiod or the 'age of Love' in Empedocles, when the goodness of man was matched by the kindly abundance of nature.[3] The coincidences, of thought and also of vocabulary, between the various authors[4] strongly suggest a common source, which may possibly have been Xenophanes, the long-lived poet and philosopher who probably survived until about 470 (vol. 1, 362f.). At least the lines (fr. 18) in which he says that 'the gods did not reveal all things to men from the beginning, but in course of time,

---

[1] *Origin of Inequality*, Everyman ed. 188. Cf. the quotation from Grotius about Ceres Legislatrix on p. 217.

[2] See especially the passages of Moschion, Diodorus (13.26.3) and Isocrates on 82, 83, 84 below. Agriculture does of course imply the change from a nomadic to a settled form of life, though this is not expressly mentioned in our sources. The connexion was helped by the associations of the word ἥμερος, meaning (*a*) cultivated as opposed to wild crops, (*b*) gentle or civilized as opposed to savage, a combination which no English word provides. Cf. esp. Moschion fr. 6.23 Nauck καρπὸς ἡμέρου τροφῆς with 29 ἥμερον βίον, and Diod. 13.26.3: the Athenians shared their τροφῆς ἡμέρου with other Greeks and brought them εἰς ἥμερον καὶ δικαίαν συμβίωσιν.

On the relationship between θεσμός and νόμος see Ehrenberg, *Rechtsidee*, ch. 3, esp. p. 123.

[3] A more detailed description than can be given here, together with some interesting attempts to combine the two, like that of Dicaearchus in the fourth century, will be found in my *In the Beginning*, chs. 4 and 5.

[4] See the translations on pp. 79ff. below, with notes drawing attention to some of the repeated key-words or -phrases.

by searching, they find out better' show him to have been a believer
in progress, not degeneration, and seem to foreshadow the detailed
expositions of the advancement of civilization which we find in the
younger writers.[1] Whether or not he expanded his statement on these
lines, he certainly passed on the idea, which fitted well with his tirades
against the religious outlook of Homer and Hesiod.[2] Wherever it
came from, it gained wide currency in the secular atmosphere of the
fifth century.

The adherents of these historical theories were obviously on the
side of *nomos*, while at the same time rejecting any idea of it as innate
in human nature from the beginning or divinely ordained. Critias,
Isocrates and Moschion all name *nomoi* as the means of raising human
life above the level of the beasts. The climax of the *Antigone* chorus
is the declaration that technical achievements in themselves are
neutral: they may bring man to evil as well as to good. The essential
is that he observe *nomoi* and follow justice. Unlike the characters in
Critias and Moschion, Euripides's Theseus is pious: he attributes
man's progress from brutality to civilization to an unnamed god,
though from indications elsewhere one may doubt whether Euripides
himself did. In any case his moral is the same: avoid pride (τὸ γαυρόν);
the ideal is the man of middle status who 'preserves the *kosmos* which
the state ordains' (*vv.* 244f.).

(*b*) *Protagoras on the original state of man*

A holder of the progress theory who can claim to be a philosopher in
his own right is Protagoras, the first and greatest of the Sophists. In
the list of his works appears a title which may be translated 'On the
Original State of Man',[3] and it will be assumed here that when Plato

[1] For a full (perhaps too full) commentary on these lines see Edelstein, *Idea of Progress*,
ch. 1.

[2] One word which must have stood in the original, if there was one, is θηριώδης (p. 80, n. 2,
below). This tells against the expansion occurring in the context of fr. 18, which is purely
hexametric, but it could have come in one of his iambic or mixed poems. It should be added,
however, that the idea of progress as a human achievement may be traced back to the early
sixth century. See O'Brien, *Socr. Paradoxes*, 59f., on the stories of Phoroneus and Palamedes.

[3] περὶ τῆς ἐν ἀρχῇ καταστάσεως, D.L. 9.55. The title would be unsuited to a cosmogony, even
if we did not know that Protagoras's main interest was in humanity. (Lesky also translates it as
referring to man, *HGL*, 345.) The words of Democritus fr. 278 are sometimes compared: to
have children is believed to be a necessity for men ἀπὸ φύσιος καὶ καταστάσιός τινος ἀρχαίης.

puts into his mouth a speech on that topic he is substantially reproducing Protagoras's own views, most probably as given in the work so named.[1] The passage in question is *Prot.* 320c ff. Protagoras has made his claim to teach political *areté* (pp. 38f. above), and Socrates has expressed doubts whether it can be taught. He objects (*a*) that on subjects which are taught and learned, like architecture or naval design, the Athenians will only accept the advice of experts, but on general policy they allow anyone to give advice, evidently because they do not think of this as a technical subject calling for training; (*b*) that good and wise statesmen prove unable to impart their political gifts to others, even their own sons. Protagoras offers to give his views either as a reasoned argument or in the form of a story or parable, and, when his audience leave it to him, chooses the story as likely to give more pleasure. This warns us plainly that the introduction of the gods is not to be taken seriously, but can be stripped away as adornment to the tale. Plato knew well that Protagoras was a religious

More to the point is Moschion's announcement (fr. 6.2) that he will explain ἀρχὴν βροτείου καὶ κατάστασιν βίου, which seems to be an echo of Protagoras. Nestle plausibly suggested (*VM₇uL*, 282) that the original was a public lecture (ἐπίδειξις), which would have included even the mythical form, like Prodicus's 'Choice of Heracles' of which Xenophon says (*Mem.* 2.1.21) πλείστοις ἐπιδείκνυται. Note that Plato's Socrates too speaks of Protagoras as τοσαῦτα ἐπιδειξάμενος (*Prot.* 328d). See also p. 319 below.

[1] This is the opinion of a large majority of scholars. For summary of opinions see Untersteiner, *Sophs.* 72, n. 24, who agrees with it, and Havelock, *L.T.* 407–9, who does not; also O'Brien, *Socr. Paradoxes*, 62f. To those in favour may be added Heinimann, *N. u. Ph.* 115, Schmid, *Gesch. gr. Lit.* 1.3.1,17, n. 10, Versényi, *Socr. Hum.* 23, and Bignone, *Studi* 22, n. 2; to those against, Capizzi, *Protagora*, 259. Cf. also von Fritz in *RE*, xlv. Halbb. 917.

The opposition of Havelock is to some extent based on the rhetorical question (*L.T.* 88): 'Why ... should a genius take the trouble to advertise in his own writings a system already in circulation and put out by a representative of a school of thought which he distrusted?', which in turn rests on his general belief that 'no philosopher in his senses will take the trouble to report with historical fidelity views which intellectually he cannot accept' (p. 165). What he does is to make a 'critical examination' of them. It is not explained how one can properly criticize views without taking the trouble to report them accurately first. It is possible to think better of philosophers than that. The books in the excellent *Pelican* series of historical studies of individual philosophers of the past are written by active philosophers who would certainly not subscribe to all the views of their subjects. A rhetorical question can usually be countered by another, in this case M. Salomon's (*Savigny-Stift.* 1911, 136): 'What interest could Plato, who speaks with no little respect of Protagoras, have had in foisting on him views which would have distorted and falsified our picture of him?'

The question has been exhaustively discussed, and there is little point in reopening it. Two arguments used against authenticity may be dismissed at once: (i) internal inconsistencies, for, as examination of the content will show, there are none of any seriousness; (ii) the contention that it is a parody or distortion designed to discredit the Sophist, for an open-minded reading of the myth and the *logos* which follows it leaves one only with feelings of deep respect for their author.

agnostic (cf. *Theaet.* 162d), and had no wish to deceive. In fact the myth is followed by a rational explanation of the main points, from which divine agents are wholly absent.

Protagoras has a difficult position to defend, and he does it with astonishing skill. If he admitted that virtue (to use the common English translation of *areté*) is a natural endowment of the whole human race, rather than something acquired by training, he would argue himself out of his job, for training in virtue is what he has just claimed as his métier. On the other hand he has undertaken to justify the principle underlying Athenian democracy, that questions of public policy are in no sense technical, so that the advice of 'smith or shoemaker' may be as good as any other's, which seems to imply that the necessary virtues are innate in every man rather than imparted by instruction. Both positions are maintained in the myth and the explanation which follows it.[1]

Technical sagacity (ἔντεχνος σοφία) is innate in man from the beginning, for in the myth it is bestowed by Prometheus at the moment when the first men see the light. It is only another expression for the practical intelligence (σύνεσις in Euripides) which is the first divine gift in Euripides and Aeschylus. Original also was the instinct for worship, because, as the myth puts it, men 'share in the divine'. This they would do both in the sense that reason was the gift of Prometheus, a divine being, and because the possession of reason was thought to be a mark of kinship with the gods. Protagoras himself probably recognized worship as something peculiar, and perhaps necessary, to man, without committing himself on the existence of its object.[2]

Using their native ingenuity, men soon provided themselves with food, houses and clothing, and learned to speak; but they still lived 'scattered', without cities, because although they had the 'craftsman's

---

[1] What follows is based on the fuller account in my *In the Beginning*, 85 ff.

[2] Protagoras did not deny the existence of the gods, but refused to discuss the question on the grounds that certainty was impossible (fr. 4 and Plato, *Theaet.* 162d–e). His friend Pericles said that our belief in gods rests on the honours that are paid to them as well as the benefits they confer (Stesimbrotus *ap.* Plut. *Per.* 8). Protagoras probably thought this evidence hardly sufficient. So Nestle, ed. of *Prot.* pp. 19 f. See further below, pp. 234 f. Similar language occurs in Xenophon, *Mem.* 1.4.13 (man is the only race that worships gods) and 4.3.14 (the soul of man τοῦ θείου μετέχει).

art'[1] they lacked the 'political art'. Consequently many were killed by wild beasts, against which the only defence for the physically weaker human species lay in combined action. Fearing, therefore, that the whole race would be wiped out, Zeus (in the story) sent Hermes to bring men two moral virtues, *aidōs* and *diké*, 'to make political order possible and create a bond of friendship and union' (322c). *Diké* is a sense of right or justice, *aidōs* a more complicated quality combining roughly a sense of shame, modesty, and respect for others. It is not far from 'conscience'. These gifts are not to be restricted to selected individuals, as with the arts, where one can be a doctor, another a musician and so on, and life be conducted on a principle of division of labour. All must share them, because 'there could never be cities if only a few shared in these virtues as in the arts'. Even Zeus, however, cannot ensure that they are universal, for they were no part of the original nature of man, so he adds the rider that, if anyone prove incapable of acquiring them, he must be put to death as a cancerous growth in the body politic.

Zeus's decree stands for what in the non-mythical anthropologies (and in Protagoras's mind) was the work of time, bitter experience, and necessity.[2] The story teaches two things about the 'political virtues': (*a*) in the civilized world they are possessed to some degree (ἀμῶς γέ πως, 323c) by everybody, but (*b*) they were not innate in men from the beginning. In the explanation following the myth he takes up both these points. The first one justifies the Athenians in demanding expertise in the technical arts but not in the art of politics, for which the prime requisites are justice and moderation. Everyone in fact believes that these virtues are shared by all. A man entirely

---

[1] δημιουργικὴ τέχνη, 322b. Comparison with ἀρετῆς... δημιουργικῆς at 322d affords a striking demonstration of the practical associations of *areté* and explains the (to an English reader) rather illogical way in which the account seems to treat technical skills and moral qualities as much the same sort of thing. The craftsman's art calls for technical *aretai* and the political man's for political *aretai*, which happen to be moral virtues. Cf. 322b ἠδίκουν ἀλλήλους ἅτε οὐκ ἔχοντες τὴν πολιτικὴν τέχνην. On statesmanship as τέχνη in the fifth century some interesting material is collected in O'Brien, *Socratic Paradoxes*, 67ff.

[2] Since writing the above I find that this point, which even now escapes most scholars, was made long ago by Kaerst in the *Zeitschr. f. Pol.* 1909, 513, n. 1: 'Der Umstand, dass im Mythos des Protagoras erst durch Hermes die δίκη und αἰδώς an die Menschen verteilt werden, soll natürlich nur die unbedingte Notwendigkeit der Allgemeinheit der Rechts- und Schamgefühle für das Bestehen des Staates veranschaulichen.'

without an artistic gift—say music—is a commonplace, but a man entirely without moral qualities could not lead a human life, and anyone who declared that this was his own case would be thought mad (322a–c). If Socrates ever met such a one—who *ex hypothesi* would be living in isolation, without education, courts of justice, laws or any other of the restraints of civilized life—he would regard the most hardened criminals of Athens as virtuous by comparison. Secondly, however, though the Athenians like everyone else believe that all have some share of the political virtues, they do not think of them as innate or automatic, but as acquired by teaching and effort (323c: these therefore correspond in reality to the decree of Zeus in the myth). The education starts in infancy, with mother, nurse and father, and is continued by schoolmasters, and in adult life by the state, which provides in its laws a pattern of how to live. Moreover the citizens prompt each other, for it is in our interests that our neighbours should understand the rules of organized social life (327a–b). In this continuous process it is difficult to single out a class of teachers of virtue, but this is no more proof that it cannot be taught than the lack of instructors in our native tongue would prove the same about speech.[1]

It is in this connexion that Protagoras produces his justly celebrated theory of punishment, with its enlightened rejection of the motive of vengeance or retribution. The passage is worth quoting in full (324a–c):

In punishing wrongdoers, no one concentrates on the fact that a man has done wrong in the past, or punishes him on that account, unless taking blind vengeance like a beast. No, punishment is not inflicted by a rational man for the sake of the crime that has been committed (after all one cannot undo what is past), but for the sake of the future, to prevent either the same man or, by the spectacle of his punishment, someone else, from doing wrong again. But to hold such a view amounts to holding that virtue can be instilled by education; at all events the punishment is inflicted as a deterrent.

Protagoras's view of *areté*, *diké* and *nomos* does certainly imply that raw human nature contains the possibility of moral advance,

---

[1] Echoed in Eur. *Suppl.* 913–15:   ἡ δ' εὐανδρία
διδακτός, εἴπερ καὶ βρέφος διδάσκεται
λέγειν ἀκούειν θ' ὧν μάθησιν οὐκ ἔχει.

though its realization is a matter of experience and education. As Aristotle said later, 'we are equipped by nature to acquire the virtues, but we achieve them only by practice (ἔθος)' (*EN*, 1103a24). Protagoras himself said (fr. 3, DK): 'Teaching needs both nature and practice (ἄσκησις: i.e. in the pupil).' It is this antecedent capability, varying between individuals, which he invokes against Socrates's other argument, that some good statesmen seem unable to impart their virtue even to their own sons. If virtue were distributed on the same principle as the other arts (326e ff.), with one practitioner to many laymen, the case might be different, though even there the sons of many artists, trained by their fathers, cannot hold a candle to them (328c). But as it is, everyone has some talent for virtue and everyone is continually having it developed by various, sometimes unnoticed, educative processes. In this situation, the advantages of contact with an outstanding father cannot have so much effect as the natural capabilities of the son, which may be very inferior.

As to his own claims as a Sophist, given that virtue can be taught, and is continually being instilled in an infinite variety of ways simply by the experience of being brought up in a well-governed state, we must, he modestly concludes, be content if we can find someone rather better than the rest at advancing us along the road, and that is all I claim to be.

(c) Other equations of 'nomos' with the just and right

For Protagoras, then, self-restraint and a sense of justice are virtues necessary to society, which in its turn is necessary for human survival; and *nomoi* are the guidelines[1] laid down by the state to teach its citizens the limits within which they may move without outraging them. Neither *nomos* nor the political virtues are 'by nature', but a 'return to nature' is the last thing that is wanted. The state of nature was uncomfortable and savage, with every man against his neighbour, and if persisted in would have led to the destruction of the race. Critias was on the same side, if we may take the quotations from his plays as

---

[1] At 326d Protagoras compares them to the lines ruled in children's copy-books when they are being taught to write. E. G. Turner in *BICS*, 12 (1965), 67f., is probably right in referring the words to parallel lines and not to a tracing of the letters themselves.

reflecting his own views.[1] This is plainly stated in the *Sisyphus* (fr. 25), and the interesting lines from the *Peirithous*, which belittle law in favour of character[2] as a guarantee of right conduct, do so only on account of its comparative weakness. 'The upright character no orator can pervert, but the law he often turns upside-down and dishonours with his talk.' In the *Sisyphus* too he pointed out that laws, relying on compulsion, could prevent open but not secret misdemeanours (fr. 25.9–11), a weakness which is also remarked on by Democritus (fr. 181). Democritus was another upholder of *nomos*, of which he offered an even more exalted conception. Law exists for the benefit of human life, and by obeying it we become aware of its excellence (*areté*). One should establish 'the *nomos* in the soul', the law of self-respect or shame which makes wrongdoing impossible even in secret. (See further vol. II, 495 f.)

Greek recognition of the supremacy of law, as opposed to the will of a king or tyrant, was something of which Greeks were proud. This is illustrated by the well-known story in Herodotus (7.104) of the reply made by Demaratus, the deposed king of Sparta, to Xerxes who had given him asylum. Before invading Greece, Xerxes asked him if the Greeks would fight, giving it as his own opinion that they would not, because of their vastly inferior numbers and because they had no overlord who could compel them to face such odds.

'They are free, yes,' replied Demaratus, 'but not entirely free; for they have a master, and that master is Law, whom they fear even much more than your subjects do you. Whatever this master commands they do, and his command is always the same. He does not permit them to flee in battle, against whatever odds, but compels them to stand firm, to conquer or die.'

[1] This is usually done without question, or even mention of the fact that the relevant passages are in the mouths of *dramatis personae*. The view of laws as man-made, to replace 'brutish disorder' with justice, is the prelude to an atheistical account of the gods as another human invention, delivered by the impious Sisyphus. Only Wilamowitz remarks (*Glaube* II, 216) that doubtless he received later in the play (which is lost) the traditional punishment. But when all is said, the motive was probably that which Aëtius attributes to the author (who he thinks is Euripides), namely to be able to disclaim responsibility for views which are really his own. (See Aët. 1.7.2, DK, 88 B 25: Euripides made Sisyphus the champion of his views for fear of the Areopagus.)

[2] Fr. 22 τρόπος δὲ χρηστὸς ἀσφαλέστερος νόμου. The same contrast between νόμος and τρόπος occurs in the funeral oration of Pericles (Thuc. 2.39.4 μὴ μετὰ νόμων τὸ πλέον ἢ τρόπων ἀνδρείας ἐθέλομεν κινδυνεύειν).

As a loyal Spartan, he claims only to speak for his own city, but Xerxes applies his answer to the Greeks, and the story is told with a truly Hellenic pride.[1] For an Athenian expression of pride in *nomos* one can quote the words of Theseus in Euripides, *Suppl.* 429 ff., beginning:

A city has no greater enemy than a tyrant, under whom in the first place there are no common laws, but one man rules, having taken the law into his own possession. There is no fairness in this. But under written laws justice is meted out impartially to the feeble and the wealthy, the weaker if slandered may speak on equal terms with the prosperous, and the lesser man prevails against the greater if his cause is just.

Pericles utters a similar encomium of law in the Funeral Speech (Thuc. 2.37).

Socrates was another who felt that the laws must in all circumstances be upheld. In a conversation which Xenophon reports him as having had with the Sophist Hippias, it is first agreed between them that laws are covenants made by the citizens themselves concerning what must be done and what not, and that they can at any time be amended or rejected. They are not therefore 'by nature', yet Socrates argues strongly that the essence of justice consists in keeping them, and that a state whose members obey the laws is both happiest and strongest.[2]

Law-abidingness begets concord, without which a city cannot prosper, while individually the law-abiding man is the most trusted, respected and sought as a friend. Even more striking is the scene in Plato's *Crito* where Socrates bases his refusal to evade execution on the ground that it has been decreed by the laws of Athens. 'Do you think a state can exist and not be overthrown, in which the law's decisions are of no force, but are disregarded and nullified by private individuals?' Here again his duty to the laws rests on nothing more fundamental than agreement—there is no hint of divine ordinance or

---

[1] A more lyrical appreciation of the Demaratus episode can be found in Gigante, *Nom. Bas.* 115–17. That Greeks fight better than Asiatics because they are not despotically ruled is also argued in Hippocr. *De aere etc.* 16 (II, 64 L.), a work possibly of the late fifth century.

[2] *Mem.* 4.4.12 ff. Cf. 4.6.6, where Socrates argues that those who know and do what is lawful in human affairs are just.

bond of nature—but Socrates has had the benefit of the agreement all his life, and to break it now would show base ingratitude.[1]

Another champion of *nomos* and *eunomia*, law and order, is the so-called 'Anonymus Iamblichi', a writer apparently of the late fifth or early fourth century.[2] His advice is aimed frankly at worldly success, and may be summed up as 'virtue is the best policy' and 'be what you would seem'. He has taken a hint from Socrates, who, says Xenophon (*Mem.* 1.7.1), 'always said that the best way to acquire a good name was to become what you wished to be thought to be'. Socrates however would hardly have included 'a ready tongue' among worth-while ambitions, nor made fame the end and virtue only a means to attain it.

The first necessity for success, says the writer, is to be born with natural gifts, but he is no aristocratic advocate of birth and breeding, for he immediately adds that this is a matter of chance. What is in a man's own power is to show that he really desires the good, and to devote the time and labour necessary to acquiring it, for in contrast to 'the art of speaking', which can be quickly mastered, *areté* demands long time and effort. Like Protagoras he sees both nature and practice as necessary, but he would evidently not have followed Protagoras in using *techné* (art, acquired skill) and *areté* interchangeably (see p. 66, n. 1), and his dismissal of the art of speaking as something in which 'the pupil can in a short time rival the master' is an almost Platonic hit at Sophists who made rhetoric the staple of their curriculum. *Areté* on the other hand is a matter of long nurture, of growing up in avoidance of evil in speech and action and pursuing and achieving good by protracted effort. *Areté* is here given the moral content which Socrates and Plato gave it.[3] It consists in using one's other gifts—ready speech, cleverness, bodily strength—in the interests of law and justice; if they are put to a contrary use, it would be better

---

[1] This magnificent passage is cited again in connexion with the social compact on pp. 140, 143 below.

[2] On these extracts and their author see pp. 314f. below.

[3] *Pace* Nestle, who says (*VMₜuL*, 425): 'That ἀρετή still has absolutely no moral sense is clear from the very fact that all these capacities may be put to the service either of the right and good or of the wrong and evil.' His following sentence weakens this one considerably, and in fact it is not ἀρετή but glibness, cleverness and physical strength which can be put to these contrary ends (DK, II, 401.16). These capacities have been *distinguished* from ἀρετή at the beginning of the extract (*ibid.* 400.3–4).

not to have them. To achieve perfect *areté* is to be useful to, or confer benefit upon, the largest possible number of people,[1] and this is best done, not by such crude and in their outcome dubious methods as indiscriminate charity, but by assisting the laws and justice, for it is they which create and preserve the union of human lives in political organizations. To achieve this calls for indifference to wealth, power and life itself. The reward will be an unfailing good name.[2]

To think (he continues) of power-seeking as virtue and obedience to the laws as cowardice is pernicious. (This attacks the kind of view represented by Plato's Callicles, but it was all too common in the late fifth century, and is equally exemplified by the assertion of Thucydides, 3.82.4, that in the general transmutation of values reckless aggression was reckoned courage, and moderation a screen for cowardice.) The reason for this is Protagorean: necessity forced men to combine for survival, and communal life is impossible without submission to law. Hence law and justice must be supreme: 'their strength is established by nature' (DK, 402.29f.). On the surface this seems to resolve the *nomos–physis* antithesis by identifying the two on the basis of the same facts which Protagoras had adduced: men's nature (physical weakness) would have brought them to destruction without political organization; therefore laws are an ordinance of 'nature'. But the reconciliation could only be accepted by a superficial mind. Protagoras, like other evolutionary theorists more conscious of the ages of suffering and experience endured in the gradual and painful advance towards civilization, could not see law itself as a provision of nature. Nature gave men only the intelligence which enabled them, as a tardy

[1] ὁ πλείστοις ὠφέλιμος ὤν, DK, II, 401.23. Kaerst (*Ztschr. f. Pol.* 1909, 516, n. 5) compares the Benthamite principle of the greatest good of the greatest number.

[2] The equation of virtue and goodness with τὸ ὠφέλιμον, the characterization of other 'goods' as indifferent and capable of serving bad ends (DK, II, 401.16–23; cf. Plato, *Meno* 87e), and the picture of the good man as self-controlled (ἐγκρατέστατον), indifferent to wealth, power and even life (on the grounds that no man can live for ever), make it difficult to resist the impression that the author was an admirer of Socrates and writing after his death. For himself, it is true, Socrates would have put εὐδοξία among the indifferents, but he recognized it as a general and legitimate human aim (Plato, *Symp.* 208c), and his death may have strengthened the opinion that it would accrue anyway from a life of virtue. The sentence at DK, II, 402.12, ὅστις δέ ἐστιν ἀνὴρ ἀληθῶς ἀγαθός, οὗτος οὐκ ἀλλοτρίῳ κόσμῳ περικειμένῳ τὴν δόξαν θηρᾶται ἀλλὰ τῇ αὑτοῦ ἀρετῇ, has a Socratic ring. I can hardly express strongly enough my disagreement with what H. Gomperz says on p. 84 of *Soph. u. Rhet.* about 'unerträgliche Tautologie und Selbstverständlichkeit', etc. In general he seems to have developed an unreasonable prejudice against this unfortunate author.

alternative to destruction, to organize themselves in this way. There is no disagreement of substance between the two accounts, and a genuine reconciliation between *nomos* and *physis* could only be effected, as Plato effected it, by seeing in nature not a series of accidents but the product of a supreme designing mind.[1]

Suppose, goes on the Anonymus, that a superman could exist. Grant him 'a body and soul of steel', exemption from the ills of the flesh, and a total lack of human feeling. Even such a one could not continue to tyrannize with impunity, for all men would be his enemies, and through their allegiance to law would overcome him by combined force or skill. It is not, as many believe, the strength and violence of the tyrant that bring him to power, but the folly of the citizens them-selves, for only a city that has already lost its respect for law and order can fall into his clutches. The extract concludes with a eulogy of the blessings of good government. Mutual trust (which Socrates also saw as the fruit of obedience to law) encourages commerce and the free circulation of money, the rich can enjoy their wealth in tranquillity and the poor are helped by the more fortunate,[2] men enjoy peace of mind and freedom to follow their private pursuits, untroubled by war or internal dissension and protected from tyranny. Law, says this democratic sympathizer, 'benefits the whole people'.

Most scholars would probably agree with the verdict of W. C. Greene (*Moira*, 251 f.), that the chief value of this composition lies in showing 'how far the stock ideas and arguments of the age penetrated into rather ordinary minds'. Echoes have been detected not only of Protagoras, Socrates and Democritus but also of Prodicus, Critias, Antisthenes, Thucydides, and even those stout opponents of *nomos* Hippias and Antiphon. Many of the supposed resemblances are commonplaces (e.g. the idea that to hazard one's life for one's country wins fame, repeated in Thuc. 2.43.2—but how often elsewhere?),

---

[1] The reconciliation also seems to be attempted in an interesting and difficult passage of the *Bacchae* (pp. 113 f. below).

[2] The idea of the rich helping the poor in a state of unity and trust recurs in Democritus fr. 255 (vol. II, 495), of which Cyril Bailey wrote (*Gk. Atom. and E.* 212) that, 'considering the general state of class feeling in most of the Greek cities, this is perhaps the most remarkable of all Democritus's sayings'. On the other hand it looks as if such a protest against class hostility was becoming common, for it is repeated also in Archytas fr. 3 (vol. I, 336) and Isocrates, *Areop.* 31–2.

and one can say little more than that ideas are here reflected which were widely current, though Protagoras and Socrates certainly seem to have been among the models. At the same time the passage offers some interesting points which are not matched in other sources: the attempted reconciliation of *nomos* and *physis*, the idea of the 'man of steel' and his fate,[1] and the combination of democratic ideals with a horror of mob-rule as the breeding-ground of tyranny.

The foregoing passages illustrate a respect for, and pride in, the rule of law as something firmly entrenched in the Greek, and perhaps especially the Athenian, mind, irrespective of whether laws were regarded as a product of nature or strongly contrasted with it. If the latter, they were hailed as a triumph of reason *over* nature, the symbol of man's ability to raise himself by his own efforts out of a 'natural' state of mutual conflict and destruction. Laws were not 'by nature' to Protagoras or Socrates, and Herodotus was fully aware of the variety and inconsistencies between the *nomoi* of different societies. Two passages which make these points, and afford further evidence of their wide currency, have been left to the last owing to certain doubts about their authorship and date, which however do not (at least in my opinion) seriously affect their value for our purpose.

(i) The second oration of Lysias, which purports to be a funeral speech for Athenians who fell in the Corinthian war, is an inept production, written probably as a mere rhetorical exercise and unlikely to be by Lysias.[2] Certain coincidences with the *Panegyricus* of Isocrates suggest that one imitated the other, but it is not so easy to say which was the imitator.[3] In §§ 18–19 the writer, eulogizing the early Athenians, says:

They conducted the city's affairs in the spirit of free men, by law honouring the good and punishing the wicked, for they thought it the action of beasts

[1] But see H. Gomperz, *Soph. u. Rhet.* 86, n. 187. There is a certain confusion (which Gomperz should have mentioned), at least as we have the passage in Iamblichus, between DK, 403.3 (*not even* a man of steel could overthrow the laws) and 404.27ff. (to do it *would need* a man of steel, not of flesh).

[2] Dobson, *Gk. Orators*, 92–4. Such judgments are admittedly subjective, and, although in this case I agree, it should be mentioned that Grote thought it 'a very fine composition' and Cope agreed with him. See Cope's ed. of Arist. *Rhet.* III, 120, n. 1.

[3] Blass, thinking pseudo-Lysias the imitator, put his speech after 387, but the argument can be used the other way. See Plöbst in *RE*, xxvi. Halbb. 2537.

to prevail over one another by violence; human beings should make law the touchstone of what is right and reasoned speech the means of persuasion, subjecting themselves in action to these two powers, with law for their king and reason their teacher.

(ii) Among Demosthenes's speeches is included one against Aristogeiton (no. 25) which, though some in the past have defended its authenticity, is generally thought to be spurious.[1] Behind certain sections of this speech Pohlenz (in *Nachrichten... Gesellschaft*, Göttingen, 1924, hereafter *NGG*) claimed to have discovered, as their source, a single lost discourse, of unknown authorship, enjoining obedience to the laws on theoretical grounds. This he dated to the end of the fifth century, remarking in particular that there was no trace of Platonic or Aristotelian doctrines. His conclusions won general acceptance, and 'Anon. π. νόμων' was freely cited, until in 1956 M. Gigante argued (*Nom. Bas.* 268–92) *first* that the passages in question cannot be isolated from the rest of the speech (which is indiscriminately eclectic) and assigned to a single model, and *secondly* that the speaker, both here and elsewhere, betrays an acquaintance with Plato, Aristotle and even Stoicism, and cannot be dated earlier than 300. His first thesis is convincing, and the 'Anon.' ought probably to be dismissed as a phantom, but the second is much less securely based.[2] The following passage from the speech is pertinent to the present theme:

(15) The whole life of men, be their city great or small, is governed by nature and by laws. Of these two, nature is disorderly [ἄτακτος like the

---

[1] Its authenticity was contested in antiquity. For the chief names on both sides see Gigante, *Nom. Bas.* 269. On the negative side may be added those of Untersteiner and Gigante himself.

[2] It is not obvious, for instance, why inconsistent definitions of *nomoi* in §16 should necessarily imply late date, and Gigante is apt to rely too much on single words or phrases, as when a mention of σωφροσύνη causes him to exclaim (p. 281): 'Socrate—Platone!' Again, he says that the sections could not have been written by a Sophist because the definition of law as a συνθήκη is not held to condemn it as a plot of the weak to defend themselves against the strong or the strong to oppress the weak, and in fact the definition itself presupposes 'the whole of the *Crito*' and Lycophron! In the preceding pages we have seen sufficiently plainly both that the definition of law as a compact was current in the fifth century and that not all the Sophists rejected it on that account. It does not appear that Lycophron himself did, nor in an earlier generation did Protagoras. When Socrates is portrayed by both Xenophon and Plato as holding that law was a συνθήκη the only sensible conclusion is that he did so, not that Plato inserted it gratuitously and falsely in the *Crito*. In protesting that the distinction between voluntary and involuntary faults betrays Stoic influence, G. does not even mention the strong possibility, noted by Pohlenz, that the correct text of the speech does not contain it. His postponement of this point until four pages later is hardly fair, nor are his arguments on p. 276 fully relevant to the theory of a gloss upheld by Blass and Pohlenz.

primitive state of nature in Critias and Diodorus] and varies with the individual, whereas the laws are common, agreed, and the same for all. Nature may be corrupt, and often has base desires, and men with such a nature will be found doing wrong; (16) but the laws aim at what is just, good and beneficial. This they seek, and when it is found it is published as a common injunction, applying equally and impartially to all. So there are many reasons why it should be obeyed by all, and in especial because it is a discovery and gift of the gods, decided on by men of wisdom, the corrector of faults both voluntary and involuntary,[1] and established by common agreement of the city as that by which every citizen should regulate his life ... (20) What I shall say is nothing new or clever or original, but what you all know as well as I do. From what cause does the Council meet, what brings the whole people to the Assembly, what mans the law-courts, causes last year's magistrates to make way voluntarily for their successors and everything to take place so as to ensure the good government and safety of the city? It is the laws, and the general obedience to them. Remove them, give every man licence to do what he will, and not only is the constitution abolished but life itself is reduced to the level of the beasts.

The threefold character of legal sanction, as described in §16, has naturally attracted considerable attention, and is universally criticized as an unintelligent juxtaposition of three mutually exclusive and contradictory accounts of 'the origin of law'. These are enumerated by Pohlenz as 'the age-old belief in the divine origin of the *nomoi*, the more modern one according to which individual legislators instituted them by virtue of their practical insight, and finally the latest and most widely accepted, according to which all *nomoi* owe their existence to a collective agreement of the community'. Further consideration of these views will give us a better insight into the Hellenic mind, and may reveal that to call them, as Pohlenz and others do, 'mutually exclusive' is to import our own viewpoint rather than enter into that of a Greek. It is unfortunate that Pohlenz should mention Lycurgus as his example of the second stage, for every Greek knew that, though a human being himself, he received his constitution for Sparta from

---

[1] Or 'faults of commission or omission'. So Pohlenz took the alternative text τῶν εἰς ἀμφότερα. The idea that ἑκουσίων καὶ ἀκουσίων ἁμαρτημάτων is a gloss on εἰς ἀμφότερα is attractive, for in themselves the words would naturally appear ambiguous and puzzling (as they still do). An alternative rendering is 'offences against both gods and men', which I do not find so grammatically incredible as Pohlenz did. (See *NGG* 29 = *Kl. Schr.* II, 324.)

Apollo. The Cretan who at the opening of Plato's *Laws* says that the laws of Crete and Sparta were owed to Zeus and Apollo respectively was not denying the work of Lycurgus.[1]

For the belief in the divine origin of laws (which he calls 'uralt'), Pohlenz gives references in a footnote (*NGG* 28, *Kl. Schr.* 313, n. 2) to five passages of the literature of the fifth and fourth centuries, but without quoting, still less discussing, the texts. Let us take a look at them, and see how far they indicate a general belief in the divine origin of laws as such.

1. Sophocles, *OT* 863 ff. Here the chorus are speaking solely of *nomoi* governing religious purity (ἀγνείαν ... ὧν νόμοι πρόκεινται), of which they very reasonably say that 'Olympus is their sole begetter, not did any mortal human nature bring them to birth'. What have these to do with the constitution of a *polis*? They belong to the so-called unwritten ordinances (ἄγραφα νόμιμα), of which Plato says that they ought not really to be called *nomoi*.[2]

2. Euripides, *Ion* 442. Ion, the idealistic young servant of Apollo, is shocked to learn that his lord has betrayed a mortal woman. Virtue should go with power. If a man sins, the gods punish him. 'How is it right for you, who have written the *nomoi* for men, yourselves to be guilty of lawlessness?' This comes nearer to supporting the generalization about 'a divine origin for *nomoi*', but, apart from the requirements of the dramatic situation, what is in question is a moral principle rather than positive law. This too, in spite of the metaphorical language about the gods 'writing' such laws, belongs rather to the 'unwritten ordinances' which were indeed believed to come from heaven. It recalls the conversation between Hippias and Socrates in which positive law as a human compact is distinguished from the unwritten laws which Hippias believes to be divinely sanctioned (pp. 118 ff. below).

3. Euripides, *Hipp.* 98. Hippolytus's servant asks him if he does not think an affable, courteous nature preferable to a proud and haughty one. When Hippolytus agrees, he continues: 'And do you hope to

---

[1] For further discussion of this point, with references to Tyrtaeus fr. 3 Diehl, Hdt. 1.65, Plato, *Laws* 624a and Plut. *Lyc.* 5 and 6, see my *Gks. and their Gods*, 184f.

[2] *Laws* 793a, to which Jebb pertinently calls attention in the note in his edition of the *Oedipus*.

find the same in the gods?' 'Yes,' replies Hippolytus, 'for we mortals adopt the *nomoi* of the gods.' This is simply an instance of the wide coverage of the word *nomos*, for it clearly means ways or manners rather than laws, and has no bearing on the origin of law.

4. Demosthenes 23 (against Aristocrates), 70, speaks of 'those who from the beginning fixed these usages [the word is not even *nomoi* but *nomima*], whoever they were, whether heroes or gods'. This is vague enough, but, apart from that, the reference is by no means general. It occurs in a high-flown eulogy of the court of the Areopagus, in which the orator has begun by mentioning 'many mythical traditions' about it (§65), for instance that the gods themselves once settled their quarrels there, or acted as judges, as in the dispute between Orestes and the Furies. Great emphasis is laid on the religious character of this ancient and revered institution, and the passage ends with the distinction between 'written *nomoi*' and 'unwritten *nomima*'.

5. Isocrates, *Panath.* 169. In this section leaving the dead unburied is condemned as 'spurning the ancient custom (ἔθος) and ancestral *nomos* which all men observe as not laid down by men but ordained by divine power'. This is the very sin which Sophocles's Antigone described as transgressing 'the sure unwritten ordinances (*nomima*) of the gods', and *contrasted* with the law that Creon as a mere human ruler had laid down!

The lesson of these passages is not that 'laws are of divine origin' but that there are certain divinely appointed ordinances (more often designated by the vaguer term *nomima* than as *nomoi*) covering religious observance or moral principle, which are distinct from the great body of positive law in a city like Athens.[1] Positive law itself, however, as the traditions about Lycurgus and other lawgivers show, could be regarded as the work of a man inspired by heaven and so of divine as well as human origin. This was an old belief, which admittedly was under heavy fire in the age of enlightenment. We need not suppose that when Pericles invited Protagoras to draw up a constitution for his new colony of Thurii either of them genuinely believed that he would be acting under divine guidance. Nevertheless the combination of 'gift of the gods' and 'decision of wise men' would by no means

---

[1] They are fully discussed on pp. 117ff. below.

appear inconsistent to a Greek as it does to us, and in the mouth of an orator would seem only proper. As for the third of Pohlenz's 'mutually exclusive' stages, what inconsistency is there in stating the truth that, although in a democracy like that of Athens a law could only come into force by the consent of the whole *demos*, it must inevitably have originated from the proposal of a single man? The author of the speech against Aristogeiton may have his faults, but the concentrated attack of scholars on this particular target is astonishing. To a fifth-century Athenian who still respected the traditions of his race, good law was a gift of providence, conveyed through the decisions of wise statesmen, and ratified by the consent of the whole city.

APPENDIX

Some passages descriptive of human progress

Aeschylus, *Prometheus Vinctus* 442–68, 478–506. (Aeschylus died in 456 B.C. and the *Prometheus* was probably his latest play. The speaker is Prometheus.) But hear the sufferings of mortals, how aforetime they were witless but I gave them sense and made them masters of their minds. At first they had eyes but saw to no purpose, heard but took no heed. Like dream-shapes they lived their long lives in utter confusion. They knew no houses of brick to face the sun, nor working of timber, but lived like crawling ants deep in the sunless recesses of caverns. They had no sure sign of winter or flowery spring or fruitful summer, but acted all without judgment until I showed them the risings and obscure settings of the stars. I discovered for them also number, that supreme device, and writing which is the universal memory and mother of culture. I first brought beasts under the yoke, that with bodies bowed to the collar they might relieve mortals of their greatest toil, and brought horses to the chariot, obedient to the reins, to be the glory of wealth and luxury. None but I invented the sea-borne, canvas-winged craft of sailors ... If one fell ill, there was no healing food, unguent or draught, but for want of medicines they pined away until I taught them to mix soothing remedies to drive away all diseases. I devised many systems of prophecy, I first judged which dreams were true visions and made known to them the secrets of omens and chance-met portents. I explained clearly the flight of crook-clawed birds, those on the right and on the left, the habits of each and their mutual hates, loves and gatherings; the smoothness of entrails also, what colour of gall-bladder is most pleasing to the gods, the subtle formation of the liver; and burning the limbs wrapped in fat, and the long loins, I brought men to a difficult art, and made plain the dim tokens of fire. So much for that. But as for those buried aids to human life, copper and iron, silver and gold, who could claim to have discovered them before myself? None, I well know, unless in vain talk. In one short word you may know all at once: all arts men owe to Prometheus.

Sophocles, *Antigone* 332–71. (Produced about 440. The lines are from a chorus.) There are many wonders,[1] but nothing more wonderful than man. This creature ventures over the grey sea when the stormy south wind blows, crossing in the teeth of the roaring billows. Earth, eldest of the gods, indestructible and inexhaustible, he harries as the ploughs year after year go to and fro, turning up the soil with the progeny of horses. The carefree race of birds he hunts and catches, and the hosts of wild beasts, and the tribes of the salt sea in the coils of woven nets—this cunning creature man. By his devices he tames the beasts of the fields and hills, he brings the horse and the tireless mountain bull to bend their necks beneath the yoke. He has learned speech and soaring thoughts and law-abiding ways in cities, and refuge from the tempestuous arrows of inhospitable frosts in the open air. Inventive always, never does he meet the future unprepared. Death alone can he not flee, but for dire diseases he has contrived the remedies. Skilful beyond expectation are the contrivances of his art, and he advances—now to evil, and again to good when he carries out the laws of the land and the just decrees of heaven to which he is sworn, proud of his citizenship. But an outlaw is the man whose reckless spirit leads him to consort with wickedness.

Euripides, *Supplices* 201–13. (Produced about 421. The speaker is Theseus, who represents Athenian humanity, democracy and rule of law against the claims of tyranny in the person of Creon's herald.) I bless the god who brought our life to order out of beastlike confusion,[2] implanting in us first of all intelligence,[3] then giving us a tongue to be the messenger of speech, that words might be distinguished, and crops to feed us and for the crops rain from heaven, to raise the fruits of earth and give us drink; defences too against winter's cold, to ward off the chill of the sky, and sea voyages

---

[1] The word is *deina*, on which see p. 32 above.

[2] θηριώδους. Also in Critias fr. 25.2, Diod. 1.8.1, Hippocr. *VM* 3 (1, 576 L.), Isocr. (*Paneg.* 28, *Antid.* 254, *Bus.* 25) and Ditt. *Syll.* 704 (vol. II, 324), have θηριωδῶς, and Mosch. 6.4 θηρσίν ἐμφερεῖς. In the Homeric Hymn to Hephaestus (20.4) men lived in caves ἠΰτε θῆρες until Hephaestus and Athena taught them better. With πεφυρμένου cf. ἔφυρον εἴκη πάντα in the Aeschylus passage (*v.* 450).

[3] σύνεσιν. Prometheus in Aeschylus says ἔννους ἔθηκα καὶ φρενῶν ἐπηβόλους (*v.* 444).

to exchange with others what our own land lacks.[1] And the hidden things, that we discern not clearly, prophets declare by looking into fire and the folds of entrails, and from the flight of birds.

Diodorus, bk. 1.8.1–7. (For the date of Diodorus's material see vol. 1, 69, n. 1, 11, 210, n. 1, and 389, n. 1. This passage follows an account of cosmogony and the origin of life from the action of heat on damp and putrefying matter.) So much for what our predecessors have said about the first beginnings of all things. As for the first generations of men, they say that they lived in an unorganized and beastlike way, scattering[2] out into the fields and gathering the most appetizing plants and the wild fruits from the trees. Warred on by wild animals, expedience taught them to help each other, and being herded together[3] by fear they gradually became aware of each other's characters. From meaningless and confused cries by slow degrees they articulated[4] forms of speech, and by agreeing among themselves on expressions for every object, created a comprehensible mode of communication about everything. Similar groups of men collected all over the inhabited world, so that all did not have a language that sounded the same, for each group composed its words as they chanced to come. Hence all sorts of languages exist, and the first groups to be formed became the archetypes of all nations.

Now the earliest men, since nothing useful for life had been discovered, led a painful existence, bare of clothing, unused to house or fire, and altogether ignorant of cultivated food. Not knowing how to harvest the wild food, they made no store of fruits against times of want, so that many of them died in the winter from cold and famine. From this state, little by little they learned from experience to retire to caves in the winter and to lay by such fruits as would keep. Once fire and other useful things were discovered they gradually invented techniques and whatever else was conducive to life in common. In general, men's teacher in everything was sheer need, instructing appropriately in every branch of learning a creature well endowed by nature, and possessing, to assist him in everything, hands, rational speech, and a shrewd intellect.

Moschion, fr. 6 Nauck. (Moschion's date is uncertain. He is now thought to belong to the third century B.C., but this passage is certainly in the spirit

---

[1] Cf. the reference to trade in Isocr. *Paneg.* 42 (p. 84 below), and the connexion between lawful government and trade in Anon. Iambl. (DK II, p. 403.16–18, p. 73 above).

[2] σποράδην as in Plato, *Prot.* 322b, Isocr. *Paneg.* 39.

[3] ἀθροιζομένους. ἀθροίζεσθαι in Plato, *Prot.* 322a.

[4] διαρθροῦν. So we have φωνὴν καὶ ὀνόματα διηθρώσατο in Plato, *Prot.* 322a.

of the late fifth or fourth century. The name of the play and the speaker are unknown.)

First I will go back and unfold in speech how human life began and was established.[1] There was once a time when the life of men resembled that of beasts. They dwelt in mountain caves and dark ravines, for as yet there was no roofed house nor broad city fortified with stone towers. Nor did the curved ploughs cleave the black clod, nurse of the grain, nor the busy iron tend the fruitful rows of bacchic vines, but earth was barren. In mutual slaughter they dined on food of flesh. Law was of small account, and violence shared the throne of Zeus.[2] But when time,[3] begetter and nurturer of all things, wrought a change in mortal life—whether by the solicitude of Prometheus, or from necessity, or by long experience, offering nature itself as teacher—then was discovered holy Demeter's gift, the nourishment of cultivated grain, and the sweet fount of Bacchus. The earth, once barren, began to be ploughed by yoked oxen, towered cities arose, men built sheltering homes and turned their lives from savage ways to civilized. From this time they made it a law to bury the dead or give unburied bodies their portion of dust, leaving no visible reminder of their former impious feasts.

Critias, fr. 25.1–8 DK. (Critias was killed in 403. The extract is from the play *Sisyphus*, and Sisyphus is the speaker.) There was a time when the life of men was disorderly and beastlike,[4] the slave of brute force, when the good had no reward and the bad no punishment. Then, as I believe, men laid down laws to chastise, that justice might be ruler and make insolence its slave, and whoever sinned was punished.

Sisyphus continues by expounding the theory of religion as the invention of an early legislator to prevent secret wrongdoing by instilling a fear of all-seeing gods. (See pp. 243 f. below.)

[1] ἀρχὴν βροτείου καὶ κατάστασιν βίου. Cf. the title of Protagoras's work Π. τῆς ἐν ἀρχῇ καταστάσεως. Moschion begins his story with the words ἦν γάρ ποτ' αἰών and Protagoras his story in Plato with ἦν γάρ ποτε χρόνος (320c).

[2] The reading Διί is not absolutely certain (Lloyd-Jones in *JHS*, 1956, 57, n. 24), though in my opinion extremely probable. The difference between the primitive and civilized eras is emphasized by the unspoken contrast here with the traditional belief that it is Law or Justice which sits enthroned with Zeus: Hes. *Op.* 259; Pind. *Ol.* 8.21 Διὸς Ξενίου πάρεδρος Θέμις; [Dem.] *In Aristog.* 11 (citing Orphic literature) Δίκην... παρὰ τὸν τοῦ Διὸς θρόνον καθημένην; *Oxy. Pap.* 2256 fr. 9 (A), v. 10 (Lloyd-Jones, *loc. cit.* 59f.).

[3] Cf. Philemon (Meineke, *CGF* IV, 54; Philemon was born c. 361 and lived to be a centenarian):

ὅσαι τέχναι γεγόνασι, ταύτας, ὦ Λάχης,

πάσας ἐδίδαξεν ὁ χρόνος, οὐχ ὁ διδάσκαλος.

[4] The same pair of Greek words as in Diod. 1.8.1; ἄτακτος of φύσις in [Dem.] *In Aristog.* 15 (p. 75 above).

On Ancient Medicine 3 (I, 574–8 L.). (This treatise probably belongs to the late fifth or early fourth century. See G. E. R. Lloyd in *Phronesis*, 1963. His conclusion is on p. 125.) Sheer necessity caused men to seek and discover the art of medicine . . . I believe that in the beginning men used the same sort of nourishment [*sc.* as the beasts]. Our present way of life, I think, has been evolved by discoveries and inventions over a long period of time. Many and terrible were the sufferings of men from their strong and brutish diet when they lived on raw and uncompounded foods of strong qualities . . . and it is reasonable to suppose that the majority were of too weak a constitution and died, while the stronger put up a longer resistance . . . So from wheat, after steeping, winnowing, grinding and sifting, kneading, and baking, they produced bread, and from barley, cake. Experimenting with many other foods in this way, they boiled, baked and mixed, combining the strong and uncompounded with weaker components, adapting everything to the constitution and power of man.

Isocrates, *Panegyricus* 28 ff. Isocrates (436–338) here puts the theories of progress to a patriotic use: the Greek world owes its civilization to Athens, for Demeter, in gratitude for the kindness she received there when searching for her daughter, granted to the city her two gifts of the cultivation of corn and celebration of the mysteries, with their hope of a future life. The first ensured that we should not live 'like the beasts', and he goes on (§ 32):

If we leave all this aside and look at things from the beginning, we shall find that the first men to appear on the earth did not lead straight away the kind of life that we now enjoy, but reached it gradually by their own joint efforts . . . (38) This was the beginning of our city's benefactions, to find for those in want the kind of sustenance which men must have if they are going to live a well-ordered life in other respects. For she believed that life that was mere subsistence was not worth living, and took thought for the rest, so that none of the benefits which men now enjoy, and which we owe to each other and not to the gods, is unconnected with our city, and of most of them she is the direct cause. (39) She took over the Greeks living in scattered groups, without laws, some groaning under tyranny, others perishing for lack of leadership, and rid them of these evils, taking some under her protection and acting as an example to others; for she was the first to lay down laws and establish a constitution . . . (40) As for arts and techniques, both those useful for life's necessities and those devised for enjoyment, some were invented and others tested by our city, which then handed them over to the rest of mankind to use ... (42) Moreover not every land is self-sufficient. Some are poor, others produce more than the inhabitants need, and it is a problem for them, in the one case to dispose of their surplus and in the other to find imports. In this difficulty too Athens came to their aid by establishing the Peiraeus as the emporium of Greece, so abundantly provided that everything can be obtained here which in any other single place it would be difficult to buy.

With the above passage of Isocrates compare

(a) Diod. 13.26.3 (speech of Nicolaus the Syracusan recommending mercy to the Athenian captives of 413 B.C.). The Athenians it was who first introduced the Greeks to cultivated food, which they had received from the gods for themselves and offered for the common use. They are the inventors of laws, through which our common life was transformed from a savage and wicked existence into a civilized and just society.

(b) to indicate the persistence of this idea, Ditt. *Syll.* 704 (vol. II, p. 324), an inscription of the second century B.C. containing a proposal of the Delphic Amphictyony to honour the Athenian *technitai* (theatrical artists). It states that the Athenian people brought men from a 'beastlike' state to civilization, admitted them to the mysteries, and gave them the boon of agriculture, laws and civilization.

(3) THE REALISTS

(a) *Thucydides*

To understand the temper of the age in which the Sophists lived, one cannot do better than start with the philosophic historian Thucydides. He is writing of the great inter-state war which was the background of Greek life for the last thirty years of the fifth century, and divided not only city from city but factions within each one. In his own words (3.82):

War, destroying the ease of everyday life, is a violent schoolmaster, and assimilates most men's tempers to the conditions around them ... The customary values of words were changed as men claimed the right to use them as they pleased to justify their actions: an unreasoning daring was called courage and loyalty to party, a prudent delay specious cowardice; moderation and self-control came to be reckoned but the cloak of timidity, to have an understanding of the whole to be everywhere unwilling to act . . . Applause, in a word, went to one who got in first with some evil act, and to him who cheered on another to attempt some crime that he was not thinking of.[1]

Thucydides has primarily in mind the effects of internal strife, but his narrative, especially in the speeches, shows these traits to have been equally marked in the dealings of one Greek state with another. It is remarkable how seldom even his orators, aiming at persuasion, see any point in appealing to considerations of right, justice or other normally accepted moral standards: it is taken for granted that only an appeal to self-interest is likely to succeed. Thucydides had an impressive insight into the minds of his fellow-Greeks, and may be trusted when he claims that he has heard some of the speeches himself and had first-hand reports of others, and that he has reproduced the kind of thing that they were bound to say on each occasion, while keeping as close as possible to the gist of what they actually said (1.22.1).[2] His reports supply the necessary background to an outburst like that of Thrasymachus in the *Republic*, and throw light on the current interpretation of such conceptions as human nature, law, justice, advantage or interest, necessity, and their mutual relations. Some illustrations from his work will therefore be very relevant to our theme.

The most famous example of amoral 'realism' is the discussion which he represents as being held between Athenian envoys and the small island of Melos, which the Athenians wished to force into their confederacy (5.85–111). The Athenians begin by saying that they will neither use moral arguments nor expect them from the Melians, because both sides know that by human standards *justice* depends on equality of power: the strong do what they can and the weak submit. Very well, say the Melians (ch. 90). To confine ourselves, as you wish, to considerations of *interest* (τὸ ξυμφέρον) rather than *justice*, we

---

[1] Trans. based on Gomme, *Comm. on Thuc.* 2. 384, with slight alterations.

[2] This sentence takes a pretty fierce bull by the horns. On the thorny question of the historicity of Thucydides's speeches, scholars seem a little inclined to have it both ways. Ehrenberg says (*S. and P.* 42) that he agrees with most scholars 'in taking not only the "form" but to some extent also the "spirit" as Thucydidean . . . but there remains the certainty that truthful reproduction (τὰ ἀληθῶς λεχθέντα) lies at the bottom of the speeches'. Can both halves of this statement be true?

claim that it is useful (χρήσιμον) as a general principle that those in danger should meet with fairness and justice (τὰ εἰκότα καὶ δίκαια) —a principle that you yourselves may need to invoke some time... (98) Since you forbid us to talk of *justice*, and bid us give in to your *interest* (ξυμφόρῳ), we will tell you what is good (χρήσιμον) for us, and, if it agrees with your interests, try to persuade you.

Later however (ch. 104) the Melians do venture to introduce moral considerations, claiming that in spite of their weakness they may hope for divine favour because they stand for right against injustice (ὅσιοι πρὸς οὐ δικαίους). The Athenians retort that this is unrealistic:

Our belief about the gods, and certain knowledge about men, is that universally, by *natural* necessity (ὑπὸ φύσεως ἀναγκαίας), he who is superior rules. We did not make this law (νόμον)... We merely use it and shall leave it to exist for ever. You would do the same in our position... Nor will the Spartans help you. More than any others they equate pleasant with good and *interest* with *justice*.[1]

Similarly in addressing the Spartans themselves (1.76.2), the Athenian representatives declare:

It has been established from all time that the weak should be subject to the strong. You Spartans, while really calculating your own *interests*, make use of the argument of *justice*, which never yet deterred anyone from seeking aggrandizement if he had the opportunity of obtaining it by superior strength. Those are deserving of praise who, while their *human nature* leads them to accept power, nevertheless display more justice than they are compelled to in their superior situation.

Closely parallel to this are the words of Hermocrates the Sicilian warning his countrymen against the Athenians (4.60.1):

Under the *legal* name of alliance they speciously turn their *natural* hostility to their own advantage... (61.5) It is wholly excusable that they should plot thus for their own aggrandizement. It is not those who seek to dominate that I blame, but those who too readily give in to them. It is universal human *nature* to dominate the unresisting, but equally to guard against attack.

Pericles told the Athenians frankly that they held their empire 'like a tyranny' (2.63.2): it might have been wrong to acquire it, but it

---

[1] Ch. 105: τὰ μὲν ἡδέα καλὰ νομίζουσι, τὰ δὲ ξυμφέροντα δίκαια.

would now be dangerous to let it go. Cleon, in advocating condign punishment for the rebellious city of Mytilene, repeats this more emphatically.[1] In his speech, which is more notable for audacity than logic, he does not shun the concept of *justice* but blandly accuses the Mytilenaeans of subordinating it to power (ἰσχύς, 3.39.3). By proposing to kill all their adult males and enslave the women and children, he claims to *reconcile justice* with *interest* (δίκαια with ξύμφορα, 40.4), since the Mytilenaeans have deserved their fate; but, even if it is wrong, he immediately continues, Athenian interest demands that they carry out the deed in defiance of decency (παρὰ τὸ εἰκός) unless they are willing to abandon their empire and turn philanthropists. He repeats that it is human *nature* to despise conciliators and admire the iron hand (39.5). The three things most fatal to an empire are pity, love of discussion, and humanity (fair-mindedness, decency: ἐπιείκεια, 40.2).

Diodotus, who opposed the atrocity, makes no more appeal to the finer feelings than Cleon. That would evidently not have served his case. He distinguishes *justice* and *interest*, and advocates consulting only the latter: this is not a law-court but a political assembly, and the sole point is how the Mytilenaeans may be best made use of (44.4). To take vengeance might be strictly *just*, but would not be in Athenian *interests*. Cleon misjudged when he thought the two coincided in the present case (47.5). It is the *nature* of everyone, state or individual, to do wrong, and no *law* can prevent it. Poverty induces recklessness, wealth leads to pride and lust for more (45.4). It would be simpleminded to deny that human *nature*, once set upon a certain course, will be deterred from it by force of *law* or any other threat (45.7).

The Mytilenaeans themselves, in appealing to Sparta for help, seem to know that appeals to justice or pity will not get them far. They begin (3.9.1) by saying that they well know what is the rule in

[1] 3.37.2. The same expression is taken off by Aristophanes, when his chorus of knights congratulate Demos (*Knights* 1111) because

καλήν γ᾿ ἔχεις
ἀρχήν, ὅτε πάντες ἄν-
θρωποι δεδίασί σ᾿ ὥσ-
περ ἄνδρα τύραννον.

The irony of a democracy which behaved like a τύραννος was not something which Aristophanes would miss.

Greece when a subject state revolts in a war: the other side accept it in so far as it is useful to them, but think the worse of it for deserting its allies. They go on to say (unusually for speakers in Thucydides) that they will next speak of justice and honesty (10.1), but in fact they say little about them, and are soon remarking (11.2) that the only trustworthy basis for an alliance is an equality of mutual fear.

Other instances of the relation between justice and interest occur in the speech of the Corinthians at Athens (1.42.1: 'Do not suppose that though what we say is *just*, your *interest* points in another direction, should it come to war') and of the Plataeans to the Spartans after surrendering (3.56.3). If, they say, you are going to estimate what is just by the standard of your immediate *advantage* (χρήσιμον), you will show yourselves no true judges of *right* (τὸ ὀρθόν) but rather servants of *expediency* (τὸ ξυμφέρον).

(b) Thrasymachus in the 'Republic'[1]

The theme of the *Republic* is the nature of justice or what is right. After some preliminary discussion of current definitions ('giving every man his due', 'benefiting friends and harming foes'), Thrasymachus bursts out that they are talking nonsense and, pressed to state his own opinion, asserts that 'Justice is nothing but the interest of the stronger'. Expanding this, he says that, whether a state is ruled by a tyrant, an aristocracy or a democracy, the ruling powers make laws with a view to their own benefit. By making these laws, they declare that to be right for their subjects which is beneficial to themselves, and punish whoever departs from them as a law-breaker and wrongdoer. Justice in all states is the same, namely what benefits the established government. Since the government holds the power, justice everywhere is what benefits the stronger.

In answer to questions from Socrates, Thrasymachus adds that, although he has said it is just for subjects to obey the laws laid down by their rulers, this does not imply that they should obey even if those in power happen, mistakenly, to ordain what is not in their interests. Like any other expert or craftsman, he claims, a ruler is not,

---

[1] *Rep.* 1.336b ff. The question whether the account in the *Republic* represents the views and character of the historical Thrasymachus is not raised here. For that see pp. 296ff. below.

strictly speaking, a ruler when he acts ignorantly or mistakenly, but only when he exercises his skill correctly. It is only then that he will command what is best for himself, and that the ruled should obey.

Socrates takes advantage of the fact that Thrasymachus has introduced the analogy between government and crafts like medicine, and, borrowing his phrase 'strictly speaking', claims that a craft as such does not seek its own advantage but that of the subject on which it is exercised (ἐκείνῳ οὗ τέχνη ἐστίν, 342b), which Socrates identifies as the body in the case of medicine, the horse in the case of horse-training and so forth. He concludes that the art of government, strictly conceived, legislates not for the advantage of those who practise it but for that of its subjects.[1]

You might as well say, retorts Thrasymachus, that shepherds study only the well-being of their flocks, whereas, if they keep them healthy and fatten them up, it is for the ultimate benefit not of the sheep but of their masters or themselves.[2] Similarly justice means serving another man's good: for the obedient subject it is a *dis*advantage. Injustice is the opposite: it rules over the genuinely[3] simple and just, who act for its benefit because it is the stronger. The just man always comes off worse than the unjust, both in private transactions and in his relations with the state (tax-paying, selfless service, incorruptibility). The advantage of injustice is best seen in its extreme and most successful form. When a tyrant has seized power he robs, plunders, and tramples on all that is sacred, but instead of being punished like the small-scale transgressor, he is congratulated and called happy by the people he has enslaved. Thus injustice is shown to be stronger, freer and more

---

[1] Joseph (*A. and M. Phil.* 24 and 22) notes that Socrates is right to claim that the purpose of an art as such is not to benefit its practitioner, even if he earns his living by it, but wrong in assuming that the purpose of all arts is to benefit others on whom it is practised. A hunter exercises his art on game, but not for its benefit, a dancer on his own body, which he may strain or injure to reach perfection.

[2] Cross and Woozley (*Comm. on Rep.* 48f.) say that, since Socrates's claim about government is deduced from a generalization based on an imperfect induction, Thrasymachus attacks it legitimately by producing a counter-instance. But it was Thrasymachus who introduced the notion of an art in the strict (that is, ideal) sense, to make his point that no ruler errs when acting as such; and Socrates is therefore entitled to retort that the work of a shepherd, *qua* shepherd, is concerned solely with the welfare of his flock. Cf. especially 345 b–c. For a contrary view see also Kerferd, *D.U.J.* 1947, 22.

[3] ὡς ἀληθῶς, 343 c. Cornford strangely translates 'who are called just', and Lee omits the phrase.

powerful than justice and the original thesis is proved, that justice is what benefits the stronger.

Asked whether this means that he considers injustice a virtue[1] and justice a vice, he replies that he would rather call injustice good policy (or prudence, εὐβουλία) and justice 'a noble simplicity'.[2] Later he calls the just man 'a well-bred simpleton' and the unjust 'sensible and good'. This is a tougher proposition, says Socrates. He could understand Thrasymachus maintaining that injustice paid in spite of being discreditable, but evidently he will call it honourable and good and everything else that is usually associated with justice. If so, they cannot argue on any generally accepted grounds. Moreover, Thrasymachus now appears to be speaking his own mind and believing in the truth of what he says. Instead of simply agreeing to this, Thrasymachus replies, 'What does it matter to you whether I believe it or not? Just refute the doctrine'—words which acquire significance in the light of his later behaviour.

Socrates proceeds to do this by several arguments,[3] and to determine Thrasymachus's position it is important to notice the nature of his responses to them. After the first proof that the just man is good and wise and the unjust stupid and bad, we have the following exchange (350d):

Th. I don't agree with what you say, and I could reply to it; but if I did, you would accuse me of claptrap. So either let me say what I wish, or if you prefer, question me, and I'll say 'all right' and nod and shake my head like someone listening to old wives' tales.

S. But not against your real opinion.

Th. Yes, to please you, since you won't let me speak. What else do you want?[4]

---

[1] ἀρετή, usually so translated, but not necessarily having the moral implications usually attached to 'virtue'. It means the characteristic excellence which enables any creature, organ or instrument to perform its specific function. (See p. 252 below.) At 353a–b Socrates speaks of the ἀρετή of eyes and ears: even a knife has it if it is well designed and sharp. Immediately after this, Thrasymachus agrees with Socrates that he would call the unjust tyrant 'sensible and good', using the adjective (ἀγαθός) which corresponds to ἀρετή. No moral judgment need be involved, though Socrates takes it into the moral sphere by adding words like καλόν and αἰσχρόν, and Thrasymachus incautiously agrees.

[2] Cf. Thuc. 3.82.4 on the way words changed their meaning (p. 84 above). 83.1 provides a striking parallel to the present passage: τὸ εὔηθες, οὗ τὸ γενναῖον πλεῖστον μετέχει, καταγελασθὲν ἠφανίσθη.

[3] The first of which appeared to Joseph 'absolutely convincing' (*A. and M. Phil.* 31) and to Cross and Woozley 'almost embarrassingly bad' (*Rep.* 52).

[4] Lee, by turning Socrates's words μηδαμῶς κτλ. into positive form ('please answer as you really think'), makes Thrasymachus's reply mean that he will act as Socrates wishes, instead of

S. Nothing. If that's what you are going to do, do it. I'll get on with my questions.

It follows that neither the immediately preceding argument nor anything later can be said to have Thrasymachus's agreement,[1] except 351c1–3, where he distinguishes between 'If you are right' and 'If I am right', and Socrates thanks him for it; and the conclusion 'if I am right' is that a strong state owes its power to injustice. Contrast the following expressions of Thrasymachus: 'Let it be so,[2] since I don't want to contradict you' (351d); 'You may enjoy your argument without fear: I shan't oppose you for I don't want to offend the company' (352b); 'So it appears according to your argument' (353e); and his final words: 'Well, this can be your holiday treat.' Socrates, it is clear, is pursuing his own train of thought irrespective of whether Thrasymachus is following him, and Thrasymachus is not committed to any of it.

In discussing the view here attributed to Thrasymachus the most recent practice has been to consider all possible alternatives as they appear to a philosopher today, and by exhaustive examination of the dialogue endeavour to decide which of them is being maintained by Thrasymachus.[3] Such clarification can be most valuable, yet may err by neglecting (as it is never wise to do with Plato) the dramatic situation and emotional tension between the speakers, and the fact that the driving-force behind Thrasymachus is passionate feeling rather than philosophical inquiry. None of this emerges from a summary of the argument, but it is emphasized by Plato at every

as he said he would act. Cornford's 'Anything to please you' is a little ambiguous but was probably intended to mean the same. Jowett and Shorey however translate in the sense given above, which is surely the obvious one. Thrasymachus will *not* speak his own mind, since he cannot do so by Socrates's method of question and answer. Socrates's οὐδὲν μὰ Δία amounts to 'Have it your own way'.

[1] For this reason I cannot agree with Cross and Woozley (*Rep.* 58) that 'Thrasymachus's mistake was to have agreed with Socrates that justice is the excellence of the soul', for he immediately withdraws his agreement (350d).

[2] ἔστω. Similarly ἔστω at 354a means 'Have it your own way' rather than 'I grant that' (Lee).

[3] Thus Kerferd (*D.U.J.* 1947, 19) sees them as (1) Ethical Nihilism, (2) Legalism, (3) Natural Right, (4) Psychological egoism. To Cross and Woozley (*Rep.* 29) they present themselves as (1) Naturalistic Definition, (2) Nihilist View, (3) Incidental Comment, and (4) Essential Analysis. References for the most important earlier discussions may be found in Kerferd's article, except that he makes no mention of Max Salomon's acute analysis in *Ztschr. d. Savigny-Stiftung*, 1911.

turn. Under the stress of powerful emotion, Thrasymachus throws his challenge into deliberately, bitterly paradoxical form: 'Justice? It's nothing but the interest of the stronger!' This need not mean literally what it says, any more than a man does if, appalled at the success of wickedness and the wretchedness of many good men, he exclaims 'There is no justice, justice is non-existent'. What he in fact means is that there *is* such a thing as justice and he knows very well what it is, but in this life he has looked for it in vain. The shock of the paradox lies in the fact that to every Greek the words justice and just (*dikaion*) conveyed an impression of positive moral worth: indeed they embraced such a wide field that the conception of *dikaion* might almost be said to be co-extensive with that of moral worth.

Since *dikaion* is a word so strongly charged with moral approval, it was difficult for any Greek to say openly that he meant by it simply the interest of the stronger party. The critics of strong-arm tactics in Thucydides usually contrast the two in some such accusation as 'You follow your own interests while pretending to follow justice'. Yet, besides the accusation of putting power before justice (3.39.3), we actually hear, in a speech of Brasidas, of 'the justification that lies in superior power' (ἰσχύος δικαιώσει, 4.86.6). In the Melian dialogue the Athenians accuse the Spartans of identifying justice with their own interest, but themselves come close to Thrasymachus when they claim (ch. 105): 'What we deem just (δικαιοῦμεν) is consistent with religious belief and human purpose: human and divine alike hold to a law, based on natural necessity, that the stronger subdues others.' Here we have the reversal of values, of which Thucydides speaks in book 3, in all its nakedness, though more often, as he says, the odious deed was cloaked under a fine phrase. Thrasymachus's purpose, as I see it,[1] is to unmask the hypocrisy and show how the meaning of justice is being perverted. Men and cities act as if it were just for the weak to be oppressed and the strong to have their way by no other

---

[1] It is necessary to be personal, since this is now a minority view and others have much to be said for them. Those who have in the past taken a view similar to that put forward here include, among others, Grote, Barker, Joseph, Burnet and Taylor. More recently Kerferd has maintained that Thrasymachus is preaching a doctrine of natural right, and Cross and Woozley that he holds it to be the moral duty of the weaker to serve the stronger but then cynically recommends us not to behave in the way in which we ought to behave.

right than their power to do so, while for the most part denying that this is true and accusing their opponents of acting as if it were.

This is the background against which the interplay of actual and ideal, 'is' and 'ought', in Thrasymachus's assertions must be seen. It accounts for a certain confusion which strikes a reader at once, though scholars have claimed to resolve it by subtle analysis. Thrasymachus begins by making, in scorn and anger, a factual statement: 'I maintain that justice is nothing but the interest of the stronger', later narrowed to 'the interest of the established government'. This could be called either a reversal of current morality—the word 'justice' still conveying approval, but standing for something that hitherto no one would admit to approving—or a draining away of moral content from the word itself: what goes by the name of justice nowadays has nothing to do with right or wrong; it is simply used to stand for the interest of whoever, at a particular moment, holds the reins of power. All governments make laws in their own interest, and call that justice. Those are the facts: praise or blame does not enter into it. One can fill in the rest from Thucydides: it is a matter of human nature, of necessity, so that, as Hermocrates said (p. 86 above), the strong are not to be blamed for seeking to rule, nor on the other hand is there anything morally praiseworthy in their action. To keep others under is simply profitable, and for a ruling power to indulge pity and humanity is dangerous. This is what Pericles and Cleon, and many others, were preaching in Thrasymachus's lifetime.

Justice, then, is the interest of the stronger, and the just subject will, to his own disadvantage, serve the ruler and obey his laws. Later, however, Thrasymachus says that to judge the advantages of injustice one should look at it in its most extreme form, that of the tyrant who has seized power by a combination of force and treachery. Wrongdoers on a small scale are punished and disgraced, but this man is fawned on and called happy and blessed. Yet 'he robs and plunders, not on a small scale but wholesale, respecting neither sacred nor profane, public nor private property'. His is 'the complete, the supreme example of injustice'[1] and this, concludes Thrasymachus, proves my point that injustice is 'stronger, freer and more lordly than justice,

---

[1] 344a τὴν τελεωτάτην ἀδικίαν, 344c τὴν ὅλην ἀδικίαν ἠδικηκότα.

and the interest of the stronger is justice, whereas injustice is the profit and interest of oneself'.

All this illustrates the historical fact to which Thucydides is witness, that in the troubled circumstances of the late fifth century established moral canons were ignored and men altered the accepted meanings of moral terms to conform to their actions. Such alteration suits the rough-and-tumble of politics and war (e.g. the label of cowardice or weakness fastened on a man who opposes an act of unjustified aggression), but can hardly stand up to philosophical examination.[1] The moral associations of the word *dikaion*—right or justice—are too strong for its equation with 'the interest of the stronger' to be consistently maintained in the face of questioning. It has been argued[2] that Thrasymachus is looking at the matter only from the point of view of the ruled, that for him justice consists in the subject seeking the interest of the ruler or, as he puts it, 'another man's good' (343 c); and that this rescues him from inconsistency and is indeed the key to understanding his thesis, which is a form of the doctrine of natural right. But what consistency, it may be asked, is there in contending that (*a*) justice is the interest of the ruling power (which Thrasymachus states simply and without qualification), but (*b*) it is not just for the ruler to seek his own interest, i.e. justice?[3]

Almost every commentator has noted the contrast in the discussion between the ideal and the actual, fact and value, 'is' and 'ought', but there has been disagreement about the places in which one or the other standard is introduced. In one of the most acute treatments of the question, M. Salomon noted that the difference between the descriptive and the normative was still *in nuce*. We find it obvious, but to maintain the distinction may not have been so easy for either Plato or the

[1] Though I do not agree altogether with Bignone's estimate of Thrasymachus, there is force in his remark (*Studi*, 38) about him and Callicles: 'But behind these two names one is more conscious of the politics than of the philosophy of the time.'

[2] By Kerferd in his article in *D.U.J.*

[3] Both sides of the thesis are clearly stated by Adimantus at 367 c, where he speaks of 'agreeing with Thrasymachus that justice is another man's good, being the advantage of the stronger, and injustice is the advantage and profit of oneself, but the disadvantage of the weaker'. Thus justice consists in obedience to laws which the ruling power (Thrasymachus's chosen example of 'the stronger') has laid down in his own interest, i.e. unjustly. A more consistent view is that referred to by Plato in *Laws* 10 (890a), of those (whoever they may be; not Thrasymachus apparently) who say εἶναι τὸ δικαιότατον ὅτι τις ἂν νικᾷ βιαζόμενος.

historical Thrasymachus. Salomon himself saw Thrasymachus as engaged in purely descriptive sociology[1] down to the place (344a) where he comes to a change in the ruling power and characterizes the man who has successfully overturned the former laws as 'the greatest criminal'. 'Here Thrasymachus not only explains, he judges': an attentive reader cannot overlook the scorn and bitterness with which he speaks. As he sees life, the greatest possible reversal of values is going on before his eyes. The most unjust man becomes the justest; i.e. people will call him just when once he is in power.[2]

With this interpretation of the latter part of Thrasymachus's remarks we may agree, but in maintaining that up to then he has simply been giving 'sociological information', Salomon ignores the fact that Thrasymachus himself introduced the concept of the ruler 'in the strict sense', who is infallible, that is, an ideal, not an actual ruler. It was this which gave Socrates the opening for his argument that no practitioner *as such*, whether of the art of government or anything else, exercises his art in his own interests. In claiming that Socrates cannot refute Thrasymachus by speaking of what happens when a man rules *rightly* (καλῶς, 347a), since Thrasymachus was asking not how a man legislates when governing rightly but how in fact people do govern in this world, Salomon invited contradiction, for no government is in fact infallible. Nevertheless the infallible or ideal ruler is still for Thrasymachus the one who legislates unerringly *in his own interests*, and he did not intend his admission to lead to the moral conclusion in which the ingenuity of Socrates lands him. His rejection of the alternative offered him by Clitophon (that what he meant by the interest of the stronger was what the stronger *thinks* to be his in-

---

[1] 'Sätze, die ... lediglich soziologische Erkenntnisse geben wollen' (*Savigny-Stift.* 1911, 143). A clarification of ideas is undertaken, but no norm set up such as, e.g.: 'Act justly, act according to the law.'

[2] In this last sentence Salomon goes beyond the text. In fairness to Kerferd's exposition it must be said that Thrasymachus nowhere calls the man or party in power 'just', or says that he is so called by others. (They call him 'happy' and 'blest'.) What he says is that justice 'is' their interest, and the just man is the subject who in his simple-heartedness is content to subordinate himself and serve that interest. Yet what Salomon says would seem to be only a legitimate inference from Thrasymachus's words, and helps to show up the inconsistency in Thrasymachus's emotionally charged assertions: justice is the interest of the stronger (equated with the established government), but for the stronger to seek his own interest is unjust. Glaucon in his reinforcement of Thrasymachus's argument does say (361a) that the perfectly unjust man will see to it that he acquires the best reputation for justice.

terest, whether rightly or wrongly) put him at the mercy of Socrates's dialectic.[1]

On the interpretation here put forward Thrasymachus, exasperated by what he regards as the unreality and childishness of the discussion so far, bursts out with an angrily paradoxical statement of what he believes to be the facts of real life: 'There's your vaunted justice for you!' He is not prepared to see this somewhat rhetorical statement undergo a Socratic examination, to which he responds with insults (such as the suggestion that Socrates needs a nurse), outbursts of bad temper, and an unsuccessful attempt to escape (344d). In so far as he represents a doctrine, it is that called by Kerferd ethical nihilism. As Joseph wrote:

He holds, like Hobbes, that every man acts only with a view to his own private interest—if he makes laws, as thinking them in his own interest; if he obeys them, as thinking it is in his own interest rather to obey than to pay the penalty of disobedience, though the act itself required of him brings benefit not to him but to the ruler

to which may be added Taylor's remark that

unlike Hobbes, Thrasymachus feels no need to justify the absolutism of the 'sovereign' by appeal to the 'social contract' by which he has been invested with his sovereign powers; since he does not regard 'right' as having any meaning, he has not to show that the sovereign has any right to obedience;

---

[1] So Joseph, *A. and M. Phil.* 18: 'Thrasymachus' defence ... introduces a contrast between the actual and the ideal which is ultimately fatal to his position.' Cross and Woozley also say (p. 46) that he 'might have done better to have accepted the suggestion' of Clitophon, though Kerferd denies this on the hypothesis (not very different from theirs) that Thrasymachus is preaching a doctrine of the natural right of the stronger.

Salomon should also have forestalled an objection that normative language is introduced at 339c and 341a, where Thrasymachus agrees that what the ruler decrees is not only 'just' (i.e. according to Socrates that that man is *called* just who obeys the law) but also ποιητέον τοῖς ἀρχομένοις. This, it might be argued, shows that in Thrasymachus's own view the subject *ought* to obey. In reply it might be said: (*a*) At this stage of thought, and in the absence of resources of vocabulary for making philosophical distinctions such as are available to twentieth-century philosophers, some confusion between descriptive and prescriptive language was unavoidable and the complete divorce from the word δίκαιον of any suggestion of obligation impossible; (*b*) that the compulsion implied by verbal adjectives of this form was by no means exclusively moral: it could refer to force of circumstances or to what must be done to achieve a specified aim (what Aristotle was later to call hypothetical necessity: examples of this use appear at 361c).

E. L. Harrison, in his interesting article in *Phoenix*, 1967, expresses the opinion that this is one of the points at which Plato 'manipulates' Thrasymachus, that is, makes the Sophist speak out of character for the sake of his own artistic design in the *Republic*.

it is sufficient to observe that his *power* to enforce obedience is guaranteed by the simple fact that he *is* the sovereign.

The theory is also, as Grote perceived, essentially different from that of Callicles in the *Gorgias*, who preaches the right of the stronger to seek unlimited power and enjoyment for themselves as 'nature's law', which the strong and powerful not only do follow but ought to follow.[1]

Finally, this interpretation of the Platonic Thrasymachus accords with one of the few pieces of independent testimony about the man himself. A scholiast to the *Phaedrus* says that he 'wrote in one of his own speeches something to this effect: The gods do not see what goes on among men. If they did, they would not neglect the greatest of human goods, namely justice, yet we see men making no use of it' (Hermias = Thrasymachus fr. 8 DK).[2] Here speaks the disillusioned moralist, who in Plato's dialogue, by his ill-judged, ill-tempered[3] and paradoxical expression of what is essentially the same view lays himself open to the rigours of the Socratic elenchus. In the general neglect of justice, the man who tries to practise it can only be described as a 'noble simpleton' (348c).

(c) Glaucon and Adimantus

After the foregoing episode Glaucon (at the beginning of book 2) complains that Thrasymachus has been too easily put off. He himself wants to hear Socrates prove his contention, that justice is good both in itself and for its consequences. He wants an explanation of 'what justice and injustice *are*, and what effect each has in and by itself, by its presence in the soul', irrespective of rewards or other extraneous consequences. He wants to hear justice praised for its own sake, but in order to elicit this he must first face Socrates with the case against it in

[1] Joseph, *A. and M. Phil.* 17; Taylor, *Plato*, 268; Grote, *History*, ch. 67, 1888 ed. vol. VII, p. 72. Similar to Grote's is the more recent statement of J. P. Maguire, *Yale Class. Stud.* 1947, p. 164: 'Unlike Callicles, neither Thrasymachus nor Glauco admits the existence of a natural right at all.' For Popper *both* Thrasymachus *and* Callicles are 'ethical nihilists' (*Open Soc.* I, 116).

[2] Similarly Adimantus, a little later in the *Republic* (365d), represents the young as saying, 'Why should we bother about the gods, since they either don't exist or don't take any notice of human affairs?' It is difficult to detect in this statement of Thrasymachus the 'obvious exaggeration' and 'manifest hyperbole' which made H. Gomperz think it impossible to take it seriously, so that it must be assigned to a παίγνιον or agonistic speech (*S. u. Rh.* 50).

[3] Thrasymachus's fiery temper is also independently attested, Arist. *Rhet.* 1400b19. For our knowledge of the historical Thrasymachus see further pp. 294ff. below.

its full strength, putting before him all that 'people say' about its origin and nature.

They say that to do wrong is in itself desirable, but to suffer it is not, and the harm of suffering injury outweighs the advantage of doing it. Experience has proved the difficulty of seizing the fruits of wrongdoing and escaping the harm, so, as a compromise, men made laws and agreements binding themselves to do neither. What these prescribed they called lawful and just. This is the origin and nature of justice, and it is valued not as good in itself but through lack of the power to do wrong with impunity.[1] A man capable of practising injustice with consistent success would be mad to allow himself to be bound by such pacts. Imagine a man endowed with the fabled ring of Gyges, which by conferring invisibility on the wearer at his pleasure enabled him to escape the consequences of his acts. It would completely obliterate the distinction between the good and the wicked, for *no one* could resist the temptation to steal, commit adultery, and indulge in every sort of profitable or pleasurable wickedness. Goodness, or justice, is never practised from choice, but only from necessity, under the fear of suffering injury oneself.

Thus what matters is not in fact to be, but to appear, just. To compare the lives of the just and unjust man, we must look at them in their pure form, each perfect in his way. The one who has perfected his wickedness will obviously not be caught—that would brand him as a botcher—but will go through life with an untarnished reputation for integrity. Conversely the perfectly just man must not have the credit for his virtue: that would bring him honour and riches, and one could never be sure that he was not virtuous for the sake of these perquisites rather than of virtue itself. His virtue must be tested by suffering throughout life an undeserved reputation for wickedness. It is not hard to predict the fate of the two men. The perfectly just will be taught by prison, torture and execution that he has chosen the wrong path, while the perfectly unjust will be blessed with wealth, friends and prosperity of every kind, and even enjoy the favour of the gods through being able to offer them the most lavish sacrifices.

[1] For a comparison with Hobbes see Bignone, *Studi*, 41 f., especially the quotation from *De cive* 1.2: 'Statuendum igitur est originem magnarum et diuturnarum societatum non a mutua hominum benevolentia sed a mutuo metu exstitisse.'

Here Adimantus joins in to add that Glaucon's case is only strengthened by the arguments of those who counsel justice, since they commend it not for its own sake but only for the reputation and rewards that it brings—honour from men and blessings from heaven in this world and the next—and deprecate injustice as leading to punishment and misery, including posthumous torments in Hades. Everyone pays lip-service to justice as a fine thing, but they add that it is hard and laborious, whereas self-indulgence and injustice are easy to practise and only apparently and by convention (*nomos*) disgraceful. Even the gods give a miserable life to many just men, and can be swayed by sacrifices, rites and incantations into condoning, and even assisting, the injuries inflicted by the wicked.

These views are offered as those of the ordinary run of mankind. We should not therefore expect to find any heroic Calliclean advocacy of the powerful and unscrupulous superman, nor do we. Instead we have a rather sordid mixture of greed, envy, pettiness and fear. Everyone would take an unjust advantage of his fellows if he could, but, though to live justly is an evil, it is a necessary one. True, the only important thing is to *appear* just, but, since the ring of Gyges is only a fairy-tale, this involves keeping on the whole within the bounds of law and conventional morality. The 'perfectly unjust man' is an unattainable ideal.

(d) *Nature and necessity*

Self-interest, says Glaucon (359c), is what every nature (*physis*) naturally pursues as a good, though law or convention (*nomos*) constrains it to diverge into respect for equality. This is the kind of realism or fact-facing which we meet in Thucydides, in the often-repeated statement that it is human nature to do wrong and dominate others wherever possible,[1] and in the Sophist Gorgias (*Hel.* 6, DK, II, 290): 'It is not in nature for the strong to be thwarted by the weaker, but for the weaker to be ruled and led by the stronger, for the strong to lead and the weak to follow.' The factual or amoral character of the current attitude to human behaviour is emphasized when, as often, we

---

[1] E.g. 4.61.5 πέφυκε γὰρ τὸ ἀνθρώπειον διὰ παντὸς ἄρχειν; 3.45.3 πεφύκασί τε ἅπαντες... ἁμαρτάνειν (cf. the reference in §7 to ἡ ἀνθρωπεία φύσις); 3.39.5 πέφυκε...ἄνθρωπος τὸ μὲν θεραπεῦον ὑπερφρονεῖν τὸ δὲ μὴ ὑπεῖκον θαυμάζειν; 1.76.3, χρησάμενοι τῇ ἀνθρωπείᾳ φύσει ὥστε ἑτέρων ἄρχειν.

find nature coupled with the idea of necessity. In the Melian dialogue (Thuc. 5.105.2) the Athenians claim that the rule of the stronger occurs 'by natural necessity' (ὑπὸ φύσεως ἀναγκαίας), and this and similar phrases are a reminder of the influence on ethics of the natural science of the day. Necessity (*ananké*) as a cosmological force runs right through Presocratic thought, in the Western tradition (Parmenides, Empedocles, the Pythagoreans) with almost mystical or theological overtones, but in Ionian rationalism, which reached its culmination in Leucippus and Democritus, appearing as a mindless natural force equated with the chance collisions of the atoms and the cosmic vortices which they form.[1] Two passages in the *Clouds* of Aristophanes parody the jargon of the scientists and illustrate the way in which it was transferred to human life as a justification for immorality. *Ananké* fills the clouds with moisture and governs the motions by which they collide and cause thunder; and the author of this necessity is no longer a personal Zeus but 'the celestial whirl' (*Clouds* 376ff.). Later in the play (1075) the Unjust Argument speaks of 'the necessities of nature' with reference to adultery, and calls shamelessness and self-indulgence 'exercising one's nature'. Democritus himself made the transfer to human life in a less provocative way when he said (fr. 278) that the begetting of children is looked upon as one of the necessities arising from nature.[2]

This association of necessity with nature is used as an argument by the opponents of *nomos*, which they represent as an attempt to thwart natural forces that is rightly doomed to failure. Thus in Antiphon we read, in a passage setting forth the advantages of breaking the law if one can escape detection, that the dictates of law are artificially imposed by human agreement, whereas those of nature are necessary just because they have grown up naturally; and in emphasizing our common humanity against the artificiality of racial distinctions he speaks of breathing and eating as activities which are 'naturally necessary to all men'.[3] In a fragment of Euripides 'the necessary'

[1] See vol. II, 415.

[2] References in the Hippocratic writers to the φύσις ἀνθρώπου no doubt also helped in the transfer of the word from the constitution of the universe to the nature of man, though they used it in a physiological rather than an ethical sense. For more on this topic see vol. II, 351–3.

[3] Antiphon, fr. 44 A, col. 1, 23ff. (DK II, 346f.) and 44 B, col. 2, 15ff. (*ib.* p. 353). These are dealt with fully on pp. 107ff. below.

simply replaces *physis* as the contrary of *nomos*.[1] The conclusion to be drawn is that since the laws of nature are inexorable, and apply to humanity no less than to the world at large, men will inevitably follow them unless prevented by the intervention of *nomos*. For some, like Thucydides and (if I am right) Thrasymachus, this was simply a fact which had to be accepted. Others drew the positive and practical conclusion that to contravene 'nature's laws' must inevitably be harmful, and they ought to be actively followed whenever possible.[2]

(4) THE UPHOLDERS OF 'PHYSIS'

Those who attacked *nomos* as an unjustified curb on the operations of *physis* did so from two quite different points of view, which may be called the selfish or individualistic and the humanitarian.

(a) Selfish

Side by side with those who saw in history proof of the fact that it was human nature for both states and individuals to behave selfishly and tyrannically, if given the chance, were those to whom this seemed not only inevitable but right and proper. For them the tyrant was not only an inescapable fact but an ideal.

(i) *Callicles: 'physis' as the right of the stronger.* The outstanding exposition of this ethic is that presented by Plato in his *Gorgias* under the name of Callicles, and summarized in the *Laws* in the words (890a):

These views are held by men who in the eyes of the young appear wise, both prose-writers and poets, who say that the height of justice is a conquest won by force.[3] Hence young men fall into irreligion, as if there were

---

[1] Fr. 433 Nauck,   ἔγωγε φημὶ καὶ νόμον γε μὴ σέβειν
                                    ἐν τοῖσι δεινοῖς τῶν ἀναγκαίων πλέον.

The quotation is from the earlier *Hippolytus*, and whoever speaks the words (see on this Heinimann, *N. u. Ph.* 126, n. 5), they no doubt refer to Phaedra's guilty passion, so that τὰ ἀναγκαῖα correspond to the φύσεως ἀνάγκαι of *Clouds* 1075.

[2] Cf. Heinimann, *N. u. Ph.* 125f. (though I cannot agree when he says (126, n. 4) that the use of ἀνάγκη as a cosmogonical force by Leucippus and Democritus is irrelevant to its employment by the Sophists). It should be noted that 'necessary' can be applied quite differently to *nomos* itself, the compulsion imposed by law and convention. This, says Glaucon in the *Republic*, is submitted to by most men as *necessary*, but not accepted as *good* (from the point of view of the individual's self-interest). The compulsion of nature is absolute, that of *nomos* contingent.

[3] These, then, are men of a different stamp from Thrasymachus, for whom tyranny was ἡ τελεωτάτη ἀδικία and the tyrant τὴν ὅλην ἀδικίαν ἠδικηκώς (p. 94, n. 3, above).

no gods such as the law enjoins us to believe in. Hence, too, outbreaks of civil discord as men are attracted to the 'right life according to nature', which plainly expressed means a life of domination over one's fellows and refusal to serve others as law and custom (*nomos*) demand.

Callicles is a somewhat mysterious figure, for apart from his appearance as a character in Plato's dialogue he has left no trace in recorded history. Yet he is described with an amount of authentic detail which makes it difficult to believe that he is fictitious. Probably he existed, and was known to have held views of the kind which Plato ascribes to him, though, in his anxiety to present in all its brutality the case that he wishes to demolish, Plato may well have taken elements from different sources and built up in the person of Callicles a somewhat stylized presentation of the doctrine 'might is right' in its most extreme form.[1] He is a wealthy and aristocratic young man, just entering on public life (515a), and, though acting as host to Gorgias, no Sophist himself. He dismisses those 'who profess to educate men in *areté*'[2] as a worthless lot, and would certainly blush as hotly as young Hippocrates in the *Protagoras* at the thought of joining their profession. His aristocratic and oligarchic connexions are indicated by his liaison with Demos,[3] the son of Plato's stepfather Pyrilampes, and friendship with Andron, who was one of the Four Hundred set up in the oligarchic revolution of 411,[4] and his pride in his descent is mentioned at 512d.

[1] By 'authentic detail' I mean that he is assigned to a real deme and given historical characters as his friends and acquaintances. Three views are possible and have been held: (1) he is purely fictitious, (2) the name is a mask for a well-known character like Critias or Alcibiades, (3) he is a historical figure. The last is the most probable. See Dodds, *Gorgias*, 12f., and for various opinions also Untersteiner, *Sophists*, 344, n. 40. Dodds conjectures that a man 'so ambitious and so dangerously frank' may well have lost his life in the troubled years at the end of the fifth century, before he had time to make his mark on history.

[2] 520a. Gorgias himself, though certainly to be classed as a Sophist (p. 39, n. 1, above), laughed, it was said, at those who made this profession (*Meno* 95c). Callicles may have been thinking especially of Protagoras, who emphatically did so, and whose moderation and respect for *nomos* would not have commended themselves to him.

[3] Most Greek names have a transparent meaning, and they can be very puzzling. Some seem too appropriate to be true, e.g. Thrasy-machus of a hot-tempered character (cf. Ar. *Rhet.* 1400b19), Aristo-teles of a teleological philosopher, Demo-sthenes of the most famous orator of his day, Dio-peithes of an atheist-hunter. Why, on the other hand, should a man of ancient and noble family call his son Demos?

[4] Possibly also by his championship of φύσις itself. Dodds remarks (*Gorgias*, p. 13) that 'praise of φύσις is usually associated with an aristocratic bias, from Pindar onwards', but the situation was perhaps rather more complex. See ch. x below.

Callicles

Callicles takes up the argument with Socrates after the discomfiture of Gorgias's young and impetuous pupil Polus, who had tried to maintain the same thesis as Thrasymachus, that 'many achieve happiness through injustice' (470d). Like Thrasymachus also Polus chose tyrants (Perdiccas of Macedon, the Great King of Persia) as his examples: they are without doubt evil-doers (ἄδικοι, 471a), but if the wicked can escape punishment they are prosperous and happy. By calling them wicked, as Callicles points out, he has played into Socrates's hands, for he has enough conventional morality left in him to agree that, whereas wickedness is a good thing for the wicked man, it is nevertheless dishonourable and blameworthy. Nonsense, says Callicles. Polus was wrong to grant Socrates his contention that to commit injustice was more blameworthy than to suffer it. That is the conventional view, but to put it forward as the true one is vulgar and mean. Nature and convention are generally in opposition, so that, if a man is prevented by shame from saying what he thinks, he is compelled to contradict himself. Those who establish the conventions and make the laws[1] are 'the weaker, that is, the majority'. It is they who say that self-advancement is disgraceful and unjust, and equate injustice with the wish to have more than others. Nature says it is *just* for the better to have more than the worse, and the more powerful than the less powerful.[2]

We may note here the formal contradiction of Thrasymachus, who said that those who make the laws are the stronger party, whether tyrant, oligarchy or democracy (*Rep.* 338e). Adimantus came nearer to Callicles when he argued that it is the weak who uphold justice (in the conventional sense of course) and censure injustice, not through conviction but because of their own impotence, and that the disgrace attached to injustice is only a matter of *nomos*. But both of these would earn Callicles's censure, as Polus did, for using justice and injustice

[1] οἱ τοὺς νόμους τιθέμενοι. It must be remembered that Callicles is using the word *nomos* for both conventional behaviour and positive law. See pp. 56f. above.

[2] (At 488b–d, Callicles says he is using βελτίων, κρείττων and ἰσχυρότερος—better, superior and stronger—as synonymous.) This sentence and the next (483c–d) show clearly the influence of Callicles's association with Gorgias (if indeed at this point he is more than a mouthpiece through which Plato is reproducing the unscrupulous rhetoric of Gorgias himself). Cf. Gorg. *Hel.* 6 πέφυκε γὰρ οὐ τὸ κρεῖσσον ὑπὸ τοῦ ἥσσονος κωλύεσθαι ἀλλὰ τὸ ἧσσον ὑπὸ τοῦ κρείσσονος ἄρχεσθαι καὶ ἄγεσθαι.

in their conventional senses.[1] Many things, he continues, point to the fact that the criterion of justice is for the stronger to get the better of the weaker, for example the behaviour of animals and of men collectively as states and races. Darius and Xerxes in invading other people's territory were acting according to the nature of justice—according to law too, if you mean the law of nature, though not according to the laws we men lay down. In this first appearance of the phrase 'law of nature', it is used as a deliberate paradox, and of course in neither of its later senses, neither the *lex naturae* which has had a long history in ethical and legal theory from the Stoics and Cicero down to modern times nor the scientists' laws of nature which are 'simply observed uniformities'.[2] But it epitomized an attitude current already in the late fifth century, and the Athenians in Thucydides's Melian dialogue came close to it even verbally, when they put forward the principle that he should rule who can as a matter of 'natural necessity' and at the same time an eternal law.[3] The bestial criterion of natural behaviour (taking the animals as models) was also known in the fifth century. Herodotus in quoting an instance expressly excludes the Greeks (2.64), but it is parodied more than once in Aristophanes (*Clouds* 1427 ff., *Birds* 753 ff.).[4]

Our unnatural laws, Callicles goes on, mould our best men from their youth up, teaching them that equality is fine and just, but, if a character naturally strong enough were to arise, like a young lion he would shake off these fetters, break his cage and turn master instead of slave. Then nature's justice would shine forth in all its glory. Socrates tries to make him retreat at least to the position of the Platonic Thrasymachus by pointing out that in a democracy, since 'the many' make and enforce the laws, they are the stronger and better element (Callicles having equated these two epithets himself), and therefore on Callicles's argument what they decree is naturally right; but it is

[1] Thrasymachus, we may remember, would not admit that he deemed injustice not only profitable but also honourable and virtuous (p. 90 above). The very different views of someone who was prepared to apply the word 'just' to what the world considers unjust may be some additional evidence that his avoidance of committal was deliberate.

[2] See Dodds's note on *Gorgias* 483e3.

[3] Thuc. 5.105.2, p. 86 above.

[4] Here also the natural philosophers may have made a contribution. Compare Democritus's theory that men learned certain arts by imitation of the beasts (vol. II, 474).

the many who insist that justice means equal rights for all and to inflict injury is more dishonourable than to suffer it, therefore all this must be right according to nature and not only to *nomos*.

Callicles replies in a burst of anger that Socrates is talking nonsense and tripping him up over words. When he said that the stronger were the better he *meant* better—naturally better men (492 a), not a non-descript and slavish rabble. Invited by Socrates to amend his statement of who should be master and get their own way he says he means the better and wiser, that is, those who display courage, and good practical sense in regard to the affairs of the state (491 c). Such men should rule, and it is just that the rulers should be better off than the rest. The idea that they should 'rule themselves', that is, display self-control, is ridiculous. Natural goodness and justice decree that the man who would live rightly must not check his desires but let them grow as great as possible, and by his courage[1] and practical sense be capable of gratifying them to the full. The common run of men condemn this indulgence only out of shame at their own incapacity for it. For a man with power over others nothing could be worse or more disgraceful than self-control and respect for the laws, arguments and reproaches of others. The truth is this: luxury, wantonness and freedom from restraint, if backed by strength, constitute excellence (*areté*) and happiness; all the rest is fine talk, human agreements contrary to nature, worthless nonsense. We need not for the present concern ourselves with the rest of the discussion, in which Socrates first gets Callicles to agree that his doctrine is the extreme hedonism which actually identifies pleasure and the good, then drives him from his position by shock tactics until he makes a shameless volte-face and says he has not been in earnest: of course he believes that some pleasures are good and others bad.

Here then at last is the championship of *physis* against *nomos* in its extreme form, fervently and eloquently preached. There *is* such a thing as natural justice, and it consists simply in this, that the strong

[1] In the sense given to ἀνδρεία here Plato is again introducing an idea that was already current in the fifth century. Cf. Thuc. 3.82.4 τόλμα μὲν γὰρ ἀλόγιστος ἀνδρεία φιλέταιρος ἐνομίσθη... τὸ δὲ σῶφρον τοῦ ἀνάνδρου πρόσχημα, and the words of Eteocles in Euripides, *Phoen.* 509 f. ἀνανδρία γὰρ τὸ πλέον ὅστις ἀπολέσας τοὔλασσον ἔλαβε. It is referred to again by Plato at *Rep.* 560 d σωφροσύνην δὲ ἀνανδρίαν καλοῦντες.

man should live to the utmost of his powers and give free play to his desires. Might is right, and nature intends him to get all he wants. Existing human *nomoi* are utterly unnatural, because they represent the attempt of the weak and worthless many to thwart the purpose of nature that the strong man should prevail. The truly just man is not the democrat, nor the constitutional monarch, but the ruthless tyrant. This is the morality against which Plato resolutely and undeviatingly set his face, from the time when as an eager young follower of Socrates he learned from him that 'no man voluntarily does wrong' (in the ordinary sense) to the end of his life when he opposed it once again in the *Laws* and, since its roots were in the natural science of the time, turned cosmogonist himself in the *Timaeus* to undermine its deepest foundations. It is necessary to emphasize this because there is a curious theory that Plato felt a secret sympathy for Callicles, who stood for something deeply implanted in his own nature, which perhaps only his acquaintance with Socrates had repressed. Callicles is 'a portrait of Plato's rejected self'. 'Although he is fundamentally opposed to the views of Callicles, he states them with the ease and sympathy of a man who has suppressed them in himself, or has yet to suppress them', or as G. Rensi put it, 'the conflict Socrates–Callicles in the *Gorgias* is not a conflict between two individuals but one which occurs within a single mind'.[1] Dodds agrees with this to the extent that, because Plato felt 'a certain sympathy' for men of the Calliclean stamp, his portrait of Callicles 'not only has warmth and vitality but is tinged with a kind of regretful affection'.[2] One may more easily associate oneself with the mild protest of Levinson (*Defense of P.* 472) that 'it is not sound to identify Plato with those of his characters

[1] The quotations are from H. Kelsen as cited by Levinson, *Defense of P.* 471, and Highet and Rensi quoted by Untersteiner, *Sophists*, 344, n. 40.

[2] Dodds, *Gorgias*, 13f. The subjective character of such judgments may be shown by comparing the impressions made by the same passage on two critics, Dodds and Jaeger. At 486a–b Dodds sees Callicles expressing a sincere concern for Socrates's safety, whereas to Jaeger the same words are 'a scarcely concealed threat of state sanctions against him' (*Paideia* II, 140). Dodds takes at its face value Socrates's praise of Callicles at 486d–487b as 'the true touchstone', honest and frank, and a man of culture: to Jaeger all this is 'bitter irony'. In contrast to the 'affection' in the portrait (which is indeed difficult to detect), Jaeger speaks of 'the brutally menacing tone of Callicles', which 'shows the seriousness of the situation here, and the irreconcilable spiritual enmity between the protagonists of each side' (*ibid.* 141). H. Neumann again sees Socrates's 'unfeigned affection for his young friend' in such expressions as ὦ φίλη κεφαλή in 513c2 (*TAPA*, 1965, 286, n. 9).

whom he abhors'. It is instructive to compare the tone of the conversation here with that in the *Protagoras*, where Socrates is talking to a man for whom, though he disagrees with him on fundamentals, he has a real respect. When Protagoras occasionally, and justifiably, gets irritated, Socrates relaxes his pressure, and friends of both are at hand to put things right between them with soothing words. The criticism is good-humoured, the atmosphere one of friendliness and tolerance, and the dialogue ends with mutual expressions of esteem. Here on the other hand is unmistakable bitterness and ill-temper. Drivelling nonsense, mob-oratory, quibbling, small-mindedness, violence, and the cheap scoring of debating points are some of the accusations which Callicles hurls at Socrates, and Socrates returns as good as he gets. Psychologically considered, all this is no doubt compatible with the existence of a repressed Callicles in Plato himself, but seen in the context of his whole philosophy it appears highly improbable. Dodds sees even greater significance in 'the powerful and disturbing eloquence that Plato has bestowed on Callicles', but it should be no news to us that Plato was a superb dramatic artist. This eloquence, adds Dodds, convinced the young Nietzsche, while Socrates's reasoning left him cold. That is not surprising, but scarcely relevant. The apostle of the *Herrenmoral*, the *Wille zur Macht* and *Umwertung aller Werte* did not need much convincing, for he was blood-brother to Callicles, whereas Socrates became for him, to quote Dodds again, 'a fountain-head of false morality'.[1]

(ii) *Antiphon: 'physis' as enlightened self-interest.* We are not at the moment concerned with the question whether the following views, which occur in some papyrus fragments of Antiphon's *On Truth*, are his own, or whether he is simply setting forth for examination 'different

---

[1] Dodds, *Gorgias*, 388. What Nietzsche called the Sophist-culture was for him 'this priceless movement in the midst of the moral- and ideal-swindle of the Socratic schools'. 'The Sophists', he said, 'were Greeks: when Socrates and Plato took the side of virtue and justice, they were Jews or I do not know what.' No wonder it was Callicles who appealed to him. These passages are quoted on p. 146 of A. H. J. Knight's book, *Some aspects of the life and work of Nietzsche, and particularly of his connexion with Greek literature and thought*, which might perhaps have been mentioned by Dodds when, at the beginning of his informative appendix on Socrates, Callicles and Nietzsche (*Gorgias*, 387–91), he says that the link between Nietzsche and Callicles has received little attention from the exponents of Nietzsche. On pp. 147f. Knight quotes a long extract from Callicles's speech in the *Gorgias*. See also Nestle, *VMzuL*, 341f.

views of the just taken from tradition or contemporary polemics'. This has been argued because they seem to many scholars to contradict the more conventional morality advocated by Antiphon elsewhere. Alternatively it has been maintained that there is no contradiction, because the passages that we are about to consider do not reveal their author 'as the immoral foe of *nomos* and social control, but as its critic, a realistic but socially minded utilitarian'. The first question may be left because for the present discussion it is enough that they represent views current in the fifth century. Whether or not they are immoral and hostile to *nomos* should emerge as we look at them.[1] It may seem rather that hostility to *nomos* is their one constant feature, which in practice may lead sometimes to a selfish precept ('ignore *nomos* in your personal behaviour if you can avoid being found out'), sometimes to a large humanity ('the distinction between Greeks and barbarians is only a matter of *nomos*').

The following is a paraphrased version of the papyrus fragments.[2]

OP 1364, fr. 1 (DK, 87 A 44 A):[3] Justice consists in not transgressing the laws and usages (νόμιμα) of one's state. Therefore the most profitable means of manipulating[4] justice is to respect the laws when witnesses are present but otherwise to follow the precepts of nature. Laws are artificial compacts, they lack the inevitability of natural growth. Hence to break the laws without detection does one no harm, whereas any attempt to violate the inborn dictates of nature is harmful irrespective of discovery by others, for the hurt is not merely, as with the law-breaker, a matter of appearance or reputation but of reality. Justice in

---

[1] That the papyrus fragments are throughout discussing the views of others is argued by Kerferd in *Proc. Camb. Philol. Soc.* 1956–7. That they contain nothing directly hostile to *nomos* is the opinion of, among others, Greene (*Moira*, 240; for similar interpretations see *ibid.* n. 122). Antiphon himself will be considered in detail later (pp. 285 ff.).

[2] Omitting 1364 fr. 2, which is discussed on pp. 152 f. To translate in full Antiphon's spate of rhetorical antitheses, and his repetitions of a point in different words, would caricature rather than reproduce his style, and tend to obscure the argument. Tolerable in Greek, they can scarcely be rendered in anything like natural English. The papyri are translated into English by the editors of the *OP* and into Italian (with textual notes) by Bignone, *Studi*, 56 ff., 101 ff.

[3] That *OP* 1364 is an extract from Antiphon's work *On Truth* is fortunately established by an attested quotation in Harpocration. See *OP*, xi, 92, or note at bottom of DK, ii, 346.

[4] χρῆσθαι. To call this inconsistent with the advice to follow nature (Kerferd, *loc. cit.* 27 f., and cf. Havelock, *L.T.* 269) is surely hypercritical. If not strictly logical, it is at least natural and practical to advise overt conformity so long as one lives in a community governed by law, on nature's own principle of maximizing one's personal pleasure and comfort and minimizing pain and inconvenience. Cf. p. 290 below.

the legal sense is for the most part at odds with nature. The laws prescribe what we should see, hear or do, where we should go, even what we should desire [one thinks of the tenth commandment], but so far as conformity to nature is concerned what they forbid is as good as what they enjoin.

Life and death are both natural, the one beneficial to men, the other unprofitable.[1] But 'benefit' as the law understands it is a drag on nature; in its natural sense it means freedom. Pains do not assist nature more than pleasures, and what is truly beneficial ought to help, not harm. It cannot be said that what causes pain is more beneficial than what brings pleasure[2]... [gap of seven lines in the papyrus]...those who, though they defend themselves, never take the offensive, those who cherish parents who have treated them ill,[3] and those who give their opponents the opportunity to bind themselves with an oath while refraining from doing so themselves.[4] Many of these actions are against nature, because they involve more pain than pleasure, and ill treatment when the reverse is possible. If the laws protected such behaviour and inflicted loss on those who did otherwise, it might be worth while to obey them; but as it is, legal justice is not strong enough for this. It does not prevent the attack nor the victim's suffering, and when redress is sought it favours the oppressor as much as the oppressed. A victim must persuade the court that he has been injured, and his attacker has equal facilities to deny it...

[1] Taking ἀπό as partitive in sense. (See LSJ, *s.v.* I 6.) Admittedly it is more usually understood as causative ('results from things beneficial...'). Kerferd notes (*loc. cit.* 31) that evidently not everything that is φύσει is advantageous, and Antiphon's norm must be restricted to τὰ φύσει ξυμφέροντα. (Cf. also Heinimann, *N. u. Ph.* 137.) This seems more reasonable than Stenzel's contention (*RE* Suppl. IV, 36) that all the emphasis is on life, and death is only introduced as a 'polar expression' and for the sake of rhetorical antithesis. The argument seems to be that both nature and law may produce harm or good (even an upholder of nature like Antiphon could hardly deny the occurrence of natural disasters like earthquakes and floods), but that they have different standards of what is good and bad, and nature's are to be preferred.

[2] A similarly hedonistic doctrine is criticized as Antiphon's in Xen. *Mem.* 1.6. As Croiset says, one can imagine what havoc Socrates would make with such imprecise language!

[3] Kerferd (*loc. cit.* 29) says, with special reference to this clause, that what is mentioned here goes beyond what the laws require, and represents therefore a third standard of action distinct from both nature and the laws. But there would be no third standard in Antiphon's mind, for a socially recognized duty like that of adult sons and daughters to support their parents (one of the most deeply rooted of any in Greek society) was a *nomos* as much as any positively enacted law. (Cf. p. 56 above.)

Bignone, in his attempted demonstration that there is a close affinity between the doctrines of the two works *On Truth* and *On Concord*, both representing a 'philanthropic utilitarianism', completely ignores this passage. In the whole of his essay in *Studi sul pensiero antico* there is no mention of this statement that such behaviour as refusing to attack others except in self-defence, and treating undeserving parents well, is inimical to that 'nature' which was Antiphon's ideal.

[4] For the procedure of oath-taking, and the advantages or disadvantages of adopting a particular course, see Arist. *Rhet.* 1377a8ff. (the relevance of which was brought to my notice by Mr J. S. Morrison).

OP 1797 (still a part of fr. 44 in DK, II, 353):[1] Justice is believed
to be something good, and to bear true witness about each other is
normally considered just, as well as helpful in human relations. But it
will not be just, if[2] the criterion of justice is that one should inflict no
injury on another unless first injured oneself. The witness, even if truthful,
inflicts injury on the man against whom he testifies, though that man has
not injured him, and may suffer injury in return. At least he will have to be
on his guard against the hatred of the other, whom he has made his enemy.
Thus wrong is involved on both sides, and to call such acts just cannot be
reconciled with the principle that it is just neither to inflict nor to suffer
injury.[3] One must conclude that trial, judgment and arbitration are not
just, whatever their outcome, for a decision which benefits one side injures
the other...

These fragments are invaluable as a source for contemporary moral
views, though their incompleteness makes it difficult to say how far
they represent the opinions of Antiphon himself. One has only to think
what impression we should have of Plato if our knowledge of the
Republic were limited to some fragments of Glaucon's speech (for
example, the sentence at 359c: 'It is natural for every man to pursue
selfish ambition as a good, but *nomos* seduces us into a respect for
equality') without the explanation that he is temporarily acting as
devil's advocate in order to have the case demolished by Socrates.
Here we are presented with three notions of justice, which have
sometimes been thought to be irreconcilable and so necessarily of
diverse origins.

[1] There is no conclusive external evidence for the authorship of this fragment, as there is
for the previous one, and it is in a different hand, though it belonged to the same find and the
editors suggest (*OP*, xv, 119f.) that the same hand may have added breathings, accents and marks
of quantity in both, and that 1797 may even be a later part of the same roll as 1364. Its subject
and style leave no reasonable doubt of the author, and very little of the work in which it
occurred. Untersteiner (*Sophists*, 267, n. 127) thinks that the fragment came between the two
fragments of 1364, but it is not clear to me how the cosmopolitanism of 1364 fr. 2 (for which
see p. 153 below) 'represents the conclusion of the theory developed in *OP* 1797'. On the
identification of the fragment see also Bignone, *Studi*, 98–100.

[2] ⟨ἐπείπε⟩ρ Wilamowitz, Kranz. Diels and Bignone preferred ⟨εἴπε⟩ρ as corresponding
better to the space to be filled. (The original editors supplied ⟨καὶ γὰ⟩ρ.) Sinclair wrote (*Gr. Pol.
Th.* 72, n. 1): 'It makes all the difference to our knowledge of Antiphon's own doctrine whether
the missing letters are to be restored εἴπε⟩ρ or ἐπείπε⟩ρ.' But either can equally well introduce
the writer's own opinion, and if εἴπερ is correct I am sure it does so.

[3] This, it will be remembered, is what Glaucon in the *Republic* (359a) describes as the ordinary
man's view of the nature of justice, a compromise solution based on a 'social compact': συνθέσθαι
ἀλλήλοις μήτ' ἀδικεῖν μήτ' ἀδικεῖσθαι (p. 98 above).

1. Conformity to the laws and customs of one's state. These, as in Glaucon's account, are belittled as matters of human agreement. Self-interest demands that a man conform only when he would otherwise be found out and punished. Law and nature have different ideals. In nature, life, freedom and pleasures are beneficial, and death is not, but law enforces things that are painful and imposes artificial restraints on nature. These are not truly beneficial. In the view outlined by Glaucon, the accepted virtues should be practised for fear of worse, though given the ring of Gyges no one would or should be virtuous, but here it is obviously believed that opportunities for defying *nomos* undetected do occur and should be seized. This is supported by a further argument, that the law cannot protect its own. It only acts after the event, and the arrival of *pede Poena claudo* is of small use to a murdered man. Worse than that, the courts in fact give an equal chance to offender and victim.

The definition of justice here criticized sounds at first exactly like that quoted with strong approval by Socrates in Xenophon's *Memorabilia* (4.4.12–13), namely that 'lawful and just are the same thing'.[1] There too laws are admitted to be created simply by the citizens agreeing on what ought to be done and what not, yet the merits of this conception of justice are argued for at some length. Corporately, obedience to the laws makes for unity, strength and happiness, and for the individual it wins friendship and trust and (in direct contradiction to Antiphon) affords the best chance of victory in the courts. All this applies to positively enacted laws, but in contrast to Antiphon Socrates goes on to include the 'unwritten laws' which are of universal application and agreed by him and Hippias to be divinely ordained. These are certainly not Antiphon's 'dictates of nature', for they include the duty of honouring one's parents and the requiting of benefits, yet Socrates claims that obedience to them is profitable and rewarding to the individual, and (like Antiphon with *his* decrees of nature) that unlike human laws they cannot be flouted with impunity (p. 119 below).

[1] Cf. also Lysias, 2.19 ἀνθρώποις προσήκει νόμῳ ὁρίσαι τὸ δίκαιον. The equation of νόμιμα and δίκαια by Protagoras (in Plato, *Theaet.* 172a) is rather different: the laws of a city are δίκαια for that city as long as they are in force, but are not necessarily συμφέροντα. Cf. 167c, and pp. 137, 172 below. Bignone (*Studi*, 74f.) thought Protagoras was the object of Antiphon's criticism.

2. To do no injury except in requital for an injury received.

3. Neither to do nor to suffer injury. It has been held[1] that these two definitions of justice conflict, and cannot therefore have been adhered to by the same people. But it cannot have seemed so to Antiphon, for the way in which he introduces them at the beginning and end of his argument that to testify against a man is 'not just' implies they are identical or closely similar. Complete freedom from wrongdoing, either as doer or sufferer, is the ideal, but it is not in anyone's power to ensure that no other man wrongs him, so the best practical expression of justice is never to take the initiative in wrongdoing; and obviously if this were universally observed the other would follow: if no one acted save in self-defence, there would be no attacks to make self-defence necessary. Very probably the third description of justice was in Antiphon's mind equivalent also to the first, since Plato makes Glaucon say that in the general opinion law was 'a mutual agreement neither to inflict nor to suffer injury'.

The general impression made by these fragments is of a single writer determined to show up the inadequacy of current conceptions of morality. His own consistent standpoint is that a morality enforced by law and custom is contrary to nature, and nature's way is to be preferred. In *OP* 1364, he claims that to refrain from doing an injury except in self-defence is against nature, but this does not prevent him from pointing out in 1797 that, if, like most people, you accept it as a principle of right action, you immediately find yourself in conflict with another generally accepted principle, that whoever has information that will cause a criminal to be brought to justice is in duty bound to produce it.

Bignone and Untersteiner both hold that the last definition ('neither to do nor to suffer injury') is 'the true definition of justice according to Antiphon'.[2] For Untersteiner the state in which injustice is neither inflicted nor suffered 'corresponds to the highest goal of the spirit', in support of which he refers to *Republic* 500c, where not men, but the objects of the philosopher's contemplation (i.e. the Forms), are said to be in this state. It might be more apt to compare 359a, where

[1] By Bignone and Untersteiner. See the latter's *Sof.* IV, 100 and *Sophs.* 251.
[2] Reference as in previous note.

'neither to inflict nor to suffer injustice' is the compact entered into by ordinary men as a second-best to having their own way individually. For men, the highest goal of the spirit is surely a conception of justice not mentioned here at all, namely to do no injury even in return for injury suffered. This brings us to the level of Socrates or Jesus, and Socrates argues for it explicitly more than once, e.g. in the *Republic* (335 d, 'Then it is not the part of a just man, Polemarchus, to harm either his friend or anyone else') and *Crito* (49b, 'Then we must not inflict injury for injury, as most people believe', and c, 'Then one must not use any man unjustly in return, or harm him, whatever we may suffer at his hands').[1] The present fragments offer no evidence that Antiphon was a moralist of this calibre. He was clearly a serious thinker, and much of what he says here can be interpreted altruistically: the statement that pleasure is more beneficial than pain might represent a hedonistic utilitarianism of a universal kind, advocating conduct which will ensure the maximum of pleasure in the world at large. Elsewhere, however, as when he deprecates refraining from unprovoked agression as contrary to that 'nature' which is his ideal, it appears that the hedonism is selfish and individualistic.[2]

(iii) *Other witnesses*. The antinomian view is reflected in many passages of contemporary literature. It is probably in the isolated line of Euripides (fr. 920):

> 'Twas Nature willed it, who cares nought for law,

and elsewhere in his plays an ostentatious reconciliation of the two itself bears witness to the existence of the view which he is contradicting. At *Ion* 642, Ion counts himself happy because both his own nature and *nomos* together make him good in the service of Apollo, and there is a similar union of the two at *Bacchae* 895 f., on which Dodds re-

---

[1] To appreciate the revolutionary character of the Socratic ethic, one must remember how deeply rooted in Greek morality was the doctrine that 'the doer shall suffer', which made the exaction of retribution or vengeance not only a right but often a religious duty. Cf. Aesch. *Ag.* 1563 f., *Cho.* 144, 306–14, Eur. *H.F.* 727 f. Other passages are quoted by Thomson, *Oresteia*, II, 185.

[2] So far as Antiphon is concerned these comments are of course made on the assumption that the views in question are his own. In spite of Bignone's and Kerferd's arguments, this is still my impression. Naturally, in dealing with such fragmentary extracts, accidentally preserved, conclusions can only be drawn with caution, and the purpose of the present chapter is only to show that such views were current in the fifth century.

marks that 'the chorus anticipate in principle Plato's solution of the *nomos–physis* controversy, viz. that when the two terms are properly understood *nomos* is seen to be founded upon *physis*'. It is the poet's privilege to *pronounce*, as an eternal truth, what the philosopher feels he has to *prove* by argument.[1]

The new morality is a favourite butt of Aristophanes, especially in the *Clouds*. The Unjust Argument claims (1039f.) that he was the first to bring counter-arguments against the *nomoi*, and declares self-control to be an evil, challenging the Just Argument to name anyone for whom it did any good (1060ff.). It deprives one of the pleasures which make life worth living, and opposes 'the necessities of nature'. 'Indulging nature' should be the aim, and if caught in wrongdoing (e.g. adultery) there are always arguments to prove your innocence. The philosophy here pilloried is that of Callicles, and the argument of Antiphon is recalled that the law favours the guilty as much as the innocent. The whole plot of the *Clouds* turns on the claim of 'Socrates' to teach his pupils how to escape the legal penalties of wrongdoing. Instructed by him, Pheidippides defends father-beating: it is good 'to slight the established laws' (1400), and this, though 'nowhere *nomos*',[2] is 'just' (1405). (It is 'nature's justice' as upheld by Callicles.) The author of the *nomos* was only a man like you and me, so why shouldn't I make a new *nomos*, that sons may beat their fathers in return for the beatings they had from them? This is parody, but in Antiphon we found it maintained in all seriousness that the sacred duty to respect one's parents was 'against nature'.

Since 'nature' and 'natural necessity' figured so largely in these antinomian tirades, it is not surprising that, as we have already noted,[3] they owed much to the professed writers 'On Nature', the Presocratic natural philosophers. Aristophanes caricatures the logic of this in an argument brought by Strepsiades against one of his creditors: 'How can you deserve to get your money back if you are so ignorant of meteorological phenomena?'[4] One can hardly do better

---

[1] Dodds *ad loc.* 179. For the *nomos–physis* contrast cf. also fr. 433, quoted on p. 101, n. 1 above.

[2] οὐδαμοῦ νομίζεται (1420). Cf. *Birds* 757 f. εἰ γὰρ ἐνθάδ' ἐστὶν αἰσχρὸν τὸν πατέρα τύπτειν νόμῳ, τοῦτ' ἐκεῖ καλὸν παρ' ἡμῖν.

[3] Pp. 58f., 100 above.

[4] *Clouds*, 1283. The practice of taking the animals as our models has already been mentioned (p. 104 with n. 4 above), and Aristophanes has the answer to that too. When Pheidippides

than close this account of the immoralist champions of nature against law with Plato's summary of their arguments in the *Laws*.[1] The greatest and best things in the world are the work of nature, or chance (which is the same thing). The four elements, and the earth, sun, moon and stars which are made of them, are lifeless matter. Moving in accordance with their chance-got properties, the elements somehow came together suitably—hot with cold, dry with moist, soft with hard —and combining by the inevitability of chance[2] generated the whole cosmos and everything in it. Animals, plants and the seasons of the year all owe their existence to these causes, namely nature and chance: no god, intelligence or art had any part in it. Art, or design (*techné*),[3] came later, a more insignificant force of purely human origin whose creations have little substance or reality in them. The only arts worth anything are those which, like medicine, agriculture and physical training, assist the forces of nature. Political skill has some slight connexion with nature, but is mostly a matter of art, and legislation has nothing to do with nature at all. It is entirely artificial, and its postulates are untrue.

The gods themselves have no existence in nature, but are a product of human artifice, and vary in different places according to local conventions. Goodness is one thing in nature and another by *nomos*, and as for justice, nature knows nothing of it. Men are for ever disputing about it and altering it, and every change is valid from the moment it is made, owing its existence to artificial conventions rather than to nature. It is by theories like these that agitators incite the young

---

justifies father-beating by reference to the unfilial habits of cocks, his father retorts: 'If you want to imitate the cocks, why not eat dirt and roost on a perch?' (*ibid.* 1430). It is only fair to add that stories of the gods (e.g. Zeus's frequent adultery) could be equally invoked on the side of the wicked (*ibid.* 1080). The crudity of popular religion, based on Homer, made its own contribution to the growth of irreligious humanism. (Cf. Plato, *Laws* 886b–d.) This will be discussed later (ch. IX below).

[1] 889 a ff. The first part of the passage is translated in full in vol. I, p. 144.

[2] κατὰ τύχην ἐξ ἀνάγκης. For the relationship between τύχη and ἀνάγκη, with special reference to the atomists, see vol. II, 417–19. Besides the atomists, the cosmogonical views here summarized recall in particular Empedocles, frr. 59 and 35, *vv.* 16f. (vol. II, 203).

[3] No English word produces exactly the same effect as the Greek *techné*. 'Art' suffers from its aesthetic associations, and also from the opposition between 'the arts' and the natural sciences. Those who know no Greek may be helped by the word itself: its incorporation in our 'technical' and 'technology' is not fortuitous. It includes every branch of human or divine (cf. Plato, *Soph.* 265 e) skill, or applied intelligence, as opposed to the unaided work of nature.

to irreligion and sedition, urging them to adopt the 'right life according to nature', by which they mean a life of selfish ambition instead of service to their fellow-men and to law.

I have cited this passage from Plato as the best account of the way in which selfish antinomianism of the Calliclean type was founded on, or at least appealed for confirmation to, contemporary natural science. The juxtaposition attributed to Archelaus ('living creatures first arose from slime, and justice and baseness exist not naturally but by convention', p. 58 above) was less incongruous than it sounds. The cosmogonic theories are described in general terms which apply to most of the Presocratic systems. Empedocles and the atomists[1] are perhaps most vividly recalled, but the undesigned mingling of the 'opposites' to produce first the framework of the cosmos and then the creatures within it is a common feature from Anaximander onwards. The general non-theistic foundations of Presocratic science were enough for Plato's humanistic opponents; they did not trouble to discriminate too nicely between them.

It would be equally misguided to look for a single author of the ethical views which are Plato's chief target. Protagoras, Critias, Prodicus, Antiphon and even the youthful Aristotle have all had their champions, and the variety of names put forward by reputable scholars is sufficient evidence of the futility of the search.[2] Plato is speaking of beliefs which, when he wrote, had long been current in influential and progressive Athenian circles. The Sophists had much to do with their promulgation, and were in general agreement with their scientific premises. The selfish ethical conclusions, however, which Plato found so shocking, were, as we have seen, neither common to all the Sophists nor exclusive to the profession.

[1] J. Tate (*CR*, 1951, 157) objected that since most of Plato's opponents in *Laws* 10 asserted that motion had a beginning they cannot have been atomists. Not all, however (895a 6–7). cf. also England's note on 889b 5.

[2] For a summary of the various attempts at identification, see Untersteiner, *Sof.* IV, 180f. He himself favours Antiphon, a view which is criticized by Burkert in *Gött. Gel. Anz.* 1964. The latest discussion of the passage (in date of publication) is Edelstein's in *The Idea of Progress* (1967), 27ff.

(b) Humanitarian: written and unwritten law

Criticism of law, and of a legal conception of justice and right, in favour of so-called 'nature' or 'freedom', nearly always has two sides. It can be selfish and brutal, as we have seen it in its Calliclean form, or on the other hand it can be wholly well-intentioned, for in the words of a modern authority who describes himself as a 'moralizing anarchist' (not a bad description of Antiphon?),

> We cannot maintain the complacent positive belief that only the law of the State is law properly so-called ... We know that the law can be used as an instrument of policy ... We have heard of, we may have met, the victims of laws that are oppressive, brutal and degrading. We believe that ... Human Rights may stand above positive law.[1]

Similarly Antisthenes, the pupil of Gorgias (p. 306, n. 2, below), who became a devoted follower of Socrates, is said to have held that 'the wise man in his activity as a citizen will be guided not by the established laws but by the law of *areté*'.[2]

This altruistic championship of *physis* against *nomos* can have various applications. It can, and did, give birth to ideas of equality,

[1] A. H. Campbell, 'Obligation and Obedience to Law', in *Proc. Brit. Acad.* for 1965. Most of the questions he raises appear in the ethical debate of the fifth century, and it will be interesting to have them in mind while we are investigating it. He states as his main theme the question: Is there a moral obligation to obey every rule of the law, just because it is the law? Among the questions he asks are these:

1. Can security exist without a common morality? (He is arguing against Lord Devlin's negative answer, which was also that of Protagoras, p. 66 above.)

2. If so, does this mean that the existence of a common opinion, which is what those who advocate it seem to mean by 'morality' (it is one side of what a Greek meant by *nomos*), justifies its legal enforcement?

3. Can one discover a common stock of ideas of right and wrong, and, if one does, will it be coterminous with the jurisdiction of a legal system? (In Greek terms, does νόμιμον = δίκαιον?) And he lays it down that:

1. Disapproval of my conduct by others does not prove that I am wrong, still less that I deserve criminal punishment.

2. 'Morality' (= public opinion, i.e. *nomos*) may be different at different places and times. He instances the moral values of the West Highlands as compared with those of London, and the so-called 'new morality' of sex, current in the 1960s. (Cf. p. 16 with n. 1 above.)

3. Law may forbid what I think beneficial, and either allow or command what I think wrong.

Campbell's lecture was prompted by Devlin's on 'The Enforcement of Morals', originally in *Proc. Brit. Acad.* for 1959. In the same year that it appeared, however, Devlin republished his own with six others, taking into account the criticisms which it had aroused and which he lists in a bibliography. (*The Enforcement of Morals*, 1965.)

[2] D.L. 6.11. For Antisthenes see pp. 304ff. below.

and of cosmopolitanism and the unity of mankind. There were now people (of whom Antiphon was one, see pp. 152ff. below) ready to declare that distinctions based on race, noble birth, social status or wealth, and institutions such as slavery, had no basis in nature but were only by *nomos*. These were revolutionary ideas of incalculable potency, and deserve to be treated independently. This chapter will conclude with a closer look at the concept of 'unwritten law' which has been mentioned earlier (pp. 22 f., 55 f.) and is an integral part of the general relationship between *nomos* and *physis* which is our present subject.[1]

It is impracticable and artificial to make a break between the centuries, at 400 B.C. or the death of Socrates. When the same questions were being raised in the same terms over perhaps a hundred years, we cannot ignore the evidence of Aristotle or Demosthenes any more than that of Hippias or Euripides. What we are seeing in this period is the birth of the concept of natural law as it was later understood by thinkers ranging from the Stoics to Rousseau.[2] The first use of the actual term (by Plato's Callicles, p. 104 above) was perhaps unfortunate, and a verbal association of 'unwritten laws' with *physis* only occurs, among extant sources, in fourth-century authors. Speaking of the propriety of punishing deliberate crime but not involuntary error, Demosthenes says (*De cor.* 275): 'Not only will this be found in the [positive] laws, but *nature herself* has decreed it in the *unwritten laws* and in the hearts of men.'[3] Aristotle first equates unwritten with universal laws, and then calls universal laws 'according to nature' (*Rhet.* 1368b7, 1373b6, 1375a32). But fifth-century supporters of the unwritten laws were themselves at the same time on the side of *physis* against the limitations and errors of positive *nomoi*.

Such a one was the Sophist Hippias, who according to Plato (*Hipp. Maj.* 285d) was an authority on 'ancient history in general, and in particular how cities were founded in the early days'. In Plato's

---

[1] On the 'unwritten laws' in general see Hirzel, Ἄγραφος νόμος; Cope, *Introd. to A.'s Rhet.*, App. E to book I, pp. 239–44; Ehrenberg, *S. and P.* ch. 2 and App. 4.

[2] Cf. Salomon, *Savigny-Stift.* 1911, 129ff.; the historically important and influential formulation of the concept first appears in post-Aristotelian times, above all in the Stoa, but the age of the Sophists must be considered first because it was then that questions were first raised in a sharp and urgent form which concern natural law and prepare the way for its formulation.

[3] For Demosthenes cf. also the contrast between written and universal law in *In Aristocr.* 61, and the use of ἄγραφα νόμιμα to describe the unwritten traditions of the Areopagus court (*ibid.* 70, p 78 above).

Protagoras he praises *physis* as destroyer of the barriers which *nomos* has erected between man and man (p. 162 below), and Xenophon (*Mem.* 4.4.14ff.) represents him as questioning the equation of justice with keeping the law, on the grounds that laws are no more than temporary agreements which cannot be taken seriously because they are often rejected and amended by the very men who made them. Socrates, having countered this argument, goes on to ask him whether he knows also of unwritten laws. He does, and designates them (like Aristotle after him) as those which are observed in every country. Since all who observe them cannot possibly have met, and would not speak the same language if they did, they must have been made by the gods. The first examples that occur to him and Socrates are to worship the gods and honour one's parents.[1] Concerning avoidance of incest and the duty to requite a benefit he is doubtful, since such laws are not universally observed,[2] but Socrates argues that to say that a law is sometimes broken is no disproof of its validity, and suggests a new criterion: transgression of man-made laws may escape punishment, but of the divine laws never. The two in question pass this test (he claims) because incest is dysgenic and ingratitude leads to loss of friends. It is noticeable that these arguments would apply equally to a world ruled not by gods but by an impersonal nature, and indeed Antiphon made the same point about punishment, that for a transgression of nature's decrees it is inevitable but not for an ordinary lawbreaker.[3] However, this hardly justifies the surprising conclusion of Levi that 'it goes without saying that the unwritten laws of which

[1] This was traditional. See G. Thomson, *Oresteia*, I, 52, and II, 270. For universal laws as divine cf. also Eur. fr. 346.

[2] It is worth reminding ourselves that Hippias may have believed in the unity of mankind (p. 162 below). Incest was repugnant to the Greeks, and its practice among non-Greek peoples was considered evidence of their barbarity. Hermione intends a cruel taunt when she reminds Andromache of her race, a race among whom parents and children, brother and sister have intercourse, 'and no law prevents it' (Eur. *Andr.* 173–6). Socrates speaks as if it were only a question of occasional breaches of a law by individuals, but Hippias knew that there were whole societies where such a law did not exist.

[3] Xen. *Mem.* 4.4.21 ἀλλὰ δίκην γέ τοι διδόασιν οἱ παραβαίνοντες τοὺς ὑπὸ τῶν θεῶν κειμένους νόμους, ἢν οὐδενὶ τρόπῳ δυνατὸν ἀνθρώπῳ διαφυγεῖν, ὥσπερ τοὺς ὑπ' ἀνθρώπων κειμένους νόμους ἔνιοι παραβαίνοντες διαφεύγουσι τὸ δίκην διδόναι, οἱ μὲν λανθάνοντες οἱ δὲ βιαζόμενοι. Cf. Antiphon fr. 44 A, col. 2, τὰ οὖν νόμιμα παραβαίνων εἰὰν λάθῃ τοὺς ὁμολογήσαντας, καὶ αἰσχύνης καὶ ζημίας ἀπήλλακται, μὴ λαθὼν δ' οὔ. τῶν δὲ τῇ φύσει ξυμφύτων ἐάν τι παρὰ τὸ δυνατὸν βιάζηται, ἐάν τε πάντας ἀνθρώπους λάθῃ, οὐδὲν ἔλαττον τὸ κακόν.

Hippias speaks are, because of their naturalistic, non-religious significance, utterly different from those mentioned by Sophocles in a famous text of the *Antigone*, 450 ff.'[1] It is admittedly not clear how the denial of burial to a brother could be said to bring its own punishment in the natural course, as (according at least to Socrates) incest and ingratitude do, but this is also true of neglecting one's parents, which Hippias agrees is among the unwritten laws. There is no reason why he should not have believed what Xenophon puts into his mouth, that 'the gods made these laws for men' and 'this does suggest the work of gods, for the idea that laws should contain their own punishment for those who disobey them must, I think, come from a better legislator than man'. It is not easy for us, with a different theological tradition, to understand the place in Greek thought of divine powers, who might have personal names and characters or might equally well be what we should class as abstractions: Necessity, Persuasion, Justice. For many of their most thoughtful minds it was a matter of indifference whether some beneficent force was ascribed to a divinity or simply to natural processes. We have seen already how the same account of human progress was referred indifferently to the agency of Prometheus or of necessity, experience and time. Hippias therefore would see no inconsistency in contrasting positive with divine laws, and at another time saying that 'law is a tyrant which often does violence to *nature*' (Plato, *Prot.* 337d).[2]

In the tragic poets, as is appropriate, the unwritten laws are unequivocally of divine origin, the 'unwritten ordinances of the gods' in whose name Antigone defies the power of King Creon.[3] In Sophocles

[1] Ad. Levi, *Sophia*, 1942, 450, n. 13, quoted by Untersteiner, *Sof.* III, 69. Levi also follows Dümmler (*Ak.* 255) and Bignone (*Studi*, 132, n. 1) in the curious view that Xenophon has put much of Hippias's doctrine into the mouth of Socrates. Dümmler's chapter is in parts a rather fantastic edifice of hypotheses built on hypotheses.

[2] For a good example of the equation of natural with divine laws see Hippocr. *De victu* 11 (VI, 486 L.): Men have laid down *nomos* for themselves but the *physis* of all things has been ordered by the gods. What men have laid down, be it right or wrong, is never constant, but what the gods have laid down is right for ever. (On the date of *De victu* see Kahn, *Anaximander*, 189, n. 2.)

This is not of course confined to the ancient world. Locke in his second treatise, §135, says that legislation 'must be conformable to the law of nature, i.e. to the will of God of which that is a declaration'.

[3] P. 22 above. Leaving a body unburied is again said to flout the laws of the gods at *Ajax* 1343 and Eur. *Suppl.* 19.

again, a chorus of the *Oedipus Tyrannus* (863 ff.) speaks of holiness in words and deeds 'for which laws are appointed on high, brought to life in the clear air of heaven, whose father is Olympus alone, for no mortal man[1] begat them, nor will forgetfulness ever put them to sleep'. Metaphorically, these unwritten laws may be said to have been 'written by the gods', as when Ion in Euripides's play rebukes Apollo for his sin against a mortal woman (440 ff.): how can it be right for the gods, who have written the laws for mortals, themselves to disobey them? In Aeschylus, respect for parents (cited as one of the unwritten laws in the conversation between Socrates and Hippias) is described by a chorus as 'written in the statutes (θεσμίοις) of Diké (Justice) highest in honour'.[2]

In the famous funeral oration (Thuc. 2.37.3), Pericles, like Socrates, praises observance of both the positive and the unwritten laws: 'We Athenians obey the laws, especially those which are designed for the protection of the oppressed, and those which are unwritten but bring acknowledged shame on those who break them.'[3] The generally acknowledged unwritten laws were those that enjoined reverence towards the gods, respect for parents, requital of benefactors, and also hospitality to strangers. Religious duty is particularly in question in another quotation from Pericles reported in the speech against Andocides attributed to Lysias (pseudo-Lys. *Or.* 6, 10):

Pericles, they say, once advised that in cases of impiety you should invoke not only the written laws about it but also the unwritten in accordance

---

[1] No special significance should be attached to the use of φύσις here. Θνατὰ φύσις ἀνέρων is simply a periphrasis for θνατὸς ἀνήρ. See vol. II, 352. On this passage see also p. 77 above.

[2] *Suppl.* 707, on which George Thomson justly comments that 'written in the statutes of Justice' is only another way of saying that they are unwritten in the statutes of mortal legislators (*Oresteia*, II, 270). Cf. the δελτογράφος φρήν of Hades at *Eum.* 275. Thomson's long note on *Eum.* 269–72 is excellent, and I owe some of my own references to it. Note only (p. 269) that in the conversation between Socrates and Hippias it is Hippias, not Socrates, who argues that the unwritten laws could not have been made by men and must therefore be the work of gods.

[3] Gomme (*Comm. on Thuc.* II, 113) mentions as a difference between Sophocles and Pericles that for the latter the unwritten law was hardly divine. But his audience would certainly believe it to be divine, and he was speaking in a way that they would understand. For a comparison between the *Antigone* and the *epitaphios* of Pericles, see Ehrenberg, *S. and P.* 28–44, and the criticism of it in Gomme, *loc. cit.* Another difference between Sophocles and Thucydides, says Gomme, is that for the former the unwritten law is universal, whereas Thucydides is 'probably' thinking of Greek νόμιμα only. To the Greeks this distinction was blurred: the same law, enjoining burial of the dead, is called τὸν Πανελλήνων νόμον and νόμιμα θεῶν in Eur. *Supplices* (526 and 19). The fact is that up to the fifth century the Greeks largely *ignored* the barbarian world: 'the world' was the Greek world and 'the gods' were the Greek gods.

with which the Eumolpidae [hereditary priests at Eleusis] give their decisions, laws which no one has been able to invalidate nor dared to contradict, nor do they know their author; for in this way they believe that an offender will pay the penalty not only to men but to the gods.

Thomson has noticed the striking parallel between the orator's 'nor do they know their author' and Antigone's words about unwritten laws, that 'no one knows from whence they come'.[1]

Plato's opinion of a democracy, in the degenerate and extreme form in which it leads to tyranny, is that the people 'disregard all laws written or unwritten, in their determination to have no master over them'.[2] In the *Laws* he speaks again of the unwritten laws.

All that we are now discussing [says the Athenian (793a)] is what people in general call 'unwritten laws', and all such injunctions amount to what they call the 'laws of our ancestors'.[3] And what we said recently, that one should neither call them laws nor yet pass them over, was well said. They are the bonds that hold a political society together,[4] links between laws already on the statute book and those still to be enacted, in truth a body of ancestral and age-old precepts which if rightly conceived and put into practice protect and safeguard the written laws of the time, but if they swerve from the right path they cause everything to collapse like a building when the builders' supports give way. With this in mind we must bind your new city together with everything possible that goes by the name of law, custom or usage.

---

[1] I feel inclined to question Ehrenberg's view of this passage when it leads him to say that for Pericles 'even the sacred laws of Eleusis were not part of a divine world contrasted with a man-made order' (*S. and P.* 47).

[2] *Rep.* 563 d, ἵνα δὴ μηδαμῆ μηδεὶς αὐτοῖς ᾖ δεσπότης, probably a deliberate reminder of Demaratus's boast in the great days of Greece: ἔπεστι γάρ σφι δεσπότης νόμος (p. 69 above). Hirzel pointed to this passage of Plato as a direct contradiction of Pericles's euology of Athenian democracy, but Plato is speaking of a state in which the democratic ideal of liberty has reached the stage of ἀπληστία which is its downfall. There is no hint that Athens had reached this stage in the days of Pericles, before Plato was born.

[3] ἄγραφα νόμιμα and πατρίους νόμους. While νόμιμα could be a vaguer term than νόμος, it is obvious that they could sometimes be used interchangeably. Cf. νόμιμα θεῶν at Eur. *Suppl.* 19 with τοὺς θεῶν νόμους at Soph. *Aj.* 1343 (both referring to burial of the dead), and the variations in Dem. 23 (*In Aristocr.*), 61 and 70. In saying that they should not be called νόμοι Plato is recalling his remark at 788a that the education of children is a matter for instruction and admonition rather than law.

[4] Cf. Devlin, *E. of M.* 10: 'Society is not something that is kept together physically; it is held by the invisible bonds of common thought. If the bonds were too far relaxed the members would drift apart. A common morality is part of the bondage. The bondage is part of the price of society; and mankind, which needs society, must pay its price.' (There is something of Protagoras here too.) To Plato δεσμοί were a necessity, to Antiphon an incubus (fr. 44 A, col. 4).

Sexual indulgence in public is an example of the kind of thing which Plato suggests should be discouraged by 'unwritten law', habituating the citizens to a sense of shame, rather than by legal prohibition (*Laws* 841b); and (like Xenophon's Socrates) he cites incest as a case where such unwritten law is already an adequate deterrent (*ibid.* 838a–b).

Aristotle attacks the subject with his characteristic zeal for classification. He first, in *Rhetoric* 1, ch. 10 (1368b7), divides law into particular and universal: 'particular' is the written law of an individual state, 'universal' embraces everything that is unwritten but agreed upon by all. In ch. 13, however, after the same initial division (1373b4) into particular and universal (and an equation of 'universal' with 'natural' law), he proceeds to divide the law of particular states itself into written and unwritten. At this point it should be stated that the object of the chapter is to classify just and unjust actions. The division of the laws is subordinate to this end, because just and unjust acts 'have been defined relatively to two kinds of law'.[1] The law of nature exists because 'there really is a natural and universal right and wrong, apart from any association or covenant'; and he quotes as examples Antigone's famous claim and Empedocles fr. 135. There are then (1374a18) two kinds of right and wrong, the one laid down in writing and the other not, and the second is again divided into (*a*) virtue and vice in excess of that which the law takes note of, which are visited with praise, honours and gifts or reproach and dishonour respectively (i.e. non-legal rewards and penalties; examples of the former are gratitude for and requital of benefits and readiness to help friends), (*b*) acts which, though they might be the subject of positive law, are omitted by it owing to the impossibility of allowing for every variety of case within the framework of general rules: here what is not written is simply a supplement to what is. It is known as equity (τὸ ἐπιεικές).[2]

---

[1] In the *Ethics* (1134b18ff.) Aristotle argues that there is both a natural and a legal form of political justice. Some, he says, have doubted the existence of a φύσει δίκαιον, because what is natural is constant (fire burns everywhere and always), whereas τὰ δίκαια κινούμενα ὁρῶσιν. These are the doubts of the sophistic age, questioning the certainties of a Solon or an Aeschylus. Aristotle counters them by a somewhat obscure and unsatisfactory argument, reflecting the conflict between Platonist and sophist in his own mind and ending lamely with the statement that there is 'only one natural, universal constitution, namely the best'. Barker has an interesting but probably over-subtle commentary on this passage in his introduction to Gierke's *Natural Law*, xxxv.

[2] On the meaning of equity in Aristotle see also W. von Leyden in *Philosophy*, 1967, 6–8.

A passion for reducing everything to classified or tabulated form is always dangerous, and Aristotle has not escaped its snares. As Hirzel pointed out,[1] the divisions are inconsistent, and the passages in ch. 10 and chs. 13–14 probably belong to different discussions. Yet, although there are two kinds of unwritten law, they are not contradictory, and Aristotle held both views: (*a*) the *nomoi* of a particular community are both written and unwritten, the latter (based on its customs and traditions) not contradicting but supplementing the former; (*b*) 'unwritten laws' signifies also the universal, natural laws as in the *Antigone* and Demosthenes.

It must be remembered that Aristotle is writing a handbook of rhetoric, based on earlier handbooks. His object is not to see that the eternal law of nature prevails, but to show how a pleader can juggle with the notions of written and unwritten law as will best suit his case. So in ch. 15 he goes on to show how the theories which he has expounded may be applied in practice. If the written law is against him, the advocate must appeal to the universal law, insisting on its greater equity and justice. The words of the juror's oath, 'according to my honest opinion', mean that he will not slavishly follow the

[1] Hirzel, Ἄγρ. νόμ. 10. Aristotle's classifications can be put in tabular form thus:
Rhet. A 10, 1368b7ff.

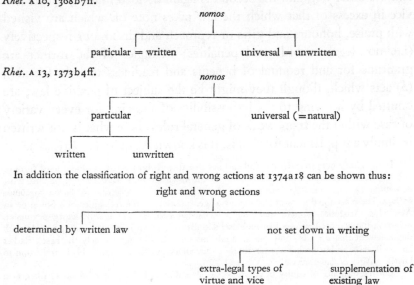

In addition the classification of right and wrong actions at 1374a18 can be shown thus:

written law. The universal law is the law of equity, the unchanging law of nature,[1] whereas written laws are unstable. He will quote the *Antigone*, and declare that the written laws do not fulfil the true purpose of law, and so on. If on the other hand the written law supports his case, he will explain that the juror's oath is not meant to absolve him from following the law, but only to save him from the guilt of perjury if he misunderstands it; that no one chooses absolute good, but only the good for himself;[2] that not to use the laws is as bad as not having any; and that it does not pay to try to be cleverer than the doctor.

These are the tricks that Gorgias and his like were already teaching their pupils and writing in their *technai*, and the passage shows how the growth of rhetoric and the passion for litigation among the Greeks contributed to the unscrupulous subordination of ethical concepts to the expediency of the moment. In itself, the doctrine of unwritten laws, valid at all times and for all men—*nomoi* which are rooted in *physis* and at the same time divinely ordained and of a lofty moral tone—stands for the archaic traditions, both philosophical and popular, which were now being challenged by the new morality.

For Hesiod justice rested on the law of Zeus, as for Heraclitus all human laws were emanations of the divine (p. 55 above), and Empedocles (fr. 135) could speak of a law for all, 'extending through the wide air and the immense light of heaven'. The religious background to this is seen at its best in the words of Solon at the end of the seventh century. What the immortal gods give, no man can escape. Prosperity based on evil conduct is inevitably insecure, for Zeus is guardian of the moral law. Soon or late the blow will fall, though Zeus may be slow to punish and the sufferers may be the offender's children. It is the old

[1] Bignone (*Studi*, 129, n. 1) sees in these words a clear reminiscence of Antiphon. It might as well be Hippias or others, but at least his remark is further evidence, if that were necessary, that Aristotle is simply repeating notions already familiar in the heyday of the Sophists. Hirzel ("Αγρ. νόμ. 8) finds it difficult to understand how Aristotle could say here of τὸ ἐπιεικές that it ἀεὶ μένει καὶ οὐδέποτε μεταβάλλει in view of the variety which he has earlier ascribed to it. It is astonishing how previous scholars seem to have solemnly analysed this passage as a serious statement of Aristotle's views, whereas it is one of a pair of contrasting ἀντιλογίαι to be used as occasion demands in the interests of victory in the courts. (Skemp is an exception, *Plato's Statesman*, 198.) On the notion of ἐπιεικές see Cope, *Introd. to Rhet.* 190–3.

[2] '*Sc.* and our written laws, which were made for us, may not reach the abstract ideal of perfection, but they probably suit us better than if they did.' (Rhys Roberts, Oxf. Trans. *ad loc.*)

doctrine, which we see also worked out in Aeschylus, that 'the doer shall suffer', *hybris* is inevitably followed by *até*, doom, under the authority of Zeus who 'watches over the end of everything'. In a striking simile Solon compares the judgment of Zeus to a spring gale which stirs the sea to its very bottom, ravages the crops on earth and at the same time sweeps the clouds from the sky so that the sun shines out once more in all its strength.

Several scholars have pointed out that in this passage 'the vengeance of Zeus falls with the weight and inevitability of a natural phenomenon', that 'Solon gives us our first intimation of the lawfulness of nature'[1]— surely an additional reason against supposing that the 'naturalistic' unwritten laws of which Hippias speaks are necessarily different from those upheld as divine in the *Antigone* (pp. 119 f. above).

Aristotle has shown how the unwritten laws could be invoked by an unscrupulous advocate in the interests of a particular case. There was indeed a danger of their abuse, especially when the ideal of a benevolent and paternal aristocracy had given place to the crowning achievement of Greek political genius, the *polis* or city-state, in which the written constitution was the guarantee of a citizen's rights and the bulwark against tyranny or oppression, and the watchword was *isonomia*, equality before the law.[2] Just as *physis* could be invoked either to uphold humanitarian ideals or in the interests of aggression and the overthrow of constitutional government, so the idea of un-written law, which originally emphasized the moral government of the universe, could, in a more democratic society, appear simply as retrograde and a menace to the hard-won assurance of human rights that now was written into the statute-book. The restored democracy at the end of the fifth century decreed that 'the magistrate should in no case make use of unwritten law', that the laws should treat all citizens alike without distinction, and that they must be displayed in public for all to see (Andocides, *De mystt.* 85). Theseus, condemning tyranny in the *Supplices* of Euripides (429 ff.), says that 'under written laws

[1] Lesky, *Hist. Gr. Lit.* 125; Snell, *Disc. of Mind*, 212. Solon, says Snell, is using the Homeric type of simile, but for a new purpose, to express 'not so much the individual explosions of energy but the necessity which prompts them, not the unique event, but the continuous condition'. This insight 'places him on the threshold of philosophy'. One might compare the cosmic δίκη of Anaximander. (The passages of Solon referred to occur in fr. 1 Diehl.)

[2] On ἰσονομία and democracy see p. 150, n. 2, below.

justice is meted out impartially to the feeble and the wealthy, the lesser man overcomes the greater if his cause is just'. This happens 'when the *demos* is master in the land'.

The difference between Sophocles and Euripides here is interesting. It would seem that Sophocles in the *Antigone* is a passionate upholder of the unwritten law, and Euripides of the written.[1] Yet both are equally opposing the tyrant, and Sophocles, who took his full share of public duties, was no less a champion of constitutional and legal safeguards. In the *Antigone* itself (367 f.), the chorus declare that the amazing ingenuity of man will only lead to good if he remain within the framework of the *polis* and respect the laws of the land,[2] and in the *Oedipus at Colonus* Theseus rebukes Creon because, 'having come to a city which observes justice and determines nothing without law, you reject the legitimate authorities' (912 ff.). We do not need the word 'written' here to tell us that Sophocles is thinking of positive, formulated law as it was understood in the Athens of his day. Conversely the Theseus of Euripides, in the very same play in which he insists on the need for written laws, is asserting the same sacred duty as Antigone, the duty of burying the dead. By doing this, he says, I shall preserve the common *nomos* of Greece (526 f.), and his mother Aethra accuses Creon of 'flouting the *nomima* of the gods' (19).

That there is a difference of mood and emphasis between the two poets no one could deny. It cannot be explained on chronological grounds,[3] yet in a way they do stand for two generations, because Euripides was so much more attracted than Sophocles to the modern, sophistic currents of thought. Like Protagoras, he knew that there were two sides to every question, and he enjoyed as much as Hippias the 'contest of words' in which his characters indulge.[4] The debate

---

[1] So Hirzel, Ἄγρ. νόμ. 69–71, in an interesting discussion with which on some points I am venturing to disagree.

[2] Pohlenz (*Kl. Schr.* II, 352) likens Sophocles to Protagoras in his respect for law as man's highest cultural achievement.

[3] So far as can be judged, the *Antigone* was produced about 440, the *Supplices* of Euripides about 420, and the *Oedipus Coloneus* posthumously in 401.

[4] Cf. fr. 189 (from the Antiope):

ἐκ παντὸς ἄν τις πράγματος δισσῶν λόγων
ἀγῶνα θεῖτ' ἄν εἰ λέγειν εἴη σοφός.

For ἅμιλλαι or ἀγῶνες λόγων see *Suppl.* 195, 427 f., *Med.* 546, *Or.* 491. On the agonistic character of sophistic see p. 43 above.

between Theseus and the herald as to whether the dead warriors should be buried develops into a set piece on absolute monarchy *versus* democracy. Although it is clear where Euripides's sympathies lie, the herald is no caricature of a bombastic tyrant's minion, but an accomplished sophist and orator. My city, he says, has no use for mob-rule. No one can sway it this way or that by playing on its vanity, pleasing it for the moment but in the long run harming it.[1] Since a whole *demos* cannot judge arguments correctly, how can it direct a city? Education takes time, and even if a labouring man is no fool, his work prevents him from giving proper attention to public affairs. (Why have these arguments a familiar ring? It is Socrates in the *Gorgias* who complains that orators in a democracy lay themselves out to flatter the *demos* rather than tell it what will be for its good, and Socrates again who said, like Hume, that 'poverty and hard labour debase the minds of the common people' and unfit them for politics, which was a matter for trained experts.)[2] Failure (continues the herald) to comply with Creon's demands means war. You may hope to win: hope has been the cause of many a conflict. Everyone thinks that its misfortunes will fall on others, not himself. (Just so did the Athenians warn the unfortunate Melians of the snares of hope in Thuc. 5.103.)[3] If, when the vote is taken, each citizen could visualize his own death in battle, Greece would be safe from war-madness. We all know how much better peace is than war, yet we renounce it in our lust to enslave one another, as men and as cities. A wise man thinks of his children, his parents, and the safety of his country. A rash leader is a danger: true courage lies in forethought.[4]

Here is a man who has studied the *technai* of Gorgias and others and mastered all the rhetorical tricks. Any argument you like can be

---

[1] In similar vein Hippolytus—a very different character—says proudly (*Hipp.* 986): 'I have no skill to speak to the mob; my wisdom is rather for the few, my equals. And this is fitting. Those who in the eyes of the wise are of no account—it is they who are more accomplished in the art of mob-oratory.'

[2] Hume, *Essays and Treatises* (Edinburgh, 1825), p. 195. For Socrates see e.g. Xen. *Mem.* 1.2.9, *Oec.* 4. 2–3, Plato, *Rep.* 495 d–e, Arist. *Rhet.* 1393 b 3. More of this on pp. 409 ff. below.

[3] It seems to have been a commonplace of the time. Antiphon wrote (fr. 58): 'Hopes are not always a good thing. They have brought many to irreparable disaster, who in the end have suffered themselves what they thought to inflict on their neighbours.'

[4] Cf. Polynices (another unsympathetic character) at *Phoen.* 599:

ἀσφαλὴς γάρ ἐστ' ἀμείνων ἢ θρασὺς στρατηλάτης.

subordinated to the opportunism of the moment. Even the case for pacifism (and no one surpassed Euripides in his horror of war; see for instance the chorus in the *Helen*, 1151 ff.) can be vividly presented in the interests of a ruthless ultimatum.

To sum up a complex situation, the term 'unwritten laws' was applied in the first place to certain moral principles believed to be universally valid, or alternatively valid all over the Greek world.[1] Their authors were the gods, and no breach of them could remain unpunished. They were already closely connected with the natural world, for to contrast man with nature instead of seeing him as a part of it is a modern rather than a Greek habit. So for instance Heraclitus, who spoke of all human laws being nourished by the one divine law, also said that if the sun left his course the Furies, agents of Diké, would find him out. In contrast to these ordinances of heaven, each country or city had its own *nomoi*. It made laws to suit its own beliefs and needs, laws which had no force elsewhere and in their own land might be altered to suit changed circumstances. In general it would be thought just or right to observe these laws, but they had not the scope or force of the divine or natural laws, and to the questing minds of the sophistic age it was matter for debate how far *dikaion* and *nomimon* coincided, the answer depending very much on whether or not a speaker was prepared to include the divine *nomoi* under the latter head.

A second meaning of 'unwritten law' derived from the ambiguity of the word *nomos* (p. 56 above). Since it meant the customs of a country as well as its law, 'unwritten *nomoi*' stood for what was believed in that country to be right and equitable but could not in practice be included in a corpus of written law. Yet it would be taken into account in judging a particular case (Ar. *Rhet.* 1374a26ff.).

By the middle of the fifth century a secular trend of thought is gaining ground at the expense of the theistic, which did not however by any means disappear completely. Side by side with it appears an

---

[1] See p. 121, n. 3, above. On the so-called 'Three Commandments' see Ehrenberg, *S. and P.* 167–72, who rightly claims that the situation was much more fluid than this phrase suggests. It is of some interest that three of Pericles's unwritten laws (to worship God, to obey parents, and to show gratitude to benefactors) recur in a modern writer's list of commands which 'Locke and most other theorists' would include in the law of nature (von Leyden, *Philosophy*, 1956, 27).

impersonal 'nature', whose decrees are as absolute, and their neglect as inevitably punished, as those of the gods had been. But they do not necessarily follow the precepts of traditional morality, for under the influence of mechanistic scientific theories the natural world is no longer subject to moral government. The effect is seen in Antiphon, for whom pleasure is the natural goal and the old divine unwritten law that parents should be honoured is 'often contrary to nature'. For Callicles the 'law of nature', which every man should follow who has the strength and determination to do so, justified the crudest hedonism and the most outrageous tyranny.

The decline of religious sanctions coincided with the rise of democratic government, for which positive, written law appeared as a safeguard against the return of tyranny or oligarchy based on the new conception of 'nature's law'. The latter was perforce unwritten and so, finally, the concept of 'unwritten law' took on a sinister meaning and was banished from the modern, more nearly egalitarian society.

This was the state of the question when Plato took it over: at one extreme the equality of all citizens under a written and published code of law, at the other the ideal of the strong man, nature's hero, who spurns the law in his march to absolute and selfishly exercised power. To both of these Plato opposed first his conception of nature itself as an intelligent and moral force, and secondly (*Politicus* 292 ff.) his vision of the wise, enlightened and trained ruler, master of the science of government, whose rule would inevitably benefit his people. Such a one would do better without written laws, imposing the fruits of his scientific understanding on subjects willing or unwilling, killing or banishing when necessary for the health of the city as a whole. (Even the docile Young Socrates is moved to a protest at this point.) Codified law is only a set of clumsy rules of thumb, which cannot allow for the infinite variety of particular cases. A magistrate who governs by it, as compared with the true statesman, will be like a layman trying to cure a patient by looking up the disease in a book compared to a skilled and experienced physician using his expert judgment. This drastic conclusion is considerably modified when Plato goes on to admit that in the absence of the ideal statesman a good code of laws provides the best 'imitation' of his rule and in all ordinary states must be drawn up and enforced with the utmost rigour.

Finally, to remind ourselves how lasting has been this dilemma which the Greeks were the first to face, we have only to look again at the passages from Rousseau and Locke quoted earlier (p. 23), and the twentieth-century judgment of Mr Campbell, to which may be appended as a comment what Ernest Barker wrote of the Natural Law school of the seventeenth and eighteenth centuries:

To begin with, there was the current conception that Natural Law somehow overbore law positive, so that enactments and acts of State which ran contrary to its prescriptions were strictly null and void, even if in actual practice, owing to the absence of any machinery for their disallowance, these acts and enactments retained their validity. Such a conception—applied in various forms, sometimes with a greater and sometimes with a less degree of reverence for actual law—was a ready solvent of political obligation. The rebel against constituted authority could easily plead obedience to the higher law, and could readily allege that he was only exerting, or defending, the natural rights which he enjoyed under that law ... An English judge had uttered the *obiter dictum*, in 1614, that 'even an Act of Parliament made against natural equity ... is void in itself; for *jura naturae sunt immutabilia*, and they are *leges legum*'.

This concept was invoked indifferently in the cause of popularism and of absolutism, for 'nature could be used to consecrate the monarch as well as the people'. In the American War of Independence, 'it was the *Law of Nature* which, more than any other force, exploded the authority of the British Parliament and the British connexion'.[1]

APPENDIX

Pindar on 'nomos'

No discussion of the *nomos–physis* antithesis would be complete without a mention of Pindar's famous allusion to '*nomos* king of all, mortals and immortals alike', but there is no agreement as to its meaning. I can only set out the alternatives and indicate what appears to me to be most probably its purport.

The relevant passage is fr. 152 Bowra, 169 Schr. Plato at *Gorg.* 484b quotes the first $4\frac{1}{2}$ lines and gives the sense down to *v.* 7; *vv.* 1–4 occur also

[1] Barker, introduction to Gierke's *Natural Law*, pp. xlvi–xlviii.

in schol. Pind. *Nem.* 9. 35, and 5–7 in schol. on Ael. Aristides (III, 408, 19 Dindorf). A great gain has been the publication in 1961 of a papyrus (*OP* XXVI, 2450) of the greater part of the poem from *v.* 6 onwards.[1] I quote *vv.* 1–8:

νόμος ὁ πάντων βασιλεύς
θνατῶν τε καὶ ἀθανάτων
ἄγει δικαιῶν τὸ βιαιότατον[2]
ὑπερτάτᾳ χειρί. τεκμαίρομαι
ἔργοισιν Ἡρακλέος
ἐπεὶ Γηρυόνα βόας
Κυκλώπειον ἐπὶ πρόθυρον Εὐρυσθέος
αἰτητάς[3] τε καὶ ἀπριάτας ἔλασεν.

The poem continues with Heracles's theft of the horses of Diomedes, including a gruesome description of a man's bones being crunched by the horses.

Plato's Callicles quotes the passage in support of his own doctrine that might is right: Pindar's *nomos* is not man-made law but the supreme law of nature which justifies the most extreme violence (or alternatively does violence to accepted notions of justice). The irony of this interpretation is apparent, but it still remains a question whether *nomos* has its usual meaning of ordinarily accepted custom or stands for a higher law of the gods. Herodotus (3.38) associates Pindar's words with his own view of the relativity of *nomos* as illustrated by the experiment of Darius (p. 16 above). This is certainly the sense of fr. 203 B (215 Schr.)

ἄλλο δ' ἄλλοισι νόμισμα, σφετέραν δ' αἰνεῖ δίκαν
ἕκαστος,

which is in keeping with Herodotus's remark that each would choose his own *nomoi* as the finest, and shows that Pindar certainly could, on occasion, speak of *nomos* as human and relative.[4] Wilamowitz and Theiler both give *nomos* in our passage the sense of ordinary custom or usage (*Brauch*):

---

[1] See also Page in *Proc. Camb. Philol. Soc.* 1962 and Theiler in *Mus. Helv.* 1965.

[2] This is universally agreed to be correct, though the manuscripts of Plato have βιαίων (for βιαιῶν) τὸ δικαιότατον. We need not here consider whether this is a copyist's error or a deliberately ironic misquotation on Plato's part. See on that Dodds, *Gorg.* 270–2, and Theiler, *Mus. Helv.* 1965, 68f.

[3] αἰτητάς Theiler, comparing Plato's paraphrase οὔτε πριάμενος οὔτε δόντος τοῦ Γ. and Soph. *O.T.* 384 δωρητὸν οὐκ αἰτητόν. Aristides's paraphrase (II, 68 Dind.) is οὔτε αἰτήσας whence Boeckh's ἀναιτήτας which Schr. and Bowra follow. ἀνατεί ('unpunished') Page *loc. cit.*

[4] Few, I imagine, will wish to follow Heinimann (*N. u. Ph.* 71) in arguing that even this does not imply the relative (and hence not universally obligatory) character of laws and customs because each is an expression of the will of Zeus and therefore binding.

it is *customary* to accept the violence of Heracles without comment or criticism, and though Pindar has a higher ethical insight he prefers to say no more, as he makes clear in fr. 70 B. (quoted below: see Theiler, *loc. cit.* 75). According to Aelius Aristides (II, 70 Dind.) Pindar's lines are an indignant protest (σχετλιάзων) against a *nomos* which approves such violent deeds as those of Heracles; and he confirms this by quoting another passage (fr. 70 B., 81 Schr.) in which Pindar says: 'I am on your side, Geryones, but I will never say what is displeasing to Zeus.' The continuation of the present poem is in the same sense, for Pindar says that Diomedes in trying to save his horses acted 'bravely, not wantonly, for it is better to die protecting one's own than to be a coward' (*vv.* 14–17).

The fullest discussion is that of M. Gigante.[1] He believes Herodotus wilfully misrepresents the quotation in the sense of fr. 203 B., and that to translate *nomos* here by custom closes the way to correct understanding. *Nomos* is 'the absolute principle of divinity'. Pindar intuits 'God as the Absolute': to quote his own words, God becomes 'idea e forza del mondo, non piú ideale della purezza e della pietà, ma ideale della giustizia che nel suo compiersi si servì della forza'. Pindar admits the right of the stronger, but only as the law and will of Zeus, not for human and contingent interests. The most violent action is justified because, being realized by the will of Zeus, it leads to justice and well-being. Gigante quotes fr. 48 B. (57 Schr.), in which Zeus is addressed as δαμιοργὸς εὐνομίας καὶ δίκας. (But why should not fr. 203 B., ἄλλο δ' ἄλλοισι νόμισμα, be equally apt?)

Untersteiner and Ehrenberg, though they eschew mention of the Absolute, come to not dissimilar conclusions in their own ways. Untersteiner agrees that in Pindar *nomos* is 'an inviolable and sacred order',[2] and Ehrenberg says (*Rechtsidee*, 119f.) that, though not a 'Schicksalsgottheit' as Schroeder thought, it is 'ancient and sacred custom', a usage which can turn violence itself to justice, making holy even what is opposed to the human sentiment of what is right. Dodds too thinks it unlikely that by *nomos* Pindar meant merely custom. It is 'the law of Fate, which for him is identical with the will of Zeus', and he too compares fr. 70 B.: 'I will never say what is displeasing to Zeus.'

All these interpretations seem to ignore what Pindar plainly says: not that *nomos* is the will of Zeus but that even Zeus is subject to *nomos*, which lords it over gods as well as men. Fr. 70 is capable of a less lofty reference than to 'the law of fate'. Heracles was Zeus's son, so naturally

---

[1] *Nomos Basileus*, chs. 5–7, pp. 72–108. On pp. 79–92 he gives a useful review of previous discussions of the fragment, to which H. Volkmann, in *Gnomon*, 1958, 474f., adds E. Wolf, *Gr. Rechtsdenken*, II (1952), 190ff.

[2] *Sophs.* 297, n. 30. He puts the words between quotes.

Zeus favoured him, and (gods being the jealous creatures they are) it would be unwise for a mortal to take his victim's side too openly. A similar reply may be made to Heinimann's comment on *Pyth.* 2.86, where *nomos* = form of government. The changes between tyranny, democracy and aristocracy (for Pindar 'the rule of the wise') are enumerated, and it is said that 'the god' favours now this one, now that. This, Heinimann thinks, shows that although *nomos* changes it depends not on human caprice but on Zeus (*N. u. Ph.* 71). What it does show is that a god can be as capricious as a man. Pindar was pious in the sense that he thought mortals must submit to the will of the gods, but his religion retains much of the Homeric. He was defender rather than critic of the Olympians. The more slanderous stories about them must be rejected and their honour upheld (*Ol.* 1.28f., 52), but they were still the wilful, amorous, powerful beings who fathered mortal heroes and must have their way. In general he holds to the traditionally prudent attitude of the Greeks that the gods are jealous and 'mortal things befit mortals'. 'It is meet that a man speak fair things of the gods, for so the blame is less.'[1]

To know what was in Pindar's mind in this poem is obviously very difficult, but I would venture the following: Recognized custom (usage, tradition) has immense power. Both gods and men conform to it, and any act, however wrong or terrible it may seem in itself, will, if only it becomes sanctioned by *nomos*, appear to be justified. What could be more violent and seemingly unjust and cruel than the theft of Geryon's cattle or the horses of Diomedes? Yet the power of *nomos* makes both men and gods accept it.[2] Pindar may well be shaking his head over this state of affairs, as Pohlenz said (*Kl. Schr.* II, 337), but more probably he prefers to make no judgment. That is the prudent course.

---

[1] *Isth.* 5.16, *Ol.* 1.35. There are similar sentiments in *Ol.* 5.27, *Pyth.* 2.34 and 3.39.

[2] Dodds's comment (*Gorg.* 270) that 'the deeds of Heracles are no apt symbol of the customary' is beside the point. What custom has done is to *justify* them (δικαιῶν τὸ βιαιότατον). To illustrate the universal truth expressed in the first three lines the most appropriate act was one that was (*a*) extremely violent, and (*b*) perpetrated by a divine being, the son of Zeus who became a god himself.

V

THE SOCIAL COMPACT[1]

Opinions differ as to how far the theory of the social contract, or compact, as understood in the seventeenth and eighteenth centuries A.D., was anticipated in our period of Greek thought, and the differences spring largely from the different meanings which scholars have given to the phrase. We shall look at the evidence first (briefly in some cases where it has already been touched on), and may then, if we wish, see how close the Greek conceptions were to those of later Europe.

One ancient belief about law attributed it ultimately to the gods. The human lawgiver or constitution-maker (whose existence was not denied) was only the channel through which the commands of heaven became known and effective. In Tyrtaeus's poem (seventh century, fr. 3 Diehl) Lycurgus's constitution for Sparta is actually dictated in detail by Apollo at Delphi. Later, men tended to say that Lycurgus drew up the constitution himself but went to Delphi for assurance that it had the god's approval (Xen. *Rep. Lac.* 8.5). Herodotus (1.65) finds two versions side by side, the traditional one

[1] More usually known as the 'social contract theory', largely through the influence of Rousseau's *Contrat Social*, though Hume also wrote on *The Original Contract*. But both Rousseau and Hume use more general terms like 'compact' and 'pact' indifferently, and as Peter Laslett has pointed out (*Locke's Two Treatises*, 112), Locke scarcely applies the word 'contract' to political matters at all; it is 'compact' or 'agreement' which creates a society. In speaking of the Greeks at least, the less specific and legal term is probably to be preferred.

It goes without saying that there were differences in the concept and its application arising out of differences in historical situation. The people who were discovering their identity and determining the place of monarchy after the wars of religion and the Reformation were in a very different position from the Sophists. One thing that both have in common is the transition from a religious to a secular view of law, from the agency of God to that of man. Kaerst rightly pointed out (*Ztschr. f. Pol.* 1909, 506) that the contract theory has two elements which must be kept distinct, though they are combined in some modern formulations. These are (*a*) the doctrine of a social contract or compact proper, i.e. an agreement of association between equals, (*b*) the *pactum subiectionis*, whereby the ordinary citizen is bound in subjection to a higher authority or sovereign. Only the former has its origin in Greek speculation. (For the history of the concept from the ancient world onward see Kaerst's article; M. D'Addio, *L'idea del contratto sociale dai Sofisti alla Riforma*; and J. W. Gough, *The Social Contract*.)

of a religious origin for the laws, and a rationalistic—based on the similarity of Spartan and Cretan laws—that Lycurgus copied the constitution of Crete. The Cretan laws in their turn were said to have been the work of Zeus (Plato, *Laws*, *ad init.*). Even Cleisthenes, making his democratic reforms at the end of the sixth century, received the names for his new tribes from the Pythia (Arist. *Ath. Pol.* 21–6), and probably therefore sought the oracle's ratification of his whole scheme.[1]

By the fifth century an impersonal nature had in some men's minds replaced the gods as the worldwide power that produced the whole order of which men are a part. For others, like Hippias, the two can exist comfortably side by side, and Euripides, when he speaks in 'Presocratic' language of the 'ageless order of immortal nature',[2] and elsewhere in his poetry, shows a desire to keep them united. When therefore, as we have seen, the view was gaining ground that law is a purely human institution designed to meet particular needs, with nothing permanent or sacred about it, it could be contrasted with either a divine or a natural order or both. In drawing this contrast the act of legislation is usually said to be the outcome of an agreement or compact (συνθήκη) between the members of a community, who have 'put together', composed, or agreed upon certain articles.[3]

The records of Protagoras do not contain the actual word 'compact', but when the gods are removed from his parable (as in view of his agnosticism they must be), we have a picture of men perishing for lack of the art of living together in cities and by hard experience learning to act justly and respect the rights of others and so founding

---

[1] See further Guthrie, *Gks. and their Gods*, 184–9.

[2] ἀθανάτου φύσεως κόσμον ἀγήρω, fr. 910 N. Burnet (*EGP*, 10, n. 3) says that ἀγήρω is genitive, which, though it sounds tautologous, could be right. Anaximander B 2 has ἀίδιον καὶ ἀγήρω, which, while it suggests that the tautology could go back to Anaximander himself, also shows that the form ἀγήρω could be used for the accusative, as appears also from examples in LSJ. Nauck arbitrarily alters it to ἀγήρων to settle the matter.

[3] The prefix συν- in compound verbs has two uses: (*a*) objective, as in συντίθημι (act.), to put two or more things together, thus constructing a composite whole; (*b*) subjective, to do something conjointly or in harmony with someone else, as in σύμφημι, which does not mean to say two or more things together or at the same time, but to say something in unison with another person, i.e. to agree with him. The middle voice of συντίθημι was used in both ways. It meant, first, 'to put together for oneself', or organize, and also to hear and understand ('put two and two together'); secondly to agree with others, and (with an infinitive) to agree to do something. When the object was laws, a treaty or the like, it is probable that both meanings were present: the constituent articles are composed or put together, and they are mutually agreed upon (the reflexive force of the middle assisting).

political communities. This is a matter of 'self-control and justice' (*Prot.* 322e). Protagoras, said Ernest Barker, was 'no believer in the doctrine of a social contract'. This is partly because of Barker's mistaken conviction that he 'conceived the state as an ordinance of God, as existing *jure divino*, rather than as a creation of man, existing *ex contractu*', partly because 'a contract issuing in an artificial unity maintained by artificial laws would be no sooner formed than broken. What is needed and what is everything, is . . . a common mind to pursue a common purpose of good life.' That is true, but is such artificiality implied by the contract theory? Is not Popper right when he claims that 'the word "contract" suggests . . . perhaps more than any other theory, that the strength of the laws lies in the individual's readiness to accept and obey them'?[1] The moral virtues which made a common life possible (αἰδώς, δίκη, σωφροσύνη) were necessary preconditions for the founding of a *polis*, but since Protagoras did not believe that laws were the work of nature or gods he must have believed, like other contemporary progressive thinkers, that they were formulated as the result of a consensus of opinion between the citizens who henceforth considered themselves bound by them.

In the 'defence of Protagoras' undertaken by Socrates in the *Theaetetus* (167c) we find a theory which refers only to present conditions, though it is not inconsistent with a belief in an original contract in the past. 'Whatever acts appear just and fine to a particular state *are* so for that state so long as it believes in them; but when in a particular case they are burdensome for the citizens, the wise man substitutes others that appear and are beneficial.' This dictum follows from Protagoras's doctrine of 'man the measure' (pp. 183 ff. below), and, as Salomon said, it is factual, not normative: what is agreed upon by a city is just for that city so long as it continues to regard it as valid (νομίζῃ —hold it as *nomos*). The compact has made it just and right for the citizens to keep the laws until they are altered, even though the

---

[1] The quotations are from Barker's *Gr. Pol. Theory* (first published 1918), 63, and *Pol. Thought of P. and A.* (first published 1906), 73; and Popper, *Open Soc.* 115. Barker's censure might be valid against Hobbes, but not against Rousseau or others who spoke of a social contract. Here too one sees how misleading it is to speak of '*the* Social Contract theory' (p. 142, n. 1, below). What I have said of Barker applies equally to a number of critics who have started from the assumption that Protagoras believed political institutions and laws to be gifts of God or 'nature', e.g. Loenen, *P. and Gk. Comm.* 50f., 65 ff.; Mewaldt, *Kulturkampf,* 11.

city might prosper better under different laws. Similarly Aristotle later, in distinguishing between natural and legal justice, equates the latter with 'justice by agreement'.[1] The first words of Antiphon fr. 44 A ('I say that justice consists in not transgressing the laws and usages of one's own state') and the identification of just with lawful by Socrates in Xenophon (*Mem.* 4.4.12, p. 111 above) suggest that this legal conception of justice was in vogue among the advanced thinkers of the time, and the various conclusions to be drawn from it were under lively discussion. It left open the question whether justice so defined was 'beneficial' (συμφέρον) or not. At any rate we may safely include Protagoras among those who explained the rise of political communities in terms of a contract or agreement.

Hippias, for whom law and nature were strongly contrasted (Plato, *Prot.* 337 d), defined laws explicitly as 'covenants made by the citizens whereby they have enacted in writing what ought to be done and what not' (language reminiscent of Antiphon, pp. 108 f. above), and pointed to the rapidity with which they may be changed as a reason for not taking them very seriously (p. 119). Antiphon, in the same context of opposition between nature and law, also calls laws the result of agreement, which for him (unlike Protagoras) justifies ignoring them in favour of the commands of nature. Untersteiner perceived the idea of the social contract again in the words 'neither to inflict nor to suffer injury', which formed the content of the compact according to Glaucon in the *Republic*.[2] Something like it is also, as Dodds said (*Gorg.* 266), implicit in the *Sisyphus* of Critias, where laws and their sanctions are instituted by men to check the savagery of the state of nature.

Of slightly later writers, we have seen (p. 76 above) how the author of the speech against Aristogeiton combines, in a way natural at the time though impossible before or since, the conceptions of law as a

---

[1] *EN* 1134b32, νομικὸν καὶ συνθήκη. The *Theaetetus* passage is dealt with more fully on pp. 183 ff. below.

[2] Antiphon, fr. 44, DK, II, 347 and 355 (pp. 108, 110 above); Untersteiner *Sof.* IV, 100. Heinimann (*N. u. Ph.* 139) says that since Antiphon speaks of transgression bringing αἰσχύνη as well as ζημία, he must be including the 'unwritten laws' and so his doctrine is not only one of the social contract as origin of law, but also of morality as originating in deliberate agreement. But (*a*) I do not feel so certain that Antiphon would not associate disgrace with purely legal punishment; (*b*) it is a question whether Antiphon intended his words in a historical sense. (See pp. 143, 145 below.)

human compact and a gift of divine providence. But for some reason pride of place is always given to Lycophron, known to Aristotle as a Sophist and thought to have been a pupil of Gorgias. He is even claimed as the founder of the social contract theory in its earliest form, though, since he was probably not writing until the fourth century, the evidence already reviewed makes this impossible.[1] Our authority is Aristotle in his *Politics* (1280b 10). Discussing the perennial question of the relation between law and morals, he claims that the end and aim of a state is to promote the good life and therefore it has a right and a duty to concern itself with the moral goodness of its citizens. 'Otherwise', he goes on, 'the political society becomes a mere alliance, differing only in respect of locality from alliances between distant countries; and law becomes a compact, and as Lycophron the Sophist said, a guarantor of men's rights against one another, not a means of making the citizens good and just.'

The only words which Aristotle here ascribes to Lycophron as a description of law are 'a guarantor of men's rights against one another',[2] not the actual noun 'compact', though no doubt their contractual nature follows and his definition comes close to that mentioned by Glaucon in the *Republic* as one commonly held. The limitation of law to the negative role of protecting the citizens against each other had been put forward earlier as an ideal by Hippodamus, the remarkable town-planner and political theorist who lived in Athens in the middle of the fifth century, rebuilt the Piraeus on a grid plan and laid out the new colonial city of Thurii for Pericles. In his ideal state he would allow three indictable offences only, which may be translated as insult, injury (to person or property) and murder.[3] He was moreover the first to propose a supreme court of appeal against wrong judgments. The passages are chiefly interesting as showing how lively in the Greek world was a controversy that is receiving so much attention from leading authorities on jurisprudence at the present day, namely

[1] For Lycophron see pp. 313 f. below. As founder of the social contract theory, Popper *O.S.* 114.

[2] ἐγγυητὴς ἀλλήλοις τῶν δικαίων. The brevity and neatness of Lycophron's definition, rather than any originality, may have been what caused Aristotle to single it out for quotation.

[3] ὕβρις βλάβη θάνατος. Our authority is again Aristotle, *Pol.* 1267b 37 ff. On Hippodamus see the references in Bignone, *Studi*, 43, and the brief but lucid account of him in Barker, *Pol. Theory of P. and A.* 44–6.

that concerning the degree to which morality should be enforced by law. Lycophron and Hippodamus would have agreed with J. S. Mill that the only purpose for which law could rightly be enforced against a member of the community was to prevent harm to others; his own good, physical or moral, was not sufficient warrant. In Aristotle's eyes this ignores the real purpose of political association, which is to ensure not simply life but the good life. He would have sided with Lord Simonds, who in 1962 pronounced it 'the supreme and fundamental purpose of the law to conserve not only the safety and order but also the moral welfare of the State', and his general conception would be close to that of Lord Devlin, that 'what makes a society is a community of ideas, not political ideas alone but also ideas about the way its members should behave and govern their lives'.[1]

In Plato's *Crito* Socrates expounds in his prison cell the doctrine of an agreement between himself and the laws of his city as an argument against attempting to evade the judgment which those laws have passed upon him. He says nothing about the origin of law, but there is no suggestion that it was divine. The argument is that, since the time when his parents were married under the laws of Athens, Socrates has owed his birth, education and livelihood to those laws. Moreover they gave him freedom, should he find anything objectionable in them, to leave Athens with all his property and settle elsewhere. Since he had not chosen to do so, he should consider himself their child and their servant. It was 'just' for him to abide by their decisions, and as he had risked his life in battle at their commands so he should give it up now that they demanded it from him. That was the agreement between them (50c, 52d), and it was necessary to the very existence of the state. If private individuals could set aside the law's judgments at their own caprice, the whole foundation of the city's life would crumble.

In Plato's works we have also seen the conception of law as a compact put forward by witnesses hostile to it, Callicles and the 'they' of

---

[1] See Devlin, *Enforcement of Morals*, 86 and 88, and cf. p. 117, n. 1, above. On Aristotle's side is also pseudo-Dem. 25 (*In Aristog.*), 16–17: the laws aim not only at τὸ δίκαιον but also at τὸ καλὸν καὶ τὸ συμφέρον. They have a twofold purpose, to prevent injustice and by the punishment of transgressors 'to make the others better'. For Democritus's view see vol. II, 496 (fr. 245).

Glaucon (pp. 103 ff., 98 above). Those who laid down the laws, said Callicles, are the weak majority; and again, justice and self-control and everything that militates against a life of wantonness and licence are 'human agreements contrary to nature'. Against them Callicles exalts the superman who will burst their bonds and live the life of a self-indulgent tyrant. 'They', on the other hand—the mass of mankind as depicted by Glaucon—entertain no such heroic ideas. They accept the existence of the compact as a second-best to being able to do exactly what one likes, since for everyone to behave so is a practical impossibility. Selfish behaviour is limited to evading of the law when it can be done without fear of detection. Plato himself is of course an advocate of *nomos*, as the *Crito* shows, and in his later years mounted a powerful attack against those who maintained that it could be in any way opposed to *physis*. He therefore opposes both the ideal of the superman who by being a law to himself is following 'nature's justice', and the more commonplace idea that the laws should be accepted as a necessary evil but broken whenever it is safe to do so.[1]

Can we say how far the theory in Greece was a 'historicist' one, asserting or implying that in the remote past the first laws took shape in something like a formal contract between members of an original political community? Barker wrote that the social contract theory, 'which is not only that of Glaucon but also that of modern writers such as Hobbes, has been met by modern thinkers point by point. In the first place, there never *was* any actual or explicit "contract": there *is* and always will be a condition of things, which is a condition of tacit and implied contract.'[2] Popper on the other hand claims that

---

[1] It will be seen that I do not follow Popper when he sees 'a complete change of front' in Plato between the *Gorgias* and the *Republic*. See Popper, *O.S.* 116.

[2] *G.P.T.* 160. It may be relevant to mention Barker's own position, which is a reconciliation of *physis* and *nomos*, at least on the human plane. Government is for him 'an essential attribute of political society, which is itself in turn an essential attribute of human nature'.

In fairness to Barker it must be added that in his introduction to Gierke's *Nat. Law* (1934) he was more cautious in his expression. He said there (p. xlix): 'Natural-law thinkers were apt to talk of an unhistorical "state of nature" and of an unhistorical act of contract by which men issued from it ... On the other hand ... the natural-law thinkers were not really dealing with the historical antecedents of the State: they were concerned with its logical presuppositions; and there is still a case to be made for the view that the State, as distinct from society, is a legal association which fundamentally rests on the presupposition of contract.'

this objection is not applicable to Lycophron's theory because it did not take a historicist form. The theories mentioned in the *Gorgias* and *Republic* are to be identified with Lycophron's, but have been given this form by Plato.

Cross and Woozley, whose criterion for a theory of social contract is that it must express a moral obligation to obey the laws consequent on the individual's own undertaking to do so, and that any supposedly historical fact about the origin of law is irrelevant to it, insist that what Glaucon propounds is not 'the Social Contract theory' for the very reason which made Barker assert that it was, namely that 'the emphasis is entirely on the factual, or would-be historical, proposition supposedly giving an account of what induced men to emerge from a state of nature into the organization of a social community'.[1]

Perhaps the first thing to note is the widespread acceptance at this time of the historical theory of the evolution of society from a primitive state in which everyone was for himself alone, until the fatal consequences of such an 'unordered and brutish life' compelled men to subdue their savage instincts in the interests of a common defence against hostile nature. This we have already looked at, and *prima facie* it would seem, if not to necessitate a theory of a historical social contract, at least to provide a setting highly conducive to it.[2] As we noted, it went with Presocratic scientific theories about the origin of physical life, and constituted a reaction against earlier mythical accounts of human degeneration. Protagoras and Critias both held this theory, and both believed in the social compact as a historical

---

[1] *Comm. on Rep.* 71 ff. As there defined, the theory would certainly exclude Glaucon's account, but is it not misleading to speak of '*the* Social Contract theory'? (The capitals but not the italics are theirs.) What the authors themselves say of Hobbes, Locke and Rousseau, all of whom they admit as contractualists, shows that it is rather a question of this or that philosopher's theory of a social contract, each one holding it in a somewhat different form; and it can hardly be denied that Glaucon's *is* a contractualist theory (359a συνθέσθαι ἀλλήλοις... νόμους τίθεσθαι καὶ συνθήκας). To say that the only social contract theory is one that does not rely on a historical statement, and is therefore immune from the objections brought against it in that form, is surely to beg a big question. It seems more helpful to start with the fact that there are two main forms of the theory, as Popper does when he distinguishes the theoretical form, concerned solely with the end of the state (which he himself sees in Lycophron), from the 'traditional historicist theory of the social contract' (*O.S.* 114).

[2] For this theory see pp. 60 ff. and Appendix (79 ff.) above. Even Sophocles in the *Antigone* chorus (355) mentions the legal regulation of social life as something which man 'developed for his own benefit, by his own efforts'. (So Jebb explains ἐδιδάξατο.)

fact. The views of Antiphon and (as reported) of Hippias make no explicit reference to historical origins, but neither do they fulfil the Cross–Woozley conditions for 'the Social Contract theory' by affirming a moral obligation to obey the law. In their eyes the fact that laws are not natural but *merely* agreements releases the citizen from a duty to obey them in all circumstances. In the fourth century the author of the speech against Aristogeiton drew the opposite moral: laws were instituted against nature because nature is 'disorderly' and law introduces impartiality and equal justice for all. As the decisions of wise men guided by the gods, they have been accepted by common agreement and must be obeyed. The evidence for Lycophron is slight, but in calling the laws 'a guarantor of mutual rights' he must have had a similar view in mind.

If one accepts as essential marks of a social contract theory that it should make no historical statement about the origin of law but hold that every member of a state has a moral obligation to obey its laws because he himself has contracted or undertaken, at least implicitly, to do so, then the one unmistakable adherent of it at this period is Socrates.[1] It can hardly be doubted that the *Crito* is true to his convictions, which Plato shared when he wrote it. He held that his whole life, like that of every other citizen, had been the acting-out of a contract and agreement according to which, in return for their benefits, he was under obligation to regard the laws as masters to be obeyed. Infringement of this principle would tear apart the whole fabric of society.

There is another possibility to be considered, that a philosopher may put his theory in historical form without intending it to be literally so understood. He may intend only a 'genetic definition', an analysis of a state of things into its constituent elements, believing that the best way to make its structure clear is to represent it as being built up bit by bit out of the elements without implying that such a

---

[1] Hume noted this, calling the *Crito* 'the only passage I meet with in antiquity, where the obligation of obedience to government is ascribed to a promise'. 'Thus', he comments, 'he [Socrates] builds a *Tory* consequence of passive obedience on a *Whig* foundation of the original contract.' (*Of the Original Contract, ad fin.* W.C. ed. p. 236.) The attribution to Socrates is undoubtedly historical. As De Strycker has justly pointed out (*Mélanges Grégoires*, 208), his attitude is confirmed not only by the manner of his death but by his solitary championship of the law against an infuriated *demos* in the case of the generals after Arginusae (p. 379 f. below).

process of construction ever took temporal form.[1] A geometrician may explain the structure of a cube in terms of *constructing* a square out of four equal straight lines and then a cube out of six squares without meaning that straight lines existed prior in time to plane figures, nor plane figures to solids. From Plato's immediate pupils onwards, commentators have disputed whether he intended his cosmogony to be understood in this way, or whether he believed in a literal process of creation. The idea of genetic definition was extended from physics to political theory by Hobbes. In general, 'if one wants to "know" something, he must constitute it himself; he must cause it to develop from its individual elements'. *Ubi generatio nulla . . . ibi nulla philosophia intelligitur.*[2]

Yet as we read the writings of the social-contract theorists we find that the distinction between literal and instructional use of genetic exposition is by no means clear-cut. While claiming on the one hand that the historical proposition, that before the contract men lived in a state of nature, is irrelevant to their theory, they seem anxious to give it all the historical foundation they can. Thus Hobbes himself: 'It may peradventure be thought there never was such a time nor condition of war as this; and I believe it was never generally so all over the world, but there are many places where they live so now'; and he proceeds to give examples. Rousseau in the preface to the *Discourse on the Origin of Inequality* calls the state of nature a state which 'perhaps never did exist, and probably never will exist; and of which it is nevertheless necessary to have true ideas, in order to form a proper judgment of our present state'. He says that facts do not affect the question, and that his investigations 'must not be considered as historical truths, but only as mere conditional and hypothetical reasonings, rather calculated to explain the nature of things than to ascertain their actual origin'. This seems a perfect example of a genetic definition, and in the *Social Contract* we find: 'I assume, for the sake of argument, that point was reached in the history of mankind . . .' and 'by the social compact *we have given* life and existence to the body politic' (my italics). Yet later in the *Origin of Inequality* he writes:

---

[1] The nature and value of genetic definitions is lucidly set forth by Cassirer in *P. of E.* 253 ff.

[2] Hobbes, *De corpore*, pt. 1, ch. 1, §8, as paraphrased and quoted by Cassirer, *loc. cit.*

'Such was, or may well have been, the origin of society', and on the next page, after repeating that the actual originating cause of political societies is indifferent to his argument, he proceeds to give reasons why the one he has put forward is 'the most natural' and to defend it against others. Similarly with Locke, Cross and Woozley say (with no reference given) that 'as Locke saw more clearly than Hobbes, the factual proposition, even if it were true, would provide no support for the theory'. Yet §§99–100 of the *Second Treatise* show plainly that for Locke it *was* a historical fact. He not only makes the unequivocal statement: 'This is that, and that only, which did or could give beginning to any lawful government in the world', but goes on to state and rebut the objection that no historical instances can be quoted of the setting up of a government in this way. Recorded history, he points out, can only begin when civil society has already been in existence long enough to allow the development of lettered leisure.[1]

Of the Greek theorists, Protagoras seems the most likely to be giving a genetic definition. His aim is not a historical account of the origin of civilization but an answer to Socrates's question, whether political virtue can be taught; and it is a matter of indifference to him whether he conveys this answer in the form of a reasoned argument or of a narrative. Moreover the narrative, when it comes, has a fairy-tale flavour[2] and many mythical elements. Yet it takes so much from seriously held theories of history that, like his post-Renaissance successors, he probably kept a foot in both camps.[3] Of the others whom we have considered, Hippias, Antiphon and Lycophron, so far as our evidence goes, give no sign of propounding a historical theory of the origin of law, nor is it apparent in the speech against Aristogeiton or in Plato's Callicles.[4] Socrates's is emphatically not a

---

[1] References for this paragraph: Hobbes, *Leviathan*, pt. 1, ch. 13 (ed. Waller, p. 85); Rousseau, *Origin of Inequality*, trans. Cole (Everyman), 169, 175 f., 221 f., *S.C.* (W.C. ed.), 254. Cross and Woozley, *P.'s Rep.* 72.

[2] The beginning, ἦν γάρ ποτε χρόνος (once upon a time), echoes the legendary poets Linus and Orpheus and was used again in verse by Critias and Moschion. (References in Kern, *Orph. Frr.* p. 303.)

[3] All that he says on the subject in the *logos* that follows the *mythos* is: 'The State sets up the laws, which are the inventions of good lawgivers of ancient times, and compels the citizens to rule and be ruled in accordance with them' (326 d).

[4] Popper (*O.S.* 116) says that Plato here puts the theory in historicist form, but I do not find it so. At *Gorg.* 483 b the present tense is used throughout.

historicist doctrine.¦ Only Glaucon in *Rep.* 2 claims to be giving a historical account.

Finally, in asking whether the Greeks believed in the social contract theory, we are putting to them a question which they did not ask themselves. The question they did ask was whether 'just' was the same as 'lawful'. The answers were of two types, normative and factual. Either justice retained its meaning of an ethical ideal, and this ideal was equated with keeping the laws, or it was claimed that when men used the high-sounding word 'justice' all they meant by it was observance of the existing laws, which could in fact be an unwise or harmful course. Protagoras is represented in the *Protagoras* as taking the first line: justice, which is an essential element in 'human excellence' as a whole (325 a), is identified with 'political excellence', the respect for law which has raised man from a state of savagery and without which society would collapse. In the *Theaetetus* he appears to adopt the second, factual interpretation, as his theory of 'man the measure' demands: what is just is only what one's state declares to be just. The state may be persuaded that it was at fault and amend its laws, whereby the content of just action in that state will be altered. But he would still hold that observance of those faulty laws, until they were altered by proper constitutional processes, was morally right as an alternative to the chaos which would ensue if every citizen felt free to disregard them. Antiphon and Hippias on the other hand maintained that, because all that was meant by justice was conformity to *nomos*, it carried no moral obligation and one might do better to follow the contrary precepts of *physis*. Such a belief could, though it need not, lead to the brutal selfishness exemplified by Callicles.

Socrates agreed with Protagoras that it was just (in the sense of morally obligatory) to obey the laws or else get them changed by peaceful persuasion (this alternative is mentioned in the *Crito*), and that failure to do so would disrupt society. But two further points may be noted. First, there is a hint in the *Crito* of something which does not occur elsewhere, namely a distinction between the laws themselves and their administration. In Socrates's imaginary conversation with the laws of Athens, they say that, if he abides by the decision of the court and agrees to be executed instead of trying to escape, 'you will be the victim of a wrong done to you not by us, the laws, but by your fellow men'. If on the other hand he runs away, he will be behaving dishonourably by breaking his agreements and contracts with the laws themselves. In other words, once a verdict has been legally given there is no legal alternative to its execution. Socrates saw nothing wrong with this even in the case of his own death-sentence, but it seems that there was room for Hippodamus's proposal for a court of appeal. Secondly, in saying that 'just' was identical with 'lawful', Socrates was including the universal and divine unwritten laws and taking into account judgment in a future life as well as in this. For the unwritten laws we have the evidence of Xenophon, and in the *Crito* the laws go on immediately from the point just mentioned to say that the laws in the next world will not receive him kindly if they know that he has tried to destroy their brothers in this.[1]

[1] That Socrates believed in a future life is disputed, but this must be left till later (pp. 476ff. below). For the idea of judgment pursuing a man from this world to the next cf. Aesch. *Suppl.* 228–31.

VI

EQUALITY

(I) POLITICAL EQUALITY

In the fifth century democracy, both as an established political constitution and as an ideal, reached its climax in Athens and some other Greek cities. Against it stood oligarchy, by no means a spent force, and whether in power or in opposition always a foe to be reckoned with. Naturally therefore an ideological conflict developed[1] which led men on beyond constitutional questions to larger problems of human nature and human relations. Democracy was part of a general movement towards equality, and the need to defend democracy was a spur to further arguments in its favour. Thucydides provides some of the best examples of this, for instance in the speech of Athenagoras, democratic leader of Syracuse, who says to the young oligarchs of his city (6.38.5):

Do you dislike being politically on an equality with a large number? But how is it just for members of the same state to be denied the same rights? I shall be told that democracy is neither sensible nor fair [literally 'equal'], and that the wealthy are also the best fitted to rule; but I reply, first, that *demos* means the whole state, oligarchy only a part; secondly, that the wealthy may be the best guardians of property, but the best counsellors are the intelligent, and the best at listening to and judging arguments are the many. And in a democracy all these, whether acting separately or together, have an equal share.

Here we have the ideal of a democracy, in which the rich have their place, but it is for the most intelligent to give counsel—possibly conflicting counsel, for there are two sides to every question—and the decision is in the hands of the whole people, when they have listened to the arguments and sized them up. In practice it did not

[1] A classic statement of it is the debate which Herodotus somewhat incongruously represents as taking place between the three Persian usurpers on the respective merits of monarchy, oligarchy and democracy. So far as the latter two are concerned, it is cast in an entirely Greek mould. (Hdt. 3.80–2.)

always work out like that, for *demos* no less than *oligoi* could be applied to a section only of the population—could mean *plebs* as well as *populus*[1]— and as such could be ruthless in its treatment of the rich or intellectual.

More even than democracy, the concept most closely connected with equality was perhaps *homonoia*, concord (literally 'being of one mind'). In the thought of this period, the notions of justice, concord, friendship[2] and equality were seen as interdependent if not identical, and essential to the preservation of the political order. Euripides (to be quoted in context shortly) sees equality as a bond of union, uniting friend to friend, city to city, ally to ally. For Protagoras, it is justice that 'brings order into our cities and creates a bond of friendship and union' (Plato, *Prot.* 322c), and Socrates in the course of demonstrating that the just is coextensive with the lawful says that concord is the best of all things for a city and its object is to secure obedience to the laws (Xen. *Mem.* 4.4.16). In the *Republic* (351d) the pursuit of justice leads to concord and friendship, and Aristotle says that if the citizens are friends justice may wither away. Legislators are even more concerned with friendship that with justice, for their aim is to replace faction by concord, and concord resembles friendship. Elsewhere he defines concord as 'friendship in the political sphere'. To inculcate friendship is the statesman's chief end, for friends do not commit injustice against each other. Indeed, 'justice and friendship are either the same or nearly so'. Concord does not mean simply community of beliefs. That could exist between strangers, or merely on an academic subject like astronomy. No, concord is a word applied to cities when the citizens agree about their common interests, make

---

[1] Cf. Vlastos, 'Ἰσ. πολ. 8, n. 1: 'The ambiguity in δῆμος (*pleps* or *populus*) is all to the good. Opponents of democracy can take it in the first sense...while thoughtful democrats can invoke the second.'

[2] *Philia*, a word of remarkably wide application. Among human beings it is friendship or affection, but it extends beyond the human sphere. Aristotle (*EN* 1155a18) saw it among birds and animals as well, in the relation between parents and offspring, and Theophrastus even among plants. In the earlier and more mythical cosmogony of Pherecydes (fr. 3) the world was created by a conflation of the opposites through *philia*, and in Plato (*Tim.* 32c) cosmic *philia* resulted from the geometric structure of the world. Similarly in the *Gorgias* (508a) 'the wise' say that heaven and earth and gods and men are all held together by community, *philia*, orderliness, temperance and justice. It is connected with the old doctrine of 'like to like', for 'the wise men who have written about nature and the whole say that like must always be *philon* to like' (*Lysis* 214b). In Empedocles the cosmic spirit of *philia* unites unlikes, but only because it has the power of *assimilating* them to each other (fr. 22.5), as the opposites were made to blend in Pherecydes.

the same practical choices and carry them out.[1] Down to the time of Plato and Aristotle, *homonoia* was mainly conceived as confined within the *polis*, being in fact the virtue by which it kept its unity and maintained itself against outsiders, a preventive of that *stasis* (faction, civil strife) which so bedevilled the life of the Greek city states. 'Waging war' is for Democritus (fr. 250) among the 'great deeds' which concord alone makes possible for a city. Gorgias however seems to have used it in a pan-Hellenic sense, when he chose it as the subject of his oration to the inter-state assembly at Olympia (fr. 8a), and this accords with his declaration that victories of Greeks over Greeks were matter for sorrow (p. 162 below).

At a time when democracy might in practice mean not the equal participation of the whole city in government but the seizing of power by the hitherto poor and underprivileged at the expense of the rich and well-born, the ideal of *homonoia*, of a *concordia ordinum*, might well seem to offer a better and truer conception of equality. *Equal* or *equality* itself is the most frequent catchword in the middle and late fifth century, and the ideal is equal political and judicial rights.[2] Pericles puts it (Thuc. 2.37.1) that in the Athenian democracy power is in the hands of the people, in private disputes everyone is equal before the law, and public responsibilities are allotted not according to

---

[1] Ar. *EN* 1155a22ff., *EE* 1241a32ff., 1234b22ff., *EN* 1167a22. For references to ὁμόνοια see further Schmid, *Gesch.* 163. Bignone (*Studi*, 87ff.) argued for a close relation between the moral doctrine of concord in Antiphon's π. ὁμονοίας and his doctrine of justice as developed in the ᾿Αλήθεια. In the *Clitopho*, he noted, one of Socrates's pupils is said to have maintained that φιλία was the product of δικαιοσύνη and ὁμόνοια the truest manifestation of φιλία (409a–e, adding that it is not ὁμοδοξία, so that the whole passage stands in a very close relation to Aristotle, especially *EN* 1167a22ff.). Bignone might have added *Rep.* 351d, where Socrates tells Thrasymachus that injustice leads to hatred and fighting but justice to ὁμόνοια and φιλία. In spite of the interesting passages which he adduces for comparison, Bignone hardly makes his point. Unfortunately, the extant fragments of the π. ὁμ. make no reference to ὁμόνοια at all, so we are quite in the dark as to what Antiphon said about it. Moreover, in reconciling ᾿Αλ. and π. ὁμ. he completely ignores col. 5 of *OP* 1364 fr. 1 (DK, II, 349f.), where Antiphon says that people who do not attack others unless provoked, and who return the bad treatment of their parents with kindness, are acting contrary to nature.

[2] ἴσος, ἰσότης, ἰσονομία, ἰσονομεῖσθαι. For the meaning of ἰσονομία see Ehrenberg s.v. in *RE*, Suppl. VII, 293ff. Vlastos has argued against Gomme that, although not synonymous with democracy, it was always identified with it in the fifth century. (Vlastos, ᾿Ισον. πολιτική. Jaeger agreed, *Paid.* I, 101, n. 1.) This seems to be in general true, though I cannot go all the way with Vlastos when he claims that the mention of ὀλιγαρχία ἰσόνομος at Thuc. 3.62.3 fits his theories perfectly. If, as he says, the connotations of the two words are different, it is not surprising if their denotations too should occasionally differ, if only to gain a special effect. Cf. Ehrenberg, *loc. cit.* 296.

any class system but solely on merit, nor is poverty ever a bar to office. The new emphasis on equality as an ideal is perhaps best seen in the plays of Euripides. On democracy itself his Theseus echoes the sentiments of Athenagoras and Pericles (*Suppl.* 404): 'The city is free, the people rule in yearly turns of office, and the poor man is given an equal share with the rich.' For the praise of equality as such we have the *Phoenissae* (531 ff.), where Jocasta pleads with her son to renounce the pernicious *daimon* Ambition, and honour instead Equality,

who unites friend to friend, city to city and allies to their allies. What is equal is a stable element in human life, but the less is always foe to the greater and ushers in the day of hatred. Equality it is who established measures and weights for men and delimited number. Equal in the year's circuit are the path of dark night and of the sun's light, and neither grudges the other his victory. Shall day and night serve mortals and you not brook to give your brother equal share in the dynasty with yourself? Where in this is justice?

One notices again the readiness with which the Greek calls on nature at large to endorse a course of human action; and as a reminder that we are in the age of ferment where every argument has two sides we may notice that in the *Ajax* of Sophocles (668 ff.) the yielding of winter to summer and night to day is used to support the contrary moral that everywhere there are rulers and subjects, and submission of one to the other is necessary. (Shakespeare too thought that the course of nature confirmed the indispensability of 'degree'.) Interesting also is the connexion in thought between equality in the social and political field and in the field of metrical standards and mathematical calculation. Evidently it was in the air before Archytas the Pythagorean made his claim that the art of calculation 'ends faction and promotes unanimity' (see vol. 1, 336), and (as we see from Plato and Isocrates) led to a controversy between the 'two equalities', the geometrical (anti-tyrannical but aristocratic) and the arithmetical (democratic).[1]

[1] Isoc. *Areop.* 21, Plato, *Gorg.* 508a, *Laws* 757a–758a. It is interesting that to describe democratic equality in the *Laws* Plato uses the same three words as Euripides in the same order: it is τὴν μέτρῳ ἴσην καὶ σταθμῷ καὶ ἀριθμῷ, and in her praise of Ἰσότης Jocasta says (541 f.):

καὶ γὰρ μέτρ' ἀνθρώποισι καὶ μέρη σταθμῶν
Ἰσότης ἔταξε κἀριθμὸν διώρισε.

See also Soph. fr. 399 N. The phrase οὔτ' ἀριθμῷ οὔτε σταθμῷ at Xen. *Symp.* 4.43 suggests a proverbial element.

(2) EQUALITY OF WEALTH

As to wealth there is, in its context, something almost Christian in Jocasta's designation of it as a trust from heaven (555): 'We mortals do not hold our wealth as a private possession; it is the gods', and we have the care of it, but when they wish they take it back again.' Actual redistribution of wealth on an egalitarian basis, even if in a, to us, imperfect form, was first proposed by a certain Phaleas of Chalcedon, probably about the end of the fifth century. (On his date see Gomperz, *Gr. Th.* I, 578.) Aristotle (*Pol.* 1266a39ff., our only source) says he was the first to affirm that the citizens of a state ought to have equal possessions.[1] By abolishing want he hoped to abolish crime, but Aristotle comments that cold and hunger are not the sole incentives to crime, and in fact the greatest crimes are caused by excess and not by necessity: it is not men's possessions but their desires and ambitions that must be equalized, and this needs suitable education. Phaleas had thought of this too, and was modern enough to propose that not only wealth but also education should be provided 'equally' by the state: but, says Aristotle, it is no use everyone having the same education if it is of the wrong sort, and Phaleas should tell us what *kind* of education he proposes.

(3) SOCIAL EQUALITY

The spirit of egalitarianism led to a questioning of distinctions based not only on wealth but on birth or race, and even to that between master and slave, which hitherto had seemed to most Greeks natural and fundamental. Antiphon, the opponent of *nomos* in all its forms, issued his challenge on both noble birth and race in an important paragraph so far omitted from our summary of the papyrus fragments.[2] It runs thus:

[1] ἴσας εἶναι τὰς κτήσεις τῶν πολιτῶν. Later however (1267b9) Aristotle says that he limited this to the possession of land. Of course the equality, as would be expected at this time, applied only between citizens, and Phaleas even proposed that all artisans should be publicly owned slaves (1267b15).

[2] *OP* 1364, fr. 2, DK, fr. 44 B. It is thus from the fragment whose authenticity is guaranteed, though its relation to fr. 1 is unknown. (See *OP*, vol. XI, 93.) Considerable restoration has been necessary in the first few lines, but their sense can be taken as certain.

The sons of noble fathers we respect and look up to, but those from humble homes we neither respect nor look up to. In this we behave to one another like barbarians,[1] since by nature we are all made to be alike in all respects, both barbarians and Greeks.[2] This can be seen from the needs which all men have. [They can all be provided in the same way by all men, and in all this][3] none of us is marked off as either barbarian or Greek; for we all breathe the air with our mouth and nostrils and [eat with our hands?]. . .

If the logic of this passage appears strange ('We pay great attention to high birth, but this is to behave like barbarians, for (ἐπεί) in reality there is no difference between barbarians and Greeks'), that may be due to the fragmentary state of the text,[4] and at least Antiphon's message is plain, that in nature there is no essential distinction either between high and low birth or between different races.[5] Another who at about the same time or rather later (there is much uncertainty about his date) castigated distinctions based on birth was the Sophist Lycophron. We know of this from Aristotle,[6] who in a dialogue *On Nobility of Birth* made one of the speakers confess his bewilderment as to the application of the term. His companion replies that this is very natural, for there is much division and obscurity about its significance, even more among philosophers than among ordinary men.

[1] *Barbaroi* strictly means all non-Greek-speaking people, and is often used to make this factual distinction with no derogatory implication. Nevertheless the Greeks had a strong sense of their superiority to other men, and more often the derogatory implication was prominent. In ordinary speech the word carried an imputation of ignorance, stupidity, or lack of moral sense. It is an insult when Tyndareus says to Menelaus (Eur. *Or.* 485) βεβαρβάρωσαι, χρόνιος ὢν ἐν βαρβάροις.

[2] If this is the translation, the Greek is rather unusual. Grenfell and Hunt render: 'we are all by nature alike fully adapted to be either barbarians or Hellenes', which is probably more accurate. Nevertheless the following sentences show that the intention is in fact to obliterate the distinction between the two. The double emphasis in φύσει πεφύκαμεν is lost in English.

[3] Of the words in square brackets little is left in the Greek, and the translation follows Bignone's restoration in *Studi*, p. 65, for which he finds hints in a passage of Porphyry's *De abstinentia* (3.25, p. 221 Nauck).

[4] And no doubt also to a sophistic straining after rhetorical effect by means of the double (factual and pejorative) significance of βάρβαρος. The whole argument may have been something like this: 'We pay too much attention to a man's race or, within our own race, to his descent. We call the rest of mankind *barbaroi*, and use the term to mean ignorant or uncivilized; and at the same time we respect or despise people according to their ancestry. If *barbaros* means stupid, are we not the real *barbaroi* here? In point of fact there is no difference in nature between Greeks and non-Greeks. All men are the same at bottom, with the same needs and means of satisfying them. Nor is there an essential difference between high and low born.'

[5] Tarn's point that only biological equality is in question has been adequately dealt with by Merlan, *CP* (1950), 164, and Baldry, *Unity*, 43 ff.

[6] Fr. 91 Rose, p. 59 Ross (Oxf. trans.). For Lycophron see pp. 313 f. below.

Equality

Is it a precious and good thing, or as Lycophron the Sophist wrote, something altogether empty? Comparing it with other goods, he says that its splendour is not apparent, and its dignity lies in words, maintaining that to prefer it is a matter of opinion, whereas in truth there is no difference between low born and high born.

Similar sentiments on the subject of noble birth are frequently on the lips of the characters in Euripides, and it is typical of him that in his *Electra* he marries the daughter of Agamemnon to a poor peasant remarkable for the courtesy and nobility of his character.[1] His virtues provoke Orestes to reflections like these (367ff.): 'About manly virtue nothing is clear, for there is confusion in the natures of men. I have seen a worthless son of a noble father, and fine children sprung from the unworthy, poverty in the wit of a rich man and a great mind in a poor man's body.' More outspoken is an unidentified character in the *Dictys* (fr. 336): 'Of high birth I have little good to say. In my eyes the good man is the noble, and the unjust base-born though his father be a greater than Zeus.' In keeping with this are several passages on bastardy which insist that the bastard is by nature the equal of the legitimate, and only inferior by *nomos*, or in name.[2] The subject of the *Alexander* (Prince Priam disguised as a slave-herdsman) gave Euripides an opportunity of raising the questions of birth and of slavery from both sides.[3] On birth the chorus sing (fr. 52):

We go too far if we praise noble birth among mortals. When first, long ago, the human race was born, and Earth our mother brought them forth,[4]

---

[1] In the interests of accuracy it must be said that in the prologue the peasant proclaims himself the descendant of a noble line, who has come down in the world, but as he says, 'poverty wipes out nobility', and in view of Orestes's remarks it seems that little significance is to be attached to the fact. In Greece, even in Euripides's time, noble lineage and material possessions still went together more than they do with us (Nestle, *Euripides*, 323), and the helplessness of the first without the second is emphasized elsewhere in Euripides (frr. 22, 95, 326). For his attitude to money in general, see Nestle, *Eur.* 334ff. That poverty need not destroy inherited nobility of character is repeated in a fragment of his *Archelaus* (fr. 232). But one must never forget that his lines are spoken in character. Fr. 235 expresses utter contempt for wealth, but fr. 248 appears to revile poverty, and all three fragments are from the same play.

[2] *Androm.* 638, frr. 141, 168, 377. That the well-born are the virtuous is said to have been maintained by Antisthenes (DL, 6.10).

[3] For the plot of the play and context of fragments see Vogt, *Sklaverei*, 16f.

[4] The choice of verb here (διέκρινε) betrays the poet's interest in natural science, for to his contemporary Anaxagoras and other philosophers the process which gave birth to the cosmos and all living creatures in it was one of continuous 'separation'. This primal uniformity of mankind appears also in Sophocles's *Tereus* (fr. 532).

the land engendered all to look alike. We have no peculiar traits, high and low born are the same stock, but time through *nomos* has made birth a matter of pride.

The obscurity and confusion which Euripides and Lycophron found in this topic were natural enough at a time when the division aristocrat–commoner by no means necessarily coincided with the political division oligarch–democrat. 'The whole development shows that up to the end of the fifth century in Athens the nobility formed a power which could make its influence strongly felt as much on the side of the democratic constitution as occasionally in vehement opposition to it.'[1] For Euripides the test is moral. No longer can noble and good, base-born and bad, be interchangeable terms as they were for a Theognis, whose words are obviously adapted to a moral sense in the lines 'Nobility consorts not with the bad, but with the good' (*Alex.* fr. 53).

(4) SLAVERY

For most Greeks society without slavery was unthinkable. The treatment of slaves, and the work they were given to do, varied widely.[2] At Athens they were employed in domestic service, in privately owned factories, in mines (where the conditions might be hard indeed), and to a smaller extent on the land,[3] which in Attica was mostly cultivated by small peasant holders. The lot of domestic slaves naturally varied, but Aristophanes depicts them as speaking freely, and sometimes impudently, to their masters. The intelligent were given posts of responsibility as secretaries or bank-managers, and might ultimately be freed by their owners. In the fourth century Archestratus bequeathed his bank to his former slave Pasion, who in turn leased it to his own freed slave. A common practice was for owners of industrial slaves to allow them to work independently, paying a fixed sum from their earnings and keeping the rest, and these might save enough to buy

---

[1] Nestle, *Euripides*, 324. Cf. p. 38, n. 1, above.
[2] For authorities see A. H. M. Jones in *Slavery*, ed. Finley. The other essays in this collection are also to be recommended; also Nestle, *Euripides*, 348 ff., and J. Vogt, *Sklaverei und Humanität*, 1–19. V. Cuffley in *JHI*, 1966, deals with it under four heads: (1) as an imposition of fate, (2) as the justifiable position of inferiors, (3) communal slavery, with, as a fourth, metaphorical slavery of a man to his own base desires.
[3] But see Finley in *Slavery*, 148 f.

their freedom. The complaint of the 'Old Oligarch' (pseudo-Xen. *Ath. Pol.* 1.10) is well known: slaves at Athens are an insolent lot who will not get out of your way in the street, and you are not allowed to strike them for the simple reason that there is nothing in their dress and general appearance to distinguish them from free Athenians. Demosthenes too says that slaves at Athens have greater rights of free speech than the citizens of other states, and there was a law under which anyone could be prosecuted for an act of *hybris* against slave as well as citizen.[1] In spite of all this the hard fact remained that the slave was a chattel to be bought and sold. Some wealthy men bought large numbers and made a good income by leasing them out as labourers.

If slavery as an institution was accepted, there was a general feeling against enslaving Greeks,[2] and most slaves were obtained, by war or raids, from non-Greek countries. In this way the question of slavery was connected in the Greek mind, as in the American, with that of racial inferiority. As Iphigenia says in Euripides (*I.A.* 1400): 'It is right for Greeks to rule over barbarians, but not barbarians over Greeks, for they are slaves, but we are free.' It is likely therefore that Antiphon, who denied any natural distinction between Greek and barbarian, also opposed the doctrine of 'natural slaves' which predominated at the time and was later defended by Aristotle;[3] but the fact is not explicitly recorded. Colour was given to the idea of barbarian inferiority by the Greek victory over the Persians and by the tendency of other peoples to be despotically ruled, for submission to a human despot rather than to law was in Greek eyes equivalent to slavery. Moreover the moral and intellectual inferiority of their slaves was a fact, the inevitable effect, not of nature, but of the complete deprivation of initiative through being employed as 'living tools', a life of 'always appeasing the masters, for this is best for slaves, and to please their lords in whatever task is assigned them'.[4]

[1] Demosth. *Phil.* 3.3, *In Meid.* 46–8. Cf. Eur. *Hec.* 291 f. On the laws of slavery at Athens see Harrison, *The Laws of Athens* (1968), pt. 1, ch. 6.

[2] For further information, see Newman, *Politics*, vol. 1, 142 f.

[3] So Nestle, *VMzuL*, 377. But on Aristotle's description of the slave as a 'living tool', see Harrison, *The Laws of Athens*, 163, n. 2.

[4] Eur. fr. 93. This enforced deterioration was already recognized in Homer. *See Od.* 17.322f.: slavery robs a man of half his ἀρετή.

According to R. Schlaifer, of all criticism of slavery as an institution (as distinct from errors and abuses in its application) 'there are only three surviving scraps: a sentence of Alcidamas, a reference in Aristotle, and an echo in Philemon'. None of these belongs to the fifth century. Schlaifer however has excluded Euripides on the ground that, though he proclaims that the slave may be better than his master and therefore wrongly enslaved, he shared the common belief that some were by nature fitted only for slavery.[1] To isolate his own views is difficult, since he was a dramatist and his characters utter opposing sentiments, but at the very least he provides evidence of a mounting tide of protest against slavery in his lifetime. The theme of the *Alexandros*, as we have seen, made it a natural forum of opposing views, on the one hand the splendid affirmation of the equality of all men (pp. 154f. above), and on the other sentiments like these:

fr. 48: 'There is no greater burden, no more worthless and useless possession in a house than a slave with thoughts above his station' (cf. fr. 216).

fr. 49: 'So evil is the race of slaves, all belly, never looking to the future.'

fr. 50: 'Slaves who are well disposed towards their master's house incur great hostility from their equals.'

fr. 51: 'It is a bad thing to have slaves who are too good for their masters.' (Cf. fr. 251.)

Fr. 86, from the *Alcmaeon*, says that anyone who trusts a slave is a fool.

From other passages we can be sure that these words were uttered by unsympathetic characters. The frequency with which a slave is shown as sympathetic, and the relationship between slaves and their masters described in favourable, even touching, terms, does not of itself prove an antipathy to slavery as such,[2] but is nevertheless striking. The wretchedness of a slave's lot was alluded to in the *Archelaus* (fr. 245): 'One thing I advise: never let yourself be taken alive into slavery if you have a chance of dying as a free man.' But it need not always be so: 'How pleasant it is for slaves to find good masters, and for the

[1] See Schlaifer's informative essay in Finley, p. 127. But for Euripides's belief in natural slavery he relies entirely on fr. 57, whereas (*a*) it is completely without context, and sounds as if it were spoken by a tyrant or other unpleasant character, (*b*) the text itself is uncertain and the word φύσει an emendation.

[2] Plato, who was no abolitionist, says that slaves have often proved better than brothers or sons, and have saved their masters' lives, property and whole families (*Laws* 776d).

masters to have a well disposed slave in the home' (fr. 529). The slaves of Alcestis are distraught with grief at the death of her who was a mother to them (*Alc.* 192ff., 769f.), though they admit it is not everywhere thus (*ibid.* 210f.), and there are many other passages in the same strain.[1] Hippolytus listens and replies seriously when his slave offers advice, and the same slave does not shrink from defending him against his father's anger (*Hipp.* 88ff., 1249ff.). Both the faithfulness and the pathos of a slave are reflected in the words of Andromache's handmaid agreeing to go on a dangerous mission for her mistress (*Andr.* 89): 'I will go, and if anything happens to me—well, the life of a slave-woman is of little worth'; and in the *Helena* (1639) another handmaid defends her mistress with the words: 'Kill not your sister but me, for to noble slaves it is a glory to die for their lords.' The freedom of speech allowed to slaves in Euripides was brought against him by Aristophanes (*Frogs* 949), and the general lack of it is repeatedly mentioned in his plays as a feature of the slave's hard lot.[2]

If in these passages Euripides does no more than show sympathy for slaves, and perhaps reflect an actually existing relationship when at its best, elsewhere he goes further in claiming that a slave may be the equal or superior of the free. At *Helena* 730 a slave claims to have 'the mind, though not the name, of a free man',[3] just as in a fragment from the *Melanippe* (511) it is said that 'the name of slave will not corrupt a good man, and many slaves are better than the free', and from the *Phrixus* (831): 'to many slaves the name brings disgrace though in heart they belong more to the free than those who are not slaves'.[4] In the *Ion* the statement is given universal form. The old slave-tutor of Creusa's father, whom she hails as a friend and well-wisher and promises to cherish as her own father (730ff.), after de-

---

[1] *Ion* 725–34, 566; *Med.* 54, *Bacch.* 1027. Slaves share the joys and sorrows of the household.

[2] *Phoen.* 392, *Ion* 674, fr. 313.

[3] Even Sophocles was prepared to let a character go as far as this. See fr. 854 εἰ σῶμα δοῦλον, ἀλλ' ὁ νοῦς ἐλεύθερος; and the accidental character of slavery, at least in a special case, is brought out by the chorus in Aeschylus's *Agamemnon* (1084), when they say of Cassandra's gift of prophecy μένει τὸ θεῖον δουλίᾳ περ ἐν φρενί.

[4] Fr. 495.41ff., seems to mean that the brave and just, even if of slave stock, are nobler than others who are full of vain fancies; but I do not find the text altogether clear, nor does the literal translation in Nestle's note (*Eur.* p. 546) seem to correspond very well with his version in the text (p. 358). Contrast fr. 976 ἀκόλασθ' ὁμιλεῖν γίγνεται δούλων τέκνα.

claring that he is ready to die in her service adds (854): 'One thing alone brings shame upon slaves, the name. In all else the slave, if he be a good man, is no worse than the free.' In these passages, taken with fr. 52, or a line like fr. 336, 2—'the well-born man is the good man'—it would be perverse not to recognize an outright denial of natural divisions within the human race whereby one can be born to serve and another to rule, with the corollary that slavery is wrong in itself. A slave as such is of no less worth than a free man. If he is morally inferior, that is due either to his own individual character or to slavery itself, which has ruined an originally good man.[1]

Apart from Euripides (who died in 406), the only surviving affirmation of this before the time of Aristotle is a quotation from a pupil of Gorgias named Alcidamas: 'God has set all men free; nature has made no man a slave.' This occurred in a speech to the Spartans recommending them to liberate Messene, whose inhabitants had been serfs of theirs for centuries, but no reference to the historical context can weaken the universality of the principle as enunciated. That is guaranteed by the words 'God', 'all' and 'nature'.[2] Slavery was already, as Newman pointed out (*Politics*, I, 143), 'undergoing a rigorous examination, in the course of which one form of it after another was being weighed in the balance and found wanting, and first enslavement for debt, then the enslavement of Greeks, then enslavement through war, were successively being eliminated, so that a total condemnation of the institution might well seem to be at hand'. Now it has been

---

[1] This is well and forcefully put by Nestle, *Eur.* 359.

[2] I therefore confine such reference to a footnote. The actual words (ἐλευθέρους ἀφῆκε πάντας θεός· οὐδένα δοῦλον ἡ φύσις πεποίηκεν) are quoted by a scholiast on Ar. *Rhet* 1373b, where Aristotle is arguing for the existence of a natural as distinct from a merely legal justice. After quoting the familiar lines of the *Antigone* about the eternal unwritten laws, and a passage in the same strain from Empedocles, he adds: 'and so also Alcidamas in his Messenian speech'. Thus Aristotle himself had no doubt that Alcidamas was speaking of a universal law of nature. Zeller however (quoted by Newman, *Politics*, I, 141, n. 1) thought that to have attacked the whole institution of slavery would not have served the purpose of his speech, therefore he would not have done so, and Levinson agrees (*D. of P.* 142): it is 'extremely unlikely that he would have been led on to make a universal application of his principle' (an excellent example of the textbook rhetorical argument ἐκ τοῦ εἰκότος. See pp. 178 f. below). But the fact is that the statement *is* universal, and no conjectures about what was prudent or tactful can stand up against the words themselves. The Sophist's sincerity, or his capacity for double-think, do not enter the question. Brzoska (*RE*, I, 1536) supposed that the work was not a genuine speech for the occasion but only a 'Schulstück'. The scholiast's use of the verb μελετᾶν (ὑπὲρ Μεσσηνίων μελετᾷ καὶ λέγει) supports this. For Alcidamas see pp. 311 ff. below.

uttered, and surely a great step forward in the history of human relations has been taken. Of course men's exasperating ability to keep their thoughts in separate compartments persisted. Levinson points out that the Justinian code, after laying down as a principle that 'slavery is contrary to natural law', proceeds to expound the rights of the slave-owner in minute detail; and in the nineteenth century an American slave-owner could happily acquiesce in the words of the Declaration of Independence, 'that all men are created equal'. The struggle was destined to be long, but it had begun, and a powerful weapon for the opponents of slavery had been forged, when the assertion that it had no foundation in nature was first openly made.

Alcidamas wrote his Messenian speech about 360. Late in the same century the affirmation recurs in a play of Philemon (fr. 95 Kock): 'Even if a man be a slave, he has the same flesh; no one was ever a slave by nature, though chance enslaves the body.' The currency of the idea in the second half of the fourth century is also attested by Aristotle, who writes in the *Politics* (1253b20): 'Some however hold that slave-ownership is unnatural. It is only by *nomos* that one is slave and another free, for in nature there is no difference. Neither, then, is it just, for it is based on force.' By this time, then (probably after 335), these liberal sentiments were well known, but it is a matter of lively controversy whether they were already current in the time with which we are now chiefly concerned, in the Athens of Euripides and Socrates, and are to be attributed to an earlier generation of Sophists than Alcidamas. How true is the claim of Nestle in 1901 that 'it will redound for all time to the glory of Greek sophistic that, starting from the conception of natural law, it opposed the existence of slavery on theoretical grounds, and the Socratic school, Plato and Aristotle, represent on this point a decidedly retrograde step'?

(5) RACIAL EQUALITY

The answer lies in the growth of the cosmopolitan idea, for, since the enslavement of Greek by Greek was generally unpopular, slavery could only be theoretically defended on the ground that barbarians (non-Greeks) were naturally inferior. This was the view of Plato,

who would only admit the enslavement of barbarians (*Rep.* 469b–c).[1]
He was prepared to be more specific: only Greeks were characterized
by good intellect and love of learning, northerners like Thracians and
Scythians were bold and irascible by nature, Phoenicians and Egyptians
avaricious (435e–436a). All this had a basis in contemporary science,
for the fifth-century Hippocratic treatise on *Airs, Waters and Places*
gives a detailed account of the effects of climate on character and
intellect as well as physique. Conditions in Asia Minor produce people
of good physique but pleasure-loving and lacking in courage and
industry, dwellers in the hot marshes of the Phasis region are fat,
sluggish and unfit for work, and so on. Greeks, living in an intermediate geographical position, possess both intelligence and courage,
which makes them a natural master-race.[2] When, in spite of this
scientific veneer, it began to be claimed that racial distinctions were
unnatural, existing only by *nomos*, the last theoretical prop of slavery
was removed, and this claim, as we have seen, was already made by
Antiphon. Some more general statements may also be noticed which
tend in the same direction. In a fragment of Euripides (902) we find:
'The good [in some authorities "wise"] man, even if he live in a far-
off land, even if my eyes never light on him, I judge my friend',
and there seems to have been a proverbial expression to the effect that
a good man's fatherland was the whole world.[3]

It is important to distinguish between pan-Hellenism and a wider
cosmopolitanism which embraced the barbarians.[4] The relations be-

---

[1] Plato defended slavery to the end of his life, in *Laws* as well as *Rep.* The passage in the
Politicus (262c–e) where he gives Greeks and barbarians as an example of a faulty classification,
because one non-Greek race differs from another as much as either from the Greek, has been
cited as evidence of a temporary change of mind (Schlaifer, *op. cit.* 98). Whether the illustration
is meant to have more than formal logical significance is perhaps doubtful. In spite of Skemp
ad loc. it is difficult to fit 'biting sarcasm' here into Plato's general view, which lasted until the
Laws, and Plato's point involves no necessary denial that all the different barbarian races are
in some respects inferior to the Greek. It is noteworthy however that in the *Phaedo* (78a) he
recommends searching not only the whole of Greece but also the barbarian nations to find a
cure for the fear of death.

[2] Hippocr. *A.W.P.* chs. 12ff. (II, 52 L.) The last point, about the Greeks, is added by Aristotle
(*Pol.* 1327b29), but obviously in dependence on earlier sources.

[3] Eur. fr. 1047, Democr. fr. 247 (again in the form of an iambic trimeter, on which DK[10]
II, *Nachtr.* p. 424, is inadequate), Lysias *Or.* 31.6. It is adapted in Aristoph. *Plut.* 1151 and
Thuc. 2.43.3.

[4] For a brief account of the growth of the Greek sense of unity and superiority to other
races, see Schlaifer, *op. cit.* 93ff. On the pan-Hellenic outlook of the Sophists, pp. 43 f. above.

tween the Greek city-states were paradoxical. Independent and jealous, they made constant war on one another, yet the sense of Hellenic unity was strong, and fostered by the great pan-Hellenic festivals at Olympia, Delphi and the Isthmus, for which quarrels were temporarily set aside and a sacred truce proclaimed. At these times the ties of a common language (even if split into dialects), religion and culture (typified by the Homeric poems) overruled the differences between the states. In the fifth and fourth centuries the fragmentation of the Greek-speaking world came more and more to be regarded as folly, and writers who use the language of cosmopolitanism may mean only to commend pan-Hellenism, which in itself accentuated rather than softened the distinction between Greek and barbarian. The ideal was the union of Greeks against the non-Greek world which had been achieved with such success in the Persian wars. Gorgias wrote (fr. 5b) that victories over barbarians called for hymns of thanksgiving, but those over fellow-Greeks for dirges. Hippias in the *Protagoras* (337c) calls the whole company, from different states, 'my kinsmen and family and fellow-citizens—by nature, not by *nomos*, for by nature like is kin to like, but *nomos*, tyrant of mankind, violates nature in many ways'. It would therefore be scandalous if they, the wisest of the Greeks, fell out among themselves. Here opinions have differed on the question whether Hippias is preaching the unity of mankind or simply of Greeks, or indeed of philosophers, for it could well be they whom he means to call 'naturally alike' (ὅμοιοι).[1] Does Hippias here 'recognize', as Untersteiner thinks, 'as friends and kinsmen the men of all cities and all nations'? His actual words are the same as those of Plato's Socrates at *Rep.* 470c when he says that the Greek race is 'one family and one kin', but immediately adds that Greeks and barbarians are not only alien but natural enemies.[2] The fact that Hippias, like Antiphon, distinguished *nomos* from *physis* and rejected the former does not, of itself, prove that he would have joined him in assigning distinctions of race and class to it, nor does his acquiescence in the existence of certain universal unwritten laws in Xenophon.

---

[1] For various opinions see Untersteiner, *Sophs.* 283f., *Sof.* III, 104f.; Bignone, *Studi*, 29; Baldry, *Unity*, 43; Strauss, *J. of Metaph.* 1959, 433.

[2] συγγενεῖς τε καὶ οἰκείους Hippias in *Prot.* of the assembled (Greek) company; τὸ Ἑλληνικὸν γένος αὐτὸ αὑτῷ οἰκεῖον καὶ συγγενές *Rep.*

The relations between Greeks and barbarians were complex, and cannot be adequately discussed here.[1] Plato might in one place dismiss the Egyptians as avaricious, but in the *Timaeus* he makes them the repositories of ancient wisdom in contrast to the 'childlike' Greeks. The debt of Greek science and mathematics to non-Greek peoples was freely acknowledged by Herodotus and others. Hippias himself said that in writing a work of his own he had made use of the poets 'and the prose-writers both Greek and barbarian' (fr. 6). Here we are simply concerned with the question whether the idea later known as the unity of mankind or the brotherhood of man was already mooted in the fifth century. It was, by Antiphon, and probably by Hippias and others too. Though our knowledge is lamentably scanty, it would be strange if belief in universal, 'natural' laws of human behaviour were not accompanied by a conviction that the human race is fundamentally akin. The idea of the basic equality of mankind was firmly rooted in anthropological theory. Since all men originally came from the earth, a by-product of the fermentation of mud or slime, nature gave no one the right to vaunt himself as sprung from better stock than anyone else.[2] That sort of distinction came on the scene later as a product of *nomos* only. This anthropological basis for the *nomos–physis* antithesis means that its justification of equality is universal, and it is reasonable to suppose that a man with any pretensions to philosophy who found it relevant to one distinction would apply it to all—high and low born, master and slave, Athenian and Spartan, Greek and non-Greek.

[1] Volume VIII of the *Entretiens Hardt* (*Grecs et Barbares*) is devoted to a discussion of them.
[2] We have just seen this applied to distinctions of birth in Euripides (fr. 52, pp. 154 f. above). See also p. 58 (Archelaus) and vol. II, pp. 207, 315 with n. 4, 343, 472.

VII

THE RELATIVITY
OF VALUES AND ITS EFFECTS ON
ETHICAL THEORY[1]

If physical philosophy begins in wonder, ethics may be said to have begun in scepticism.

Grant, *Ethics*, I, 155.

The chapter on the Sophists (p. 49) mentioned Sir Alexander Grant's division of morality into three stages, corresponding in a nation to childhood, adolescence and maturity in the individual. In one respect his division would not pass unchallenged today. He calls the second, sceptical or sophistic era 'transitional', and implies that only the third, that is, a return to earlier beliefs more deeply held because attained by independent thought, represents maturity. In Greek thought the transition was to the idealism of Plato, a philosophical reaffirmation and defence of those absolute values which are accepted by the 'simplicity and trust' of childhood as they are in the pre-critical stage of society. The second or sceptical stage might equally well be called positivist, and it is by no means generally accepted that belief in absolute values is more mature than positivism. Not every adult re-covers the convictions of his childhood. The positivist rejects the view that positive law must set out from the ideal of a natural, i.e. universally valid, standard of right: there is only a relative right or goodness, which is derived from the positive law prevailing at a particular time. The positivist knows that the search for goodness is a chimaera-hunt. Similarly beauty, as it was for Hume, is 'no quality in things themselves, it exists merely in the minds which contemplate them, and each mind perceives a different beauty'.[2] In statements like these the modern positivist would not wish to be told that his standpoint was either pre-Platonic or adolescent, but he is in fact repeating the Sophists' assertions in the controversy of the fifth and fourth centuries B.C.

[1] Cf. pp. 59 f.
[2] See Cassirer, *Phil. of Enlightenment*, 307.

Value for him, as for Archelaus, exists by *nomos* only, not by *physis*. For Ayer there is not even a controversy:

Talking about values is not a matter of describing what may or may not be there, the problem being whether or not it really is there. There is no such problem. The moral problem is: What am I to do? What attitude am I to take? And moral judgments are directives in this sense. We can now see that the whole dispute about the objectivity of values, as it is ordinarily conducted, is pointless and idle.[1]

Pointless and idle though it may be, the dispute has reappeared many times, and in speaking of the positivism of fifth-century Greece one can hardly claim that it was rendered obsolete by Plato. In Euripides a character asks rhetorically, 'What action is shameful if it seem not so to the actor?', which drew from Aristophanes the parody, 'What action is shameful if it seem not so to the audience?', and both Plato and Antisthenes were credited with the retort: 'Shameful is shameful, seeming or no seeming'.[2] Eteocles in the *Phoenissae*, asserting his lust for power in truly sophistic terms, says (499 ff.):

'If the same thing were to all men by nature fair and wise, there would be no disputes or quarrels among us. But as it is there is no consistency or impartiality where mortals are concerned: it is all names, without reality', and when Hippias claims to know what justice is, Socrates congratulates him ironically on a discovery which will cause juries to cease differing over their verdicts and put an end to litigation, rebellion and war (Xen. *Mem.* 4.4.8). Again, in Plato he remarks that when we utter words like 'iron' or 'silver' we all know what we mean, but when we say 'just' or 'good' we disagree with one another and even in our own minds.[3] These quotations give an idea of the sceptical atmosphere of the time, to which Socrates himself was so strongly opposed, holding that agreement on the meaning of moral terms was an essential preliminary to morality in practice.

The most distinguished advocate of the relativity of values (though, as inevitably happens, his thought was often distorted as it filtered

---

[1] Ayer, *Philosophical Essays*, 242.

[2] Eur. fr. 19, Ar. *Frogs* 1475. The retort is attributed to Antisthenes by Plutarch, *De aud. poet.* 33 c, and to Plato in Stobaeus, *Flor.* 5.82 (both quoted by Nauck on the fr.).

[3] *Phaedr.* 263 a. Cf. *Euthyphro* 7 c–d, *Alc. I* 111 e–112 a. Nestle (*VMʒuL*, 271) says that the lines from the *Phoenissae* 'unmistakably reproduce the doctrine of Protagoras', but are we not rather reminded of Socrates?

through other, less gifted minds) was Protagoras, and his philosophical challenge to traditionally accepted norms was in its turn based on relative and subjective theories of ontology and epistemology. As applied to values, relativity may mean one of two things. (*a*) There is nothing to which the epithets good, bad or the like can be applied absolutely and without qualification, because the effect of everything is different according to the object on which it is exercised, the circumstances of its application and so on. What is good for A may be bad for B, what is good for A in certain circumstances may be bad for him in others, and so on. The objectivity of the good effect is not denied, but it varies in individual cases. (*b*) When a speaker says that good and bad are only relative, he may mean that 'there is nothing either good or bad, but thinking makes it so'. Any investigation of the *nomos–physis* antithesis turns up plenty of examples of this: incest abominable in Greek eyes, normal in Egyptian and so on. With aesthetic values the case is even more obvious.

Heraclitus had earlier adduced the first type of relativity as one justification of his paradox of the identity of opposites: 'Sea water', he said, 'is at the same time purest and most polluted, being drinkable and salutary for fishes, undrinkable and deadly to men.'[1] Protagoras develops the theme in answer to a suggestion of Socrates that 'good' may be equated with 'beneficial to men':[2]

Even if things are not beneficial to men, I still call them good . . . I know plenty of things—foods, drinks, drugs and many others—which are harmful to men, and others which are beneficial; and others again which, so far as men are concerned, are neither, but are harmful or beneficial to horses, and others only to cattle or dogs. Some have no effect on animals, but only

[1] Fr. 61; see vol. I, 445.

[2] Plato, *Prot.* 333e–334c. The utilitarian equation of ἀγαθόν with ὠφέλιμον was a favourite one with Socrates. (See ch. xiv, §8, below.) Nor can it be doubted that the speech of Protagoras represents his actual view. Xenophon (*Mem.* 3.8.7) shows Socrates saying something similar (what is good for a hungry man is bad for one in a fever, etc.), and on this account has been accused of fathering on him the ideas of Antisthenes (Caizzi, *Stud. Urbin.* 1964, 65; not, oddly enough, of Protagoras). What Socrates is arguing there, however, is that the goodness of anything lies in its fitness to perform its proper function—an unimpeachably Socratic tenet (cf. *Rep.* 352e–353d). His thought was intensely practical: what is good must be *useful*, and the same thing can be useful or harmful according to circumstances (*Meno* 87e–88c and Xen. *Mem.* 4.6.8). Precisely how his thought differed from that of a Sophist like Protagoras must be considered later, but it is not correct to say as Caizzi does that the passage in Xenophon is 'fortemente antiplatonico' (by which he means against the Platonic Socrates).

on trees, and some again are good for the roots of trees but injurious to the young growths. Manure, for instance, is good for all plants when applied to their roots, but utterly destructive if put on the shoots or young branches. Or take olive oil. It is very bad for plants, and most inimical to the hair of all animals except man, whereas men find it of service both to the hair and to the rest of the body. So diverse and multiform is goodness that even with us the same thing is good when applied externally but deadly when taken internally. All doctors forbid the sick to use oil in preparing their food, except in the smallest quantities.

This able little speech has come in for a surprising amount of criticism on the ground of irrelevance.[1] Since Socrates has virtually asked Protagoras what he means by the concept 'good', it is hardly irrelevant for him to reply with his own theory of its diversity. That a Sophist should at the same time show off his miscellaneous knowledge is only in character. Hackforth[2] objected that, the point being ethical, the irrelevance lies in taking the meanings of 'good' beyond the ethical sphere. But not only was Socrates's question purely general, concerning the equation of 'good' with 'beneficial to men'; for the Sophists the connexion between ethics, politics and rhetoric on the one hand and hygiene or medicine on the other was important, as two branches of the art of improving human nature, moral and physical. In the *Theae-tetus* (167b–c) Protagoras says, 'When men exercise their skill on bodies I call them physicians, when on plants, husbandmen. These too, if a plant is sick, give it sound, healthy and true sensations instead of bad; and similarly good and skilful orators make good instead of evil courses appear just to cities.' Versényi has pointed out the close parallels that exist between Protagoras and the Hippocratic treatise *On Ancient Medicine*:[3]

Both stress the facts that their arts are human inventions rather than original endowments, that their arts are necessary because of the difference between one man and another and between men and animals, and that there is a resulting relativity of what is good for each. Both hold that 'our present

---

[1] Adam and Grube both call it irrelevant. To H. Gomperz (*S. u. R.* 162) it was a 'disturbing interruption', and he took its intrusiveness to be evidence that it was an extract from one of Protagoras's own books. That it may well be, but Plato is not the sort of writer to push something in where it is not wanted simply in order to introduce a verbatim quotation.

[2] In an unpublished lecture.

[3] *VM* 3 (quoted in part on p. 83 above): Versényi, *Soc. Hum.* 33–5, 43.

way of life' (laws, customs, regimen) is not by nature but 'has been discovered and elaborated during a long period of time'.

The aim of both [*sc.* the political and the medical arts] is to find what is useful, appropriate, fitting, or due to the nature of what each has in his care so as to promote healthy, harmonious and undisturbed life. This similarity of aim, method, and (almost) subject not only leads to constant association of the two, but at times makes it exceedingly difficult to draw a sharp dividing line between them.

'Speech', said Gorgias (*Hel.* 14), 'bears the same relation to the mind as drugs to the body. As drugs draw off different humours from the body, and some put an end to disease and others to life, so words can induce joy or grief, fear or confidence, or by evil persuasion drug and bewitch the mind.' This theory was actually put into practice by Antiphon in his 'psychiatric clinic' as reported in the *Lives of the Ten Orators*: hiring a special room in Corinth, he 'developed an "art of consolation" parallel to the therapy of the body by physicians'.[1]

Protagoras sees a close parallel not only, like Gorgias, between medicine and oratory, improving respectively the physical and moral conditions of men, but also between both and husbandry, the care of men and that of plants. This reappears in Antiphon (fr. 60):

Primary among human concerns is education, for in any enterprise when the beginning is right, the outcome is likely to be right too. As is the seed that is ploughed into the ground, so must one expect the harvest to be, and similarly when good education is ploughed into young persons, its effect lives and burgeons throughout their lives, and neither rain nor drought can destroy it.

This analogy is applied specifically to the teaching of medicine in the Hippocratic *Law*:[2]

The learning of medicine may be likened to the growth of plants. Our natural ability is the soil. The views of our teachers are as it were the seeds.

---

[1] [Plut.] *Vitae* 833c, Antiphon A 6. On this and the identity of Antiphon see further below, pp. 290f. Psychological insight is also suggested by his dictum (fr. 57) that illness is a holiday for the work-shy, for then they do not have to go out to work. I have assumed here that the story in the *Vitae* is true, but see p. 290, with notes.

[2] Ch. 3, trans. Jones. Jones (Loeb ed. 257f.) cites D.L. 7.40 as evidence that the *Law* is late enough to have been written under Stoic influence. But, apart from the fact that, as he says, 'the resemblance may not appear striking', he seems to have overlooked the extract from Antiphon.

Learning from childhood is analogous to the seeds' falling betimes upon the prepared ground. The place of instruction is as it were the nutriment that comes from the surrounding air to the things sown. Diligence is the working of the soil. Time strengthens all these things, so that their nurture is perfected.

These passages should increase our insight into the mind of a Sophist and assist an understanding of Protagoras's use of medical and agricultural examples in answering Socrates's question. It was the medical writers above all who insisted (as success in their craft demanded) on the relativity of 'good' and 'bad' to the individual. Comparison between what is good for man in health and man in sickness, and between man and animals, is made in *Ancient Medicine* (ch. 8), and in ch. 20 it is argued that, far from a knowledge of the whole nature of man being a prerequisite of the medical art (as certain philosophers maintained), a knowledge of medicine is necessary to the knowledge of man and indeed of nature in general. What the physician needs to answer is not a general question like 'what man is', but what man is in relation to different foods, drinks and ways of life, and what will be the effect of each on each individual.[1]

We have already seen how widespread was the tendency to substitute the concepts of interest and advantage, the useful or the beneficial (συμφέρον, χρήσιμον, ὠφέλιμον), with which goes naturally the appropriate or fitting (ἐπιτήδειον), for the universal standard of 'justice' or 'right'. As 'the interest of the stronger' (Thucydides, Thrasymachus) it became a doctrine of self-aggrandizement and neglect of the rights of others, but in itself it was simply utilitarian and practical. Bound up with it was the notion of necessity (*ananké*), and to the examples already cited (pp. 100f. above) may be added another extract from *Ancient Medicine*, ch. 3, which emphasizes the connexion

---

[1] It is sometimes supposed that *VM* was written under the influence of Protagoras (e.g. Versényi, *Socr. Hum.* 11, but denied by Longrigg in *HSCP*, 1963). Its date is uncertain. If Festugière were right in putting it anywhere between 450 and 420, Protagoras might have been acquainted with it, but it was probably later (Lloyd in *Phronesis*, 1963). Even so, its conclusions spring more from the exigencies of medical practice than from the influence of any non-medical thinker, and that Protagoras himself was influenced by the more empirical of contemporary physicians seems to me beyond doubt. That according to Sextus he 'introduced' the 'man–measure' doctrine (Versényi, *op. cit.* 11, n. 9) is no evidence against this. Perhaps a more accurate way of putting it would be that Protagoras's own empirical turn of mind led him to take an interest in medicine and similarly practical subjects.

between practical activity and a relative conception of values: 'The fact is that sheer necessity caused men to seek and discover medicine, because sick men did not, and do not, profit by the same regimen as do men in health.' This again is bound up with the whole evolutionary view of human progress (p. 83 above).

In all this it is not easy to find references to specifically aesthetic values, though in any discussion of the relativity of values these might be the first to occur to us. Needless to say, the Greeks were not insensitive to beauty, but as the ambiguity of their word for it, *kalon*, suggests, did not speak much of it in isolation. One reason for this was the close association in their minds of beauty with appropriateness and fitness for function.[1] C. T. Seltman put the point well (*Approach to Greek Art*, 29):

Beautiful is a misrendering of *kalos*. We can perhaps get nearest to the meaning by using Fine and Fineness, for these may be employed in most of the senses of the Greek words. To say that for the Greeks Beauty and Goodness were one and the same is an error. But put it, that to the Greeks Fineness automatically included excellence, because what is fine must be fitted to its purpose and therefore good, and we are on the right track. Fineness could become the ultimate Value by which all other Values could be measured.

A delightful illustration of this association in the Greek mind is the 'beauty contest' in Xenophon's *Symposium* (ch. 5). Socrates undertakes to prove to the company that he is more beautiful than the young and handsome Critobulus. Critobulus gives his case away at the outset by saying that anything is beautiful (*kalon*) if it is well constructed for the purpose for which we have acquired it, or is adapted by nature for our wants. Then, replies Socrates, if we have eyes for seeing, mine are more beautiful than yours, since being prominent and bulging they can see far to the side and not simply straight in front of them; and so on. (The passage is fully translated on pp. 387 f. below.)

Did Protagoras also believe in the relativity of values in the second sense, i.e. that all value-judgments are purely subjective? At first sight

---

[1] According to Aristotle, the difference between ἀγαθόν and καλόν is that καλόν is the more inclusive term. ἀγαθόν refers to actions only, but καλόν is used *also* where no action or movement is involved. (See *Metaph.* 1078a31.)

at least this would seem an inevitable conclusion from his famous saying that man is the measure:[1]

'Man is the measure of all things, of the things that are that they are, and of the things that are not that they are not.' In the *Theaetetus* (152a), Socrates asks Theaetetus if he has read this. 'Often', is the reply. 'Then you know that he puts it something like this, that as every single thing appears to me, so it *is* to me, and as it appears to you, so it *is* to you—you and I being men.' Since this addition is made in practically the same words in the *Cratylus* (386a), it too must be a part of Protagoras's own argument, and this is borne out by Aristotle, who adds the information that the 'things' in question include values (*Metaph.* 1062b13):

Protagoras said that man is the measure of all things, meaning simply and solely that what appears to each man assuredly also *is*. If this is so, it follows that the same thing both is and is not, and is both bad and good, and whatever else is asserted in contrary statements, since often a particular thing appears good (or beautiful, *kalon*) to some and the opposite to others; and the criterion (μέτρον) is what appears to each individual.[2]

All the direct sources agree on the general meaning of Protagoras's saying, namely that what appears to each individual is the only reality and therefore the real world differs for each; and this is all the more likely because he would find similar ideas in contemporary natural philosophers. Anaxagoras told his pupils that 'things would be for them such as they supposed them to be', and Empedocles and Parmenides emphasized the connexion between a man's physical condition and his thoughts.[3]

So far so good, but now there comes a remarkable development. As Socrates says (*Theaet.* 161cff.), on the thesis as so far propounded no man can be wiser than another, and there could be no sense in Protagoras or anyone else setting himself up as a teacher. Socrates therefore offers a defence which he says Protagoras would have given

---

[1] Fr. 1. A detailed interpretation is reserved for the discussion of its epistemological implications, pp. 183ff. below.

[2] If it is admitted that the 'Double Arguments' (pp. 316ff. below) reflect Protagoras's teaching, they provide further evidence that his relativity included such concepts as good and bad, right and wrong, laudable and blameworthy.

[3] Aristotle has collected the passages in *Metaph.* 1009b15ff. See on them vol. II, 319, 229, 67. The use of ἄνθρωπος is discussed more fully on pp. 188ff. below.

if he were alive.[1] It consists in maintaining that, though all beliefs are equally true, not all are equally good (*agatha*).[2] The wise (*sophos*) man is he who can change what appears and is bad (*kakon*) to any one of us and make it be and appear good. (*a*) A sick man's food *is* bitter (for him): he cannot be called mistaken when he says it is, nor more ignorant than the healthy. But the doctor, the *sophos* in the healing art, can so change his condition that it both appears and is sweet and pleasant. (*b*) In education, the Sophist does with words what the doctor does with drugs (compare Gorgias, p. 168 above), namely change the pupil to a better state. He does not make him exchange false beliefs for true, for false beliefs are impossible; but, when a man has a depraved (*ponēron*) state of mind and corresponding thoughts, he makes his mind sound and so gives him sound (*chresta*) thoughts— not truer but better. (*c*) Such things as a whole city thinks just and honourable (*kala*) are so for it as long as it thinks they are; but in each case where they are injurious (*ponēra*), the wise man substitutes others which are and appear sound (*chresta*). In this way it is allowed that some men are wiser than others, although no man thinks falsely.

Here is a paradox: two men's beliefs can be equally true, but not equally valuable, *even though* they are beliefs about the goodness or badness of something. In the case of physical sensations, at least with Plato's example, there is no difficulty. The sick man dislikes what he tastes, and will be glad when the doctor, as we should say, restores his normal appreciation of good food or, as Protagoras would have it,

---

[1] Evidently what follows was not to be found in Protagoras's writings, but it is unlikely that it departs from the sense of what he taught. As Cornford says, he must have reconciled his profession as a Sophist with his claim that all beliefs are equally true, and there is no other way in which he could have done it. The point is argued fully by H. Gomperz, *S. u. R.* 263 ff., and for other references see Untersteiner, *Sophs.* 70f. (n. 1). S. Moser and G. L. Kustas, in *Phoenix*, 1966, claim that 'reading the *Protagoras* in the light of the *Theaetetus*' has been a prime cause of misinterpretation of the earlier dialogue. This claim depends on accepting Th. Gomperz's assumption (*Gk. Th.* I, 457f.) that the one presents a 'genuine', the other a 'sham' Protagoras— a highly arbitrary procedure.

[2] Plato uses a variety of words in this passage, all of which are sometimes simply translated 'bad' or 'good'. I have inserted them in Roman letters and append a rough approximation to the different senses which they conveyed to a Greek. *Kakon*: the most general word for *bad*; *agathon*: the most general word for *good*, with the overtone of *conducive to efficient performance of function* which was commonly present in Greek terms of approbation; *ponēron*: causing toil, distress, pain or grief (from noun *ponos*, labour, trouble, suffering); *chreston*: useful, serviceable, effective, wholesome (coupled with *hygieinon*, healthy, at 167c1); *kalon*: fine, beautiful, of good quality, laudable, honourable.

makes his unpleasant food both seem and be pleasant to him. But with moral values the case is different. If what a city thinks just and fine *is* just and fine for it so long as it thinks so, it will not want its views or its laws changed nor, one would have thought, ought they to be changed. They should be like the olive oil of the *Protagoras* speech, good for that city though not perhaps for others. It seems however that the city may not be *wise*, nor its judgments sound and profitable, but useless and likely to cause harm. How then can they be, as well as seem, both just and fine (*kala*) for the city?

Protagoras is seeking his own solution to that burning question of the day, the relation between *nomimon* and *dikaion*, positive law and morality. It was said:

(1) That the two were identical by definition, and the statement of their identity simply analytic. This might be (*a*) the old religious idea, going back to tribal days, that laws came from the gods, and so could not err and must be obeyed ('all human laws are nourished by the one divine law'); or (*b*) a criticism consequent on the equation of the two: given the definition, that 'justice' includes only what is enjoined or sanctioned by the laws, then, as Antiphon pointed out, a man has a right to observe it only in so far as it coincides with his own interests, and a duty to ignore it when it conflicts with a fact of nature like the equality of Greek and barbarian, noble and commoner, rich and poor.

(2) As a result of (*b*), the identity of just and legal was denied. 'Just' and 'right' represented moral values, which could not be equated with the dictates of positive law, for the law might be unjust and conversely what was just extended beyond the field of legal enactment.

(3) There was the doctrine of the social compact as held by Socrates, according to which, though the legal machinery might lead to an unjust judgment in an individual case, it was still right for the citizen to accept it because his membership of the state implied a promise to obey the laws in return for the many legal benefits of citizenship.

The topicality of the controversy, and the still fluid state of opinion, led to a certain amount of confusion, which is reflected in Protagoras. He held that, though laws were not 'by nature', their institution and observance were necessary for the preservation of society. The whole function of our sense of justice (*dikē*) is 'to make political order possible' (p. 66 above). Naturally therefore he inclines to those who equate *dikaion* with *nomimon*. Yet in the middle of the fifth century it was impossible for a thinking man to ignore the existence of bad laws, and he has attempted a solution which will take account of them. If the result is an inconsistent or circular argument,[1] its interest lies in the state of the question at the time, which led Protagoras to take such a tortuous course. It is, after all, a question which has not even now been resolved.

Since Protagoras was famous for his claim to 'make the weaker argument the stronger', H. Gomperz (*S. u. R.* 269) suggested that he may have used these epithets here, rather than 'worse' and 'better' which Plato uses in his defence and which make the circularity particularly glaring. They would not essentially alter the case, but give the appearance of a more objective standard. Gomperz's explanation of the paradox is that each man is right because each sees one facet of the truth, that which his disposition allows him to see, but (as with bodily health) there are normal and abnormal dispositions, and the most normal man, whom Protagoras calls the wise, has the most normal, strongest and best belief. His theory corresponds to his rhetorical practice, is in fact an epistemological justification of the importance of rhetoric. The rhetor must be able to defend opposing points of view with equal success but finally to bring one to victory as the 'stronger'. Just so the epistemologist proves that all views are equally true because each grasps one facet of the truth, then decides for one as the 'better'. For Protagoras, the rhetor is identical with the wise man because he has been trained to see both sides, whereas the layman sees only one—truth but partial truth (p. 275).[2]

What this amounts to is that Protagoras's criterion is quantitative: all judgments are equally true, but not equally valuable because, according as they grasp more or less of reality, so they are more or less normal or abnormal and thus stronger or weaker. The explanation

---

[1] 'That there is a logical circle here cannot be denied . . . If value judgments are only valid for the individual, how can a judgment that two beliefs are of unequal value be valid for more than the individual who makes it?' (Gomperz, *S. u. R.* 269.) As von Fritz remarks (*RE*, XXIII, 917), if Protagoras's moral doctrine contains an inconsistency and contradiction of his fundamental premise, he shares this inconsistency with most modern relativists, who like him try to combine their relativism with positive doctrines and precepts for human action.

[2] For a criticism of Gomperz's interpretation of Protagoras see ZN, 1357, n. 1.

has its attractions, but is weakened by its reliance on the concepts of 'normal' and 'abnormal', for as Cornford said (*PTK*, 73) 'sounder' for Protagoras 'does not mean "normal", for that would set up the majority as a norm or measure for the minority'. It can only mean more useful or expedient, a belief that *will* produce better effects in the future; that is, for the individual, effects that will both be and seem better to the Sophist's pupil after his training. He will then prefer his new beliefs. For a state, its laws and customs are right and laudable so long as they are enforced or socially approved, but a statesman may persuade it that others would be of greater advantage to it. (The point is made explicitly at 172a.) Capital punishment, we may say, is right and proper so long as it has the backing of public opinion and is legally enforced. If these conditions are altered, it is likely to be because in the first place a few advanced thinkers (*sophistai* as a Greek might call them) succeed in initiating the diffusion of different ideas; and this they can only do (according to the theory) by convincing the citizens that the alteration will be of practical advantage (*chreston*)— that, for instance, crimes of violence will diminish rather than increase. Behind this tortuous argument is Protagoras's conviction that *diké* exists for the preservation of social order, and that therefore the maintenance of existing laws, even though they are not the best, is just and laudable because the alternatives of disobedience or subversion would destroy the 'bond of friendship and union' on which our very life depends (*Prot.* 322c4). Only if new laws are enacted by common consent and constitutional processes can the change be for the better.[1]

[1] Cf. p. 146 above. By thinking out this matter on independent lines, I hope I have resolved the difficulty felt and expressed by A. T. Cole in *Yale C.S.* 1966, which led him to the conclusion that Plato's 'Apology of Protagoras' was in fact 'not one Apology but two', containing respectively 'a "subjectivist" conception compatible with the man–measure principle as stated in 166d and a "utilitarian" one not so compatible' (pp. 112 and 114f.). In particular I do not agree that Plato has misinterpreted or misunderstood the doctrine of 167a–b (p. 116). The contention that 169d is inconsistent with it is untrue. All that Plato says there is that, according to Protagoras, 'some men are superior in the matter of what is better or worse, and these, he said, were wise' (Cornford's translation). He does not say that these better judges are the healthy as opposed to the sick. They are of course the doctors (or in their respective spheres the husbandmen, orators or Sophists).

VIII

RHETORIC AND PHILOSOPHY

(Seeming and being, believing and knowing, persuading and proving)

(1) GENERAL

Rhetoric has already been mentioned in these pages (20, 50f.), but demands a closer look. Obviously we are not here concerned with appraisal of the works of Lysias, Andocides or other Attic orators, nor with questions of manner and style;[1] but the theory behind Greek rhetoric had philosophical implications, with which not only the Sophists but Plato himself felt that they had to come to grips. Plato could even describe his own dialectical philosophy as the substitution of good rhetoric for bad, and it has been contended that rhetoric alone was the distinguishing mark of a Sophist.[2] That this is an exaggeration will have already appeared, but all the leading Sophists were deeply concerned with it, in its forensic, political and epideictic branches, both as active practitioners and as teachers, systematizers and writers of rhetorical handbooks.[3] Plato, who knew his Sophists, distinguishes sophistic and rhetoric by an elaborate analogy, designed to show how 'though they differ in nature, yet they are so closely related that Sophists and orators, working in the same sphere and on the same subject-matter, are confused, and know not what to make of themselves, nor others of them'. It must be read in the light of his own doctrine of the superiority of knowledge, reality and teaching to belief, appearance and persuasion. As gymnastic keeps the body fit, so legislation keeps a state sound and healthy. If the body falls

---

[1] Which may be studied in such works as Blass's *Attische Beredsamkeit*, Norden's *Antike Kunstprosa* and Dobson's *Greek Orators*. One should also mention Kroll's article in *RE*, Suppl. VII, 1039–1138, and G. Kennedy, *The Art of Persuasion in Greece*.

[2] By H. Gomperz in his *Sophistik u. Rhetorik*. The thesis is denied in the *Prodikos* of H. Mayer, who refers to the rebuttals of Wendland in *Gött. Gel. Anz.* (1913), no. 1, and Drerup, *Lit. Zentralbl.* (1913), Sp. 681 f.

[3] τὰ βιβλία τὰ περὶ τῆς τῶν λόγων τέχνης γεγραμμένα (Pl. *Phaedr.* 266 d) or simply τέχναι (p. 44, n. 4, above).

sick, medicine will cure it, and the corresponding art in the state is the execution of justice. All these arts have their counterfeits. To gymnastic corresponds make-up, giving the appearance of health, and to legislation sophistic, claiming to impart what keeps a state sound, but without real knowledge. The counterfeit of the doctor is the chef, who claims to know the best diet for the body but in fact aims only at pleasing the palate, and similarly rhetoric corresponds to the due execution of justice in that it aims at cajoling an audience and producing the semblance, not the reality, of justice. It can be said, then, that sophistic and rhetoric are 'pretty nearly the same thing', but, for what the difference is worth, sophistic is superior in so far as the art which it imitates is superior, that is, in so far as prevention is better than cure.[1]

The rhetorical art was also known as 'the art of *logoi*', and the wide meaning of this word (from talking or speech-making to argument, reason, thought) made possible very different conceptions of the art of which it was the subject. Plato's aim was to get it out of the hands of superficial persuaders and special pleaders, and show that, properly applied and based on knowledge of the truth, it was coextensive with philosophy. This is the lesson of the *Phaedrus* (see especially 278b–d), and in the *Phaedo* (90bff.) Socrates attributes the evil of 'misology'— an aversion from *logoi* of every kind—to lack of proper training in 'the art of *logoi*'. Without it a man believes whatever he is told, then later discovers it is false, and in his disillusionment falls to abusing, not his own lack of experience, but *logoi* themselves, and so misses the path to knowledge and truth. The worst offenders are the men who deal in contradictions (ἀντιλογικοί) and think it the height of cleverness to have discerned that there is no soundness or certainty in anything or any argument, but everything goes up and down like the current in the Euripus and never stays the same for a moment. Plato may have had Protagoras and his *Antilogiai* (p. 182 with n. 1 below) particularly in mind, but his censure extends to all rhetoricians and Sophists, the 'uncultured whose desire is not for wisdom but for scoring off an opponent' (91a), the very people, in fact, who considered

---

[1] *Gorg.* 465c, 520a. The comparison between mind and body, rhetoric and medicine or drugs, as we have seen (pp. 167ff.), was not new. Plato refines on it.

themselves masters of 'the art of *logoi*' and the best teachers of it to others.[1] In Plato's eyes, as in actual fact, Socrates was the real master of this art. He put it to a different use from the Sophists, but, although he was no rhetorician, if Critias in making it illegal to teach the art of *logoi* had Socrates particularly in mind,[2] this was not altogether unreasonable. He was convinced that if one understood a thing one could 'give a *logos* of it', and his demand for definitions was a demand that people should prove that they understood the essence of courage, justice or whatever else was under discussion by finding a verbal formula which would cover all cases of it. 'He held that those who know what any given thing is must also be able to expound it to others' (Xen. *Mem.* 4.6.1). The following words which Xenophon puts into his mouth are characteristic (*Mem.* 3.3.11; he is arguing that a good cavalry commander must be a good speaker):

Has it not occurred to you that all the best things that we learned according to custom, by which we know how to live, we learned through speech, that any other good lesson that may be learned is learned through speech, and that the best teachers make the greatest use of speech and those with the deepest knowledge of the most important matters are also the best speakers?[3]

The 'invention' of rhetoric is attributed to two Sicilians of the first half of the fifth century, Corax and Tisias. Invention in this connexion had a specific meaning,[4] namely the introduction of the appeal to probability instead of fact, the drawing up of rules for its application, and their embodiment in written handbooks. If a man accused of assault can produce facts showing incontrovertibly that he did not commit it, he has no need of the art, but, if he cannot, he must invoke the argument from probability. If he is smaller and weaker than his victim he will say, 'Look at me; is it likely that someone like me should go for a big strong man like him?' If on the other hand he is a Samson, he will

---

[1] Taylor has pointed out (*VS*, 92, 98) that Plato makes two things clear about *antilogikē* and eristic: they were rife in Socrates's time and not due to a perversion of his elenchus, and their ancestry is Eleatic.

[2] Xen. *Mem.* 1.2.31. Gigon (*Komm. ʒ. erst. Buch* 58) doubts the historicity of the incident.

[3] Cf. Stenzel in *RE*, 2. Reihe, v. Halbb. 821 f. Stenzel goes so far as to say that language is the starting-point of Socrates's teaching.

[4] To be a good speaker as well as a man of action had, as Lesky points out (*HGL*, 350), been the ambition of a Greek since Homeric times (*Il.* 9.443).

argue, 'Would I be such a fool as to attack him when I am the first person on whom suspicion would fall?' These arguments are preserved as a sample from Corax and Tisias.[1] A good modern one was reported in the *Sunday Times* for 21 May 1967. An accusation of exceeding the 70 m.p.h. speed limit on a motorway was brought by police who claimed to have followed the defendant for nearly a mile with their speedometer registering 80–85. The defence was not counter-evidence from the accused's own speedometer. It was that the police-car had a flashing blue light, hence that it was easy for him to see that it was following him, and 'Would I be such a fool as to drive at over 80 with a police-car on my trail?' Rhetoric teaches from the first that what matters is not what is the case, but what appears, what men can be persuaded of (*Phaedrus* 267a). It is 'the art of *logos*', which is not only speech and argument but also appearance or belief as opposed to fact (*ergon*), and its goal is persuasion. On the credit side it may be said that persuasion is better than force,[2] and rhetoric is *par excellence* the democratic art which cannot, either in its political or its forensic form, flourish under tyranny. Its birth in Syracuse, Aristotle noted (*ap.* Cic., see n. 1), coincided with the expulsion of the tyrants and the establishment of democracy.

The Sophists, then, were not the pioneers of rhetoric, but they were certainly ready to step in and supply the demand for it which accompanied the development of personal freedom all over Greece.[3] A distinction may be drawn between the Sicilian school, carried on after Corax and Tisias by Empedocles (vol. II, 135), Gorgias and Polus and aiming mainly at fine speaking (εὐέπεια), and that of other Sophists who congregated at Athens, Protagoras of Abdera, Prodicus of Cos and Hippias of Elis. These latter, besides being interested in

[1] Aristotle (*Rhet.* 1402a 17) connects it with Corax. Plato (*Phaedr.* 273a–b) attributes it in a somewhat garbled and caricatured form to Tisias, who was said to be his pupil. See also Arist. *ap.* Cic. *Brut.* 12.46 (presumably from the Συναγωγὴ τεχνῶν) for Corax and Tisias as the first to have written handbooks on rhetoric after the expulsion of the tyrants from Sicily, and in general Aulitzky in *RE*, XI, 1379–81.

[2] A point noted by Democritus, fr. 181 (vol. I, 496), and claimed by Gorgias in favour of his art (Plato, *Phileb.* 58a).

[3] It is not to be thought that, because Gorgias on the embassy of 427 is said to have amazed the Athenians by his art, they were unacquainted with artistic and professional oratory. They were already in love with it (φιλόλογοι), and what took them by surprise was Gorgias's exotic and artificial style, which then appealed by its novelty, though later it was seen as cloying and affected (Diod. 12.53).

education in its widest sense, emphasized the correct use of language όρθοέπεια, όρθότης όνομάτων) and so were led on from their concern with public speaking to initiate the studies of philology and grammar, etymology and the distinction of synonyms. (See §6 below.)

The essential theoretical basis of rhetoric was that which distinguished it from the beginning, and which so shocked the absolutist Plato, namely that (as he put it of Tisias and Gorgias, *Phaedr.* 267a), 'they held the probable (or likely-seeming, plausible, εἰκότα) in more honour than the true'.[1] The justification of this was that, to a Sophist and rhetorician, truth and knowledge were illusion.

Since all human inquiry moves within the realm of opinion, where deception is easy, all persuasion (philosophic, 'scientific', legal or other) is a result of the force of eloquence rather than of rational insight...If men *knew*, there would be a great difference between deception and truth. As it is, we can only distinguish between successful and unconvincing, persuasive and fruitless arguments.[2]

Turning Parmenides upside-down, Gorgias claimed that nothing exists (or is real), that if it did we could not know it, and if we could know it we could not communicate our knowledge to another. The philosophical basis is the same as that of Protagoras's 'What seems to each man *is* as far as he is concerned'.[3] 'If', says Gorgias (fr. 11a, 35 DK), 'it were possible through words (*logoi*) to make the truth about reality (*erga*) pure and clear to the hearers, judgment would be easy as simply following from what was said; but since it is not so...'

The *logos* has supreme power, and it is neutral. It can do great good, banishing fear and grief and fostering joy and compassion (Gorg. *Hel.* 8, DK II, 290). Even when deceptive, the deceit may be a just one and the deceived go away wiser than before, as happens with the

---

[1] Plato must have enjoyed the irony of imagining Protagoras as protesting against precisely the methods of argument which he himself found objectionable in the Sophist and his kind: 'You adduce no compelling proof at all, but rely on the probable' (*Theaet.* 162e).

[2] Versényi, *Socr. Hum.* 47f.

[3] Sicking (*Mnem.* 1964, 245) appears to think otherwise; but it can hardly be denied that if nothing has real existence, nor can be recognized or communicated, the only alternative is that each man's private sensations and beliefs are alone valid, and valid for him alone. That Gorgias's polemic is not aimed *solely* at the Eleatics ('nicht *nur*', Sicking p. 232, though on p. 245 he drops the qualification) cannot alter this.

fictions of tragedy, which to Gorgias was only rhetoric in verse.[1] But in itself it is simply 'the art of persuasion', armed with which a man can convince of whatever he likes 'a jury in court, senators in the Council, the people in the Assembly, or any other gathering of citizens' (Plato, *Gorg.* 452e). This art of speaking Gorgias claimed to teach, and nothing more. Though it concerned right and wrong, he disclaimed the teaching of *areté* (*Meno* 95c) and maintained that the rhetorician is not to be blamed if his pupils employ their skill for wicked ends, any more than a boxing instructor if his pupil goes away and knocks his father down. Rhetoric, it appears, is concerned entirely with means, not ends,[2] and his teaching had different effects on pupils according to their character. Xenophon (*An.* 2.6.16ff.) contrasts Proxenus the Boeotian, who paid Gorgias's fees because he longed for greatness, fame and money, 'but had no desire to win them unjustly', with the unscrupulousness of Meno the Thessalian (whose connexion with Gorgias is known from Plato). If Socrates's pupils did not all do him credit, it was not for the same reason.

(2) PROTAGORAS

Protagoras's subjectivism has already been introduced in connexion with the relativity of values, and its close relation to his activities as a teacher of rhetoric is obvious.[3] He taught his pupils to praise and

---

[1] Frr. 23 and 11.9 (λόγον ἔχων μέτρον). Deceit then is possible. In spite of his denial of absolute truth, Gorgias would not maintain that it is all the same whether a murder takes place on the stage or in reality. But what is death? Whatever we are persuaded it is. There is a nice bit of rhetorical effrontery in Gorgias's *Palamedes*, where, after playing the argument from probability throughout his speech, Palamedes towards the end (§34) exhorts his hearers μὴ τοῖς λόγοις μᾶλλον ἢ τοῖς ἔργοις προσέχειν τὸν νοῦν.

[2] *Gorg.* 456c–457c. When Socrates presses his argument, Gorgias does indeed admit, in an offhand way, that if his pupil doesn't know about right and wrong he supposes he can teach him (the subjects for which Socrates and Plato found a lifetime of philosophy inadequate!), but, when Socrates goes on to draw the conclusion that in fact rhetoric cannot be used for wrong ends, it is time for the old and respected man to be released and his brash pupil to take over. The whole discussion with Gorgias throws an invaluable light on current conceptions of rhetoric, and bears no marks of caricature. See also *Phileb.* 58a for his conviction of the superiority of persuasion to every other art, and on his disclaiming to teach ἀρετή pp. 271f. below.

[3] Nestle (ZN, 1358 n.) says it is nothing but a *petitio principii* to regard rhetoric as the source of Protagoras's philosophy. It is of course unpardonably crude. The scepticism and subjectivism of which he was such a notable representative were rooted in the previous history of philosophy, if only as a reaction from its universal assumption of an unperceived reality underlying pheno-

censure the same case, was notorious for his claim 'to make the weaker argument the stronger' (see e.g. Ar. *Rhet.* 1402a23ff.), and wrote two books of 'Contrary Arguments' which must have been a rhetorical textbook. 'There are', he said, 'two opposite arguments on every subject',[1] and in the *Euthydemus* (286b–c) Socrates attributes to 'Protagoras and even earlier thinkers' the thesis that it is impossible to contradict, which, he says, amounts to saying that it is impossible to speak falsely.[2] Aristotle (*Metaph.* 1007b18) speaks of the thesis 'that contradictory statements about the same thing are simultaneously true' and 'it is possible either to assert or deny something of every subject' as one that must be accepted by those who accept Protagoras's dictum. Lower down, at 1009a6, he says (after mentioning denial of the law of contradiction): 'What Protagoras says originates in the same opinion, and they must stand or fall together; for if all that appears and is believed is true, everything must at the same time be true and false, for many people hold opinions opposite to each other.'[3]

mena or even (in the case of the Eleatics) denying them their right to exist (cf. p. 15 above). It is best to avoid dogmatizing about cause and effect, and say only that, just as the democratic freedom of Athens favoured the rapid rise of rhetoric in practice, so the philosophical situation provided a background suited to its theoretical justification; and this the best of the Sophists, who were very much more than demagogues or soapbox orators, were anxious to provide.

[1] Eudoxus ap. Steph. Byz. (DK, A 21; cf. Aristoph. *Clouds* 112ff.), D.L. 9.55 ('Αντιλογιῶν α'β'), D.L. 9 51, of which an equally possible translation would be: 'Of every thing two contrary accounts can be given.'

[2] The 'earlier thinkers' need not be taken too seriously. Plato would chiefly be thinking of Heraclitus and his doctrine of the identity of opposites (vol. 1, 442ff.), which no doubt influenced Protagoras's views but contained them only in embryo. Plato liked to bring in not only earlier philosophers but even poets as *soi-disant* parents of philosophical doctrines, as, for example, at *Theaet.* 152e and *Crat.* 402b he carries the Heraclitean flux-doctrine back to Homer. Nor, in view of many Platonic examples to the contrary, can we suppose οἱ ἀμφὶ Π. intended to exclude Protagoras himself. The thesis of the impossibility of contradiction is usually ascribed to Antisthenes on the evidence of Aristotle (*Metaph.* 1024b32, *Top.* 104b20). D.L. (9.53, cf. 3.35) calls it the thesis of Antisthenes, but adds, citing Plato, that it was first argued by Protagoras. Aristotle's words certainly do not exclude this, and Plato's language suggests that it may have been well known in sophistic circles of the fifth century. A papyrus from an author of the fourth century A.D. ascribes it to Prodicus. This may be simply a mistake, but Prodicus was acquainted with both Protagoras and Antisthenes (Xen. *Symp.* 4.62). See Binder and Liesenborghs in *Mus. Helv.* 1966.

[3] Untersteiner (*Sof.* 1, 49f.) and H. Gomperz (*S. u. R.* 225f.) have argued from these passages that the impossibility of contradiction was not a tenet of Protagoras himself, since Aristotle represents it as an *inference* from what he said. The most that can be claimed is that they do not prove that it was, and other evidence makes it practically certain. There is however this qualification to be made, that what cannot be contradicted must 'appear to, or be believed by', at least one man. Protagoras would not agree with Aristotle that everything that can be uttered must be true and false (1007b20), for after all nobody believes that men are triremes or walls.

Protagoras: 'Man the Measure'

The theoretical foundation for all these statements lies in the thesis with which he opened his work on *Truth*,[1] and which has already been quoted for its bearing on concepts of value (fr. 1 DK):

Man is the measure of all things, of the things that are that they are, and of the things that are not that they are not.[2]

The continuation shows that he had chiefly the individual in mind, though unless Plato goes beyond him in this he would have extended it to the corporate opinion of a state as embodied in its laws. (See p. 172 above.) Besides Plato and Aristotle, the statement is quoted by Sextus, who also understands it of the individual, explaining: 'truth is something relative because everything that has appeared to, or been believed by, *someone* (τινί) is at once real in relation to *him*'.[3]

The word 'measure' (*metron*) was probably chosen by Protagoras for the epigrammatic flavour which it gives to his very quotable saying, and there is no reason to doubt that Plato, followed by Sextus, was right in explaining it as *kriterion*, standard of judgment.[4] Its meaning is also brought out by a criticism of Aristotle's. At the end of a discussion of *metron* in the *Metaphysics* (1053a31) he says (to paraphrase and expound a difficult passage) that, in addition to its more usual meanings, the word is applied to knowledge and sensation because they are a means of learning about things, as a standard measure enables us to learn their size, quantity, weight, value, etc. This however is a misuse of the term which makes it mean the opposite of what it should. Far from our knowledge and sensations being the measure of reality, it is reality which must measure the amount and worth of our cognition.[5] Knowledge cannot determine the nature of things; its job is to adapt itself to their nature as already determined, in order to

---

[1] The position of this sentence in his work is vouched for by Plato (ἀρχόμενος τῆς Ἀληθείας, *Theaet.* 161c) and Sextus (ἐναρχόμενος τῶν καταβαλλόντων, *Math.* 7.60). καταβάλλοντες appears to have been an alternative title for the Ἀλήθεια (Bernays, *Ges. Abh.* 1, 118). A metaphor from wrestling, it means arguments which overthrow others. Cf. Eur. *Bacch.* 202 (of ancestral traditions) οὐδεὶς αὐτὰ καταβαλεῖ λόγος.

[2] On the translation of this fragment, see the Appendix, pp. 188–92.

[3] Sext. *Math.* 7.60; cf. *P.H.* 1.216 (DK, A 14).

[4] Plato, *Theaet.* 178b (and cf. κριτής, 160c); Sextus, *P.H.* 1.216.

[5] The analogy that he uses to illustrate this is not particularly happy but rather as Bonitz calls it 'exemplum parum feliciter adhibitum': it is, he says, as if we thought we were measuring ourselves when someone else measures us and we learn our own height from the number of times that he applies the foot-rule.

reach the truth. So, he adds, when Protagoras says that man is the measure of all things, meaning the man who knows or perceives, he is talking nonsense, though it sounds clever.

Aristotle is speaking from the point of view of his own and the Platonic philosophy, according to which there exists a reality beyond and independent of our knowledge or beliefs, and contrasting with it the doctrine of Protagoras that nothing exists save what each of us perceives and knows. (Since our perceptions on this theory are infallible, they may be given the name of knowledge, *Theaet.* 152c.) It is our own feelings and convictions that measure or determine the limits and nature of reality, which only exists in relation to them and is different for every one of us. Aristotle's opposition shows that for him Protagoras's was a doctrine of pure subjectivism or relativism. Was this a correct assessment of it? Two views have been taken. To put it in the terms of Plato's example (*Theaet.* 152b), if the wind *is* cold to me who feel it cold, and *is* warm to you who feel it warm, does this mean that the wind in itself is both warm and cold, or that the wind in itself is neither warm nor cold? In general terms, are we to say (*a*) that all properties perceived by anybody coexist in a physical object, but some are perceived by one man, others by another, or (*b*) that the perceptible properties have no independent existence in the object, but come to be as they are perceived, and for the percipient?

Cornford (*PTK*, 34ff.) favoured the first view: Protagoras was supporting 'the naive realism of common sense',[1] as well as the Ionian tradition, that the senses were to be trusted and things were mixtures of the opposites apprehended by sense, against the Eleatics, who denied the evidence of the senses and the reality of the opposites. He was also in accord with Heraclitus's belief in the coexistence of opposites and took his side against Democritus. ('Because honey seems bitter to some and sweet to others, Democritus said it is neither sweet nor sour,

---

[1] Von Fritz says similarly (*RE*, XLV. Halbb. 916f.) that Protagoras's statement does not express full sensualism, relativism or phenomenalism, but aims at opposing a 'Philosophie des gesunden Menschenverstandes' to the philosophies of the Eleatics, Heraclitus, etc., which are so far removed from *communis opinio*. He claims that this is borne out by the *Theaetetus*: Plato goes on to point out that, if Protagoras's statement is carried to its logical conclusion, it does lead to absolute relativism and subjectivism, but makes it clear that this conclusion was not drawn by Protagoras (166dff.). Cf. also Cherniss, *ACP*, 369.

Heraclitus that it is both', Sext. *P.H.* 2.63.) This, Cornford claimed,
is supported by Sextus, who wrote (*P.H.* 1.218) that 'the *logoi*
("grounds", Cornford) of all appearances subsist in the matter, so
that matter, in itself, can be all things that appear to all men'. He concludes that for Protagoras contrary sense-objects, like the hot and the
cold, exist independently of any percipient, and to call his doctrine
'subjectivist', or even 'relativist', is misleading.[1] But his arguments
are not strong. The thesis that no man has the right to contradict
another because each man's sensations and beliefs are true for him has
little to do with 'the naive realism of common sense', and little more
with Heraclitus, who urged men to follow the *logos* which was
common to all and despised them for living as if each had his own
private wisdom (fr. 2; see vol. I, 425). The language of Sextus is so
entirely that of a later age as to cast suspicion on its substance, and his
conclusion—'Thus according to Protagoras man proves to be the
criterion of what exists'—does not follow from his premises. Although
he denies it, 'things' on his interpretation (that is, properties) exist
(as Cornford says) whether they are perceived or not: a jar of honey
has its sweetness none the less because nobody is tasting it. The theory
of a substance or matter containing properties which may or may not
be perceived is specifically denied for Protagoras by Aristotle. When
discussing the Megarian theory that there is no such thing as a potentiality that is not actualized, i.e. that nothing is cold, hot, sweet or in
general perceptible when no one is perceiving it, he identifies this
theory with Protagoras's.[2] According to Cornford the second view,
that perceptible properties have no independent existence, corresponds
to the 'secret doctrine' (*Theaet.* 152cff.) which everyone agrees is
not Protagorean; but, in quoting Sextus, *P.H.* 1.218, as support for
the first, he omits the previous sentence, in which Sextus attributes to
Protagoras the doctrine that 'matter is in flux' (τὴν ὕλην ῥευστὴν
εἶναι). This, surely, belongs to the 'secret doctrine', and Sextus
proves an untrustworthy witness of genuine Protagorean ideas when

[1] Protagoras would thus be in agreement with the contemporary philosopher Diogenes of
Apollonia. For this, and for a similar theory in our own time, see vol. II, 381, n. 3.

[2] *Metaph.* Θ, ch. 3, especially 1047a 4–7. It has to be remembered that δύναμις, besides its
Aristotelian sense of potentiality, was quite commonly used to mean a property like hot, sweet
or red. See vol. I, 325, n. 1.

he tries to go further than the 'man–measure' statement itself and its obvious implications.[1]

We may conclude that Protagoras adopted an extreme subjectivism[2] according to which there was no reality behind and independent of appearances, no difference between appearing and being, and we are each the judge of our own impressions. What seems to me *is* for me, and no man is in a position to call another mistaken. If what I feel as warm you feel as cold, we cannot argue about it: it is warm for me and cold for you. No natural philosopher went as far as this, for it is a denial of the very meaning of *physis*. Democritus too said that all sensations are subjective, that hot and cold, sweet and bitter, have no existence in nature, but this was because they were to be explained as due to the interaction between the atomic structure of our bodies and that of the perceived object. There *was* a permanent *physis* or reality, namely atoms and void (vol. II, pp. 438, 440). For Protagoras there is none, and for this Democritus attacked him, objecting that on his view 'nothing was any more *such* than *such*'.[3] He was in the vanguard of the humanistic reaction against the natural philosophers, whose contradictory speculations were bringing them into disrepute among practical men—each one, as Gorgias said (p. 51 above), claiming to possess the secret of the universe, but in fact only pitting one opinion against another, each more incredible than the last. Like all the Sophists, he was acquainted with their theories, but turned away from them to teach the one thing that mattered, how to take care of one's own affairs and the business of the state (Plato, *Prot.* 318e–319a).[4] There is not much profit, therefore, in debating which of the

---

[1] The view attributed by Cornford to Protagoras seems rather to resemble that which Socrates in the *Cratylus* (386d) distinguishes from his and assigns to Euthydemus, namely πᾶσι πάντα ὁμοίως εἶναι ἅμα καὶ ἀεί.

[2] If a label is wanted, this is a better one than sensualism or phenomenalism, for the theory applied to what was thought or believed as well as what was perceived, to notions of right and wrong as well as sensations of hot and cold. The conclusion here reached as to Protagoras's subjectivism agrees with that of Ad. Levi's article in *Philosophy*, 1940, though it will be evident that I do not accept his further claim that it applied only to knowledge of nature and that Protagoras did not extend it into the ethical field. The difference between us rests on a different interpretation of his speech in the *Protagoras*.

[3] μὴ μᾶλλον εἶναι τοῖον ἢ τοῖον τῶν πραγμάτων ἕκαστον, Democr. fr. 156 (Plut. *Adv. Col.* 1109a). He also, it would seem, anticipated Plato (*Theaet.* 171a) in arguing that the doctrine is self-refuting (DK, A 114, Sext. *Math.* 7.389).

[4] Cf. Vlastos, *Ph. Rev.* 1945, 591.

philosophers he borrowed from or reacted against, especially as we know so little of the content of his writings: they were all chasing chimeras, though his direct polar opposite was of course Parmenides, who taught that all sensations and opinions were to be rejected as false.

We have seen that his relativism extended to the field of ethics. Our information relates only to states, but obviously, if a man sincerely believes that it is good to steal, then for him, so long as he believes it, it *is* good. But, just as it is worth while for a doctor to change a sick man's world by his drugs (*Theaet.* 167a) so that what appears and is to him sour appears and is sweet, so it is worth while for the majority, or their appointed representatives, to whom stealing both seems and is bad, to work upon him by persuasion until his view—that is, the truth for him—is changed. The logical conclusion of Protagorean subjectivism is moral and political anarchy, but this was far from his thoughts, and morals and the social order were saved by this curious doctrine, typical of its period, whereby the standard of truth or false-hood is abandoned, but replaced by the pragmatic standard of better or worse. 'Some appearances are better than others, though none is truer' (*Theaet.* 167b). Here, undoubtedly, the epistemological-ontological[1] doctrine of complete subjectivity breaks down: the appearance of the moment is subordinated to a higher standard, the end or purpose of human nature and society. At the same time the other kind of relativity comes in:[2] men and societies differ widely, and so therefore do their needs. There is no all-embracing 'good for man'. To diagnose the particular situation and prescribe the best course of action for a man or a state under given conditions, as a doctor does for his patient, is, as Protagoras saw it, the task of the Sophist.[3] To ensure

[1] A clumsy expression, which may nevertheless bring home the point that, however it may be today, in Greek thought epistemology and ontology, knowing and being, are not to be separated.

[2] That which is described under (*a*) on p. 166 above.

[3] The relation of Socrates and Plato to the Sophists is subtle. It is generally said that, whereas the Sophists were empiricists who denied the possibility of a general definition of 'good' on the grounds that it differed relatively to individual men or societies and their circumstances, Socrates (and Plato after him) insisted that there was one universal good, knowledge of which would give the key to right action for everybody everywhere. Thus Aristotle (like Plato in the *Meno*) depicts him as insisting on a general definition of *areté* in contrast to Gorgias who preferred to enumerate separate virtues (*Pol.* 1260a27). Yet in the *Phaedrus* it is the 'true rhetorician', that is, the dialectically trained philosopher, who is compared to a qualified doctor who not only knows how to administer various treatments but understands also which is appropriate to a particular patient, and when and for how long—a man, it would seem, in the empirical tradition of the best

that that course is followed is the concern of the rhetorician. Protagoras was both, and taught both arts. His own integrity, perhaps, prevented him from seeing that his art of defending both sides, and making the weaker argument appear the stronger, was a two-edged sword in the hands of less scrupulous men. The average rhetorician was satisfied with the means and careless of the end. He turned the heads of the young by telling them that if they only mastered the art of persuasion they could have the world at their feet: what they did with it was their affair.

APPENDIX

Protagoras fr. 1, DK: some points of translation

Controversy has flourished for many years over the translation of three words in this sentence: ἄνθρωπος, ὡς, χρήματα.

1. ἄνθρωπος. Is Protagoras using it in (*a*) an individual or (*b*) a universal sense, or is he (*c*) unaware of the distinction? For older authorities see ZN, 1357, n. 1. In the past at least the majority of scholars have supported (*a*), e.g. Zeller himself, H. Gomperz (*S. u. R.* 222f., 234ff., in spite of saying on p. 217 that no one would have been more astonished at the question than Protagoras), Nestle (with some qualifications; see his edition of the *Prot.*, p. 14), Grant (*Eth.* I, 135f.), R. G. Bury (Sextus, Loeb ed. I, xiv), Burnet (*Th. to P.* 115), Campbell (ed. of *Theaet.* xxix), Heinimann (*N. u. Ph.* 117), Calogero and Ad. Levi (for whom see Untersteiner, *Sophs.* 86 with nn.).

Grote is always quoted as the originator of (*b*), but in his *Plato*, II, 322ff. (to which Zeller refers) I do not find this interpretation. The pages must be read entire, but one may quote 328–9: 'However multifarious the mental activities may be, *each* man has *his own peculiar* allotment and manifestation thereof, to which his cognitions must be relative . . . *Each* man's mind, with its peculiar endowments . . . is still the limit or measure or limit of his cognitions.' (My italics.) T. Gomperz on the other hand held the universalist view unambiguously (*G.T.* I, 451): 'Man . . . was obviously not

Greek medical teaching. In contrast, the ordinary rhetorician, who 'through ignorance of dialectic is unable to define the nature of rhetoric', resembles a quack who has learned from a book how to give an emetic or a purge, but has no idea when its use will be appropriate (*Phaedr.* 268a–c, 269b). It may be that the Socratic search for definitions, and its offspring the Platonic dialectic of 'collection and division', rather include and transcend than undo the work of Sophists and rhetoricians. Their teaching is, after all, described in the *Phaedrus* as being, though not the art of rhetoric proper, a necessary propaedeutic to it (τὰ πρὸ τῆς τέχνης ἀναγκαῖα, 269c). Such questions will call for careful consideration later. See especially ch. xiv, §8.

the individual, but mankind as a whole.' If Zeller (ZN, 1357) is correct in describing this view as meaning that according to Protagoras 'Things present themselves to us as under the limitations and according to the disposition of human nature they must present themselves', then it fits none of the evidence.

Holders of interpretation (*c*), which has gained favour recently, include Joël (*Gesch.* 703–5), Untersteiner (*Sophs.* 42, 86f.), Classen (*Proc. Afr. Cl. Ass.* 1959, 35) and Cornford (unpublished). Some who hold this view combine it with (*a*): Protagoras was thinking of the individual, but the distinction was probably not present to his mind. This seems likely enough, provided it is taken to exclude (*b*). H. Gomperz, in his argument that Protagoras would have made no distinction, claims that there is no contradiction between the two, because, if what appears to an individual exists for him, then what appears to all men exists for all men. True enough, if Protagoras believed that there was anything at all that appeared the same to all men. But was it not the essence of his teaching that this was not so?

After all this it is refreshing to turn to the common sense of a historian of Greek literature, Lesky, who says in his *Hist. Gr. Lit.* p. 345 : 'Certainly the sentence refers to the individual. Anyone who doubts it must hold that Plato is lying or mistaken . . . If we are determined to disbelieve Plato, we have still to reckon with other authors [Aristotle, Sextus] whose use of the word ἕκαστος shows that they also took the sentence as referring to the individual.'

2. ὡς ἔστιν. Does it simply mean 'that they are', ὡς being the equivalent of ὅτι, or does it contain the idea of 'how they are', the *manner* of their existence? Gomperz father and son both spoke for the former, citing the analogy of fr. 4 on the existence of the gods. (See Th. G., *G.T.* 1, 452; H. G., *S. u. R.* 204.) Heinrich's arguments seem decisive, though he adds that the question is of little importance for the substance of the statement. Von Fritz (*RE*, XLV. Halbb. 914) takes the same view, noting that classical scholars tend to the meaning 'that', philosophers to 'how'. Zeller (ZN, 1355, n. 1) thought it more correct to include both meanings. So did Joël (*Gesch.* 708), who denied the validity of fr. 4 as an argument the other way. Untersteiner agrees (*Sophs.* 84), though his interpretation is connected with his curious conception of μέτρον as 'mastery', which has not found general acceptance. (It involves translating Soph. *El.* 236, τί μέτρον κακότητος ἔφυ, as 'what way will there be [*sic*] to *get the better of* wickedness?' The italics are his.) Calogero (see Untersteiner, *Sophs.* 90, n. 34) thinks it unhistorical to pose the question because the distinction between existence and essence could not have been consciously present to Protagoras's mind.

This is rather like saying that, because the distinctions between all the different senses of λόγος could not have been consciously present to the mind of a writer of the fifth century, therefore when Herodotus says ἔλεξε λόγον (1.141.1) there is no sense in asking whether he meant a story or any of the other things the word could mean: argument, pretext, proportion, definition or whatever. What decides is the context.

That ὡς can mean 'how' is undeniable, but it is also used interchangeably with ὅτι. That it is so used here is made overwhelmingly probable by its setting (especially in the negative clause ὡς οὐκ ἔστι) and by comparison with fr. 4, to which should be added the sophistic Hippocratic treatise *De arte*, ch. 2 (VI, 4 L.), τῶν γε μὴ ἐόντων τίνα ἄν τις οὐσίαν θεησάμενος ἀπαγγείλειεν ὡς ἔστιν, where 'that' is certainly the most natural translation of ὡς.

Discussion has concentrated on the word ὡς in this phrase, but the word ἔστι is equally worth comment. Like other scholars I have hitherto written on the assumption that the primary, if not the only, sense of εἶναι when used without predicates is 'to exist', but C. H. Kahn is very persuasive in his claim that its fundamental value is 'not "to exist" but "to be so", "to be the case", or "to be true"'. This, as he points out, fits Plato's explanation of the sentence: '*as* each thing seems to me, *such* is it for me', etc. 'Plato's exegesis becomes entirely natural and intelligible if we understand the absolute use of *einai* as . . . an affirmation of fact in general, as "what is so" or "what is the case". The existential use, e.g. for an affirmation such as "there are atoms and void", would then be included as a special case of the general factual assertion intended by Protagoras's statement *hōs esti*. If man is the measure of all things, "that they are so or not so", then he is the measure of the existence or non-existence of atoms just as he is the measure of the being-cold or not-being-cold of the wind.' See his article in *Foundations of Language*, 1966, especially p. 250.[1] (It will have appeared, however, that I do not entirely agree with him when on p. 262 he calls Protagoras 'a philosopher of common sense'.)

3. χρῆμα. This is a word of very wide application, meaning anything from an oracle to money (so in sing. Hdt. 3.38.3, though commonly in pl.). Recently there has been a tendency to overstress its etymological connexion with χρῆσθαι and narrow it down to 'something one uses', and so something in close relationship to man (Nestle, *VMzuL*, 271), or according to Untersteiner (*Sophs.* 79) 'the totality of things understood as action or experience'. He professes to give a review of its possible meanings, but it is

[1] The use of εἶναι and πρᾶγμα in Aristotle's discussion of ψεῦδος (*Metaph.* 1024b17ff.) may lend some support to his view.

a very partial one. (On Untersteiner's interpretation of the saying in general R. F. Holland in *CQ*, 1956, is severe but just.) The following (all easily available in LSJ) find no mention.

(*a*) In plural anything useful or good for man. See Xen. *Oec.* 1.7–8, the passage which affords the strongest support to Nestle's thesis, though not cited by him in this connexion. In any case it is only one of many meanings, and seems to be confined to the plural.

(*b*) Cases where it might be omitted: δεινόν τι χρῆμα ἐποιεῦντο, 'they thought it dreadful' (Hdt. 8.16.2); πικρόν τι μοι δοκεῖ χρῆμα εἶναι, 'it seems to me disagreeable' (Plato, *Gorg.* 485b); τί χρῆμα λεύσσω; 'what do I see?' (Aesch. *Cho.* 10 and elsewhere); at Eur. *Alc.* 512 τί χρῆμα means 'why?', 'for what cause?'.

(*c*) In periphrasis: ὑὸς μέγα χρῆμα, 'a great boar' (Hdt. 1.36.1); λιπαρὸν τὸ χρῆμα τῆς πόλεως 'what a fine city!' (Aristoph. *Birds* 826); and so frequently: τὸ χρῆμα τῶν νυκτῶν ὅσον, 'how long the nights are!' (*idem*, *Clouds* 2).

(*d*) As the English 'business' in its wide colloquial sense. ἅπαν τὸ χρῆμ' ἥμαρτε, 'she mismanaged the whole business' (Soph. *Tr.* 1136); κακὸν τὸ χρῆμα, 'it's a bad business' (*idem*, *Ph.* 1265; Untersteiner does give both these references, but explains them as an '*event* ... which one undergoes (χρῆται)').

(*e*) Cases where 'thing' is the only possible translation: κοῦφον χρῆμα ποιητής ἐστιν καὶ πτηνὸν καὶ ἱερόν, 'a poet is a light, winged and holy thing' (Plato, *Ion* 534b). In explaining Protagoras's sentence Plato (*Crat.* 385a–386e) equates it with πρᾶγμα, a word which also had become estranged from its parent verb and was used to mean simply 'an existing thing'.

(*f*) Number, amount: χρῆμα πολλὸν νεῶν, 'a large number of ships' (Hdt. 6.43.4), χρῆμα πολλόν τι χρυσοῦ, 'a lot of gold' (*idem*, 3.130.5).

No doubt it is possible to represent χρῆμα in all these cases as having *some* relation to mankind (what thing of whose existence we are aware has not?), but it would be fanciful to suppose that this relation is in the writer's mind, and we may conclude that no word more specific than 'thing' will serve as its translation in the dictum of Protagoras. That 'things' include heat and cold, justice and injustice is undeniable, but *Prot.* 330c and d show that these were still commonly regarded by the Greeks as existing things (πράγματα). χρήματα will have been for Protagoras what they were for his contemporary Anaxagoras: that is, they will have included the 'opposites' and concrete things alike (vol. II, 285). We need not dismiss the latter from the argument on the grounds that man cannot be a measure of the existence of trees and stones (as Nestle does, *VMₓuL*, 271): according to a philosophy of *esse est percipi* he can. But there is little point in pursuing this line, since all the examples given by Plato and Aristotle are of properties or attributes. These are what would concern Protagoras as a teacher of politics, ethics and rhetoric.

(3) GORGIAS

Gorgias was primarily a teacher of rhetoric, associated with his countryman Tisias in the use of the argument from probability.[1] He wrote manuals of the art (p. 44, n. 4, above), which may have consisted largely of model declamations to be learned by heart, since Aristotle (*Soph. el.* 183b36) says that this was his method of instruction. Of these the *Helen* and *Palamedes* (frr. 11 and 11a) will be surviving examples,[2] and the *Helen* has been well described as 'an essay on the nature and power of *logos*' (Versényi, *Socr. Hum.* 44), proving that 'the word is a mighty despot', and that (as Plato says Gorgias repeatedly declared, *Phileb.* 58a–b): 'The art of persuasion far surpasses all others and is far and away the best, for it makes all things its slaves by willing submission, not by violence'. So irresistible is its power that if Helen was peruaded into adultery she was as guiltless as if she had been abducted by force. The epistemological implications of this have already been mentioned (pp. 50f.), and we must now face the problems of that remarkable *tour de force*, the treatise *On the Non-Existent*, or *On Nature*.

The Eleatics, by their primitive limitation of the term 'being'

[1] Plato, *Phaedr.* 267a. Lesky (*HGL*, 351) says Tisias 'certainly accompanied him to Athens in 427' on his mission for Leontini. Perhaps he did, but the sole evidence is an unsupported statement in Pausanias's handbook for travellers in Greece in the second century A.D. (6.17.8). See Stegemann in *RE*, 2. Reihe, ix. Halbb. 140. Gorgias and Tisias must have been almost exact contemporaries, born in the decade 490–480.

[2] On the character and genuineness of these two speeches see Dobson, *Orators*, 17; H. Gomperz, *S. u. Rh.* 3ff.; Joël, *Gesch.* 657ff.; Schmid, *Gesch.* 72, n. 2; Untersteiner, *Sophs.* 95 and other references in his n. 54 on p. 99. The general opinion is now favourable to their genuineness. As to date, see Calogero in *JHS*, 1957, 1, p. 16 with n. 23. The *Pal.* was dated by E. Maass before 411 (*Hermes*, 1887, 579). The *Hel.* was put by Preuss in 414, between the *Troades* and *Helen* of Euripides (*De Eur. Hel.* Leipzig, 1911) and by Pohlenz before the *Troades* (*Nachr. Gött. Ges.* 1920, 166). I should not be surprised if Helen's speech in the *Troades* (914–65) owed something to what Gorgias makes her say on the same subject. In Euripides she takes the offensive at once by saying her troubles were Hecuba's fault for bearing Paris (!), and goes on to blame Aphrodite. The chorus appeal to Hecuba to destroy the πειθώ of this 'evil woman who knows how to speak'.

Gorgias himself calls the *Helena* a παίγνιον, on which the best comment is probably Versényi's (*Socr. Hum.* 43f.): it is certainly not serious in its ostensible purpose (Gorgias does not mind whether Helen's memory is vindicated or not), which however he is using as a vehicle for his general views on the nature of λόγος and πειθώ.

to what is one, unchanging and timeless, had driven practical people like Protagoras to the opposite extreme of subjectivism, a denial of all being in the Eleatic sense. Plato, convinced that any explanation of phenomena must still allow for an eternal and changeless being over and above them, contrasted Sophists as 'those who take refuge in the darkness of not-being' with philosophers who are 'devoted to the nature of being' (*Soph.* 254a). He meant, as Aristotle pointed out (*Metaph.* 1026b14), that the Sophists recognized only accidental as opposed to essential being, that is, the conditional and relative as opposed to the self-existent or absolutely existent. The way to these useful distinctions had been closed for a time by the blunt antithesis of Parmenides, and they were only established by Plato and Aristotle. Obviously Protagoras's 'what appears to me and is for me' had no existence in the Eleatic or Platonic sense (in which 'what is' was completely inaccessible to the senses), and Gorgias brought this opposition fully into the open, and took the Eleatic bull by the horns, by boldly proclaiming that 'nothing exists'.

The treatise itself has not survived, but we possess two paraphrases of its arguments, one in the little work *On Melissus, Xenophanes and Gorgias* attributed to Aristotle, and one in Sextus. They are not always in agreement, and the relevant section of *MXG* contains lacunae and corruptions, but between them they give a good idea of the type of argument which Gorgias employed.[1] He set out to prove three things: (*a*) that nothing exists, (*b*) that even if it does it is incomprehensible to man, (*c*) that, even if it is comprehensible to anyone, it is not communicable to anyone else. A great deal of ink has been spilt over the question whether this was intended as a joke or parody, or as a serious contribution to philosophy,[2] but it is a mistake to think that parody is

---

[1] *MXG* 979 a 11–980b21, Sextus, *Math.* 7.65 ff. Both texts are available with Italian translation in Untersteiner, *Sof.* II, 36 ff., Sextus in DK, Gorgias fr. 3. See Lloyd, *Pol. & An.* 115, for a succinct judgment on their relationship, and references to some of the many earlier discussions; also Untersteiner, *Sophs.* 96 f. and Sicking, *Mnem.* 1964, 227 ff. For *MXG* in general, vol. I, 367 and 370. W. Bröcker in *Hermes*, 1958 endeavoured to show that Sextus has no independent value as a source when compared with *MXG*.

[2] For orientation in the discussion see Untersteiner, *Sophs.* 163–5, Kerferd, *Phronesis*, 1955, 3, n. I, Sicking, *Mnem.* 1964, 225–7. Sicking says rightly that 'es doch keineswegs von vornherein feststeht, dass man mit der Alternative Scherz–Ernst dem Charakter des Werkes gerecht werden könne'; and Calogero in *JHS*, 1957, I, 16, n. 22, referring to the chapter on Gorgias in his *St. sul Eleat.*, claims that 'it is neither a joke nor an exercise, but a highly ironical *reductio ad*

incompatible with serious intention. Gorgias's purpose was negative, but none the less serious. To show up the absurdity of Eleatic, and particularly of Parmenidean, logic (the absurdity of arguing from 'it is' and 'it is not' as such) was of the utmost importance both to common sense and to the theory of rhetoric. Gorgias would hardly wish to deny the existence of everything in the sense in which the ordinary man understands existence; his aim was to show that, by the sort of arguments that Parmenides used, it was as easy to prove 'it is not' as 'it is'. The inversion of Parmenides's arguments is undoubtedly amusing, reminding one of Gorgias's advice to his pupils 'to destroy an opponent's seriousness by laughter, and his laughter by seriousness' (fr. 12).

The title of the work is itself sufficient indication of parody. Simplicius, who shows first-hand knowledge of the books of both Parmenides and Melissus, says that both gave them the title 'On Nature', and Melissus 'On Nature or That Which Is' (*Cael.* 556, 557; see vol. II, 102). Considering the subject of Parmenides's work, it is safe to say that that was its full title too. The name 'On Nature' was given to the works of most of the Presocratic natural philosophers either by themselves or by their contemporaries (vol. I, 73), and by saying that 'nothing is' Gorgias was denying the assumption underlying all their systems, that behind the shifting panorama of 'becoming' or appearances there existed a substance or substances, a *physis* of things, from the *apeiron* of Anaximander to the air of Anaximenes, the four 'roots' of Empedocles and the atoms of Democritus. All such permanent 'natures' would be abolished on Gorgias's thesis, but the form of his arguments shows that their irony was aimed especially at Parmenides and his followers, to demonstrate that on their own reasoning it is as easy to prove the contrary of x as x itself.[1]

---

absurdum of the Eleatic philosophy (especially of Zeno)'. Except that I see more of Parmenides in it than his parenthesis suggests, I am sure that this explanation of it as ironical is correct.

[1] This applies at least to the first part of the treatise proving the thesis that 'nothing is', which to judge from the summaries was the longest and most important. Kerferd (*loc. cit.* 15) finds it hard to believe that Gorgias could have argued in a certain way because having appealed to a 'decisive agreed principle' he then turns round and denies it: one argument depends on the impossibility of saying that what is does not exist, yet the very next one begins 'Neither does what is exist, for . . .' and proceeds to argue it. But the 'decisive agreed principle' comes from Parmenides, and considered as parody the idea of arguing from it as a premise and then disproving it is a good one.

There is one witness who, if only on account of his contemporaneity, cannot well be ignored, though the significance of his tirades for the character of *On the Non-Existent* has been variously judged. Isocrates, though a much younger man than Gorgias, was his pupil when in his early twenties (Münscher in *RE*, IX, 2152). At the beginning of his *Helen* he attacks paradox-mongers and eristics of all kinds. They are not even original, for Protagoras and other 'sophists' of his time could do the same thing better.

Who could outdo Gorgias, who had the audacity to say that nothing is, or Zeno who tried to show that the same things were possible and impossible, or Melissus who amid the infinite profusion of things tried to find proofs that all is one? What they did demonstrate was that it is easy to trump up a false argument about whatever you like to put forward.

Again in *Antid.* 268–9 he issues a similar warning against the 'old sophists', of whom one said there was an infinite number of beings, Empedocles four (with Strife and Love among them), Ion three only, Alcmaeon two, Parmenides and Melissus one, and Gorgias none at all. He compares their efforts to conjuring tricks which serve no useful purpose but are gaped at by fools. It has been argued that, since in these attacks Isocrates has no qualms in grouping Gorgias with the Eleatics and philosophers like Empedocles, his 'nothing exists' must have been meant as a serious philosophical thesis. Probably however more weight should be laid on the fact that Isocrates treats even the philosophers as tricksters ready to maintain the most absurd hypotheses.[1] In his own view, expounded on a number of occasions, philosophy should turn its back on all such idle speculations, and Gorgias condemned himself by stooping to use their own arguments.

Sextus classes Gorgias with those who abolished a constant standard of judgment (*kriterion*), but adds that he used a different method of attack from Protagoras; and after summarizing his arguments he concludes: 'These are the difficulties raised by Gorgias, and they do

---

[1] See Dodds, *Gorg.* 8, who reproduces the views of H. Gomperz, *S. u. Rh.* 30f. I confess to a slight feeling of uneasiness, because, if Isocrates knew Gorgias's treatise as an ironical exposure of Eleatic reasoning, he would surely have claimed him as an ally rather than attacked him along with the rest. He was, however, above all things an advocate, ready to press anything into the service of his immediate case. His criticism of Gorgias would be that by bothering at all about the philosophers and refuting them with their own weapons he put himself in the same class.

away with the criterion, for there can be no criterion for what neither exists nor can be known nor is of a nature to be described to another person.' In their conclusions Gorgias and Protagoras were at one, and, if there is anything that may be spoken of as a general sophistic view, it is this, that there is no 'criterion'. You and I cannot, by comparing and discussing our experiences, correct them and reach the knowledge of a reality more ultimate than either, for there is no such stable reality to be known. Similarly in morals, no appeal to general standards or principles is possible, and the only rule can be to act as at any moment seems most expedient. This positivism is important both for its own sake and for the reaction which it produced in thinkers of the calibre of Socrates and Plato.

We may now look at some of the arguments of *On the Non-Existent*. The following is not a complete account, but sufficient to convey their character.[1] It should be said as a preliminary that Parmenides's thesis depended on one and the same Greek verb (εἶναι) meaning both 'to be' (which may refer to the relation of subject to predicate, individual to species, identity, etc.) and 'to exist'. Where either is used in the English version, they stand for the same word in Greek.

(*a*) *Nothing exists.* If anything exists, it is either the existent or the non-existent or both. The non-existent does not exist ('what is not is not'). This might be thought obvious, but Gorgias solemnly argues it in ultra-Parmenidean terms: in so far as it is conceived as not-being it is *not*, i.e. does not exist; but in so far as it *is* non-existent, it *is*, i.e. exists. But to be and not to be at the same time is absurd, therefore the non-existent is not. The purpose must be to bring in the point that by saying that something 'is *x*', whatever the predicate, you are allowing being to it; and since according to Parmenides 'is' has only one meaning, namely 'exists', you can prove on his own premises the opposite of what he says. At the same time Gorgias turns against him his criticism of the stupid crowd who claim that to be and not to be are the same as well as different (fr. 6.6).

Neither does the existent exist. If it does, it must be either eternal or

---

[1] There is a full summary in Untersteiner, *Sophs.* 145–58. See also Freeman, *Comp.* 359–61, and Bröcker, *Gesch. d. Phil. vor Sokr.* 115–18. One of the best essays on the subject in English, never noticed nowadays, is that of Grant, *Ethics*, I, 137–42.

generated or both. The argument that it cannot be eternal depends on identifying temporal with spatial infinity and then contending that 'what is' cannot be infinite. Since Melissus had said that it was, and moreover reached this conclusion by the same confusion of temporal with spatial (vol. II, 107 ff.), it seems likely that at this point he is the butt of Gorgias's sophisticated wit. The argument that it is not generated follows the lines of Parmenides fr. 8.7 ff., by denying in turn that it could be generated from what is or what is not. Again, it must be either one or many. If one, it must have quantity, discrete or continuous, size and body, but then it will be divisible and so not one. Yet for anything to exist without magnitude is absurd. For this too an Eleatic proof was available, since it had been argued by Zeno (frr. 1 and 2; vol. II, 391, n. 2), and according to a fragmentary part of *MXG* (979 b 36) Gorgias seems to have referred to this. Nor can it be many, for a plurality is composed of ones, so if the one does not exist, neither can the many.

Neither do both exist.[1] This would seem fairly obvious by now, but Gorgias is enjoying his game with Parmenides. Although he has already shown that (*a*) what is not and (*b*) what is do not exist, he now 'proves' that both do not exist together. If both exist, they are identical so far as existence is concerned; and since what is not does not exist, and what is is identical with it, what is will not exist either.[2]

In proving his second and third hypotheses, Gorgias goes beyond the Eleatics, and his arguments are perhaps more interesting.

(*b*) *If anything exists it cannot be known or thought of by man.* We certainly think of things that do not exist, e.g. chariots crossing the sea

---

[1] It was of course Leucippus and Democritus who, trapped in the net of Parmenidean language, said that both being and non-being existed, meaning by these terms solid body and void (vol. II, 392). Gorgias may have had them in mind, but the nature of his 'proofs' shows that the Eleatics are his main target all the time. Cf. Mondolfo, *Problemi*, 180, quoted by Untersteiner, *Sophs.* 168, n. 32.

[2] Untersteiner, *Sophs.* 146, interprets thus: 'The attribution of existence to both Being and Not-being leads to their identification "so far as existence is concerned": therefore Being merges into that existence of Not-being which is Non-existence; Being therefore, like Not-being, will not exist.' This is probably the best that can be done. It is all, of course, engaging nonsense. That what is not does not exist is said in Sextus's summary to be ὁμόλογον (admitted, or common ground) and would seem to follow from the expression itself, though this has not prevented Gorgias from 'proving' it earlier.

and flying men,[1] and according to Sextus Gorgias stated and defended the converse, that, if things thought are not existent, then the existent is not thought. He may have been parodying someone who was guilty of this, but more probably his argument was that, if our thought of something is not sufficient to prove its existence, then, even if we think of something real, we have no means of distinguishing it from the unreal.[2] Gorgias has indeed 'abolished the criterion'. *MXG* (980a 9ff.), if its corruptions are suitably emended, gives a better sequence of thought. If everything that can be thought of exists (as Parmenides had repeatedly said, frr. 2.7; 3; 6.1), then nothing is untrue, even the statement that chariots cross the sea. [This we may assume to be absurd.] We cannot fall back on the senses, for they are unreliable unless checked by thought, which has already failed us.

(*c*) *Even if it can be apprehended, it cannot be communicated to another.* This thesis rests chiefly on a point insisted on by Gorgias's master Empedocles, that each sense has its own objects and cannot distinguish those of another (Theophr. *De sensu* 7; vol. II, 231). If there are things existing outside ourselves, they will be objects of sight, hearing, taste and so forth. Our means of communication is speech, which is none of these external objects, and is understood differently. Just as a colour cannot be heard, or a melody seen, so 'since what is subsists externally, it cannot become our speech, and without becoming speech it cannot be communicated to another' (Sext. *Math.* 7.84; that cognition can only be due to the interaction of similars is another Empedoclean doctrine, vol. II, 229). 'Sight does not distinguish sounds, nor hearing colour; and what a man speaks is speech, neither a colour nor an object' (*MXG* 980b1). According to *MXG* 980b9ff. Gorgias added that the hearer cannot have in his mind the same thing as the

---

[1] That Gorgias had the ἀπάτη of tragedy in mind is probable. Cf. fr. 23. (Gercke, followed by Untersteiner, restored ἀπατᾶν for ἄπαντα at *MXG* 980a9.) Untersteiner (*Sophs.* 171, n. 71) mentions the Oceanides of Aeschylus crossing the sea in winged chariots πτερύγων θοαῖς ἁμίλλαις (*P.V.* 129; *MXG* 980 a 12 has ἁμιλλᾶσθαι ἅρματα) and Bellerophon in Euripides. (Why not Daedalus? Sophocles wrote a play of that name, and after all it was Pegasus who flew, not Bellerophon except *per accidens*.)

[2] So Ad. Levi; see Untersteiner, *Sophs.* 152f. The probability is strengthened by *P.H.* 2.64, where in close proximity to a mention of Gorgias, and possibly still dependent on him, Sextus says: εἰ δέ τισιν [*sc.* αἰσθήσεσι καὶ διανοίαις κρινοῦσι τὰ πράγματα], πῶς κρινοῦσιν ὅτι ταῖσδε μὲν ταῖς αἰσθήσεσι καὶ ⟨τῇδε⟩ τῇ διανοίᾳ προσέχειν δεῖ, ταῖσδε δ᾽ οὔ, μὴ ἔχοντες κριτήριον ὁμολογούμενον δι᾽ οὗ τὰς διαφορὰς αἰσθήσεις τε καὶ διανοίας ἐπικρινοῦσιν;

speaker, for the same thing cannot, without losing its identity, be present in more people than one. Even if it could, it need not *appear* the same to them both, since they are different from one another and in different places. Even the same man does not apprehend things similarly at different times, or as presented by different senses.

Finally one may quote a pregnant saying of Gorgias, appropriately called by Untersteiner 'Gorgias on the tragedy of knowledge'. It has come down to us without context or any indication of its place in his works:

Existence is unknown unless it acquire appearance, and appearance is feeble unless it acquire existence.[1]

NOTE. From the arguments used by Gorgias it should be clear that the main weight of his irony fell upon the Eleatics, and in particular on Parmenides, though the thesis itself is equally cogent against all those Presocratics who had posited the existence of a non-sensible reality (or realities) behind the changing panorama of the sensible world. (See G. Rensi, *Fig. di filos.* 99, n. 1, quoted by Untersteiner, *Sof.* II, 36.) This was in essentials the view of Grote (*Hist.* 1888 ed. vol. VII, 51 f.). Gorgias, said Grote, is using the word 'to be' in the Eleatic sense, according to which it did not apply to phenomena but only to ultra-phenomenal (noumenal) existence. 'He denied that any such ultra-phaenomenal Something, or Noumenon, existed, or could be known, or could be described. Of this tripartite thesis, the first negation was neither more untenable nor less untenable than that of those philosophers who before him had argued for the affirmative: on the last two points his conclusions were neither paradoxical, nor sceptical, but perfectly just, and have been ratified by the gradual abandonment, either avowed or implied, of such ultra-phaenomenal researches among the major part of philosophers.'

Grote's view has been criticized by several later scholars, e.g. by A. Chiappelli, on the ground that the distinction between noumenal and phenomenal is foreign to all Greek thought before Plato. It may have been Plato who first formulated it explicitly in those or similar terms, but the contrast between appearance and (non-sensible) reality is a leitmotiv of Presocratic thought, and the whole basis of the present volume, and particularly its account of the Sophists, is that the question of their relations was at the

[1] Fr. 26 (from Proclus on Hesiod's *Erga* 758) ἔλεγε δὲ τὸ μὲν εἶναι ἀφανὲς μὴ τυχὸν τοῦ δοκεῖν, τὸ δὲ δοκεῖν ἀσθενὲς μὴ τυχὸν τοῦ εἶναι. The implication no doubt was that existence *is* unknowable, and appearance non-existent, and the Greek would bear the translation 'Existence is unknowable *for* it does not acquire appearance', etc.

centre of fifth-century philosophical controversy. (Cf. p. 4.) For Heraclitus eyes and ears were untrustworthy unless the mind could interpret their message and discover the underlying truth. Parmenides made the distinction clearly, saying that only the objects of *nous* existed and the phenomenal world was illusion. Democritean atomism also taught the doctrine of a reality behind appearances, a noumenal (the object of 'legitimate' as opposed to 'bastard' cognition) behind the phenomenal. (For the relation of this to Plato's philosophy see vol. II, 462.) This was the legacy which the Sophists inherited and made the most of for their own purposes. Zeller also criticized Grote (ZN, 1367, n. 2), saying that even the Eleatics themselves did not distinguish appearance from what lay behind appearance, but only the true view of things from the false. In fact, however, Parmenides distinguished τὸ ὄν—what exists or is real (or if we follow Kahn, p. 190 above, what is the case)—from τὰ δοκοῦντα, what appears but does not exist, which is what Grote said he did.

(4) OTHER VIEWS: SCEPTICISM EXTREME AND MODERATE

A certain Xeniades of Corinth, whom we know only from a brief reference in Sextus,[1] also adopted an extreme scepticism at about this time. According to Sextus 'he said that everything was false, that every impression and opinion is false, and that everything which comes to be comes to be from what is not and everything which is destroyed is destroyed into what is not'. What arguments, if any, he used to support this thesis we do not know, and his assertion is worth quoting simply as another example of the disrepute into which the rival theories of the natural philosophers and especially the logic of Parmenides had brought the whole subject of the nature of reality and the possibility of change. It was Parmenides who expressly attacked the idea that anything could come into being from what is not (fr. 8.6ff.), but the whole of Presocratic philosophy and indeed all Greek thinking up to now had been based on the unquestioned assumption that *ex nihilo nihil fit*.[2]

[1] *Math.* 7.53. Mentions of him in §388 and *P.H.* 2.76 add nothing. The only indication of his date is that according to Sextus he was old enough to have been mentioned by Democritus. On Xeniades in the context of his time see now Lloyd, *Pol. & Anal.* 113, and in general von Fritz in *RE*, 2. Reihe, XVIII. Halbb. (1967), 1438f., who has misgivings about the trustworthiness of Sextus's report.

[2] For the Parmenidean thesis οὐδ' εἶναι πολλὰ ἀλλὰ μόνον αὐτὸ τὸ ὄν as the logical conclusion of archaic thought based on the principle ἐκ μὴ ὄντος οὐδὲν ἂν γενέσθαι see Ar. *Phys.* 191a 23–33.

Cratylus, a younger contemporary of Socrates (Plato, *Crat.* 429 d, 440 d), carried to extremes the Heraclitean doctrine of the flux or impermanence of everything in the sensible world. Aristotle, discussing in his *Metaphysics* the sceptical doctrines that every statement is both true and false, or alternatively that no true statement can be made, attributes them to a belief that there is no existence outside the sensible world, in which (i) contraries emerge from the same thing, and (ii) everything is constantly moving and changing.[1] The latter observation, he goes on (1010a10), blossomed into the most extreme of these doctrines, that of the 'Heraclitizers' and Cratylus, who finally decided that he ought to say nothing at all, but only moved his finger, and criticized Heraclitus for saying that one cannot step twice into the same river on the ground that one could not do so even once. He evidently thought (as one would expect from what is put into his mouth in Plato's *Cratylus*) that to utter any statement is to commit oneself to the affirmation that something *is*.[2]

In the fifth-century controversy about *nomos* and *physis*, it has now become clear that two positions must be distinguished among those who were sufficiently serious philosophers to trouble about the ontological and epistemological implications of their views. (This did not include all the controversialists, for the argument itself arose in the context of practical human action and was used primarily to advocate a certain attitude to law and morality.) It was possible to think that law and custom, and with them the totality of sense-impressions, were to be contrasted as mutable and relative with a *nature* which was stable, permanent and knowable, opposing like Democritus what was 'by *nomos*' to what was 'in reality'. It may be that 'we really know nothing, for truth is in the depths' (Democr. fr. 117), but there the truth is, if we can dive deep enough to find it. Alternatively it was held

---

[1] For these characteristics of the sensible world cf. especially Melissus, fr. 8.3: 'It appears to us that hot becomes cold and cold hot, hard becomes soft and soft hard, the living dies, and is born out of the non-living; that all these things change, and what was and what is now are in no way alike: iron which is hard is worn away by contact with the finger, as are gold and stone and every other tough-seeming substance, while out of water come earth and stone. It follows that we do not see or recognize what is real (τὰ ὄντα).' See vol. II, 105, and Morrison in *Phronesis*, 1963, 38.

[2] *Crat.* 429 d. (Presumably he did not carry consistency so far as to deny himself speech in making the criticism of Heraclitus.) This argument is attributed explicitly to Antisthenes; see p. 210 below.

that there was no objective and permanent reality behind appearances and therefore, since these were purely subjective, no possibility of scientific knowledge. No natural philosopher believed this, but sophists seized on the inconsistencies between their accounts as evidence that they were not to be trusted. (Cf. Gorgias, *Hel.* 13, p. 51 above.) It was these sceptics whom Aristotle criticized for making every statement true and false, or true statements impossible, and they included Protagoras and Gorgias. It has been claimed that Antiphon was also of their number.[1] The evidence is scanty and dubious, but so far as it exists it points to a different conclusion. It is confined to fr. 1, a passage in Galen which exists only in a corrupt form and has been variously restored.[2] The most thorough examination, with the most convincing result, is that of Morrison.[3] Galen first says (Critias fr. 40, p. 302 below) that Critias in the second book of his homilies frequently opposes the mind to the senses, then adds that Antiphon does the same in the first book of his *Truth*. There follows the quotation, which therefore, whatever its precise import, must express a contrast between thought and sense. In Morrison's translation it runs: 'When a man says a single thing there is no corresponding single meaning (νοῦς), nor is the subject of his speech any single thing either of those things which the most powerful beholder sees with his sight or of those things which the most powerful knower knows with his mind.'[4]

No reading or interpretation can put the meaning completely beyond

---

[1] So Schmid, *Gesch.* 1.3.1, 160: 'Antiphon joins in the epistemological scepticism of Protagoras and Gorgias, in that he also contests the possibility of real knowledge and confines himself within the limits of δόξα. Within this framework he distinguishes two levels of cognition: a higher one through the mind (γνώμη) and a lower one through the senses, which in his view as in that of the Eleatics and the atomists cannot communicate any valuable cognition.' Yet every other contemporary thinker who distinguished between mental and sensual perception associated the one with real knowledge and the other with δόξα, and so far as I can see Schmid produces no evidence at all for the surprising idea that Antiphon, though he accepted both modes of cognition, saw the functions of both alike as confined within the limits of δόξα.

[2] *In Hipp. De med. off.* XVIII B., 656 K. Besides the attempts given by DK in their apparatus, that of H. Gomperz (*S. u. R.* 67) and the interpretation of Untersteiner, who accepts Bignone's text (*Sophs.* 235 and 258), may be noted. Cf. also Stenzel in *RE*, suppl. IV, 37.

[3] *Phronesis*, 1963, 36ff. His text of the fr. itself is as follows: ἐν τῷ [or better τοι] λέγοντι οὐδέ γε νοῦς εἷς, ἔν τε οὐδὲν αὐτῷ οὔτε ὦν ὄψει ὁρᾷ ⟨ὁ ὁρῶ⟩ν μακρότατα οὔτε ὦν γνώμη γιγνώσκει ὁ μακρότατα γιγνώσκων.

[4] Literally 'the man who sees farthest' (or most deeply, μακρότατα) with his sight and 'the man who has the deepest insight (or power of recognition, γιγνώσκων) with his mind (γνώμη).' I have altered Morrison's 'seer' to 'beholder' to avoid the former's misleading associations with prophecy.

doubt, but Antiphon seems to be criticizing the ambiguity of language and the shifting meaning of words, which renders them incapable of expressing reality, with the implication that such a constant reality does exist. Even phenomena, if the senses are keen enough, can be 'a sight of the unseen', as Anaxagoras and Democritus held (vol. II, 459), though both were emphatic in contrasting the powers of sense and intellect and insisting on an unseen reality behind the perceptible flux of becoming. (It was of course an aspect of physical body no less than the phenomena, not a *noumenon* in the Platonic or Aristotelian sense.) They would agree with Heraclitus that the senses delude unless subject to an understanding mind. Antiphon seems to have followed them rather than the Eleatics who denied that the senses could assist in any way whatsoever towards the apprehension of 'what is'.

It is in keeping with this that Antiphon, unlike Gorgias who threw doubt on all the theories of the *physici* alike, made his own study of the natural world, which took up a large part of the second book of his *Truth*. The fragments show him speaking in traditional Presocratic style of cosmogony (the 'ordering' of the world) and of the cosmic whirl, of the nature of the sun and moon, eclipses, hail, earthquakes and the sea, and of biological matters.[1] The contrast between natural and artificial he illustrated, in a passage criticized by Aristotle, by saying that if one were to bury a wooden bed and the rotting wood sent out a shoot, what came up would be simply wood, not another bed.[2] Nor does fr. 1, as here interpreted, conflict with the ethical views expounded in the papyrus fragments of *Truth*, where the reality and inevitability of nature are opposed to the artificiality of *nomos* as truth to appearance, and *nomos* is stigmatized as a shackle imposed on nature.[3]

---

[1] Frr. 23–36 (fr. 15, on the origin of life from putrefying matter, is referred to book 1). Not that his recorded observations on these topics show any originality. So far as the scanty fragments go, they seem to be a hotchpotch of Presocratic ideas, going back to Heraclitus and Empedocles, and common to Anaxagoras and Diogenes of Apollonia. On the influence of Anaxagoras cf. Momigliano in *Riv. di Filol.* 1930, 134f., and for a summary Freeman, *Comp.* 395f.

[2] Ar. *Phys.* 193a9, cited also more briefly by Harpocration. See fr. 15 in DK. On Aristotle's criticism of Antiphon here see Guthrie in *CQ*, 1946.

[3] Fr. 44 A, pp. 108f. above. For a fuller discussion of the bearing of these fragments on Antiphon's ontological views, and their relation to the use of language, see Morrison's valuable article in *Phronesis*, 1963. Of Antiphon's remarks in fr. 44 B (*Oxy. Pap.* 1797, p. 110 above, about the inconsistency of applying the name 'justice' to the bearing of true witness), Morrison says (p. 44): 'This argument, again, tends to the rejection of common names, which have no single meaning, and adopting instead concepts which are based on nature.'

(5) LANGUAGE AND ITS OBJECTS

No doubt Antiphon was not a profound philosopher, but one may regret the scantiness of our knowledge of him because what we have gives us one brief glimpse of a much-debated theme: the relation of language to its subject-matter. His reference to the equivocal use of words in Galen's quotation is obviously disapproving, and in another place Galen, commenting on the fact that 'each one of those concerned with *logoi* thinks fit to coin new names', adds that this is made sufficiently plain by Antiphon, 'who teaches how they ought to be made'.[1] Presumably his teaching was that they should be made to fit the concepts which they were intended to express. The problem of the correctness of words or names (ὀρθότης ὀνομάτων) aroused widespread interest at this time, and Morrison has clearly shown the importance of this debate 'in the wider investigation of the problem of how ὄντα (existing things) are to be known' (*loc. cit.* 49). Antiphon's position in this debate was perhaps not far from that taken up by his sparring-partner Socrates, at least with reference to moral terms: on the meaning of 'just' and 'good' we disagree with each other and even with ourselves, and this is a state of things that calls for remedy.[2] Morrison (*loc. cit.* 42f.) gives good reasons for supposing that even the method by which, in Plato, Socrates proposes to rectify it, namely 'division according to natural kinds' (κατ᾽ εἴδη διατέμνειν ᾗ πέφυκεν, *Phaedr.* 265e, cf. *Rep.* 454a), was not invented by Plato but current in the fifth century. He cites the *Clouds* of Aristophanes (740f.), and the Hippocratic *De arte* 2 (quoted by DK after fr. 1 of Antiphon). There the writer says that the arts, or sciences (*technai*, p. 115, n. 3, above), take their terminology from the kinds (εἴδεα), not *vice versa*, for words are an attempt to impose legislation on nature (νομοθετήματα φύσεως), whereas the kinds are not conventionally imposed but natural growths (βλαστήματα). One is reminded also of Antiphon's contrast between nature as a matter of growth and law as conventional agreement.[3]

---

[1] Galen, *Gloss. Hipp. prooem.* v, 706 B., XIX, 66, 7 K., quoted by Morrison, *Proc. Camb. Philol. Soc.* 1961, 49. οἱ περὶ λόγους ἔχοντες sounds very general, but λόγων τέχνη referred particularly to rhetoric (pp. 177f. above). [2] Plato, *Phaedrus* 263a; see p. 165 above.

[3] Fr. 44 A, DK II, 347: τὰ τῆς φύσεως φύντα οὐχ ὁμολογηθέντα. See p. 108 above. On the *De arte* passage Heinimann, *N. u. Ph.* 157; and cf. *Nat. hom.* 5 (*ibid.* p. 159). Also relevant is Xen. *Mem.* 4.5.11–12 (pp. 439f. below).

Instruction in 'the correctness of names' is ascribed by Plato to Protagoras, Prodicus, and the Sophists in general.[1] It is sometimes taken to mean simply the correct, or effective, use of language as we should understand it, and we may be sure that for most of the Sophists, as teachers of rhetoric, it included that. But Plato's *Cratylus* shows that the question at issue was whether the names of things had an inherent, or natural, fitness or were merely conventional signs. Two expressions have to be considered, *orthoepeia*, of which the nearest possible translation is perhaps 'correct diction', and 'the correctness of names' (ὀρθότης ὀνομάτων). Both have been thought to be the titles of books by Protagoras, but this is at least uncertain.[2] They do not necessarily mean the same. *Onoma* is a single word, a name or a noun. *Epos* may mean a word, saying or speech, but was also a current term for poetry (not only epic); and Fehling has drawn attention to the significance of *Prot.* 338eff., where Protagoras claims that an educated man ought to be skilled in this subject so as to understand when a poet is composing correctly and when not,[3] and challenges Socrates to interpret a poem of Simonides. Moreover in his grammatical pronouncements the target of his criticism is the Iliad. (See pp. 220 and 221, n. 2, below.) Fehling concludes that he had no systematic programme to offer, but suggestions for the right use of language set in the framework of a criticism of poetry. That *orthoepeia* had this reference is indicated by the title of Democritus's work 'On Homer, *orthoepeia* and unusual words', from which a comment on Homeric

[1] Protagoras, *Crat.* 391c; Prodicus, *Crat.* 384b, *Euthyd.* 277e; the Sophists, *Crat.* 391b.

[2] At *Phaedr.* 267c Plato introduces ὀρθοέπεια in connexion with Protagoras, and Hackforth translates it as the title of a book. Murray (*Gk. Stud.* 176) assumed that π. ὀρθ. ὀνομ. was an alternative title for it, presumably (though he gave no reference) on the strength of *Crat.* 391c, where Hermogenes is recommended to ask his brother τὴν ὀρθότητα περὶ τῶν τοιούτων [*sc.* the nature of names] ἣν ἔμαθε παρὰ Πρωταγόρου; Classen on the other hand (*P. Afr. C.S.* 1959, 34f.) thinks ὀρθοέπεια was no more than a slogan or catchword, but it is at least vouched for as a title among the works of Democritus (fr. 20a, from a scholium on Dion. Thrac.), though not among Protagoras's as listed by D.L. (9.55). Actually the reply of Hermogenes at *Crat.* 391c shows clearly enough that whatever Protagoras wrote on the subject occurred in the Ἀλήθεια.

Prodicus is usually connected with ὀρθότης ὀνομάτων, but a late writer (Themistius, *Or.* 23, p. 350 Dindorf) says that he taught ὀρθοέπεια and ὀρθορρημοσύνη. The catch-phrase is brought in by Aristophanes in connexion with Euripides (τῆς ὀρθότητος τῶν ἐπῶν, *Frogs* 1181).

[3] περὶ ἐπῶν δεινὸν εἶναι· ἔστι δὲ τοῦτο τὰ ὑπὸ τῶν ποιητῶν λεγόμενα οἶόν τ' εἶναι συνιέναι, ἅ τε ὀρθῶς πεποίηται καὶ ἃ μή. The association of the words ἔπη and ὀρθῶς surely is suggestive. See Fehling in *Rh. Mus.* 1965, 213.

vocabulary has survived.[1] Like the study of the 'correctness of names' it probably included speculation on the natural fitness of names to what they signified, for Socrates introduces Homer as an authority on the latter subject, citing first of all his practice of mentioning two names for a thing, one used by men and the other by the gods: 'obviously the gods must call them by the names which rightly and naturally belong to them' (*Crat.* 391 d).

'Correctness of names' is the subject of the *Cratylus*, which discusses two opposing views.

1. The fact that a group of men have agreed what they will call a thing does not make that its name: indeed a word which has no further warranty is not a name at all. Belonging to each thing is one natural and proper name, the same for Greeks and foreigners alike. It must be supposed to have been bestowed by an original name-giver or legislator who had complete insight into the nature of the thing itself, doubtless as a result of superhuman powers.[2]

2. To this thesis of Cratylus Hermogenes opposes his own that correctness of names is determined solely by convention and agreement, and differs for different people. Asked for his own opinion, Socrates at first supports Cratylus. To maintain the completely arbitrary character of names leads inevitably to accepting the Protagorean thesis that there is no objective reality but things too are different for each individual, or else that of Euthydemus that all things possess all attributes together and all the time. This they agree is wrong. Putting it in his own teleological terms, Socrates argues that actions (πράξεις) like things (πράγματα) have a fixed nature and must be performed with the proper instrument, as cutting with a knife. This includes speech, whose instruments, namely words or names (ὀνόματα), have the func-

---

[1] He approved the use of ἀλλοφρονεῖν as a term for mental derangement. See vol. II, 452, n. 1. That this occurred in the above-mentioned work is not expressly stated, but it seems the obvious place.

[2] νομοθέτης, 429 a, ὁ θέμενος (τιθέμενος) τὰ ὀνόματα, 436 b–c, 438 a. Hence as Fehling has pointed out (*Rh. Mus.* 1965, 218 ff.), the later contrast between a φύσει and a θέσει theory of names is not appropriate at this date. (Perhaps one should not overlook the attribution of it to Democritus by Proclus, in Democr. fr. 26, but in all probability Proclus is importing the categories of his own time. See Momigliano, *Atti Torino*, 1929–30, 95 f.) The opposition is between θέσις (κατὰ φύσιν) by a single, mythical divine or heroic εὑρετής and the collective action (ὁμολογία or συνθήκη) of an evolving society. (For the place of speech in evolutionary theories of society cf. Diod. p. 81 above, and Soph. *Ant.* p. 80; and for the divine teacher Eur. *Suppl.* p. 80.)

tion of teaching about, and distinguishing, the essences of real things. They are given by *nomos*, and hence by a legislator or word-maker who (on the analogy of other crafts, e.g. a shuttle-maker who subserves the work of the weaver) must produce the name naturally fitted for its object, working under the direction of the skilled user, that is, the dialectician, or expert at discussion.

In what, then, does the correctness of names consist? Socrates disclaims knowledge—this is the province of the Sophists and poets—but is induced to expound a theory. A name is a vocal imitation of an object—not in the crude sense in which one imitates a cow by saying 'moo', but conveying the nature of the thing, as, if we had not speech, we might convey the nature of heaviness by a downward movement of the hand. Words being compound or simple, this applies most directly to the simple, and still more directly to the letters and syllables of which they are composed. These are like the pigments which the painter may use either singly or in combination to build up his picture. The form of the word will sometimes show it obviously enough, e.g. the letter *r* imitates motion or violent action, *l* smoothness; but many words have become so battered and distorted in the course of history that the intention of the original name-maker is no longer recognizable. Socrates then proceeds to illustrate his point by a series of etymologies most of which are obviously fanciful, making evident his own sceptical attitude towards them by several ironic remarks.[1] He is parodying a current practice,[2] and keeping his own opinion to himself.

Names, then, are not arbitrary labels, but a form of imitation of their objects. Nevertheless (turning to Cratylus) it must be said that, as with painters, some will be better imitators than others, and so will be their products, the names. Cratylus disagrees. Either the names are right, or they are nothing, simply unmeaning noises like the banging of a gong. (It is in keeping with this that Cratylus avows himself one of those who hold that it is impossible to speak falsely.) Socrates

---

[1] E.g. the references to Euthyphro at 396d–e, 400a, 407d. Under his influence Socrates has become possessed, and is uttering his etymologies under divine inspiration. He will let it run today, but tomorrow will find someone, 'either a priest or a Sophist', to purge it away. Elsewhere (426b) he describes his etymological guesses more straightforwardly as 'presumptuous and ridiculous'.

[2] A practice with which Euripides shows himself familiar when his Hecuba connects the opening syllables of 'Aphrodite' with ἀφροσύνη, 'folly'. (*Tro.* 989f.: note the inevitable ὀρθῶς.)

counters that an imitation can never be exactly like the original in all respects, or it would *be* the original, but Cratylus remains unconvinced, and falls back on the superhuman power of the original inventor of names.[1]

These linguistic theories have an obvious connexion with current theories of knowledge and of reality. The thesis of Hermogenes, that words are of purely arbitrary and conventional origin, is agreed in the dialogue to lead to the Protagorean doctrine that there is no reality behind appearances. The opposite view of Cratylus allows for a reality (*physis*) to which the name is essentially united (383 a), so that 'he who knows the names knows the things also' (435 d). False opinion or statement is impossible, but for the opposite reason to that given by Protagoras. Whereas he dissolved reality in appearance, this more paradoxical theory (which as we shall see immediately was that of Antisthenes) holds that there is a *physis* for everything and no possibility of naming or describing it wrongly. To apply to it what others would call the wrong name or *logos* is to utter no name at all but merely unmeaning noises (430a, 438c). Only Socrates puts forward an explanation of language based on the antithesis commonly called sophistic, and maintained especially clearly by Democritus and Antiphon, between *physis* and *nomos*. Things have a fixed nature, and words are an attempt to reproduce that nature through the medium of sound; but such imitation is never perfect, and in some cases very imperfect, even from the beginning, besides which the words have become corrupted through use and the passage of time (421 d). Nor are the imitations attempted in different parts of the world the same. (The possibility of a non-Greek origin for some words is mentioned at 409 d–e, 416a, 425 e.) Further, just as a picture of Smith may be wrongly identified as a picture of Jones, so a word too may be wrongly identified with something other than that of which it is the image (430c). On such a theory it could well be true, as Antiphon said, that

---

[1] Aristotle in the first chapters of *De interpr.* obviously has his eye on the *Cratylus*. He sides with Hermogenes in maintaining (16a19) that a name is φωνὴ σημαντικὴ κατὰ συνθήκην and that this means (a27) ὅτι φύσει τῶν ὀνομάτων οὐδέν ἐστιν, ἀλλ' ὅταν γένηται σύμβολον. He distinguishes between inarticulate sounds, common to early man and animals, which are natural and convey meaning but are not yet language, from 'names' which are conventional (a28, δηλοῦσί γέ τι καὶ οἱ ἀγράμματοι ψόφοι, οἷον θηρίων, ὧν οὐδέν ἐστιν ὄνομα). See on this L. Amundsen in *Symb. Osl.* 1966, 11f.

men usually or conventionally apply the word 'justice' to what is not truly, correctly or naturally just. The end of the *Cratylus* affords another fascinating glimpse (cf. p. 187, n. 3, above) of the way in which Socrates turned sophistic arguments to his own purposes. He suddenly asks Cratylus if, granted that words are images of things, it is not better to learn of the reality which an image expresses rather than only of the image. Cratylus cannot dispute this, and Socrates leads him on from it to his own 'dream' of absolute and unchanging forms of beauty, goodness and the rest, which alone can be said to be real and knowable, and are different from their fleeting representations in a fair face or a good action. Cratylus is still inclined to stick to his own Heraclitean position, and the dialogue ends, like so many, in an agreement to give the matter further thought. But in a reader's mind the seed has been sown.

Antisthenes, a disciple of Socrates who was among the intimate circle present at his death, showed his sense of the importance of language by entitling a work 'On Education, or on Names', and declaring that 'the foundation of education is the study of names'. Caizzi says truly: 'The problem of the relation between things and names, or better the close connexion of the one with the other, is fundamental to Antisthenes's thought and will have important consequences.'[1]

Unfortunately we are still dealing with fragmentary quotations, and it is difficult to be certain what Antisthenes's teaching was. As we have seen (p. 182, n. 2, above), he like Protagoras was credited with the thesis that it is impossible to contradict or to speak falsely, and it is commonly thought that he was one of those who held that to predicate one thing of another was erroneous: it is not admissible to say 'man is good', but only 'man is man' and 'good is good'. In fact the two doctrines are held to be inseparable,[2] but recent work has shown that this need not necessarily be so. We must look at the evidence.

---

[1] ἀρχὴ παιδεύσεως ἡ τῶν ὀνομάτων ἐπίσκεψις, fr. 38. (References are to Caizzi's edition of the fragments.) The title of the work occurs in D.L.'s list (6.17). See also Caizzi in *Stud. Urb.* 1964, 31. For Antisthenes in general see pp. 304ff. below.

[2] Grote, *Plato*, III, 521: '"Man is good" was an inadmissible proposition: affirming different things to be the same, or one thing to be many. *Accordingly* it was impossible for two speakers really to contradict each other.' (My italics.)

In his 'philosophical dictionary' (*Metaph.* Δ),[1] Aristotle deals with the concept 'false'. It may refer (*a*) to things or facts, if they are non-existent (e.g. a diagonal commensurate with the side) or produce the appearance of something non-existent (e.g. dreams, or illusionist painting); (*b*) to *logoi*. Here Aristotle will have had in mind the classic difficulty, often referred to by Plato and used by Antisthenes himself in support of his thesis of the impossibility of contradiction: 'Every *logos* (statement) is true, for he who speaks says something, he who says something says what is, and he who says what is speaks truth.'[2] Speaking absolutely ('*qua* false'), says Aristotle, a false *logos* is of what is not, therefore in practice when we speak of a false *logos* we mean one which belongs to something other than that to which it is applied, e.g. the *logos* of circle is false if applied to a triangle. (A triangle every point on which is equidistant from a given point does not exist, yet the *logos* 'plane figure every point on which is equidistant from a given point' does exist; i.e. it describes something which is; it has only been misapplied.) Further, although there is in a sense only one *logos* of each thing, namely that which describes its essence, in another sense there are many, since the thing itself and the thing plus certain non-essential attributes are somehow the same, e.g. Socrates and educated Socrates (or Socrates the educated man). This is the reason, he goes on, why it was foolish of Antisthenes to suppose that a thing can only be spoken of by its proper *logos*, one to one; from which it followed that it is impossible to contradict, and practically impossible to speak falsely.

The meaning of *logos* here emerges from the context. It has been understood as a single word or term,[3] but clearly means a description, or statement of what a thing is. This accords with D.L. 6.3: Antisthenes said 'a *logos* is that which sets forth what a thing was or is'.[4]

---

[1] 1024b17ff. The reference to Antisthenes comes at line 32.

[2] Procl. *In Crat.* 37 Pasq. (Antisth. fr. 49): Ἀ. ἔλεγε μὴ δεῖν ἀντιλέγειν. πᾶς γάρ, φησι, λόγος ἀληθεύει. ὁ γὰρ λέγων τι λέγει, ὁ δέ τι λέγων τὸ ὂν λέγει, ὁ δὲ τὸ ὂν λέγων ἀληθεύει. Caizzi (*Stud. Urb.* 34f.) detects a discrepancy between Aristotle's witness and Proclus's, and suspects that Proclus has given a current justification of Antisthenes's paradox without going back to the original source.

[3] Campbell, *Theaet.* xli: 'There is only one term applicable to one thing.' He refers not to Aristotle but to Isocr. *Hel.* οὐδὲ δύο λόγω περὶ τῶν αὐτῶν πραγμάτων ἀντειπεῖν, where the rendering 'terms' seems even more improbable in the context. According to Plato in the *Sophist* (262aff.) a *logos* must contain at least a noun and a verb.

[4] Fr. 45. Caizzi notes (*Stud. Urb.* 29) that its authenticity is confirmed by Alexander, *In Top.* 42, 13ff. (fr. 46). Alexander, commenting on Aristotle's definition of a definition as λόγος ὁ τὸ

The 'foolishness' of Antisthenes is enlarged on by pseudo-Alexander in his commentary (Antisth. fr. 44 B), who explains how the assertion that each thing has only one *logos* led to the impossibility of speaking falsely or of two people contradicting each other. To contradict, they must say different things about the same thing, but since each thing has only one *logos* (which after all, in addition to any more specialized uses, means simply 'one thing which can be said—λέγεσθαι—about it') this is impossible. If they say different things they must be speaking about different things and hence not contradicting each other. None of our authorities gives examples, and modern scholars have been similarly reticent.[1] Presumably Antisthenes would have claimed that 'one cannot say' 'man is a winged and feathered animal', for that is to say what is not, i.e. to say nothing (οὐδὲν λέγειν).[2] He who says nothing cannot contradict or be contradicted, and the only alternative is that, although uttering the sound 'man', the speaker is really talking about birds and so, once again, is not contradicting another who gives a different *logos* of man.[3]

Such theories of language are made more comprehensible by the probability that they owed their origin to the prestige enjoyed by rhetoric, the art of persuasion. For Gorgias persuasion was sovereign because there was no truth over and above what a man could be persuaded to believe, and Protagoras was already teaching his pupils that on every subject opposite positions could be argued with equal

τί ἦν εἶναι σημαίνων, defends the insertion of εἶναι on the grounds that without it the formula might apply equally to a statement of the genus (it is an answer to the question 'What is man?' to say 'He is an animal'; or, in the Peripatetic terminology of Alexander, genus is a predicate in the category of being), which however does not by itself constitute a definition. 'The ἦν, then, is not sufficient by itself as some have thought, of whom Antisthenes appears to have been the first.'

[1] My discussion of these matters owes much to Caizzi's lucid interpretations in *Stud. Urb.* 1964. Nevertheless more concrete examples would have been welcome there too, especially in the discussion of essence and accidental attributes on pp. 33 f. For Antisthenes (says the author), to say 'Socrates is black' would be to say nothing at all, whereas for Aristotle it is to say Socrates with an untrue predicate. One would welcome a similar illustration of a *logos* of the essence of Socrates which would maintain the difference between the two philosophers. Field gives the example of a triangle (*P. and Contemps.* 166). This is helpful, but mathematical definitions are a special case, and the application of the theory to natural objects is not so obvious to us.

[2] For the effect on problems of this kind of the ambiguous Greek phrase οὐδὲν λέγειν cf. vol. II, 20. The doctrine expounded here is that parodied by Plato at *Euthyd.* 285 d ff. and referred to πολλοί δή, and in particular to οἱ ἀμφὶ Πρωταγόραν.

[3] If this sounds implausible, I can only say that I see no alternative explanation, and that others have interpreted Antisthenes similarly but softened the implausibility by refraining from illustrating their interpretations with examples. Cf., in its context, Arist. *Metaph.* 1006 b 20.

validity, what a man believed was true for him, and no man could contradict another in the sense of opposing a true view to a false. Antisthenes may have gone further than Protagoras in attempting a philosophical explanation of how this could be so. In connexion with the last paragraph it is interesting that Plato (*Phaedrus* 260b) examines the effects of applying the name 'horse' to the *logos* of donkey ('tame animal with the largest ears'), and persuading someone that the creature signified by this *logos* possesses the virtues generally ascribed to horses, in order to compare them to the harm done by rhetoricians who, ignorant themselves of the nature of good and evil, advocate evil as being really good.[1] Antisthenes himself wrote rhetorical exercises, of which we still possess speeches of Odysseus and Ajax, contending for the arms of Achilles.[2]

But Aristotle has more about Antisthenes (or his followers). Elsewhere in the *Metaphysics* (1043b23) he says: 'Therefore the difficulty which was raised by the Antistheneans and other such crude thinkers is not inapposite, that you cannot define what a thing is, because a definition is an extended *logos*.[3] You can explain what it is like, e.g. of silver you cannot say what it is, but only that it is like tin. There *is* a class of substance of which definition (ὅρος) or *logos* is possible, namely composite substance, whether sensible or intelligible; but its elements cannot be defined, since definition predicates one thing of another, and the one must be matter and the other form.'

As an example, pseudo-Alexander *ad loc.* (Antisth. fr. 44 B) takes 'man'. 'Man' is a name. We may say he is a rational mortal animal, but this in turn is only a string of names. We are simply listing, enumerating or naming his elements, but neither separately nor collectively do they provide a definition,[4] for a definition is different from

[1] There is a story in D.L. (6.8) that Antisthenes taunted the Athenians with the ignorance of their *strategoi* by saying that they ought to vote that donkeys are horses (or 'vote donkeys into the position of horses', τοὺς ὄνους ἵππους ψηφίσασθαι).

[2] Frr. 14 and 15 Caizzi. He is said to have been a pupil of Gorgias before he met Socrates (p. 306, n. 2, below), and to have adopted a rhetorical style in his dialogues.

[3] λόγος μακρός. That this phrase was used by Antisthenes himself is vouched for by pseudo-Alexander, *In Met.* 554.3 Hayd. It suggests evasion, and Warrington renders it *ad sensum*, 'circumlocution'. Ross on *Metaph.* 1091a7 gives some evidence from literature that the word had a contemptuous flavour.

[4] Aristotle was speaking a little carelessly, or from his own point of view, when at 1043b29 he used the two words ὅρον καὶ λόγον to describe Antisthenes's view.

a name. What is 'rational' or 'animal'? Even if we can divide them into further pluralities of names, yet ultimately we shall come to a simple, elemental entity which cannot be so divided, and this will be indefinable. But how can we claim to have defined, or explained the being of, something if we have simply described it as composed of elements which are themselves indefinable?

Plato in the *Theaetetus* (201 d ff.) describes a similar doctrine anonymously. There can be no *logos* of the first elements of which we and everything else consist; they can only be named. But the compounds made up out of them, being complex themselves, can have the names belonging to them combined to make a *logos*, for this is just what a *logos* is, a combination of names. Elements, then, are inexplicable and unknowable, but can be perceived, whereas complexes are knowable and explicable and comprehensible by a true opinion.

The theory assumes that a complex whole is no more than its parts put together in a certain way. To this Aristotle opposes his own view (inspired by Plato) that the essence or substance of anything, which is expressed in its definition (the 'what it was to be the thing'), is not simply elements-plus-combination but a new, unitary 'form'. For him a definition must include an expression of the cause (see e.g. *An. Post.* 2 ch. 10, *Metaph.* 1043 a 14 ff.), that is, the final cause, for in fact Aristotle's theory of substance amounts to an assertion of his faith in teleology. A house is not to be defined as bricks enclosing a space and covered by a roof. If that were all that could be said, Antisthenes would be right, for that is merely an enumeration of (ultimately indefinable) elements and their arrangement. It is defined by saying that it is a shelter for man and his possessions, and this type of definition applies to natural objects also, for 'nature makes nothing without a purpose' (*De caelo* 291 b 13, *De an.* 432 b 21, etc.).[1]

As far as can be judged from these second-hand and hostile reports, it does not seem likely that Antisthenes supported the doctrine that none but identical predication is possible. This is referred to contemp-

---

[1] Hence Antisthenes's mistake of saying that, when one thing is predicated of another, 'one must be matter and the other form'. All the elements stated in a definition are formal constituents. (This is explained by pseudo-Alexander, *In Metaph.* 554, 11 ff.) For Aristotle individuals *are* indefinable: only definitions of species and genera are possible. The mistake, in his view, resulted from a confusion between the particular and the universal references of a noun like 'horse'. (Cf. p. 215, n. 3, below.)

tuously by Plato in the *Sophist* (251 b) as something that is seized on by 'youths and old men of retarded intellect', 'who object that it is impossible for many things to be one or one many, and enjoy insisting that we must not say a man is good, but only man is man and good is good'. Some have identified this with the thesis ascribed to Antisthenes by Aristotle that 'a thing can only be spoken of by its proper *logos*, one to one', but in the light of other evidence, including that of Aristotle himself, it is plain that *logos* here is not limited to a single term. It is not the same thing as ὄνομα (a name),[1] which in view of the current uses of *logos* would in any case be improbable. If it is true that Antisthenes said 'a *logos* is that which sets forth what a thing was or is', he evidently went on to claim that such a *logos* could only substitute for the name of the thing a collection of the names of its elements, which themselves could only be named. Grote called him the first nominalist, because he denied the existence of those forms or essences (εἴδη or οὐσίαι) of particular things, which Socrates sought to define and Plato was already proclaiming as independent realities. (Antisthenes lived till about 360.) The rivalry between the two philosophies is suggested by the anecdote that Antisthenes said to Plato: 'I see a horse, but I don't see horseness', to which Plato replied: 'No, for you have the eye with which a horse is seen, but you have not yet acquired the eye to see horseness.' This is told by Simplicius, whose teacher Ammonius also quoted the *mot* of Antisthenes as an illustration of his view that 'the kinds or forms existed only in our thoughts' (ἐν ψιλαῖς ἐπινοίαις).[2]

---

[1] Grote (*Plato*, III, 521) was one who thought that Aristotle was crediting Antisthenes with the proposition that none but identical propositions were admissible, but had to admit (on p. 526) that in that case the doctrine which Aristotle attributes to οἱ Ἀντισθένειοι at *Metaph.* 1043 b 23 is not in harmony with that which he ascribes to Antisthenes himself. He also thought it probable (p. 507, n. x) that in the *Sophist* Plato does intend to designate Antisthenes as γέρων ὀψιμαθής. (He may have been some 20 years older than Plato.) Apart from the plural, such commentators ignore the fact that the theory is ascribed equally to οἱ νέοι. Contrast Campbell, *Theaet.* xxxix: the doctrine of *Theaet.* 201 d ff. (which we have seen to be the same as that ascribed to Antisthenes at *Metaph.* 1043 b 23 ff.) 'is surely very different from such crude nominalism [*sc.* as that described in the *Soph.*] ... The opinion quoted, if properly examined, is not a denial of predication, but rather a denial that anything can be predicated *of the prime elements* ... which is by no means the same thing.'

[2] Simpl. *Cat.* 208, 28; Ammon. *In Porph. Isag.* 40, 6 (Antisth. frr. 50 A and c). The story is told in a slightly different form of Diogenes the Cynic, naturally enough considering that he was Antisthenes's pupil and Antisthenes himself came to be regarded as the founder of the Cynic

If however nominalism is the doctrine that assumes, as a recent definition has it, 'that language imposes its own structure upon a reality which by itself lacks any such distinctions',[1] it does not appear that Antisthenes was its advocate. His teaching does not resemble the convention-theory of names maintained by Hermogenes in Plato's *Cratylus*, so much as the nature-theory of Cratylus[2] according to which names have a natural affinity with their objects (or, if they do not, they are not names, and the man who utters them 'says nothing', 429bff.): they 'reveal the things' (433d), and he who knows the names knows the things also (435d). A complex object can be analysed by naming its elements, but the elements can only be named or described analogically (silver like tin). They are grasped by intuition or perception ('I see a horse'; cf. *Theaet.* 202b), but cannot be explained, or known as knowledge was understood by Socrates and Plato, for whom it meant the ability to give a *logos* of the essence of the thing known. If we may judge by the criticisms of Plato and Aristotle, Caizzi is right in saying that Antisthenes's theory of 'one, and only one, proper *logos* for each thing' is based on a lack of the distinction between essential and accidental predication plus a confusion between proper and common names.[3] Predication is not impossible, but it must

school. Whether historically true or not, it is certainly *bien trouvé*. Other stories were also current testifying to the ill will between him and Plato, against whom he wrote a dialogue under the opprobrious name of Sathon. (See p. 310, n. 2, below.)

[1] Lorenz and Mittelstrass, *Mind*, 1967, 1. They themselves add (p. 5) that realism and nominalism can be recognized as variants of the nature-theory and the convention-theory of the *Cratylus*. It might be interesting to compare the latter with the conventionalist theory of necessary truth as it appears in Hobbes, who like the fifth-century philosophers saw a close connexion between names and truth: 'the first truths were arbitrarily made by those that first of all imposed names upon things'. See W. and M. Kneale, *Dev. of Logic*, 311f.

[2] A similar conclusion was reached by von Fritz in *Hermes*, 1927: it is Antisthenean doctrine, 'gleichgültig, ob dort Antisthenes persönlich oder allein gemeint ist oder nicht' (p. 462). See also Dümmler, *Akad.* 5. Field, however, in a carefully reasoned account, concluded that 'there is no real evidence for associating him with either view' (*P. and Contemps.* 168).

[3] *Stud. Urb.* 34. (The confusion would be facilitated by the fact that at this primitive stage of grammatical study the one word ὄνομα had to do duty for both 'name' and 'noun'. According to Lorenz and Mittelstrass (*Mind*, 1967, 5), it persists in the *Cratylus* and throughout Plato's writings.) Cf. 32: 'For Plato [and, one might add, for Aristotle] the object of definition is not the particular but the universal... Therefore... the denial of ποιότης implies also the denial of the definition of what a thing is. According to Antisthenes we not only see but know the individual horse, in whose name is included all that is proper to it. He does not seem to have realized that this would imply the necessity of a name for every single thing, not only for every class.' And on p. 31: 'The problem of predication, which the thesis that only names can express the essence seemed to have rendered impossible, is therefore to be resolved on this plane, i.e. basically the descriptive.'

be assumed that whatever follows the copula is essential to the subject (a part of 'what it is'), and if any of the elements named is inapplicable to the subject the whole *logos* must be dismissed as meaningless. (He was misled, says pseudo-Alexander, *In Metaph*. 435, 1, by the fact that a false *logos* is not absolutely or primarily (μὴ ἁπλῶς μηδὲ κυρίως) the *logos* of anything into saying that it was nothing at all.)

On those who denied the possibility of predicating one thing of another, Aristotle has this to say:

The more recent of previous philosophers were disturbed by the thought of making the same thing one and many. For this reason some abolished the word 'is',[1] as Lycophron did, while others altered the form of the expression, saying not 'the man is white' but 'the man has-been-whitened' [λελεύκωται, one word in Greek], not 'is walking' but 'walks', lest by adding 'is' they should make the one many, as if 'one' or 'being' had only one sense.[2]

Simplicius (*Phys.* 91) explains that Lycophron simply omitted the verb 'is', saying 'white Socrates'[3] for 'Socrates is white', as if to state the attribute in this way did not involve the addition of anything real; but if it did not, he adds, then there would be no difference between saying 'Socrates' and 'white Socrates'. It was to avoid the consequence that no significant statement was possible that the 'others' (whom neither he nor Aristotle identifies) tried using other verbs instead of the offensive copula. If Lycophron thought it admissible to say 'white Socrates' he cannot, any more than Antisthenes, have been one of those at whom Plato is tilting in the *Sophist* (251b). The only other thing known about his thory of knowledge is that he described knowledge as 'an intercourse (συνουσία) of the *psyche* with the act of knowing'. So Aristotle puts it (*Metaph.* 1045b9ff.), and pseudo-Alexander explains (563, 21; DK, 83, 1): 'Lycophron when

---

[1] *Sc.* as copula. Simplicius (*Phys.* 91) adds that Lycophron allowed its existential use. For Lycophron see pp. 313f. below.

[2] *Phys.* 185b25. To say that Socrates is (*a*) white, (*b*) a philosopher, and (*c*) an Athenian would be to make the one subject, Socrates, many (Philop. *Phys.* 49, 17).

[3] Actually Σ. λευκός in the Greek, not λευκός Σ. One cannot fully understand these people without reference to current idiom. The copula frequently *was* omitted in speech and writing, so that Σ. λευκός is as much a complete sentence, meaning 'Socrates is white', as if the ἐστι were expressly inserted. Lycophron was a little naive if he thought that those who omitted it were correcting a logical fault. Themistius's comment on his procedure was κακῷ τὸ κακὸν ἰώμενος (*Phys. paraphr.* 7.2 Schenkl, not in DK).

asked what it was that caused knowledge and the *psyche* to be one, would reply that it was their intercourse'. This 'intercourse' or 'coexistence'[1] of the mind with knowledge suggests a view like that of Antisthenes, not scepticism but belief in knowledge by direct acquaintance. One cannot say 'Socrates is white' (himself plus whiteness), but one experiences 'white Socrates' as a unitary essence.

The only people specifically mentioned as qualifying for Plato's condemnation by confining speech to identical propositions ('man is man', 'good is good', etc.) are Stilpo the Megarian and the Eretrians.[2] Since Stilpo was probably born *c.* 380 and the Eretrian school was founded by Menedemus who was born after Plato's death, it is improbable that the former, and impossible that the latter, could have been Plato's target. But Euclides who founded the Megarian school was a friend of Socrates, and the Eretrian was closely linked with it, Menedemus having been a pupil of Stilpo. Plato stayed with Euclides at Megara after the death of Socrates, and they may well have differed and had lively discussions of these questions. A doctrine which could lead to the same conclusion as that in the *Sophist* is ascribed to them by Simplicius (*Phys.* 120). After quoting from Eudemus that the mistakes of Parmenides were excusable owing to the inchoate state of philosophy at his time, when no one had suggested that a word could have more than one sense or had distinguished essence from accident, he goes on:

Out of ignorance of this even the philosophers known as Megarians assumed as an obvious premise that things having a different *logos* were different, and that different things were divided from each other, and so thought to prove that everything is divided from itself, e.g. the *logos* of 'educated Socrates' is different from that of 'white Socrates', therefore Socrates is divided from himself.

[1] In ordinary language συνουσία meant intercourse or association, but it could also, and more literally, be understood as 'co-being'. In the late commentators, the verb συνουσιόομαι is used to express the idea of being essentially united. See LSJ *s.v.*

[2] For Stilpo see Plut. *Adv. Col.* 1119 c–d, and for the Eretrians Simpl. *Phys.* 91, 28. It might be interesting to compare their doctrine with that which has been derived in modern times from a strict interpretation of Bishop Butler's dictum: 'Everything is what it is and not another thing', quoted by Moore as the motto of *Principia Ethica*. This, it has been claimed, appears to rule out not only a definition of 'good' (the 'naturalistic fallacy'), but all definitions of any term whatsoever, on the grounds that they must be the result of confusing two properties, defining one by another, or substituting one for another. See the discussion by Frankena reprinted in the Foot essays, pp. 57 ff.

The same doctrine is opposed by Aristotle in *Soph. el.* (166b28ff.) without attribution: 'Coriscus is a man [but note that Greek has no indefinite article], "man" is different from "Coriscus", therefore Coriscus is different from himself.' It bears a resemblance to the 'one *logos* to each thing' of Antisthenes, but was brought to a more radical conclusion.[1]

In the foregoing account an attempt has been made to attach the various theories to individual authors. Such assignment has been the subject of intensive research in the past, but the evidence is not always sufficient for certainty, nor is the matter of great importance for the history of thought, since some of the possible authors are now little more than names. The important thing is to know that in the lifetime of Socrates and Plato these questions of language and its objects were being zestfully thrashed out by a group of contemporaries who in the course of their debate threw up a number of related or rival views which were all ultimately the result of wrestling with the crude but effective logic of the Eleatics. The thought of Socrates and Plato, whose influence on the subsequent history of philosophy has been profound, must be seen against this background, as an integral part of the debate and an attempt to find a definitive solution to its problems. That in Plato's hands it became only an element in a great moral and metaphysical synthesis does not alter this fact, which a reading of the *Cratylus* and *Euthydemus* alone (not to mention more important dialogues like the *Sophist*) puts beyond all doubt.

Summary of results. During the lifetimes of Socrates and Plato the following positions were held. Names of some who held them are given in brackets where either certain or probable.

　1. It is impossible to speak falsely, for that is to say what is not, and what is not cannot be uttered. (Protagoras, Antisthenes. The thesis depends on Parm. fr. 2.7–8.)

　2. As a corollary, no one has a right to contradict another. (Protagoras, Antisthenes.)

[1] See on this Maier, *Syllogistik*, 2. Teil, 2. Hälfte, 7ff., where the relevance of Arist. *Metaph.* Γ 4 is discussed, and it is suggested that in Aristotle's time the eristic of Antisthenes and the Megarians was undergoing a certain fusion.

3. Truth is relative to the individual. (Protagoras, Gorgias.)

4. We use words inconsistently and with no correspondence to reality. This is wrong, for there is a reality (ὄν, φύσις) and there are natural kinds (εἴδη), to which our terms should correspond univocally. (Socrates, Antiphon, Hippocr. *De arte*.)

5. Definition of the essence of a thing is impossible, for one can only list its elements and they themselves, not being subject to further analysis, are indefinable, and can only be described analogically. (Antisthenes, probably Lycophron.)

6. To every object belongs one and only one proper *logos*, which says what it is by naming the elements of which it is composed. If any of them do not apply to it, there is no *logos*. (Antisthenes.)

7. Names have a natural affinity with their objects, which are known by direct contact of mind with object as in sense-perception (αἴσθησις). A name which has no such affinity is not wrong, but no name at all. (Antisthenes, Lycophron, 'Cratylus' in Plato.)

8. Names are labels arbitrarily chosen, having no natural connexion with the objects to which they are applied. (Democritus, 'Hermogenes' in Plato.)

9. The use of 'is' to join subject and predicate is illegitimate because it makes one thing many, though one may perceive and speak of a subject and its attribute (e.g. white Socrates) as a unity. (Lycophron.)

10. On the same Eleatic grounds that a thing cannot be both one and many, only identical predication is possible. (Megarians, and probably others.)

(6) GRAMMAR

The intense interest in the possibilities and limitations of language led to the beginnings of grammatical study (distinction of genders, parts of speech and so forth), of which there are traces from Protagoras onwards. The foregoing sections, however, as well as the treatment of these topics themselves, should make it clear that in contemporary minds they were not divorced from wider questions, whether of the philosophy of language or of rhetorical practice. The aim was not in fact scientific, to sort out and codify existing usage, but practical, to reform language and increase its effectiveness by a closer correspond-ence with reality.[1]

Protagoras, we are told, was the first to divide speech (*logos*) into four basic kinds (πυθμένες λόγων): request (or prayer), question, answer, command; or according to other authorities into seven: narration, question, answer, command, report, request, summons. A little later Alcidamas said that the four *logoi* were affirmation, nega-tion, question and address.[2] This comes from a late source, but Aristotle refers to the division when in the *Poetics* (1456b15) he records that Protagoras criticized Homer for writing 'Sing, goddess', because this was to command when what was wanted was a prayer.

The distinction between noun and verb (*rhēma*) occurs in Plato, and as Cornford remarks (*PTK*, 307), it is introduced in the *Cratylus* (425a) without explanation as something familiar, so was probably made earlier by Protagoras or some other Sophist.[3] It is true, never-theless, that in the *Sophist* they are carefully defined and illustrated by examples. A combination of noun with verb yields a statement (*logos*).[4] *Rhēma* is here defined as 'what signifies actions', which seems definite enough, but at this early stage terminology is by no means fixed, and elsewhere (*Crat.* 399a–b) we find Plato saying that if the name Diphilus is split into its component parts (Διὶ φίλος, 'dear to Zeus') it becomes a *rhēma* instead of a name. Literally *rhēma* means only a 'thing said', and a name or noun is contrasted with it as that of which things are said. Even Aristotle with his more technical vocabu-lary, for whom *rhēma* is most often a verb and is so defined (*De int.*

---

[1] 'Ancient Greek *grammatikē* was a τέχνη, an art or craft, a study aiming at practice; modern philology is not a τέχνη but a physical science. It takes the worldwide phenomenon of human speech as its object, and is concerned merely to ascertain and co-ordinate the facts.' This is from Murray's highly readable essay on *The Beginnings of Greek Grammar* (in *Gk. Stud.*), in which he also points out the enormous difference resulting from the fact that γραμματική was concerned solely with Greek speech: 'The phenomenon that lay before the Greek *grammatikoi* was not all human language. It was the *Logos.*'

[2] D.L. 9.53f. His words might mean that others, not Protagoras, divide into seven, and so Hicks translates. The second list looks dubious, and it is difficult to see on what grounds, in such a general classification, διήγησις was separated from ἀπαγγελία. Unfortunately there is no more nearly contemporary authority.

[3] The classification of letters as vowels, sonants and mutes, which precedes it at 424c, is ascribed to οἱ δεινοὶ περὶ τούτων.

[4] ὄνομα plus ῥῆμα = λόγος, *Crat.* 425a, 431b–c, *Soph.* 262cff. 'Theaetetus sits' is an example of the simplest λόγος. On these two parts of speech as the sole essentials of a λόγος see the comments of Cornford, *PTK*, 307.

16b6), uses it also to mean an adjective (*ibid.* 20b1–2), and the wider term 'predicate' must sometimes be the best translation.

Stenzel noted (*RE*, xxv. Halbb. 1010f.) that, if Plato's definition of a statement by its simplest grammatical form seems primitive, we must bear in mind that his concern is not in fact with the grammatical form but with such questions as how, of two grammatically equally correct propositions ('Theaetetus sits', 'Theaetetus flies'), one can be true and the other false. The exalted position of the *logos* in a Greek mind is well brought out by the build-up which Plato gives it at *Crat.* 425a. Nouns and verbs are constructed out of letters and syllables, and from nouns and verbs we compose 'something great and beautiful and complete, the *Logos*, formed by the art of naming or rhetoric or whatever it be, just as a living figure is composed by the art of the painter'. This Greek attitude to Logos (in some contexts the capital letter seems to impose itself) must never be forgotten when as cold-blooded grammarians or logicians we find ourselves growing exasperated by the looseness and ambiguity with which it appears to be used.

Protagoras's interest in the gender of nouns is vouched for by a contemporary. Aristotle tells us that it was he who divided nouns into masculine, feminine and neuter,[1] and this is reflected in the *Clouds* of Aristophanes. The play contains, under the name of Socrates, an attack on Protagoras's claim to make the weaker ('unjust') argument the stronger, and Strepsiades, who has come to Socrates to learn the unjust argument in order to avoid payment of his debts, is dismayed to discover that he must first learn 'about names, which of them are masculine and which feminine'. His failure (in common with all his fellow-Greeks) to distinguish animals of different sex by different terminations, and his use of the masculine article with nouns which have what is usually a feminine ending, earn him a sharp rebuke from 'Socrates'. This castigation of the grammar of ordinary language as illogical or imprecise appears again in Protagoras's contention that the Greek words for 'wrath' and 'helmet', which are feminine, ought to be masculine.[2]

---

[1] Or things (σκεύη), Ar. *Poet.* 1407b7. Aristotle himself called them μεταξύ (*Rhet.* 1458a9, *Soph. el.* 166b12, 173b28). The word οὐδέτερον (Lat. *neuter*) came into use with later grammarians.

[2] Arist. *Soph. el.* 173b19. Some have supposed that this was on account of the warlike or 'unfeminine character' (Murray) of the conceptions which the words signified. More probably

Prodicus[1] is mentioned in the *Euthydemus* (277e) as one who insisted on the primary importance of 'the correctness of names', which Socrates there calls the first stage of initiation into the mysteries of the Sophists. His speciality was precision in the use of language and the accurate distinction of the meaning of words commonly regarded as synonymous. He rebukes me, says Socrates in the *Protagoras* (341a), for using an expression like 'terribly clever'. 'Terrible' (*deinos*, see p. 32) must qualify unpleasant things like poverty, disease or war. The same dialogue contains a parody of his teaching, a somewhat pompous speech in which he distinguishes between discussion and dispute, esteem and praise, pleasure and enjoyment. In the *Laches* (197d) he is mentioned, in connexion with the distinction between courage and fearlessness, as 'the best of the Sophists at drawing such distinctions'.[2] Aristotle shows him listing enjoyment, delight and gladness as subdivisions of pleasure, and in connexion with this a late commentator credits him with the 'invention' of 'verbal accuracy'.[3]

Perhaps the most interesting thing about all this is the evidence for a personal relationship between Prodicus and Socrates, who refers to himself several times in Plato as Prodicus's pupil or friend.[4] Prodicus's insistence on distinguishing precisely between words of closely related

Protagoras was moved by purely morphological considerations connected with their terminations. See T. Gomperz, *Gr. Th.* I, 444f. and Fehling, *Rh. Mus.* 1965, 215, and cf. the argument about κάρδοπος at *Clouds* 670ff. Note that once again his target is Homer, and indeed his criticism of the concord μῆνιν οὐλομένην belongs to the same context as that of the mood of ἄειδε, viz. a critique of the opening lines of the *Iliad*. See Fehling's imaginative reconstruction, *ibid.* 214, and, for his conclusions from this, p. 205 above.

[1] For Prodicus in general see pp. 274ff. below.

[2] Other Platonic references to Prodicus in this connexion are *Prot.* 340aff., *Meno* 75e, *Charm.* 163d, *Crat.* 384b.

[3] τέρψις, χαρά and εὐφροσύνη, Ar. *Top.* 112b22; cf. schol. on *Phaedr.* = Hermias, p. 283 Couvreur (not in DK but added by Untersteiner, *Sof.* II, 173f.): Prodicus τὴν τῶν ὀνομάτων εὗρεν ἀκρίβειαν. According to the scholiast, τέρψις was pleasure through the ears, χαρά pleasure of the mind, and εὐφροσύνη visual pleasure; a classification which, if really Prodicus's, shows once again the normative rather than descriptive character of this kind of teaching, for it hardly corresponds to ordinary usage. (In Prodicus's speech in the *Protagoras*, εὐφραίνεσθαι is *contrasted* with ἥδεσθαι, and is defined as the enjoyment resulting from exercising the intellect.) The scholiast, however, has very likely introduced a Stoic classification. Cf. Alex. in DK, 84 A 19, and see on this Classen in *Proc. Afr. C.A.* 1959, 39f. Classen thinks that even Aristotle has confused Prodicus with Platonic διαίρεσις.

[4] See pp. 275f. below. I agree with H. Gomperz (*S. u. R.* 93) that these allusions cannot be dismissed as jokes without any historical foundation.

meaning has obvious affinities with the Socratic habit of pinning down an interlocutor and making him say precisely what courage, temperance, virtue, or whatever be the subject of their discussion, *is*—what is its form or being; and the teaching of Prodicus may well have been an influence directing his thought along these lines. Whether, as Calogero has written, 'the difference between the two approaches is very sharp', Prodicus caring only for 'correct speaking' and Socrates interested in 'the real thing' or whether, as W. Schmid has it, Prodicus's art of division was a 'scientific fertilization of the Socratic sphere of thought' and 'his attempt to sharpen and regularize the use of language through logical demands an undoubtedly valuable preparation for the conceptual clarification of literary language', is a question that will be taken up later.[1] One may add here, however, that Prodicus like other Sophists had a high reputation as a political orator and gave paid public displays of eloquence, and also, like Protagoras, undertook to teach the art of success in politics and the management of private estates. It is likely therefore that his insistence on precise language occurred in the context of rhetorical instruction.[2]

ADDITIONAL NOTES

(1) *Prodicus and Thucydides.* Antiphon, Gorgias and Prodicus were all mentioned in late antiquity as teachers or models of Thucydides. (See DK, 84 A 9, H. Mayer, *Prodikos*, 61.) In Mayer's own opinion the 'Schärfe und Prägnanz' of Thucydides's style is a combined inheritance from Gorgias's antitheses and Prodicus's 'Synonymik'. It is not easy to see in Gorgias a teacher of 'Schärfe und Prägnanz', but in any case I do not wish to enter here on a discussion of influences on Thucydides in general but simply to follow Mayer in drawing attention to some places where the distinction between near-synonyms

---

[1] See pp. 275 ff. For some further assessments of the value of Prodicus's linguistic work see Grant, *Ethics*, I, 124f. ('We must acknowledge the merit of this first attempt at separating the different shades of language, and fixing a nomenclature', etc.); H. Gomperz, *S. u. R.* 124–6 (the aim of his instruction was rhetorical—otherwise young men would not have paid 50 dr. a time to hear him!—yet 'aus der Bedeutungslehre des Prodikos ist die Begriffsphilosophie des Sokrates erwachsen'); and other authorities referred to in Untersteiner, *Sophs.* 225, n. 66. Untersteiner is not quite correct in saying on p. 215 that 'all scholars are agreed' on the question.

[2] Plato, *Hipp. Maj.* 282c, *Rep.* 600c, and see pp. 41 f. above.

is drawn in a way so strikingly reminiscent of Prodicus in the *Protagoras* that they must surely owe their inspiration to him.

In 1.23.6 we have the famous distinction between the true but disguised *cause* (πρόφασις) of the war and the *reasons* (αἰτίαι) which were openly given.

1.69.6, αἰτία and κατηγορία. 'Please do not think that our remonstrance arises out of any hostile feelings. *Remonstrance* (αἰτία) is what one employs against friends who have erred, *accusation* (κατηγορία) against enemies who have wronged one.'

2.62.4, αὔχημα and καταφρόνησις. 'Any coward can be *boastful* out of ignorance and luck, but a proper *disdain* comes from reasoned confidence in one's superiority over the enemy.'

3.39.2, ἐπαναστῆναι and ἀποστῆναι. The Mytileneans are 'not so much *revolutionaries*—a word which applies to people who have suffered harsh treatment—as deliberate *insurgents* plotting with our enemies to destroy us'.

4.98.6, ἁμάρτημα and παρανομία. 'Involuntary *faults* [the Athenians claimed] earned sanctuary at the altars of the gods, and the name *crime* should be reserved for wrongful acts committed gratuitously, not under the pressure of circumstances.'

6.11.6, ἐπαίρεσθαι and θαρσεῖν. 'What matters is not to feel *elation* at any chance setback of our enemies, but rather *confidence* in our own superior planning.'[1]

All but one of these instances occur in a speech, direct or reported, and the use made of them by Thucydides is further evidence of the rhetorical purpose of such nice distinctions. They can indeed be remarkably effective.

(2) *Synonymic and philosophy*. Momigliano has an interesting theory of the possible bearings of Prodicus's discrimination of synonyms on both philosophy of language and ethics. The words 'theory' and 'possible' are my own, for Momigliano presents his conclusions as certain. On the evidence that we have, it is difficult to be so confident, but even on a more cautious view the interpretation is too interesting to be passed over. It is as follows (in *Atti Torino*, 1929–30, 102 f.). Democritus had

---

[1] Not all the examples cited by Mayer seem relevant. At 1.84.3 the rhetorical effect is gained by using αἰδώς and αἰσχύνη indistinguishably rather than differentiating between them, and at 1.36.1 φοβοῦμαι and δέδοικα seem to be used simply to avoid clumsy repetition. Nor is any difference of meaning between ἴσος and κοινός suggested at 3.53.1–2.

said that words do not reflect reality because (among other reasons) not every word has an object corresponding to it. (See vol. II, 475.) The only way to refute him was to show that it did, i.e. that of so-called synonyms (like τελευτή, πέρας, ἔσχατον, *Meno* 75 e) each has in fact its own separate object. What Prodicus is doing with his apparent pedantry is to oppose the prevailing scepticism. And, since theoretical scepticism led to practical relativism, he is equally in reaction against 'the army of Thrasymachuses and Callicleses'. This explains how Prodicus the hair-splitter is also the author of the moralizing fable of the Choice of Heracles (pp. 277 f. below). The art of distinguishing synonyms had important bearings on ethics, involving the separation of ἀγαθός from κρείττων, δίκαιον from συμφέρον. (These particular examples do not, so far as I am aware, occur in the surviving record of Prodicus's activity.) His reaction, continues Momigliano, is the more interesting for not being simply a defence of traditional beliefs. On the dangerous subject of the gods he was both bold and original (see on this pp. 238 ff. below), yet he felt the need of upholding sound moral principles in daily life. He thus (concludes Momigliano) occupies a special place among the Sophists, different on the one hand from the scepticism of Gorgias, Protagoras and Thrasymachus, and on the other from Antiphon and Hippias with their antithesis between natural and conventional morality.

IX

RATIONALIST THEORIES
OF RELIGION: AGNOSTICISM
AND ATHEISM[1]

(1) CRITICISMS OF TRADITIONAL RELIGION

The Presocratic philosophers, whether or not they retained a belief in a divine force or forces, all alike promulgated conceptions of religion which were far removed from the anthropomorphism of the popular or state cults based on the Homeric pantheon. Xenophanes openly attacked them, and substituted a non-anthropomorphic monotheism or pantheism, while others tacitly abandoned them in favour, first, of an ever-living world-stuff described vaguely as governing or steering the motions of the cosmos and everything in it, and later, in Anaxagoras, of a single Mind separate from the matter of the universe and the cause of the rational order which it displays. We have seen Heraclitus condemning phallic and other cults for their unseemliness and Democritus (doubtless under the influence of already existing evolutionary theories) claiming that it was only the alarming nature of thunder, lightning and similar phenomena that made men think they were caused by gods. As 'enlightenment' grows, it shows itself under two main aspects (whether in ancient Greece or Europe since the Renaissance): first, the determination to believe only what is reasonable and a tendency to identify reason with positivism and the progress of natural science, and secondly a genuine concern with morality. Morality is identified with the amelioration of human life and the elimination of cruelty, injury and all forms of exploitation of human beings by their fellows, and is based on purely humanistic and relative standards, for it is held that absolute standards claiming supernatural

---

[1] For a general aperçu of the criticism of traditional religion in Greece, a subject which far exceeds the scope of this history, see P. Decharme, *La critique des trad. rels. chez les Grecs.*

authority not only have led in the past, but must inevitably lead, to cruelty, intolerance and other evils. The Greek gods were very vulnerable in both these aspects, and as soon as conventional piety began to yield to a more thoughtful attitude—when *nomos* in all its aspects was no longer taken for granted but rather contrasted with what was natural and universal[1]—scepticism and disapproval began to make themselves felt in increasing volume.

The attack on religion was indeed closely bound up with the *nomos–physis* antithesis. Plato (*Laws* 889e) complains of people who claim that 'the gods are human contrivances, they do not exist in nature but only by custom and law, which moreover differ from place to place according to the agreement made by each group when they laid down their laws'.

When Plato wrote, such contentions were nothing new. The Aristophanic Socrates rejected the gods as an out-of-date currency (*nomisma*, p. 56 above), and in Euripides Hecuba calls *nomos* superior to the gods because it is by *nomos* that we believe in them as well as in standards of right and wrong (p. 23). There is plenty of evidence that the hold of religion over men's minds was weakening in the intellectual ferment of the Periclean age, and also that Athenian officialdom was nervous and touchy about it. The cult of the gods was integral to the life of the state and a powerful cohesive force. It may be claimed that all that was necessary was conformity with cult-practices,[2] and that thought was free; but it must have been as obvious to an Athenian traditionalist as it was to Cicero's Cotta that those who deny outright that the gods exist 'non modo superstitionem tollunt ... sed etiam religionem, quae deorum cultu pio continetur' (*N.D.* 1.42.117). Hence the impiety trials and the decree of Diopeithes against atheism and cosmic speculation.

---

[1] The conventional attitude is exemplified by the reply of Socrates in Xenophon (*Mem.* 4.3.16) to Euthydemus, who acknowledges divine providence but is worried by the thought that no adequate return can ever be made to the gods by men. The gods themselves, he says, have provided the answer, for whenever the Delphic oracle is approached with this problem, it always replies: 'Follow the *nomos* of your city', which means propitiating the gods with sacrifices just as far as is in your power. Such an answer would scarcely satisfy the more progressive and inquiring spirits of the fifth century.

[2] 'Even if we concentrate on the religious controversy which occasioned the trial [of Socrates], the problem of faith never became an issue.' (Snell, *Disc. of Mind*, 26.) See also p. 237, n. 2 below.

They did not tolerate [says Plutarch (*Nicias* 23)] the natural philosophers and star-gazers,[1] as they called them, dissolving divinity into irrational causes, blind forces and necessary properties. Protagoras was banished, Anaxagoras put under restraint and with difficulty saved by Pericles, and Socrates, though in fact he had no concern in such matters, lost his life through his devotion to philosophy.

And in his life of Pericles (32):

About this time [*sc.* just before the outbreak of the Peloponnesian War] Aspasia was prosecuted for impiety... and Diopeithes[2] introduced a bill for the impeachment of those who denied the gods or taught about celestial phenomena, directing suspicion at Pericles through Anaxagoras.

The motives might be political, but the state of opinion was such that imputations of atheism and natural science were a sure way to secure a prosecution, as Socrates's accusers knew well. No distinction was drawn between the scientific writers and the paid teachers whom we call Sophists. They shared the same religious scepticism, which for the Sophists was often the result of reading the works of the scientists, and at the time the word *sophistes* was applied as naturally to Anaxagoras as to Protagoras or Hippias (p. 30 above).

Criticism of the gods on moral grounds came early. It needed no scientific speculation or logical subtlety to be scandalized by Zeus's castration of his father or his many amours, the thefts and deceit of Hermes, or the jealousy of Hera and the malicious and vengeful character of the immortals in general. Myths in which the gods appeared as thieves, adulterers, seducers and gluttons were already rejected by Xenophanes and Pindar. In the age of enlightenment we find Euripides everywhere giving rein to such criticism. It can take different forms—reproach of the gods for their behaviour, declarations that gods exist

[1] μετεωρολέσχας, lit. 'chatterers about things in the sky'. The word occurs in Plato (*Rep.* 489c), coupled with the adjective ἀχρήστους, to illustrate the kind of abuse that was levelled at philosophers.

[2] Not much is known about the appropriately named Diopeithes. The name is mentioned several times in Aristophanes (*Knights* 1085, *Wasps* 380, *Birds* 988), but all that emerges is that the holder of it was a soothsayer. Fragments of other comic poets depict him as a fanatic and as a drummer in the Corybantic rites (Ameipsias 10 K., Teleclides 6 K. and Phrynichus 9 K.; see Lobeck, *Aglaoph.* 981). The prosecution of 'Anaxagoras the Sophist' is mentioned (but not Diopeithes or his ψήφισμα) by Diodorus (12.39.2). For the connexion of the Sophists with the natural philosophers cf. pp. 45 ff. above, and for the supposed connexion between 'sky-gazing' and immoral sophistic teaching *Clouds* 1283 (pp. 114f.).

but do not and cannot behave like that, or assertions that, since these are the gods we are taught to believe in, either they do not exist—it is all lies—or they are heedless of human affairs and do not merit or need our worship. As a dramatist Euripides could reflect all points of view through his various plots and characters. In the *Ion* we see the disillusionment of a pious young acolyte who learns that the god he serves has stooped to seduce a mortal woman. The *Heracles* contains a vehement denial that the gods could behave wickedly (1341 ff.):

I do not believe that the gods take pleasure in unlawful intercourse, nor have I ever thought nor can be persuaded that they load each other with fetters, nor that one is lord over another. God, if he be truly god, lacks nothing. These are the wretched tales of bards.[1]

Complete disbelief in the gods, based on the prosperity of the wicked and the sufferings of the just, is voiced in a passionate outburst in the *Bellerophon* (fr. 286): There are no gods in heaven. To believe in such old wives' tales is folly. You have only to look around you. Tyrants murder, rob, cheat and ravage, and are happier than the pious and peaceful. Small god-fearing states are overwhelmed by the military might of those larger and more wicked. More in the vein of the *Heracles* passage is the line, again from the *Bellerophon* (fr. 292.7): 'If gods act basely, they are no gods.' That the example of the gods could be invoked to excuse human failings is also pointed out by Euripides, for instance when Phaedra's old nurse condones her illicit passion by pointing out, with the examples of Zeus and Eos, that Aphrodite is a power too strong for the other gods themselves to resist, and again by Helen in extenuation of her own conduct (*Tro.* 948). The same point is made in comic vein by Aristophanes, when the Unjust Argument claims that without his rhetorical skill a sinner will be lost, but with it he will confound his accusers (*Clouds* 1079):

Suppose you are caught in adultery, you will argue that you have done nothing wrong, and point to Zeus, who could never resist love or women. How, you will say, could you, a mortal, show greater strength than a god?

---

[1] Yet so strong was the force of tradition that the whole plot of the *Heracles* depends on the jealous wrath of Hera, of whose unspeakable cruelty the hero himself, who speaks these words, has been the victim. Some have thought that the paradox was deliberate, to bring out the inherent absurdity of the situation, but Lesky (probably rightly) sees it as a product of the tension between the subject-matter, imposed by tradition and mythology, and the intellect of the dramatist. See Lesky, *HGL*, 382.

In contrast to the homely traditionalism of the nurse, the moralist could claim that a god might be simply the product of psychological transference: men gave the name to their own evil passions. 'My son was handsome,' says Hecuba to Helen (Eur. *Tro.* 987), 'and at sight of him your mind became Cypris. All foolish acts are called Aphrodite by mankind.'[1] The kind of criticism which sought to absolve the gods from the unethical behaviour attached to their names in the myths must not be thought of, and was not thought of at the time,[2] as an attack on religion as such, or even the established state-religion. One of its most vigorous exponents was Plato, who in the *Republic* firmly accused Homer and Hesiod of lying, yet was an implacable opponent of unbelief either in the gods or in their providential care for mankind, and an upholder of the official cults.

Besides moral probity, self-sufficiency was being demanded as an essential property of deity. Aided perhaps by Xenophanes and Eleatic notions of God as 'unmoved' and 'impassible', the rationalism of the time saw the godhead as 'lacking nothing'. These words of Euripides's Heracles can hardly be unconnected with the pronouncement of Antiphon: 'For this reason he has need of nothing, nor does he expect anything from anybody, but is infinite and all-sufficient.'[3] Belief in the

---

[1] Cf. also fr. 254 N.:

> A. Often the gods lead mortal men astray.
> B. You take the easy line, and blame the gods.

G. Devereux has pointed out that Helen's defence is anticipated by what Penelope says about her at *Od.* 23.222. See his *From Anxiety to Method*, 344, n. 2. (The comparison is made by Stanford *ad loc.* in his edition.) But whereas Homer accepts, Euripides, in the person of Hecuba, criticizes.

[2] Decharme (*Critique*, p. vii) has pointed out a reason why no suspicion of impiety attached to this purgation. Fundamentalism was a phenomenon unknown to the Greeks because there was nothing in their religious literature corresponding to the 'word of God'. 'Ils ne crurent point que les dieux eux-mêmes eussent été les auteurs de leur théologie, où ils virent seulement l'œuvre des poètes.'

[3] (*a*) Fr. 10. With Antiphon's οὐδενὸς δεῖται cf. δεῖται γὰρ ὁ θεὸς... οὐδενός in Euripides.

(*b*) There is so much uncertainty about the date of Antiphon's writings (see p. 286, n. 2, below) that it is impossible on external grounds to say whether Euripides is copying this passage from the Ἀλήθεια or not. Some have used 'echoes' of Antiphon in Euripides as actual evidence of his date, but this is a dangerous criterion. Such statements as 'God lacks nothing' could be common to more than one writer of the time, and neither Euripides nor Antiphon need have said it first.

(*c*) The quotation is given in a lexicon (the Suda) to illustrate the meaning of ἀδέητος. Since context is lacking, the reason referred to in διὰ τοῦτο is unknown. It is not even stated (but can scarcely be doubted) that the subject is θεός. (For the consensus of scholarly opinion on this point see Untersteiner, *Sophs.* 259, n. 10.)

self-sufficiency of the deity leads naturally to doubts about the reality of any divine providence or care for mankind. The idea which Plato deplored, that 'there are gods, but they take no thought for human affairs' (*Laws* 885 b, 888 c), was current in the fifth century. Xenophon (*Mem.* 1.4.10) represents a man called Aristodemus as protesting to Socrates, when taxed with refusing to give the gods their customary meed of sacrifice and prayer, that far from contemning the divine, he thought it was too great to need his service, and moreover that the gods could have no thought for mankind. Antiphon is said to have denied providence in the same work *On Truth* in which he declared the self-sufficiency of God and spoke of the advisability of conforming to conventional morality only when under observation;[1] and Thrasymachus saw in the prevalence of wickedness evidence that the gods are blind to what goes on among men (p. 97 above).

The rationalism of the natural philosophers was not completely atheistic (as we should use the word) but none the less destructive of the traditional and official pantheon. In the Ionian tradition divinity for long was identified with the living *physis* of the world, until Anaxagoras separated it as a remote Mind which started the cosmic process in the beginning. More important to his contemporaries than the existence of this Mind was his reduction of the all-seeing Helios, who traversed the sky every day in his flashing chariot and was the awful witness of men's most sacred oaths, to the status of a lifeless lump of glowing stone. Euripides was bold enough to introduce this description into his tragedies and it made such a deeply unfavourable

---

(*d*) I have translated ἄπειρος by infinite. Luria suggested that there was a double meaning: (i) infinite, (ii) untried, and Untersteiner has followed him (*Sophs.* 259, n. 13). But in the passages which he cited as parallel (Plato, *Phil.* 17 e and *Tim.* 55 d), the second meaning is active (ignorant, inexperienced). LSJ give no example of the passive sense (unexperienced, unknown or untried), nor do I know of any.

(*e*) Untersteiner (*Sophs.* 260, n. 13 a, *Sof.* IV, 42 f.) thinks Xen. *Mem.* 1.6.10 is proof that Antiphon was not giving his own view but one that he was opposing. Schmid (*Gesch.* 1.3.1, 160) takes the fr. at its face value and includes *Mem.* 1.6.3 among his references without comment. The reader may take his choice. Personally I think even Xenophon's Socrates was capable of a bit of raillery. What he says is: 'You seem to imagine that happiness consists in luxury and extravagance, ἐγὼ δὲ νομίζω τὸ μὲν μηδενὸς δεῖσθαι θεῖον εἶναι', slyly bringing up his own words against him.

[1] Fr. 12, from Origen. For references to modern opinions about this see Untersteiner, *Sophs.* 264, n. 74. It should be noted that Untersteiner is one of those who believe that the whole passage *Laws* 888 d–890 a reproduces the doctrine of Antiphon. See *Sophs.* 231, n. 17, 263, n. 70, 265, n. 91, and *Sof.* IV, 178 ff.

impression on the Athenian mind that not only was it said to have been the occasion of Anaxagoras's banishment but Meletus thought it worth while to try to implicate Socrates in it at his trial.[1] But the most popular philosophic theology was that which identified divinity with the air or *aither*, revived as a scientific theory at this time by Diogenes of Apollonia and easily absorbed by popular thought owing to its affinities with ancient beliefs.[2] Its familiarity is shown by the invocation of Socrates to the 'Lord and Master, measureless Air' in the *Clouds*, and the identification of air or *aither* with Zeus in the prayer of Hecuba in Euripides's *Troades*. *Aither* also takes the name of Zeus in two other places in Euripides. The atomic gods of Democritus were even farther removed from official religion.[3]

It is hard to arrive at the mind of Euripides himself, beyond saying that he was intensely interested in the most advanced thinking of his day. He speaks through his characters, who mirror almost every point of view,[4] and it is as such a mirror of his time that he is (for our present purposes, naturally) best regarded. A woman in the *Thesmophoriazusae* accuses him roundly of atheism (450f. 'In his tragedies he persuades men that the gods do not exist'), but the comic poet has hardly made her an impartial witness. Plutarch (*Amat.* 756b–c) says that, when the *Melanippe* was first performed, the line (fr. 480) 'Zeus, whoever Zeus may be, for I know not save by hearsay' caused such an uproar in the theatre that for a second production he altered it to 'Zeus, as truth itself has said'.[5] A similar phrase, 'whatever the gods may be', occurs in the *Orestes* (418) in a context of outspoken criticism of divine powers.[6]

---

[1] See vol. II, 307, 269 and 323, Plato, *Apol.* 26d.   [2] Vol. II, chapter VII, and vol. I, 128 ff.

[3] See vol. II, 310 f., and Eur. frr. 877, 941 (quoted from unknown plays and without context); also Euripides's αἰθήρ ἐμὸν βόσκημα at *Frogs* 892. For Democritus vol. II, 478 ff., esp. p. 480, n. 1. There may be a flavour of Democritus in *Tro.* 886, but the idea was widespread. Ἀήρ and αἰθήρ were interchangeable in these contexts (vol. II, 480). In the *Clouds* it is ἀήρ who ἔχεις τὴν γῆν μετέωρον, and γῆς ὄχημα at *Tro.* 884 must be the same, whereas in fr. 941 it is αἰθήρ which 'holds the earth in its buxom arms'.

[4] Though Lucian, *Zeus trag.* 41, quotes both fr. 941 and fr. 480 as places where Euripides is speaking his real mind, not bound by the exigencies of the dramatic situation.

[5] It is curious that the same line occurred in the *Peirithous*, now generally attributed to Critias (Eur. fr. 591.4 N. = Critias fr. 16.9 DK).

[6] The expressions of Euripides show a quite different spirit from some in Aeschylus which superficially might be thought to resemble them.

(i) The famous fr. of the *Heliades* (fr. 70),

Ζεύς ἐστιν αἰθήρ, Ζεὺς δὲ γῆ, Ζεὺς δ' οὐρανός,
Ζεύς τοι τὰ πάντα, χὦτι τῶνδ' ὑπέρτερον,

A striking choric passage which must surely express his own outlook is fr. 910 where he speaks of the happiness of a man who has learned the ways of scientific inquiry and observes 'the ageless order and beauty¹ (*kosmos*) of immortal nature, and how it was put together'. Such a man, he says, will have no part in wicked or injurious deeds. This praise of *historia* is not necessarily inconsistent with the disparagement of *meteorologoi* in fr. 913: 'Beholding these things, who is not conscious of god?² Who does not cast far from him the deceitful wiles of the star-gazers, whose mischievous tongues, void of sense, babble at random of matters unknown?' Misguided probing into the secrets of nature has brought some to atheism, but for a wise man the ageless *kosmos* which she reveals can only lead to the conclusion that there is a god, an intelligent orderer, in or behind it. Fr. 913 can stand beside the air- or *aither*-god of the *Troades* and frr. 877 and 941, and the god of Diogenes from whom they doubtless derive, the air which is also a conscious planning mind (vol. ii, 369). If it does not preach the Olympian religion, it is far from being atheism. Lacking the context, we do not know for certain what 'these things' are, the sight of which makes one aware of the divine, but, if we assume them to be natural, and especially celestial, phenomena, the lesson of the passage is the same as Plato's in the *Laws* (967a–c): understanding of the *taxis* (orderly arrangement) of the stars does not lead to atheism but to an awareness of the mind that brought about this *kosmos*. Astronomers (says Plato) got the name of atheists because some of the earlier ones thought that the heavenly bodies were mere dead masses carried round by necessity. But even among these the keener minds suspected that

does not reflect any rationalistic theories about an air-god, but clearly conveys the idea that Zeus is present in all the manifestations of nature and at the same time transcends them. It is deeply felt pantheism—the poet is conscious of a living spirit in earth and sky and everything else—and something more besides. Comparison with the last lines of Sophocles's *Trachiniae* (Lloyd-Jones in *JHS*, 1956, 55) misses the mark badly, for τούτων there refers to the changes and chances of human life, not to 'aither, earth, sky and all things'.

(ii) At *Ag.* 160 the chorus invoke Ζεύς, ὅστις ποτ' ἐστίν, but the following words show that this is the familiar case of a piety apprehensive lest it offend by addressing a god by the wrong name or one that is displeasing to him (as in Euripides himself, fr. 912, where ὁ πάντων μεδέων is addressed with the words Ζεύς εἴτ' Ἀίδης ὀνομαζόμενος στέργεις); and, as in the *Heliades* fr., the feeling expressed seems to be that Zeus is omnipresent: 'All things have I measured, yet nought have I found save Zeus.'

¹ The complex force of *kosmos* cannot be rendered by one word. Cf. vol. i, 110 and 206.
² θεὸν οὐχὶ νοεῖ. For the meaning of νοεῖν see vol. ii, 17 ff.

their perfectly calculated movements could not have been achieved without intelligence, and decided that, although the stars themselves might be lifeless clods and stones, there was a mind behind them directing their movement and the whole cosmic order.

(2) AGNOSTICISM: PROTAGORAS

According to Diogenes Laertius (9.24), the Eleatic philosopher Melissus said that it was wrong to make any pronouncement about the gods, because knowledge of them was impossible. But the classic case of an agnostic in this century is his contemporary Protagoras, who was famous for having written:

Concerning the gods I am unable to discover whether they exist or not, or what they are like in form; for there are many hindrances to knowledge, the obscurity of the subject and the brevity of human life.

The full text is quoted by Diogenes Laertius and Eusebius, and the major part by Sextus,[1] and much nearer his own time it is referred to by Plato, who in the *Theaetetus* (162d) imagines the great Sophist as objecting to the introduction of gods into the discussion, 'whose existence or non-existence I expressly refuse to discuss in my speeches and writings'. The form of the statement as one of personal opinion ('I am unable...') contrasts significantly with an expression like that of Xenophanes fr. 34, that no man has seen, nor will any man ever know, the truth about the gods. Some believed in gods and some did not, and so, in accordance with the 'man the measure' principle, gods existed for some and not for others; but for Protagoras himself suspension of judgment was the only possible course.[2] Sextus and the Epicurean Diogenes of Oenoanda indefensibly ranked him with the atheists, but Cicero carefully distinguishes them.[3] The sentence is said to have stood at the opening of a work (or section of a work)

[1] See Protagoras fr. 4 and A 12 DK. It is also referred to by Timon of Phlius (quoted by Sextus, *loc. cit.*), Philostratus (*V. Soph.* 1.10.2 = A 2), Cicero (*N.D.* 1.1.2, 12.29 and 23.63), and Diogenes of Oenoanda (A 23).

[2] Cf. Jaeger, *TEGP*, 189. This disposes satisfactorily of T. Gomperz's contention (*GT*, I, 457) that if Protagoras had believed, as Plato said he did, that 'every man's truth is the truth which appears to him', he could not have said what he did about the gods.

[3] *N.D.* 1.1.2, 'Dubitare se Protagoras, nullos esse omnino Diagoras Melius et Theodorus Cyrenaicus putaverunt'. Cf. *ibid.* 23.63, 42.117.

234

called 'On the Gods',[1] and scholars have naturally wondered what could have followed on such an unpromising beginning. We shall never know, but 'there is nothing against supposing' (to adopt a phrase from the latest commentator)[2] that it upheld religious worship and cult according to the ancestral *nomoi*. Not only was this an integral part of the life of the *polis*, that civilized social and political community of whose value, and indeed necessity, he was firmly convinced, but also the instinct for worship was probably in his view an original and ineradicable trait of human nature.[3] (Cf. p. 65 above.)

(3) ATHEISM: DIAGORAS, PRODICUS, CRITIAS; PLATO'S TWO TYPES OF ATHEIST

'As a dogmatic creed, consisting in the denial of every kind of supernatural power, atheism has not often been seriously maintained at any period of civilized thought.' So A. C. Pearson, in a brief article whose main merit is to demonstrate the difficulty of establishing beyond doubt that any Greek thinker was an atheist in the full sense.[4] There is first the need to distinguish a rejection of traditional polytheism from denial of the whole idea of divinity, secondly the fragmentary and sometimes untrustworthy character of our authorities for this period, and thirdly the tendency to use a charge of atheism as a weapon against any public

[1] D.L. 9.52 and 54, Eus. *P.E.* 14.3.7 = Prot. fr. 4, Cic. *N.D.* 23.63 (without title). For σύγγραμμα applied to part of a work see Untersteiner, *Sof.* 1, 78, von Fritz, *RE*, xlv. Halbb. 919. The 'title' of a prose work at this time often consisted, as in this case, of the opening words. (See C. W. Müller, *Hermes*, 1967, 145.)

[2] 'Nichts spricht gegen die Vermutung', C. W. Müller. Earlier conjectures were collected by Nestle, *VMzuL*, 278–82. Untersteiner (*Sophs.* 38, n. 47) criticizes Nestle's, partly because it does not fit his own conviction that π. θεῶν was part of the 'Αντιλογίαι (in which he follows H. Gomperz, *S. u. R.* 131). Müller (*Hermes*, 1967) also thinks Nestle's suggestion neither demonstrable nor probable, but his own is of course, like everyone else's, no more than 'Vermutung'. Nestle's idea (see also his edition of the *Protagoras*, p. 18) was that the work was directed against popular proofs of the existence of gods and their care for men, and he adduced in support the official anger which there is some evidence that it aroused at Athens.

[3] Müller (*Hermes*, 1967, 143f.) offers a new and subtle interpretation of *Prot.* 322a. ὁ ἄνθρωπος θείας μετέσχε μοίρας κτλ. is a mythical reversal of the 'homo mensura' dictum: man's 'kinship with the gods' means, when stripped of mythical clothing, that the gods are simply projections or reflections of humanity. This interpretation, he says, removes the objection to regarding the Platonic passage as genuinely Protagorean. I doubt if it is necessary for that purpose (cf. p. 65 above and my *In the Beginning*, 88f. and 141f., nn. 10 and 11), but it has its attractions nevertheless.

[4] 'Atheism (Greek and Roman)', in Hastings, *ERE*, vol. 11, 184f.

figure whom on other grounds it was desired to discredit. As the case of Socrates shows, we must be careful about accepting such an imputation at its face value, and conversely one or two of his contemporaries whom later antiquity regarded, with some reason, as out-and-out atheists seem never to have been brought to trial. That such atheists ('complete disbelievers in the existence of the gods', 908b) were common by Plato's time is certain from his mentions of them in the *Laws*, where he carefully distinguishes them from those who hold (*a*) that gods exist but have no interest in human conduct, (*b*) that they can be bought off by offerings.

In later writers we find a kind of stock list of atheists, that is, those who denied outright the existence of the gods.[1] It included Diagoras of Melos, Prodicus of Ceos, Critias and (of a later date) Euhemerus of Tegea and Theodorus of Cyrene. Diagoras in particular never appears without having 'the atheist' tacked on to his name. Yet, if he defended his atheism by any philosophical arguments, we know nothing at all of what they were.[2] The only reason alleged for it, and that in late sources, is moral: he is said to have begun as a god-fearing dithyrambic poet, who later became convinced of the non-existence of gods by the spectacle of successful and unpunished wrongdoing, in this case a specific injury done to himself, though its nature is variously reported. Besides his unbelief, the only other fact recorded about him by contemporaries is that he was convicted on a charge of impiety by the

---

[1] They φασι μὴ εἶναι θεούς (*Aët.* 1.7.1) or 'omnino deos esse negabant' (Cic. *N.D.* 1.42. 117f.). Cic. *ibid.* 118 adds, though without naming him, the theory of Critias, who appears by name in Sextus's list (*P.H.* 3.218) and with Diagoras in Plutarch, *De superst.* 171c. See also Sext. *Math.* 9.51–5. On the origin of the list in the περὶ ἀθεότητος of the Academic Clitomachus (second century B.C.) see Diels, *Dox.* 58f., and Nestle, *VMℓuL*, 416. For Hippon, known as ἄθεος and occurring in the list of Clem. Alex. (DK, 38 A 8), see vol. II, 354ff.

[2] All the sources of information on Diagoras are printed in full by Jacoby, *Diagoras ὁ ἄθεος* (*Abh. Berl.* 1959), 3–8. (He is omitted from DK.) For modern literature see *ibid.* 31f., n. 2, and Woodbury, *Phoenix*, 1965, 178, n. 1. Perusal of the different arguments and conclusions of Jacoby and Woodbury will tell a reader all he needs to know about Diagoras-problems. The Suda (Jacoby, p. 5) calls him a philosopher (as well as a lyric poet) and says that he wrote a book, with the unintelligible title of Ἀποπυργίζοντες λόγοι, describing his abandonment of religious belief. Jerome (see Woodbury, *op. cit.* 178, n. 5) makes him out to have been a φυσικός with a following. His book was already known to Aristoxenus in the fourth century (*ap.* Philodemus, Jacoby, p. 5 = Aristoxenus fr. 127a, Wehrli, *Schule des Ar.* vol. x, p. 198), which, *pace* Woodbury (p. 207), is more significant than the fact that Aristoxenus wished to athetize it. The book, or one called Φρύγιοι λόγοι (which may be the same), is mentioned in a number of late sources, but beyond the meagre words of the Suda we have no clue as to its contents.

Athenians, and a price put on his head in his absence from the city. Aristophanes (*Birds* 1071 ff.) does not specify the charge, and pseudo-Lysias (*Andoc.* 17) says merely that he 'committed impiety against the rites and festivals in words'. Later writers say that he insulted the gods by mocking and divulging the Eleusinian mysteries. This is not the same as a charge of intellectual atheism, but puts him more in line with Alcibiades and his friends who parodied the mysteries, or with the unknown mutilators of the Hermae. The evidence of Aristophanes suggests that his trial took place about the same time, shortly before the launching of the Sicilian expedition, when nerves were taut and the city prone to take instant alarm at anything which might offend the gods or be of evil omen.[1] Nevertheless, though it may have been some such irreverent frivolity that led to his actual prosecution, the fact of his out-and-out atheism cannot be doubted. Jacoby is right when he says that all witnesses alike attribute to him 'a repudiation pure and simple of the whole concept of gods, an atheism radical, extreme and uncompromising'. This goes back to his contemporary Aristophanes, for whom (and for his audience) Socrates could be immediately branded as an atheist by calling him 'Socrates the Melian'.[2]

Since nothing is known of Diagoras's mind save the fact of his disbelief in the gods, he cannot claim much space in a history of philosophy. More interesting are those who are known to have held a

[1] At *Birds* 1071 f. Aristophanes introduces a quotation from the actual decree outlawing Diagoras (which is known also from other sources: see Jacoby, p. 4) with the words τῆδε θἠμέρᾳ ἐπαναγορεύεται. The allusion would have had little point if it were not topical, and the *Birds* was produced in 414. I do not see that any other evidence can stand against this, and Jacoby's attempt to make Diagoras a victim of the decree of Diopeithes in 433/2 has been countered by Woodbury in his *Phoenix* article.

[2] The ousting of Zeus by Dinos does not mean that Socrates is here accused of introducing δαιμόνια καινά, but that he agrees with those who were substituting natural (ἀναγκαῖα) forces, like the vortex of the atomists and others, for gods. Woodbury (*op. cit.* 208) contends that before the Hellenistic age (i.e. at the time when the label was first attached to Diagoras) ἄθεος did not mean 'atheist' but only 'godless' or 'god-forsaken', but this is not so. Plato, *Apol.* 26c, does not 'show the transition from one meaning to the other'. When Socrates says καὶ αὐτὸς ἄρα νομίζω εἶναι θεοὺς καὶ οὐκ εἰμὶ τὸ παράπαν ἄθεος, he shows that ἄθεος already means 'not believing in the existence of the gods'. Nor can Woodbury's argument from the use of νομίζειν be allowed. It *may* occasionally be possible to translate νομίζειν θεούς as 'pay respect, or customary worship, to the gods' (as at Aesch. *Pers.* 497–8, though even here the meaning 'believe in' would be equally appropriate), but never of course with εἶναι, and usually (as in the same sentence of the *Apology*) νομίζειν and νομίζειν εἶναι are used interchangeably. There is no need to go into this, or cite once again examples like Hdt. 4.59.1 or Plato, *Laws* 885c, because the point was demonstrated, it is to be hoped finally, by J. Tate in *CR*, 1936 and 1937.

particular theory of the natural and human origin of the belief in gods. Democritus saw it, partly at least, in fear of the more violent manifestations of nature (vol. II, 478). Prodicus, like many of his contemporaries, was interested in the origins of things. This included cosmogony (for the comic cosmogony of the birds in Aristophanes, *Birds* 684ff., is offered as an alternative to Prodicus) and more particularly, as befitted a Sophist, anthropology. Unlike Democritus, he saw the origin of religious belief in gratitude, not fear. We have the following reports:[1]

(*a*) Philodemus (Epicurean of first century B.C.) *De piet. c.* 9, ed. Gomperz p. 75: 'Persaeus[2] shows himself destructive, or utterly ignorant, of the divine when in his book on the gods he declares not improbable what Prodicus wrote, namely that the things that nourish and benefit us were the first to be considered gods and honoured as such, and after them the discoverers of foods and shelter and the other practical arts such as Demeter, Dionysus and the . . .' [*break in papyrus*]

(*b*) Minucius Felix (second to third century A.D.), *Octavius* 21.2 (text omitted by DK but given in Untersteiner, *Sof.* II, 192, and Nestle, *VMʒuL*, 354, n. 22): 'Prodicus says that those were accepted as gods who in their journeyings discovered new crops and so contributed to human welfare.'

(*c*) Cicero, *N.D.* 1.37.118: 'What sort of religion did Prodicus of Ceos leave us, who said that things useful to human life were accounted gods?'

(*d*) *Ibid.* 15.38: 'Persaeus says that those were considered gods who had discovered what was especially useful for civilized life, and that things useful and salutary were themselves called by the names of gods.'

(*e*) Sext. *Math.* 9.18: 'Prodicus of Ceos says, "The ancients considered as gods the sun and moon, rivers, springs, and in general all the things that assist our life, on account of the help they give, just as the Egyptians deify the Nile." He adds that for this reason bread was called Demeter, wine Dionysus, water Poseidon, fire Hephaestus, and so on with everything that was of service.' (This is repeated in slightly different words in chapter 52.)

(*f*) *Ibid.* 51 includes Prodicus in a list of atheists 'who say there is no god'.

(*g*) *Ibid.* 39–41 criticizes 'those who say that the ancients supposed that all the things which benefit life are gods—sun and moon, rivers and lakes and the like', on the grounds (*a*) that the ancients could not have been so stupid as to ascribe divinity to things they saw perishing or even ate and destroyed themselves, and (*b*) that on this argument one ought also to believe

---

[1] Some of the passages are in DK (Prodicus fr. 5), and all in Untersteiner, *Sof.* II, 191 ff.
[2] Stoic and pupil of Zeno, *c.* 306–243 B.C.

that men, especially philosophers, are gods, and even animals and inanimate utensils, for all these work for us and improve our lot.

(*h*) The thirtieth oration of Themistius (fourth century A.D.) is an encomium of husbandry containing the kind of exaggerated claims that had been commonplace at least since the days of Isocrates,[1] about agriculture not only providing the means of subsistence but being the mother of all civilized life, the begetter of laws, justice, peace, cities, temples, philosophy and much else. In the course of this he speaks (p. 422 Dindorf) of 'the wisdom of Prodicus, who derived all religious practices, mysteries and initiations from the benefits of agriculture, believing that the very notion of gods came to men from this source and making it the guarantee of piety'.[2]

These passages, the authors of which range in date from 400 to 800 years after Prodicus, exemplify the wretchedly inadequate material at our disposal for reconstructing the thoughts of a fifth-century Sophist. But we must do our best. Philodemus presents a theory, rather like some in the nineteenth century, of the development of religion from the cult of inanimate objects to the deification of culture-heroes, the supposed discoverers of the amenities and arts which raised mankind from the beasts to civilization. It has been disputed whether the second half of the statement, and so the two-stage theory of religion, should be credited to Prodicus or only to Persaeus. The former not only conforms better to the run of the sentence[3] but also accords with Minucius Felix (passage *b*) and Cicero (*d*). The important thing about the latter is not that he attributes the theory to Persaeus (for we know from Philodemus that Persaeus accepted it) but that he puts both halves together as parts of one and the same theory. Sextus, it is true (passage *g*), ridicules the idea that beneficial objects or products were ever deified on the grounds (among others) that it would be as reasonable to believe in the deification of men. I hesitate to adopt Untersteiner's solution of this difficulty, namely that the 'dis-

---

[1] *Paneg.* 28. See p. 62 with n. 2 above.

[2] θεῶν ἔννοιαν is probably right, though since it is a correction by Diels of εὔνοιαν (which Dindorf printed) it is misleading of DK and Untersteiner to adopt it with no comment. See Nestle, *VMzuL*, 352, n. 14. In the last phrase, καὶ πᾶσαν εὐσέβειαν ἐγγυώμενος, Untersteiner prints the widely different conjecture of Kalbfleisch, ἐγγενέσθαι. As will appear, a point of some substance could depend on this. Diels, followed by Untersteiner, supposed a lacuna after ἀσέβειαν.

[3] See Untersteiner, *Sophs.* 221, n. 9, or *Sof.* II, 191 f., Nestle, *VMzuL*, 354.

coverers' whom Prodicus supposed to have been deified were never in fact men, because I am not convinced that it is right or even that I understand it correctly.[1] On the other hand, even if Sextus had Prodicus chiefly in mind, he is casting his criticism in general form, and although the unexpressed conclusion of his argument might seem most naturally to be 'and nobody believes that', this is impossible, for Sextus was well aware of the belief that gods were deified men. He speaks of the theory of Euhemerus more than once.[2] This however lands us in a further difficulty, because in chapters 51 and 52 Prodicus's theory is not only described (repeating chapter 18) as a theory of the deification of sun, moon, rivers, springs, and other beneficial objects, but expressly distinguished, as a different form of atheism, from that of Euhemerus who believed in the deification of 'men of power'. It must be said then that the evidence of Sextus is decisively against a 'Euhemeristic' theory for Prodicus, though that of Philodemus and Minucius Felix is in favour of it (if Minucius was only paraphrasing Philodemus, at least he took him in this sense), and to a lesser extent that of Cicero, *N.D.* 1.15.38. Taking all things into account (including Cic. *N.D.* 1.37.118), it must at least be agreed that the feature of Prodicus's theory which made the greatest impression was that the origin of religion lay in the tendency of primitive man to regard things useful to his life—including sun, moon and rivers as well as bread and wine—as gods.[3] This theory would come easily to the mind of a rationalizing Greek, for in his literature from Homer onwards he would find the name of the appropriate god used for the substance itself, as Hephaestus for fire ('They spitted the entrails and held them over Hephaestus', *Il.* 2.426), and the sun, moon and rivers *were* gods.

[1] His n. 27 on pp. 222f. of *Sophs.* I find very obscure. If the discoverers were not originally men, what were they before they 'were received among the gods' (p. 211)? His language here does not suggest that he thinks they were purely mythical for Prodicus, and I cannot reconcile p. 210 and p. 223 at all.

[2] *Math.* 9.17, 34 (without name), 51. He would know, too, that the theory was older and went back to Prodicus's time, for there are traces of it in Herodotus. (See Nestle, *VMzuL*, 354f.) He must also have known that even man-made σκεύη, like the hearth (Hestia), were worshipped as gods.

[3] The theory of two stages of religious development is claimed for Prodicus by Nestle (*VMzuL*, 353f.), whom others follow including Untersteiner (*Sof.* II, 92, *Sophs.* 211 and 222, n. 7) and Versényi (*Socr. Hum.* 59f.). None of these takes into account the way in which Sextus contrasts the theory, as that of the deification of useful objects, with that of Euhemerus.

'My suitor was a river', says Deianeira quite naturally (Soph. *Trach.* 9), and, being a god, he could take any form he wished—a bull, a serpent or a man, as well as water. Empedocles gave the names of gods to the four elements, and (for what it is worth) Epiphanius says that Prodicus called them gods, as well as the sun and moon, 'because the life of everything depends on them'.[1]

A remarkable passage in the *Bacchae* (274ff.) shows how easily the Greek mind could slip from the idea of a substance as embodying a living god to that of the god as its inventor or discoverer. Attempting to soften the impious hostility of Pentheus to Dionysus, Tiresias tells him that

two things are primary in human life: first, the goddess Demeter—she is Earth, but call her by which name you like [and of course Ge, the earth, was a great goddess by that name too]. She gives men all nourishment that is of a dry nature. To balance this came Semele's son, who *discovered* the flowing liquor of the grape ... He, being a god, is poured out to the gods.[2]

Here Dionysus, the god of wine, is described at the same time, with no sense of incongruity, as the discoverer of wine and the wine itself. Here, therefore, in all probability, is the key to Prodicus's doctrine. In the pious prophet Tiresias he would see a perfect example (and, since Euripides is sure to have known his teaching, he too saw an example) of the mentality out of which religion arose: to ask whether men imagined their food, drink and other life-giving or life-enhancing things as gods, or alternatively the beings who discovered and provided them, was to make a psychologically unreal distinction. Dionysus was at the same time wine and the giver of wine, Hephaestus fire and the giver of fire.

Was Prodicus an atheist?[3] Certainly all antiquity thought so.

---

[1] Epiph. *Adv. haer.* 3.21 (*Dox.* 591 and Untersteiner, *Sof.* II, 194, not in DK). Too much attention should not be paid to this. The Christian writer is running hastily through all the philosophers, one sentence to each, and commits some glaring blunders.

[2] There is no need to translate the perfect participle γεγώς as 'when he had become' ('zum Gott geworden', Nestle *VMzuL*, 354) and so see two chronological stages. The perfect forms of γίγνομαι mean rather 'to be'. For the god who is wine cf. the Indian parallel in Dodds, *Bacch.* 100f., who quotes Sir Charles Eliot on Vedic hymns addressed to Soma: 'It is hard to say whether they are addressed to a person or a beverage.'

[3] In trying to reconstruct Prodicus's outlook on religion and human life, I have thought it best not to follow scholars like Cataudella and Untersteiner in using the *Birds* of Aristophanes as a source. (See Untersteiner, *Sophs.* 221, n. 3, and 223, n. 33.) They may be right, but the only

Dodds (*ad loc.*) identifies Tiresias's speech with the doctrine of Prodicus, and then says that the reason why it can be put in the mouth of a pious and believing character is that Prodicus's doctrine was not in fact atheistic. I have already offered a different explanation: to believe that wine and bread are gods is of course not atheistic, it is precisely the belief which Prodicus said 'the ancients' had and from which religion arose. To Prodicus himself they were just wine and bread. The relevant passages in Sextus, of which Dodds quotes one, are offered as explanations of his atheism. Dodds translates the last words of the Themistius passage (*h*) as a claim that Prodicus had 'put piety on a sound foundation', but even if the verb is not corrupt (see p. 239, n. 2, above), it need not mean that, and the claim that the very conception of gods resulted from the practice of agriculture does not sound as if it came from a believer in them. Prodicus may be justly hailed as one of the earliest anthropologists, with a theory about the purely human origin of belief in gods which would not have disgraced the nineteenth century. In this theory, as the passage from Themistius shows, he laid especial stress on the evidential value of agricultural practices. This was entirely natural and reasonable when one considers, first, the belief already current that not only our food but all the benefits of a settled and civilized life are owed to this source, and secondly the number and variety of religious cults that in fact owe their existence to the fertility of the soil. Prodicus, as was to be expected of one who was both Sophist and natural philosopher, and wrote on cosmogony, evidently subscribed to a 'progress', not a 'degeneration', theory of human development (pp. 60 f. above); and, like Protagoras, he thought of religion, along with settled conditions, the building of cities, the rule of law and the advancement of knowledge, as one of the fruits of civilization and essential to its preservation. To hold these views it is not necessary to believe in the existence of gods as the objects of worship independently of men's conception of them.[1]

certain inference from the mention of Prodicus at *v.* 692 is that he produced a cosmogony of some sort, perhaps the very latest. It may equally be true that his name is simply being used to stand for any μετεωροσοφιστής (*Clouds* 360): the birds can do better than any of these.

[1] In my *In the Beginning* (p. 142, n. 11) I quoted the case of Frederic Harrison, who 'regarded all religions as false, but insisted on the human necessity of worship'. Versényi (*Socr. Hum.* 60) points out that 'giving a psychological foundation to religion ... is not tantamount to saying that religion has no legitimate basis'. It is true that a modern Christian can accept such an origin

Critias[1] was a wealthy aristocrat who would have disdained to be a professional Sophist, yet he shared the intellectual outlook which came to be known as sophistic. In his play *Sisyphus*[2] he depicted religious belief as a deliberate imposture by government to ensure an ultimate and universal sanction for the good behaviour of its subjects. Although the speech is put into the mouth of Sisyphus himself, the notorious sinner who no doubt received his well-known punishment by the end of the play, this is a fairly obvious device of the author's for promulgating an atheistic view without giving too much offence.[3] It starts with a brief account, which has already been quoted (p. 82 above), of the progress of human life from lawless brutality to the introduction of laws, punishment and justice. This we know from other sources to have been a seriously held current view. It continues (fr. 25.9ff.):

Then when the laws prevented men from open deeds of violence, but they continued to commit them in secret, I believe that a man of shrewd and subtle mind invented for men the fear of the gods, so that there might be something to frighten the wicked even if they acted, spoke or thought in secret. From this motive he introduced the conception of divinity. There is, he said, a spirit enjoying endless life, hearing and seeing with his mind, exceedingly wise and all-observing, bearer of a divine nature. He will hear everything spoken among men and can see everything that is done. If you are silently plotting evil, it will not be hidden from the gods, so clever are they. With this story he presented the most seductive[4] of teachings, concealing the truth with lying words. For a dwelling he gave them the place whose mention would most powerfully strike the hearts of men, whence, as he knew, fears come to mortals and help for their wretched lives; that is,

for human belief in God without abandoning his conviction of its truth, but this seems to me to represent a stage of thought well ahead of the pioneers of rationalism. (Drachmann (*Atheism*, 43 f.), like Dodds and Versényi, thought Prodicus believed in—indeed 'took for granted'—the existence of gods, and did not connect the question of their existence with that of the origin of the conception of them.)

[1] See below, pp. 298ff.

[2] Our sole source for the extract is Sextus (*Math.* 9.54), who attributes it to Critias. Some ancient authorities gave Euripides as the author. On the authorship see ZN, 1407, n. 2.

[3] On this, of course, two views are possible. For the opposite one see Drachmann, *Atheism*, 45 f., which goes against Sextus (*P.H.* 3.218, *Math.* 9.54) and Plutarch (*De superst.* 171c). Schmid (*Gesch.* 180f.) thought that in any case no Athenian archon would have allowed the play to be performed, and Critias must have intended it only for reading.

[4] ἥδιστον is strange in this context of fear, and Nauck's suggestion of κέρδιστον (*TGF*[2], 773) is tempting. Though he does not say so, Nauck doubtless had Eur. *El.* 743f. in mind (quoted on p. 244, n. 3, below).

the vault above, where he perceived the lightnings and the dread roars of thunder, and the starry face and form of heaven fair-wrought by the cunning craftmanship of time; whence too the burning meteor[1] makes its way, and the liquid rain descends on the earth. With such fears did he surround mankind, and so by his story give the godhead a fair home in a fitting place, and extinguished lawlessness by his ordinances ... So, I think, first of all, did someone persuade men to believe that there exists a race of gods.

This is the first occurrence in history of the theory of religion as a political invention to ensure good behaviour, which was elaborately developed by Polybius at Rome and revived in eighteenth-century Germany.[2] There is no other mention of it at this time, so it may well have been as original as it was daring,[3] and ingenious in the way in which it subsumes under a more general theory the teaching of both Democritus and Prodicus that belief in gods was a product of either the fear or the gratitude produced by certain natural phenomena. At the same time the theory reverses the increasing volume of criticism which attacked the gods on moral grounds, insisting that if they existed, or deserved the name of gods, they ought to be the guardians of the approved moral code. It was the demand for a supernatural sanction for moral behaviour, says Critias, which brought the gods into being in the first place.

This exhausts the list of those known to have argued, on some

[1] Or the sun (DK, Untersteiner). I have hesitantly followed R. G. Bury in the Loeb Sextus (against DK) in taking λαμπρὸς ἀστέρος μύδρος to refer to meteors or meteorites. (He gives no note.) Critias, it is true, was writing after Anaxagoras had called the sun μύδρος διάπυρος, and sun and rain make a natural pair as two of the ὀνήσεις of mortal life. This seems to me slightly outweighed by the difficulty of taking ὅθεν with both rain and sun: rain comes *from* the sky, but not, surely, the sun. In pseudo-Ar. *De mundo* (395 b 23) μύδροι διάπυροι are the stones thrown out by volcanoes, and after all it was probably the fall of the meteorite at Aegospotami that gave Anaxagoras the idea that sun and stars might *also* be μύδροι. (If Wecklein's στίλβει, not the MS στείχει, is what Critias wrote, this would obviate the difficulty of ὅθεν.)

[2] See H. Trevelyan, *Popular Background to Goethe's Hellenism*, 28, n. 2. It is however not the same as theories of the exploitation by politicians of already existing religious beliefs, current in and after the Renaissance and culminating in Marxism, which are identified with it by Nestle (*VMzuL*, 419).

[3] Eur. *El.* 743 f. φοβεροὶ δὲ βροτοῖσι μῦθοι κέρδος πρὸς θεῶν θεραπείαν may echo it, though to say 'fear is conducive to worship of the gods' is not the same as saying that worship based on fear is conducive to good behaviour and was invented to that end; and to express disbelief in the more incredible of the myths (λέγεται, τὰν δὲ πίστιν σμικρὰν παρ' ἔμοιγ' ἔχει v. 737) was certainly not atheism. There is absolutely no evidence for Nestle's contention (*VMzuL*, 416) that Diagoras's atheism was based on the same theory as that of Critias, and was indeed its source.

kind of theoretical ground, that the gods were fictions of the human mind, for of Hippon's atheism we know no more than of Diagoras (vol. ii, 355). But it is hard to believe that the immoralist upholders of *physis* against *nomos*, like Callicles and Antiphon (or those whose views he depicts), held any sort of religious beliefs. At the most, they could have subscribed to Plato's second type of error, that gods exist but have no interest in human kind, but it is unlikely that they thought there was much difference between gods that were totally ineffective and no gods at all. Antiphon indeed, with his advice to heed *nomos* before witnesses, but disregard it when unobserved, exhibits precisely the attitude which on Critias's theory prevailed before the gods were invented. Such irreligion must have been common among the intelligentsia of the time. The profanation of the mysteries and the mutilation of the Hermae were not the work of believers. Another instance was Cinesias, a butt of the comic poets of the time on many counts— his inflated verse, unconventional music, physical emaciation, and impiety or 'atheism'. The orator Lysias named him with three others as forming a kind of 'Hell-fire club' or band of Satanists ('Kakodaemonists' as they called themselves), who deliberately chose unlucky or forbidden days on which to dine together and mock the gods and the laws of Athens. He was also said to have defiled a statue of Hecate, an exploit parallel to that of the mutilation of the Hermae.[1] All this may have little direct connexion with the history of philosophy, but together with the rationalism of natural philosophers and Sophists it contributed to the atmosphere in which Plato grew up, and which moved him to construct in opposition a philosophical theology based on a theory of the origin and government of the whole universe and of man's place within it.

---

[1] For the κακοδαιμονισταί see Lysias *ap.* Ath. 12.551e. The defilement of the statue is mentioned by Aristophanes in the *Frogs* (366, cf. *Eccl.* 330), where the scholiast says Cinesias was the perpetrator. For further information about them, Maas in *RE*, xi, 479–81, Dodds, *Gks. and Irrat.* 188f., Woodbury in *Phoenix*, 1965, 210. Woodbury (p. 199) makes the interesting point that such offences of sacrilege and blasphemy 'presuppose the authority of something holy. A black mass implies the authority and validity of the sacrament.' This can be so. Medieval Satanists no doubt believed themselves to be giving allegiance to one of two opposed, and equally real, powers. But it is also possible to commit offences which might bring down the wrath of the gods, if they existed, simply to demonstrate one's confidence that they do not. This, on the evidence, is more likely to be the explanation of the antics of Cinesias and his dining club, and of the perpetrators of other outrages against religion at Athens.

It is of interest that Plato, commonly regarded as the most bigoted and ruthless of theists, distinguishes two types of atheist, one much more dangerous than the other and deserving much more severe treatment. He admits that atheism does not necessarily lead to immoral conduct, and recognizes a type something like the ethical humanists of our own day. The relevant passage is *Laws* 908 b–e:

> Though a man may be a complete unbeliever in the existence of the gods, if he have a naturally upright character he will detest evildoers, and out of a repugnance to wickedness will have no desire to commit wrongful acts, but will shun the unrighteous and be drawn to the good. But there are others who in addition to their belief that there are no gods anywhere are characterized by a lack of self-control in pleasures and pains, combined with a vigorous memory and keen intellect. Both sorts have in common the malady of atheism, but in respect of injury to others the one does far less harm than the other. The one will no doubt have a very free way of speaking about gods, sacrifices and oaths, and by ridiculing others may perhaps make some converts if he is not restrained by punishment; but the other, holding the same opinions but with the reputation of being a gifted man, full of craft and treachery—this is the kind which breeds your diviners and experts in all sorts of quackery. Sometimes also it produces dictators, demagogues, generals, contrivers of private mysteries, and the devices of those called sophists. There are thus many types of atheist, but two which deserve the attention of the legislator. The sins of the hypocrites deserve more than one death or even two, but the others call for admonition and confinement.

In Plato's eyes the first and greatest crime against religion is not open atheism but the encouragement of superstitition. Earlier too, in the *Republic* (364 b–e), he had arraigned the pseudo-priests and prophets who fleeced the gullible rich with spurious Orphic books promising immunity from divine punishment to all who would pay for their rites and incantations. A character in Euripides calls prophecy 'a thing of naught, and full of lies'. The flames of sacrifice, he thinks, and the cries of birds, have nothing to teach us. Good sense and good counsel are the best prophets.[1] But this is not an attack on the gods,

---

[1] From the messenger's speech in the *Helena*, *vv.* 744ff. With 757 γνώμη δ' ἄριστος μάντις ἥ τ' εὐβουλία cf. fr. 973 μάντις δ' ἄριστος ὅστις εἰκάζει καλῶς. According to a late source Antiphon made a similar remark, that μαντική was ἀνθρώπου φρονίμου εἰκασμός (*Gnomol. Vindob.* DK, A 9). This is anecdote, and, according to Plutarch, *Pyth. Or.* 399a (who also quotes Eur. fr. 973 at *Def. or.* 432c), the saying became proverbial. The attack on μαντική goes back to Xenophanes. See Cic. *Div.* 1.3.5 and Aët. 5.1.1 (in DK, 21 A 52).

for he adds: 'Let us sacrifice to the gods and pray for good, but leave prophecy alone.' Nor is Plato condemning all prophecy alike. He fully respected the Delphic oracle, the mouthpiece of Apollo himself, but the mantic art had its higher and lower forms, and there was a whole tribe of mercenary diviners, claiming to tell the will of the gods from the appearance of sacrifices, the flight of birds, or written collections of forged oracles (such as are ridiculed by Aristophanes in the *Birds*) who were bringing religion into contempt. Plato gives yet further evidence of the need to distinguish attempts to purify religion from attacks on religion itself.

(4) MONOTHEISM: ANTISTHENES

To detect and isolate any expressions of pure monotheism in Greek writings is as difficult as to pin down unadulterated atheism. The question of one god or many, so central in the Judaeo-Christian tradition, hardly troubled the Greeks at all. This is manifest even in the works of so philosophical a theologian as Plato, who uses the expression 'god'[1] and 'the gods' indifferently, and often in the closest proximity. Many philosophers were convinced of the existence of a single spirit or intelligence in or behind the universe, but they would not necessarily deny that there was either practical value or an element of truth in the polytheistic beliefs and cults of the cities and the ordinary man. This single godhead, living and intelligent, could be identified, as we have seen in many authors, with a physical element, especially the air or *aither*. An idea which came easily to the Greek mind was that the divine spirit entered, in a higher or lower degree of purity, into creatures of a lower order such as *daimones*, men or even animals. One form of this belief was that the living and divine *aither*, in its less pure form of air, was breathed in and so assimilated by mortals, a doctrine shared by religious mystics and physical philosophers from the time of Anaximenes or earlier.[2] In a climate of thought which saw the problem of 'the one and the many' in these terms, it

---

[1] More often 'the god', for Greek regularly, though not invariably, uses the article, which gives the word less of the character of a proper name than our 'God'. This applies to the New Testament also.

[2] It has occurred frequently, and recently, in these pages, but see especially vol. I, 128 ff.

was not difficult for a philosopher to take the popular gods under his wing by supposing them to be genuine manifestations of 'the divine' (τὸ θεῖον: the abstract expression is frequent) in different aspects. On one point however the philosophers are agreed: 'the divine' itself is not anthropomorphic, whether it be the Logos-fire of Heraclitus, the 'one god' of Xenophanes fr. 23 (vol. I, 374) who is 'in no way like mortals either in body or in mind', the god of Empedocles who is pure thought and expressly denied all bodily parts (fr. 134, vol. II, 256), or the original cosmopoeic Mind of Anaxagoras. Some of these thinkers might be classified, if we wished, as monotheists or pantheists, especially Heraclitus and Xenophanes with their scathing attacks on popular beliefs and cults. No such attacks by Anaxagoras are recorded, but his expression of his own doctrine was extremely outspoken and his prosecution for impiety not surprising. Empedocles on the other hand found room for a number and variety of gods in his unique amalgam of physical science and religion (vol. II, 257ff.). On the whole it is better to avoid these labels, which though made up from Greek roots were alien to the Greeks themselves.

Nevertheless in the period of the Sophists and Socrates which we are now considering there does seem to be one unmistakable expression of a monotheistic view, couched in terms of the current antithesis between *nomos* and *physis*. It is that of Socrates's disciple Antisthenes, whose theory of the relation of language to reality we have already examined, and as usual we have only tantalizing little fragments of indirect testimony. Said to come from a work on Nature, they are to the effect that 'according to *nomos* there are many gods, but in nature, or in reality, there is one' (κατὰ δὲ φύσιν ἕνα). So Philodemus the Epicurean reports, and Cicero's Epicurean (all our other versions are in Latin) puts it that 'Antisthenes, in the book called *Physicus*, by saying that there are many gods of the people, but only one in nature (*naturaliter unum*), does away with the power of the gods'. The Christian Lactantius adds that the one 'natural' god is the supreme artificer of the whole, and phrases it that he alone exists although nations and cities have their own popular gods. Christian writers also quote Antisthenes as saying that the god is like no other thing (or person; the dative could be either masculine or neuter) and that for this reason no one can learn of him from an image.[1] If Lactantius is correct in saying that for Antisthenes the one god was the creator of the world (which in the absence of better qualified witnesses cannot be taken as certain), then this is a remarkably early example in Greece of a pure monotheism. The contrast between the many gods of *nomos* or popular belief and the one real god is clear and emphatic. Without this addition, however, the emphasis on the unity of God and the impossibility of representing him by any visible image is reminiscent of Xenophanes and consistent with a pantheistic, rather than a monotheistic credo.[2]

[1] The testimonies are collected by Caizzi as frr. 39 A–E and 40 A–D. They are Philod. *De piet.* 7, Cic. *N.D.* 1.13.32, Min. Felix 19.7, Lact. *Div. inst.* 1.5.18–19 and *De ira Dei* 11.14, Clem. *Strom.* 5.14.108.4 and Protr. 6.71.1, Euseb. *P.E.* 13.13.35, Theodoret. *Graec. aff. cur.* 1.75.

[2] Caizzi, the most recent scholar to make a special study of Antisthenes, describes it cautiously as 'una fede monoteistica, forse in germe panteistica'.

X

CAN VIRTUE BE TAUGHT?

'Can you tell me, Socrates, whether virtue can be taught? Or is it a matter of practice, or natural aptitude or what?' The urgency with which this question was debated in the fifth century has been mentioned in an introductory chapter (p. 25), where the meaning of *areté* was briefly outlined and it was suggested that it had powerful social implications inclining a writer to answer in one sense or another on grounds not purely rational. The debate reflected the clash between older aristocratic ideals and the new classes which were then rising to prominence under the democratic system of government at Athens and seeking to establish what would today be called a meritocracy.[1] The claim of Sophists that *areté* could be imparted for fees by travelling teachers, instead of being freely transmitted by the precept and example of family and friends, and by association with 'the right people', coupled with the qualities of character native to any young man of good birth, was to the conservative-minded profoundly shocking. Philosophically, the question whether it was a matter of natural talent, or could be acquired by either teaching or assiduous practice, is chiefly important because, as a commonplace of the time, it was caught up in the thought of Socrates and Plato, who tried to answer it at a deeper level. Since the present chapters are intended in part as preparation for meeting these two great figures we may take a brief look at the kind of answers offered in and before their time. Afterwards, of course, the topic became more commonplace still, till we get to Horace's 'fortes creantur fortibus et bonis ... doctrina sed vim promovet insitam'.[2]

The old idea is typified by Theognis in the sixth century. To his

---

[1] I fear it is too late to kill off this ugly and bastard term and replace it by its legitimate half-brother 'axiocracy'.

[2] *Odes* 4.4.33. For other passages in Latin literature see Shorey in *TAPA*, 1909, 185, n. 1, who rather surprisingly does not mention this one. In general his article (Φύσις, Μελέτη, Ἐπιστήμη) should be consulted on this topic.

young friend Cyrnus he writes (*vv.* 27 ff. Diehl; the rest of his poetry makes it abundantly clear that for him 'good' and 'noble' mean 'of the right class'):

Out of the goodwill I bear you I will tell you what I myself learned from good men when I was still a child. Consort not with bad men, but always cling to the good. Drink, eat and sit with the great and powerful, and take pleasure in their company, for from noble men you will learn noble ways, but if you mingle with the bad you will lose what sense you have. Understand this and consort with the good, and some day you will say that I am a good counsellor to my friends.

This idea of having virtue 'rub off on one' through the right associations was still a commonplace in the fifth century and later, its connexion with social class becoming more tenuous with time. It was as a conservative member of the governing democratic party[1] that Anytus expressed his contempt for the professionals and claimed that 'any Athenian gentleman' would fit Meno for political life better than a Sophist. In Euripides (fr. 609) it sounds more like the moral commonplace which it became in Menander's 'Evil communications corrupt good manners'. A bad companion, he says, educates his fellows to be like himself, and a good one similarly, therefore young men should pursue good company; a sentiment repeated in an actual Sophist, Antiphon (fr. 62): 'A man necessarily comes to resemble in his ways whomsoever he consorts with for the greater part of the day.' Pindar's exaltation of natural gifts (φυά) is aristocratic,[2] and the contexts in which he expresses it show how the question whether *areté* is teachable is a part of the general antithesis between *physis* and art, or *physis* and *nomos*.

Ol. 2.86: 'Wise are they to whom knowledge of many things comes by nature; but those who learn, vehement and garrulous as crows, utter idle words.'
Ol. 9.100: 'What is natural is always best, but many have leaped to seize fame through accomplishments (*aretai*) got by teaching.'[3]

---

[1] See pp. 38, n. 1, and 39 above.
[2] Though the Anon. Iambl. shows that by the end of the fifth century an emphasis on φύσις had lost this association. For him it is a matter of chance (p. 71 above).
[3] For an example of the antithesis in prose, see Thuc. 1.121.4 (speech of the Corinthians at Sparta): 'The good qualities which we possess by nature, they cannot acquire by teaching.'

This does not mean that native talent cannot be improved by training. As he says in another Olympian ode (10.20), the man born to achievement (φύντ' ἀρετᾷ) is raised to great glory when training has put a keen edge on his *areté* and the gods are on his side. Pindar's poems were commissioned, and just as he conformed to the aristocratic outlook of his patrons, so (as his editor Gildersleeve reminds us) some praise of the trainer, whom in this passage he has just mentioned by name, was part of the contract.

This ode was in praise of a boy boxer, which is a reminder that besides its general sense, in which it stood for the type of excellence most valued in the period of its use, *areté* could be qualified as excellence in a particular accomplishment or art. Just as we (and the Greeks) speak not only of a good man, but also of a good runner, fighter, scholar or carpenter, so *areté*, suitably qualified, stood for excellence or proficiency in these and other pursuits. This is natural enough, but needs to be said in view of the traditional but misleading English translation 'virtue'. In the *Iliad* Polydorus as a swift runner 'displayed *areté* of the feet' (20.411), and Periphētes (15.641 f.) excelled his father in 'all kinds of *areté*, both in fleetness of foot and in fighting'. This application persists in Pindar, who in the tenth Pythian (*v.* 23) writes of someone who 'conquering by his hands or the *areté* of his feet wins the greatest prizes by his daring and strength'.[1] In this sense horses too can have it (*Il.* 23.276, 374; Xen. *Hieron* 2.2, 6.16), and inanimate objects or substances like soil (i.e. fertility, Thuc. 1.2.4, Plato, *Critias* 110e, *Laws* 745d) or cotton (Hdt. 3.106.2). Plato applies it frequently to particular skills, as when he makes Protagoras speak of '*areté* of carpentry or any other craft' (*Prot.* 322d), and of course of his own speciality 'political *areté*'. In the *Republic* (353b ff.) Socrates claims that there is a proper *areté* belonging to whatever has a particular function or job to perform, namely the condition in which it will be best able to perform that function, and as examples he mentions pruning-hooks, eyes and ears. He then goes on to make his own point

---

[1] This linguistic usage could lead to what we cannot but regard as a slightly comic confusion. Arguing in the *Meno* that *areté* cannot be taught, Socrates (at 93c–d) comments on the fact that Themistocles was unable to impart his statesmanlike virtues to his own son, and with no hint of irony points to the young man's ability to throw a javelin while standing upright on horseback as proof that he was not lacking in natural talent.

by claiming that the *psyche* of man also has its function, namely to govern the lower elements, to deliberate and in general to ensure a life lived to the best of human capacity, and that its own *areté* is to be identified with justice or righteousness.

It might therefore be said that it was Socrates who enlarged the meaning of *areté* from talent or proficiency in a particular art or function to something like virtue in our sense, the prerequisite of a good human life. There is some justification for this, but it needs qualification. The absolute use of the word had always existed, alongside its particularization by means of a genitive or an adjective, to stand for what its users thought was human excellence in general. It is so used in Homer, though we may translate it 'valour', that being the virtue most prized in a heroic age. Used thus it was liable to 'persuasive definitions' by reforming spirits who claimed that excellence 'really' consisted in this or that, as when Heraclitus (fr. 112) declared that 'the greatest *areté* is self-control'. The general use is seen in the title of a work of Democritus 'On *Areté* or Manly Virtue' (ἀνδραγαθίας, D.L. 9.46).[1] The originality of Socrates did not lie in recognizing the general use, but in (*a*) the emphasis which he laid on it as a moral quality, rather than simply the prerequisite of success, and (*b*) his attempt to give it philosophical justification by demanding a universal definition. In his eyes a general term was only valid if it corresponded to a single 'form' or reality whose 'essence' could be defined in a single verbal formula. Here he was on controversial ground. When he asks Meno to tell him 'what *areté* is', Meno thinks it an easy question, for he can say what is the virtue of a man, a woman, a child, a slave, or anyone or anything else. But he is puzzled when Socrates replies that he does not want a list of virtues but a statement of the essence, form or being of the one thing, virtue, which in his view must be common to them all to justify calling them by the one name. It looks like a lesson in elementary logic, and so in Meno's case it is, for he is no philosopher but an impetuous young aristocrat who genuinely does not understand the difference between enumerating a string of instances and drawing an inductive generalization from them. But he

[1] See also p. 71 with n. 3, on the Anon. Iambl., which however may have been influenced by Socrates. Connexion between this work and Democritus may be more than fortuitous. See A. T. Cole in *HSCP*, 1961, 154.

is introduced as an admirer of Gorgias, and we know from Aristotle that Gorgias did not approve of attempting a general definition of *areté*. After mentioning Socrates by name as holding that self-control, courage and justice are the same for a woman as for a man, Aristotle goes on (*Pol.* 1260a 25): 'Those who speak in general terms, saying that virtue is "the well-being of the soul" or "right action" or the like, are wrong. To enumerate the virtues, as Gorgias did, is much nearer the mark than to make this kind of definition.'[1] To Socrates it is as legitimate to ask for a general definition of virtue as it is to ask for a definition of an insect and to object when a list of insects is offered instead; and Meno is perhaps not altogether to be blamed when he says that he can understand the question as applied thus to a natural genus but does not grasp it so easily when it is transferred to virtue, which he feels is not altogether parallel to the other cases mentioned by Socrates (72d, 73a). Gorgias would no doubt have claimed that Socrates was trying to extend a method appropriate to natural science beyond its proper sphere. The opening of his *Helen* is a good example of his own practice. To explain the meaning of *kosmos*, where Socrates would have looked for an all-embracing definition, he writes: '*Kosmos* is for a city the manliness of its citizens, for a body beauty, for a soul wisdom, for an action virtue, for speech truth. *Akosmia* is the opposite of these.' This reluctance to give a general definition is a consequence of the sophistic belief, shared by Protagoras, in the relativity of values.[2]

Although Meno puts his question to Socrates in the form of clear-cut alternatives, it is not likely that anyone believed *areté* to be attainable *solely* by the bounty of nature or by personal effort or by another's instruction. Even Pindar admitted that natural endowment can be sharpened by training, and although Hesiod spoke as a peasant, not an aristocrat, when he uttered his famous line about the gods putting sweat on the path of achievement (*Erga* 289), his poem became a part

---

[1] For the same view in Isocrates see *Helen* 1, and cf. *Nicocles* 44.

[2] Compare Protagoras's miniature lecture on the relativity of goodness in the *Protagoras* (pp. 166f. above). This point is made by Versényi (*Socr. Hum.* 41f.), who comments that 'in Protagoras, this reluctance leads not to the denial of the unity of virtue but to a formal rather than a material definition (the equation of the good with the useful, fit, appropriate, etc.)'. On the difference between Socrates and the Sophists in this matter, which will be dealt with under Socrates, Versényi is helpful. See his pp. 76ff.

of the Greek heritage, and no one was so unrealistic as to suppose that greatness could be achieved without effort. There was nevertheless great difference in the emphasis laid on the three elements of natural endowment, practice or personal effort, and teaching respectively.

That 'virtue' could be taught was the basis of the Sophists' claim to a livelihood, and its justification lay in the close connexion in the Greek mind between *areté* and the special skills or crafts (*technai*). Protagoras's references, in Plato, to 'the craftsman's *techné*' and 'the craftsman's *areté*'[1] show that for him they meant much the same. He himself considers instruction in the special *technai*, which some Sophists offered, to be beneath him, and the 'political art' or 'political virtue'[2] which is his own speciality is much closer to moral virtue, for it has its roots in the ethical qualities of justice and a respect for oneself and others. Without these, he considers, life in an organized society is impossible. (Cf. p. 66 above.) Nevertheless this political art is capable of precise definition as 'prudence in personal affairs and the best way to manage one's own household, and also in the affairs of the State, so as to become a most powerful speaker and man of action' (318d–e), a subject practical and utilitarian and at the same time obviously suitable for a course of instruction. Protagoras's view on whether virtue is natural or acquired can be extracted from his long and brilliant speech in the *Protagoras* when its mythical elements are thought away. This has been done already (pp. 65 ff.), and a brief summary is all that is necessary here. It was not, in the beginning, a part of human nature as such. Hence, although primitive men had the intelligence to learn various arts such as the use of fire, the working of metals and so forth, they treated each other savagely and could not co-operate sufficiently to protect themselves within walled cities from the attacks of animals fiercer and more powerful than they. Gradually and painfully some of them learned to exercise self-denial and fair play sufficiently to enable them to take joint action and so survive. No one completely without these virtues, therefore, is alive today, and even the most villainous characters in our civilized societies have some elements of virtue. They have been acquired by teaching since early childhood, first from parents and nurse, then from schoolmasters, and finally from the state, whose

---

[1] 322b and d. See p. 66, n. 1.   [2] τέχνη 319a, 322b, ἀρετή 322e.

system of laws and punishments has an educative purpose. Admonition and punishment are only appropriate in the absence of such good qualities as may be acquired through 'care, practice and teaching': they are not employed against natural deficiencies which a man can do nothing to alter. All that the Sophist can claim is to carry the teaching a little further and do it a little better, so that his own pupils will be somewhat superior to their fellow-citizens. This does not mean of course that everyone has an equal talent for learning political virtue, any more than for mathematics or piano-playing. It is an obvious fact that all men are not equally endowed by nature, and this is no less or more true of virtue than of any other accomplishment.

For all this we rely on Plato, but it accords well with the meagre quotations from Protagoras himself that have any bearing on the subject. Successful teaching, he said, requires that the pupil contribute both natural ability and assiduity in practice (ἄσκησις), and he added that to learn one must begin young (fr. 3). Elsewhere he said (fr. 10) that art and practice, or study (μελέτη), were inseparable. Plato, again (*Theaet.* 167b–c), makes him compare the influence of the orator on cities and the Sophist on individuals to that of the husbandman on plants, recalling what seems to have been a commonplace, the comparison between education and husbandry in which the soil represents the natural capacity of the pupil. We have seen it recurring in Antiphon and the Hippocratic *Law* (pp. 168f. above).[1]

The claims of training or practice (ἄσκησις) were preferred to those of nature by Democritus (fr. 242), and his comment on the relation between natural ability and teaching was less superficial than most and in modern terms might be said to have an existentialist tendency. The two were complementary, because a man's nature is not irrevocably fixed at birth: he can be altered by teaching, which is therefore a factor in the formation of his nature.[2] A line of Critias is also quoted (fr. 9) to the effect that more men become good through study (μελέτη) than by nature. Iamblichus's anonymous writer puts 'nature' first, followed

[1] As Shorey pointed out (*TAPA*, 1909, 190), Euripides in the *Hecuba*, 592ff., uses this simile to make an entirely different point, that human nature cannot be changed by circumstances, whether from bad to good or good to bad.

[2] Democr. fr. 33. Hazel Barnes, *An Existentialist Ethics*, 33f., speaks of Sartre's pronouncement 'that human nature is not fixed, that man is indeed a creature who makes himself by a process of constant change'.

by sustained hard work and willingness to learn, begun in early youth. *Areté* is only to be acquired by applying oneself diligently to it over a long period of time. (See p. 71 above.) The 'Double Arguments' devoted a chapter to the same well-worn theme of whether virtue is teachable (pp. 317ff. below), Isocrates summed up the position, and Plato himself in the *Phaedrus* speaks of it in much the same vein, indeed so similarly to Isocrates that it is usually supposed that one of these was acquainted with the other's writing.[1] As will have appeared by now, much of what was said on the subject was sententious and trivial, yet at the time it seemed of paramount importance to know how *areté* was acquired. In the competitive society of the day ambitious young men like Meno and Hippocrates (in the *Protagoras*) were willing to spend fortunes on Sophists who might be able to impart the secret, and the suggestion that no teacher could communicate it was in Socrates's day an attack on a large vested interest. In this discussion Socrates and Plato took a vigorous part. In the *Euthydemus* Plato ridicules two charlatans who claim to teach it in the face of Socrates's doubts whether it can be taught at all. In the *Protagoras* he expresses the same doubts, and Protagoras counters them with skill and force. The *Meno* is wholly devoted to the topic. Sometimes, as in the discussion of rhetoric in the *Phaedrus* already mentioned, Plato joins in the argument at the same rather banal level as the rest.[2] At other times he makes it the starting-point for developing his own or the Socratic philosophy.

For Socrates—surely the most uncompromisingly intellectual of all ethical teachers—what one man could give to another by teaching was knowledge. If then virtue (in which he certainly included the moral virtues) could be taught, it must be a form of knowledge (*Meno* 87c). As to the teaching of it, his answer was neither crude nor simple, and must be investigated later; but that it was a form of knowledge he

---

[1] For references to, and discussion of, the relevant passages in Isocrates and Plato, see Shorey's article in *TAPA*, 1909.

[2] Of certain passages in Plato and Isocrates, Shorey points out (*op. cit.* 195) that 'there is nothing in either of which the sufficient suggestion is not found in the apologetic and protreptic literature of the day'. Plato may be summarizing the opinions of Isocrates, a conclusion which may be unpalatable 'on account of our natural tendency to regard Plato as the more original thinker', but, as Shorey rightly adds, 'the originality of a work so surpassingly rich in suggestion as the *Phaedrus* does not depend on these links of commonplace lightly assumed in passing'.

was convinced. But if virtue is knowledge, vice or wrongdoing can only be due to ignorance and it follows that 'no one sins deliberately'. Right action will follow automatically on knowledge of what is right. Socrates was judging others by himself for, astonishing as it may seem, in his case it was true. His calm assurance that he was following the right course was unshaken by the fact that its outcome was the cup of hemlock, which he tossed off in complete confidence that 'no harm can come to a good man'. Such heroic doctrine was not for most men. Aristotle said bluntly that it was 'in flat contradiction to experience' (*EN* 1145b27). Plato makes Socrates recognize the prevalence of the opposite view in the *Protagoras* (352d–e). 'You know', he says, 'that most men don't believe us. They maintain that there are many who recognize the best but are unwilling to act on it. It may be open to them, but they do otherwise.' Since the struggle between conscience and desire, or weakness of will, is essentially dramatic, it is not surprising that some of the most striking expressions of the opposite point of view occur in Euripides, quite possibly in conscious contradiction of Socrates. This has been suspected of Phaedra's words in the *Hippolytus*:[1] 'We know, we recognize the right, but do it not, some of us from idleness, others through choosing some pleasure rather than the good.' Faced with the prospect of killing her own children, Medea cries (*Medea* 1078ff.): 'I understand the evil I am prompted to commit, but my passions (θυμός) are stronger than my counsel, passion which is the cause of men's greatest crimes.' In this connexion 'nature' with her 'necessity', that despairing resort of the weak-willed, makes an appearance once again. (See p. 100 above.) 'All that you warn me of I know well', says another character (fr. 840), 'but though I know it, nature compels me.' Nor is the other parner of the antithesis, *nomos*, lacking. 'Nature willed it, who cares nought for law' is the excuse of an erring woman: women were made like that.[2] Again (fr. 841): 'Alas, this is a heaven-sent curse for mortals, that a man know the good but pursue it not.' ('*Heaven*-sent?' comments the moralizing Plutarch, 'Nay, rather bestial and irrational.' See *De aud. poet.* 33e–f.) 'To be

[1] 380ff. See Snell in *Philologus*, 1948; Dodds, *Gks. & Irrat.* 186 with n. 47; O'Brien, *Socr. Paradoxes*, 55, n. 78.
[2] Fr. 920, and see Dodds, *op. cit.* 187 with n. 55.

overcome by pleasure' was a phrase of the day,[1] a phrase which is subjected to a critical investigation by Socrates in the *Protagoras* (352 d ff.). For him the natural course was to act as reason and knowledge dictated, though it does not follow (indeed there is some evidence to the contrary)[2] that he was entirely without emotions and would not have qualified for Antiphon's description of a temperate (σώφρων) man. 'He who has neither felt the desire for, nor come in contact with, what is foul and evil', said Antiphon (fr. 59), 'is not temperate, for there is nothing that he has had to overcome in order to show himself well-behaved (κόσμιον).'[3] Antiphon also brought in the idea of 'mastery of self', where 'self' stands for the lower self or base desires[4] (fr. 58 *ad fin.*): 'The best judge of a man's temperance is one who[5] makes himself a bulwark against the momentary pleasures of the passions and has been able to conquer and master himself. Whoever chooses to yield to his passions at every moment chooses the worse instead of the better.' This self-mastery however is not recommended by Antiphon on any purely moral grounds, but rather as a piece of calculated self-interest. He has just said that 'temperance' or self-restraint (it is the same word, *sophrosyne*, or its adjective *sophron*, which unfortunately cannot be fully covered by any single English one)[6] consists in admitting the truth of the old Greek adage that the doer shall suffer. 'Whoever thinks he can injure his neighbours without suffering himself is not a temperate man. Such hopes have brought many to irrevocable disaster, when they have turned out to suffer exactly what they thought to inflict on others.' Therefore think before you give your passions rein. There is here at least the germ of the 'hedonic calculus' which Socrates advocates in the *Protagoras* and which obviously played an important part in the formation of his thought. Everything depends

---

[1] See e.g. Lysias 21.19, Thuc. 3.38.7. In the *Gorgias* Socrates calls it 'the popular notion' (ὥσπερ οἱ πολλοί, 491 d).

[2] See pp. 393 ff. below.

[3] Scholars have made much of the moral tone of this, which is indeed sufficiently remarkable. See the quotations in Untersteiner, *Sof.* IV, 144 f. When Phaedra opposes Socratic doctrine in the words (*Hippol.* 358) οἱ σώφρονες γὰρ οὐχ ἑκόντες ἀλλ' ὅμως κακῶν ἐρῶσιν, Euripides may have had Antiphon in mind.

[4] As is explained in the *Republic*, 430e–431a.

[5] Jacoby's alteration of ἄλλος to ἄλλου, adopted by DK, seems unnecessary. See Untersteiner's note, *Sof.* IV, 142 (where ἄλλον is presumably a misprint).

[6] A full-scale study of the history of the concept has now been made by Helen North (*Sophrosyne*, 1966).

on making the right decision, i.e. on the correct calculation and weighing up of one's own interests. This brings us close to Socratic intellectualism. What is wanted for a correct choice of pleasures is, in Socrates's phrase, an "art of measurement".[1] The difference between them is that for Socrates no pleasure could exceed that of a good conscience, and no pains, though they might include poverty, disgrace, wounds and death, could outweigh it. It is better, and to the man who knows less painful, to suffer injury than to inflict it, for what matters is the soul, the *psyche*, not the body or appearances, and to prosper and enjoy what are vulgarly called pleasures by selfish and unjust means is to maim and injure one's own *psyche*.

[1] So K. Gantar in *Živa Ant.* 1966, 156, discussing Antiphon fr. 58. His reference is to Plato, *Prot.* 356d–357b. See further on this pp. 462ff. below.

XI

THE MEN

INTRODUCTION

In the foregoing chapters many of the views of Sophists and their contemporaries have been introduced in a discussion of the main topics of philosophical interest in the fifth century. The priority given to this discussion over a treatment of each thinker individually may be justified by the reflection that on the whole this was a debate of contemporaries eagerly exchanging views and that the subjects of perennial human interest on which they argued do not admit of the same linear progress from one thinker to the next which can be detected in the more scientific theorizing of the Presocratics. It seemed best therefore to reproduce, so far as possible, the interplay of their minds on this topic or that. There is the further consideration that, as I have tried to bring out more than once during the discussion, it is not always possible on the evidence available to assign a particular view to its author with certainty. Salomon went so far as to say (*Sav. Stift.* 1911, 131) that 'the picture of the individual Sophists which we construct on the basis of such of their dicta as are preserved is, in so far as it is determined by the vicissitudes of the tradition, the result of pure chance.' At the same time there is something in Nestle's reasons (in the preface to *Vom Mythos zum Logos*) for choosing an arrangement by persons rather than by subjects, namely that 'otherwise much repetition would have been necessary and the contributions of the great personalities, whose unitary vigour was in fact responsible for the intellectual progress achieved, would have been dismembered'. An attempt to have the best of both worlds will obviously increase the risk of repetition, a point which must be borne in mind. One reason why, if the advantages of arrangement by subject seemed too great to miss, it is nevertheless advisable to attempt a short unified account of each individual is that in scattering the views of one man through several widely separated chapters—here his remarks on law or ethics, and far removed from these a dictum on epistemology and another on the gods—it would be all too easy to overlook inconsistencies and attribute to the same philosopher views which no sane man could have held simultaneously. It will be salutary to see if together they add up to a credible character, and at the same time there remains some detail to be filled in about the evidence for the dates of these people, the events of their lives, and in some cases aspects of their teaching which in the previous general discussion have been omitted or dismissed with a bare mention. In what follows therefore I shall try to sum up what is known of each individual, with the briefest reference possible to what has already been said. I have confined myself to those who have appeared in the previous chapters, and omitted one or two minor figures about whom everything necessary has been said there.

(1) PROTAGORAS

Protagoras was a native of Abdera, the city in the remote north-east of Greece which also gave birth to Democritus.[1] Since for our purposes relative dates are more important than absolute, we may note first that Plato makes him say, before a company which included Socrates, Prodicus and Hippias, that he is old enough to be the father of any one of them (*Prot.* 317c). In the *Hippias Major* (282e), too, Hippias describes himself as a much younger man than Protagoras. This suggests a date of not later than 490 for his birth (which would make him about twenty years older than Socrates, probably the eldest of his auditors), and in the *Meno* (91e) he is said to have died at the age of about seventy after forty years as a practising Sophist. His death, therefore, may be assumed to have occurred about 420.[2] There was a story that he was a child at the time of the invasion of Xerxes (480), who in return for his father's hospitality ordered the magi to give him

---

[1] An isolated reference to him as Π. ὁ Τήιος occurs in the comic poet Eupolis (*ap.* D.L. 9.50). Abdera was colonized from Teos (Hdt. 1.168), and the continuous long syllables of Ἀβδηρίτης would have been difficult to accommodate to the metre.

[2] The chronologist Apollodorus followed Plato (D.L. 9.56), and gave Ol. 84 (444–441) as his *floruit*, probably in allusion to his drafting of the constitution of Thurii in 444–443. According to D.L., some said he lived till nearly 90, but see on this Davison in *CQ*, 1953, 35. For references to other discussions of his date see Untersteiner, *Sophs.* 6, n. 7, and for his life in general Morrison in *CQ*, 1941 and Davison in *CQ*, 1953.

instruction. This may be some corroborative evidence for a date of birth about 490.[1] The cause of his death is said by a number of late authorities (with some differences in detail) to have been drowning by shipwreck after leaving Athens where he had been tried and banished (or alternatively condemned to death) for the impiety of his agnostic assertion about the gods.[2] Plato says in the *Meno* (91e) that throughout his professional life, and indeed ever since, his high reputation had been continuously maintained, which is not necessarily inconsistent with trial and conviction: he would have said the same about Socrates.[3]

Protagoras was the most famous, and perhaps the earliest, of the professional Sophists, who trained others for the profession as well as for public life.[4] He was well known in Athens, which he visited a number of times,[5] and became a friend of Pericles. Plutarch tells a story that the two men spent a whole day discussing an interesting point of legal responsibility involving also, in all probability, a more philosophical question of causation. In an athletic contest a man had been accidentally hit and killed with a javelin. Was his death to be attributed to the javelin itself, to the man who threw it, or to the authorities responsible for the conduct of the games?[6] A more practical

---

[1] Philostr. *V. Soph.* 1.10.1 (DK, 80 A 2), probably taken from the *Persica* of Dinon in the late fourth century B.C., who also says that he was a pupil of Democritus, which is chronologically impossible. See vol. II, 386, n. 2. The same story of education by magi was told of Democritus himself (D.L. 9.34). For its evidential value see Davison, *loc. cit.* 34.

[2] D.L. 9.54, 55; Philostr. 1.10.3 (A 2); Hesychius (A 3); Sext. *Math.* 9.56 (A 12). D.L. and Eusebius (A 4) add the picturesque detail that copies of his books were collected from their possessors and publicly burned. The whole story is, perhaps rightly, rejected by Burnet, *T. to P.* 111f.

[3] See however Vlastos in Plato's *Protagoras* (1956), p. viii, n. 6, who thinks it compatible with prosecution but not condemnation.

[4] See pp. 35 and 37 above. That he was the first to demand fees for his teaching is repeated by D.L. 9.52 and Philostr. 1.10.4. (The latter approved it, on the sensible ground that we value what we pay for more than what is free.)

[5] Plato in the *Protagoras* (310e) mentions two visits, and Eupolis in a play produced in 422–421 spoke of him as then present in Athens, i.e. later than the dramatic date of the *Protagoras*, which in spite of one anachronism must have been about 433. See Morrison, *CQ*, 1941, 2 f., and Davison, *CQ*, 1953, 37. The reference to the *Kolakes* of Eupolis occurs in Athenaeus 218c (A 11). The best summing-up of the evidence for the dates in Protagoras's life (not all mentioned here) is that of von Fritz in *RE*, XLV. Halbb. 908–11.

[6] Plut. *Per.* 36 (DK, A 10). At Athens both animals and lifeless instruments which had been the cause of death were tried in the court of the Prytaneum. See Demosthenes 23 (*In Aristocr.*), 76, and cf. Aristotle, *Ath. Pol.* 57.4, Plato, *Laws* 873d ff.; and for the prevalence of the custom Frazer's long note, *Pausanias*, vol. II, 370–2. On the philosophical character of the discussion see Rensi and Untersteiner in the latter's *Sophs.* 30f.

outcome of their relationship was the invitation to Protagoras to collaborate in an exciting new enterprise. After the sack and destruction of Sybaris in South Italy by the Crotoniates, the surviving Sybarites appealed to Athens and Sparta to assist their return and share in the refounding of the city. Sparta refused, but the Athenians accepted with enthusiasm, and invited volunteers from any Greek city to join the new colony, which thus became a truly pan-Hellenic enterprise. All this is told by Diodorus, but Heraclides Ponticus in a study of the laws of Greek states added that Protagoras was the man chosen to draft a legal code for Thurii.[1] He was a familiar figure to the Western Greeks, for he also lived for a time in Sicily, where he made a reputation in his profession (Plato, *Hipp. Maj.* 282d-e).

There is little point in trying to list the titles of his separate works. Diogenes Laertius (9.55) gives a catalogue, but many of the names will have been arbitrarily attached in later centuries. In the fifth century the custom of attaching titles to prose works was in its infancy, and for a long time those who quoted them would attach a descriptive name to what was only a section of a longer continuous work. There were at least two main treatises: (1) *Truth* (known alternatively, at least in later times, by a wrestling term as the 'Throws' or arguments to floor an opponent), which is cited as such by Plato several times; it opened with the 'man the measure' pronouncement; (2) *Antilogiae* or contrary arguments. *On the Gods* also sounds like a separate work, and it is certainly ineffective to argue that after the agnostic first sentence there would have been nothing left to say on the subject. It might, as already suggested (p. 235), have dealt with the value of religious cults as a part of civilized life, or alternatively have been an anthropological treatise describing the forms of belief and worship current among various peoples. There is also reference to a 'Great Logos', which may be the same as *Truth*, and a number of other titles.[2]

---

[1] Diod. 12.10, Heracl. Pont. Π. νόμων, fr. 150 Wehrli (*ap.* D.L. 9.50). There seems no reason to doubt Heraclides's information, though it is a little curious that Diodorus does not mention Protagoras with the others at 12.10.4. On the foundation of Thurii see Ehrenberg in *AJP*, 1948, 149–70. He speaks of the part played by Protagoras on pp. 168f.

[2] For the Ἀλήθεια in Plato see *Theaet.* 161c, *Crat.* 391c. The alternative title Καταβάλλοντες occurs in Sextus, *Math.* 7.60 (Prot. fr. 1). That Eur. *Bacch.* 202 is an allusion proving that it was already current in the fifth century has been denied outright by Wilamowitz (*Plat.* 1.80 n. 1), and asserted by Gigante (*Nom. Bas.* 216, n. 2) to be 'not merely possible but certain'. On

Protagoras: Plato's Evidence

Much of our information about Protagoras's thought comes from Plato's dialogues, and our assessment of his philosophic achievement therefore depends to a considerable extent on the historical value which we are prepared to grant them. Many scholars have joined in the debate, and complete agreement will probably never be reached. One thing, however, which cannot be argued against Plato's veracity is that his aim was to blacken or destroy Protagoras's reputation. The respect with which he treats his views is all the more impressive for his profound disagreement with them. In the dramatic setting which is one of the chief charms of the dialogue *Protagoras*, the great Sophist is certainly portrayed as fully conscious of his own merits, with a harmless vanity and love of admiration which amused Socrates and tempted him to a little good-tempered leg-pulling; but in the discussion he remains consistently urbane in the face of considerable provocation, including fallacious and unscrupulous argument, on the part of Socrates, displaying at the end, as Vlastos well expresses it, a magnanimity which is 'self-conscious but not insincere'. His own contributions to the discussion are on a consistently high level both intellectually and morally, and leave no doubt of the high esteem in which Plato held him. Even Grote, the arch-castigator of Plato for his unfairness and animosity towards the Sophists (pp. 11 f. above), had to agree that 'that dialogue is itself enough to prove that Plato did not conceive Protagoras either as a corrupt, or unworthy, or incompetent teacher', and concluded that, on the evidence of the *Protagoras* itself, the ethical code of Protagoras appears as superior to that of the Platonic Socrates. 'Protagoras', said Grant, 'is represented by Plato throughout the dialogue as exhibiting an elevated standard of moral

Π. τῆς ἐν ἀρχῇ καταστάσεως see p. 63 above. For those interested in opinions on this minor and insoluble question here is a selection. Nestle identified the Μέγας Λόγος (fr. 3) with the Π. ἀρετῶν, Frey with the Προστακτικός, DK and Untersteiner with the Ἀλήθεια. See Nestle, *VMzuL*, 296 (but cf. his edition of the *Prot.* p. 31); DK, II, 264 n.; Unterst. *Sophs.* 14. Von Fritz (*RE*, XLV. Halbb. 920) thinks it an independent work. For Π. τοῦ ὄντος see p. 47 with n. 1 above. Untersteiner (*op. cit.* 10 ff.) has an elaborate theory (charitably characterized by Lesky, *HGL*, 344, as 'too sweeping to be fully demonstrable') that all the titles in D.L.'s catalogue refer to subsections of the Ἀντιλογίαι, which contained four main sections: (1) on the Gods, (2) on Being, (3) on the Laws and other problems concerning the *polis*, (4) on the Arts (τέχναι, including π. πάλης and π. τῶν μαθημάτων). One of D.L.'s titles is Π. πολιτείας, commonly assigned to the Ἀντιλογίαι because of the scandalous story of Aristoxenus (*ap.* D.L. 3.37, and cf. 3.57) that almost all of Plato's *Politeia* was to be found in the latter work.

feelings', and no unprejudiced reader of the dialogue could disagree. Von Fritz, after pointing out the fairness with which Plato treats the 'man-the-measure' doctrine in the *Theaetetus*, adds: 'In other ways also Plato, in spite of all his opposition, has treated Protagoras with more justice than have other of his opponents.' Unlike Aristophanes, who interpreted 'weaker' as 'unjust' in Protagoras's claim to make the weaker argument prevail, Plato never accused him or other Sophists of flouting the established moral rules.[1]

For many people one of the chief obstacles to believing in Plato's veracity has been the speech in which Protagoras gives a brilliant account of the origins of human society deliberately cast in the form of a myth (*Prot.* 320c–322d), though, as he has said (320c), it could equally well have been told as a rational *logos* without the mythical accretions.[2] What sticks in their throats is the statement that man is the only creature who believes in the gods and practises religious cult 'because of his kinship with the divine'. I hope I have disposed of this objection. That the instinct to believe and worship is fundamental to human nature is plain fact, and to attribute it to divine kinship no more than is to be expected in an account confessedly cast in the form of popular mythology to make it more entertaining (320c).[3] That Plato reproduced Protagoras's teaching with complete accuracy is something we shall never know for certain, but with this proviso, so long as what he says is both internally consistent and not in conflict with the rest of our scanty information (and this I believe to be true), I shall prefer to make use of it as I have done in the earlier part of this book rather than assume, as we should have to do if Plato's testimony is rejected, that we know very little indeed about this stimulating and influential figure.

Protagoras's innovation was to achieve a reputation as a political and moral thinker without supporting any political party, attempting political reform, or seeking power for himself, but simply by lecturing and speaking and offering himself as a professional adviser and educa-

[1] Grote, *History* (1888 ed.), VII, 59–62; Grant, *Ethics*, I, 144; von Fritz, *RE*, XLV. Halbb. 917.

[2] For views on the authenticity of the myth see the references on p. 64, n. 1, above, especially, for objectors to the mention of divine kinship, Havelock, *L.T.* 408f.

[3] See pp. 88ff. above and *In the Beginning*, 88f. If my explanation is unsatisfying, readers have the choice of C. W. Müller's (p. 235, n. 3, above).

tor to make others better and more successful in both their personal and political careers. It was a brilliant solution for an able and ambitious man born in an unimportant city in the remote north-east who longed for wealth, reputation and the company of his intellectual equals but could only find them in the leading cities of Greece, where his alien status debarred him from active participation in political life. His character evidently seemed to overcome, in the minds of many prominent Athenian citizens, the prejudice against his professionalism, and it was not long before others followed his example. (Cf. pp. 40 f. above.) The aim of his teaching was above all practical, and in accordance with the needs of the day he based it largely on the art of persuasive speaking, training his pupils to argue both sides of a case and providing examples to prove his point that there are contrary arguments on every subject. The art of *logoi* was acquired by various exercises, including study and criticism of the poets (the Sophists' predecessors in education for life), and analysis and criticism of current forms of speech. The legitimacy of taking either side in an argument according to circumstances was founded on theories of knowledge and being which constituted an extreme reaction from the Eleatic antithesis of knowledge and opinion, the one true and the other false. There was no such thing as falsehood, nor could anyone contradict another or call him mistaken, for a man was the sole judge of his own sensations and beliefs, which were true for him so long as they appeared to be so. Since there was no absolute or universal truth, no one needed to consider, before attempting to make an individual, a jury or a state change its mind, whether or not he would be persuading them of a truer state of affairs. The personal nature of our sensations did not mean that all perceptible properties coexist in an external object but I perceive some and you others. It meant rather that they have no objective existence, but come to be as they are perceived, and for the percipient. Consistent with this was his attack on mathematicians for dealing in abstractions, describing straight lines, circles and so forth as no man perceives them and as, therefore, they do not exist. (See vol. II, 486.)

If each of us lives like this in a private world of his own, the attempt to change another man's world might be thought not only unobjectionable but impossible. This difficulty is overcome by substituting a standard of advantage and disadvantage for that of truth and falsehood, and extending by analogy the case of sensations in health and sickness. The food that to a sick man tastes unpleasant *is* unpleasant, for him, but a doctor can change his world so that it will both appear and be pleasant to him. The doctrine becomes more difficult when applied to values in general. To be consistent, Protagoras must hold an extreme relative theory of values according to which not only may the same thing, or course of action, be good for *A* but bad for *B*, but also, just as what a man believes to be true is true for him, so also what he believes to be good is good for him, so long as he believes it. We have no record of how Protagoras applied this doctrine to individual morality, but of a state he certainly said that whatever customs or policies it believed in and embodied in its laws were right for it so long as it held them to be right. This difficulty he got over by equating 'just' or 'right' with 'lawful' but distinguishing it from 'the expedient', which was that belief or course of action which *will* produce better effects in the future. As the doctor, with the patient's consent, administers treatment which will improve the patient's condition (cause pleasanter sensations both to appear and be for him), so a wise Sophist or orator may, with the city's goodwill, convert it by argument and not by violence to genuine belief in the virtues of a new policy which will lead (e.g. by promoting a sounder economy or better relations with its neighbours) to a happier life for its citizens. At the root of this curious argument is Protagoras's invincible respect for the democratic virtues of justice, respect for other men's opinions and the processes of peaceful persuasion as the basis of communal life, and the necessity of communal life to the very survival of the human race. Law and order were not in our nature from the beginning, but the agreement which brought them into being was the fruit of bitter experience, for they are essential to our preservation. It follows that all men now living in society possess the capacity for moral and intellectual virtue, and those in whom it is inadequately developed may be punished, if persuasion fails, provided that punishment is designed to be one means among others of education in virtue.

One would hardly expect a religious spirit in a man of these views, and Protagoras confessed that on the existence of gods he personally could only suspend judgment. This would not preclude an interest in the phenomena of religious belief and worship, and with his conviction of the value to society of established custom and law, he probably believed that this *nomos* ('for', as Euripides said, 'it is by *nomos* that we believe in the gods') was to be encouraged as much as others. Gods, after all, existed for those who believed in them.

A word may be added about Protagoras as a literary critic. There is evidence independent of Plato and Aristotle that his criticism of poetry was not confined to grammatical pedantry or moralizing. A papyrus of about the first century A.D., containing comment on *Iliad* XXI, shows him examining the poet's purpose and the structure of the poem in a surprisingly modern way. 'Protagoras', runs the comment, 'says that the purpose of the episode immediately following the fight between the river Xanthus and mortal men is to divide the battle and make a transition to the theomachy, perhaps also to glorify Achilles and ...'[1]

(2) GORGIAS

The other great member of the first generation of Sophists, almost exactly contemporary with Protagoras, was Gorgias son of Charmantides. Though a Western Greek, he too was an Ionian, for his city Leontini in Sicily was a colony of Chalcidian Naxos in the east of the island. He was born about 490 or a few years after, and all authorities are agreed that he lived to a great age: their reports vary between 105 and 109.[2] Tradition says he was a pupil of Empedocles (vol. II, 135), and this is likely, though he could have been only a very few years younger. Plato (*Meno* 76c) connects his name with the Empedoclean theory of pores, and he would also owe to Empedocles an interest in the arts of persuasive speech and of medicine. His brother Herodicus too was a doctor, and he claimed to be of service to medicine by bringing his powers of persuasion to bear on recalcitrant patients

---

[1] *Oxy. Pap.* II, 221. See Gudemann in *RE*, 2. Reihe, III. Halbb. 640.

[2] For the sources see Untersteiner, *Sophs.* 97, n. 2. Plato (*Apol.* 19e) speaks of him as still active in 399, and from Pausanias (6.17.9, DK, A 7) it would seem that he ended his days at the court of Jason, who became tyrant of Pherae in Thessaly about 380. (Plato, *Meno* 70b, shows him as already a familiar figure in Thessaly by 402.) Athenaeus (505d, A 15a) tells a story which if true would mean that he lived long enough to read Plato's characterization of him in the *Gorgias*, written probably *c.* 385 (Dodds, *Gorg.* 24ff.).

of his brother or other practitioners.[1] Nor could he have failed to be in touch with the Syracusan rhetoricians Corax and Tisias (with whom Plato associates him, *Phaedr.* 267a), and his own oratory was of the flowery Sicilian type: his name is not connected, as were those of Protagoras and Prodicus, with the linguistic studies of *orthoepeia* and 'the correctness of names' (p. 205 above). Like other Sophists he was an itinerant, practising in various cities and giving public exhibitions of his skill at the great pan-Hellenic centres of Olympia and Delphi, and charged fees for his instruction and performances. Besides Thessaly, there are reports of visits to Boeotia and Argos (where he was badly received and his lectures banned).[2] A special feature of his displays was to invite miscellaneous questions from the audience and give impromptu replies. When he came to Athens in 427, on an embassy from Leontini, he was already about sixty, and took the city by storm with his novel style of oratory, as well as earning large sums by special performances and classes for the young (pp. 40 and 179, n. 3 above).

His written works included *Technai*, manuals of rhetorical instruction, which may have consisted largely of models to be learned by heart, of which the extant *Encomium of Helen* and *Defence of Palamedes* (frr. 11 and 11a) would be examples.[3] Then there were his own speeches, epideictic, political and other. Aristotle quotes from the introduction to his Olympian oration, the subject of which was Hellenic unity (frr. 7–8a), which he also touched on in his funeral oration for Athenians fallen in war (frr. 5a–6). Also in Aristotle is a brief quotation from an *Encomium on the Eleans* (fr. 10), and the Pythian oration is mentioned by Philostratus (1.9.4, A 1). The only considerable extant fragment is one from the funeral oration, quoted by a late writer to illustrate his rhetorical style (fr. 6), which Aristotle stigmatizes more than once as being in bad taste (frr. 15 and 16). Apart from the speeches, we have paraphrases of the argument of the ironic

---

[1] There is not the slightest evidence for Schmid's topsy-turvy idea that Empedocles owed his fame as a teacher of rhetoric (see vol. II, 135) to his brilliant pupil (*Gesch.* 1.3.1, 58, n. 4). See Classen in *Proc. Afr. Cl. Ass.* 1959, 37f. For Gorgias's assistance to the doctors by his 'master-art' of rhetoric see Plato, *Gorg.* 456b. His interest in the πόροι theory is also mentioned by Theophrastus (Gorg. fr. 5 DK).

[2] See Untersteiner, *Sophs.* 93 with notes, and Schmid, *Gesch.* 1.3.1, 59, n. 10.

[3] On these two works see p. 192 with n. 2 above.

treatise *On Nature or the Non-existent,* in which he turned the Eleatic thesis upside-down.

All the Sophists indulged in disparagement of their competitors. Protagoras accused them of wasting their pupils' time on useless specialization, and Gorgias (no doubt with an eye particularly on Protagoras) disclaimed any intention of teaching *areté.* 'What about the Sophists,' Socrates asks Meno, 'the only people who profess to teach it? Do you think they do?' And the reply is (*Meno* 95 c): 'What I particularly admire about Gorgias is that you will never hear him make this claim; indeed he laughs at the others when he hears them do so. In his view his job is to make clever speakers.' In any case there was no one thing, *areté,* whose essence could be known and defined (pp. 253 f. above). What was virtue in a slave would not be virtue in a statesman, and the same course of action would in one set of circumstances exhibit *areté* and in another not. But if his sole accomplishment was to make his pupils masters of the art of persuasion, this, he claimed, was the queen of sciences and had all the rest in its power. Of what use was the surgeon's skill if the patient would not submit to the knife? Of what use was it to know the best policy for the city if the Assembly could not be persuaded to adopt it? Skill in *logoi* was the road to supreme power. It may be an art of deceit, but deceit, said Gorgias, can itself be employed in a good cause, as poetry—especially tragedy—shows (fr. 23). It can be, but it may not. This is the essence of Plato's complaint, the truth of which emerges not only from his criticisms but from Gorgias's own surviving compositions, namely that the art of Gorgias is morally neutral, concerned with means not ends. He himself was an upright man, who would not wish to see his instruction put to a bad use,[1] and so, after he has disclaimed responsibility for this, Plato's Socrates is able to force him into a contradiction. He cannot deny that right and wrong are part of the subject-matter of rhetoric itself, so he supposes he will tell a pupil about them 'if he happens

---

[1] Calogero in *JHS,* 1957 even claims to have found the Socratic principle that no one does wrong willingly, and the idea of the *psyche* as seat of consciousness and moral principle, in those egregious documents of the persuader's art, the *Helen* and *Palamedes.* As to the former, Socrates's position was that wrongdoing can only be due to ignorance of the good, for which the certain cure is knowledge; Gorgias's, that there is no such thing as knowledge and a man's conduct was in the hands of the most powerful persuader, however unscrupulous. I do not see much resemblance.

not to know already'—an admission which makes nonsense of his denial that he teaches *areté*.[1] He makes it only, of course, because he has been driven into a corner, and we cannot be certain that he would have said such a thing in real life. At any rate, whereas rhetoric was in the curriculum of every Sophist, Gorgias must have put it more prominently in his shop window than any of the others. He saw the power of persuasion as paramount in every field, in the study of nature and other philosophical subjects no less than in the law-courts or the political arena. One essential to the art was the sense of occasion, *kairos*, the right time or opportunity, for, as Disraeli also knew, 'the opportune in a popular assembly has sometimes more success than the weightiest efforts of research and reason'.[2] The speaker must adapt his words to the audience and the situation.[3] He was, said Dionysius of Halicarnassus, the first to write about this, though neither he nor anyone later had yet developed it as a *techné*.[4]

His rhetorical practices were based on, and justified by, a relativistic philosophy similar to that of Protagoras. If there were any universally valid truth which could be communicated to another, then no doubt only that truth, backed by incontrovertible evidence, ought to be conveyed.

[1] Gorgias's disclaimer has naturally aroused discussion. Joël (*Gesch.* 669) drew attention not only to Plato, *Gorg.* 460a, but also to the epitaph written by his great-nephew Eumolpus for his statue at Olympia (mentioned by Pausanias, 6. 17.7 = DK, A 7, and discovered in 1876). This speaks of him as having 'invented the best τέχνη for training the soul for the lists of virtue' (ἀρετῆς ἐς ἀγῶνας). Rensi, quoted by Untersteiner (*Sophs.* 182), forces this into agreement with the disclaimer by a (for its time) rather artificial distinction between theoretical exposition and practical training. Schmid (*Gesch.* 66f.), relying on a high-flown bit of rhetoric in the *Epitaphios*, claims Gorgias believed ἀρετή to be 'im vollen und höchsten Sinn' a gift of the gods, yet in the same paragraph says that, whereas for Protagoras αἰδώς and δίκη were part of a divine order, for Gorgias they were human and mutable! Were they not in his eyes ἀρεταί? I have ventured to connect the disclaimer with his denial that any single thing, *areté*, existed.

[2] Quoted by Robert Blake, *Disraeli*, 266.

[3] In vol. II of his autobiography Lord Russell describes his visit to Russia soon after the First World War. He speaks of the utter horror with which he observed the cruelty, persecution and poverty, the spying and hypocrisy that prevailed. The shock, he says, was almost more than he could bear. Later in the same year, when he was on his way to China, the English on the boat asked him to give a lecture about Soviet Russia and, he continues (p. 125), 'in view of the sort of people they were, I said only favourable things about the Soviet Government'. This seems a good illustration of the Gorgian attitude to truth and *kairos*.

[4] Dion. Hal. *De comp. verb.* 12 (Gorg. fr. 13). In Philostratus 1.1 (A 1a) ἐφιεὶς τῷ καιρῷ refers only to his gift of improvisation—'trusting to the inspiration of the moment', as the Loeb translation has it. Some have made a great deal of this 'καιρός-Lehre', in which among other things they see medical influence. See Schmid, *Gesch.* 1.3.1, 58, n. 5, 65 with n. 2, 24, n. 3 (Protagoras); Nestle, *VM ʒu L*, 316f.; Shorey, *TAPA*, 1909.

If everyone had a memory of all that is past, a conception of what is happening at present and a foreknowledge of the future ... [1] But as it is, there is no easy way of either recollecting the past or investigating the present or divining the future, so that on most subjects most men have only opinion to offer the mind as counsellor; and opinion is slippery and insecure (*Hel.* 11).

To express, with all the intellectual force at his command, this thesis that we are all at the mercy of opinion and the truth is for each of us whatever we can be persuaded to believe, because there is no permanent and stable truth to be known, he cast it into the philosophical form of a challenge to the Eleatic assertion of a single changeless being grasped by an infallible reason as opposed to the changing world of appearance, or opinion, which was unreal. Nothing *is* as Parmenides used the verb, that is, exists as at the same time an immutable reality and the object of human knowledge. If there were such a reality we could not grasp it, and even if we could, we could never communicate our knowledge to others. We live in a world where opinion (*doxa*) is supreme, and there is no higher criterion by which it can be verified or the reverse. This leaves the Sophist-orator, master of the art of persuasion both private and public, in command of the whole field of experience, for opinion can always be changed. Only knowledge, based on unshakeable proof, could withstand the attacks of *peitho*, and there is no such thing. This was, in Plato's eyes, the arch-heresy which he must do his utmost to destroy. He must show, first, that there is such a thing as true and false opinion. Next, because if they are *only* opinions the true one will be as vulnerable as the false to the wiles of the persuader, he must restore the criterion of judgment and demonstrate how opinion can be converted to knowledge by 'thinking out the reason' (*Meno* 98a).

The influence of Gorgias was considerable, especially of course on literary style, where it was felt by writers as diverse as the historian Thucydides and the tragic poet Agathon. (For Agathon see Plato, *Symp.* 198c.) His most famous pupil was Isocrates. Among others who are said or thought to have been either his pupils or subject to his

---

[1] The apodosis, omitted here, is uncertain in text and meaning. For different solutions see DK *ad loc.* and Untersteiner, *Sof.* II, 101f. It does not affect the main point, that knowledge is in general impossible and fallible opinion the only guide. Cf. fr. 11a, §35, quoted on p. 180 above.

influence are Antisthenes and Alcidamas, and more doubtfully Lycophron, Prodicus, and Hippocrates the great physician; and among
active politicians Pericles, Alcibiades, Critias, Proxenus and Meno.

(3) PRODICUS

To any reader of Plato the name of Prodicus inevitably recalls, before
anything else, the picture of the unhappy professor, 'suffering grievous
pains' as the sobriquet Tantalus suggests, lying on his bed wrapped in
sheepskins and blankets ('and plenty of them'), his words drowned by
the reverberations of his droning voice in the small room in the house
of Callias where he holds forth to a select group of listeners. To draw
such a picture, thought Sidgwick, was an act of 'refined barbarity'
on Plato's part, whereas Joël, taking Plato's picture for the truth,
denied that this miserable creature could possibly have been the
author of the heroic fable of Heracles at the crossroads.[1] In Joël's
psychology, a writer about Heracles should himself be wrapped in
lion's skin, not sheep's. However that may be, since there is no other
evidence for Prodicus's personal idiosyncrasies, we are free to accept
Plato's if we wish as a not unkindly exaggeration (so at least it seems
to me) of genuine traits.

He was a native of the Ionian city of Iulis on Ceos in the Cyclades,
the home of the poet Simonides, as Socrates reminds him when that
poet's works are under discussion (Plato, *Prot.* 339e ff.). The Suda
(DK, A 1) calls him rather vaguely a contemporary of Democritus and
Gorgias, which allows anything between 490 and 460 for his birth; but
it must have been nearer the second, for the *Protagoras* tells us that
he was much younger than Protagoras. One cannot do better than
put it, with Mayer (*Prod.* 3) and others, between 470 and 460. He was,
then, a few years older than Socrates, and all that can be said about the
length of his life is that he outlived him, for with Gorgias and Hippias
he is mentioned in the present tense at Plato *Apol.* 19e. Plato says that
he often came to Athens on official missions from Ceos, and like
Gorgias took the opportunity to earn some money by declaiming his
compositions in public and giving instruction to the young men. If

[1] Plato, *Prot.* 315 c–d; Sidgwick in *J. Philol.* 1873, 68; Joël, *Gesch.* 689.

we accept the obvious dramatic date for the *Protagoras*, he must have been well known in Athens before the beginning of the Peloponnesian War, and Aristophanes could raise a laugh by mentioning his name in 423 and 414.[1]

He was a Sophist in the full sense of a professional freelance educator, whose name is coupled with that of Protagoras as teaching the art of success in politics and private life. There seems to have been a standing joke about the difference between his one-drachma lecture and his fifty-drachma lecture (or course? See p. 42, n. 1) on semantics. In the *Cratylus* (384b) Socrates says that if he could have afforded the fifty drachmas he would now be fully expert on the 'correctness of names', but unfortunately he had to be content with the one-drachma lecture. Aristotle (*Rhet.* 1415b12), giving hints on how to recall the wandering attention of an audience by some striking pronouncement, says this is what Prodicus called 'slipping in a bit of the fifty-drachma when the audience begins to nod'.

As one of those present at the gathering of Sophists described in the *Protagoras*, he takes part in the conversation at various points, where the main emphasis is on a somewhat ironic treatment of his insistence on fine distinctions of meaning between words commonly regarded as synonyms. Socrates (of whose relations with Prodicus something has already been said, pp. 222f.) calls himself his pupil in this skill, and elsewhere in the dialogue speaks of him as a man of 'inspired wisdom', which he thinks may be 'ancient and god-given, going back to Simonides or even earlier'. In the *Meno* also he speaks of himself as having been trained by Prodicus as Meno by Gorgias, and in the *Charmides* says he has listened to 'innumerable discourses' of Prodicus on the distinction of names. In the *Hippias Major* he calls him his friend or companion. In the *Theaetetus*, after explaining his maieutic skill in aiding the birth-pangs of men whose minds are big with ideas, he adds that when he has judged that people are not pregnant (that is, presumably, are without a good idea in their heads), and so have no need of him, he has passed many of them on to Prodicus and other 'wondrously wise men' who are more likely to help them. The inference is not flattering. Undoubtedly Socrates thought of his own dia-

---

[1] Plato, *Hipp. Maj.* 282c; Aristophanes, *Clouds* 361 and *Birds* 692.

lectic, whereby one man helps another to mature and formulate his own ideas, as the only genuinely philosophic method, and the implication is that sophistic education, as exemplified by Prodicus, treats the pupil rather as a passive receiver of ready-made facts or theories. In the *Laches*, on the other hand, it is Laches who, in opposition to Socrates, disparages Prodicus's accomplishment as 'the sort of cleverness that befits a Sophist rather than a statesman'. To extract from the nuances of Plato's literary portraits a prosaic and agreed account of the relations between the two men is practically impossible, or at least very much at the mercy of subjective impressions. There is no doubt that Socrates had close personal relations with him, attended his lectures on the importance of using words precisely, and (I should say) felt a certain affection for his donnish gullibility. To Socrates, as to Confucius (p. 488, n. 1, below), correct language, 'the rectification of names', was the prerequisite for correct living and even efficient government, and it may well be that this truth first dawned on him while listening to the one-drachma discourse of Prodicus. But Prodicus, though his linguistic teaching undoubtedly included semantic distinctions between ethical terms, had stopped at the threshold. He was like the orators who 'when they have learned the necessary preliminaries to rhetoric think they have discovered the art itself, and that by teaching them to others they have given them complete instruction in rhetoric' (*Phaedr.* 269b–c). The complete art of *logoi* embraces nothing less than the whole of philosophy.[1]

One would suppose from Plato that the essence of Prodicus's teaching was linguistic. 'The correctness of names' was the foundation of all else (*Euthyd.* 277e). The Suda however (A 1, DK) classifies

[1] Other references for this paragraph: Plato, *Prot.* 341a, 315e, *Meno* 96d, *Charm.* 163d, *Hipp. Maj.* 282c, *Theaet.* 151b, *Laches* 197d. Whether or not one agrees with Joël and Momigliano (see the latter in *Atti Torino*, 1929–30, 104) that the 'myth' of Prodicus as master of Socrates is Cynic in origin depends, of course, on how one chooses to interpret the many references to their relations which, since they come from Plato, are free from suspicion of such an origin. However, Momigliano does go further than I have ventured to go here in attributing to Prodicus an awareness of the consequences of his semantic teaching as it affected both ethics and epistemology, thus bringing him much closer to Socrates. (For more on this see pp. 224f. above.) To say that it led him to renounce the scepticism and relativism of his brother-Sophists is to pay him a compliment which I should be inclined to reserve for Socrates. For a summing up of the Socratic–Platonic picture of Prodicus see also Mayer, *Prod.* 18–22, who thought that the *Prot.* gives distortion, caricature and irony; elsewhere Plato acknowledges the scientific value of Prodicus's procedure.

him as 'natural philosopher and Sophist', and Galen (see DK, 24 A 2) includes him in a somewhat indiscriminate list of 'writers on nature', with Melissus, Parmenides, Empedocles, Alcmaeon, Gorgias 'and all the rest'. This finds some contemporary confirmation in Aristophanes, who in the *Clouds* (360) calls him μετεωροσοφιστής, an 'astronomical expert',[1] and in the *Birds* (692) implies that he produced a cosmogony. Galen mentions a work 'on the nature of man', in which he brought his linguistic interests to bear on physiological terms, insisting that the word *phlegm* should be applied to the hot humour because of its etymological connexion with the verb 'to burn', and assigning the name *blenna* to the cold humour commonly called *phlegm*.[2]

We possess at least the content, if not the actual words, of an *epideixis* of Prodicus, which seems to guarantee its genuineness by being exactly the sort of thing that one would expect a Sophist to compose for recital before a popular audience, conveying elementary moral commonplaces through the easily absorbed medium of a fable about one of the most popular figures of legend. Its influence has been surprisingly great. Xenophon describes it as 'the composition about Heracles which he delivered before the largest crowds', and puts the report in the mouth of Socrates as a counterweight to the hedonism and sensuality of Aristippus. At the end Socrates says that what he has given is 'approximately Prodicus's story of the education of Heracles by Virtue, though he clothes its sentiments in even more magnificent words than I have now'. It is presumably the work referred to by Plato when he speaks of 'the good Prodicus' as having written a prose encomium of Heracles (*Symp.* 177b). Impeccable as are its sentiments, few would nowadays accord it the enthusiastic eulogy of Grote, beginning:

Who is there that has not read the well-known fable called 'The Choice of Heracles'...? Who does not know that its express purpose is to kindle the

---

[1] One cannot altogether discount this on the ground that he applied the same word to Socrates, for there is every likelihood that Socrates's earlier years were in fact marked by an interest in natural philosophy sufficient to give some factual basis to the description. (See pp. 420ff. below.) For Cicero's reference to Prodicus, together with other Sophists, as having written *etiam de natura rerum*, see p. 46 above. Gellius on the other hand contrasts him with Anaxagoras as a *rhetor*, not a *physicus* (15.20, DK, A 8).

[2] Galen, *De virt. phys.* 3.195 Helmreich (Prodicus fr. 4). Galen adds a reference to his linguistic innovations as described by Plato.

imaginations of youth in favour of a life of labour for noble objects, and against a life of indulgence? If it be of striking simplicity and effect even to a modern reader, how much more powerfully must it have worked upon the audience for whose belief it was specially adapted, when set off by the oral expansions of the author?

It is, Grote thought, a vindication of Prodicus and a warning against putting confidence in the sarcastic remarks of Plato. One might rather say that if all sophistic teaching were like this it would confirm the view expressed by Plato in the *Republic* (493a) that the so-called wisdom of the Sophists boils down to a rehash of the conventional opinions of the crowd.[1] There is no need to repeat every detail of the well-known tale. When Heracles as a young man is pondering which path of life to take, he is accosted by two tall women representing Virtue and Vice, who compete for his allegiance. Each is suitably described, Virtue handsome and noble in mien, her body clothed in purity and her eyes in modesty, her whole appearance suggesting self-control, and Vice plump and soft, with a complexion not left to nature, a wandering eye, and a dress revealing rather than concealing her charms. She speaks first, and the pleasure and ease that she promises can be imagined. Virtue by contrast promises a life of severe training, hard work and simplicity, which will however be rewarded with honour, true friendship and, if he wishes it, wealth and power, which can only be won by toil and sweat. Idleness, pleasure and vice on the other hand will weaken his body and destroy his mind. His later years will be a burden to him, whereas if he has followed virtue he can bask in the memory of past glories and enjoy the happiness that his efforts have merited.[2]

---

[1] Grote, *History* (1888 ed.), VII, 57. For a more balanced criticism see Grant, *Ethics*, I, 145 f., who makes some telling points. This is not to deny that it may have become, as Schmid calls it, 'One of the most influential pieces of world-literature' (*Gesch.* 41; see his n. 9 for bibliography). Its basic idea of the choice of two ways in life, the primrose path and the arduous climb to virtue, was already in Hesiod (*Erga* 287–92). Schultz's article *Herakles am Scheidewege*, in *Philol.* 1909, goes further into the mythical affinities of the tale, especially its relation to the Y symbol as (*a*) crossroads and (*b*) tree of life.

[2] The full text, from Xen. *Mem.* 2.1.21–34, is printed as fr. 2 of Prodicus in DK. It appeared in a work called *Horai*, a title of dubious meaning which if it was the author's own (Lesky, *HGL*, 348) was doubtless explained somewhere in the work itself. On this work see especially Nestle in *Hermes*, 1936 and H. Gomperz, *S. u. R.* 97–101. Joël took the extreme view, which has not been generally followed, that the fable was not by Prodicus at all, but an Antisthenean work Cynic in character. (See his *Gesch.* 686–9.) This is refuted by the reference to it in a scholion

Prodicus

Prodicus's outlook, like that of other Sophists, was humanistic, and he took a purely naturalistic view of religion (pp. 238 ff. above). His theory was that primitive man, to whom many aspects of nature must have appeared hostile, was so impressed with the gifts that she provided for the furtherance of his life, welfare and enjoyment—such as the sun, earth and water, air and fire, foodstuffs and the vine—that he believed them either to be the discovery and especial benefaction of divine beings or themselves to embody the godhead. This theory was not only remarkable for its rationalism but had the additional merit of discerning a close connexion between religion and agriculture. This was based on observed fact, since fertility-cults are not only widespread at an early stage of civilization but were especially common in Greece, where moreover it was customary to trace all the benefits of civilized life to an origin in the invention of agriculture.

The only recorded titles of works by Prodicus are *On Nature, On the Nature of Man*, and *Horai*, and about these we must remind ourselves of what was said earlier (p. 264) about the dubious authority of such titles in general. Some have thought that the *Horai* was a universal work including as internal sections his views on nature, human and otherwise, his theory of the origin of religion, a panegyric on agriculture leading to thoughts on moral virtue and the education requisite to attain it, and even the doctrine of synonyms.[1]

to Aristophanes (Prodicus fr. 1), whose independence seems assured by its mention of the title and final choice of Heracles, which are not in Xenophon. There is of course no means of knowing how close Xenophon has kept to the original. I have ventured what can be no more than an opinion. Grote, Grant and Untersteiner (*Sophs.* 207) also regard it as authentic in substance; others (Wecklein, Blass, Schacht, Mayer in *Prod.* 8 f.) suppose him to have handled the tale very freely. In this connexion attention has been drawn to the use of words of closely related meaning which some have connected with Prodicus's 'synonymic' while to others they have appeared as mere stylistic variations *à la* Gorgias and entirely unlike Prodicus, who insisted that no two words ought to be used as if they had identical meanings. See Spengel in Gomperz, *S. u. R.* 101, n. 225, Mayer, *Prod.* 10 f. Although such arguments can never lead to certainty, there is more to be said for Spengel and Gomperz. The first set quoted (κατασκοπεῖσθαι, ἐπισκοπεῖν, θεᾶσθαι, ἀποβλέπειν) neither have nor appear intended to have the same meaning, but give the impression of being carefully chosen for their context.

[1] See Untersteiner, *Sophs.* 207 and (for Nestle's reconstruction) 225, n. 74. For Untersteiner the *Horai* was 'his greatest work, in which the cycle of things and the ethical law which governs all found one of their unifying visions'. This would be difficult to substantiate. His insistence on the correct use of words naturally permeated all his work, but it is plain from Plato that instruction in the subject was given in an independent lecture or course of lectures. The inclusion of the Heracles fable involves, as Gomperz frankly says (*S. u. R.* 100 f.), assuming that much in Xenophon's description of it as an *epideixis* is fiction.

Finally one may mention references to Prodicus in two pseudo-Platonic dialogues. Their date is uncertain, and the views attributed to him cannot be regarded as certainly authentic. In the *Eryxias* (397 d ff.) he is reported as saying that wealth, like everything else, is a blessing to a good man who knows how to use it properly, but a curse to the ignorant and evil. If he did say this, he was remarkably in harmony with Socrates, who argues for it in the *Meno* (87 e ff.), though the author of the *Eryxias* makes him take part in the discomfiture of the Sophist, who, he says, seemed to everybody to be talking nonsense. But the thesis itself was perhaps a commonplace, and something very like it appears in the 'Anonymus Iamblichi' (DK, II, 401, 16–19). In the *Axiochus* (366 c ff.) 'Socrates', after some boorish and ill-phrased criticism of Prodicus's greed for fees, says that he has heard him, in an *epideixis* delivered at the house of Callias, give vent to such depressingly pessimistic comments on the worthlessness of life that he himself felt a strong urge for death. The mention of an *epideixis* is circumstantial, and the allusion to Prodicus as Tantalus in the *Protagoras*, together with his bedridden state (until he was hauled out of it by the others), may suggest that he was inclined to a gloomy view.[1] When all is said, however, the only facets of his teaching about which we know enough to make it of philosophic interest are his passion for the exact use of language and his theory of the origin of religion.

(4) HIPPIAS

Hippias son of Diopeithes was another of the younger generation of Sophists, contemporary with Socrates rather than with Protagoras and Gorgias. His widowed daughter married Isocrates in the latter's old age.[2] The only authority for his date is Plato, who simply says that he was much younger than Protagoras,[3] and implies that he was alive

---

[1] H. Gomperz has a long discussion of both these passages in *S. u. R.* 102–10. For the first, see also the references in Untersteiner, *Sophs.* 226, n. 82.

[2] For authorities see DK, A 3 and 4.

[3] *Prot.* 317 c, *Hipp. Maj.* 282 d–e. Untersteiner's belief that he was not born until about 443 depends on his theory that he wrote the proem to Theophrastus's *Characters*. (See *Sophs.* 272 and 274, n. 3.) Untersteiner also claims that he is the Anonymus of Iamblichus and wrote Thucydides 3.4 (on events in Corcyra). I cannot follow his argument (*Sof.* III, 76) that, because according to Pausanias 5.25.4 (*a*) Hippias wrote an inscription for the statues by

in 399. Coming from Elis, he was, as Nestle has pointed out (*VMₓuL*, 360), unlike most Sophists in being a Dorian, and hence travelled more to Dorian cities than to Athens, most often to Sparta (Plato, *Hipp. Maj.* 281 b) but also to Sicily (*ibid.* 282 e). He boasts (in Plato) that the Eleans always turn to him as the ideal man to represent them abroad, and of the vast sums of money which he has earned on these visits by his outstanding virtuosity as a Sophist, which he also displayed at Athens and Olympia and no doubt elsewhere. At Olympia, 'at the festival of all Hellas', he offered both prepared discourses and extempore answers to questions put to him on the spot (*Hipp. Min.* 363 c–d).

Most of our information about Hippias comes from Plato, who in two dialogues made him the only interlocutor of Socrates[1] as well as including him in the *Protagoras*. Those therefore who are convinced that Plato was possessed by a hatred of the Sophists which blinded him to their real character may ignore it and conclude that we know little or nothing about him. On the other hand there is a marked difference between his treatment of them as individuals. When one thinks of the respect which he accords to Protagoras, his tactful handling of Gorgias, whereby the real onslaught on what to Plato were the disastrous effects of his teaching was reserved for other, less sympathetic characters, and even his mildly ironical attitude to the pedantic side of Prodicus's semantic distinctions, the consistency with which he makes broad fun of Hippias surely justifies a suspicion that he was in fact a somewhat bombastic, humourless and thick-skinned character.[2] He is given to breath-taking remarks like 'I have never found any man who

Calon of the drowned Messenians which was later than the statues themselves, (*b*) the inscription on the base of a different statue by Calon (which has been excavated) shows lettering of 420–410, therefore the inscription by Hippias is to be assigned to that decade. This is not the inference of Frazer, to whom Untersteiner refers.

[1] I will not at this point enter into the question of the genuineness of the two *Hippias* dialogues. For modern authorities pro and con see Friedländer, *Plato*, II, 101 with 316 n. 1, 146 with 326 n. 6, and for the *major* D. Tarrant's ed. pp. ix–xvii (she believed it to be probably by a pupil of Plato) and E. Edelstein, *X. u. P. Bild*, 24, n. 7. The *minor* is quoted by Aristotle, *Metaph.* 1025 a 6, though without mention of its authorship.

[2] Nestle drew a different conclusion from the variety of treatment (*VMₓuL*, 360): because Plato liked Protagoras but felt a deep antipathy for Hippias, the picture of him in the *Hippias* dialogues *is* just a caricature, though (Nestle admits) Plato does take him more seriously in the *Protagoras*. This, he thought, makes Hippias's character the most difficult to grasp of any Sophist's, but the difficulty seems to be of his own making.

was my superior in anything', and the unsuspecting innocence with which he laps up the most blatantly ironical flattery from Socrates is almost attractive. Certainly he is a man with whom it would be difficult to be angry.

That he had something to boast about is equally certain. Plato speaks of his Macaulay-like memory, whereby he could retain a list of fifty names after a single hearing, and his astonishing versatility. Well might Xenophon call him a polymath. He was evidently one of those who absorb learning easily and quickly, some of it such as to demand high intellectual gifts. Subjects that he was prepared to teach included astronomy, geometry, arithmetic, grammar, rhythm, music, genealogy, mythology and history, including the history of philosophy and mathematics.[1] He also wrote declamations on the poets, which in the hands of a Sophist were more likely to deal with moral questions than with what we should call literary criticism. In the *Protagoras* (347a) he lays claim to a *logos* on Simonides (which he will recite to the company if requested), and at the beginning of the *Hippias Minor* he has just finished an epideixis on Homer. Most of his subjects are listed by Plato without any illustrations, a few of which have come down in later writers. He spoke of Thales drawing from the behaviour of amber and the loadstone the conclusion that inanimate objects had soul,[2] and of Mamercus, brother of the poet Stesichorus, as a successor of Thales in geometry. As a historian he noted that the word *tyrannos* was not used before the time of Archilochus, spoke of Lycurgus's military talent, and published a list of Olympic victors, as Aristotle did later of the Pythian victors. (Olympia was of course on his home territory.) Anthropological interests are suggested by a work called *Nomenclature of Tribes*. In mythology he differed from Pindar over the name of Phrixus's stepmother and claimed that the continents of Asia and Europe were called after Oceanids of these names. The only astronomical pronouncement that has come down is that he put the

---

[1] Xen. *Symp.* 4.62, Plato, *Prot.* 315c, 318e, *Hipp. Maj.* 285c–e.

[2] Aristotle introduces this cautiously at *De an.* 405a19 in the form: 'Thales too seems to have supposed, from what is reported about him . . .', and D.L. (1.24) attributes the information to both Aristotle and Hippias. Snell, and following him Classen, have deduced that for this and all his other references to Thales Aristotle made use of the work of Hippias mentioned by Clement in fr. 6, of which they have detected further traces in Plato *Crat.* 402b and *Symp.* 178a. See Classen in *Philol.* 1965.

number of stars in the Hyades group at seven.[1] His prodigious memory was cultivated by a deliberate technique of mnemonics which he also taught to others.[2] Not content with all this he wrote tragedies and dithyrambs as well as prose, and was as clever with his hands as his brain, according to the story in Plato that he appeared at Olympia wearing nothing that he had not made himself, not only clothes but also a ring, oil-flask and strigil (*Hipp. Min.* 368b–d). The Suda says (A 1, DK) that he set up self-sufficiency as the goal of life, and this passage would certainly bear it out if it is not in fact the basis of the tradition.

He was an omnivorous reader, and incorporated the results of his reading in a comprehensive work called the *Synagogé*, that is, collection or miscellany. The title is mentioned by Athenaeus, and an interesting quotation in Clement of Alexandria (the only one extant which claims to give anything like Hippias's own words) must surely be his own description of this work.[3] It runs:

It may be that some of this has been said by Orpheus, some briefly, here and there, by Musaeus, some by Hesiod and some by Homer, some in other poets and some in prose-writers both Greek and foreign. For my part, I have collected from all these writers what is most important and belongs together to make this new and composite work.

The only bit of its contents vouchsafed to us concerns a certain Thargelia of Miletus, a 'wise and beautiful woman' who had fourteen husbands.

One mathematical discovery is attributed to Hippias which, if the attribution is correct, 'differentiates him', as K. Freeman says (*Com-*

---

[1] Mamercus, Hipp. fr. 12 (Proclus); *tyrannos*, fr. 9 (schol. Sophocles); Lycurgus, fr. 11 (Plut.); Olympic victors, fr. 3 (Plut.); Phrixus, fr. 14 (schol. Pind.); Ἐθνῶν ὀνομασίαι, fr. 2 (schol. Apoll. Rhod.); Hyades, fr. 13 (schol. Arat.).

[2] Besides the reference to his μνημονικὸν τέχνημα in *Hipp. Min.* 368d, see Xen. *Symp.* 4.62 (Callias learned τὸ μνημονικόν from Hippias). *Diss. Log.* 9 (DK, II, 416) may be an echo of Hippias. (According to Cicero, *De or.* 2.86.351–4, the first to evolve a mnemonic technique was Simonides. He and Hippias are mentioned together by Aelian, *Hist. Anim.* 6.10 and Amm. Marcell. 16.5.8, both quoted by Tarrant, *Hipp. Maj.* xxvii.)

[3] Fr. 6, from Clem. *Strom.* 6.15 (II, 434 St.). Clement commits himself to no more than ὧδέ πως λέγοντα, but gives it as a direct quotation. (His object is to prove that Greeks are incorrigible plagiarists.) The phrase ἐν συγγραφαῖς τὰ μὲν Ἕλλησι τὰ δὲ βαρβάροις is interesting. Even if, as Nestle thought (*VMzuL*, 364), Hippias only knew the latter at second hand, perhaps from Hecataeus, it challenges the oft-repeated but improbable claim that Greek writers knew no language but their own. For the title see fr. 4 (Ath. 608f).

panion, 385), 'from all other Sophists and places him in the ranks of the scientific discoverers'. This is the curve called *quadratrix* (τετραγωνί-ӡουσα), which as its name implies was used for squaring the circle, and also for trisecting an angle or dividing it according to any given ratio.[1] In mentioning it as Hippias's work Proclus does not add 'of Elis', and since the name is not uncommon (there are eighteen in the *Real-Encyclopädie*) some have been sceptical, thinking it scarcely credible that our universal virtuoso could have achieved such original work in any single field. Others argue that Proclus had earlier in his work attributed the remark about Mamercus to Hippias of Elis, and if he now meant a different man would have said so. This is not very cogent (particularly as the Mamercus passage comes nearly 200 Teubner pages before the earlier of the two references to the *quadratrix*), but most modern opinion is in favour of the attribution to the Sophist.[2]

Grote remarked (*History*, 1888 ed., VII, 63 f.) that Plato, for all his 'sneer and contemptuous banter', never accuses Hippias, as he did some other Sophists, of preaching 'a low or corrupt morality'. In the *Hippias Major* (286a) Hippias mentions a *Trojan Discourse* which he has recited at Sparta and intends to repeat at Athens. Its theme is a discourse by Nestor in reply to Neoptolemos, who has asked him (as Grote puts it) 'what was the plan of life incumbent on a young man of honourable aspirations', and Grote suggests that for high moral purpose it was probably not unworthy to be set beside Prodicus's *Choice of Heracles*. That may or may not be so (we know nothing of its content), but in any case Hippias has better claims to be accepted as a serious ethical thinker. He was one of those who contrasted law and nature and upheld the latter on moral and humanitarian, not selfish and ambitious, grounds. He held a form of the social-contract theory of law: positive law, being a matter of human agreement and frequently

---

[1] The sole authority is Proclus, *Eucl.* pp. 272 (= Hipp. fr. 21) and 356 Friedländer, whose source is Eudemus.

[2] Among the sceptics were Wilamowitz (*Platon*, 1, 133, n. 3) and Schmid (*Gesch.* 54f.). Björnbo in *RE*, VIII, 1708f., mentions four objections to the attribution to Hippias, and finds none of them cogent; but he makes no reference to the silence of Simplicius, who at *Phys.* 54ff. seems to be giving as complete an account as he can of attempts to square the circle, and says nothing of Hippias. This might be thought significant. The authorship of Hippias was accepted by Heath, *Hist. Gr. Math.* 1, 23. For details of the *quadratrix* see Freeman, *Comp.* 386–8, or Björnbo, *loc. cit.*

altered, was not to be regarded as providing fixed and universal standards of conduct. It could be 'a tyrant doing violence to nature'. He believed however that there were unwritten laws, divine in origin and universal in application, concerning such things as the worship of the gods and respect for parents. With belief in universal, natural laws (and for Hippias natural and divine appear to be the same) went belief in the fundamental unity of the human race, whose divisions are only a matter of *nomos*, i.e. positive law and established, but mistaken, conventions or habits (p. 163 above).

As witness to his ethical views we have, finally, some remarks on envy and slander which were quoted by Plutarch.[1] There are, said Hippias, two sorts of envy, a right and a wrong. It is right to feel envy when honours go to bad men, wrong when they go to good. Moreover the envious have a double share of suffering: they are grieved, like all men, by their own troubles, but also by the good fortune of others. Of slander he said that it is a curse because the law prescribes no punishment for it as it does for robbery, though in fact it is robbery of the best thing in life, namely friendship or goodwill (*philia*). Its underhand nature makes it worse than open violence. Here is a concrete instance of his censure of *nomos*, and in this respect at least he would regard today's laws as an improvement.

(5) ANTIPHON

Antiphon was a very common name,[2] especially in Attica, and the identity of Antiphon the Sophist, whose views have been discussed in earlier chapters of this book, has been the subject of endless scholarly controversy. The main question is whether he is the same man as the orator Antiphon of Rhamnus who figures in Thucydides as a member of the Four Hundred and was the author of an extant collection of oratorical exercises called the *Tetralogies* and three forensic speeches. The position is further complicated by references to Antiphon as a

[1] Frr. 16 and 17. Actually we have them from Stobaeus, who found them in a work of Plutarch *On Slander*, now lost.

[2] For instance Plato had a half-brother called Antiphon, whom he introduces as narrator of the dialogue *Parmenides*. Blass (*Att. Bereds.*[2] I, 93 ff.) distinguishes six in addition to the orator (summarized in Loeb Plut. vol. x, 346 note *d*).

tragic poet, as the author of a work on dreams, and as a soothsayer. Thus Heinimann (*N. u. Ph.* 134) pronounced: 'It must be taken as certain that the Sophist, the oligarchic orator and the tragedian are three different people.' It has even been suggested that the works *On Truth* and *On Concord* are by different men.[1] Whatever the answer, one thing must be borne in mind throughout: references in our authorities to 'Antiphon the Sophist' do not suffice to distinguish a Sophist from an orator, since in ancient times the word *sophistes* would be applied equally to both. In any case Origen says that the Antiphon who wrote *On Truth* was known as an orator (Antiphon, fr. 12). The question is of minor interest for the history of philosophy, and discussion of it has been relegated to a note (pp. 292–4 below), which may be thankfully omitted by all but classical specialists.

The oratorical works, whoever wrote them, are not our present concern. About the external circumstances of the Sophist's life (if he is different from the orator) nothing is known, nor is there any precise information about his date, though he was obviously a contemporary of Socrates. The orator is said (pseudo-Plut. *Vit. or.* 832f) to have been born about the time of the Persian Wars, and to have been a little younger than Gorgias, and this certainly does not militate against their identity.[2] Antiphon never appears in Plato's dialogues, possibly because, as Schmid suggested (*Gesch.* 159), Plato thought him only second-rate.

There is another problem to be faced. Twenty-nine fragments are grouped by DK under the title *On Concord*, but few of them are

[1] Schmid (*Gesch.* 100) said 'Die grösste Wahrscheinlichkeit spricht dafür' that the Sophist wrote both. Nestle (*VMzuL*, 1942, 387f.) does not mention Schmid, but says with a choice of phrase that is surely deliberate, 'Es spricht daher die grösste Wahrscheinlichkeit dafür', that the author of *Concord* is not the Sophist, who wrote *Truth*, but the orator.

[2] Attempts have been made to date the Sophist's writings. Π. ὄμ. has been put close to 440 on the rather shaky ground of 'echoes' in Euripides (Altwegg and J. H. Finley), and Π. ἀλ. about a decade later also on echoes of his ethical doctrines in drama plus Aly's analysis of the relation of his mathematical work to that of contemporaries. See Greene, *Moira*, 232 with n. 74 and 236 with n. 94. Heinimann (*N. u. Ph.* 141f.), adding to the other arguments one from the style of the papyrus fragments, puts Π. ἀλ. in the twenties. He rejects the idea (see p. 114 above) that it is satirized in the *Clouds* in 423. Antiphon was not of course '*the* Sophist against whom Aristophanes is *especially* tilting', but that he as well as Protagoras (and perhaps others) contributed to the Sophistic morality which is the target does seem at least likely. Schmid (*Gesch.* 159) says that the conversation of Antiphon with Socrates in Xenophon is to be dated in the last decade of the century (i.e. after the orator's death) and his writings should be put no later than the thirties.

explicitly attributed to that work, and none of them deal with the subject of concord.[1] The strength of the case for so assigning them may be judged from Schmid's contention (*Gesch.* 163, n. 1) that, because some of them (those in Stobaeus) are in the form of maxims, and Philostratus says in his life of Antiphon (of *Rhamnus*) that his work on concord included collections of maxims (*gnomologiai*), therefore we may safely assign these fragments to the Sophist's work of that name. Even if we could, the word *gnomologia* does not give much encouragement to suppose that they express his original thought, but in fact the genuineness of these snippets from John of Stobi's anthology (there are twelve of them, each headed simply 'from Antiphon') has been challenged.[2] Comparison with the papyrus fragments, thinks Havelock (*LT*, 419), makes their rejection inevitable, with the partial exception of fr. 49.[3] W. C. Greene, on the other hand (*Moira*, 239), saw no real inconsistency between the ethical doctrines in the supposed fragments of *Concord* and those of *Truth* as seen in the papyri.[4]

Most of the 'fragments' expressly attributed to *Concord* come from the lexicon of Harpocration and consist of single words.[5] Three of them (frr. 45–7) refer to mythical tribes, the Sciapods, Macrocephali and dwellers under the earth or Troglodytes, which with fr. 48 ('man calls himself the most godlike of animals') show an anthropological

---

[1] Some have thought Antiphon intended the word (which does not occur at all in the fragments) in the sense of *inner* harmony (what Iamblichus many centuries later, and with Plato behind him, called τὴν ἑνὸς ἑκάστου πρὸς ἑαυτὸν ὁμογνωμοσύνην, *ap.* Stob. 2.33.15), which they equate with his emphasis on σωφροσύνη and self-mastery. See Stenzel in *RE*, suppl. IV, 40f. Nestle denied this (*VMχuL*, 381), while Praechter (Ueberweg-P. 129) thought to have it both ways.

[2] Compare the case of Democritus, vol. II, 489ff.

[3] This fragment deals with the cares of marriage, and appears to Havelock to be compatible with the outlook of Antiphon, provided we assume that a later writer has contaminated what he wrote with 'moralizing reflections borrowed from the *Medea* and the *Phaedo*'. It does indeed contain phrases reminiscent of both these works (some have thought Euripides was influenced by Antiphon), and (as Havelock also notes) remarkable coincidences with frr. 275–7 of Democritus, but this does not deter him from dissecting the passage in confidence that we know the mind of the Sophist well enough to sift the true from the false.

[4] That there were two separate works is undoubted, but we must remind ourselves at some stage, as Havelock (*op. cit.* 418) pertinently does, that the titles of pre-Platonic works were probably bestowed not by the author but by Alexandrian scholars with the conceptions of the Academy, Lyceum and other schools in mind.

[5] An astounding amount has been built on the entries in Harpocration, especially frr. 4–8, which afford no justification at all for crediting Antiphon with an Eleatic belief that all things are one, and sense-experience (sight, smell etc.) is illusory, as Freeman does (*Comp.* 395, cf. Untersteiner, *Sophs.* 258, n. 5).

interest.[1] Fr. 52 makes the 'philosophical' observation that you can't take back your life like a move at draughts,[2] others comment in a commonplace vein on misplaced hesitation (55) and on consorting with flatterers instead of true friends (65). Fr. 63 reads 'When they know the *diathesis* (setting in order, arrangement) they listen', and Momigliano in his article in *Riv. di filol.* (1930) built on this, in conjunction with certain fragments of the *Truth*, an interesting and very probable reconstruction of a basic tenet underlying and uniting Antiphon's philosophy of the universe and of man. In fr. 24a we read: 'Antiphon applied the word *diathesis* to mind (γνώμη) or intelligence... In the second book on Truth he also uses it for the ordering of the universe (διακόσμησις)'; and in fr. 2: 'For all men mind (γνώμη) controls their body in matters of health and disease and everything else.' With these goes fr. 14: 'Deprived of material she would order (διαθεῖτο) many good things badly.' (The subject is generally taken to be nature, but could now equally be mind or γνώμη.) Momigliano's conclusion is that Antiphon saw a single active rational principle at work in both man and nature, an idea which he could well have taken from the *Nous* of Anaxagoras.[3] I feel some difficulty in reconciling this with his alleged denial of providence (fr. 12), but from such sorry fragments we cannot hope for anything like a complete insight into his thoughts. Momigliano himself thinks this active principle, which otherwise would be a completely autonomous *natura naturans*, must be distinct from the supremely self-sufficient being mentioned in fr. 10, and it is just conceivable that this possibility may conceal (for one cannot say it reveals) the solution.

Of the Stobaeus extracts, three express deep pessimism. Fr. 49

[1] θεειδέστατον, not θεαιδέστατον ('god-fearing'), must surely be correct (*pace* Nestle *VM₂uL*, 382), in view of Photius's lemma. Momigliano (*Riv. di filol.* 1930, 129) thought that in 45–7 Antiphon was giving examples of those living closest to the state of nature, his ideal, whereas for Altwegg (see Greene, *Moira*, 233, n. 78) they were 'types of man's wretchedness'. (Both views existed earlier, Nestle, *VM₂uL*, 382, n. 50.) Bignone (*Studi*, 86) connected them with Antiphon's assertion in *O.P.* 1364 that there was no difference between Greeks and barbarians: Antiphon's purpose, he thought, was probably to bring out that among the most barbaric peoples there were traces of humanity and social life. The names in Harpocration afford not the slightest evidence for any of these conjectures.

[2] From Harpocration. The worthy anthologizer Stobaeus quotes a longer version of the same sentiment under the name of Socrates! See Untersteiner, *Sof.* IV, 131.

[3] Antiphon's interest in cosmology and natural philosophy has already been noted (p. 203 above).

is on marriage (see p. 287, n. 3, above). If a wife proves unsuitable, divorce is tiresome and makes enemies of friends, but keeping her is painful. A good wife brings joy, but pain lurks rounds the corner. It is bad enough to have to look after one's own health, daily needs and good name, but care is doubled when there are two. Children bring nothing but worry, and soon take the spring out of your step and the bloom from your cheeks. Life, says fr. 50, is like a day on watch-duty— just a single day to look at the light, then we hand it over to our successors; and fr. 51 abuses it roundly: it has no greatness or nobility, nothing but what is small, weak, short-lived and shot through with grievous pains. 53 and 53a attack misers and those who live in the present life as if preparing for another, and so let the time slip by (and 'time', he says in fr. 77, 'is the most costly thing that one expends'), and 54 simply retells a fable of Aesop on the same theme and concludes that if God gives a man wealth but not sense he in fact deprives him of both. Two more are merely commonplaces, 62 (character formed by the company kept) and 64 (old friendships more necessary than new). Fr. 58, already noted (p. 259 above), has more individuality, with its warning that indulgence in the immediate impulse may get one into greater trouble than self-mastery. (A young man's urge to marry might be an example of this, as well as the urge to assault a neighbour.) It could well have stood in the same context as 59, that a man cannot be called self-controlled if he has never been tempted. Fr. 61 is the strongest card in the hand of those who want to argue that the teaching of *On Concord* (from which they assume it to come, though Stobaeus does not say so) is irreconcilable with that of the *Truth*, but it is hardly a trump. It begins by paraphrasing a line of Sophocles which says that there is no greater evil than anarchy,[1] but goes on to apply this solely to the upbringing of children: it is the reason why 'the men of old' accustomed children from the start to submit to control and do as they are told, to save them from getting too great a shock when they grow to manhood and find things very different. Hence the importance of education (fr. 60), for a good ending depends on a good beginning.

[1] *Ant.* 672. Bignone (*Studi*, 140) thought Sophocles dependent on Antiphon. We shall never know.

If we may assume the fragments to be genuine, or at least those which bear an individual stamp, one thing that seems certain about Antiphon is that, for his time, he was a considerable psychologist. He was certainly ahead of the advocates of the 'do-as-you-like' theory of education, especially popular with the intelligentsia of the 1930s, in realizing that this was no preparation for adult life, in which if one does not submit to the discipline imposed by the community one is in for some harsh experiences. His philosophy of life is a refined and intellectual hedonism. One must plan to get the maximum of pleasure and the minimum of suffering from our brief and imperfect existence, and this could not be achieved in a completely anarchic society, where everyone was free to act on the impulse of the moment, and assaulted his neighbour at every opportunity. Such behaviour would very soon bring its own nemesis. To acknowledge this is not to deny that (as he says in fr. 44 A) laws are artificial and often bad, or that while living in such a way as not to destroy their framework a man may disregard the law for his own ends whenever he can do so undetected and with impunity.

It is in this psychological connexion that one must see the 'art of painless living' (τέχνη ἀλυπίας), as to which I should like to go on the assumption (deviating perhaps, as an occasional luxury, from the strictest standards of scholarly criticism)[1] that the story in the *Lives of the Orators* (ps.-Plut. 833 c, DK, A 6) is founded on fact and refers to the same Antiphon who wrote *On Truth*.[2] If there were several Anti-

---

[1] I was seriously taken to task by a reviewer of vol. 1 for reporting without comment Cicero's statement that Anaximander gave the Spartans warning of an earthquake, and suggesting that he might have done it by a method still employed (according to *The Times*) in modern Greece. I confess that in this comparatively unimportant matter I thought readers might like to know the titbit about the storks without caring too much about the verification (no longer possible) of Cicero's remark.

[2] H. N. Fowler (Loeb Plut. x, 347 n.) and most others have supposed that the Sophist is meant. There is no other authority except that Philostratus, also in a life of the Rhamnusian, says that he 'announced a course of sorrow-assuaging (νηπενθεῖς) lectures, claiming that no one could tell him of a grief so terrible that he could not expel it from his mind'. 'Consolation-literature' later became a regular genre (cf. Greene, *Moira*, 232), and many have supposed the word τέχνη in τ. ἀλυπίας to have been used in the sense of a written work, which Altwegg even identified with Π. ὁμονοίας ('irrig' Stenzel, 'haltlos' DK), but the context makes this highly improbable, and in Plato (*Symp.* 186e) συνέστησεν τὴν ἡμετέραν τέχνην means 'founded our (the physicians') art'. (Cf. συνεστήσατο in pseudo-Plut.) Morrison (*Proc. Camb. Ph. Soc.* 1961, 57) conjectures that the 'clinic' was originally a comic invention like the *phrontisterion* of the *Clouds*.

phons, the writer has probably confused them. His subject is Antiphon of Rhamnus, and, after saying that sixty orations are ascribed to him, he adds that he also wrote tragedies and 'invented an art of painlessness comparable to the medical therapy of the diseased. In Corinth he fitted up a room near the agora and advertised that he could cure the distressed by words. What he did was to bring consolation to those in trouble by questioning them as to the causes.' To suggest that Antiphon set up the first psychiatric clinic is at any rate no more improbable than some proposed explanations, e.g. that the *techné* in this case was a written work. He knew, after all, that the roots of physical illness were to be sought in the mind (fr. 2) and that it could sometimes be explained as an escape-route from active life (*praxis*, fr. 57). It is in keeping with Antiphon's philosophy of the hedonic calculus, his advocacy of self-mastery and deprecation of yielding to the pleasures and impulses of the moment, that the ideal sought should be a negative one, freedom from pain. Bignone (*Studi*, 83) justly compares this state of calm content (*alypia*) with the *euthymia* of Democritus and the *ataraxia* of Epicurus. A utilitarian hedonism, he adds, was undoubtedly the basis of Antiphon's ethics, but in the moderate form upheld by these two other philosophers.

Of the ethical doctrines of the *Truth*, which have been expounded in earlier chapters and of necessity referred to in the present account, we need only remind ourselves that they were based on a sharp contrast between *physis* and *nomos* to the advantage of the former. Nature compels us to avoid pain and seek the maximum of pleasure, for pain is harmful and pleasure beneficial. One should therefore follow the dictates of convention and the laws only in so far as flouting them for one's immediate pleasure would bring more pain in the form of punishment or disgrace. (There is no suggestion of destroying them by open rebellion.) Moreover nature knows no distinctions of class or race. So far as we know anything about *Concord*, it may seem to show a different emphasis, but nothing to make one suppose that it was not written by the same man, perhaps at a different stage of life, but involving no conversion to contrary convictions. In fact, however, in spite of many attempts, the attested fragments of this work, or testimonies to its contents, are insufficient to provide the basis of any continuous argument.

There is no need to repeat his views on language, which, like his ethics and doubtless not unconnected with them, seem to have been based on the *nomos–physis* antithesis (p. 204) and linked with an ontology allowing a place to both reality and appearances (pp. 202 f.). As yet unnoticed are his interesting observation about time (fr. 9), that it has no substantive existence but is a mental concept or means of measurement,[1] and his attempt to square the circle by a method of exhaustion which Aristotle criticized as not based on geometrical principles.[2]

ADDITIONAL NOTE: THE IDENTITY OF ANTIPHON

Hermogenes (3rd century A.D., DK A 2) is the first extant writer to distinguish two Antiphons, though he says that Didymus did so some 200 years earlier. There were several of the name, but 'two who practised sophistry', (*a*) the orator, cited as author of speeches on homicide cases, political speeches, and suchlike *logoi*, (*b*) the one who is also said to have been a diviner and interpreter of dreams, to whom are ascribed *On Truth*, *On Concord*, and a *Politicus*. Hermogenes himself is convinced on grounds of style that these are different people, but when he reads what Plato and others say (Plato, *Menex.* 236a, mentions Antiphon of Rhamnus as a teacher of rhetoric) he is again thrown into doubt. Many call Thucydides a pupil of the Rhamnusian, whom he knows as the author of the forensic speeches, yet he finds Thucydides's style more like that of the *Truth*. In any case he thinks it necessary to treat the two as separate, because the difference between the two groups of writing is so great.

Of the many modern discussions, I summarize Bignone's, which is the fullest and most judicious.[3] After citing Hermogenes, he remarks that it is strange that no contemporary distinguishes between two such famous men living in Athens at the same time. Moreover we are told the orator's deme

---

[1] This is the earliest extant Greek definition of time, for that ascribed to Archytas (Iambl. *ap.* Simpl. *Phys.* 786, 11), even if genuine, would be a little later. Aristotle (*Phys.* 223 a 21) also doubted whether there could be time without thinking beings, for time, he said, is not simply succession but 'succession in so far as it is numbered' (*ibid.* 219 b 2), and nothing can be numbered or counted if there is no one to count. He says in agreement with Antiphon that time is a measure ('the measure of motion and rest', *ibid.* 220 b 32, 221 b 22), but also that the relations between time and motion are reciprocal: 'we not only measure motion by time but also time by motion, because they are defined by each other' (*ibid.* 220 b 14).

[2] *Phys.* 185 a 14. It is explained in detail by Simplicius (*Phys.* 54, see Antiphon fr. 13 DK), whose description is summarized by Freeman, *Comp.* 397.

[3] 'A. oratore ed A. sofista', in *Studi*, 161–74.

and his father's name, but not those of the Sophist (Gomperz, *S. u. R.* 58), and pseudo-Plutarch, writing about the Rhamnusian orator (832c), says that he had conversations with Socrates as recorded by Xenophon. That Xenophon called him 'Antiphon the Sophist' is not against the identity, and Croiset supposed him to be distinguishing the orator-cum-Sophist from others including the tragedian.[1] Aristotle always refers to 'Antiphon' simply, without feeling the need for a distinguishing title. The chronology of both is about the same. The orator died in 411 (Thuc. 8.68), and the dispute with Socrates in Xenophon is probably earlier than this, because Plato, who became Socrates's follower after this date, says nothing about it. [I should not attach much weight to this argument.] The orator was born c. 480 (Blass, *Att. Bereds.* 1², 94ff.) and probably wrote the extant orations late in life, after 427, because they show the influence of Gorgias. Could he not have been Sophist-philosopher first and orator later? (Croiset thought it probable.) The orator shows marked sophistic characteristics, and both of them taught the young and had schools (for the orator of Rhamnus see Plato, *Menex.* 236a, for the Sophist Xen. *Mem.* 1.6) and took fees. (Bignone's references for this are Xen. *ibid.*, pseudo-Plut. 833 [doubtful?], Diod. *ap.* Clem. Al. 1.365, 2.66 D., Amm. Marc. 30.4 and the papyrus of Antiphon's *Apology* published by Nicole, *REG*, 1909, 55.) The orator had an active political life, and the Sophist rebuked Socrates for taking no part in politics (Xen. *loc. cit.*).

On the argument from style, already used by Hermogenes, Bignone says that the papyrus fragments, the most extensive that we have of the Sophist, do in fact suggest that he was not also the orator, but on the other hand this is a somewhat subjective criterion and the same man might have changed his style during his lifetime. However, there is also a strong historical argument. The orator was a pugnacious aristocrat and oligarch (Thuc. 8.68, 89, 90, Arist. *Ath. Pol.* 32), whereas fr. 44 B of the Sophist expresses extreme democratic sentiments. Also the orator was an emphatic upholder of the laws, as is shown by many passages in his speeches, which again contrasts strongly with the Sophist. Bignone's final conclusion therefore was that orator and Sophist were different persons (though he thought that the Sophist could well be the diviner and writer on dreams).

---

[1] As to the tragedies, it is by no means impossible that a Sophist should write them, and it is interesting that one line employs a form of the νόμος–φύσις antithesis, of which Antiphon the Sophist was such an enthusiastic exponent (fr. 4 Nauck: τέχνῃ κρατοῦμεν ὧν φύσει νικώμεθα). On the other hand the tradition associates the tragedian (as the Rhamnusian) with Dionysius I of Syracuse, which some have thought puts him later than the Sophist (*Vit. or.* and *Gnomol. Vindob.* A 6 and 9 DK), though Wilamowitz felt this no objection (*Platon*, 1, 84, n. 1.). The Rhamnusian was killed in 411, but we know nothing of how long the Sophist lived if he is a different man.

This is the conclusion which has found most favour, so that Stenzel could begin his article in the *RE* (suppl. IV, 33) 'Antiphon, of Athens, to be distinguished, as is now generally recognized, as a Sophist from the orator of Rhamnus', and Untersteiner (*Sophs.* 228 f.) simply refer to Bignone and add 'I do not think that there is any occasion to re-examine the question'. However, J. S. Morrison in 1961 reopened it, and maintained that the orator whose speeches we possess was identical with the Sophist who wrote the *Truth* and the *Concord* and is shown arguing with Socrates in the *Memorabilia* of Xenophon. This provoked a sharp retort from S. Luria, who quoted freely from the speeches to show that the orator, whom Thucydides (8.90.1) named as an extreme oligarch, and singled out among the Four Hundred as one who was particularly strongly opposed to democracy, could not possibly have held the left-wing views expressed in the papyrus fragments of the *Truth*. These are by one who rejects the laws in favour of 'nature', and is a fervent preacher of egalitarianism. The speeches reveal an ultra-conservative, who upholds the laws in the traditional manner as sacred, and all the better for having lasted through centuries unchanged (*Or.* 5.14, 6.2). 'It does not do', he continues, 'to start from the accuser's speech and ask whether the laws are well founded or not; we must rather judge the accuser's speech by the laws, and see whether he is setting forth the matter rightly and lawfully.' The speech-writer is moreover an enthusiastic supporter of the traditional religion, praising the gods and exhorting to worship and sacrifice in terms impossible (says Luria) for one who denied divine providence as did the author of *Truth* (fr. 12).[1]

(6) THRASYMACHUS

Thrasymachus came from Chalcedon on the Bosporus, a colony of Megara. The only fixed points from which to judge his date are (1) *The Banqueters* of Aristophanes, produced in 427, in which he is made fun of (DK, A 4); (2) a sentence from one of his speeches (fr. 2) which shows it to have been written during the rule of Archelaus of Macedon over Thessaly (413–399). There is an obscure hint that he may have

---

[1] Morrison in *PCPS*, 1961, Luria in *Eos* 1963. Of course, if Kerferd were right in supposing that the views expressed in the papyrus fragments were not Antiphon's at all (p. 108 above), most of Luria's argument would fall to the ground; but I find no evidence in them that Antiphon is simply setting forth the ideas of others for examination, and Kerferd seems sometimes to raise imaginary difficulties in order to dispose of them by this hypothesis (especially on p. 28). Nestle (*VMzuL*, 394) adopted an unusual division, attributing *Truth* and the tetralogies to the Sophist, and *Concord* to the Rhamnusian. For further references see Morrison, *loc. cit.* 50, n. 1, and for an excellent brief survey, culminating in a *non liquet*, Lesky, *HGL*, 353 f.

committed suicide.[1] He was known primarily as a teacher of rhetoric, in which he was something of an innovator, and most of the extant references to him are concerned with his style. In writing his handbooks and model speeches he paid great attention to the technical details of the art, and experimented with the use of prose-rhythms, as well as developing the appeal to the emotions of an audience (Plato, *Phaedr.* 267c). Aristotle (*Soph. el.* 183b31) called him a successor of Tisias, and Theophrastus named him as the inventor of the so-called 'middle style' (fr. 1). The only considerable fragment of his writing which has survived was preserved by Dionysius of Halicarnassus solely as an example of his style. He was a Sophist in the full sense, who charged for his instruction (*Rep.* 337d), travelled to foreign cities, and though specializing in rhetoric was prepared to answer ethical questions also. His teaching on justice seems to have been well known. In the *Republic* (*loc. cit.*) he claims a fee for it, and in the *Clitophon* the young man threatens to desert Socrates for Thrasymachus, who, he thinks, is better informed on this subject.

The surviving passage of his works (fr. 1) is the opening of a speech to the Athenian Assembly. As a foreigner he could not have delivered it himself, but it reads like a genuine contribution to a debate held in the later stages of the Peloponnesian war rather than a mere schoolpiece. The speaker feels it necessary to begin by apologizing for his youth.[2] The rule that young men should keep silence was a good one so long as the older generation were managing affairs competently, but those for whom the prosperity of the city is only hearsay and its disasters their own experience[3]—disasters moreover which cannot be blamed on heaven or chance but only on the incompetence of those in charge—must speak out. He cannot submit to deliberate mismanagement or carry the blame for the unprincipled plotting of others. We have seen, he says, the city pass from peace to war and peril and from internal harmony to quarrelling and confusion. Elsewhere it is pros-

---

[1] Nestle (*VMₓuL*, 348) states this as a fact, but it depends on a corrupt line of Juvenal (7. 204), in which some editors prefer the reading 'Lysimachi', with the comment of the scholiast 'rhetoris apud Athenas qui suspendio periit' (DK, 85 A 7).

[2] That the *prooimion* should engage the audience's sympathy was a textbook maxim. See Theodectes in Rose, *Arist. frr.*, Berlin ed. vol. v, 1499 a 27 and 32, and Arist. *Rhet.* 3, chapter 14.

[3] In this imperfectly preserved clause I have followed Havelock's rendering, which seems to combine Blass's τὰς μὲν εὐπραξίας with the πάσχειν of Diels. This makes good sense.

perity that leads to arrogance and faction,[1] but we kept our heads in the good times and have lost them in adversity. The parties are simply fighting mindlessly for power. They may think their policies are opposed but in fact there is no real difference between them. What, if one goes back to first principles, are both sides looking for? In the first place it is the question of the 'ancestral constitution' which throws them into confusion, though it is the easiest thing to grasp and more than anything else the concern of the whole citizen body. Then in the last sentence of the extract, presumably with his own comparative youth still in mind, the speaker says that for matters going back beyond our experience we must rely on the accounts of former generations or, when they are within the memory of older men, learn direct from them.

The speech is mainly of political interest, and the reference to the 'ancestral constitution' suggests that it was written by an oligarch, 'some young aristocrat of Spartan sympathies'. Havelock however is impressed by its 'non-partisan quality, its air of objectivity, its plea for clarity of thinking', and sees in it 'a serious intellectual position, a rationale of political behaviour and method, if not a theory of politics'. Certainly its main plea is the timeless one for efficiency and principle in government, and for reconciliation between the parties to that end.[2] Its counsel would be no less useful today, and the point that party struggle is based on the thirst for power rather than on fundamental differences of policy has an uncomfortably familiar sound.

This is the only independent passage by which we can hope to judge the fairness or otherwise of Plato's sketch of Thrasymachus in the *Republic* (pp. 88 ff. above). The speech is composed for a client to deliver, but let us give Thrasymachus the credit for not writing anything that was against his own principles. It may fairly be supposed that he could only put the argument in so convincing a form if his own mind was behind it. Everything, of course, depends on what view we

---

[1] This accords with the common Greek view that κόρος breeds ὕβρις, but Thucydides would not have agreed with the speaker. Cf. 3.82.2: 'In peace and prosperity cities and individuals behave more sensibly because they are not forced to act against their will, but war which deprives them of their daily cheer is a harsh schoolmaster and reduces the temper of most men to the level of their circumstances.'

[2] ὁμόνοια, concord or consensus. On the importance of this concept cf. pp. 149 f. above. For Havelock's analysis and appraisal of the piece see his *L.T.* 233–9.

take of the scene in the *Republic*. That Plato disliked him is plain enough from the outbursts of rudeness and bad temper in which he makes him indulge (though his pugnacity and sharp tongue are almost the only other things independently recorded of him).[1] If however my interpretation has been correct, that he speaks there in a mood of bitter disillusionment as well as opposition to what in his view is the facile optimism of Socrates, and if we allow for a certain exaggeration due to Plato's desire to present two human characters in dramatic contrast, the incompatibility between the dialogue and the speech is at least mitigated. Governments, he declares in the former, rule for their own aggrandizement and justice is the name given to obedience to their laws: it means serving the interests of others. According to his angry logic, if a subject seek power for himself, this is injustice. To be just, he should obey the laws which the rulers have laid down in their own interests. If however his 'injustice' is successful and he becomes a ruler and lawgiver himself (and the tyrant, says Thrasymachus, is the supreme example of injustice), everyone will flatter rather than blame him.

> Treason doth never prosper. What's the reason?
> For if it prosper, none dare call it treason.

Justice, then, does not pay, and the man who observes it is noble but a simpleton (348c). These, he says brutally, are the facts, and you cannot get away from them. He is only describing, with cynical realism, what he sees around him. Athens, as Thucydides constantly reminds us, reached the height of her power, and endeavoured to maintain it, by acting on the belief that 'the only law in earth or heaven is that the strong should subdue the weak' (Thuc. 5.105.2). But, by the later years of the Peloponnesian War, the pursuit of this philosophy in external relations and domestic politics was threatening to lead to defeat from outside and internal disintegration. The policy of domination and oppression no longer worked to the advantage of Athens, and, as it broke down, internal faction and struggles for power only made things worse. The Thrasymachus of the political speech does not deny that the earlier policy was right for its time, indeed he calls it *sophrosyne*[2]—'in the good times we kept our heads'—but it no

---

[1] Arist. *Rhet.* 1400b19 and 1413a7.
[2] Just as in the *Republic* he calls injustice 'good counsel', εὐβουλία (p. 90 above).

longer works. He is no less of a realist, but the Athenians must learn to adapt themselves to changed circumstances. They cannot afford the luxury of an internal struggle for power. To quote Havelock again (*L.T.* 234):

To begin with, he assumes that the purpose of government is to be successful and efficient; this is the criterion by which it should be judged ... He assumes that prosperity and disaster are not god-given but man-made; and, secondly, that it is the purpose of any government to preserve the one and avoid the other ... Traditional piety, and the archaic fatalism of the Greek temper, seem to be rejected.

The character depicted by Plato would not have quarrelled with these assumptions, nor would the man who, to quote a final bit of independent evidence (fr. 8, p. 97 above), affirmed that the gods took no heed of human affairs, or they would not allow justice to be set aside as it is. Plato has shown his worst side, perhaps relying on things that he said or wrote when Athens was at the height of her power and arrogance (the most likely dramatic date for the *Republic* is about 322), but we need feel no doubt that it was one side of the real man.

(7) CRITIAS

Critias[1] would seem to provide Plato with the perfect example of a fine nature ruined by the society of his day, and by sophistic teaching with its emphasis on the attainment of power and indifference to the moral consequences of rhetorical and debating skill. Wealthy, high-born and handsome, he was also richly endowed with philosophic and literary gifts and an eager listener to Socrates, yet deserted him to play power-politics and ended up as the most bloodthirsty and unscrupulous member of the Thirty. These men, elected at the end of the war to draw up a constitution, made themselves tyrants instead and massacred their opponents. He was personally responsible for the death of Theramenes, an oligarch like himself and a personal friend, who was unwilling to go to such extremes. In the eyes of the democracy the fact that Socrates had associated with men like Critias told strongly against

---

[1] Where references to authorities are not given in the following paragraphs they can be found in the accounts of Critias given by Diehl, *RE*, xi, 1902–12, and Nestle, *VMzuL*, 400–20.

him. He seems exactly to fit the role of a Callicles, or might, one would think, be designed to prove Plato's point in the *Republic* (491 d) that 'the finest nature given the wrong nurture will turn out worse than the commonest' and that (495 a) 'the very qualities which make a philosophic nature will, with bad upbringing, be the cause of his falling away, no less than wealth and other external advantages'. But does Plato speak of him like this? On the contrary, he shows him only as an intimate member of the Socratic circle, with no hint that he was worse than the rest, and every indication of a genuine interest in philosophy. In the *Timaeus* and *Critias* he has a leading role, and the whole story of Atlantis is told through his mouth. Though writing years after his death, Plato still thinks of his uncle Critias with respect and affection.[1]

There is a mystery here which the evidence does not allow us to solve completely. It is lessened, of course, if we believe with Sir Karl Popper that Plato 'betrayed Socrates, just as his uncles had done' (*O.S.* 194). We cannot decide that yet, but in any case no one would accuse Plato of condoning the murderous excesses of the Thirty, nor did he, if the *Apology* and the Seventh Letter (324 c–d) are any evidence at all. There are however certain points to take into account, beginning with their relationship. The family was an old and distinguished one, including Solon among its earlier generations, and family feeling would be strong. Critias was the son of Callaeschrus and cousin of Plato's mother Perictione, whose father Glaucon was Callaeschrus's brother, and when Glaucon died her brother Charmides became Critias's ward. Plato would also be attracted by his brilliant intellect and literary and artistic gifts, and undoubtedly they shared the conviction that unbridled democracy was the ruin of the state. Aristotle was of the same mind, and there is a curious discrepancy between his references to Critias and the Thirty and the account of Xenophon in his *Hellenica* which is our sole contemporary source for the leading part played by Critias. In the *Constitution of Athens* (35 ff.) he frankly

---

[1] Besides the *Timaeus* and *Critias*, he has a part in the *Charmides* and *Protagoras*, and also in the pseudo-Platonic *Eryxias*. On the question whether the speaker in the *Critias* was the same one or his grandfather see Diehl in *RE*, XI, 1901 f., Levinson, *Defense*, 359 f., and Rosenmayer in *AJP*, 1949. It is only fair to add that in Plato's picture of him in the *Charmides* M. J. O'Brien sees 'a self-assertive man more concerned with honour than with truth' (*Socr. Parad.* 124 f.).

relates the atrocities of the Thirty and the execution of Theramenes for attempting to curb them, but with no mention of Critias, and in the *Politics* (1305b26) he names Charicles as their leader. In the *Rhetoric* (1416b26), on the subject of eulogies, he says, with seemingly deliberate intent, that if you want to praise Achilles you need not recount his deeds, because everyone knows them, but in praising Critias you must, because they are little known. This may have been true.[1] Philostratus, writing in the time of the 'second Sophistic', said that his philosophy was not taken seriously by the Greeks because his words were difficult to reconcile with his character. Xenophon's account of his relations with Socrates (*Mem.* 1.2.12ff.) is that he and Alcibiades were consumed with ambition, and, knowing Socrates's mastery of argument, thought that his teaching would help them to gain their ends. They had no desire to be converted to his way of life, and left him as soon as they thought they had learned enough to attain their political ambitions. In spite of this, such was Socrates's influence that so long as they were with him their worst passions were held in check. The break came when Socrates publicly reprimanded Critias for trying to seduce a youth in their circle, a hurt for which Critias never forgave him. When the Thirty came to power, he was in trouble with Critias and Charicles for his outspoken criticism of their conduct, and as we learn from Plato's own version of his *Apology* (32c), deliberately disobeyed an order from them which was designed to implicate him in their guilt.

Considering all this, Plato may indeed have thought of him as the type of brilliant young man whom he describes in the *Republic*, with the roots of philosophy in him and an immense capacity for good but also for harm if his environment corrupted him. Unfortunately it did, and the story of his evil latter days was on everyone's lips. To redress the balance, and out of regret for one who was his relative and at one time a companion of his master Socrates, Plato on this hypothesis will have concentrated on the earlier, happier years of hope and promise. He reserved his attack for the corrupting forces which he considered responsible for the downfall of such promising young men, the licence and mob-oratory prevailing under the democracy and the rhetorical

---

[1] See Diehl in *RE*, xi, 1910f.

teachers who claimed that the art of speaking had nothing to do with moral standards.[1]

Critias died in civil war against the democrats in 403, when he is generally believed to have been about fifty. He first appears in politics in 415, when with others of his persuasion he was imprisoned for complicity in the mutilation of the Hermae. He was both a bitter opponent of democracy and violently pro-Spartan, and may have been, with his father, a member of the Four Hundred in 411.[2] However, he was not immediately exiled after their fall, and helped to engineer the recall of Alcibiades. Later the democracy did exile him and he went to Thessaly, where if he did not consort with Gorgias personally the intelligentsia were steeped in his teaching.[3] After the capitulation of Athens in 404 he returned, and was elected one of the commission of Thirty, with the consequences that have been mentioned.

Critias was not of course a Sophist in the full sense of a paid teacher, but it has been fairly said that 'in his personality we find a union of all the impulses of the sophistic movement, whose period of *Sturm und Drang* reached a symbolic end in his dramatic death' (Lesky, *HGL*, 357). We have seen that he shared with Protagoras, Democritus and others a belief in the progressive evolution of mankind by their own efforts, that he thought of laws as neither inherent in human nature from the beginning nor a gift of any gods, and of religion as a purely human invention aimed at preventing lawless behaviour. Religion was for the subject, to ensure his obedience, not for the enlightened ruler. His interest in technical progress comes out also in a set of elegiacs in which he assigns inventions to particular peoples or countries. They include chariots, chairs, beds, working in gold and bronze, writing, ships, the potter's wheel and (curiously enough) the game of *Kottabos* (fr. 2). Perhaps for this reason, coupled with the close relationship

[1] According to Philostratus, *ep*. 73 (Critias A 17), Critias learned from Gorgias but turned his teaching to his own purposes.

[2] See Diehl in *RE*, XI, 1903, Nestle, *VMʒuL*, 401. The only evidence is [Dem.] 58.67. Nestle speaks of his 'striking reserve' vis-à-vis the Four Hundred, which he interprets as a concession to the demos to facilitate Alcibiades's return.

[3] ἐγοργίαζον ἐν Θετταλίᾳ μικραὶ καὶ μείζους πόλεις, Philostr. *V.S.* 1.16 (Crit. A 1). Cf. Plato, *Meno* 70a–b. Xenophon (*Mem.* 1.2.24) claimed that it was the Thessalians that corrupted him. Plato's opinion of the country was that it was full of ἀταξία καὶ ἀκολασία (*Crito* 53d). But Philostratus concluded (*V.S.* 1.16) that it was rather Critias who corrupted the Thessalians.

between *areté* in general and the craftsman's skill, his aristocratic sympathies did not prevent him from saying that more men become good by practice than through natural endowment.[1] His literary output was large and diverse, including both poetry and prose. His poem in praise of Alcibiades revives the political elegy of his ancestor Solon and Theognis, though with characteristic boldness, since the name of Alcibiades resisted inclusion in dactylic verse, he substituted an iambic for the customary pentameter. There is no record of his speeches, but Hermogenes (see A 19) mentions a collection of 'prooemia for public speakers'. We have fragments of two sets of *Politeiai*, so called, one in prose and one in verse. The prose set included one on the Thessalians (fr. 31),[2] where he mentioned their extravagant ways, and one on the Spartans, of which the only extant fragments do not deal with their constitution but with their way of life. He mentions their drinking habits and cups (made suitable for use on campaigns), dress, furniture, dancing, and the precautions which they take against the Helots, and praises the eugenic effects of the hardy regime imposed on men and women alike (frr. 32–7). His poem on the Spartans also deals mainly with their drinking habits, emphasizing their moderation, and attributing to Chilon the saying 'nothing too much' (frr. 6–8).[3] Literary interest is shown in his hexameters on Anacreon (fr. 1) and his prose works. It is combined with aristocratic pride when in fr. 44 he takes Archilochus to task for exposing his humble birth and weaknesses in his verse.

Two books of *Homilies* must have been more philosophic in content, and a quotation from the first touches on the relation between the mind and the senses. At least the context in Galen makes it fairly certain that 'they' are the senses in the sentence (fr. 40): 'If you yourself study to become strong in intellect, you will be least wronged by them.' This comes in a passage where Galen is quoting examples to prove his point that *gnomé* in earlier times was used with the same meaning as other words for mind or thought. He adds two more quota-

[1] See pp. 251 and 256 above.
[2] The manuscripts give the author's name as Cratinus, but the alteration has been accepted since Casaubon.
[3] A prose 'Constitution of Athens' has been inferred as the likeliest home for two unassigned quotations. In one, Critias characteristically gives the exact amount of the fortunes made out of politics by Themistocles and Cleon, and in the other he has the effrontery to criticize Cimon for his pro-Spartan policy. (Frr. 45 and 52. See Diehl in *RE*, XI, 1908, and Nestle, *VMʒuL*, 405.)

tions which he says are from the *Aphorisms* of Critias (fr. 39): 'Neither what he perceives with the rest of his body nor what he knows with his mind' and 'Men have awareness when they have accustomed themselves to be healthy in their mind'. Aristotle (*De an.* 405 b 5) says he was one of those who identified the *psyche* with blood: regarding sensation as the most typical characteristic of *psyche*, they believed that it was due to the nature of the blood. Philoponus in his commentary (after identifying Critias as 'one of the Thirty') attributed to him the line of Empedocles (fr. 105.3) which says that 'the blood around the heart is thought (νόημα)'. (See Critias, A 23. He may have learned of Empedoclean theory from Gorgias.) In fact Empedocles, and evidently also Critias, distinguished thoughts from sensation, though considering both to be equally corporeal phenomena. The Hippocratic treatise on the heart uses the word *gnomé* when it declares that the mind rules the rest of the *psyche* and resides in the left ventricle. (See on this vol. II, 229 with n. 2.)

Critias also wrote dramas. We have excerpts from three tragedies, the *Tennes*, *Rhadamanthys* and *Peirithous*, and the long passage from the satyr-play *Sisyphus* containing the theory of the origin of religion.[1] The *Rhadamanthys* (fr. 15) contains a list of the various objects of men's longing. Similar lists were commonplace,[2] but Critias's has some touches of the sophistic age. Health is missing, and we have, besides high birth and wealth, the power and audacity to persuade one's neighbours of what is unsound. The speaker then declares that his own choice is to have a fine reputation. Two choric fragments of the *Peirithous* are cosmological. Fr. 18 speaks of unwearied Time endlessly bringing itself to birth in unceasing flow, and in fr. 19 the epithet 'self-born' suggests that it is again Time that is addressed as embracing all nature in the heavenly whirl, while light and darkness, and the innumerable host of stars, perform their endless dance around him. Clement of Alexandria, who quotes the passage, took 'the

[1] Pp. 243 ff. above. The reader should be warned that all were commonly attributed to Euripides in antiquity, though the *Vita Eur.* rejected the tragedies (Critias fr. 10), and the *Sisyphus* is given to Critias by Sextus. They were rescued for him by Wilamowitz, *N. Jbb.* 1908, 57; *Hermes*, 1927, 291 f.; and *Analecta Eurip.* 166. Schmid still had reservations about Critias's authorship (*Gesch.* 176).

[2] Cf. the scholion on the good things of life, Diehl, *Anth. Lyr.* no. 7 (II, 183) with the various authorities cited.

self-born' to be 'the demiurgic *nous*',[1] no doubt with Plato rather than Anaxagoras in mind, but most scholars have seen a suggestion of Anaxagoras in the passage as a whole. More prominent is the effect of Orphic cosmogonies or of Pherecydes of Syros, where Chronos (Time) appears as a primeval creative power. Evidently Critias (assuming that he and not Euripides is the author) shared Euripides's interest in cosmological speculation.[2] A few further quotations from this play in Stobaeus's anthology are easy to reconcile with Critias as we know him:[3] fr. 21 'He had no unpractised mind who first said that fortune fights on the side of the wise'; fr. 23 'Better not to live at all than to live miserably'; and fr. 22 on the superiority of character to *nomos* (p. 69 above).

We are left with the picture of a man of brilliant intellectual and artistic gifts, plunging eagerly into the philosophical discussions of his time, all the more so as many of them had a direct bearing on political life. But some of the headier theories conspired with his own ambitious, headstrong and unstable character, the product of generations of politicians and poets, to lead him away from the wisdom of Socrates to violence, cruelty, and death in civil strive.

(8) ANTISTHENES

Antisthenes is one of those interesting bridge-figures who serve to remind us how much happened in a short space of time between the manhood of Socrates and the death of Plato. As a pupil of Socrates, and reputed teacher of Diogenes and founder of the Cynic school, it might be expected that he would be left to be dealt with under 'Socratics' after an account of Socrates himself. Yet he lived in the heyday of the Sophists, probably a little older than Prodicus and Hippias, and, as we have seen, was deeply involved in the argument about the use of language and the possibility of contradiction which formed part of the theoretical background of fifth-century rhetoric, and in which Protagoras played a leading part. Since this has

[1] *Strom.* 2.403.14 Staehlin, quoted by Nauck on Eur. fr. 593.
[2] For Chronos in Orphic cosmogonies and Pherecydes see Guthrie, *O. & Gk. Rel.* 85–91 and Kirk in KR, 56.
[3] Even if we ignore our complete ignorance of the dramatic context and the speakers.

brought him into our discussion already, it seems appropriate to make some general observations about him now. Before coming under the influence of Socrates, he was himself a rhetorician and pupil of Gorgias. In recent times he has been the subject of very varied judgments. Popper's verdict, that he was the only worthy successor of Socrates, the last of the 'Great Generation' (*O.S.* 194), was foreshadowed by Grote: 'Antisthenes, and his disciple Diogenes, were in many respects closer approximations to Sokrates than either Plato or any other of the Sokratic companions' (*Plato*, III, 505). On the other hand Schmid considered that 'in spite of his enthusiasm for Socrates in Socrates's last years, his own philosophy went the way of an undisciplined free-thinking against which Plato had to be emphatically on his guard' (*Gesch.* 272f.), and to Campbell, relying on Xenophon and Aristotle, he 'seems to have been the butt of the Socratic school, a sort of mixture of Ajax and Thersites . . . He followed rather the form than the spirit of the Socratic teaching' (ed. of *Theaet.* xl–xli). Karl Joël's verdict is also interesting (*E. und X. S.* 257):

What in Socrates was an unconscious miracle of his nature became in Antisthenes a set purpose, a basis for variety and an artificial product. He copied the Socratic mode of life and fanaticized the Socratic teaching, trusting thereby to seize upon the essence of his master, to whom he stood in the relationship of flagellants imitating a genuine saint, or better of the Romantics—the poet of Lucinde—to Goethe.

Perhaps the truest statements are those of Popper (*O.S.* 277), that 'Very little is known about Antisthenes from first-rate sources', and Field, that there has been 'an immense amount of conjecture and hypothesis about him' (*Plato and Contemps.* 160).

Most of our information about his life and circumstances comes from many centuries later, and must be treated with corresponding reserve.[1] It was believed that he had founded the Cynic school and through it influenced the Stoics, and a certain amount of hindsight may have crept into accounts of his teaching written after these

---

[1] The source-material is collected in Caizzi's *Antisthenis Fragmenta*, the arrangement of which is unusual. After the title 'Frammenti' the passages are numbered continuously throughout, but divided into three parts: 'Frr. 1–121' are the testimonia and actual fragments (or what are reckoned as such), 122–44 are 'notizie biografiche' and 145–95 anecdotes. There is also a full bibliography.

schools became famous. He was said to be the son of an Athenian and a Thracian slave, and hence not an Athenian citizen,[1] and to have fought at Tanagra (D.L. 6.1), which must refer to the battle there in 426 (Thuc. 3.91). Diodorus (15.76) speaks of him as still alive in 366 and Plutarch (*Lycurgus* 30) quotes a remark which he made on the battle of Leuctra (371). Xenophon (*Symp.* 4.62) says that he introduced the Sophist-lover Callias to Prodicus and Hippias, and speaks of him in general as an older man than himself and Plato, so (although we have no certain information) about 455–360 will not be far out for the span of his long life. He was a rhetorician and pupil of Gorgias, whom he afterwards attacked, and some have seen in him the influence of other Sophists as well.[2] Later he became a friend and fanatical admirer of Socrates. That at least is certain, and Plato (*Phaedo* 59b) mentions him among the few intimates who were with Socrates in prison in the last hours of his life.

He was especially attracted by the ascetic side of Socrates's life and his independence of worldly goods, and carried this to such lengths that in later antiquity he was commonly regarded as the founder of the Cynic school, with Diogenes 'the Dog' for his pupil. (See frr. 138 A–F, 139 Caizzi.) Nowadays it is generally held that the Cynics owed their most distinctive features, as well as their name, to Diogenes. There never was a Cynic school in the literal sense in which the Academy, Lyceum and Stoa were schools. Antisthenes himself may have had a sort of school, or at least a group of pupils with a fixed place of meeting, for Diogenes Laertius (6.13) says that he used to converse (or 'use dialectic') in the gymnasium of Cynosarges,[3] but

---

[1] D.L. 6.1, 2.31; Seneca *De const. sap.* 18.5. But Field notes (*Plato and Contemps.* 160 n.) that in the *Phaedo* Plato speaks of him as an ἐπιχώριος with no hint that he was different from Crito, Aeschines and the rest. D.L. introduces the fact to give point to two probably apocryphal anecdotes.

[2] Antisthenes and Gorgias, D.L. 6.1, Athen. 220d (from the *Archelaus* of Antisthenes). For Protagoras and the impossibility of contradiction see p. 182, n. 2, above. Dümmler (*Akad.* 194) argued that Antisthenes's denial that one can call a statement false originated with Gorgias (*MXG* 980a10), and claimed also to see the influence of Prodicus and Hippias (*ibid.* 158, 161, 256, 274).

[3] This was the gymnasium assigned to bastards, or men of mixed descent (Demosth. 23.213 and later sources), which tallies with the report of his half-foreign origin. But D.L. or his source is trying by every means to represent him as the founder of Cynicism. 'Cynosarges' is brought in as an alternative origin for the name, and D.L. immediately goes on to say that Antisthenes himself was called Ἁπλοκύων (just as he was also called Κύων by Herodicus in the first century B.C.

this certainly does not bring him closer to the Cynics, who never adopted such methods. Antisthenes was probably horrified at some of Diogenes's principles and behaviour. There is every reason to think that they were acquainted, and the stories about them are all to the effect that Diogenes was far from a favourite of his, but won him over by sheer importunity and persistence. Nevertheless the portrait of Antisthenes in Xenophon's *Symposium* does show traits which, developed to an extreme, were characteristic of the Cynics.[1] He called himself the richest of men, because wealth resided in men's souls, not in their pockets, and equated poverty with independence. Men who went to all lengths to increase their fortunes he pitied as diseased. They suffered as much as men whose bodies were never satisfied however much they ate. Happiness lies not in having great possessions but in losing the desire for them. All this he claims to have learned from Socrates. There is a specially Cynic touch in his reference to sex as a purely bodily need, for whose satisfaction any woman will do (*Symp.* 4.38). Cynic also was his anti-hedonism. Later sources may perhaps be suspected, because they had already adopted him as the founder of the sect, when they report him as declaiming that he would rather go mad than enjoy pleasure (frr. 108 A–F); but the bias is already there in Xenophon (*Symp.* 4.39), when in speaking of the appetite for sex— which he regards as a natural one like that for food—he says that he would prefer to satisfy it without pleasure, since the intense pleasure derived from it is harmful. Similarly one should eat and drink solely to banish hunger and thirst. The only pleasure to be recommended is that which follows from hard work (fr. 113) and which brings no

---

ap. Ath. 216b), whereas there can be little doubt that the original Dog was Diogenes. Aristotle already knew him by that name (*Rhet.* 1411a24), but spoke of the followers of Antisthenes as Ἀντισθένειοι. The story in D.L. (*loc. cit.*) that he had few pupils because as he said he 'drove them away with a silver rod', if it has any basis in fact, implies that in spite of his Socraticism he charged high fees which many were unwilling to pay. He would have learned to do so as a rhetorician and pupil of Gorgias.

[1] Cf. p. 341 below. (Cynics were notoriously 'difficult' characters.) This has been most recently argued by Caizzi, *Stud. Urb.* 1964, 73f. Wilamowitz made a vigorous protest against the 'legend' of Antisthenes the Cynic in *Platon*, II, 162–4, and many have followed him, e.g. Taylor, *Comm. on Tim.* 306, Dudley, *Hist. of Cyn.* 1 ff., Field, *Plato and Contemps.* 162f., and the references collected in Burkert, *Weish. u. Wiss.* 197, n. 69. But see also Popper, O.S. 277, and, for an older view on the other side, Ueberweg–Praechter, 160n. For Zeller too Antisthenes was 'the founder of Cynicism' (*Ph. d. Gr.* 280–1). Chroust in his *Socrates Man and Myth* speaks of a unitary philosophy which he calls 'Antisthenean–Cynic', but not everyone would follow him.

repentance (fr. 110). The virtues of hard work he recommended through the examples of Heracles and Cyrus in books called after them (frr. 19–28).[1]

Through the Cynics he was supposed also to have been a founder of Stoicism before Zeno, and the succession-writers, represented for us by Diogenes Laertius, assumed a direct line of master and pupil: Antisthenes–Diogenes–Crates–Zeno. If, as is generally supposed nowadays, this is not strictly historical, it is probably true that he gave the impulse to an outstanding characteristic of each: that is, as Diogenes Laertius puts it, 'the indifference of Diogenes, the self-control of Crates, and the endurance of Zeno'—all traits which he himself would claim to have found in Socrates. In his doctrine of virtue as the end of life (fr. 22) he certainly anticipated Zeno. Virtue can be taught and once acquired cannot be lost (frr. 69, 71). It needs a Socratic strength, is taught by deed and example rather than argument and erudition, and is sufficient in itself to ensure happiness (fr. 70). Education is necessary (fr. 68), but it is the kind of education that Chiron gave Heracles (fr. 24). Virtue has no use for long speeches (fr. 86). The sage is self-sufficient, for his wealth includes that of all other men (fr. 80, a particularly Stoic touch). So far as our evidence goes, it seems that his ethical teaching was purely practical. There is no trace of systematic theory nor of any connexion with his logical doctrine such as we have found in some of the Sophists. The *nomos–physis* antithesis (also to be found in his theological pronouncement, p. 248 above) is echoed in the dictum that the wise man acts not according to the established laws but to the laws of virtue (fr. 101, p. 117 above). Otherwise all that one can say of his political views is that he was no egalitarian, as appears from his reference to what the lions thought when the hares made public speeches in favour of equal rights for all. (This comes from Aristotle, *Pol.* 1284a15.) His *Politikos Logos*, we are told, attacked 'all the demagogues of Athens',[2] and he made a special target of Alcibiades (frr. 43, 29, 30). His *Archelaus* attacked his former master Gorgias, a natural consequence of his conversion to

---

[1] For Antisthenes's views on pleasure Caizzi has collected references in his notes to frr. 108–13.

[2] Compare his advice that they ought to vote asses to the position of horses, p. 212, n. 1, above.

Socrates.[1] He may have argued that rhetoric was not simply the creator of persuasion, but the criterion and vehicle of truth.[2]

The foregoing account has made use of late as well as early sources, but the result is a consistent ethical standpoint. Apart from this, on the philosophical side we know of his logic and his assertion of the unity of God, which have been discussed in an earlier chapter. There is nothing else save the report of a Johnsonian riposte to Parmenides's assertion of the impossibility of motion: not being able to counter the arguments in words, he simply stood up and walked.[3]

The interpretation of poetry, usually for its ethical lessons, was part of the business of a Greek teacher, and Antisthenes was no exception. A number of quotations from his studies in Homer have survived, mainly ethical in tendency and sometimes trivial, as when he said that the reason why old Nestor was the only man who could raise the cup (*Il.* 11.636) was not that he was exceptionally strong but that he was the only one who was not drunk. In a lengthy analysis of the epithet *polytropos* applied to Odysseus, he said that it applied both to character and to speech, which gave him the opportunity of introducing the contemporary definition of a *sophos* as a clever speaker, and hence *polytropos* because master of many *tropoi* or turns of speech and argument. He also brought Homer up to date by introducing into the poems the distinction between truth and opinion. It would appear that his Homeric interpretations were set as squarely in the ambit of the fifth-century enlightenment as the argument over Simonides in the *Protagoras*, though he did not agree with Protagoras and Gorgias that opinion was everything and there was no objective criterion of truth. Dio Chrysostom, our authority here, does not enlarge on the distinction between truth and opinion in Homer, indeed he says that Antisthenes did not develop it and it was only worked out in detail by Zeno. In Xenophon's *Symposium* (3.5) he is made to laugh at the claim of

[1] Fr. 42. This Archelaus was the tyrant of Macedon whom Gorgias's pupil Polus held up to Socrates in Plato's *Gorgias* (470d ff.) as a man who was both wicked and supremely happy. He was arguing against the Socratic teaching that it is better to be the victim of wrong than to commit it. (Dümmler, in *quellenkritisch* vein, claimed to have discovered the content of the *Archelaus* in the thirteenth speech of Dio Chrysostom. See his *Akad.* 1–18.)

[2] See Caizzi, *Stud. Urb.* 1964, 54.

[3] Fr. 160. This seems worth mentioning, though it is attributed to Diogenes by D.L., 9.39. Probably the attribution of some other 'fragments' is equally open to doubt. Though a few are assigned to named writings of Antisthenes, many in Caizzi's collection are simply given as 'sayings'.

Niceratus that he is a better man because he knows the Homeric poems by heart: so does any rhapsode, he retorts, and there is no more foolish set of men than the rhapsodes. Ah, says Socrates, but Niceratus has been to school with the allegorizers and knows all the hidden meanings. Later (4.6) Antisthenes asks Niceratus ironically if he could take over a kingdom because he knows all about Agamemnon. These exchanges are in a light post-prandial vein, but it does not look as if in his references to Homer as writing now 'opinion' and now 'truth' he was beguiled either by the craze for finding allegorical meanings or by the current idea that Homer was a practical guide to all the subjects mentioned in the poems.[1]

Many scholars, particularly in Germany, have claimed to discover veiled attacks on Antisthenes in various dialogues of Plato, sometimes under other names, and by this means to reconstruct much of his teaching. Great labour and considerable ingenuity have been expended in this attempt, and there is good reason to assume hostility between the two. Apart from anecdotes, Antisthenes wrote a dialogue abusing Plato under the opprobrious name of Sathon.[2] Nevertheless the results are in no case certain, and in recent times a more cautious attitude has prevailed.[3] The same may be said of K. Joël's theory that Xenophon's portrayal of Socrates had no historical value because it made him into an essentially Antisthenean and Cynic figure. In Joël's book the importance and influence of Antisthenes grow to enormous proportions, and Plato himself is put heavily in his debt.[4] So long as we know no

---

[1] The Homeric interpretations are in Caizzi's frr. 51–62, and discussed by him in *Stud. Urb.* 1964, 51 ff. There has been controversy over the question whether Antisthenes was an allegorist: see the references in Caizzi, *loc. cit.* 59, n. 47.

[2] See Antisthenes frr. 36–7. Its second title was 'On contradiction' (D.L. 6.16), lending colour to the anecdote that he wrote it as a counterblast to Plato's criticism that his denial of contradiction could be turned against itself. Σάθων, applied to babies, was a diminutive of σάθη meaning penis.

[3] See e.g. Field, *Plato and Contemps.* 160. Such speculation went very far. In 1894 Natorp could claim it as 'proved repeatedly' that the *Theaet., Euthyd., Crat.* and probably also *Hipp. Maj.* and *Min., Ion* and *Euthyphro*, were chiefly devoted to polemic against Antisthenes, either anonymously or under another name. On the *Ion* see now Caizzi, *Antisth. Frr.* p. 109. On *Theaet., Crat.* and *Soph.* pp. 213–15 above, and for *Crat.* von Fritz in *Hermes* 1927. *Rep.* 495 c–d was supposed by Dümmler to refer to him, but see Adam *ad loc.* For the same possibility elsewhere in the *Rep.* Popper, *O.S.* 277. For Socrates's 'dream' in *Theaet.* Gillespie in *Arch. f. G. d. Phil.* 1913 and 1914.

[4] Joël, *Der echte u. d. Xenoph. Sokr.* Joël held the remarkable theory that Prodicus in both Xenophon and Plato was not Prodicus but a mask for Antisthenes, to whom even the fable of

more than we do about Antisthenes from independent sources, the only topic on which such theories can claim anything like a firm basis is his logic. Plato says no more of him than the bare mention of his name among the intimate friends who were present with Socrates in prison up to the moment of his death.

He was a prolific writer, both rhetorical and philosophical. Diogenes Laertius lists about seventy-four titles divided into ten volumes. In his rhetorical period, like his teacher Gorgias he composed declamations on mythical themes, two of which have survived, in which Ajax and Odysseus defend in turn their claims to the arms of Achilles.[1] A defence of Orestes is also mentioned. According to Diogenes Laertius (6.1), his rhetorical style overflowed into his dialogues, and Aristotle gives an example of his somewhat extravagant metaphors.[2] Of the dialogues, some, though not all, were Socratic (D.L. 2.64). The *Heracles* and *Cyrus* were ethical in content, extolling the virtues of hard work, and the *Aspasia* contained scurrilous attacks on Pericles and his sons. The *Sathon*, *Archelaus* and *Politicus* have already been mentioned, and we hear of a *Physiognomonicus* and a *Protropticus*, as well as the works on Nature, which contained the statement on monotheism, and 'On Education or on Names' (pp. 248, 209 above).[3]

(9) ALCIDAMAS

According to the Suda, Alcidamas was a native of the Aeolian city of Elaea, the port of Pergamon.[4] The only indication of his date is that, like Antisthenes and Lycophron, he was a pupil of Gorgias.[5] Gorgias

---

the choice of Heracles must be transferred. (See on this H. Mayer, *Prod.* 120.) The book has been criticized by many, including Joël himself (see his *Gesch.* 731, n. 3), and a reappraisal of the question has now been undertaken by Caizzi, *Stud. Urb.* 1964, 60–76.

[1] Their authenticity has been queried, but see Caizzi, *loc. cit.* 43.

[2] Arist. *Rhet.* 1407a 10. He compared a likeable but thin and weakly man to frankincense, which gives pleasure as it is consumed!

[3] I have mentioned some which occur outside D.L.'s comprehensive list. References will be found in Caizzi's *Fragmenta*. According to the list, the *Physiogn.* was given the subtitle 'on the Sophists'.

[4] For general information about him see Brzoska in *RE*, I, 1533–9. The surviving remains are in Baiter–Sauppe, *Orat. Att.* pt. II (1850), 155–62, and Radermacher, *Artium Scriptores*, 132–47.

[5] Shorey (*TAPA*, 1909, 196) discussed the possibility of dating him through coincidences between his work on the Sophists, Plato's *Phaedrus*, and Isocrates's *Panegyricus*, but concluded that 'these facts hardly suffice to date Alcidamas relatively to either Plato or Isocrates'.

himself had dealt both in carefully prepared written declamations and in impromptu speeches, but his 'school' evidently divided itself on this point, with Alcidamas as the champion of improvisation, emphasizing Gorgias's doctrine of *kairos* or the opportunity of the moment, and Isocrates of the written speech. We still possess a short piece by Alcidamas entitled 'on those who compose written speeches, or on Sophists', in which he begins by attacking some of those called Sophists for neglecting research and culture (or education) and having no technique of public speaking. They parade their cleverness in written words and think themselves masters of rhetoric when they possess only a small fraction of the art. He will censure them not because the written word is alien to oratory but because it should be no more than a *parergon*, not a thing to pride oneself on, and those who spend their lives on it ignore a great deal of rhetoric and philosophy and do not deserve the name of Sophists. When this is taken with passages from Isocrates's works it is evident that they are conscious rivals and foes.[1] His little treatise shows that we are among the *epigoni*, and that Sophists have changed their methods since the great days when Protagoras and Gorgias were in their prime.[2]

Alcidamas has acquired great, and perhaps justifiable, fame among the moderns for his bold assertion that 'God has set all men free, Nature has made no man a slave' (p. 159 above). He was however primarily an orator and a faithful pupil of his master in defining rhetoric as 'the power of the persuasive'. Demosthenes is said to have studied his speeches.[3] Apart from the one complete pamphlet against written speeches[4] almost all our quotations from him occur in the *Rhetoric* of Aristotle, who cites most of them not for their content but as examples of faulty style.[5] As an instance of inappropriate metaphor he mentions

[1] For their opposition see the references in Lesky, *HGL*, 353, n. 4.
[2] Cf. Morrison in *D.U.J.* 1949, 56.
[3] Plut. *Demosth.* 5, 7 (Radermacher, p. 154) and [Plut.] *Vit. orat.* 844c.
[4] There is also a speech against Palamedes, one of those exercises on mythical subjects which the teachers of rhetoric provided for their pupils to learn, but its authenticity is doubtful. It is a poor thing, and bears no relation to the *Palamedes* of Gorgias.
[5] An exception is the sentence about slavery in the Messenian oration, introduced to illustrate the difference between legal and natural justice. (The actual quotation we owe to the scholiast.) He also gives at 1397a11 and 1398b10 examples from Alcidamas of types of argument (argument from the opposite and inductive argument) as used in oratory. Elsewhere he castigates him for his use of poetical compounds (1406a1), of exotic vocabulary (1406a8), of redundant epithets or descriptive phrases (e.g. 'damp sweat', 'laws the monarchs of cities', 1406a18ff.) and in-

'philosophy, a bulwark against the laws (*nomoi*)' (*Rhet.* 1406b11), and we may take this, together with the declaration that slavery is against nature and the plea that Sophists should return to philosophy, as indications that Alcidamas aspired to be a Sophist of the old school, in which rhetoric and philosophy went hand in hand, and was comparable to Antiphon as a champion of nature against convention.[1]

Of his other works we hear of a *Mouseion* or miscellany, which included a contest between Homer and Hesiod and perhaps also the 'encomium of death' mentioned by Cicero as containing a catalogue of the ills of human life. The whole collection was probably a sourcebook of material for orators.[2] Athenaeus (592c) mentions an encomium of a hetaera called Naïs, and according to Diogenes Laertius (8.56) he also wrote a work on natural philosophy containing historical assertions which, for a champion of *historia* and *paideia*, have generally been thought rather wild, unless they have been mangled in transmission. On this however see now D. O'Brien in *JHS*, 1968, 95f.

(10) LYCOPHRON

Lycophron has already found mention in these pages for his theory that law was a means of guaranteeing an individual's rights against his fellow-citizens but had no concern with positive morality, his disparagement of noble birth, and his theory of language and epistemology. Though the challenge to aristocracy was common enough at or before his time, as we see from Antiphon and Euripides, these dicta are collectively sufficient to make him appear a highly interesting figure, and it is unfortunate that we know scarcely anything else about him. Aristotle referred to him as a Sophist,[3] and he is generally agreed to

appropriate metaphor (1406b11). Cicero thought better of him, calling his redundancy *ubertas* and judging him *rhetor antiquus in primis nobilis*, while admitting that the subtleties of philosophic reasoning were beyond him (*Tusc.* 1.48.116).

[1] Nestle (*VMzuL*, 344f.) constructs a theory of the relation between politics and philosophy in Alcidamas by translating a poorly attested reading νομίμους for νόμους in Ar. *Rhet.* 1406a23. No editor prints this, and it would weaken Aristotle's point about redundancy, but Nestle adopts it without comment or hint of another reading. (He has in fact silently taken it over from Salomon in *Savigny-Stift.* 1911, 154.)

[2] Cic. *Tusc.* 1.48.116. See Radermacher, 155.

[3] *Pol.* 1280b11. This is presumably why DK include him in the *Vorsokratiker* but not Alcidamas with his striking statement about slavery. The testimonies occupy just a page (DK no. 83, vol. II, 307f.).

have been a pupil of Gorgias, which, though it is nowhere expressly stated,[1] we may take as extremely probable, as also that he was roughly contemporary with his fellow-pupil Alcidamas. Aristotle criticizes all three for similar faults of style. Of Lycophron's birthplace, date and life-history nothing whatever is recorded.

(11) ANONYMOUS WRITERS[2]

(a) The 'Anonymus Iamblichi'[3]

Of the content of this work I have spoken above (pp. 71 ff.). The *Protrepticus* of Iamblichus is a cento of unacknowledged borrowings from earlier philosophers, as one may see from its incorporation of word-for-word extracts from the *Phaedo*. It is universally agreed (however much opinions may differ in detail) that Bywater was correct in detecting in it considerable portions of the lost *Protrepticus* of Aristotle. There is then no *a priori* difficulty in supposing that other parts are taken straight from an otherwise unknown writing of the late fifth or early fourth century, and this was demonstrated by Friedrich Blass in 1899, though that is not to say that the paragraphs in question form either one continuous extract or the whole of the work.

Many attempts have been made to assign the fragments to a known author, but none has won general assent. Blass, whose acumen first detected their origin in the period of the *Aufklärung*, thought of Antiphon the Sophist, but this was disproved by the later discovery of the papyrus fragments of Antiphon's *Truth*. For K. Joël he was Antisthenes (and it is true that Antisthenes wrote a *Protrepticus*, which Iamblichus could have plundered as he did Aristotle's); Wilamowitz surprisingly thought Critias 'not impossible' (though he had earlier considered Protagoras); Cataudella saw the work as a collection of extracts from an ethico-political treatise of Democritus,

---

[1] DK say 'vielleicht Gorgiasschüler' (11, 307n.). The argument for placing him in the school of Gorgias (and it is a strong one) depends on Aristotle's criticisms of his style. See ZN, 1323, n. 3, and Nestle, *VMzuL*, 343. On his date and relation to Alcidamas see Popper, *O.S.* 261, who frankly admits that all this, like anything to do with the circumstances of Lycophron's life, must be highly speculative.

[2] Of the 'Anon. π. νόμων' enough has been said above, pp. 75 ff.

[3] Text, from Iambl. *Protr.* chapter 20, in DK, 11, 400 ff.

Nestle thought of Antiphon of Rhamnus, Untersteiner is convinced that the author is Hippias. H. Gomperz also inclined to this view but did not, in Untersteiner's opinion, go far enough in proving it. (Contrast Nestle, *VMŽuL*, 430: the writer is 'in evident opposition to the *nomos*-doctrine of Hippias'.) Most modern critics however would admit that we cannot now hope to put our finger on the author. He could well be some pupil of Protagoras, acquainted with the teaching of other Sophists and with Socrates, and probably not himself a professional Sophist. H. Gomperz thought he was one (*S. u. R.* 79), but on shaky grounds, and Nestle (*op. cit.* 424) thought of him as an educated layman like Critias. What makes it especially unlikely that he was a Sophist is his low opinion of rhetoric.[1]

Estimates of the date of the work on which Iamblichus drew have varied from the later years of the Peloponnesian War, the time of the 'post-Periclean extreme democracy' (Nestle, *op. cit.* 430; Dodds, *Gr. and Irrat.* 197, n. 27, makes a similar guess), to some time in the first half of the fourth century. Thus Gigante (*Nom. Bas.* 177) thought of it as having already a Socratic–Platonic basis. Paul Shorey struck a note of caution in *TAPA*, 1909, 192, n. 1. He pointed out that since Blass's time the fragments have been pruned by the rejection of some material taken from Plato and Isocrates, and claimed to see echoes of Plato here and there in what remains. He thought therefore that we should limit the amount of directly quoted fifth-century prose still further, and admit the hypothesis that what remains came to Iamblichus through an intermediate Platonizing source. In making use of the extracts earlier I have tried to confine myself to indubitably fifth- and fourth-century matter.

For bibliography on the subject see ZN, 1328, n. 2; DK, 11, 400 n. (with the *Nachträge* in later editions); Untersteiner, *Sof.* III, 110f.; Gigante, *Nom. Bas.* 177; and the notes to A. T. Cole's article in *HSCP*, 1961.

[1] A. T. Cole has recently (in *HSCP*, 1961) argued strongly for a modification of Cataudella's view, according to which the writer is 'an Athenian follower of Democritus, much more influenced than his master by late fifth-century rhetoric'. His article is especially interesting about the influence of the 'Anon.' on later philosophy.

(b) The 'Double Arguments'[1]

This curious little work in a mainly Doric dialect appears at the end of manuscripts of Sextus Empiricus with no indication of author or title. It is obviously incomplete, and the ultimate purpose of the writer is not clear. Stephanus christened it the *Dialexeis*, but in recent times it has been known as the *Dissoi Logoi*, 'Double (or Twin) Arguments', from the opening words, which recur later, 'Double arguments are maintained (or 'two views are taken') concerning...'[2] It has no literary or philosophical merit, and is most plausibly thought to be a pupil's notes from a teacher who had adopted Protagoras's methods or alternatively something written by a teacher for his pupils. As such it is of interest for the type of teaching current in the second generation of Sophists and also as showing how the argument about the teachability of virtue had degenerated into a school commonplace. The date is fortunately fixed at about 400 B.C. by a reference to the victory of the Spartans over the Athenians and their allies as 'very recent'.

Protagoras, we know, maintained that there are two contrary arguments on every subject, and himself composed two books of 'Antilogies'. In this way he set his pupils to debate, reconciling the opposing views or justifying one against the other. The present lecture—or series of textbook examples—looks like an imitation of this method. Many of the chapters start off by saying that 'two views are taken' about good and evil, or justice and injustice, fair and foul, truth and falsehood: the one that they are the same, the other that they are different. The writer sets out the arguments, and adopts one view himself. Thus in chapter 1, 'On Good and Evil', we have the relativist view of good and bad set forth in a way similar to Protagoras's in Plato's dialogue (*Prot.* 334, pp. 166f. above), but with some ridiculous argu-

---

[1] For a fuller account see Taylor, *Var. Socr.* 1, chapter 3, 91–128. Attempts to assign the work to a particular author have not been successful. For various views on this, and on its general character, see Untersteiner, *Sophs.* 308, n. 2, and *Sof.* III, 148f. Further bibliography will be found in O'Brien, *Socr. Paradoxes*, 75, n. 47. Text in DK, II, 405 ff.

[2] If the conception is Protagorean, the phrase itself seems to be an allusion to Euripides, fr. 189 (from the *Antiope*):

ἐκ παντὸς ἄν τις πράγματος δισσῶν λόγων
ἀγῶνα θεῖτ' ἂν εἰ λέγειν εἴη σοφός.

For other echoes of Euripides see Taylor, *Var. Socr.* 1, 96.

ments added. The writer sides with those who say that the same thing is both good and bad, being good for some and bad for others, and for the same man in some circumstances good and in others bad. After adducing the Protagorean instance of the different effect of food and drink in health and sickness, he goes on to say things like this: a life of dissoluteness and extravagance may be bad for the dissolute man but good for trade, sickness bad for the sick man but good for the doctors, death bad for the man who dies but good for the undertakers, and so on. The identity of honourable and disgraceful is argued by appealing to the different customs and beliefs of Athenians and Spartans, Greeks and barbarians, with instances taken from Herodotus (p. 16 above).

The little work repeats all the sophistic tricks with which Plato was familiar: a talent is heavier than a mina but lighter than two talents, therefore the same thing is both heavy and light: what is here is not in Libya, therefore the same thing both is and is not, and so forth.[1] The sixth chapter is headed 'Concerning wisdom and virtue, whether teachable', and begins: 'There is a certain argument neither true nor novel, that wisdom and virtue cannot be taught or learned.' It then enumerates five arguments used by supporters of this view and proceeds to refute them.

1. If you hand over something to another, you cannot possess it yourself.

2. If it were teachable, there would be recognized teachers of it, as of music. (This appears in the *Meno*.)

3. The wise men of Greece would have taught their skill to those near and dear to them. (So Socrates argues at *Protagoras* 319 that Pericles could not teach his own sons his wisdom and at *Meno* 90 that no great statesman has done so.)

4. Some have gone to Sophists and got no good from it. (At *Meno* 92, Anytus claims that the Sophists do their pupils more harm than good.)

5. Many have become distinguished without going to Sophists.

[1] Cf. *Rep.* 479 ff., *Theaet.* 152 d, 155 b–c, and *Euthyd.* 283 c–d and *passim*. In the *Theaet.* the idea of the same thing being both heavy and light is put forward as a 'secret doctrine' of Protagoras, i.e. as a necessary consequence of his teaching even if he himself was not aware of it.

These evidently form a series of stock objections to the sophistic profession. The writer proceeds to reply to them one by one.

1. This argument, he thinks, is 'very silly' (κάρτα εὐήθη), for he knows that teachers of writing and lyre-playing do retain the knowledge they impart.

2. In reply to the argument that there are no recognized teachers of virtue, what, he asks, do the Sophists teach, if not wisdom and virtue? (In the *Meno* Socrates suggests that the Sophists are the right men to teach virtue. Anytus is furious at the idea, and Meno admires Gorgias because, unlike the other Sophists, he makes no claim to teach it.) And what, he goes on, were the Anaxagoreans and Pythagoreans? (Meaning presumably that they were pupils who learned wisdom and virtue from Anaxagoras and Pythagoras.)

3. Against the third argument, he simply says that Polyclitus did teach his sons to make statues (thereby imparting his particular *sophia* and *areté*). (Polyclitus was instanced at the very end of Protagoras's speech, *Prot.* 328c, with the suggestion that, if a man's sons did not turn out to equal him at his own *areté*, this was not necessarily for lack of teaching.) Moreover, if someone has failed to teach, this is no argument, whereas, if a single one has taught it, that is proof that it can be taught.

4. If it is true that some have not learned wisdom from Sophists, it is also true that many who have been taught to read and write have not learned these arts.

5. Against the fifth argument he says that after all natural talent (*physis*) does count for something. One who has not learned from the Sophists may do very well, if he has a gift for picking things up easily, after learning a little from those who teach us language—that is, our parents. One may learn from his father, another from his mother, one more, one less. If anyone believes that we do not learn language but are born with a knowledge of it, let him consider that, if a newborn child were sent straight to Persia and brought up there, he would speak Persian and not Greek. We learn language without knowing who are our teachers.

In the same way Protagoras at *Prot.* 327 introduces the notion of natural bent (εὐφυία , cf. εὐφυής in *Diss. Log.*), suggesting that some have a greater talent for virtue just as for flute-playing, and goes on to introduce the analogy of language, which we learn without knowing who are our teachers. A child's education in virtue begins at birth with his parents and nurse and is continued by the school and in later life by the city itself through its laws (325 c ff.). The Sophist does not claim to be the sole teacher of virtue, but only to carry this education further than others.

Since we may assume this document to have been written before Plato's *Protagoras*, it shows that the objections to the thesis that virtue is teachable, which Socrates raises in that dialogue in order to draw Protagoras out, are based on well-known material from current and earlier controversy. When we add the points in common between the writer's reply and that of Plato's Protagoras, it lends support to what one would in any case think probable, that the long speech which Plato assigns to Protagoras reproduces substantially the views of the Sophist himself.[1]

Chapter 7 argues that the use of the lot rather than election in appointment to office is neither efficient nor truly democratic, chapter 8 is an attempt to maintain that the good speaker knows everything about everything,[2] and the final, incomplete section deals with the value of a good memory. The argument that magistrates ought not to be appointed by lot because expert knowledge is as necessary for government as for any other occupation is one used by Socrates. That which follows it, however, that the lot is undemocratic because it leaves it to chance whether a friend of democracy or an oligarch is appointed, would not have commended itself to Socrates, who had grave doubts about the wisdom of democratic government. It recurs in Isocrates.[3]

---

[1] P. 64 above, with notes. Cf. Nestle in his edition of the *Protagoras*. He takes it for granted that the obvious connexions of *Dissoi Logoi*, chapter 6, with the speech in the *Prot.* are connexions of both with the original work of Protagoras on which they are based, and suggests that it was the Περὶ ἀρετῶν mentioned in D.L. 9.55, just as the story of human nature and progress in the dialogue was based on his Περὶ τῆς ἐν ἀρχῇ καταστάσεως.

[2] I cannot agree with Taylor that the purpose of this chapter is to establish the Socratic thesis that the dialectician is also the philosopher who is identical with the 'true' statesman and orator. Its claim is far more like that of Hippias (whom Taylor mentions in a footnote, *VS*, 127, n. 1) that the Sophist-orator is omniscient.

[3] See Xen. *Mem.* 1.2.9, Arist. *Rhet.* 1393b4, Isocr. *Areop.* 23, Taylor, *VS*, 123f.

PART TWO
SOCRATES

In 1894 Edmund Pfleiderer observed that, since innumerable writers, many of them men of the highest reputation, had written about Socrates and Plato, anyone undertaking the task once more must surely, *in tanta scriptorum turba*, ask himself like Livy: *Facturusne operae pretium sim?* I should not like to have to count the number of books and articles about Socrates that have appeared in the seventy-odd years since Pfleiderer wrote, but I must hope that yet another presentation of him, in the context of the history of Greek philosophy and especially of the philosophic preoccupations of his own century, will prove worth while. The enormous bulk of the scholarly literature means that my own reading in it has been even more—much more—selective than for the earlier portions of this history.[1] I have tried to make the selection representative of at least the more recent work, but it is probably inevitable that some of my readers will look in vain for their favourite items. I hope however that I have made myself sufficiently familiar with the ancient evidence to be entitled to views of my own, and it would not be safe to assume that the omission of a writer or a theory is necessarily due to ignorance. In putting Socrates into his setting in the history of Greek thought, it is impracticable to take note of every theory about him, including those which seem to me (though others may differ) to be highly improbable. I shall not, for instance, say much about what may be called the pan-Antisthenean school, who see Antisthenes lurking anonymously in many of Plato's dialogues and disguised as Socrates in Xenophon's *Memorabilia*.[2]

In a review in *Gnomon* for 1955 (259 ff.) Dr Olof Gigon, considering that in spite of over 2,000 years of inquiry the problem of Socrates had not yet been tackled in a properly methodical way, outlined what he saw as a programme of the required research. It is perhaps the best that could be devised, and I have tried to keep its principles in mind in my own work, even if not proceeding in the same order. Yet the final effect of it was a feeling

---

[1] The bibliographies of V. de Magalhães-Vilhena's two books on Socrates, published in 1952, cover about 96 pages of titles, and the literature of the last sixteen years could add considerably to their number. He also provides a survey of all previous opinion from the eighteenth century. C. J. de Vogel's article on *The Present State of the Socratic Problem* (*Phron.* 1955) deals mainly but not entirely with Vilhena and is a useful starting-point for an exploration of recent views. Useful bibliography will also be found in Coleman Phillipson's *Trial of Socrates* and Gigon's commentaries on Xen. *Mem.* 1 and 2.

[2] For Joël's theory see p. 310, n. 4, above. Perhaps the climax of pan-Antistheneanism is the description of the simple word φρόνησις in Chroust's *S. M. & M.* (128) as 'a typical Antisthenean–Cynic term'. On p. 204 the equation of σωφροσύνη with τὰ ἑαυτοῦ πράττειν at *Charm.* 161 b is said to be 'an Antisthenean definition'. The cult frequently causes its devotees to overlook completely parallels between Xenophon and Plato. For more about it see p. 347 below.

that, in spite of the application of the most scientific methods, in the end we must all have to some extent our own Socrates, who will not be precisely like anyone else's. The first step in Gigon's programme is to set apart all texts whose character makes them necessarily consider the historic Socrates alone. The remainder will be those whose aim is other than a historical report: his personal friends, comedy, the attack of Polycrates (which incidentally no longer exists) and certain later material. As to these we are to consider several questions, of which the first is how big a part is played by apologetic or polemic. It sounds perfect, until one finds that the first to be mentioned in the list of purely historical texts is the indictment of Socrates in 399. If this gives us 'the historic Socrates alone' we must accept without question that he was a corrupter of youth and a disbeliever in the city's gods. Did polemic play no part in the statement of those who wished him brought to trial and demanded the death penalty? Another is Xenophon's story of how Socrates rebuked him for asking the Delphic oracle a leading question (p. 348 below); but some scholars have seen a strong apologetic purpose behind this story. The fact is that no one was left indifferent by this altogether unusual character: everyone who has written about him was also reacting to him in one way or another. If then every man must have his own personal Socrates, I can do no more than present mine. It will be based on the fairest assessment of the evidence of which I am capable.

XII

PROBLEM AND SOURCES

(1) GENERAL

It is a bold—some will say over-bold—idea to put Socrates in one volume and Plato in another. In the dialogues of Plato it would seem that he has so blended his own spirit with that of Socrates that they can never again be separated. I thought so myself until I came to write the preceding chapters of this book; but the study which this necessitated has made me see Socrates as squarely set in his contemporary world of the Sophists, Thucydides and Euripides and an eager participant in their arguments. Certainly it has been impossible to leave him out of the previous sections describing fifth-century controversies. Plato, for all his reverence for Socrates as the inspiration and starting-point of his own reflections, is a more sophisticated philosopher and marks a new and fateful development in the history of thought. I would even claim that in reading Plato himself, without any checking or supplementation from other sources, one gets a strong impression that he was an essentially different philosophical character from the master through whose mouth he so often expresses the results of his own maturer and more widely ranging mind. He was still passionately concerned with the questions which excited the previous two generations—whether law and morals were natural or conventional in origin, whether 'virtue' could be taught, whether intelligence or inanimate nature was prior, whether all values were relative, the nature and standing of rhetoric, the relation between being and seeming, knowledge and opinion, language and its objects—and to him Protagoras and Gorgias, Prodicus and Hippias were still opponents whose challenge had not been adequately met; but to meet it called for something far more radical and comprehensive than the simple ethical intellectualism of Socrates. It called for nothing less than a new vision of the whole of reality, involving metaphysics, human psychology and not least cosmology, for the physicists' conception of a world

325

arisen from soulless matter had proved a powerful support for the sophistic denial of a scientific ethic based on anything but the exigencies of a particular immediate situation. To provide this total solution Plato, a genius of a far more universal stamp than Socrates, was supremely fitted. Since he claimed to have found what Socrates all his life was seeking, and since the personal impact of Socrates had been for him an unforgettable experience of his most impressionable years, he could see nothing improper in putting into Socrates's mouth some (not all) of the discoveries which in his eyes provided the final justification of Socrates's life and death and the answers to the questions that he had asked.

This distinction can only be maintained on the assumption that our sources of information about Socrates are sufficient to give a reliable portrait of him as a man and a philosopher. Any account must begin with the admission that there is, and always will be, a 'Socratic problem'. This is inevitable, since he wrote nothing,[1] and all that we know about him and his thoughts comes from the writings of men of the most varied character, from philosophers to comic poets, some of whom were passionately devoted to him while others thought his influence pernicious. Two things are frequently said of him which, if they both were true, would preclude us from making any significant remarks about him at all. It is claimed on the one hand that his teaching is indissolubly linked with his whole personality, and on the other that we can know nothing about the historical person Socrates because the accounts of him which we have not only are somewhat distorted, as might be thought inevitable, by being filtered through the minds of his pupils or opponents, but were actually never intended by their authors to be anything but fiction.[2] It will be the purpose of the

[1] That is, nothing philosophical. If the *Phaedo* is to be believed (60 c–d), he wrote a hymn to Apollo and versified the fables of Aesop in his last days in prison. For references to spurious Socratic works see Chroust, *Socr. M. & M.* 279, n. 791.

[2] Examples: for the first statement (*a*) Jaeger, *Paideia*, II, 36f.: 'The whole of Socratic literature, with one voice, denies that Socrates's doctrine can be detached from his individual self'; (*b*) Zeller (*Ph. d. Gr.* II. i, 44): 'There is no thinker whose philosophical importance is more closely attached to his personality than is the case with Socrates.' For the second statement: (*a*) Chroust, *S. M. & M.* xiii: 'From its very inception this [*sc.* the Socratic] tradition was intended to be fiction and nothing else'; (*b*) 'L'œuvre, la vie et la mort de Socrate sont une fiction littéraire' (quoted by Ritter, *Sokr.* 61f., from the summary of Dupréel's *La légende socr.* on its dust-cover). Ritter comments that in this way scholarly critics have happily consigned the person of Socrates, as they did that of Jesus, to the realm of myth ('mit nicht geringerem Scharfsinn—und eben so dumm').

following pages to show that the first statement is true and the second false.

The existence of the Socratic problem makes it necessary to start with an examination of our sources of information. These are for practical purposes four: Aristophanes, Xenophon, Plato and Aristotle. Of the rest of the Socratic literature which grew up in the period immediately following his death, virtually nothing has survived except a few fragments of his follower Aeschines, and the later sources say little of interest which is not taken from Plato or Aristotle. Of our four surviving writers two were philosophers of very different philosophical temperaments, one a retired general who, though endowed with a strong literary and historical bent, had been for most of his life a man of action and always remained so by temperament, and the fourth was a writer of comedies with a strong admixture of satire and farce. With these diverse characters and gifts they naturally saw different things in Socrates and have left us different impressions of him. Albert Schweitzer wrote that in the matter of historical information we are much better off with Jesus than with Socrates, because Jesus was portrayed by simple uneducated people, but Socrates 'by literary men, who exercised their creative ability upon his portrait'.[1] The idea of the 'Socratic legend' as a serious theory seems to have owed its inception to the book of E. Dupréel,[2] and by some scholars it has been taken for granted as needing no further proof. Yet the assumption that all the writers I have mentioned *intended* their accounts to be no more than fiction is so extraordinary as to require indisputable evidence before it is believed. The nearest to such evidence that can be produced is probably the *a priori* argument in the preface to A. H. Chroust's book that

Whenever we possess an ample literary tradition about a certain historical personality, but are yet unable successfully to reconstruct the historicity of that person, we are compelled to assume that the whole literary tradition was never really intended to concern itself with the historical reporting of fact.

---

[1] *The Quest of the Historical Jesus*, Eng. tr., 1954, p. 6.
[2] *La légende socratique et les sources de Platon* (1922). A similar thesis, reducing the Socratic literature to the status of romantic fiction, is put forward by Gigon in his *Sokrates* (1947), on which the comments by C. J. de Vogel in *Mnemos.* 1951 are pertinent.

We must *surmise*, therefore, that this tradition was aimed primarily at creating a legend or fiction.

On the next page this becomes '*As has been pointed out*, from its very inception this tradition *was* intended to be fiction and nothing else'.[1] Evidently therefore the theory of a deliberate fiction stands or falls by our ability or otherwise to elicit from the sources a credible historical figure. If the reader when he reaches the end of this volume thinks that we have done so, he need not trouble himself with the theory, but, until the attempt has been made, judgment must be suspended.

Should it be considered to have failed, it need not on that account have been waste of time. We shall at least have learned what Socrates meant to many people, and there remains the possibility of regarding him not as a historical but as a symbolic or eternal figure, in which guise he has been proved an incalculable influence on the history of thought. Thus A. W. Levy has written:

The problem of the historic Socrates is, I believe, insoluble, but the quest to find the meaning of Socrates for ourselves is perennial . . . One can as legitimately ask a philosopher what stand he takes on the meaning of Socrates's life as one can ask what is his theory of the nature of sense-data or his belief about the objectivity of moral values.[2]

For myself however I do not think that our position concerning knowledge of the historical Socrates is as hopeless as is sometimes alleged. The 'question' is at least in part the creation of scholars themselves, who for some reason when they hear the name of Socrates abandon the ordinary canons of comparative evaluation of evidence in favour of one-sided reliance on a single source. Disparity between the authorities is not a thing to cause despair. If they agreed exactly, then indeed we might suspect either that we were getting a very one-sided view of him, because they were all similar people looking for

---

[1] Chroust, *S. M. & M.* xii and xiii. The italics are mine. M. Treu also argues that it is *a priori* (von vorne herein) mistaken to look for the historical Socrates in the *Memorabilia* (*RE*, 2. Reihe, xviii. Halbb. 1772f.).

[2] *JHI*, 1956, 94 and 95. As an instance, Professor Ayer's claim about the controversy over the objectivity of values (quoted on p. 165 above) could certainly be described as taking a stand on the meaning of Socrates's life, for Socrates as we know him both lived and went to his death in the conviction that the moral problem: 'What am I to do?' cannot be adequately answered without an antecedent knowledge of objective standards of value. In this he has not only his contemporaries the Sophists but the whole tradition of British empiricism against him.

and admiring the same sort of thing, or that he was himself a rather simple and uninteresting figure, which he clearly was not. He was a complex character, who did not and could not reveal every side of himself equally to all his acquaintances, since by reason of their own intellectual powers and inclinations they were not all equally capable of observing and appreciating them. If then the accounts of, say, Plato and Xenophon seem to present a different type of man, the chances are that each by itself is not so much wrong as incomplete, that it tends to exaggerate certain genuine traits and minimize others equally genuine, and that to get an idea of the whole man we must regard them as complementary.[1] The important thing is that of all four main authorities we have writings sufficiently voluminous and self-revealing to leave us in no doubt about *their own* character, mentality and tastes; and this knowledge of the writers themselves is a most valuable aid in comparing and evaluating their impressions of Socrates.

To make this comparison, and neglect no one who had access to Socrates himself or to those who knew him, is absolutely essential. The earlier tendency to pick out one source as authentic, and belittle the rest, became somewhat discredited when every one of the four had found his chosen champion and been held up in turn as the only true mirror. A. Diès speaks entertainingly of how few scholars have, as he puts it, had the courage to mount the quadriga and drive all four horses. Most have preferred to disqualify all but one whom, rather than guide, they allow to run as he pleases. Plato was the first to enjoy this privilege, then Xenophon, then Aristotle; one or two backed Aristophanes, then round came the wheel to Plato again in this century with the British scholars Burnet and Taylor.[2]

[1] It is scarcely any longer possible to say anything new about Socrates. After making the above point repeatedly in lectures, I saw the following by W. W. Baker in *CJ*, 1916–17, 308f.: 'This great figure of Socrates was not one-sided but many-sided... If Socrates was many-sided, it is natural that men who themselves had different tastes and interests should have *seen* different sides. Therefore the pictures they draw, though different, may be entirely true.' It is astonishing how few scholars have taken this elementary point. (Kierkegaard argued somewhat similarly in a puckish way when he said that although we have no completely dependable conception of Socrates, 'still, we have in exchange all the various nuances of misunderstanding, and with such a personality as Socrates I believe this serves us best'. See his *Concept of Irony*, 158f. His American translator thinks he may have had his tongue in his cheek and Hegel in mind.)

[2] Diès, *Autour de P.* 157–9. See also Stenzel in *RE*, 2. Reihe, v. Halbb. 888: 'He who thinks it permissible to orientate himself from a single source must inevitably, from the standpoint of his own modern thought, intensify still further the exaggeration of his source' (and much more

One very curious argument is quite commonly found, that if something appears to have been widely asserted in the Socratic literature (the writings about Socrates of those in his immediate circle or their associates), that is evidence that it is not genuinely Socratic. This is clearly implied for instance in Chroust's reference to the refusal of Socrates to be perturbed at being condemned to death (*S. M. & M.* 23), which is found in both Xenophon and Plato:

Both Xenophon and Plato may have borrowed 'the philosopher's willingness to die' from Antisthenes; or Xenophon (*Memor.* 4.8.1) may have derived it from Plato who, in turn, is probably dependent on some Antisthenian dictum [when he was a close disciple of Socrates and present at his trial!]. The Stoics, who in this are admittedly under Cynic influence, made much of this 'readiness to die'.[1]

Again, though there are differences between Plato's and Xenophon's accounts of Socrates and his teaching, at many points they coincide. Some critics, however, will not allow us to regard this as any confirmation of the truth of what they say about him: their conclusion is simply that Xenophon has copied Plato. This is not critical method but uncritical theorizing. No doubt Xenophon read Plato's dialogues and the other Socratic writings,[2] but similarity between them is not necessarily evidence that Xenophon was a mere borrower, and it is still less justifiable to extend the argument to the rest of his Socratic writings on the ground that if he sometimes borrowed he did so always. Is it not more likely that, as Diès put it, 'Xenophon et Platon exploitent un fonds commun de Socratisme'?[3]

Before going on to consider the main authors one by one, a word is in place about the so-called 'Socratic *logoi*' or discourses featuring

that is to the point). Vilhena's massive work is once again directed to establishing Plato's dialogues, rightly understood in the context of their time, as the sole historical source. His examination of Xenophon and Aristotle leads him to an entirely negative conclusion, and a full consideration of Aristophanes is deferred.

[1] We cannot doubt that the attribution of such readiness to Socrates is historical. As De Strycker justly points out (*Mél. Grég.* 208), his attitude is confirmed not only by the manner of his death but also by his solitary championship of the law against an infuriated *demos* in the case of the generals after Arginusae (pp. 379f. below).

[2] Chroust has collected references to a number of 'suggestive similarities' between passages in Xenophon and the Platonic dialogues on p. 230, n. 39, of his *S. M. & M.*

[3] A. Diès, *Autour de P.* 228. See also Field, *P. and Contemps.* 140f., Stenzel in *RE*, 837f.

Socrates. In the *Apology* (39 d) Plato makes Socrates utter a prophecy: if the Athenians think that by silencing him they will escape future censure, they are wrong. Others will speak, of whom as yet they know nothing because his authority has restrained them, and being young they will speak all the more harshly. This was true, as Plato knew. He himself (still in his twenties when Socrates died), Aeschines, Antisthenes, Xenophon and others, poured out so many writings to his memory, mostly in the form of conversations in which he played the leading role, that these 'Socratic conversations' (Σωκρατικοὶ λόγοι) achieved the status of a literary genre. The flow was stimulated by opposition, such as that of Polycrates who, probably in the late 390s, composed an *Accusation of Socrates* which is now lost but is mentioned and criticized by Isocrates (*Bus.* 4) as well as later writers.[1] Xenophon, in writing his own version of Socrates's defence and attitude to death, speaks of 'others' who have described them before him and says that he owes his own information to Hermogenes. (Hermogenes, Aeschines and Antisthenes were all of the intimate circle who were with Socrates in his last hours. See *Phaedo*, 59 b.) We know of seven Socratic dialogues by Aeschines (*Alcibiades*, *Axiochus*, *Aspasia*, *Callias*, *Miltiades*, *Rhinon*, and *Telauges*) from which a number of quotations survive, the fullest remains being those of the *Alcibiades*.[2]

For the supposition that 'Socratic *logoi*' had the status of a literary genre of their own our main authority is Aristotle. At the beginning of his *Poetics* he introduces the subject by classifying different kinds of 'imitation' (*mimesis*), of which poetry is one, according to their media. Painters imitate through the medium of colours and shapes, others through the voice,[3] poetry through rhythm, language and harmony, dancing through rhythm alone. There is also an art which

[1] For information on Polycrates see Chroust, *S. M. & M.* chapter 4, and Dodds, *Gorgias*, pp. 28 f. Many scholars believe that, when Xenophon speaks of what 'the accuser' said of Socrates, his reference is to Polycrates rather than to the actual accusers at the trial, and that the *Gorgias* and possibly other dialogues of Plato were written in reply to his attack.

[2] For Aeschines see Field, *P. & Contemps.* 146–52, who gives a complete translation of the *Alcibiades* fragments. He seems to have looked somewhat sourly on his fellow-companions of Socrates, determined to show the worst sides of Callias (in his *Callias*, Dittmar, 193 ff.), Hermogenes and Critobulus, calling Hermogenes a slave to money and Critobulus stupid and dirty (in the *Telauges*, see frr. 40 and 44, Dittmar 290 f.). Plato and Xenophon give a different impression.

[3] Cf. Plato *Soph.* 267 a.

imitates by language (*logos*) alone, either in prose or verse. It has no
name, for (1447b9) 'we have no common name for a mime of Sophron
or Xenarchus[1] and a Socratic *logos*', and should still lack one if their
imitation were in verse. I have quoted this sentence in its context
because it is sometimes said that Aristotle is here putting the Socratic
conversations 'into the same class with' the mimes of Sophron (the
Syracusan contemporary of Plato whose *mimoi* depicted realistic
genre scenes of everyday life) in such a way as to justify the conclusion
that in substance the former could claim no more historical veracity
than the latter. In fact he is citing them only as random samples of the
whole genus of 'imitation through language alone'. All that they are
said to have in common is the medium of *logos*, as painters effect their
imitation through colour,[2] and *mimesis* could cover the whole range of
verisimilitude from Homer or tragedy ('the imitation of a serious
action') to Zeuxis's painting of grapes, so realistic that the birds pecked
at it. It is true (and this may well be what made Sophron and the
Socratic *logoi* occur to Aristotle's mind together) that Plato was said
to have been a great admirer of Sophron and to have introduced his
work to Athens.[3] Probably he saw in the form and presentation of its
material a useful precedent for the realistic setting and conversational
style which he adopted as the best medium for interpreting to the world
the character and philosophy of his master, and developing its implications. This is especially likely as the mime had up to then been a very
humble and popular form of entertainment, and its elevation to the
plane of literature seems to have been due to Sophron himself. It

[1] Xenarchus was Sophron's son, but little else is known of him. See Ziegler in *RE*, 2. Reihe,
XVIII. Halbb. 1422.

[2] The much-discussed fragment of Aristotle's dialogue *On Poets* (72 Rose, from Ath. 505 c),
with its doubtful points of reading, adds nothing. In Ross's translation (p. 73) it runs: 'Are we
then to deny that the so-called mimes of Sophron, which are not even in metre, are *logoi* [to
accept Ross's 'stories' here would be misleading] and imitations, or the dialogues of Alexamenos
of Teos, which were written before the Socratic dialogues?' (If the MS πρώτους, emended by
Kaibel to πρότερον, is correct, the only difference is that the otherwise unknown Alexamenos
is himself being called the first writer of Socratic dialogues. See on the text Natorp in *RE*, 1, 1375.)
Aristotle was evidently making the same point in his lost as in his surviving work on poetry.
His only other reference to the Σ. λ. is at *Rhet.* 1417 a 18, where he says that mathematical λόγοι
are not concerned with character or moral purpose as Socratic are.

[3] The earliest reference to Plato's interest in Sophron is a quotation from the historian Duris
(fourth–third century B.C.) in Athenaeus (504 b). See also D.L. 3.18. In later times the story was
frequently told that after his death a copy of the mimes was found under his pillow. (References
in *RE*, 2. Reihe, v. Halbb. 1100. It was said that the plays of Aristophanes were found with them.)

remains in the highest degree improbable that from the point of view of historical fidelity there was anything in common between the dialogues of Plato, in which Socrates is shown conversing with other well-known historical figures like Protagoras, Gorgias or Theaetetus, and a series of mimes with titles like *The Sempstresses*, *The Mother-in-law*, *The Fisherman and the Farmer*, *The Tunny-fisher* or *The Sorceresses*. They are 'true to life' in a different sense, and their heirs are Theocritus and Herondas, not Plato.[1] The practice among Socrates's friends of making notes of his conversations at the time, then writing them up and referring back to Socrates himself to check any doubtful points, is attested on pp. 343 f. below.

The historical value of the Socratic literature is to be judged from its own purpose and character; that is, mainly from the internal evidence of the writers—Plato and Xenophon—whose works have survived. And, as Field wisely reminded us, 'we must not fall into the error of ascribing a precisely similar purpose to all of it'.

(2) XENOPHON

Xenophon was an almost exact contemporary of Plato. Probably born within five years of him (430–425), he is known from the internal evidence of his works to have lived until after 355.[2] He was an Athenian citizen, son of Gryllus of the deme Erchia.[3] In 401, in spite of a warning from Socrates (*Anab.* 3.1.5), he joined the ill-fated expedition of Cyrus in Asia, with which his name is primarily linked in most people's minds as the author of the immortal *Anabasis*. Just how long his acquaintance with Socrates lasted we cannot say, but, since Socrates was executed in 399, it could have been almost as long as Plato's. He missed the

---

[1] Detailed comparison between the Platonic dialogues and the mime will be found in Reich, *Der Mimus*, vol. I, chapter 5. If I have not used him as an authority, it is because I find in this chapter some misunderstandings and a truly astonishing exaggeration. One example, in the face of which I find comment impossible, should suffice. Of Plato's portrait of Protagoras he writes (p. 390): 'He has become a type, matched by few in world literature, such as are—besides Hamlet, Falstaff, Don Juan and Don Quixote—above all the figures of mime, Samio and Ardalio, the stupidus, the μωρὸς φαλακρός, Maccus and Pulcinello, Hans Wurst and Kasperle and Karagöz.'

[2] See the discussion in M. Treu, *RE*, 2. Reihe, XVIII. Halbb. 1571 ff. The precise date of his birth is not now ascertainable. Gigon (*Comm. on Mem.* I, 106; but cf. *OCD*, 962) has revived an early theory that it was a few years earlier (441/0), whereas others have made him a little younger than Plato. (See Phillipson, *T. of S.* 27 with n. (q).)

[3] Authorities in *RE*, VII, 1899.

poignant last scenes of Socrates's life, the trial, the conversations in prison, and the drinking of the hemlock in the presence of his intimates, which so heightened and intensified the feelings of Plato and others about him; but his own attachment was so strong and lasting that in later years he made a point of inquiring about these events from another friend of Socrates, and wrote his own version to counteract the misleading impressions which, as it seemed to him, were being created by others already current. 'When I think', he said at the end of this little work (*Apol.* 34), 'of both the wisdom and the nobility of this man, I cannot refrain from writing of him nor, in writing of him, from praising him.' Set beside this the closing words of the *Phaedo*—'our friend, the best, as we should claim, of any of his generation known to us, and the wisest and most just'—and they afford together a moving testimony to the effect of this remarkable man on others of the most diverse character.

Xenophon might be described as a gentleman in the old-fashioned sense of the term, implying as well as a certain not ignoble type of character a high level of education and general culture. It is a plant that thrives best in an environment of wealth, especially inherited wealth, and there is a certain resemblance between Xenophon and the best among the aristocracy which occupied the great country houses of England in the eighteenth and nineteenth centuries—men whose hearts were not only in the management of their estates and the service of their country but also in the great libraries which some of them amassed with considerable discrimination and also used. He was soldier, sportsman, and lover of country life, methodical in his work, temperate in his habits, and religious with the religion of the plain and honest man. As a writer he employed a clear, easy, straightforward Attic prose on subjects which at least have the charm of variety, and as treated by him seem to put us in astonishingly close touch with the life of his period and class. In these qualities it would be difficult for anyone to surpass the man whose works include the first-hand story of the retreat of Cyrus's Greek force across the Anatolian plateau, a history of Greece from the time when Thucydides left off, a treatise on housekeeping and husbandry, a manual of horsemanship (and one on hunting if the *Cynegeticus* is a genuine work of Xenophon), another on 'ways and means' with suggestions for improving the finances of Athens, and, of course, a series of works designed to display the character of Socrates and preserve his memory from detractors.

On the debit side we must put a certain literal-mindedness and tendency to prosiness, a pedestrian outlook which is sometimes frankly dull, and little sign of any capacity for profound philosophical thought. Here we are concerned with his portrayal of Socrates, as to which it is fair to say that if Plato had been as capable as Xenophon of coping with the retreat across Anatolia or discoursing on the finer points of horsemanship or the virtues of different kinds of soil, he would have been unlikely to display at the same time the philosophic genius and the deep insight into character and motives which so obviously mark his own interpretation of Socrates's life and make one feel that it is penetrating much further than Xenophon's. Xenophon honoured and respected intellectual ability, but all the more, we may suspect, when he saw it combined, as it was in Socrates, with high physical courage, a good war record and general contempt of danger. So much of Socrates he appreciated and loved, and he felt a generous indignation at the harsh treatment that Athens had meted out to him. Much that he saw in Socrates was, I am convinced, characteristic of the real man. When however we find in the Socrates of Plato something far less commonplace, far more paradox, humour and irony and above all a greater profundity of thought, it would be wrong to suppose that these were foreign to Socrates simply because they do not appear in Xenophon's portrait. The impression of uniqueness, and the powerful impact, favourable or unfavourable, which he made on everyone who met him (and of these the most hardened sceptic can scarcely feel a doubt), are more comprehensible if we suppose that he had in him much of what Plato discovered as well as what appealed to the prosaic commonsense of Xenophon.

The works in which Xenophon introduces Socrates (apart from the story in *Anab.* 3.1) are four: *Oeconomicus*, *Apologia*, *Symposium* and *Memorabilia*. A reading of them at once makes plain that they differ considerably in character and purpose. The *Oeconomicus* is a highly practical treatise on estate management and farming, in which out of compliment to his dead teacher and friend Xenophon writes of a favourite pursuit of his own in the form of a dialogue between Socrates and a young man seeking his advice. Verisimilitude is assisted by making the last two-thirds of the work a report by Socrates of a conversation which he himself had had with a gentleman farmer, in which he questioned him about his pursuits, although even in this part we find that Socrates has something of his own to contribute. Readers of Plato, knowing their Socrates, may be amused to find this devotee of the city, who never left it of his own free will because 'trees and the open country have nothing to teach me' (*Phaedr.* 230d), singing the praises of agriculture not only as the healthiest of occupations but because it gives the mind leisure to attend to the interests of one's friends and city and is a training in the leadership of men, and solemnly declaring that 'the earth teaches justice too to those capable of learning' (*Oec.* chapters 5 and 6.9). Nevertheless Socrates knew himself to be a peculiar character marked out for a unique mission. He never claimed that his life of self-chosen poverty in the city, with no regular occupation, was the right life for others; and there are several touches in the dialogue sufficiently individualistic to show that the choice of Socrates as chief speaker is something more than an empty compliment. In making Socrates the exponent of one of his own favourite subjects, Xenophon was not neglecting what he remembered of his character or had learned from the talk and writing of others. So for instance Socrates claims to be richer than his wealthy young friend Critobulus because he has sufficient for his needs whereas Critobulus's commitments exceed his income (2.4). At 6.13 we read of his consuming interest in visiting the workshops of all sorts of craftsmen—builders, smiths, painters and sculptors.[1] At 11.3 he makes a joking reference to the comic poets' picture of him as a chatterer, a measurer of the air and a penniless beggar. At 17.15 he digresses briefly from the subject of weeds to remark on the value of an apt simile. Finally, his conversation

---

[1] In *Mem.* 3.10 Xenophon shows him conversing about their craft with a painter, a sculptor and an armourer. The precepts on management and farming, and certain other details, are obviously Xenophon's own, but it was a brilliant touch to remind a reader at this point of Socrates's insatiable eagerness to acquire information about every sort of craft and profession from the men who practised it. (Cf. also *Mem.* 2.7.6 and Plato, *Apol.* 21b–22d.) With questions about the secrets of their art he bombarded manual workers of every sort, poets and politicians: why not also farmers and estate owners?

with Ischomachus is not only a lesson in agriculture but an illustration in that particular field of the truth that one can be unaware of one's own knowledge, and that the best form of teaching is to elicit by questions this knowledge which the pupil already possesses but has been unable to formulate or use. 'Can it be, Ischomachus, that asking questions is teaching? I am just beginning to see what was behind all your questions. You lead me on by means of things I know, point to things that resemble them, and persuade me that I know things that I thought I had no knowledge of.'

Here is the Socratic method in a nutshell, question and answer, 'mental midwifery' and all. It is a clever (and again a truly Socratic) touch, that this time Socrates casts himself in the role of pupil but in reality, through narrating the conversation to one of his own young men, is acting as his guide to the method. Xenophon is not usually credited with an appreciation of the Socratic irony, the affectation that everyone else was wiser than he, but surely it is present here in double measure: in his pretence to Critobulus that he had to put himself under the instruction of Ischomachus not only in the technicalities of farming but even in the method which was peculiarly his own; and in the delighted surprise with which, in the dialogue-within-a-dialogue, he hails his discovery of what Ischomachus had been after with his questions. There is even an open acknowledgment of the Socratic theory, which Plato seized upon with such avidity, that learning is recollection, the bringing into full consciousness of knowledge that was latent in the mind already.[1] For instance, Socrates is quite sure that he does not know how big a hole should be dug when planting a fruit tree, but he has used his eyes as he walked about the fields, and in answer to Ischomachus's questions has to admit that he has never seen one more than $2\frac{1}{2}$ or less than $1\frac{1}{2}$ feet deep, nor more than 2 feet broad, and can even suggest a reason for the appropriate depth. We may well doubt whether the real Socrates was as observant of these things as he was of the characters of his fellow men, but Xenophon has simply used an example from his own sphere of interest to illustrate a pedagogic principle that he had learned from Socrates. The recollection in this

---

[1] ἐλελήθη ἐμαυτὸν ἐπιστάμενος, 18. 10. Cf. Plato, *Meno* 85 d οὐκοῦν οὐδενὸς διδάξαντος ἀλλ' ἐρωτήσαντος ἐπιστήσεται, ἀναλαβὼν αὐτὸς ἐξ αὑτοῦ τὴν ἐπιστήμην.

instance is of observations of practical, workaday life, and the author of the *Memorabilia* would be the first to admit that Socrates applied his method to more philosophical, and particularly ethical, teaching. Yet Socrates was not averse to taking his analogies from 'shoemakers, carpenters and smiths' or even, in all probability, from farmers as the Sophists did.[1] Whether he raised the theory of recollected knowledge from an educational aid to a metaphysical doctrine of an immortal soul recalling in this life eternal truths that it has learned in the Beyond, as Plato makes him do, is another question, and must be left till later. The object of the present section is simply to suggest, from an independent reading, that E. C. Marchant goes very wrong when he says (Loeb ed. xxiv): 'The thoughts and reflections . . . are so entirely Xenophon's own that we may wonder why he did not frankly produce a treatise on the management of an estate instead of a Socratic dialogue.'

The *Apologia*, a brief pamphlet of some eight pages, does not, like its Platonic counterpart, consist simply of the speeches supposedly made by Socrates at his trial. It begins with a statement of purpose. To describe once again the bearing of Socrates at the time of his condemnation and death will not be otiose. Previous writers have put beyond doubt the lofty tone of what he said, but, since they omitted to give the reason for it, it has appeared to spring from a lack of understanding of his predicament. Xenophon therefore applied to Hermogenes, one of the philosopher's closest friends who was with him at the end, and Hermogenes explained the reason, that in Socrates's opinion it was better for him to die than live because he had reached an age when he could only look forward to a gradual failing of his powers, and this would be particularly intolerable to one who had lived such a perfect life hitherto. What follows is partly in Xenophon's own words and, as he tells us himself, 'I have not tried to relate all that was said at the trial, but have contented myself with demonstrating, first, that Socrates's whole concern was to act with reverence towards the gods

---

[1] *Mem.* 1.2.37, and of course analogies from everyday crafts and their tools are frequently employed by the Socrates of both Xenophon and Plato, e.g. the shuttle and the awl at Pl. *Crat.* 388 a–b, the pruning-knife at *Rep.* 353a. The common fifth-century analogy between education and farming is used by Socrates at *Phaedr.* 276b and e and (*ex parte Protagorae*) at *Theaet.* 167 c. (See pp. 168f. above.)

and justice in his dealings with men; and secondly, that he did not think it proper to beg and pray for his life, but rather considered it time for him to die.' His method of doing this, as is obvious to anyone who takes the trouble to read this rather pathetic little work, is to put all his reverence for Socrates into the philosopher's own mouth, thus producing an impression of intolerable smugness and complacency. If Socrates had really said such things about himself,[1] far from exciting the love and admiration of men as wise as Plato and as talented and high-spirited as Alcibiades, he would have repelled them more speedily and surely than the ostracizer was repelled by Aristides the Just, who, after all, was only given that standing epithet by other people.

There are a few features in common between Plato's and Xenophon's versions of what happened at the trial, though they have been blunted and coarsened by Xenophon's less sensitive mind and by the fact that his information was at second or third hand and probably put together from various sources besides Hermogenes. In so far as they agree, however, they provide evidence that such points were in some form or another really made, or such incidents really occurred. Both agree that Socrates thought it at least possible that death was better for him than life, and there is a reference in Plato to his advanced age (38c), though this is by no means given as his reason for thinking so. Xenophon's Socrates has not prepared a speech in his own defence, Plato's says that he will speak 'at random, using whatever words come into my head' (17c). Both introduce the 'divine sign' (pp. 402ff. below), Xenophon as forbidding him to prepare a defence in advance, Plato as having uttered no warning against his coming to trial, thereby indicating that, whatever the outcome, it must be good. In both cases the effect is an indication that death will mean no harm for Socrates. Both agree on the substance of the charges brought against him, which are confirmed as

---

[1] E.g. §5: 'Do you not know that up to now I would not allow that any man has had a better life than I have, for I have had the supreme pleasure of knowing that I have lived my whole life piously and righteously'; and §18: 'If no one can disprove what I have said about myself, do I not justly deserve the praise of both gods and men?' Plato's Socrates says (*Apol.* 21 a–b) that Chaerephon asked the Delphic oracle whether anyone was wiser than he, and the oracle replied 'no one'; whereat he was astonished and incredulous, because he knew he was not wise in the least. Xenophon's, reporting (§14) only that Chaerephon 'asked the oracle about me', says Apollo told him that no man was either more liberal or more just or possessed of greater prudence and self-control (σωφροσύνη); and he accepts the reply without comment, except to say that Apollo at any rate did not call him a god, as it did Lycurgus, but only the wisest of men.

historical from an independent source (p. 382 below). Both agree that Chaerephon consulted the Delphic oracle about Socrates and received a favourable reply, though Xenophon tells the story more clumsily and makes Socrates speak about it in a different and more laboured way. Both report that an exchange of remarks took place between Socrates and Meletus, and that Socrates was unwilling to offer an alternative penalty in the ordinary sense, though only Plato refers to the suggestion of free meals in the Prytaneum and the offer of a sum of money put up by his friends. Finally, both mention his refusal of the offer of his friends to arrange his escape after condemnation, the subject of Plato's *Crito*. There is some slight internal evidence that the *Apology* of Plato was among Xenophon's sources, but the differences are too great to allow of the supposition that he simply took over these facts from Plato. Even if he had done so, we should still have been faced with the question whether Plato, who claimed to have been present at the trial, had himself invented them.

To conclude, Xenophon's *Apology* is of little or no independent value, and may be set aside in favour of a serious consideration of Plato's writings on the same subjects. It teaches us something about Xenophon, that, when he was trying to live up to the demands of a serious and solemn subject like the justification of Socrates's conduct through his trial and approaching death, he was by no means at his best.[1]

The *Symposium* is a longer and a more elaborately composed work, which naturally invites comparison with Plato's of the same name. Apart from Socrates, none of the participants are the same, but some are

---

[1] Every kind of opinion has been put forward about the *Apology*. Its authenticity has been denied (by Schenkl, Wilamowitz and others) and reasserted. The reliance on Hermogenes has been called fictitious (e.g. by Gigon and Treu; and the fact that in *Mem.* bk. 4 Xenophon repeats some of the same matter on the same authority is, oddly enough, said to confirm this), and again both genuine and Xenophon's only source (von Arnim). The *Apol.* has been said to have borrowed from Plato's as well as other Socratic 'apologies' (Treu) and again to have been written before Plato's (von Arnim, whose imagination soared to recounting how Plato's when it appeared made Xenophon ashamed of his own so that he wrote *Mem.* 1.1.4 and bk. 4 to replace it, as well as to answer the attack of Polycrates; Maier on the other hand, *Sokr.* p. 15, thought his *Apol.* itself showed knowledge of this attack). Alternatively, it was written after Plato's not in imitation but to oppose the sober truth to Plato's 'magnificent fiction', and is a highly trustworthy source (W. Schmid, *Gesch.* 224 f.). See in general Diès, *Autour de P.* 220–2, Hackforth, *CPA*, 11–21, Edelstein, *X. u. P. Bild*, 138–50, and Treu in *RE*, 2. Reihe, XVIII. Halbb. 1888–94. If it is true that Anytus lived until after 386 (Wilam. *Ar. u. Athen*, II, 374 f.) then the *Apol.*, which mentions his death, cannot have been written before that date.

known from the pages of Plato nevertheless. We meet Hermogenes the brother of Callias (known to us from the *Phaedo* and *Cratylus*), Critobulus the son of Crito (mentioned in the *Apology* and *Phaedo*), and Plato's uncle Charmides, after whom he named a dialogue. The host is Callias son of Hipponicus, whom Plato portrayed as the richest man of Athens with an extravagant passion for Sophists[1] and cast as host to the gathering of Sophists so vividly described in the *Protagoras*. Of special interest is the presence of Antisthenes, of whom we know all too little. We have seen that he was a figure of considerable importance in the context of Sophistic and Socratic thought, yet Plato ignores him completely except for the bare mention of his name among those present at Socrates's death. In Xenophon he appears as a somewhat ill-mannered, disputatious and tactless person, and at the same time quick to take offence at any suspected aspersions on himself. It is easy to believe that this was the man who quarrelled with Plato and gave an insulting title to the dialogue that he wrote against him (p. 310 with n. 2 above).

Whatever else may be said about the work, it presents a most vivid and realistic picture of that curious institution of the time, the *symposion* or 'drinking-together', a mixture of after-dinner conversation over the nuts and wine with cabaret entertainment hired by the host. Plato with his more purely philosophical interests does not give us such a typical example. At his *symposion*, as soon as dinner is over, the proposal is made and accepted that the drinking should be moderate and the entertainer dismissed, so that the company can embark immediately on a discussion of a set subject, each stating his views in turn. Xenophon's aim is to portray the whole man Socrates, not simply the philosopher, and for this, as he tells us, he decided it was important to show him in his lighter and more unbuttoned as well as his serious moods.[2] It is therefore only in the middle of a varied programme of

---

[1] The joke about the huge sums that he has spent on them (Plato, *Apol.* 20a, *Crat.* 391c) is repeated by Xenophon (*Symp.* 1.5). On Xenophon's characterization of him see Dittmar, *Aesch.* 207–10. Aeschines wrote a dialogue named after him.

[2] *Symp.* 1.1. Cf. *Mem.* 4.1.1. Dittmar noted (*Aesch.* 211) that in Plato's *Prot.* (347c ff.) Socrates appears to condemn outright the hiring of entertainers at symposia as unworthy of educated men. But he misses the irony of the passage. The point of it is that Socrates chooses to put the understanding of poetry, which Protagoras has just advocated as 'the most important part of education' (338e), on a level with such cabaret turns. (In Plato's *Symp.* the suggestion that the flute-girl be dismissed comes not from Socrates but from Eryximachus.)

entertainment that Socrates suggests turning to *logoi*.[1] Admittedly the dancing-girl's achievements inspire him to make a few observations on the comparative powers of men and women (rudely interrupted by Antisthenes with a personal remark about Xanthippe), but he breaks into the start of a discussion on whether virtue is teachable with a suggestion that they attend instead to the business in hand: the dancer is ready to begin. The humour in the dialogue, of which there is plenty, consists of personal banter, never subtle and often crude. The main subjects of more serious talk are, first, a series of speeches and discussions in which each symposiast is asked to say what is the accomplishment or possession on which he most prides himself and why; and secondly a speech by Socrates on Eros which is brought in rather suddenly and awkwardly without natural connexion with what has gone before. The Syracusan master of the boy and girl entertainers has gone out to prepare with them for a little mythological scene of Dionysus and Ariadne, and Socrates suddenly 'raised a new topic' while they were waiting, namely the praise of Love. A eulogy on Love by each of the diners in turn is of course the sole theme at Plato's symposium, which may be the reason for its sudden appearance here (there are one or two pretty clear signs that Xenophon knew Plato's),[2] but it is likely also that Love was a fairly constant theme at such gatherings in real life. The erotic element runs like a thread throughout Xenophon's conversations, much more crudely and outspokenly expressed than in Plato, and no secret is made of the intentionally aphrodisiac effect of some of the performances. As for Socrates, though as ready to join in the jokes as anyone, his theme, as one would expect, is that 'love of the soul is greatly superior to love of the body'.

Structurally the composition creaks at every joint. Rather than lead naturally from one subject to another, Xenophon will say, 'So that subject dropped. Then X said...' or 'that was the end of that conversation'. Unable to trust his readers to catch the tone of his writing, he will tell us laboriously, 'Thus they mingled jest and earnest in their

---

[1] They had already enjoyed instrumental solos by a flute-girl and boy-citharist, acrobatic dancing by a girl with hoops and among knife-blades, a dance by the boy, a comic parody of it by the professional buffoon, and an accompanied song by the boy.

[2] On the complex relation between the two see Maier, *Sokr.* 17–19, and other authorities referred to by Treu, *RE*, 1872. Perhaps predictably, an assumed but unknown dialogue of the ubiquitous Antisthenes figures prominently as a conjectural common source.

talk', or 'So then this *logos* was conducted seriously'. Nevertheless the scenes have an authentic stamp, all the more perhaps for his naivety, and few would want to miss such things as the 'beauty competition' between young Critobulus and the Silenus-like Socrates or the latter's complaint that Antisthenes loves him not for himself but only for his looks. That the *Symposium* is an imaginative work can hardly be denied, and Xenophon's claim to have been present must be taken as a transparent dramatic device. He begins: 'In my opinion, it is worth recording the behaviour of good men not only when they are serious but also when they are amusing themselves, and I wish to relate things which I know because I was present when they took place.'[1] There is no other reference to his presence, he takes no part in the conversations, and indeed, from the time in this first chapter when he describes the meeting of the friends and their adjournment to the house of Callias, it is impossible to suppose that he was among them. In any case he was probably, as Athenaeus already objected, only a child at the time.[2] What we may without undue credulity allow him is that his playlet was at least to some extent based on conversations which he had heard at different times and on his personal recollections of the characters and idiosyncrasies of its real-life actors, supplemented no doubt after his return from Asia by talk with surviving friends of Socrates and perusal of their reminiscences. Phillipson very reasonably says[3] that, if his Socratic writings were not composed until, perhaps, between 387 and 371, this is no objection to such a supposition. Memoirs and autobiographies are often written many years after the events and people to which they refer. In an age when books were less amenable to quick and easy reference, memories were better, and Xenophon, as a devoted Boswell, would no doubt have made notes at the time of conversations of Socrates to which he had listened. This practice among Socrates's pupils is mentioned by Plato. In the *Theaetetus* Euclides of Megara speaks of having been told by Socrates of a discussion he had had with Theaetetus and, when asked whether he can repeat it, replies (142d): 'Certainly not from memory, but I made some notes at the time, as

---

[1] οἷς δὲ παραγενόμενος ταῦτα γιγνώσκω δηλῶσαι βούλομαι.

[2] Ath. 216d. The dramatic date of the *Symp.* is fixed at 422 by the victory of Autolycus in the Panathenaic pancration (*Symp.* 1.2, cf. Ath. *loc. cit.*).

[3] *Trial*, 29, and cf. Schmid, *Gesch.* 231.

soon as I got home, and later on wrote out what I could recall at my leisure. Then, every time I went to Athens, I questioned Socrates upon any point where my memory had faded and made corrections on my return. In this way I have pretty well the whole conversation written down.' The narrator of Plato's *Symposium*, Apollodorus, who has been an associate of Socrates for three years, says that during that time he has 'made it his care to know what Socrates says and does every day' (172c). He learned the conversation at Agathon's house from another admirer of Socrates, obtained confirmation of some points from Socrates himself (173b), and is now ready to pass it on like a precious inheritance to others. Plato's half-brother Antiphon 'worked hard at getting by heart' the discussion between Socrates, Zeno and Parmenides (*Parm.* 126c). One may admit the dramatic value of such passages, but they would be impossible without a foundation in a known practice of the disciples. To record or commit to memory Socrates's conversations, and repeat them to one another, was obviously a labour of love among them.[1] If Xenophon included among things that he had 'heard Socrates say' conversations which in fact had been related to him in this way, or written down, by those who *had* heard them, the conventions of the time would allow it to be an innocent enough procedure.

Whatever Xenophon's sources of information and method of composition may be, we recognize in the Socrates of his *Symposium* a number of traits which can be justifiably regarded as genuinely Socratic. Such are his mock modesty (1.5); his cultivation of bodily health by exercise and avoidance of excess (2.17 and 24f.); his addiction to the method of question and answer (4.56ff.); his equation of beauty (καλόν) with practical utility or fitness for function (5.4ff.; Treu compares *Mem.* 3.8.4ff., 10.9ff., 4.6.9, to which one could add many passages from Plato); and his praise of a love which, though spiritual rather than physical, does not thereby become pallid and lacking in passion (ἀνεπαφρόδιτον, 8.15 and 18.)[2]

[1] Cf. also D.L.'s report of Simon the cobbler (2.122), who used to make notes of all he could remember of what Socrates said on visits to his shop. (For details on Simon, Zeller, *Ph. d. Gr.* 241f. with notes.)

[2] I have said nothing about the so-called 'sympotic literature', a shadowy phenomenon which some have assumed to have been already in existence in the fifth century, so that the *Symposia* of

Xenophon's 'Symposium' and 'Memorabilia'

I have left to the last the main Socratic work of Xenophon, the four books of *Memorabilia*.[1] What has just been said about the credibility of the *Symposium* applies in even stronger measure to them. Their character is governed by his motive, which he states thus (1.3.1): 'To support my opinion that Socrates benefited those who consorted with him, both by actions revealing his own character and by his conversation, I will set down what I can remember of them.' This then is the work in which he has collected all possible material bearing on his chosen subject, and it is not surprising to find occasional repetitions of what he has said elsewhere, e.g. in the *Apology* (cf. *Mem.* 4.8), and even internal repetitions and sometimes inconsistencies. The occasional claim of the author to have been present at the actual conversations he records is perhaps not to be taken more seriously than when it occurs in *Symposium* or *Oeconomicus*,[2] but his earnest desire to reproduce accurately the substance of what he has learned is, in accordance with his purpose, beyond doubt.[3] This purpose is not to write a life of Socrates, nor even to give a complete portrait of his character, but by

Plato and Xenophon represent only links in a chain ('ein Glied innerhalb der sympotischen Literatur', Treu, *RE*, 1872), or alternatively the tip of an iceberg of which the rest lies submerged beneath the waves of time. Treu refers to the article on this subject by Hug (*RE*, 2. Reihe, VIII. Halbb. 1273 ff.), but what Hug says is quite different. As a form of prose literature, the symposium is a post-classical phenomenon owing its inspiration entirely to the work of Plato and Xenophon who were not intermediaries but the originators of the whole genre. 'Aber erst durch den sokratisch-platonischen Dialog wurde die naturgemässe und bequeme Form für eine Literaturgattung gegossen, die Symposion-Literatur, welche . . . eine ununterbrochene Reihe von Plato bis Macrobius bildet.' 'Durch ihre [*sc.* Plato's and Xenophon's] häufige Nachahmung wurden die literarischen Symposien eine eigene Literaturgattung.' (See Hug, 1273 and 1274.)

[1] In Greek ἀπομνημονεύματα. Schmid (*Gesch.* 225, n. 5), distinguishes this word as 'personal recollections' from ὑπομνήματα, written notes or memoranda. The Latin title dates only from the sixteenth century, and *Commentarii*, which occurs in Gellius (14.3), has been suggested as a better translation. See Marchant, Loeb ed. vii.

[2] Schmid's attempt at a distinction, on the ground that the *Mem.* belong to a different 'Literaturgattung', has not been generally supported. The claim is however, as Treu remarked (*RE*, 1771), genuinely intended 'to legitimize the author's right to speak about Socrates'. It is in fact rarely made, unambiguously in only four places (1.3.8, 1.4.2, 2.4.1 and 4.3.2). To these are usually added 1.6.14 and 2.5.1, but I do not think that ἐμοὶ ταῦτα ἀκούοντι and ἤκουσα ἄλλου αὐτοῦ λόγον necessarily imply the presence of Xenophon at the conversation in question. Contrast ἤκουσα αὐτοῦ διαλεγομένου at 2.4.1 and the emphatic language of 4.3.2, ἐγὼ δέ, ὅτε πρὸς Εὐθύδημον τοιάδε διελέγετο, παρεγενόμην. 1.3.8 is the only occasion on which he himself takes part in the talk.

[3] For a reasoned defence of the *Mem.* as historical in intention, and an estimate of their historicity in effect, see Simeterre, *Théorie socratique*, 7–19. For the date or dates of its composition see his summary of the evidence on p. 13. On pp. 19–21 he gives a bibliography to date of works on the historical value of Xenophon.

illustrating in speech and action his inherent goodness and the beneficial effect of his companionship, example and advice, to refute his detractors and in particular those who, at his trial or afterwards, brought specific charges against him. He is not concerned to fill in the historical, biographical or local background, and however much we should now treasure such information it is pointless to blame Xenophon, as he is sometimes blamed, for not doing what he did not set out to do.

He starts by repeating the legal indictment against Socrates and refuting its two charges in turn, namely offences against the state religion and corruption of the young. Under the latter head he introduces a series of points which are not known to have been made by the prosecution and are known from Libanius to have occurred in the later 'Accusation' of Socrates by Polycrates (written some time after 393), and in dealing with these he speaks no longer of 'the prosecution' (οἱ γράψαντες) but of 'the accuser' (ὁ κατήγορος). This apologia, it appears, is a combined reply to both.[1] It occupies only the first two chapters of Book I, after which Xenophon turns from the negative task of rebuttal to the positive benefits which resulted from Socrates's teaching and example, and it has all the appearance of a self-contained pamphlet. The structure of the *Memorabilia* has given rise to wildly different opinions. To some they are a consciously and carefully constructed whole, to others a confused and clumsy collection of material for whose arrangement Xenophon is not to be blamed, since he obviously never intended it to be published and it was thrown together by a careless editor after his death.[2] Such judgments are inevitably in large measure subjective, and need not detain us here.

Enough has probably been said in estimation of the historical value of the work, which is made more probable by the feebleness of some

---

[1] The allusions to Polycrates were first detected by Cobet. The charges are partly political in character (Socrates was said to have fostered oligarchy and to have attacked the Athenian method of election by lot), and it is suggested that such matters could not be brought up at the trial owing to the amnesty of 403 (Chroust, 73). See also pp. 381–3 below.

[2] Gigon in his Commentary argued against Maier and Wilamowitz for conscious composition by Xenophon himself, and he is supported by Treu (*RE*, 1779). By way of contrast Chroust (*op. cit.* 5) speaks of 'the obvious lack of an orderly and articulate arrangement', and concludes that 'the whole *Mem.* could neither have been the result of one single uniform draft, nor have been edited by Xenophon himself'. Similar opinions are expressed by von Fritz in *Rh. Mus.* 1935, p. 20, and Schmid, *Gesch.* 229.

of the arguments used against it. If many of the ideas must be 'Xenophon's own' because they reappear elsewhere in his writings, is it not possible that he owed them to Socrates whom he so much admired? Those who like to detect 'Antisthenean elements' everywhere say for instance that, since Antisthenes's ideal was to teach by example rather than theoretical discussion, it is 'Antisthenean' when Xenophon tells us of the moral influence of Socrates's own conduct. Apart from the fact that Antisthenes claimed to be in all things following Socrates, the information is most useful as illustrating how different disciples' accounts of Socrates supplement each other to give between them a picture of the whole man: we know enough of Plato and Xenophon to be sure that it is his ideas that would especially appeal to the former, his conduct and practical advice to the latter. Again, the Antisthenes-cult can lead its devotees to ignore completely any parallels between Xenophon and Plato. At *Mem.* 1.2.53 Socrates says that once the soul has left a body, even of a near relation, it may be disposed of quickly and unceremoniously. Chroust compares this to 'Cynic lack of piety towards the dead'. No thought of the *Phaedo* enters his head, where in answer to Crito's question how they are to bury him Socrates smilingly replies (115c) 'Anyhow you like, provided you can catch me', and explains that, since the corpse will no longer be Socrates, its disposal is of no importance. Nor does he think of Aristotle, who says (*EE* 1235a39) that in Socrates's opinion corpses were useless, and could be disposed of as such.[1] Finally, when Diogenes Laertius five or six centuries later tells an anecdote in which a saying is attributed to Antisthenes, and Xenophon gives the same saying to Socrates, the same critics expect us to believe Diogenes rather than the man who was personally acquainted with Socrates and with a number of his friends.[2] There is indeed something in the claim that, in accordance with his avowed purpose of winning over the ordinary Athenian, we must be prepared to find him putting a somewhat one-sided emphasis on the conventionally virtuous side of Socrates rather than on his uniqueness

---

[1] Gigon (*Mus. Helv.* 1959, 177) assumes that Xenophon and Aristotle are both drawing on a 'Grundtext' now lost.

[2] For a treasury of such examples of the Antisthenes-cult, which was inaugurated by Joël's *Echte u. xenoph. Sokr.*, see Chroust, *S. M. & M.* chapter 5. It is to be noted that, in Chroust's own words (p. 102), 'with the exception of a few meagre fragments, all the writings of Antisthenes have been lost'.

and eccentricity.[1] Yet even this did not prevent him from letting Socrates argue for his disturbing paradox (known also from Plato) that the sinner who knows what he is doing is more righteous than the involuntary one (*Mem.* 4.2.19f.).

Before leaving Xenophon it is worth recalling a story of which the truth can hardly be doubted, and which gives a valuable insight into his personal relations with Socrates. In the *Anabasis* (3.1.4) he tells how, when he received a letter from his friend Proxenus inviting him to join the expedition of Cyrus, his first reaction was to show it to Socrates and ask his advice. Socrates was doubtful of the effect on Athenian opinion of Xenophon's linking himself with the pro-Spartan Persian prince, and advised him to consult the oracle at Delphi. Being keen to accept, Xenophon somewhat disingenuously put his question in the form 'to what god should he sacrifice and pray in order to ensure a successful outcome of the enterprise he had in mind?', and the oracle obligingly supplied the names of gods. Socrates told him frankly that he had done wrong in not asking first whether he should go at all, but added that, as he had put the question in this way, he must carry out the god's orders. The Athenians did in fact pass sentence of banishment on Xenophon, and there is something rather touching in the pains he takes to make it clear that Socrates was not in any way responsible for his unpatriotic conduct. One of the complaints against Socrates was that his young associates, of whom Alcibiades was the most notorious, had had discreditable political careers, and Xenophon elsewhere shows himself particularly anxious to exonerate him from the charge.[2] Here he does so even when the story must be against himself. It also shows that the occasions in the *Memorabilia* on which Socrates's younger friends turn to him for immediate practical advice are based on a genuine aspect of their relationship, though Plato preferred to concentrate on their more general and philosophical difficulties like the nature of names or (half-way between the two) the way in which *areté* is acquired.

---

[1] So Zeller, *Ph. d. Gr.* 2.1, 95, and Taylor, *VS*, 31: 'He carefully suppresses, as far as he can, all mention of the personal peculiarities which distinguish Socrates from the average decent Athenian.' Since Xenophon was something of an 'average decent Athenian' himself, perhaps 'was less aware of' would be truer than 'carefully suppresses'.

[2] See especially *Mem.* 1.2.12 ff. Plato in the *Symp.* shows the same desire to dissociate Socrates from Alcibiades's unprincipled conduct.

(3) PLATO

Mann kann einem Lehrer einen schöneren Dank nich abstatten, als es Platon gerade damit tat, dass er so über ihn hinausging.

The finest possible expression of gratitude to a teacher is to go beyond him in just the way that Plato did.

Julius Stenzel

In describing the intellectual ferment of the fifth century B.C. it would have been absurd to leave out the man who was probably its most important, and certainly its most controversial figure. In referring to his opinions in the first part of this volume, I have depended mainly on Plato, as I have also, to a considerable extent, for the views of the Sophists Protagoras, Prodicus and Hippias. It may fairly be said, therefore, that up to now I have prejudged, or begged, the question of Plato's trustworthiness as a source for Socrates. On their relationship as I see it I have said a little already (pp. 325 f. above). It is here that one feels most acutely the inevitable subjective element in anyone's treatment of Socrates. Perhaps this is in itself some evidence for the kind of man he was. 'This', said L. Versényi, 'was what the maieutic method aimed at: that each should come to know himself rather than Socrates.'[1] At any rate it is best to state one's position frankly at the outset. For the personal appearance, character and habits of Socrates[2] we may go with confidence to both Plato and Xenophon, and we find indeed a general agreement in their accounts of these matters. But for our chief concern, the contribution of Socrates to philosophical, and in particular ethical, inquiry, I believe it is best to rely primarily on those who were themselves philosophers and so best capable of understanding him. That means in the first place Plato, but also Aristotle in so far as he was a student and associate of Plato and had learned from him the relation of his own thought to the unwritten teaching of his master.

---

[1] *Socr. Hum.* 159. Did the author realize that even in that sentence he was accepting Plato as a reliable source? It is from Plato that we learn of the 'maieutic method' as characteristic of Socrates (pp. 378 n. 3, 444f. below). Or take the boldly sceptical remark of Schmid about the one work in which, if anywhere, most people would claim that there was a large amount of historical truth (*Gesch.* 243): 'Although Plato was present at the trial (Plato, *Ap.* 34a, 38b), to regard the *Apology* as historical is out of the question.' If it is out of the question to regard the *Apol.* as historical, why believe its statement that Plato was at the trial?

[2] Those who are wondering what place these have anyway in a history of philosophy may be referred back to the quotations from Jaeger and Zeller on p. 326, n. 2 above.

Plato, then, it is here claimed, is the chief, and Xenophon only an auxiliary, source of our knowledge of Socrates as a philosopher. But this brings us immediately to the crux of the whole Socratic question, namely the relation between the teachings of Socrates and Plato. The very fact that Plato was himself a philosopher means not only that he was better placed than others to understand the full import of Socrates's teaching, but also that in his own hands philosophy was bound to progress. His lifetime was prolonged for over fifty years after Socrates's execution, and his love and admiration for his master did not lead him to suppose that he could best honour his memory by merely writing down, as nearly as possible verbatim, what he recollected of his conversations, with no attempt to develop their implications. Piety itself demanded that he should defend the outlook of Socrates against criticisms inherent in the development of philosophy after his death, and how could this be done without adding fresh arguments to what the living Socrates actually said? This is of course the normal relationship between the work of master and follower in the philosophical world. Here however we have not only the complication that the master himself left nothing in writing by which the innovations of his successor could be checked: we have the altogether unusual situation that the successor wrote no impersonal treatises but a series of dialogues, sometimes highly dramatic in form, in many of which his predecessor is the chief speaker; and a limitless field for controversy is provided by the question how far what is ascribed to Socrates in a Platonic dialogue represents the views of the historic Socrates.

Our own answer to this question will only be completed with the completion of the whole account of Socrates, for it is bound to crop up at various points in the exposition itself. But a few principles may be briefly laid down first. I have said already that it is difficult not to think of Socrates as a man of (to use a crude distinction) the fifth century and Plato of the fourth, one who had had time and talent to think out a fuller reply to the Sophists than Socrates had done in the heat of personal contact and argument with them. Reading our authorities on Socrates gives a vivid impression of a highly individual character whom one feels one knows not only as a thinker but as a whole person. In this of course the dramatic form of Plato's writings, far from being a hindrance, is a tremendous help.[1] This feeling of personal acquaintance gives a certain encouragement (may I even say a certain right?), when a particular philosophical point is in question, to say: 'No, I can't imagine that Socrates himself would have put it like that', or 'Yes, that is just what I should have expected Socrates to say'. If this sounds an impossibly subjective criterion, I can only say that, provided it is based on a reading of all the sources, I do not believe that any better one presents itself. Indeed on this basis a large measure of agreement was being reached, at least in England, when in the first quarter of this century the subject was once more thrown into the melting-pot by the contentions of two Oxford scholars, both occupying chairs in Scotland, whose knowledge of their subject and general powers of judgment inevitably commanded respect: A. E. Taylor and John Burnet. Their thesis obtains little if any support today,[2] but reference to it may be a useful way of leading up to what I regard as a more historical approach.

The Burnet–Taylor thesis was that whatever in a Platonic dialogue is put into the mouth of Socrates must be assumed to be substantially what Socrates said in his lifetime. If this were true, much of what has through the centuries been thought of as Plato's most characteristic contribution to philosophy would not be his at all, but only a reproduction of his master's voice. This applies in particular to the famous 'Theory of Ideas', which is expounded through the mouth of Socrates in some of Plato's greatest dialogues like the *Phaedo* and *Republic*. On it Taylor wrote (*Socrates*, 162):

For my own part, I feel with Burnet that it is inconceivable that any thinker should introduce an eminently original doctrine of his own to the world by representing it as something which had long been familiar to a number of living contemporaries who were certain to read his work and detect any misrepresentation.

The main argument for this point of view might be described as 'the argument from outraged propriety',[3] and it receives its greatest support from the *Phaedo*, which purports to relate the conversation on the last

---

[1] Ritter on p. 31 of his *Sokrates* gives an admirable summing-up of the way in which Plato presents a consistent and rounded picture of a real, living and exceptional individual and makes credible both the devotion of his followers and the opposition and hatred of his enemies.

[2] For an effective reply to it see A. M. Adam's article in *CQ*, 1918.

[3] 'An offence against good taste and an outrage on all natural piety', Burnet (*Phaedo*, p. xii).

day of Socrates's life up to the last moving moment when, surrounded by his most intimate friends, he drank the hemlock. How improper it would have been for Plato at any time, but above all in describing this last solemn scene, to misrepresent Socrates as putting forward a doctrine which was in fact his own invention and not something taught by Socrates at all!

This argument errs because it looks back from the present day on all the consequences of Plato's theory, which have admittedly been tremendous. But it is no unique event in the history of philosophy and science that something which proves afterwards to have been a turning-point should have been first introduced naturally, almost unconsciously, by its author, to whom it seems no more than an inevitable consequence of things that have been said before. A parallel will be helpful. The 'Copernican revolution' is certainly such a turning-point, yet of the *De revolutionibus* of Copernicus, in which the epoch-making hypothesis was announced, T. S. Kuhn has written:[1]

It is a *revolution-making rather than a revolutionary* text ... A revolution-making work is *at once the culmination of a past tradition and the source of a novel future tradition*. As a whole the *De revolutionibus* stands almost entirely within an ancient astronomical and cosmological tradition; yet within its generally classical framework are to be found a few novelties which shifted the direction of scientific thought *in ways unforeseen by its author*.

Briefly the matter stands thus. Socrates said that you cannot discuss moral questions like how to act justly, or aesthetic questions like whether a thing is beautiful, unless you have previously decided what you mean by the concepts 'justice' and 'beauty'. (This we know from Xenophon and Aristotle no less than Plato.) Until these are fixed, so that we have a standard in our minds to which the individual actions or objects may be referred, we shall not know what we are talking about, and discussion may be frustrated because the parties are attaching different meanings to the same words. If this is right, said Plato, then we must believe that such a thing as justice or beauty really exists, for otherwise what is the use of trying to define it? It is no good looking

---

[1] *The Copernican Revolution*, 134. I have italicized words which seem to me particularly significant for our present purpose. Cf. also what is said about the relation of Platonic to Socratic forms on p. 441 below.

for a universal standard if it is only imaginary. He taught therefore the existence of a Form or 'Idea' (in Greek *eidos* or *idea*) of these and other concepts, which was not a *mere* concept existing in our minds but had an eternal and unchanging nature independent of what human beings might think it was. This is the famous *chorismos*, or affirmation of the *separate* existence of the Ideas—separate, that is, both from the particular instances of them in the world and from our thought of them; and belief in such independently existing Forms constitutes what is known as 'Plato's Theory of Ideas'. That it arose out of the Socratic demand for definitions, and went beyond it in this way, is confirmed by Aristotle.

This was seen by later philosophers, from his immediate pupil Aristotle onwards, to constitute a new conception of reality, and further reflection, and discussion with his colleagues in the Academy, revealed serious difficulties in it to Plato himself. Yet in his own mind, I am sure, it would seem to constitute no more than the obvious and only possible defence of Socrates's teaching, and to do no more than bring its implications into the open. 'Before you can know that a thing is beautiful you must be able to say what beauty is.' It could not have been long before someone raised the pertinent question: 'Yes, Socrates, but are you asking us to define what is real or not? For, if beauty, justice and such are only creations of our imagination, surely you are wasting our time.' By trying to answer this question in a sense favourable to Socrates rather than to Gorgias, how could Plato have thought that he was acting otherwise than from motives of piety, and why should he have hesitated to put the necessary defence of Socratic doctrine into Socrates's own mouth?

The justification, then, in Plato's mind for putting a doctrine into Socrates's mouth was not that the doctrine *tel quel*, in its complete form, had been taught by Socrates, but that it could appear to Plato to be based on one of Socrates's fundamental convictions, and constitute a legitimate projection, explication and defence of it. This criterion may help us to put our fingers on some of Socrates's other beliefs. Did he, for instance, believe in the immortality of the soul? Many scholars have thought that in the *Apology* Plato makes him speak as an agnostic on this point, but in the *Phaedo* he asserts it unequivocally and offers a series of elaborate and highly metaphysical proofs involving the doctrines of transcendent forms, of reincarnation, and of knowledge as recollection of truths learned in the other world. It is neither improper nor unlikely that Plato should have added these proofs on his own account, drawing them from his other great source of inspiration, the Pythagorean philosophy, *provided that Socrates was convinced of immortality in the first place.* If he was not, we must agree with Burnet and Taylor that it would have been unthinkable for Plato to have foisted the conviction on him in narrating the last hours of his life. But if Plato knew that Socrates died in the faith that his soul—his true self—would survive the death of his body, it was both natural and proper that he should make him defend that faith in what seemed to him, Plato, the most convincing manner. Again, the idea of the philosopher-kings in the *Republic*, with all the substructure of psychology, epistemology and ontology that supports it, undoubtedly goes beyond anything that Socrates ever said and develops his teaching in ways peculiarly Platonic; but it has its base in the firm conviction of Socrates, which he preached in season and out of season, that politics was no place for the amateur, because government was a *techné* and depended on expert knowledge as much as architecture, shipbuilding, shoemaking, or any other craft.

The general point is well made by Stenzel in his article on Socrates in the *RE*. He writes for instance (867): 'In my opinion the decisive question here is not "what new thing has Plato introduced?" but "what trait, what view, what tendency in Socrates gave him the objective (or at least subjective) right to strengthen a trait in this or that direction, to produce a line already drawn?"' Stenzel's own example (872) of a case where the borderline between Socrates and Plato can be detected is the nature and influence of goodness, a constant theme of Socrates's talk, which Plato took over and sought to raise to a theoretical plane as the highest object of knowledge. By comparing *Meno* 87e and 88a–b (where goodness, practical benefit and right usage are equated) with the introduction of the form of goodness in the *Phaedo* (76d) and goodness as the 'greatest object of learning' at *Rep.* 504dff., he shows how the Platonic doctrine developed out of Socrates's insistence on the identity of good with useful or profitable (ὠφέλιμον) and of virtue with knowledge. These, one may add again, are known to be Socratic from Xenophon and Aristotle as well as Plato.[1]

I will only add here the chronological fact that Plato was born in 427. We do not know when he first met Socrates,[2] but if he were eighteen he could have known him for about ten years, and only when Socrates was already in his sixties. It must be admitted, then, with Diès (*Autour de P.* 170), that 'Platon a donc, en somme, peu vu de la vie de Socrate'. But, as Diès goes on, Socrates would have talked of his earlier years to his young friends, and there were plenty of others to satisfy Plato's unquestionable curiosity about them, notably his uncles Charmides and Critias.

(4) ARISTOTLE[3]

Unlike Plato, Xenophon and Aristophanes, Aristotle, who was not born until 384, did not have the benefit of personal acquaintance with Socrates. He had however the inestimable advantage of having worked for twenty years in the Academy under Plato's headship, which must have given him an unrivalled opportunity for knowing just what we want most of all to know: the relation between the philosophies of Socrates and Plato. Xenophon has painstakingly amassed, from his own memory and other sources, recollections of Socrates and his conversations, and used them, to the best of his ability and in his own, sometimes rather heavy-footed and platitudinous way, to construct a defence of his life and example. Plato offers a series of philosophical and literary masterpieces, the dramatic dialogues in which it is not easy to distinguish what goes back to Socrates himself, what has been transformed by the sheer artistry of the writer, and what is the result of Plato's own reflections on the consequences of his master's thought and his attempt to buttress it against criticism. Aristotle, whose interest is purely

---

[1] Of the hundreds of books and articles on the subject, I would suggest, to supplement this brief essay, Diès, *Autour de P.* book II, chapter 2 (*Le Socrate de Platon*); Ritter's *Sokrates* (especially pp. 48 ff.); Stenzel in *RE*, 2. Reihe, v. Halbb. 865 ff.; and De Strycker in *Mél. Grégoire*, II, 199–230. Note especially in De Strycker's excellent article his four criteria for deciding whether a particular passage in Plato is historically Socratic or not.

[2] According to Diog. Laert. (3.6) he became his 'hearer' when he was twenty.

[3] The texts of Aristotle relating to Socrates are conveniently collected in Th. Deman, *Le témoignage d'A. sur Socrate.*

philosophical, tells us in a few crisp sentences where in his opinion the thought of Socrates ends and that of Plato begins. He if anyone ought to know, and his contribution to the problem is invaluable. I have no intention of trying to guide the reader through the extraordinary maze of conflicting views which have been put forward on this point, but it may save discussion if I allow myself to quote from one or two of those with whom I should wish to ally myself as having said the most obvious and sensible things.[1]

Sir David Ross has expressed his views in the introduction to his edition of Aristotle's *Metaphysics*, pp. xxxiii–xlv, and his presidential address to the Classical Association in 1933 (*The Problem of Socrates*). Both should be read in full, but here is a quotation from the latter:

Can we seriously suppose that in twenty years' membership of the school [*sc.* Plato's] he did not, just as he learned a great deal about Plato's later views which we find nowhere in the dialogues,[2] learn much from Plato or from older members of the school about the origin of the ideal theory? It is in the last degree improbable. And we have direct evidence that it is not true. For one thing, he could not have learned from the dialogues that Cratylus was Plato's first master; nothing in the *Cratylus* or elsewhere in Plato suggests it.[3] And, what is more important, the statement that it was Plato and not Socrates that 'separated' the universals and called them Ideas shows that he did not take at their face value the many passages in the dialogues in which Socrates does both these things; are we not bound to infer that there was a well-understood tradition in the school on the subject; that it was known that the dialogues were Plato's chosen method of expounding his own views, and not studies in biography? ... That Aristotle credited Plato and not Socrates with the introduction of the ideal theory is con-

---

[1] With Aristotle as with every other source learned opinion has swung from one extreme to the other. He is independent of Plato and Xenophon and the only source for the real Socrates (Joël); he is dependent on Plato, whose dialogues have no historical value, so that the only historical source is Xenophon (Döring); or he is dependent on both Plato and Xenophon and may therefore be omitted (Taylor and Maier). Deman (*Témoignage d'Ar.* 11–21) gives a summary of earlier scholarship which may save a reader from wading through a morass of tedious and frequently perverse argument. I am surprised that so sympathetic a critic as Ritter (*Sokr.* 46f.) should have been seduced by Taylor and Maier into leaving Aristotle out of his assessment of sources.

[2] He also learned something about the difference between Plato's and Socrates's manner and style of speaking. It was not from Plato or Xenophon, but from some other Socratic *logos* if not even more directly, that he learned of the retort of Aristippus when Plato had expressed himself somewhat too didactically: 'Our friend Socrates never spoke like that' (*Rhet.* 1398 b 31).

[3] Gigon in *Mus. Helv.* 1959, 187, suggests that Aristotle's source here was Aeschines.

firmed—though confirmation is unnecessary—by the familiar passage in the *Ethics* in which he confesses his hesitation to attack the theory because it had been introduced by his friends. Would he have spoken thus of Socrates, who died fifteen years before he was born?[1]

G. C. Field writes, referring to the influence of Socrates on Plato (*CQ*, 1923, 113f.):

In his twenty years' association with Plato, Aristotle must have had constant personal intercourse with him and with others who knew him. It is really impossible to suppose that Aristotle would be reduced to mere conjecture or to a reading of Plato's works when he wanted to know anything about him. At least for twenty years of his life he had far more direct and certain sources of information than that.

In his compilation of Aristotle's evidence, Th. Deman writes (*Témoignage*, 106): 'There is no reason to charge Aristotle with inaccuracy. It is up to us to discover his methods and use his witness in a way which consorts with our own historical demands.'

The significance of the last sentence is this. One can usually trust Aristotle to distil the essence of one of his predecessors in philosophy, as it appeared to him, in the tersest and driest terms. This is most valuable for comparison with the wordy and scarcely philosophical expositions of Xenophon or the easy conversational flow of Platonic dialogue, flitting naturally from subject to subject 'wherever the wind of the argument blows' (*Rep.* 394d). But the terms in which he sums it up are his own: he explains earlier ideas in his more advanced and analytic vocabulary. This may not be in our eyes a sound historical procedure (though common enough among philosophers today), but guided by our knowledge of his own philosophy and terminology we can without too much difficulty make allowances for it (it is not for nothing that we have enough Aristotelian material to fill twelve volumes in translation), and his purely philosophical judgments will then form an invaluable supplement to the more personal records of Xenophon and Plato. He says for instance that Socrates, when Plato

---

[1] *Class. Ass. Proc.* 1933, 18f., supported by Diès, *Autour de P.* 210–18, Robin in *REG*, 1916. As Ross says, his case is strong enough without the final reference to *EN* 1096 a 11ff., as to which a captious critic could object that Aristotle might have said the same thing (διὰ τὸ φίλους ἄνδρας εἰσαγαγεῖν τὰ εἴδη) even if Plato had taken over the theory from Socrates and given it circulation in his writings.

came in contact with him, was not concerning himself at all with natural philosophy but solely with ethics, and that he had great influence in turning the whole current of philosophy in that direction; that his method was to look for the universal and ask for definitions, but that he did not 'separate' the universals: it was Plato who assumed that the object of a definition must exist apart from its instantiations in sensible form. In the Socratic search for the universal Aristotle saw the germ of a logical method, and being himself, unlike Socrates, keenly interested in logic for its own sake, he gave Socrates credit for this in his own language by saying that we may fairly ascribe two things to Socrates: inductive argument and general definition. Socrates, who had other aims in mind, would no doubt have been surprised to hear it put in those terms, but in grasping the historical significance of the Socratic method Aristotle has shown considerable insight.[1]

Aristotle had no personal interest in Socrates. He weighed his thought as dispassionately as he could, his purpose being, as with all his predecessors, to study their ideas and test them by the touchstone of his own philosophical assumptions, in order to discover how far they might be said to have contributed to the advancement of philosophy and still be useful for incorporation in a modern system, and how far they must be discarded as mistaken. There is no emotional involvement, as there was for Plato and Xenophon, who were frankly concerned to defend the memory of their friend, 'the most righteous man of his time', and as there was for Aristotle himself in his relations with Plato. (The emotional tension crystallized in the later paraphrase of *EN* 1096a16, *amicus Plato sed magis amica veritas*, was genuine enough.) With Socrates he could always be cool and critical, as in his brief and crushing comment on the doctrine that no one does wrong except through ignorance: it is 'in plain contradiction to experience'.

For his knowledge of Socrates he had of course the writings of Plato, Xenophon,[2] Antisthenes, Aeschines and other Socratics, and the

---

[1] See the further quotations from Ross on p. 428 below.

[2] *Eud. Ethics* 1235 a 35–b2 reproduces fairly closely *Mem.* 1.2.54. When however Taylor claims that *Rhet.* 1393 b 4ff., because it refers to Socrates's disapproval of election by lot as giving power to the ignorant, shows clear dependence on *Mem.* 1.2.9, he is talking nonsense. See Deman, 58f. Joël (*E. u. X. S.* 206–10), though a little apt to see contrasts too starkly in black and white, has proved pretty conclusively that in general the Socrates of Aristotle owes nothing to Xenophon's.

'so-called unwritten opinions' of Plato to which in one place he refers.[1] Above all he had the earlier Platonic dialogues and the personal instruction of Plato himself. He came to Athens at the early age of seventeen because the fame of Plato's school had reached his northern home. As it happened Plato was away in Sicily at the time, but the dialogues were written, and nothing could be more natural than that the enthusiastic youngster should prepare for the great man's return by reading them. That he did so is confirmed by the fact that he could think of no better inspiration for his own early efforts at writing. The death of his friend Eudemus prompted him to compose a dialogue on immortality on the lines of the *Phaedo*, and the central figure of his *Nerinthos* was a farmer who had been so impressed by reading the *Gorgias* that he abandoned his field and his vines to submit his soul to Plato. In this Aristotle was probably lagging behind the rest of the Academy, who by 367 under Plato's guidance were deep in the ontological and epistemological difficulties raised by the theory of transcendent forms, and tending more and more towards mathematical solutions of philosophical problems. One may feel some sympathy for the young boy, who in his maturity was to express his regret that 'for the moderns, philosophy has become mathematics' (*Metaph.* 992 a 32), if at this stage he found their discussions a little difficult to follow and turned with relief to the more Socratic topics of ethics and immortality as treated in these dialogues. But if as a philosopher Plato had left Socrates behind, one may be sure that he had not forgotten him as the greatest single influence on his life, nor would he be reluctant to answer the eager questions of his latest recruit.

(5) COMEDY

Surely the oddest place in which serious information about a philosopher has ever been sought is the Athenian comedy of the fifth

[1] At *Phys.* 209 b 13 he says that Plato's description of the 'receptacle of being' in the *Timaeus* differs from that ἐν τοῖς λεγομένοις ἀγράφοις δόγμασιν. Ross (*Metaph.* 1, xxxv) speaks of him as drawing on these for his knowledge of Socrates as well as Plato, but it is more probable that they contained Plato's later doctrines, formed at a time when his interests had diverged greatly from those of Socrates, and would not have much to say about Socrates himself. From Aristotle's description it does not sound as if they were actually never committed to writing, but rather that they were unpublished notes for use within the school.

century, with its farcical knockabout business, broad sexual humour, and grotesque phallic costumes. But though the object was certainly to raise a laugh, many features of the plays were there because they stemmed from the ritual origin of comedy and represented a tradition which the poet was not free to abolish.[1] Within its framework he aimed his criticism at the manners and customs of the time and at specific individuals of whom he disapproved. The phenomenon has no modern parallel, though serious criticism by comic means is familiar enough in satire and the political cartoon.

Aristophanes is the only contemporary comedian of whom we still possess complete plays, but he was not the only one to make fun of Socrates, who was evidently thought of as a peculiarly good subject. He was mentioned to our knowledge by four other writers of the Old Comedy, Callias, Ameipsias, Eupolis and Telecleides, of whom Ameipsias at least brought him on to the stage in person. Aristophanes too makes passing reference to him in other plays besides the *Clouds*. Not all the remarks are uncomplimentary. Ameipsias in the *Connus* says that along with being foolish, going hungry, having no decent coat and being 'born to spite the cobblers' (since he never wore shoes), he had great powers of endurance[2] and never stooped to flattery. Eupolis spoke of him as not knowing or caring where his next meal was coming from. Apart from this he is represented as squalid (literally 'unwashed'), thievish, and as an endless talker indulging in time-wasting dialectical subtleties. His name was linked, naturally enough, with that of Euripides, in the insinuation that Socrates wrote his plays for him. Callias spoke of one who had come under his influence as acquiring a 'solemn and lofty mien'.[3] The *Connus* of Ameipsias called Sophists *phrontistai*

---

[1] Chapter 4 of Murray's *Aristophanes* gives a good account of the part played by traditional elements.

[2] καρτερικός; Xenophon uses the same word, *Mem.* 1.2.1. Socrates's one old coat (τρίβων, not χλαῖνα) was a byword. Cf. Plato, *Prot.* 335 d, *Symp.* 219 b. It became a sort of uniform for ascetic philosophers, especially the Cynics, who claimed to model themselves on Socrates. (D.L. 2.28 in quoting these lines does not say which play of Ameipsias they come from, but I agree with all scholars since Meineke (*CGF*, 1, 203) that the *Connus* is by far the most likely.)

[3] Callias *ap.* D.L. 2.18. The line τί δή σὺ σεμνή καί φρονεῖς οὕτω μέγα; is surely lifted from a tragedy. Cf. Eur. *Alc.* 773 οὗτος, τί σεμνὸν καί πεφροντικὸς βλέπεις; other references are to Ameipsias in D.L. 2.28 (poverty and endurance), Eupolis, Kock, 1, p. 251 (poverty and loquacity), Aristophanes, *Birds* 1282 (associated with long hair, hunger and dirt), 1553 (unwashed, cf. *Clouds* 837), *Frogs* 1491 (time-wasting logic-chopping; the words Σωκράτει παρακαθήμενον λαλεῖν remind one of Callicles's criticism in Plato, *Gorg.* 485 d).

(thinkers), and Socrates was nicknamed *phrontistes* and in Aristophanes presides over a private *phrontisterion* or thinking-shop.[1]

However, the main source for the Socrates of comedy is the *Clouds* of Aristophanes, in which he is the chief figure.[2] Like all other sources of information on Socrates, it has aroused the most diverse opinions. In the eyes of some it exhibits a 'passionate hatred' (Ritter); Aristophanes has heaped on Socrates's head 'everything he knew about the Sophists that was hateful and unreasonable' (Zeller). Alternatively it carefully exonerates Socrates from the immoral teaching of the Sophists: his would-be pupil comes to him *expecting* to learn how to cheat, and is encouraged in this by the chorus, but in fact Socrates only teaches him all sorts of unpractical and unworldly things. Socrates is not responsible for what the Unjust Argument says, and is accused of nothing worse than wasting time in talk and finicky argument (Gelzer). Taking a different approach we are told on the one hand that Aristophanes aimed his shafts at a general tendency of the time: warmongering (*Acharnians*), modern poetry (*Frogs*), or subversive educational ideas (*Clouds*). For dramatic purposes these must be embodied in a single individual, but the element of personal attack is subordinated to the general aim, and no one would expect to see anything but the most general resemblance to the chosen victim. Socrates in the *Clouds* is 'in effect the abstract principle of evil'. So Cornford, who argued that the characters, though bearing historical names, were made to wear one or other of a

[1] Athenaeus (218c), discussing the dates of Protagoras's sojourn in Athens, says that Ameipsias in the *Connus* οὐ καταριθμεῖ αὐτὸν ἐν τῷ τῶν σοφιστῶν χορῷ. This was for long taken (and still is by many) as evidence that the chorus of the *Connus* consisted of φροντισταί, but Rogers (*Clouds*, xxxvf.) long ago pointed out the utter impossibility of a comic chorus being composed of twenty-four named individuals or of a man like Protagoras being represented not by an actor but by a member of the chorus. (Dover, *Clouds*, l–li, does not seem to think these are impossibilities.) The word obviously has its general, semi-humorous meaning of a troop or company, as at Plato, *Prot.* 315b, *Theaet.* 173b, and elsewhere, and the explanation of the phrase is that at some point or points in the play the Sophists then resident at Athens are named, and Protagoras was omitted from the list. The *Connus* won second place in 423 when the *Clouds* (first version) came third, and as I have just said it presented Socrates in person. Connus, according to Plato (*Euthyd.* 272c and 275d, *Menex.* 235e), taught Socrates music.

Socrates is ὁ φροντιστής at *Clouds* 266 and Xen. *Symp.* 6.6 (ἆρα σύ, ὦ Σ., ὁ φροντιστής ἐπικαλούμενος;). The use at *Mem.* 4.7.6 has an obvious apologetic purpose. Cf. Plato, *Apol.* 18b.

[2] K. J. Dover's recently published (1968) edition of this play did not become available to me until I was about to deliver my completed typescript to the press. Consequently I have only been able to add a note here and there in reference to it.

set of stock masks and were 'to the almost complete sacrifice of realistic portraiture, conformed to the traditional traits of those masks'. The masks represented a few set types—the Boastful Soldier, the Learned Doctor (these have had a long history), the Cook, the Parasite—which in a particular play were attached to the name of a well-known contemporary, Lamachus or Socrates, Euripides or Cleon. In the case of Socrates, 'almost everything he had to say and do was notoriously foreign to the real philosopher's nature and pursuits'. The proper comparison is Shakespeare's Falstaff, and his relation to the real Sir John Falstaff, the 'magnificent knight' of whom Fuller wrote that 'to avouch him by many arguments valiant is to maintain that the sun is bright'.[1] In a lecture Cornford once drew a more amusing parallel.

In one of Mr Shaw's plays there is a professor of Greek who, in moments of enthusiasm, quotes his own translation of Euripides. He can be identified with a personal friend of the author, well known for his pacific and rationalist opinions, who after the war became a member of the League of Nations Assembly. Some centuries hence critics may argue, on the strength of *Major Barbara*, that this gentleman had a past lamentably inconsistent with his ostensible character. Before the war he had been the director of an armament firm and, earlier still, the adherent of an unconventional religious organization, frequenting the lower quarters of the town for the purpose of indulging in corybantic rites.[2]

On the other side we have Taylor, for whom the old comedy 'dealt throughout in personal burlesque, not in satire on generalized social "types"... A successful burlesque must be founded on notorious fact, or what is believed to be such.' It is caricature, admittedly, but we should be 'foolish not to ask ourselves what are the real facts which explain the caricature, and whether we cannot discern them reappearing from a different angle of vision in what we are told by Plato or Xenophon' (*Socrates*, 18 f.).

[1] See Cornford's *Origin of Attic Comedy*, ch. 8. That the masks in the old comedy represented types rather than actual portraits is by no means certain. Cornford argued strongly that they did (*op. cit.* 169 n. 1, 170), but the case for portraiture is probably stronger. See Schmid in *Philol.* 1948, 211, and the evidence in M. Bieber's *RE* article *Maske* (xxviii. Halbb. 2087). Add now Dover, *Clouds*, xxxiii with notes.

[2] Unpublished. The name of the professor in question will be found on the flyleaf of *The Origin of Attic Comedy*, which is dedicated to him. It is a curious coincidence that A. Diès (*Autour de P.* 160) speaks of A. E. Taylor presenting Socrates as 'le général d'une antique Armée du Salut'.

Taylor's last piece of advice is surely sound. If we can recognize, even through the veils of caricature and burlesque, some of the traits which we find in the more serious accounts of Socrates given by others of his personal acquaintance, we may regard this as confirmation of their historical verisimilitude, and perhaps even feel encouraged, with due caution, to use Aristophanes in amplification of knowledge already gained. If on the other hand there seems to be nothing in common between them, it will be the comic poet rather than the others who feels entitled by his medium to lead us into a world of fantasy.

First, then, a summary of the play. Strepsiades, a blunt, uneducated farmer, has married an aristocratic wife with expensive tastes, who abets their son Pheidippides in his extravagances. This elegant youth cherishes a passion for horses which has got his father deeply into debt. Unable to sleep for the thought of his creditors, he bethinks himself of a set of people who, if their palm is crossed with silver, will teach one how to outwit an adversary, be one's cause right or wrong. They keep on the premises both *logoi*, the stronger and the weaker, the latter of which can win an unjust cause (112 ff.). Anyone who has had the patience to read the present volume up to this point will recognize the type at once—the professors of rhetoric, Protagoras let us say (though a little unfairly), or Gorgias or Polus. But no: the people he has in mind are Socrates and his school, who combine such instruction with strange theories about the heavens. If his son will agree to go to school with them, he can soon learn the way to bilk a creditor. Pheidippides is appalled. What? Join that set of pale-faced, bare-footed impostors? He could never look his fellow-sportsmen in the eye. He refuses point-blank, so there is nothing else for it: the old man must go himself, slow-witted and forgetful as he is, and try to learn the new hair-splitting logic.

He knocks at the door, and a comic scene ensues in which the disciples of Socrates are revealed in various indecorous poses as they pursue their researches into geophysics, astronomy, geometry and geography,[1] and one of them explains (with a warning that these things

---

[1] Instruction in the special sciences like mathematics and astronomy was offered by some Sophists. Cf. Plato, *Prot.* 318e, 315c, and p. 45 above.

are religious mysteries, only to be revealed if Strepsiades is determined to join the disciples) how the Master applies his brilliant intellect to such questions as the length of a flea's jump, which end of a mosquito produces the buzz and, more practically, how to filch a supper for the school (143–79). Socrates himself is discovered suspended above the stage in a basket. He is contemplating the sun and other astronomical phenomena, and gives a scientific explanation of the necessity for the mind to be raised up from the earth's damp vapours and mingled with its kin, the air, if it is to think clearly about such matters.[1] Strepsiades explains his wishes and promises payment on oath, whereat Socrates chides him for invoking non-existent gods, and asks him if he wants to know the truth about religion and consort with 'our own deities', the Clouds. He agrees, and is put through a mock initiation ceremony, which Socrates promises will make him 'a rattling talker, a wide boy, a slippery customer' (260). Socrates then prays to Air, Aither and the Clouds, and the Clouds appear in the form of goddesses. They are genuine clouds, as they themselves make plain in one of those odes of pure poetry which so surprisingly irradiate the buffoonery of an Aristophanic comedy, and Socrates expounds their role as weather-controllers, the supplanters of Zeus, in the current scientific jargon of vortices, compression, and natural necessity. But they are also, he says, the patron deities of Sophists, and can bestow wit and cleverness, skill in debate, verbal juggling and the like (317f.). For Aristophanes atheistic natural science and dishonest debating tricks are evidently but two sides of the same thing, sophistry.

The Clouds address Socrates with respect as 'high priest of the finest nonsense', a 'meteorosophist' in his own way the equal of Prodicus,[2] and promise their favours to Strepsiades on conditions: he will need a good memory, intelligence and powers of endurance, and to achieve his aim of victory, in action, counsel and speech, must be prepared to bear cold and subdue his taste for food, wine and physical

---

[1] Kinship of the *psyche* with the air went back to Anaximenes, but the theory was being developed and popularized at the time of the *Clouds* by Diogenes of Apollonia, with particular emphasis on the connexion between pure, dry air and the power of thought. See vol. II, 374.

[2] Even if we accept Dover's interpretation of the joke here (Clouds, lv f.), which does not seem to me to be certain, there remains the fact that Socrates is addressed as a μετεωροσοφιστής.

exercise.[1] When he has promised to put up with all this and more, and to renounce all gods except Chaos, the Clouds and the Tongue, they promise to make him the best speaker in all Greece, whose words will carry the day in the Assembly more often than any other's (432).[2] But his aims are much more modest: let them only teach him how to pervert justice and give his creditors the slip. Praising his spirit, they promise him this and more. Through their teaching he will become famous and rich, for men will flock to his doors to learn the secrets of his success. They then hand him over to Socrates, whom they describe as their minister (πρόσπολος, 436), to put him through his paces, and the two retire together to the inner sanctum of the *phrontisterion*.

After the parabasis, out they come again with Socrates swearing by all the gods in the scientific pantheon that he has never met a more hopelessly stupid and forgetful pupil. But he will give him another chance. In the following scene he tries to instruct him in the more theoretical sorts of sophistic learning, of which we have seen something already—poetry, metre, rhythm, and the rules of grammatical gender.[3] When Strepsiades objects that not these, but the 'unjust argument', is what he came to learn, he is told that these are a necessary propaedeutic (658). Socrates relents so far as to set him to think out by himself something relevant to his own affairs (695), and present it for criticism, adding a little advice on method: 'Let your subtle thought go free, think out the subject bit by bit, dividing it aright and examining it, and if one of your thoughts defeats you, let go and leave it, and then again set it in motion and weigh it up' (740ff.). The old man's first idea (involving getting a witch to draw down the moon so that the end of

[1] 412ff. The last was certainly not a genuine Socratic trait, but the poor physical condition of his disciples seems to have been thought suitable material for a joke. They are pale creatures who cannot stand the open air (103, 198f.). The origin of it may have been his fanatical follower Chaerephon, noted for his emaciated appearance. He is mentioned at *v.* 104, called 'half-dead' at 504, and was nicknamed 'the Bat' (*Birds* 1296, 1564). The παρὰ προσδοκίαν is effective, and (*pace* Merry *ad loc.*) spoiled by the κάδηφαγίας of D.L. 2.27, a feeble repetition of ἀριστᾶν. According to Xenophon (*Mem.* 1.2.4) Socrates disapproved of *over*-exertion; one should take as much exercise as is agreeable to the soul. Rogers suggested that the γυμνάσια may be mentioned as places resorted to for idle or immoral purposes, and passages illustrating the connexion of pederasty with the palaestra have been collected by H. Reynen in *Hermes*, 1967, 314f.

[2] This echoes the profession of Protagoras to teach a man ὅπως τὰ τῆς πόλεως δυνατώτατος ἂν εἴη καὶ πράττειν καὶ λέγειν (*Prot.* 319a, p. 38 above).

[3] See especially pp. 205, 221 above (Protagoras). Hippias taught περὶ ῥυθμῶν (Plato, *Hipp. Maj.* 285d).

the month, when payment is due, would never come) so impresses Socrates that he consents to propose specific financial problems, and adds the lucid advice that the pupil should 'not keep his mind close to himself,[1] but slacken it off into the air like a cockchafer tied by the foot to a thread' (762). However, after one more successful attempt, he produces a solution (suicide) that even Socrates cannot stomach, and after further evidence of his forgetfulness he gives him up for good. On the chorus's advice Strepsiades makes another attempt to enlist Pheidippides by dazzling him with his new learning about the non-existence of the gods and the importance of distinguishing the names for the male and female of animals. In the end he gets him to Socrates, and begs that he be taught the Just and Unjust Arguments—or the latter at least. Socrates replies that Pheidippides will learn 'from the Arguments themselves'; he will not be present.[2]

Enter the Just and Unjust *Logoi* (also known in Protagoras's terms as the Stronger and Weaker). They have a little preliminary sparring. There is no such thing as justice, says the Unjust. Where can it be found? 'With the gods', replies the Just, to be countered with the stock reference to Zeus and his unfilial treatment of his father. The chorus intervene and persuade them to have a set debate (reminiscent of the dialogue between Vice and Virtue before Heracles in Prodicus's fable), with the tutelage of Pheidippides as the winner's reward. The Just speaks first, and commends the 'old education', when boys were taught to be seen and not heard, to walk in well-ordered troops, coatless in any weather, to have good manners, defer to their elders, be modest, chaste and hardy, avoid the baths and brothels, and train hard for athletic success. Such an upbringing produced the heroes of

---

[1] This cannot possibly mean, as some critics would like it to (e.g. Murray, *Aristoph.* 96), that Socrates is telling Strepsiades to forget his money problems and fix his mind on higher matters. His own instructions were ἐκφρόντισόν τι τῶν σεαυτοῦ πραγμάτων, and he has just set him the specific problem of how to get out of an action for damages of five talents.

[2] The absence of Socrates does not imply, as has been suggested, that he dissociates himself from the ἄδικος λόγος. Given the idea of bringing the personified arguments on to the stage, contemporary theatrical practice made it impossible for him to remain, since the same actor would be needed to play one of the *Logoi* (Dover, lxvii). The theory that the poet wishes to exonerate Socrates from the immorality of the Unjust *Logos* is far-fetched. It is Socrates who 'keeps the *Logoi* on the premises', and Socrates who personally hands back Pheidippides to his father with the assurance that he has learned his lesson well and can secure an acquittal however plain the guilt. Strepsiades is under no illusions. When his son's new morality recoils on his own head, he curses him 'along with Socrates and the worse *Logos*'.

Marathon. This, of course, is both the 'just' and the 'stronger' case, but the Unjust Argument retorts that, though he is called the weaker (simply because he taught how to confute the old rules, which has been worth a fortune to him), he will easily beat it. For warm baths he can invoke Heracles, strongest and best of all the heroes.[1] Unchastity is not only enjoyable but is indulged in by Zeus himself.[2] What matters is to follow 'the necessities of nature'.[3] So it goes on till the Just *Logos* admits defeat. The two depart, Socrates and Strepsiades enter again, and Socrates asks the old man whether he is satisfied with what his son has heard already, or wants him to have personal instruction from himself. Strepsiades begs him to take the boy in hand and sharpen his wits both for petty lawsuits and other purposes, and Socrates promises to turn him out 'an accomplished sophist' (1111).[4] A choral interlude represents the teaching period. Socrates comes out again and assures Strepsiades that the lesson is well and truly learned. Strepsiades need never henceforth be convicted in any court, though there be ten thousand witnesses of his default. He receives Pheidippides with joy and triumph, and sure enough Pheidippides can tell him a trick to avoid the day of reckoning. They go into the house to celebrate with a dinner, but Strepsiades is brought out again by the arrival of the creditors, whom he tries to worst by a marvellous mixture of the 'unjust argument' that Pheidippides has taught him with the rest of the new cleverness that he has learned from Socrates, which in his eyes is obviously all alike and ought to be equally effective. 'How can you expect to be paid when you make mistakes in your genders?' 'What right have you to your money when you are ignorant of the natural laws governing the rainfall?'[5] That natural philosophy and practical astuteness are not in fact unconnected he shows by an argument from analogy, applied by the Socratic method of question and answer (1286ff.): What is interest? The growth of a sum of money month by month.

[1] Warm springs were regularly called baths of Heracles because of the story that the first one sprang out at Thermopylae to refresh him after one of his labours.

[2] For the unprincipled use of mythology at this time as an excuse for human failings see pp. 228f. above.

[3] Cf. Antiphon, p. 108 above.

[4] Dover argues *ad loc.* that this conversation is between Strepsiades and the Unjust *Logos*, since there would be no time for the actor to change his clothes and reappear as Socrates.

[5] This has been quoted already in the general context of fifth-century thought on p. 114.

Is the sea larger now than last year? No. If then the sea, with all the rivers that run into it, grows no larger, what reason can there be for money to grow?[1]

Having rid himself of the creditors by blows rather than the persuasiveness of his arguments, Strepsiades returns within, but the chorus have just time to prophesy an unhappy ending to his affair when out he comes again, crying and lamenting as Pheidippides rains blows on his head. They have quarrelled at table over the moral tone of the old and modern poets, and armed with the New Logic Pheidippides has no difficulty in proving that it is right for sons to beat their fathers. That it is not *nomos* is no objection: he has learned the worthlessness of established *nomoi* (1400), which have no other sanction than human persuasion, and can be altered at will (1421 ff.). We should take example from the animal world.[2] The poor old man is almost convinced that his treatment is just, when Pheidippides tries to comfort him by adding that he can as easily prove the rightness of beating his mother too. Not all his marital trials can make Strepsiades swallow this culminating evidence of depravity, which finally convinces him that his whole recourse to the New Thought has been wrong. Overcome by repentance, he curses his son, Socrates and the Weaker Argument together and turns reproachfully on the Clouds who have encouraged him in his wickedness. They blandly reply that it was his own idea, and if they seem to have egged on a 'poor foolish old man', it was with the highest moral intentions: when they see someone planning evil, they let him carry on to the inevitable downfall, thus teaching repentance and a proper respect for the gods. Strepsiades (with astonishing magnanimity, one might say, but Aristophanes's old men, even if rogues, are always

[1] In thus associating, through caricature, natural philosophy with sophistic argument, Aristophanes was hardly being unfair (cf. pp. 114, 116 above), and argument by analogy in ethical contexts was in itself characteristic of the Platonic Socrates. It was common in earlier and contemporary natural philosophy (e.g. Empedocles's famous comparison of respiration to the action of the clepsydra, or the 'like-to-like' analogies for the behaviour of atoms in Democritus; see vol. II, 220ff., 409) and in the Hippocratic Corpus. See in general Lloyd, *P. & A.* part 2. These scientific analogies have already been caricatured in the *Clouds* (234), when Socrates compared the absorption of moisture by cress and by the human mind. Among the Sophists we saw analogy used in the comparison of education to husbandry (pp. 168 f., 256 above), and it was probably much more common than the scanty remains of their teaching allow us to see.

[2] The dethronement of οἱ καθεστῶτες νόμοι (*v.* 1400) at this period has been a major theme of the present volume. Socrates of course was firmly opposed to it. That the human race could learn from the animals is reminiscent of Democritus fr. 154. See p. 104 with n. 4 above.

rather endearing characters) admits that this is hard but just. The real villains are Socrates and his crew, and they must be punished. The play ends with Strepsiades setting fire to the *phrontisterion* and smoking out Socrates and his disciples, 'above all for their crimes against the gods'.

I have summarized the play at some length in the hope that it will carry its own answer to the question how far it is likely to give a true portrait of the historic Socrates, or at least to the question how far Aristophanes intended to implicate Socrates in the immoral side of sophistry. There has been a tendency of recent years to argue that Socrates is discharged without a stain on his character, that Aristophanes in fact is at pains to distinguish his teaching from immoral sophistry, and that much of the comic effect lies in the contrast between what the rascally old man hopes and expects to be taught and what he actually finds when he joins the *phrontisterion*: a band of unworldly, pale-faced students living in poverty with their heads in the clouds, studying mathematics and the secrets of nature. Instead of ways to cheat his creditors, Socrates teaches him the true explanation of meteorological phenomena and the niceties of metre and grammar. There is no attack on his honour, says Murray, and Wolfgang Schmid repeats it: Aristophanes never impugns his honour, and he never tells Strepsiades how to cheat his creditors. The worst that he is accused of, adds Gelzer, is garrulity and waste of time in finicky argument.[1] According to Erbse, the Unjust Argument does indeed use a 'Sophistic-Socratic method', but in a context in which Socrates would have allowed it. Socrates, he thinks, is doing his best to cure Strepsiades of the immoral hopes that he entertains of philosophy, and the play demonstrates the irreconcilability of Socratic teaching with the moral dangers of Sophistic. The themes are sophistic, for instance language

---

[1] Murray, p. 94, Schmid, 224, Gelzer, 92. The chief upholders of this view are Murray in his *Aristophanes* (who had been much impressed by Taylor's *Varia Socratica*), Wolfgang Schmid in *Philol.* 1948 (not to be confused with Wilhelm Schmid of Christ–Schmid's *Gr. Literaturgesch.*, whom he criticizes on p. 213, n. 2 for overestimation of Xenophon as a source), and H. Erbse in *Hermes*, 1954. Much of Schmid's article seems to be taken from Murray, and Erbse's special pleading goes too far. Socrates, he contends, is not shown as an atheist (as that was understood at Athens), nor as pursuing natural science further than Xenophon said he did. (For this purpose we are asked to assume that not only stupid old Strepsiades, but Socrates's own pupils in the first scene, have 'misunderstood' him.)

and grammar, but Socrates's aim in his questions about 'the correctness of names' is to *attack* the theory that words were symbols of realities, a theory which must have been held 'in gewissem Umfange' by all the Sophists who taught the subject. (This is a considerable oversimplification of a complicated situation. Cf. pp. 209 ff. above.)

Erbse makes much of the words of the Clouds at the end (1454 ff.). 'Why didn't you warn a poor ignorant old man?' asks Strepsiades. 'This is our way with wicked people, to lead them into trouble so that they may learn to fear the gods.' The old man has misunderstood them from the beginning. They warned him (412–19) of the necessity for perseverance, concentration, hard work, abstinence and so forth. (But they did promise him that the reward for all this would be 'victory in battles of the tongue'!) Erbse does mention that Socrates introduces the Clouds as purveyors of quick wit, verbal juggling, circumlocution and chicanery, argument and counter-argument (320 f.), and boasts of the way they support crowds of sophists and undesirables in idleness (331 ff.), but he seems oblivious to the damage this inflicts on his case. However, even if we agreed with the repentant Strepsiades that their cruel deceit was 'hard but just', that would not exonerate Socrates and his crew, whom he still regards as scurrilous deceivers to be smoked out of their nest. This in Erbse's view was no outburst of hate against philosophy on the poet's part but the trifling (*sic*: *unbedeutender*) price paid by Socrates for a clear indication of the uprightness of his teaching!

This is a highly distorted and over-subtle view which disregards much that is in the play. The Clouds are the queens of sophistry (317 f.), the patrons of oracle-mongers, quack doctors, beringed dandies, dithyrambic poets and hordes of Sophists (331 ff.), and Socrates is their minister (436). They promise Strepsiades 'You shall have your wish; it is a modest one' (435), and their astonishing *volte-face* at the end of the play can only be taken as another example of their sophistry. Likewise Socrates, who holds that all other gods are false, promises a training in dishonesty (260), regrets that Pheidippides does not yet seem capable of mastering all the weapons of litigation (874 f.), but later guarantees that he has learned the Unjust Argument and can now get his father acquitted of all his peccadilloes (1148 ff.). He is the master of 'contrary arguments',[1] for he keeps both the stronger and the weaker, the just and the unjust, on the premises (112ff.). This is not misunderstanding on Strepsiades's part, for Socrates, when asked to teach them to Pheidippides, can produce them in person and let them speak for themselves. He is in fact a replica of Protagoras, if one assumes (as Aristophanes and other conservatives did) that the rhetorical methods taught by Protagoras were bound to be employed for improper purposes. His atheism too would link him with Protagoras as well as the natural philosophers, and he has certainly turned Pheidippides into a Sophist when the latter declares that the 'established *nomoi*' were made by a man like himself and he has every right to make new ones.[2]

Amid the stresses and anxieties of the Peloponnesian War, which had already continued for eight years when he produced the *Clouds* in 423, Aristophanes was deeply concerned at the decay of the old ideals of conduct, the lowering of moral standards which was corrupting the youth of Athens. This he attributed to a variety of influences in their education and environment which all alike tended to undermine the sense of loyalty to the old-fashioned values and virtues formerly accepted without question. To attack these tendencies through the medium of comedy, they must all be embodied in a single individual, and the obvious person was Socrates. He had lived in Athens all his life[3] and would be known to everyone in the theatre since, as Xenophon said, he always lived in the public eye and was an unmistakable figure with his snub nose, bulging eyes, rolling gait and continuous, insatiable questioning. Whenever distinguished Sophists visited Athens— Protagoras, Gorgias, Hippias, Prodicus—he joined eagerly (if the evidence of Plato and Xenophon means anything at all) in their discussions and took up with enthusiasm their favourite subjects: the relation between *physis* and *nomos* and of language to its objects, the nature of virtue and whether it was teachable, or the meaning of

---

[1] ἀντιλογίαι. Cf. ἀντιλογικός in v. 1173, and pp. 177 and 264 above.

[2] Cf. p. 114 above.

[3] On p. xxi of his *Clouds*, Rogers suggests that it would not have accorded with Athenian courtesy and hospitality to make a distinguished visiting Sophist the butt of an entire comedy. But, as he notes on p. xxxv, Protagoras was at least brought on to the stage, not simply referred to, by Eupolis, and the supposition is not necessary. Socrates would be chosen for the advantage, for comedy, of having a man really well known to everyone, whose personal characteristics lent themselves readily to caricature. (James Adam in the introduction to his edition of the *Apology*, pp. xxi–xxiii, is excellent on this.)

justice. Moreover he was well known to gather the young men of Athens around him and set them arguing on any and every subject. If a single Athenian had to be chosen to embody all the influences that Aristophanes disliked, he was the obvious victim. Consequently there is something in a claim once made by Cornford,[1] that we can recognize in the Socrates of the *Clouds* at least three different types which were never united to perfection in any single person: first the Sophist, who teaches the art of making a good case out of a bad one; secondly the atheistic natural philosopher like Anaxagoras; and thirdly the ascetic moral teacher, ragged and starving through his own indifference to worldly interests. With the worship of his new deities and the initiation ceremony in mind, we may add the begging priest or seller of purificatory rites, a type castigated by Plato in the *Republic*, or the diviners and devisers of private mysteries whom he hits at in the *Laws*.[2] How much of each there was in Socrates we shall hope to see as we proceed. Both Plato and Xenophon agree that he was attracted to natural philosophy in his younger days (Plato was a child of four when the *Clouds* was first produced, perhaps seven or eight at the date of the second version); he consorted with Sophists and advocated a freedom of thought and lack of respect for conventional views which might be held to be characteristic of them; and in the ardour of his intellectual and moral mission he certainly neglected his own advancement. But (to anticipate) he turned from natural science when he found that it could teach him nothing about what he had come to see as the most important topic of all, namely the conduct of human life. He disagreed with the Sophists on fundamentals, as well as repudiating their practice of education as a paid profession, whether with private pupils or in public lectures and declamations at festivals. To the third type, the ascetic living in voluntary poverty, he probably bore a stronger resemblance, with his indifference to money, clothes and luxurious feeding, although there is evidence that he was no lover of abstinence for its own sake: it was simply that his mission must come first.

There is (*pace* Taylor) little evidence to connect him with Pythagorean or Orphic sectaries who practised private rites, though he had friends among them like the Thebans Simmias and Cebes of the *Phaedo*,

---

[1] In an unpublished lecture. [2] *Rep.* 364b, *Laws* 908d. See p. 246 above.

and this together with occasional fits of rapt withdrawal (pp. 404f. below) might lend some plausibility to the charge. Having decided that Socrates was to be the *persona* for all this, Aristophanes was not likely to leave out every trait by which he could be recognized. There is little about his personal appearance (probably because the mask was a portrait or caricature, see p. 362, n. 1, above), but lines 362f. 'You swagger along the streets and roll your eyes from side to side and go barefoot' must have called up a familiar picture to the audience. Other features also tally with the Socrates of Plato and Xenophon. He is poor and of Spartan habits. We see him teaching by asking questions on analogous examples and explaining by means of homely similes,[1] bringing people to 'know themselves' by convincing them of their ignorance (842), and acquiring both an inner circle of genuine disciples and a fringe of 'young gentlemen' who sought him out for the wrong reasons. Pheidippides's treatment of his father after instruction by Socrates can be compared with the later accusation that he undermined the respect of children for their parents.[2] Even the *phrontisterion*, or college, could be a comic version (wildly distorted, but what in Aristophanes was not?) of known features in Socrates's life. In Plato's *Apology* (33a–b) he claims, no doubt justly, that he never taught anyone privately or grudged that anyone who wished should hear him. Nevertheless he certainly had a small band of young followers linked to him by strong emotional ties. Though a familiar figure in the *agora* and other public places, he did not *always* talk there. In the *Gorgias* Callicles's criticism of a philosopher like Socrates is that he shuns the city centre and the *agora* and retires to whisper with a few young boys in a corner. Xenophon speaks of the common meal which he and his friends enjoyed, and of their habit of reading together 'the treasuries of ancient wisdom in books', and making extracts from them.[3] It has to be remembered that a meal in Greece was a ritual, probably preceded by sacrifice and certainly followed by libation to the gods. The line

[1] See 345f., 234 (cress and the human mind), 385ff. (thunder explained by analogy with abdominal disturbances). At 1286ff. Strepsiades has learned to use the method of question and analogy.

[2] Xen. *Mem.* 1.2.49, *Apol.* 20. The comparison was made by Kierkegaard (*Irony*, 209n.).

[3] *Gorg.* 485d–e, Xen. *Mem.* 3.14.1, 1.6.14. Xenophon's reference to οἱ συνιόντες ἐπὶ δεῖπνον, who each brought a contribution, suggests a regular practice. The δεῖπνον of the members of the φροντιστήριον comes in at v. 175. See also Joël, *E. u. X. S.* 254, n. 3.

373

between a band of friends joining regularly in a common meal, a religious guild or *thiasos*, and a philosophical school was a thin one, and disappeared altogether in the next generation. Both Plato's Academy and Aristotle's Lyceum were legally registered as *thiasoi* and held organized monthly dinners.[1] Although no formal foundation of this sort can be fairly assigned to Socrates, there may have been enough in the habits of him and his companions to justify turning them into a *thiasos* for comic effect and adding such picturesque details as the ban on revealing its 'mysteries' to any but the initiated disciples (140–3, 258).

Xenophon and Plato make several references to the treatment of Socrates by the comic poets, though not all are certainly to Aristophanes. In the *Oeconomicus* (11.3) he says he is 'supposed to be a chatterer and a measurer of the air and—the silliest kind of accusation— a poor man' and in the *Symposium* (6.6) Xenophon makes a direct reference to the *Clouds* when the impresario rudely asks Socrates not only whether he is 'the one they call *phrontistes*' but also whether he can tell him how many feet away a flea is, 'for this is the sort of geometry they say you do' (cf. *Clouds* 145 f.). At *Phaedo* 70b–c Socrates says drily that if, as a man condemned to death, he discusses the possibility of immortality, 'not even a comic poet could say that I am a chatterer about things that don't concern me', and the remark in the *Republic* (488e) that in the 'democratic' ship the skilled steersman will be called a 'sky-gazer, a chatterer,[2] and useless' is a fairly obvious reference to the Socrates of comedy. In Plato's *Symposium* (221b) Alcibiades quotes the actual words from the *Clouds* about his 'swaggering and rolling his eyes'. But the most striking allusion is in Plato's *Apology* (18b, 19b–c). What he has to fear, says Socrates, on trial for his life, is not the present legal accusation so much as the slander with which for many years the minds of his fellow-citizens have been misled about him. He will treat these slanderers as his real accusers and as it were read their indictment. It runs thus: 'Socrates is guilty of mischievous meddling in that he searches into the things under the earth

---

[1] See on this Festugière, *Epicurus and his Gods*, p. 25, and Jaeger, *Aristotle*, 325 f.

[2] ἀδολέσχης is the word in all three passages, and seems to have been a stock label for Socrates. It occurs in the *Clouds* (1485; the φροντιστήριον is the οἰκία τῶν ἀδολεσχῶν) and in Eupolis, Kock, I, p. 251 (Σωκράτην τὸν πτωχὸν ἀδολέσχην). Probably it was applied also to Sophists in general. Cf. Plutarch and Plato quoted on p. 228 with n. 1 above.

and the things in the sky, makes the weaker argument the stronger, and teaches the same to others.' 'That is the gist of it', he continues. 'You have seen it for yourselves in Aristophanes's play, someone called Socrates swinging around there, saying he is treading the air and a lot of other nonsense that I don't know the first thing about.' Many people have expressed astonishment that, if Socrates thought of the *Clouds* as a major cause of his ultimate condemnation, Plato, who tells us this, could also in his *Symposium* depict him with Aristophanes and the tragic poet Agathon, amicably discussing the art of drama around Agathon's hospitable board. Making all allowance for the *Symposium* as an imaginative work, we cannot doubt that the two were still on friendly terms after the writing of the *Clouds*. What the real situation was, one can only conjecture, but two things may be said. The *Clouds* was produced in 423, when no one had any thought of prosecuting Socrates,[1] and twenty-four of the most unhappy years in Athenian history had to pass before such a catastrophe could occur. Many a politician has enjoyed the cartoons about himself, and the play is extremely funny. One can well imagine Socrates taking up at the time the attitude attributed to him in an anecdote of Plutarch's. Asked if he was not angry at the way Aristophanes had abused him in the *Clouds*, he replied, 'Good heavens no. He has his joke against me in the theatre as if it were a big party of friends.'[2] Secondly, the *Clouds* is certainly not introduced in the *Apology* as an originating cause of the slander. Socrates says that he has been falsely accused by many people over many years, and that his hearers, the jury, have had it dinned into them since they were children or adolescents. He does not even know the names of the slanderers, 'unless one of them happens to be a comic poet'. As Burnet pointed out (*Euthyphro* etc., pp. 74f.), all jurors had to be over thirty, and at the end of a war that had lasted a generation, it was unlikely that many of them were under fifty. The mistaken impression of Socrates went back far beyond the *Clouds*, which is mentioned as an example because all but the comic poets were, as is the way with malicious gossips, unidentifiable.

---

[1] Only the year before, it seems, he had been the hero of the fighting and retreat in Boeotia (p. 379 below). Some have thought this difficult to reconcile with Pheidippides's sneer at 'the pale-faced Socrates and Chaerephon', but Pheidippides is hardly an admirable character, and the laugh would be one in which Socrates himself could join with the rest.

[2] Plut. *De lib. educ.* 10c, literally 'I am made fun of in the theatre as at a big *symposion*', where all sorts of freedom are allowed because it is all in jest and among friends. See also D.L. 2.36.

NOTE ON THE TWO EDITIONS OF THE 'CLOUDS'

The play as first written was produced in 423, when to Aristophanes's disappointment (cf. *Clouds* 520–6) it obtained third place after the *Wine-bottle* of Cratinus and the *Connus* of Ameipsias, although he himself thought it his best play. He then revised it, and it is the revised version which we possess. It can be dated between 421 and 418 (Merry, *Clouds*, xi; Murray, *Aristoph.* 87), and it was probably never put on the stage or even (to judge from internal evidence) completed. The extent of the revision is stated in one of the Greek 'Arguments' prefixed to the play, which I quote first in Merry's translation:

'This edition is identical with the former one; but it has been to some extent[1] recast, as though the poet had intended to reproduce it on the stage, but for some reason or other had never done so. A general revision too of nearly every part has been effected, some portions having been withdrawn, while others have been woven into the play, and alterations made in arrangement and interchange of characters. The main changes in the play, as recast, are the altered parabasis, the scene between the Just and Unjust Argument, and the burning of the house of Socrates.'

The revision was, it appears, fairly extensive, and the purport of the first clause is somewhat obscure. For our purposes it is important to decide whether the writer of the argument means us to understand that the whole contest between the Just and Unjust *Logos* and the final burning of the *phrontisterion* were additions and did not appear in the acted version at all. This is generally assumed, and some scholars suppose that Aristophanes concluded from his failure that the play had treated Socrates too kindly, and added these two scenes in the revision to make it plain that he really was against him and all the new learning. (So Murray, *Aristoph.* 87 f., 104, and Schmid in *Philol.* 1948, 225. Others, as we have seen, think that in any case Socrates is carefully dissociated from the enormities of the Unjust *Logos*. It is amusing also to note that Kaibel in *RE*, II, 977, thought the failure of the original play due to Aristophanes's error in making Socrates the scapegoat for the sins of sophistry, when the Athenian public well knew that he was neither an atheist nor a 'meteorosophist'.)

But were these two episodes absent from the earlier version? There is much to be said for the arguments of Rogers, which, as they have been generally neglected, I will quote fairly fully (*Clouds*, xv f.):

'Strange to say, some have supposed the writer of the argument to mean

---

[1] ἐπὶ μέρους. Not 'to some extent' but 'in details', Dover, lxxxii.

that the dispute between the two λόγοι had no place in the drama as acted: and some have gone so far as to contend that it contained no reference at all to the λόγοι. This would indeed have been "Hamlet, without the Prince of Denmark". The promise of Protagoras that his disciples should be able τὸν ἥττω λόγον κρείττω ποιεῖν is singled out by Aristophanes as containing the very essence of the Sophistical teaching, and he everywhere makes it the central point of his attack . . . The debate of the two λόγοι is the very core of the play. Every preceding scene leads up to it; every subsequent scene looks back to it . . . The writer of the Argument pointedly confines his statement to the existing speech of the Just Logic [This is true, and Merry's translation is at this point faulty; literally it should be, not 'the scene between the Just and Unjust Argument' but 'where the Just Argument addresses the Unjust', πρὸς τὸν ἄδικον λαλεῖ], and implies, rather than negatives, the idea of speeches by both λόγοι in the original play.

'*The part of the Play where the Phrontisterion is set on fire.* It is not the conflagration itself that is new, but the part of the written Play which describes it. No doubt the Comedy always ended with the burning of the Phrontis-terium, but the present description—the climbing up to the roof, the chopping logic with the rafters, and the actual flames—is a description of proceedings which could hardly have been presented, or described with a view to their presentation, on the Athenian stage. We may therefore readily believe that lines 1482 to 1507, or thereabouts, belong exclusively to the revised version.'

Rogers goes on to conjecture what the original may have been. Whatever may be thought about the practicability of producing the revised finale on the stage, the words of the Argument mean only 'the parabasis of the chorus has been altered, and the part where the Just Argument addresses the Unjust, and lastly the part where the house of Socrates is burned'.

Postscript. The above note was of course written before the appearance of Dover's edition of the play (p. 361, n. 2 above). According to Dover, p. lxxxiv, 'the last sentence of the Hypothesis tells us that the parabasis, the contest of Right and Wrong, and the burning of Socrates' school, belong in their entirety to the second version'. This has the support of a scholium which he quotes. Nevertheless the first version did contain a contest at this point (p. xciii, 'I suggest that in the first version the contestants were brought on as fighting-cocks'), and it is not clear to me whom he supposes the contestants to have been. A suggestion that they might have been Chaerephon and Pheidippides is discussed on pp. xcvi f., but not favoured by Dover. Conformably to a principle enunciated in his preface (p. viii), he does not mention Rogers.

XIII

LIFE AND CHARACTER

(1) LIFE

Socrates was a native Athenian, son of Sophroniscus and Phaenarete, of the deme Alopeke.[1] He was born in 470 or 469 B.C., for the records of his trial and execution put them in the spring of 399, and Plato gives his age as seventy at the time. His father is said to have been a stonemason or sculptor,[2] and references in Plato to Daedalus as his ancestor (*Euthyphro* 11b, *Alc. I* 121a) do something to confirm this. As doctors traced their descent to Asclepius as eponymous ancestor (so

[1] Apart from a number of mentions in Plato (e.g. *Laches* 180d, *Gorg.* 495d), his father and deme were recorded in the official indictment (D.L. 2.40). That his mother was called Phaenarete and was a midwife is difficult to believe but seems to be true. In Plato's *Theaet.* (149a) Socrates compares his own function in life to the midwife's art. As the midwife helps women in bringing their bodily children to birth, so Socrates practises on men, and the children which he assists into the world are offspring not of the body but of the mind. Like Greek midwives too, he is incapable of childbearing himself. That is, he has no ideas of his own, and can be of service only by assisting others to bring their brain-children to the light. This light-hearted simile he introduces by saying, 'Haven't you heard that I am the son of a fine upstanding midwife (μαίας μάλα γενναίας τε καὶ βλοσυρᾶς) called Phaenarete? Well, I also practise my mother's art.' βλοσυρός in classical usage meant 'shaggy, hairy, bristling' and so 'virile, burly' (LSJ; Lehmann, quoted by Webster, *Myc. to Hom.* 94, supposed the word to be originally connected with vultures, but its etymology is uncertain). It seems a strange word to apply to one's mother. That she was a midwife might be what made Socrates think of the joke in the first place, but that she was a midwife called Phaenarete—'she who brings *virtue* to light'—takes some believing. On the other hand (*a*) Theaetetus's reply to the question 'Haven't you heard . . . ?' is 'Yes, I have heard so'; (*b*) In the *First Alcibiades* (131e) Socrates refers to himself as 'son of Sophroniscus and Phaenarete' where the mention of her name has no special point; (*c*) Phaenarete was at any rate an Attic name, for it occurs in an inscription (Ritter, *Sokr.* 6, n. 11). It was also the name of the mother of Hippocrates of Cos (*RE*, VIII, 1802).

[2] λιθουργός or λιθοξόος (*RE*, 2. Reihe, v. Halbb. 1104), generally translated 'stonemason' but perhaps rather higher in the artistic scale. Aristotle (*EN* 1141a 10) applies λιθουργός to Phidias. λιθοξόος does not occur till later. Lucian (*Somn.* 9) speaks of a boy apprenticed to his uncle in this craft, who is told in a dream that he might become a Phidias but takes instead the advice to follow Socrates and desert it for 'culture' (παιδεία, §12). Run-of-the-mill sculptors would be wanted to turn out the herms and Apollos and such for every house and street, which would no more be original works of art than the monumental sculpture of our cemeteries. Many of these workers lived in Alopeke, which lay on the road from Athens to the marble quarries of Pentelicon (*RE*, I, 1597). There is no express mention of Sophroniscus's profession in Plato, Xenophon, Aristophanes or Aristotle, and the best evidence is probably Aristoxenus fr. 51 Wehrli. (For other late mentions see *RE, loc. cit.*) Burnet did not believe in it (*Euthyphro*, etc., p. 50).

Eryximachus in Plato, *Symp.* 186e), sculptors would naturally trace their line back to Daedalus. The justification for the mythical genealogy is that it was regular Greek practice for a craft to be handed on from father to son. Accordingly it was said that Socrates himself was brought up in the sculptor's craft, which he may have practised in his earlier years (Zeller, *Ph. d. Gr.* 52, nn. 1 and 2), before he 'deserted it for *paideia*' as Lucian later put it (*Somn.* 12). Sophroniscus seems to have been a respected citizen who could hold up his head in any company, since Plato makes Lysimachus son of Aristides speak of him as a lifelong friend whom he held in the highest esteem. It is unlikely that he was poor, or that Socrates's later poverty was anything but self-chosen, as Plato in the *Apology* (23b) says it was.

The Peloponnesian War involved him in much active service, and he earned high praise for his courage and coolness, especially in adversity, and his powers of endurance. Plato mentions three campaigns in which he took part, the siege of Potidaea at the beginning of the war, the defeat and subsequent retreat of the Athenians at Delium in Boeotia in 424 ('I was with him in the retreat,' says Laches in the dialogue that bears his name (181a), 'and if everyone were like Socrates, our city would never have come to disaster'), and the battle of Amphipolis in 422. It was during the expedition to Potidaea that he saved Alcibiades's life, and performed feats of endurance which are mentioned by Alcibiades in the *Symposium*.[1]

We next hear of him in the public eye in 406, when he resisted the demand that the generals who failed to rescue the men from ships wrecked in the victorious action of Arginusae should be tried together instead of having their cases considered separately. This was illegal, and it happened to be the turn of his 'tribe' to be *prytaneis*, which meant

---

[1] Plato mentions all three campaigns at *Apol.* 28e, Delium again at *Laches* 181a and *Symp.* 220e, and Potidaea at *Symp.* 219e and *Charm.* 153a. Whether or not he has embellished Socrates's heroic behaviour, he would hardly have invented the fact that he was present at these engagements. The doubts of Burnet and Gomme are answered by W. M. Calder III in *Phronesis*, 1961. A story known from later writers told how Socrates saved some of those retreating with him at Delium by insisting on taking a different route from the others, warned by his 'divine sign' (Plut. *Gen. Socr.* 581e, Cic. *Div.* 1.54.123). According to Strabo 9.2.7 and D.L. 2.23 he saved Xenophon's life there by carrying him when he had fallen from his horse. Some have inferred from a fragment of Antisthenes (33 Caizzi) that Antisthenes transferred the rescue of Alcibiades (Pl. *Symp.* 220d–e) to Delium, and that Alcibiades was then turned into Xenophon! (*RE*, 2. Reihe, v. Halbb. 812f.) Such stories show at least that the tradition of Socrates's military service does not depend solely on Plato.

that it was for them to decide what business should be brought before the Assembly.[1] The other members were finally intimidated into agreeing to put the illegal motion, and Socrates alone stood out.[2] He mentions this in Plato's *Apology*, where he says that he has never held any political office, though he has served on the Council as any other citizen might be called upon to do. It was well known that he avoided taking an active part in politics, though one purpose of his talks with young men was to prepare them to play their own part honourably and efficiently,[3] and he preferred to go his own way, irrespective of party, following his inner conviction of what was right. If in this instance his conscience and respect for law ran counter to the decision of a democracy, some two years later we find him resisting with equal courage a demand from the newly established oligarchy of the Thirty. These men were responsible for a series of judicial murders, especially of wealthy citizens whose property they coveted. Attempting to implicate Socrates in their violence, they ordered him with four others to arrest a certain man of substance called Leon of Salamis. Leaders of the revolution like Plato's relatives Critias and Charmides might well think that they could count on him, since they had been members of his circle and knew, too, that he was no advocate of the Athenian democratic system, but they underestimated his attachment to legality. The others obeyed and Leon was arrested and killed, but Socrates simply went home.[4]

He was saved from the consequences of his action by the counter-revolution which restored the democracy. But this only brought him into fresh danger. The times were desperate, and the democrats felt it their plain duty to prevent a repetition of the horrors that were so

---

[1] The Council (*Boulé*) of 500 was divided for convenience into panels of 50 *prytaneis*, acting in rotation for one-tenth of the year each. Their duty was to prepare business for the *Ecclesia* (assembly of the whole people), and any proposal had to be considered by them before being brought before the *Ecclesia*.

[2] Xen. *Hell.* 1.7. 12–15, *Mem.* 1.1.18 and 4.4.2, Plato, *Apol.* 32a–c. For problems connected with details of the incident see Burnet *ad loc.*, Treu in *RE*, 2. Reihe, XVIII. Halbb. 1772, De Strycker in *Mél. Grég.* II, 207ff., Dodds, *Gorg.* 247f. G. Giannantoni in *Riv. crit. di stor. della fil.* (1962) tries to reconstruct Socrates's attitude to the trial as an aid to understanding his political thought, based on fidelity to the laws, and De Strycker (*loc. cit.*) points out how it confirms the historical accuracy of Plato's *Apol.* and makes it likely that Socrates's attitude to the laws in the *Crito* is also historical.

[3] Xen. *Mem.* 1.6.15, Plato, *Apol.* 31c and elsewhere.

[4] Plato, *Apol.* 32c and *Ep.* 7. 324d–e, Xen. *Mem.* 4.4.3. The incident is also referred to without mention of Socrates by Xenophon, *Hell.* 2.3.39, Andocides, *De mystt.* 94, and Lysias, 12.52. See Burnet, *Apol. ad loc.*

fresh in everyone's mind, the reign of terror instituted in the short period of their triumph by Critias and his oligarchic associates. Leading figures in that spell of violence, as well as the traitor Alcibiades, had all been intimate with Socrates in earlier days. Moreover he was notorious for having said things which appeared incompatible with the whole democratic form of constitution as then understood. They could not feel safe until he was out of the way. These were not men of violence like the Thirty. Plato himself, who had every reason for disliking them, pays tribute to the moderation with which they conducted themselves after their restoration.

But by some mischance, some of those in power brought my friend Socrates to trial on an infamous charge, the last that should ever have been brought against him. It was impiety that some of them accused him of, and the others condemned him and put him to death—the very man who had refused to have any hand in arresting one of their own friends when they themselves were in exile and misfortune.[1]

Ostensibly, the chief accuser was Meletus, in whose name the indictment stood. In the *Euthyphro* (2b), Socrates describes him to Euthyphro, who has not heard of him, as 'an unknown young man with straight hair and a skimpy beard', and he can only have been a puppet whose strings were pulled by the powerful Anytus, possibly chosen for the enthusiasm with which he would press the religious charge.[2] Anytus was one of the most powerful democratic politicians, a leader in the fight against the Thirty, and Plato represents him in the *Meno* as abusing the Sophists and uttering dark hints of what the city might do to Socrates himself. His objections to Socrates's behaviour will have been largely political, but to bring political charges against him, or mention his earlier associations with Critias or Charmides, would have been contrary to the amnesty declared by the restored

---

[1] Plato, *Ep.* 7.325b–c. This is not the best place to discuss the authenticity of the Seventh Letter, on which equally good scholars have taken opposite sides. I cannot believe that these sentences contain anything but Plato's own judgment of the tragedy.

[2] Cf. τοὺς ἀμφὶ Ἄνυτον and πειθόμενοι Ἀνύτῳ, *Apol.* 18b and 31a (also 29c, 30b). There is some evidence of Meletus's religious zeal in the *Apol.* itself, and if (as Burnet and Taylor thought) he was the Meletus who prosecuted Andocides in the same year, there is ample proof of it in the speech for the prosecution which has survived among the remains of Lysias and is described by Burnet as 'almost the only monument of religious fanaticism that has come down to us from antiquity'. (See his *Euthyphro*, etc. p. 9.) The name is not common, but Kahrstedt denies the identity in *RE*, xxix. Halbb. 503.

democracy, to which Anytus was conspicuously loyal.¹ The accusation therefore confined itself to offences against the state religion and the vaguely worded 'corruption of youth'. There was a third accuser, an otherwise unknown Lycon, whom the *Apology* practically ignores to concentrate on Anytus and Meletus. He is said to be acting on behalf of the orators, whereas Anytus represents the crafts or trades as well as the politicians (he owned a tannery), and Meletus the poets (*Apol.* 23 e). Politicians (not really distinct from orators), craftsmen and poets are the three classes mentioned later in the speech as having been angered by Socrates's questioning, and the classification was no doubt made by Plato with that in mind. We possess the text of the indictment from two sources, Xenophon and Diogenes Laertius. Diogenes took it from Favorinus the contemporary of Plutarch, who stated that it was preserved in the Metroön in his day. Xenophon confines himself to the actual charges, in which only one word, not affecting the sense, is different in the two copies, so we may be confident that we have them correctly.² The full version runs:

This indictment is entered on affidavit by Meletus son of Meletus of the deme Pitthus against Socrates son of Sophroniscus of Alopeke. Socrates is guilty of refusing to recognize the gods recognized by the State and introducing other, new divinities. He is also guilty of corrupting the youth. The penalty demanded is death.

Both Plato and Xenophon lead one to believe that the second charge was argued in somewhat vague terms. Plato makes Socrates link it with the first, trapping Meletus into saying that he turns young men into atheists, and Xenophon (*Mem.* 1.2) defends him against all possible charges: encouraging them in licentiousness, gluttony, disrespect for parents, and immoral interpretations of the poets. He does, however, give prominence, in his account of what 'the accuser' said (i.e. probably Polycrates in his pamphlet written some years after the event, p. 346 above), to the charge that Socrates had been the educator of Alcibiades and Critias, and so was responsible for their misdeeds. His relations

---

¹ For the amnesty see Aristotle, *Ath. Pol.* 39, Xen. *Hell.* 2.4.43, and for Anytus's strict observance of it, even to his own disadvantage, Isocr. *In Callim.* 23.

² Xen. *Mem.* 1.1.1, Favorinus, *ap.* D.L. 2.40. Xenophon has καινὰ δαιμόνια εἰσφέρων for D.L.'s εἰσηγούμενος, which may have been the correct legal term (Burnet, *Euthyphro,* etc. p. 102). Paraphrases occur at Plato, *Apol.* 24b, and Xen. *Apol.* 10, and in part at *Euthyphro* 3b.

with these men, especially Alcibiades, seem to have been a focus of controversy between Socrates's attackers and defenders.[1] Anytus would have Critias very much in mind, as a strong reason for wishing Socrates out of the way, but he was prevented by the amnesty from bringing it into the open. Many years later the orator Aeschines (*In Timarch*.173) told the Athenians bluntly: 'You put Socrates the Sophist to death, because he was shown to have educated Critias.' The motive was in part political, but also wider, as Zeller has well expressed it (*Ph. d. Gr.* 217):

Socrates, it is true, fell as a sacrifice to the democratic reaction which followed the overthrow of the Thirty; but his political views as such were not the primary motive of the attack on him. Rather his guilt was sought first of all in the undermining of the morality and religion of his country, of which the antidemocratic tendency of his teaching was partly no more than an indirect result, partly an isolated offshoot.

One has to remember the licentiousness and suspected sacrilege of Alcibiades, and the atheism of Critias, as well as their politics.[2]

One need not accuse Anytus and his associates of thirsting for Socrates's blood. They would have been content—probably more content—if he had simply removed himself from the Athenian scene, gone into voluntary exile and let the case go by default. In Plato's *Apology*, Socrates quotes Anytus as having said (presumably in his speech as a prosecutor) that *either* he ought never to have come before the court at all *or*, now that he has come, the judges must award the death penalty in order to save their sons from his influence (*Apol.* 29c). Similarly his friend Crito speaks of the bringing of the case to court 'when there was no need for it to be brought' (*Crito* 45 e). Even after the verdict of guilty, it was not necessary for the judges to accept the penalty demanded by the prosecution. According to Athenian law, the accused himself could propose a lighter penalty, and the judges voted again on the question which was to be enforced. If at this point Socrates

---

[1] Diès (*Autour de P.* 166f.) calls Alcibiades the pivot on which turned the greater part of the attack and defence; and he instances the *Accusation* of Polycrates, the *Alcibiades* of Aeschines and Antisthenes, Plato's *Symposium*, Xen. *Mem.* 1.2, and the *Alcibiades* ascribed to Plato. *Republic* 494c–495b is also with good reason taken to be a reference to Alcibiades. Dittmar discusses what the various Socratics, including Plato, say about Alcibiades in his *Aeschines*, 65–177.

[2] On Critias and his relations with Socrates see pp. 298ff. above.

had proposed banishment, there is every likelihood that it would have been accepted, as according to Plato he realized himself. In his reply to Crito's offer to smuggle him out of the country, he imagines the laws of Athens saying to him, 'At the trial itself it was open to you to elect for banishment had you wished, and thus to do with the city's goodwill what you are now trying to do against it' (*ibid.* 52c). However, Socrates believed, for reasons given in the *Apology* and *Crito*, that to leave Athens would be a betrayal of his mission, and that Athens had become in any case so essential a part of his life that he could not imagine himself living anywhere else. Besides, he was convinced that he had done no harm to the city, but on the contrary a great deal of good. His counter-proposal was, therefore, that he should be granted free meals in the Prytaneum, a privilege awarded to Olympic victors and others who had brought honour and benefit to the State. However, he added, he had no objection to paying a fine, since loss of money was no hurt. He could only afford one mina himself, but some of his friends (including Plato) had offered to collect thirty,[1] and in deference to their wishes he would offer that. So at least Plato tells. According to Xenophon he showed his high spirit by refusing to name a counter-penalty at all.[2] In either case his behaviour hardly left the judges any choice, and it is not surprising that this 'miscellaneous assembly of 501 Athenians, including superannuated officials, old and decrepit artisans, little shopkeepers, and others unable to find more remunerative employment' (as Phillipson called them) voted for the death penalty by a somewhat larger majority than had secured the verdict of guilty.[3]

Normally the sentence would have been carried out at once, but a particular circumstance delayed it. Every year the Athenians sent a ship to Delos on a religious mission, in fulfilment of an ancient vow made to Apollo after the success of Theseus in putting an end to the annual

[1] Quite a respectable sum. It has been calculated that at the end of the fifth century a mina had about the purchasing power of £75 in the 1950s. See the Jowett translation of Plato's dialogues, 4th ed. vol. 1, 335 n.

[2] *Apol.* 23. Xenophon's protestation that Socrates neither proposed an alternative himself nor allowed his friends to do so, on the grounds that it would amount to an admission of guilt, must be a conscious attempt to contradict Plato. Others too have felt the offer of a fine to be an anticlimax (on which see Phillipson, 373 ff.), and its inclusion by Plato encourages the belief that he, who was present at the trial himself, was telling the truth.

[3] Phillipson, *Trial*, 241. For details of the voting, slightly differently expressed by Plato (*Apol.* 36a) and D.L. 2.41, see Phillipson, 367, and S. Erasmus in *Gymnasium* 1964.

tribute of young lives paid to the Minotaur in Crete. The ship had been dedicated on the day before the trial of Socrates, and from then until its return the city was kept in a state of religious purity which did not allow public executions to take place.[1] During this period therefore Socrates was kept in prison, where his friends were allowed to visit him, thus giving opportunity for conversations such as those related by Plato in the *Crito* and, on the last day of his life, the *Phaedo*.

Socrates was married to Xanthippe, and had three sons, of whom the eldest, Lamprocles, was a 'youth' at the time of his execution,[2] and the youngest, to judge from the *Phaedo* (60a), a small child. Xanthippe's name suggests aristocratic connexions, and she has become a byword for shrewishness, by all accounts deservedly. To omit the tales of later scandalmongers, Xenophon (*Mem.* 2.2.7) represents their son as complaining of her intolerable bad temper, and among the badinage of his *Symposium* (2.10) Antisthenes asks Socrates why, if he holds that women are no less capable of education than men, he has not trained Xanthippe, but is content to live with 'the most troublesome woman of all time'. Socrates replies in the same vein that, just as a horse-trainer must practise on the most spirited and awkward, rather than docile animals, so he, whose ambition was to be able to deal with all sorts of men, had chosen her as his wife in the knowledge that, if he could tame her, there would be no one whom he could not handle. Plato's mention of her in the *Phaedo* (60a) is not against this otherwise universal verdict. That she should remark on the day of his execution 'This is the last time that you will speak to your friends' is common-place enough ('the sort of thing women do say', as the narrator Phaedo remarks), nor is it surprising that she should be led away 'crying and beating her breast'. The thought of being left husbandless with three young sons was not a cheering one, and in any case such conduct was expected of a Greek wife.[3]

---

[1] *Phaedo* 58a–c, Xen. *Mem.* 4.8.2. Xenophon puts the delay at a month.

[2] Plato, *Apol.* 34d. It could mean anything up to twenty.

[3] This not very important question of Xanthippe's character has aroused surprisingly strong feelings, and scholars have rushed gallantly to her defence. Most of them agree that the odious Antisthenes was responsible for blackening the character of a good woman (though there are in fact no witnesses at all on the other side), and Xenophon's second reference to her is silently ignored. Ritter (*Sokr.* 64), following Joël, argues that, although Antisthenes was admittedly one of Socrates's most devoted followers, he was an insensitive sort of fellow, and his only motive

Life and Character

(2) APPEARANCE AND GENERAL CHARACTER

We must remind ourselves at this point of the impossibility, already mentioned, of separating the teaching of Socrates from his whole personality. Otherwise the reader will soon become impatient at the amount of attention given to matters apparently unimportant and remote from philosophy. As it is, however, even to discuss his personal appearance leads directly to the teleological standpoint which led him to judge the ideals of beauty and goodness by the yardstick of utility and fitness for function. By the same token the teaching itself cannot be taken apart, for whether he was demanding definitions, insisting that virtue was knowledge, claiming that no one does wrong willingly or urging men to care for their souls, whether the ostensible subject of the conversation was shoemaking or love, he was always, as he said himself, 'saying the same things about the same things'.[1]

In appearance Socrates was universally admitted to be extraordinarily ugly, but it was the kind of ugliness which fascinates. His chief features

in falsely insulting Socrates's wife to his face was to enhance the glory of Socrates himself! It should be obvious that Xenophon could never have told the story of Antisthenes's joke and Socrates's reply if the bad temper of Xanthippe were not a well-known fact.

It has been argued more than once that, if Xanthippe's shrewish reputation were deserved, Aristophanes could never have resisted such a gift of comic material. It is just possible that Socrates was not yet married when the *Clouds* was produced, but, if not, it must have been very soon after. I wonder if he did resist it. In the *Clouds* Strepsiades has a wife whose social station is above his, and who insists on an aristocratic name for their son. (Lamprocles was an aristocratic name, as Burnet points out on *Apol.* 34d6.) Her particular penchant was for names ending in -ippos, and the first to be mentioned among her favourites is Xanthippos (*Clouds* 64)! Is it not possible that this name brought the house down? One can only guess why Aristophanes did not make her the wife of Socrates himself, but unlike Antisthenes he may have been prevented by a feeling that to make fun of a friend was one thing but to laugh at his wife without disguise another. Also there is a difference between doing it on the public stage and in the easy familiarity of a private party, where a good deal of wine had already been drunk.

Late sources attribute to Socrates a second wife Myrto, daughter or granddaughter of Aristides, some say bigamously married, others as a second wife after Xanthippe, which is manifestly impossible. The truth of the story was already doubted in antiquity by Panaetius (Plut. *Aristid.* 27, Ath. 13.556b) and others, and the reports are indeed riddled with inconsistencies and justify the contempt with which most scholars regard them. Some of the ancient authorities trace them back to a lost work by Aristotle (while at the same time expressing doubts about its authenticity), but it is most likely that it originated with his younger contemporary Aristoxenus in a context of abuse of Socrates. (See Zeller, *Ph. d. Gr.* 55, n. 2, and 63, n. 5.) Some texts are collected in Deman (*Témoignage*, 38), who also cites some representative scholarly opinion, but see also Aristoxenus frr. 54a and b Wehrli. Needless to say, Joël blamed the whole story on Antisthenes.

[1] Xen. *Mem.* 4.4.6, Plato, *Gorg.* 490e. Its recurrence in the two authors (in conversation with Hippias and Callicles respectively) suggests that it was in fact a well-known reply of Socrates to people who taxed him with tedious repetition.

were a broad, flat and turned-up nose, prominent staring eyes, thick fleshy lips and a paunch, or, as he phrases it himself in Xenophon's *Symposium* (2.18), 'a stomach rather too large for convenience'.[1] He had a characteristic way of looking at people which was unforgettable but hard to describe. We hear of him 'staring with wide open eyes, as his custom was', 'glancing up, as his manner was, with lowered head like a bull', and 'casting his eyes sidelong'. He boasts humorously that with eyes so prominent he can see further to the side than most people.[2] His friends compared him to a satyr and a flatfish (the ray).[3] Xenophon in the *Symposium* (ch. v) describes an engaging 'beauty competition'[4] between Socrates and the handsome young Critobulus, who has challenged him to prove by his accustomed method of cross-examination that he is the more handsome. ('Only', he adds, 'let's have the lamp a bit nearer.') So Socrates begins:

S. Do you think beauty exists in man alone, or in anything else?
C. I believe it is found in horse and ox and many inanimate things. For instance I recognize a beautiful shield, sword or spear.
S. And how can all these things be beautiful when they bear no resemblance to each other?
C. Why, if they are well made for the purposes for which we acquire them, or well adapted by nature to our needs, then in each case I call them beautiful.
S. Well then, what do we need eyes for?
C. To see with of course.
S. In that case my eyes are at once proved to be more beautiful than yours, because yours look only straight ahead, whereas mine project so that they can see sideways as well.
C. Are you claiming that a crab has the most beautiful eyes of any animal?

---

[1] References in Xenophon and Plato to Socrates's appearance and personal habits are collected by E. Edelstein in *X. und P. Bild*, 7f. and 22. Some of their points are confirmed by Aristophanes. D.L. 2.43 speaks of a bronze statue of him by Lysippus erected by the repentant Athenians shortly after his death. Extant representations are of two types, of which one is probably based on the lost Lysippean bronze, and the other on a marble original of Hellenistic date. (They are types A and B respectively in Gisela Richter's *Portraits of the Greeks*.) The idea of a pre-Lysippean portrait, executed in the lifetime of Socrates, is conjectural. The design on the cover of the present volume is taken from a head of type A in the Vatican (*Richter, op. cit.* figs. 456–7, 459).

[2] Plato, *Phaedo* 86d (for διαβλέπω cf. Arist. *De insomn.* 462a 13), 117b, Xen. *Symp.* 5.5.

[3] Plato, *Symp.* 215b, *Meno* 80a (pp. 398, 402 below).

[4] Such competitions actually formed part of the games (ἀγῶνες) at Athens and elsewhere, under the name of εὐανδρίαι. They were a feature of the Panathenaea (Arist. *Ath. Pol.* 60.5), and the author of the speech against Alcibiades speaks of winning one ([Andoc.] 4.42). Athenaeus (565f.) says that the aim was to choose the most beautiful, and speaks of a beauty contest (κρίσις κάλλους) at Elis.

S. Certainly, since from the point of view of strength also its eyes are best constructed by nature.

C. All right, but which of our noses is the more beautiful?

S. Mine, I should say, if the gods gave us noses to smell with, for your nostrils point to earth, but mine are spread out widely to receive odours from every quarter.

C. But how can a snub nose be more beautiful than a straight one?

S. Because it does not get in the way but allows the eyes to see what they will, whereas a high bridge walls them off as if to spite them.

C. As for the mouth, I give in, for if mouths are made for biting you could take a much larger bite than I.

S. And with my thick lips don't you think I could give a softer kiss?

C. By your account I seem to have a mouth uglier than an ass's.

S. And isn't this further evidence that I am fairer than you? The Naiads, who are goddesses, are mothers of the Sileni, who resemble me much more than you.

C. I give up. Let's put it to the vote, so that I may know as quickly as possible what forfeit I have to pay.

When the votes were counted, and every one was found to be for Critobulus, Socrates protested in pained surprise that he must have bribed the judges.

True to his aim, Xenophon is letting the mind of Socrates show through even his lighter talk. The principle followed in the beauty competition appears again in Plato's *Hippias Major* (295 c):

Let us postulate that whatever is useful is beautiful. What I have in mind is this: we do not say that eyes are beautiful when they are without the power of sight, but only when they have that power and so are useful for seeing. Similarly we say that the whole body is beautifully made, sometimes for running, sometimes for wrestling, and we speak in the same way of all living things. A beautiful horse, or cock, or quail, and all utensils, and means of transport both on land and sea, merchant vessels and ships of war, and all instruments of music and of the arts generally, and for that matter practices and laws—we apply the word beautiful to pretty well all of these in the same way.

This lesson of Socrates is repeated by Xenophon in other conversations (*Mem.* 3.8.4–6, 4.6.9). For the closest parallel one must go, perhaps, to eighteenth-century England. At the beginning of his *Analysis of Beauty* Hogarth wrote:

Fitness of the parts to the design for which every individual thing is formed, either by art or nature, is first to be considered, as it is of the greatest consequence to the beauty of the whole.

After illustrations from the size and shape of chairs, pillars and arches, he goes on:

In shipbuilding, the dimensions of every part are confined and regulated by fitness for sailing. When the vessel sails well, the sailors . . . call her a beauty: the two ideas have such a connexion.[1]

Socrates gave no thought to appearances, but went regularly barefoot, the one ancient coat he possessed was a standing joke, and his critics called him 'unwashed'. Even his friends had to admit that to see Socrates newly bathed and wearing shoes was unusual, and marked a special occasion such as a party to celebrate his friend Agathon's success in carrying off the prize with his first tragedy.[2] Hardiness, temperance and self-control are the features of his character most remarked on, if one understands temperance as meaning not total abstinence or extreme asceticism, but an indifference to the presence or absence of material pleasures. On the Potidaean campaign he walked over the icy ground in the dreaded Thracian winter unshod and otherwise clad as at home; a practice (says Alcibiades in Plato's *Symposium*) which did not endear him to the soldiers, who muffled up well and wrapped their feet in felt and sheepskins, and thought he wanted to humiliate them. As for drink, he was said to be able to outdrink anyone, yet no one had ever seen Socrates drunk, nor did he drink except to comply with social custom and because he valued the conversation which flowed so easily at a *symposion*. All his appetites and passions, for sex as for food, he kept under strict control.[3] Admittedly our information has to be taken mostly from men who not only knew him well but were his devoted admirers, and may therefore be thought suspiciously partial witnesses. Yet, together with what they tell us about his teaching and his intellectual force, it builds up a portrait of an integrated and credible

[1] Ed. Burke, p. 32. See also Burke's article 'A Classical Aspect of Hogarth's Theory of Art' in *Journal of the Warburg (and Courtauld) Institute*, 1943. The utilitarian side of Socrates's teaching will be developed later (ch. XIV, §8).

[2] No shoes and one poor coat, Xen. *Mem.* 1.6.2; ἀνυπόδητος Aristoph. *Clouds* 103, 363, Plato *Symp.* 220b. His coat was a stock comic joke. Cf. Ameipsias, p. 360 with n. 2, above. For ἄλουτος see *Birds* 1554, and for his unusual party get-up Plato *Symp.* 174a.

[3] His attitude to sex is discussed in the next section.

character, and the little that we have to the contrary is, unfortunately, not impartial but bears the marks of malice and scandal. That curiously sour character Aristoxenus claimed to have heard from his father Spintharus that no one could be more persuasive than Socrates when he was in a good temper, but he was choleric, and when seized with passion was an ugly sight and would give way to the most violent language and actions. He was also passionate sexually, 'but did not add injury to his licentiousness because he only consorted with married women or common harlots'![1] That Socrates had a passionate nature there is no doubt, and those who were smarting under the lash of his anger may well have felt about it as Spintharus did. If it was rarely allowed to erupt, when it did the effect was devastating. Xenophon gives an instance. Critias had been attempting to seduce a youth in Socrates's circle called Euthydemus. When private remonstrance had had no effect, Socrates, seeing him behaving badly at a talk where Euthydemus and several others of his young acquaintance were present, said before them all, 'Critias seems to be overcome by a swinish desire to rub himself against Euthydemus like a pig on a stone'.[2]

(3) ATTITUDE TO SEX AND LOVE

Socrates's attitude to sex must be looked at more closely, in view both of his constant companionship with youth and of the central part played by *eros* in the Platonic philosophy under Socratic inspiration. The attitude to homosexual relationships in the Athens of his day was different from our own. Romance was seen chiefly in male attachments of the Achilles–Patroclus or Orestes–Pylades type, and it was seriously held that such relationships between men, with varying degrees of overtly sexual content, were far more capable of fostering heroism and other virtues, and leading to a lasting and truly spiritual connexion,

[1] Aristoxenus, fr. 54 Wehrli. It is a pity that those who mistrust the favourable accounts of Plato and Xenophon have nothing better than this sort of gossip to put forward on the other side. Aristoxenus was also the man who accused Socrates of bigamy, said that he had been the παιδικά of Archelaus, and claimed that he demanded pay for his teaching (frr. 57 f., 52, 59). He also said that the whole of the *Republic* was to be found in Protagoras's *Antilogika* and that Aristotle founded the Lyceum in Plato's lifetime as his rival (frr. 67, 65).

[2] *Mem.* 1. 2. 29–30. Mary Renault has reconstructed the scene with remarkable imaginative power in her novel *The Last of the Wine* (pp. 120 f. of the *New English Library* paperback ed.).

than was marriage between man and woman. In Plato's *Symposium* it is taken for granted that attraction between the sexes is purely physical and its object the begetting of children. The position is summed up by Demosthenes: 'We have courtesans for our pleasure, concubines for the requirements of the body and wives for the procreation of lawful issue.'[1] Different Greek states, it is true, had different codes of behaviour. Pausanias in Plato's *Symposium* says that in Elis and Boeotia there were no second thoughts about it, and Thebes is known to have been proud of her 'Sacred Band' of lovers, a model for steadfastness and courage. In Ionia and among Greeks under Persian rule it was condemned, a fact which Pausanias connects with a tyrant's natural wish to discourage intellectual and physical achievement, and strongly knit friendships and associations, among his subjects. At Athens itself, he goes on,[2] the position is more complicated and not easy to understand. It is believed that such love can be a noble thing, and much is forgiven to a lover, but at the same time fathers place their sons in the hands of tutors with orders to guard them strictly against any possible communication with suitors. The explanation, he thinks, is that there is a right and a wrong type of love, one man seeking only physical gratification and making off when his favourite's looks begin to fade, and another loving a boy's spirit rather than his body and offering him an ennobling friendship. The obstacles put in the way, taking time and effort to overcome them, serve as a test, and two things are disapproved of by Athenian society: to give in to a lover quickly, or to give in from motives of fear, greed,[3] or hope of advancement. The

---

[1] Demosth. *In Neaer.* (59) 122, quoted by Levinson, *In Def. of P.* 106, n. 81. Levinson's description of the general state of opinion in Athens is a good antidote to a theory like Kelsen's that Plato suffered from feelings of guilt, rejection and isolation induced by deviation from a socially recognized standard.

[2] And at Sparta if the text at 182b is sound. It has been questioned (see Bury *ad loc.*) on the grounds that Sparta was a completely permissive state and could not have been associated with Athens in this respect. This permissiveness is referred to by Plato (*Laws* 636b, 836b) and from a number of indications is generally accepted as a fact, though Dover has now argued learnedly that the evidence does not justify supposing that homosexual practices were more prevalent at Sparta than elsewhere or were believed to be so by the Athenians (*BICS*, 1964, 36–8). Xenophon certainly claims (*Rep. Lac.* 2.13–14) that the Lycurgan laws, while encouraging a virtuous association between a man and a boy, regarded physical relations between them as on a par with incest.

[3] Prostitution was forbidden to an Athenian citizen by law, and conviction involved loss of civic rights (ἀτιμία). The chief source of our knowledge of Attic law on homosexuality (which also throws considerable light on current νόμος in its wider sense of conventional attitudes) is Aeschines's speech against Timarchus. For a summary see Dover in *BICS*, 1964, 32f.

motive of the younger must be a belief that his association with the older man will strengthen his character and improve his mind, and the other should act in the knowledge that he can do this. Such love is of value both to states and individuals 'because it compels both lover and beloved to submit to self-discipline for the attainment of excellence'.

The speakers in the *Symposium* are in character. Though Pausanias says some things with which Plato would agree, his conception of love is not the same as the Socratic–Platonic one which comes later, and it may be taken as representative of cultivated Athenian opinion. Lagerborg is certainly right to say, in his excellent study of the subject, that 'In the eyes of the Greeks these tender friendships were by no means something to be ashamed of', and 'In his love of beautiful youths Plato is a true child of his time'.[1] The same is true of Socrates, and it disposes of any theory that either was affected by the feeling that he was a deviant from the established mores of his society. Confusion has been caused by failure to make the requisite distinctions between different forms of these attachments, which might range from romantic and high-minded affection, more easily bestowed perhaps on a youth whose good qualities included bodily beauty, to a more or less promiscuous desire for sensual gratification. The latter was certainly condemned by Athenian opinion, and no less by Socrates and Plato.[2] To deny the truth of Vergil's line 'Gratior est pulchro veniens de corpore virtus' would be hypocritical in most of us. As an instance of the accepted moral level, which yet falls far short of the Socratic, one may quote the words of Critobulus, a much sought-after young man now old enough to take an interest in those younger than himself.[3]

We who are handsome infuse something into our admirers which makes them more liberal with money, more ready to work hard and face danger with honour, and even more modest and self-controlled, since what they desire at the same time fills them with shame. Indeed, it is folly not to choose

---

[1] *Plat. Liebe*, 44 f., 31. For the moral and socially valuable aspects of the Greek code of conduct between men, see especially pp. 42 ff.

[2] In the speech of Lysias which Phaedrus reads to Socrates (*Phaedr.* 231 e) it is the non-lover who feels obliged to meet the point that the object of his desire may hesitate 'for fear of the established *nomos*'; but the whole passage shows that in any case the *flaunting* of a physical relationship was deplored.

[3] Xen. *Symp.* 4.15. For Critobulus's stage in life cf. 8.2 ἔτι καὶ νῦν ἐρώμενος ὢν ἤδη ἄλλων ἐπιθυμεῖ.

handsome men as commanders: for my part at any rate I would go through fire if I had Clinias beside me, and I know that you with me would do the same. So don't think it astonishing, Socrates, that my beauty should be a good thing for mankind, and don't despise beauty as something that quickly fades. A youth, a grown man and an old man can have beauty just as a child can. This is proved by the choice of fine-looking old men to carry the olive-shoots at Athena's festival, on the principle that every time of life has its own beauty.

Phaedrus in Plato's *Symposium* (178–9) utters similar sentiments: That which should be the ruling principle of a man's life, without which neither a city nor an individual can do any great or fine deed—namely a feeling of shame at disgraceful acts and ambition to do what is honour-able—is instilled by nothing, whether kindred, honours or wealth, so much as by love. To have his father or his comrades catch him behaving dishonourably, or suffering through his own cowardice, will hurt a man less than if it is seen by his beloved. To put it at the mini-mum, then, no one can read Plato or Xenophon—or for that matter Aristophanes[1]—without accepting as a historical fact that among the leisured classes at Athens love between males was a perfectly natural and unembarrassing topic either for serious conversation or for jesting. G. Devereux, in an interesting article written from the psychoanalytic point of view ('Greek Pseudo-homosexuality and the "Greek Miracle"', *Symb. Osl.* 1967), makes out a good case for seeing Greek homosexual behaviour as not a true perversion but an expression of adolescence prolonged into adult life. It may have been an unfortunate expression but, as the author points out, adolescence is not an opprobrious term. It is, after all, the same as youthfulness, and it is not the detractors of the Greeks who have spoken of their eternal youth. The relation of this youthfulness to the unparalleled flowering of the Greek genius is admirably brought out by the author in his concluding pages.

In all this, what was the position of Socrates? He is depicted as making free use of the language of love, declaring himself an expert

[1] Hans Kelsen, in his argument that Plato felt socially isolated because homosexuality was severely condemned at Athens, says that Aristophanes 'scourged it with the sharpest scorn and irony' (*Int. Journ. Ethics*, 1937–8, 375). It is possible to put a different interpretation on his highly obscene jokes which must have roused the audience to fits of laughter; otherwise they could not have been there. On the difference between the attitudes of Plato and Aristophanes to homosexuality see Dover, *BICS*, 1964, 36 and 38.

in 'erotics' (τὰ ἐρωτικά) and by nature a lover (ἐραστής). In the *Meno* (76c) he says that he can never resist the fair (who are, of course, not of the opposite sex), and in Xenophon's *Symposium* (8.2) that he cannot remember a time when he was not in love. It is by no means unusual, however, to find someone using the language of erotics and yet being entirely continent in his behaviour. The sexual imagery of religious mystics has often attracted attention.[1] Moreover, whereas at the present time we acknowledge (perhaps decreasingly) at least the residue of a social taboo on such language, Socrates was under no such restraint. All the evidence indicates that, on the one hand, he had his passions under complete control, and used the socially approved association of an older man with his juniors as an educational asset; but, on the other hand, he was by nature susceptible to youthful beauty and did not resist it without an effort. When he speaks of it, though it is usually in a humorous way, there is certainly something behind the jest. The most outspoken passage is the description of Socrates's meeting with the boy Charmides after a long absence in the army. All the company have been praising his beauty, and Socrates agrees that he must be quite irresistible, if only he has a soul to match his outward form. They propose to test this by engaging him in talk, and he sits down between Socrates and Critias.

But then I felt embarrassed, and my former confidence that I could make conversation with him was all knocked out of me. And when Critias told him that I knew the cure for his headache, and he turned his eyes on me with an indescribable look and made as if to question me, and everyone in the palaestra gathered round us, I caught a glimpse inside his clothes and was aflame. I was no longer master of myself, and thought how well Cydias had understood love when, speaking of a fair boy, he warned someone to take care 'that the fawn come not in sight of the lion, to be devoured by him'. Indeed I felt just as if I had been seized by a wild beast.[2]

The rest of the dialogue is devoted to the nature of *sophrosyne*, self-control or temperance.

[1] E.g. Taylor, *Socrates*, 46: 'The almost universal adoption of symbolic language borrowed from sexual passion by the mystics of all times and places seems to point to a real connexion between the mystical and the erotic temperament.'
[2] Pl. *Charm.* 155c–e. Cf. Xenophon, *Mem.* 1.3.13, where Socrates describes 'that wild beast called "youth in bloom"' as more dangerous than a scorpion, because it can inject a maddening poison without ever coming into contact with its victim.

A particular joke between Socrates and his friends seems to have been his supposed passion for Alcibiades. It is mentioned several times in Plato, and most interestingly in a fragment of the Socratic Aeschines, where it is compared to Bacchic frenzy.[1]

> For my part, the love I bore to Alcibiades brought me an experience just like that of the Bacchae. They, when they are inspired, draw honey and milk from wells which will hardly yield even water to other people. Similarly I, though I have learned nothing that I could impart to a man to do him good, nevertheless thought that, because I loved him, my company could make him a better man.

The irony is apparent. The erotic delusion of Socrates, comparable to those of frenzied maenads, is that by his love he might be able to convert the dissolute Alcibiades to a better way of life. With this goes Alcibiades's own description, in Plato's *Symposium*, of Socrates's impregnable chastity and ability to make him feel ashamed of himself. In the *First Alcibiades* Socrates is arguing generally that a man's self is his mind or spirit (*psyche*) and the body only an instrument which it 'governs' and makes use of for living. This gives him the opportunity to point out what he means by true *eros* and to denounce the current version of homosexual love; for he who loves Alcibiades's body does not love Alcibiades but only something belonging to him.[2] In lighter vein, there is a pleasant exchange in Xenophon (*Symp.* 8.4) between Antisthenes and Socrates. Antisthenes says he loves him, and the Silenus-like Socrates replies, 'But the less said about your love the better, since you love me not for myself (literally "my *psyche*") but for my looks'. Later (8.23) he says seriously, 'to consort with someone who loves the body rather than the soul is slavish'.

We may trust Plato's account of Socrates's philosophy and practice in matters of sex not only because there is no reliable evidence to the contrary, nor because, had he been given to pederasty, the conventions of the time imposed no need of concealment. It is more important that the character which Plato presents is absolutely convincing, but the most unchallengeable part of his evidence lies not in his direct praise of

[1] Pl. *Prot.* 309a, *Gorg.* 481d, *Alc. I, ad init.*; Aesch. fr. 10c, p. 273 Dittmar. At *Symp.* 217aff. Alcibiades is made to speak of his own mistaken impression that Socrates wished to sleep with him.
[2] 131c. See further pp. 470ff. below.

Socrates, but in his own philosophy. Holding the views on *eros* which he did, he could not have been such an admiring disciple had Socrates himself fallen short of them. It must indeed have been the influence of Socrates which helped him to transcend so notably the current morality of his time. He condemned pederasty both in the *Republic* and the *Laws*.[1] More important, because more positive, is the central position occupied by *eros* in his whole philosophy. Full consideration of this will come later, but briefly it means that a complete and satisfying philosophy of life must have regard to the emotions as well as the reason, since both are integral parts of human nature. Philosophy does not consist in cultivating the intellect to the neglect of everything else. It should mean the use of reason to guide the desires towards other forms of satisfaction than physical, in which they will find, not frustration, but their highest fulfilment. In this process the sexual impulses have their place, for it is through them that the *psyche* is first attracted to what is beautiful. They lead first of all, of course, to the admiration of physical beauty, and if they are indulged at this level by physical debauchery, our life is maimed. But in fact this *eros* in us is a spiritual force, and by shunning its lower manifestations and learning its true nature, we may allow it to lead us upwards (as Socrates is made to expound it in the *Symposium*) from passionate desire for a particular body to an aesthetic enjoyment of visible beauty in general, from that to beauty of character,[2] higher still to the intellectual beauty of the sciences, until by persevering to the end we are granted the sudden vision of Beauty itself, the absolute Form which is perceived not with the bodily eye at all, but with the eye of the soul or mind. On this ultimate, indeed divine level, beauty and goodness and truth are one, and the vision of this supreme reality, says Plato through the mouth of Socrates, is only possible to the man who is by nature a lover, for the power which leads to it is the power of *eros*. That, says Socrates, is what is meant by initiation into the final mysteries of *ta erotika*; and

---

[1] *Rep.* 403 a–c. At *Laws* 838 e, homosexual intercourse is condemned on the grounds of its barrenness as 'deliberate murder of the human race, sowing seed on rocks and stones where it will never take root and bear its natural fruit'. At 636 c it is called 'unnatural and the height of shameless and incontinent indulgence'. That Plato forbade this intercourse is agreed by Aristotle, *Pol.* 1262 a 32 ff.

[2] It has to be remembered that the single word καλόν, which we translate 'beauty', referred as much to moral excellence as to grace of outward form.

that is a fundamental doctrine of Platonism, a philosophy to a large extent inspired by Socrates himself.

In speaking of Plato as a source, I made it clear that I am far from those who claim that everything which he puts into the mouth of Socrates was, or could have been, said by Socrates in real life. In this magnificent central speech of the *Symposium* he certainly transcends the teaching of the historical Socrates.[1] But, just as he could not have made Socrates propound what he himself regarded as the strongest arguments for immortality if Socrates had been convinced that death was the end of everything (p. 354 above), so it is impossible to believe that he could have attributed the *Symposium* speech to Socrates if the ideas and behaviour of the real Socrates in matters of love had been on the same earthy level as those of many of his contemporaries.

All this agrees well with the testimony of Xenophon already noted (pp. 342, 344 above) that Socrates put love of the soul before love of the body, but did not believe that spiritual love need lack a passionate element. Cicero tells a story which probably goes back to a dialogue written by Socrates's young friend Phaedo. A certain Zopyrus, who professed to read character from faces, said that he saw in the features of Socrates many signs of a vicious and lustful nature—not an unnatural verdict when one thinks of those thick sensual lips. The others present laughed at him, out of their knowledge of the continence of Socrates's life, but Socrates himself stood up for him: the lusts were there all right, he said, but he had conquered them by reason.[2] He was

---

[1] At 209e the Mantinean prophetess Diotima, from whom Socrates professes to have had this lore, says: 'So far, Socrates, I have spoken of those mysteries of love into which even you could be initiated; but the final revelations, to which they lead up if properly pursued, I doubt if you will be able to grasp.' As others have seen (see Stenzel, *PMD*, 4 f.), it is most probable that with this sentence Plato marks the limit reached by the philosophy of his master. It has included the notion of the union of minds, resulting in pregnancy and parturition in the realm of ideas, linking up with the mental labour-pains which the maieutic skill of Socrates relieves by his successful delivery of other people's mind-children, as described in the *Theaetetus*. This involves the characteristically Socratic pose of knowing nothing himself, and justifies a strong presumption that the whole complex belongs to the historical Socrates.

[2] Cic. *Tusc.* 4.37.80, and cf. *De fato* 4.10. Phaedo's dialogue *Zopyrus* is mentioned as genuine by D.L. (2.105). The story has been called 'schwerlich geschichtlich' by Zeller (*Ph. d. Gr.* 64 n.) and 'well substantiated' by Friedländer (*Plato*, Eng. tr. I, 45). Phaedo is the obvious source, and this guarantees that it is historical at least in the sense that it fitted the Socrates he knew. Henry Jackson (quoted by Adam, *Apol.* xxii) remarked that in outward appearance Socrates 'seemed the embodiment of sensuality and even stupidity'. (Cf. 'stupidum et bardum' in *De fato* 4.10.)

a good man in the sense defined by Antiphon (p. 259 above) and had sympathy and understanding for those weaker than himself. As Zeller well expressed it (*Ph. d. Gr.* 68), he was no impersonal ideal of virtue, but an Athenian Greek of flesh and blood.

Handsome young men then, we know, had a powerful attraction for Socrates, and he was never so happy as when in their company. But they knew that the only stimulus they would get from him was the excitement of his friendship and conversation, of experiencing his intellectual midwifery which made their thoughts seem to flow ten times as fast as before.

(4) EFFECT ON OTHERS

If Socrates was fascinated by youthful beauty, it is no less true that the young were fascinated by him. This ugly, flat-nosed, pot-bellied and pop-eyed man exerted an uncanny power of personal magnetism. Such power is difficult to understand without experiencing it, but his young friends have done their best to communicate it, and may be left to speak for themselves. Alcibiades in Plato's *Symposium*, after comparing him to Marsyas the satyr, who contended with Apollo in flute-playing, and commenting on the remarkable resemblance in personal appearance, goes on:[1]

But you don't play the flute, you say? No, indeed; the performance you give is far more remarkable. Marsyas needed an instrument in order to charm men by the power which proceeded out of his mouth . . . But you, Socrates, are so far superior to Marsyas that you produce the same effect by mere words without any instrument. At any rate, whereas most of us pay little or no attention to the words of any other speaker, however accomplished, a speech by you, or even a very indifferent report of what you have said, stirs us to the depths and casts a spell over us, women and men and boys alike. I myself, gentlemen, were it not that you would think me absolutely drunk, would have stated on oath the effect which his words have had on me . . . Whenever I listen to him, my heart beats faster than if I were in a religious frenzy, and tears run down my face, and I observe that numbers of other people have had the same experience. Nothing of this kind ever used to

[1] 215 b ff., trans. W. Hamilton. Michael Joyce's more racy version of the brilliant young rake's speech (in the Hamilton–Cairns volume of the collected dialogues) is also well worth looking at.

happen to me when I listened to Pericles and other good speakers; I recognized that they spoke well, but my soul was not thrown into confusion and dismay by the thought that my life was no better than a slave's.

Such language is not to be explained away by any reminder of Plato's apologetic purpose of exonerating Socrates from responsibility for Alcibiades's misdeeds. What it describes goes deeper than mere charm of conversation or power of argument, and is less easy to explain. Meno also is made to describe it in the language of spells and magic, and it can only have sprung from Plato's own experience of an effect exerted almost unconsciously by Socrates and in part independently of the words he used. The most remarkable description of it is in the *Theages*, which, if not written by Plato, is generally agreed to be a production of the early fourth century by one of the Socratic circle. If those who deny it to Plato are correct, its witness is the more valuable for its independence, and Plato's own descriptions justify confidence in what it relates. When all allowance is made for Socrates's *eironeia*, there remains something extraordinary which calls for explanation.[1]

A father, worried about his son Theages[2] who is pestering him with his longing to be trained for political life, brings the boy to Socrates. Theages would like Socrates himself to take him on, but Socrates suggests that the proper instructors are the Sophists, men like Prodicus and Gorgias and Polus. They have something definite to teach and know what they are about. He has no skill or knowledge to impart save in the one art of love, and whether or not young men who consort with him make good progress is not in his control; it is a matter of divine providence. Sometimes his heaven-sent premonitory voice forbids him to take a pupil, and even when it does not, success is not guaranteed. Some acquire lasting benefit, but with others the

---

[1] For the best short account of the *Theages* see Friedländer, *Plato*, Eng. tr. II, 147–54. He sees no good reason against assigning it to Plato, and dates it on grounds of style to c. 400. W. Janell (in *Hermes*, 1901), who thought it spurious, would identify it as the work of a Socratic composed in Plato's lifetime, between 369 and 366. Other references are in *RE*, XL. Halbb. 2366f. Some have doubted Platonic authorship simply on the grounds of what they see as an irrational, superstitious element, in the treatment of the *daimonion* and the reference to physical contact in Aristides's speech. So Dorothy Tarrant in *CQ*, 1958, 95. If this must always remain a matter of opinion, Friedländer has at least given the opposite opinion a good foundation. See especially his p. 152. (J. M. Rist disagrees, *Phoenix*, 1963, p. 17.)

[2] Theages is also mentioned in the *Rep.* (496b) as one who would have deserted philosophy for politics if ill-health had not prevented him.

improvement lapses as soon as they leave his society.[1] He will tell a story to prove it (130a):

It is the story of what happened to Aristides, the son of Lysimachus and grandson of the great Aristides. This boy spent his time in my company and made great progress in a short while. Then he sailed off on some military expedition, and when he returned he found that Thucydides, Melesias's son, had attached himself to me. The day before, Thucydides had taken offence at something in our conversation, so when Aristides caught sight of me, after he had given me his greeting and so forth he said, 'I hear Thucydides is taking a high line with you and complaining to you as if he were somebody.' 'Quite true', I said. 'Why,' said Aristides, 'didn't he know before he took up with you what a slavery it was?' 'Apparently not', said I. 'No, I'll swear he didn't.' 'And what about me, Socrates?' he said. 'My own position is ridiculous.' 'Why so?' 'Because before I sailed I could talk to anybody and show myself their equal in argument. I even sought out the company of the cleverest people. Now it's just the opposite. If I feel that someone is a man of culture, I run away from him, so ashamed am I of my inadequacy.' 'Did this power leave you suddenly or gradually?' I asked. 'Gradually', was his reply. 'And when you had it', I went on, 'did you get it from anything you learned from me, or in some other way?' 'I will tell you something, Socrates', said he, 'something quite incredible but true. *I never learned a single thing from you*, as you know yourself; but whenever I was with you I improved, even if I was only in the same house but not in the same room, though more so when I was in the same room; and it seemed to me that the effect was much greater if, being in the same room, I kept my eyes on you while you were speaking rather than looking in another direction. But the greatest progress of all I made when I actually sat next you and could touch you. But now it has all leaked away.'

One can imagine the solemn youth as he meditates round-eyed on the magical effect of Socrates's presence.[2] What Plato really thought of 'education by contact' (not an impossible belief for a Greek, as

---

[1] Similar points are made in the *Theaetetus* (150dff.), where they are expressly related to the midwife metaphor, and Aristides is mentioned in passing. There however it is said only that, if the *daimonion* permits a pupil's return, he again improves. The possibility of a second lapse, in spite of the god's consent, is not mentioned.

[2] The *Theages* is not devoid of character-drawing or humour. Friedländer (*op. cit.* 326) pointed out that the stiff and heavy style of Demodocus's opening speech, which has been stigmatized as un-Platonic (e.g. by Shorey, *WPS*, 429), might be intentional, as appropriate to the worthy farmer. Inevitably he brings out the stock comparison between plant-rearing and education (pp. 168f. above) including the delightful remark that 'planting' children is much easier work for a man than planting trees! It is in the rearing that the hard work begins.

Dorothy Tarrant pointed out in *CQ*, 1958), he shows in the *Symposium* (175 c–d), where Agathon calls to Socrates to sit beside him, so that by contact with him he may have the benefit of his latest inspiration. Socrates replies that it would indeed be a fine thing if by touching each other we could make wisdom flow from the emptier to the fuller by a sort of capillary attraction. There was nothing physical or magical about Socrates's educational powers, as his wide-eyed young admirers might think, but there was nevertheless more than the mere inculcation of facts or ideas. Friedländer (*op. cit.* 152) rightly contrasts Socratic education through love[1] with sophistic education without love, and the sophistic practice of offering intellectual wares to all and sundry with Socrates's *daimonion* which told him whether there was likely to be the requisite mental and moral affinity between himself and a young man to make the teacher–pupil relationship successful. This is also connected with his maieutic art. Since he teaches nothing but only draws out what is there, he can do nothing with one who has not already conceived in his mind. The others he sent to the Sophists (*Theaet.* 151 b). The freedom to choose only those whom his instinct (or his *daimonion*) told him would be able to respond to his 'advances' was his main motive for declining to accept payment (p. 39 above). He certainly taught them to be anyone's equal in argument, but only because he was convinced that clear thinking was the necessary prerequisite of right moral action. Dialectical skill was for him only the means to moral reform, which will always fail unless there is an initial current of sympathy between teacher and disciple.

If Socrates had no literal magic in his touch, Plato nevertheless makes it indisputable that the effect of his personality on his hearers was something unique and uncomfortable. Only those of the right temperament could respond to it, and only if they were prepared to persevere. The first contact induced not the self-confidence of which Aristides speaks, but a depressing sense of helplessness. His method was rooted in his belief that before anyone could be helped on the path to wisdom he must first be convinced of his own need, that is, of his present ignorance and foolishness. Some only waited for this first, negative

[1] Although Friedländer does not mention it here, the passage of Aeschines quoted on p. 395 is highly relevant to this.

stage, and left him in what a psychoanalyst might call a state of negative transference, angry with Socrates but also with themselves. Many, he says (*Theaet.* 151c), 'are ready to bite me' when they see their brain-children discarded as phantoms. This aspect of him comes out in the *Meno* (80a), joined, as Alcibiades joined it, with an uncomplimentary reference to his face.

It seems to me that you are exercising magic and witchcraft and spells against me till I am a mass of helplessness. To be flippant, I think that in outward appearance and everything else you are exactly like the flat sting-ray in the sea. Whoever goes near and touches it, it numbs, and numbness is just what you inflict on me. My mind and my lips are literally numb, and I have nothing to reply to you... In my opinion you are well advised not to go abroad. If you behaved like this as a foreigner in another country, the chances are you would be arrested as a wizard.

Together with the *Symposium* and *Theages* this does suggest something that goes further than the force of rational argument. At the same time his method in itself explains much. To be inexorably compelled to recognize one's ignorance is not a pleasant or comfortable process. That some of the young should have enjoyed trying out on their elders and betters what they had been put through themselves is understandable even if not laudable.

(5) THE DIVINE SIGN: SOCRATES AND THE IRRATIONAL

There is other evidence for a less rational side to Socrates. Both Plato and Xenophon refer frequently to what he called his *daimonion*, divine sign or spiritual guide, often simply 'the customary sign'.[1] In Plato's *Apology* (31c–d) he describes it thus:

I experience a certain divine or daemonic something, which in fact Meletus has caricatured in the indictment. It began in childhood and has been with me ever since, a kind of voice, which whenever I hear it always turns me back from something I was going to do, but never urges me to act. This is what has prevented me from taking part in politics.

---

[1] τὸ δαιμόνιον, τὸ δαιμόνιον σημεῖον, τὸ τοῦ θεοῦ σημεῖον, τὸ εἰωθὸς σημεῖον, ἡ εἰωθυῖά μοι μαντική, φωνή. Stress is sometimes laid on the adjectival character of τὸ δαιμόνιον and it is of course different from δαίμων or θεός. This assists the defence in Plato and Xenophon against the accusation that it is a 'new god'.

(Two points in this passage are repeated by Plato elsewhere. In the
Euthyphro (3b) Euthyphro surmises that the *daimonion* is the basis of
Meletus's accusation of introducing strange gods, and in the *Republic*
(496c) Socrates says it is the *daimonion* that has kept him from a
political career.) After his condemnation he tells his friends (40a–c):

In former times my customary prophetic sign has opposed me assiduously
even in quite trivial matters, if I was going to do anything amiss. Now there
has befallen me, as you see, what would commonly be considered the worst
of all evils; yet neither when I left my house nor when I was taking my place
in the court nor at any point in my speech has it opposed me.[1] On other
occasions it has checked me in the middle of a sentence, but this time and in
this affair it has not opposed me in a single word or action.'

From this he concludes that death, which now awaits him, cannot be an
evil.

Of the 'more trivial' occasions of its intervention, Plato tells in the
Phaedrus (242b) how 'the customary sign' occurred, and he 'seemed
to hear a voice' which forbade him to leave after his first discourse on
love before he had delivered a palinode; and in the *Euthydemus* (272e)
how, as he got up to go from the dressing-room in the palaestra, it made
him sit down again, and rewarded him with an exhibition by an egregious pair of Sophists. In the *First Alcibiades* he gives its veto as his
reason for having shunned Alcibiades's company.[2] Perhaps its most
important function was that mentioned in the *Theages* and *Theaetetus*
(151a), of dissuading him from accepting or taking back pupils who
could not profit from his highly personal teaching methods. In the
former it is even said that this daemonic power contributes to, or col-
laborates in, the success of the pupils whom he takes, and this is distinguished from a merely negative attitude of non-opposition.[3]

Xenophon is more inclined to attribute a positive as well as negative function to the *daimonion*, and some of his references have a more
definitely apologetic purpose. He evidently took seriously the suggestion that in accusing Socrates of rejecting the gods of the state and

[1] According to Xenophon (*Apol.* 4, *Mem.* 4.8.5), it did intervene *before* the trial, by preventing him from preparing a defence in advance.
[2] 103a. Similarly in Xenophon (*Symp.* 8.5), Antisthenes complains that Socrates makes the
daimonion an excuse for not speaking to him.
[3] *Theages* 129e. Cf. ἐφῆκεν at *Alc. I* 106a, and Friedländer, *Plato*, I, 34f.

introducing new divinities Meletus and his associates had the *daimonion* in mind, and he is at pains to show that the inner voice was simply the way in which one of the known gods revealed his will to Socrates, as others were shown it through omens, oracles and the other approved channels of prophecy. He is also bothered by the fear that the divine voice might be thought a delusion because Socrates made a point of having received no warning from it about his approaching trial, when in fact he was condemned to death. Xenophon's reply to this is that Socrates was already so old that death was not far off, and that his execution saved him from the diminution of powers which would otherwise have awaited him, and brought him instead the glory due to a noble end.[1]

The exact nature of the 'divine sign' may be left to students of psychology or religious experience.[2] At this distance of time, and on the evidence available, it probably cannot be decided with certainty. We may be content with knowing that it was something that Socrates himself took seriously, and that therefore his educational activities were for him a matter of genuine vocation. More generally, belief in a special, direct relation between himself and divine forces must be accepted in any account of his mentality which lays claim to completeness.

Other evidence adduced in favour of a less rational streak in Socrates's nature is perhaps less certain. In the *Symposium* (220c) Alcibiades, who was with him on the Potidaean campaign, describes how one day he stood still from dawn, apparently fixed in thought. By noon, he began to be noticed. In the evening he was still rooted to the spot, and some of the Ionians, out of curiosity, brought their bedding outside to keep an eye on him and see if he would stand there all night as well. 'And he stood until it was dawn and the sun rose; then after a prayer to the sun he walked away.' It may be said that, being a profound philosopher, he was all this time engaged in following out a normal train of thought; but even the knottiest of philosophical problems could hardly keep him on his feet, oblivious of his surroundings, for twenty-four hours, and the story, if true, is hard to explain without

---

[1] See *Mem.* 1.1.2ff., *Apol.* 12–13, *Mem.* 4.8.1, *Apol.* 5. The *daimonion* is also mentioned as a compliment to Socrates by Euthydemus at *Mem.* 4.3.12.

[2] Good accounts in English are those of Phillipson, *Trial*, 88–98, and Friedländer, *Plato* (Eng. tr.) I, 32–6. See also H. Gundert in *Gymnasium*, 1954 and the references in his notes.

some element of trance. In any case, this power of complete abstraction or withdrawal from his surroundings must partly account for his notorious hardiness and indifference to physical conditions and fatigue.

Less striking perhaps is the incident which caused embarrassment to his friend Aristodemus, whom he met when he was on the way to dine with Agathon (*Symp.* 174a ff.). He suggested that Aristodemus should join him, and he himself would take the responsibility for having invited him. As they neared the house, Socrates stopped and asked Aristodemus to go ahead. He entered the house thinking Socrates was just behind, but he was nowhere to be seen. A servant of Agathon's, sent to fetch him, reported that he was standing in a neighbour's porch and refused to stir when spoken to. Aristodemus, who knew his odd habit of 'going apart and standing still wherever he happens to be', recommended that he be left alone, and he turned up about half-way through dinner.

(6) SOCRATES AND THE DELPHIC RESPONSE

Not unrelated to all this is another event in his life which must be mentioned before we turn to consider more specifically his teaching and its significance. That is, the reply which the Delphic oracle gave concerning him to his ardent and impetuous[1] young follower Chaerephon. We know of it mainly from Plato's *Apology*, though it is also mentioned, in exaggerated form, by Xenophon.[2] We cannot know exactly when it happened, but although Taylor's argument from the *Charmides*, that it must have been before 430, is weak, to suppose it an

---

[1] *Apol.* 21a καὶ ἴστε δὴ οἷος ἦν Χαιρέφων, ὡς σφοδρὸς ἐφ' ὅτι ὁρμήσειεν.

[2] Plato. *Apol.* 21a ff., Xen. *Apol.* 14. The two versions are compared on p. 339, n. 1, above. For some opinions on the historicity and significance of the incident see Edelstein, *X. u. P. Bild*, 34, n. 13, Schmid, *Gesch.* 240 with nn., Ritter, *Sokr.* 62f., Hackforth, *CPA*, 88–104, Deman, *Témoignage*, 45–7. Wilamowitz, *Platon*, II, 52–4, is particularly sensible. It is impossible that Plato (who makes Socrates offer to produce the dead Chaerephon's brother as witness) should have invented it, though opinions may differ about the extent to which it was responsible for Socrates's 'mission'. On the reported statement of Aristotle that it was the Delphic precept 'know thyself' that gave Socrates the impulse to inquire into the nature of man, see Deman, *op. cit.* 44–8. Aristotle also (according to D.L. 2.23) spoke of a personal visit of Socrates to Delphi, and in Gigon's opinion (*Mus. Helv.* 1959, 176) we may 'confidently' put these statements together and assume that Aristotle was telling a story in deliberate rivalry to Plato's.

event of Socrates's early middle age is consistent with what he says in the *Apology*, and some time in his thirties would suit well.[1] His story is that Chaerephon went to Delphi and had the effrontery (ἐτόλμησε) to ask the oracle if anyone was wiser than Socrates, and the Pythia replied that no one was. 'This', wrote J. B. Bury (*Hist. of Greece*, 580), 'showed a strange insight which we should hardly have looked for at the shrine of Delphi.' Taylor was nearer the mark when he said (*Socr.* 77) that the oracle, which liked to please, naturally gave the answer which the eager young man with his very leading question wanted to receive. It was not even necessary (though the necessity is generally assumed) that Socrates should already have achieved a wide reputation as a wise man for the question to have been asked. He need only have had a small but devoted band of disciples, of whom the lean and earnest Chaerephon, 'the Bat', was fanatical enough to take the question to the oracle. Such a following he had even before he abandoned his enthusiasm for natural science: Chaerephon figures prominently in the *Clouds*.[2]

Socrates himself chose to take the oracle very seriously, and regarded it as a turning-point in his life. Some scholars have doubted this, for two reasons, both fallacious. First, they do not believe that Socrates, though a man of undoubted religious feelings, was the sort of orthodox pietist to allow his whole life to be influenced by the Delphic oracle. Secondly, his first reaction was to say that he was sure he was not wise at all, and to set out immediately to find someone who was wiser than he, so that he could point to him and refute the plain meaning of the god.[3] This he describes as acting in obedience to Apollo, but, they say, that is a contradiction: to set out to prove the god a liar would be a strange way of obeying him.

---

[1] Taylor, *Socrates*, 78. J. Ferguson in *Eranos*, 1964 argues for a date *c.* 421.

[2] Parke (*CP*, 1961) suggests that the oracle may have been given by lot—the drawing of a white or black bean—and the question of motive may not have arisen. (Amandry published an inscription showing that this method was sometimes used. See his *Mantique Apollinienne*, pp. 33, 245.) This however is doubtful. Parke refers to Xenophon's addition that the response was given πολλῶν παρόντων, and says that this detail (not mentioned by Plato) is likely to be historical even though other details in Xenophon's account are not. I cannot see that it has any better claim than the rest. On the contrary, it is just the sort of thing that Xenophon would add to make the story sound better in the telling. In any case, the oracle's reply as Xenophon gives it is inconsistent with the simple 'yes' or 'no' which could be conveyed by the drawing of a white or black bean respectively. [3] ὡς ἐλέγξων τὸ μαντεῖον, *Apol.* 21 b.

The first point is a matter of opinion,[1] but granted such a view of his general attitude, there could be a good psychological reason for his response to the oracle in this case. There is plenty of evidence that as a young man he was an enthusiast for the natural science of his time, but later condemned it for its irrelevance to human problems and its neglect of final causes. Presumably he was already feeling dissatisfied with this type of inquiry, perhaps already telling his young friends that it was barren and urging them rather to 'care for their souls', but the change would not be made without doubts and mental struggle. In such a state he could well accept the impulsive act of Chaerephon and its consequences as a sign that he was on the right track, and allow it to make up his mind for him. If the mind is already prepared, the actual occasion for such a call to action need only be trivial, just as, if it is not so prepared, the most solemn adjurations in the name of Heaven may fail to take effect.

The second objection rests on a misunderstanding of the way in which Delphic responses were regularly regarded and acted on. Socrates's description of his first reaction to the oracle is this (*Apol.* 21 b): 'What can the god mean? What is his riddle? I know very well that I am not the least bit wise. What does he mean by saying that I am the wisest? He can't be lying: that would not be right for him.' What he set out to refute was the obvious meaning of the oracle, its words taken at their face value, in order to discover the answer to its riddle. Everyone knew that it spoke in riddles, and any sensible man or city would look past the obvious meaning for what was hidden underneath. When the Athenians, threatened by Persian invasion, were advised to rely on a wooden wall, they did not set about building one: they held a consultation, and many opinions were expressed as they sought to solve the riddle, until finally the interpretation of Themistocles was accepted that by 'wooden wall' the god meant the navy.[2] In this case Socrates's solution of the riddle was that the god took advantage

---

[1] Dodds (*Gks. & Irrat.* 185 and 198, n. 36) gives chapter and verse for the statement that 'he took both dreams and oracles very seriously'.

[2] Hdt. 7.142, cf. vol. 1, 418. Hackforth (*CPA*, 94) argues that Socrates's procedure in testing the oracle was incompatible with a serious acceptance of its authority because he rationalizes it, saving Apollo's face 'by ingeniously imputing to him what he did not say'. But this was a recognized procedure, entirely compatible with acceptance of the oracle's authority. (Hackforth is also criticized by J. A. Coulter in *HSCP*, 1964, p. 303, n. 33.)

of Chaerephon's question to inculcate the lesson that no human wisdom was worth anything. He simply took Socrates as an example and used his name in order to say that the wisest thing a man could do was to be aware of his own unwisdom (23a–b).

(7) HIS SERVICE TO THE GOD

His method of investigating the oracle's meaning was a tireless interrogation of Athenians in different walks of life in order to discover whether any of them were wiser than he. In this practice he continued after as before his discovery of its lesson, because having learned the lesson himself he felt it to be the god's will that he should impart it to others. This took up so much of his time that he had little left for public or private affairs, 'and my service to the god has brought me into great poverty' (23b). It also, not unnaturally, brought him a considerable amount of ill-will. Whether he really believed himself singled out by Heaven for a special mission, or its dependence on the oracle was simply a playful conceit (and it certainly sounds serious enough), may remain, if one likes, a moot point; but at least his cross-questioning and the odium it brought him are facts, and we may continue the story as we have it in the *Apology*. He first sought out a politician with a reputation for wisdom, and talked to him; and as a result of the talk he decided that, whereas the man appeared both to himself and others to be wise, in reality he was not so. He continued the quest, in spite of animosity and abuse, testing the claims of various professions in turn. After the politicians he tried the poets, those traditional repositories of wisdom and knowledge, 'the educators of grown men', only to conclude, regretfully, that they must indeed, as they claimed, have written by divine inspiration rather than their own wisdom, since left to themselves they seemed to have no understanding of what they had done. Yet because of their poems they laid general claim to a knowledge and wisdom denied to other men. Finally he tried the artisans or handworkers. They had not the same reputation for wisdom as politicians or poets, but the wisdom of these had melted away under examination, and at least the craftsmen must be wise in what pertained to their craft, or they could not carry it out. There was no question of divine inspiration here, and, since Socrates, as he says, was convinced that he knew nothing at all, they could not fail to have more *sophia* than he.[1] Nor was he disappointed. 'And in this I was not deceived: they knew things which I did not know, and in this respect were wiser than me' (22d). But they did not know their own limitations. Because of their command of a small field of technical skill, they imagined themselves qualified to give an opinion on greater matters too, and laid claim to a wisdom which they did not possess. This fault, similar to that of the poets, overshadowed what wisdom they had.

(8) POLITICAL VIEWS

Socrates's opinion of the skilled practitioners of any art or craft is as good an introduction as any to the subject of his attitude to democracy. His appreciation of their skills is genuine. One has only to think of the admiration which he expresses in the *Gorgias* (511cff.) for the pilot who asks a mere two obols to carry a man, his wife, children and goods from Aegina to the Piraeus, and only two drachmas from Egypt or the Black Sea, for which sum he has preserved lives and goods from all the dangers to which the sea exposes them. But his virtue is in his modesty, which realizes that he is in no way capable of improving, in body or soul, those whom he has landed, or even of knowing whether, in their circumstances, a safe landing is better than drowning. He had the same admiration for skill and good workmanship wherever he saw them, in a shoemaker, an armourer, or a farmer.[2] But he objected to the assumption that mastery of a particular skill qualified a man to give a judgment outside his own sphere. The practice of some modern newspapers, which assist their circulation by publishing the opinions of famous footballers, actors or singers on political and social questions,

[1] The Greek words in question are of course *sophos* and *sophia*. For the way in which these straddled the meanings of our 'knowledge', 'skill' and 'wisdom', see pp. 27f. above.

[2] For some interesting passages illustrating Socrates's opinion of such occupations see Schlaifer's article reprinted in Finley, *Slavery*, p. 102, n. 6. It is likely that he distinguished some trades as especially banausic on the ground that they stunted or deformed the body, with a consequential effect on the personality (Xen. *Oec.* 4.2–3). That he believed honest labour was nothing to be ashamed of, even among those of gentle birth, is most strikingly illustrated by his advice to the impoverished Aristarchus and his family in Xen. *Mem.* 2.7.3ff. Yet in *Alc. I* (131b) he calls medicine, physical training, agriculture 'and other crafts' all banausic on the grounds that they do not, in and by themselves, impart self-knowledge or σωφροσύνη.

would have seemed to him pernicious. But at Athens every citizen had an equal right to discuss high policy in the popular Assembly, which was a universal, not a representative body. As Socrates says in the *Protagoras* (319b), in questions requiring technical knowledge—architecture, shipbuilding or the like—the Assembly calls on experts, and shouts down anyone who tries to speak without professional experience, but where the conduct of government is concerned, it is ready to listen to anybody, 'builder, smith, shoemaker, merchant, sea-captain, rich or poor, of good family or none'.

That the shoemaker should stick to his last was not such an un-political statement as it may sound. Everyone, in Socrates's view, was by nature and training fitted for a particular job, and the mind and way of life of a good artisan were inevitably such as to preclude him from acquiring the knowledge, character and powers of judgment which would make him an adequate guide in political affairs. Such a view contravened the whole basis of democracy as then understood at Athens, where the dogma that one man's opinion is as good as another's was acted on so unreservedly that anyone not a slave or a metic might be appointed to office by lot. Politics, said Socrates, was a craft like any other. It needed natural gifts, but above all things study and applica-tion.[1] Class came into it accidentally, and by no means exclusively. In Xenophon (*Mem.* 3.6) we find Socrates thoroughly deflating Glaucon, Plato's half-brother, who had political ambitions and the right personal connexions to gratify them, by asking him a few pertinent questions. How can he propose to take a leading part in government when (as quickly proves to be the case) he is ignorant of such essential facts of life as the source of the city's revenues, the amount of its income and ex-penditure, its naval and military strength, the state of its frontier garrisons, or how far it is self-supporting and how far dependent on imports?

However, Glaucon had the contacts and the leisure to put that right if he wished. In general Socrates would have agreed with David Hume that 'poverty and hard labour debase the minds of the common

---

[1] It will be seen that I would slightly modify Popper's statment (*O.S.* 1, 128) that the wisdom needed for ruling was only the peculiarly Socratic wisdom of knowing one's own ignorance. This would be like saying that a doctor would be σοφός if he confessed his ignorance of medicine but continued to treat patients. So much is plain from many passages in the Platonic dialogues, and especially from Xen. *Mem.* 4.2.3–5.

people, and render them unfit for any science or ingenious profession'.[1]
In a conversation with Charmides he is said to have described the
Assembly as made up of 'dunces and weaklings, fullers, cobblers,
joiners, smiths, farmers, merchants, traffickers in the market whose
minds are on buying cheap and selling dear . . . men who have never
given a thought to public affairs'.[2] Such contempt for the common
people was so repugnant to Euripides that he put pure Socratic doctrine
into the mouth of a tyrant's lackey, to be refuted by Theseus as the
champion of popular power. 'A poor labourer', says Creon's herald
(*Suppl.* 420), 'even though he be no simpleton, is by his work made incapable of giving heed to the common good.' Like the writer of
Ecclesiasticus (ch. xxxviii), Socrates believed of artificers and work-
masters that 'each becometh wise in his own work', and no city can
become inhabited without them; but like the same writer he would add,
'They shall not be sought for in the council of the people, and in the
assembly they shall not mount on high . . . neither shall they declare
instruction and judgment.'

The significance of this was not lost on his enemies.

The accuser claimed [writes Xenophon] that he led his associates to treat the
established constitution with contempt, declaring that it was folly to appoint
the rulers of the city by lot, when no one would be willing to employ a
navigator or builder or other technician who had been selected in this way,
although the mistakes of such people would have far less disastrous consequences than political mistakes. Arguments like these, the accuser claimed,
incited young men to despise the established political order and turned them
into violent revolutionaries.[3]

[1] See p. 128 above.

[2] Xen. *Mem.* 3.7.6. Since Xenophon himself was no democrat, he may have been inclined
to exaggerate Socrates's contempt for the mob. But, as with Plato, one has to account for the
devotion of such men to him in the first place.

[3] (*a*) *Mem.* 1.2.9. Arist. *Rhet.* 1393 b 4 may be a reflection of this passage, as Taylor noted.
If so, Taylor's suggestion that ἀθλητάς in the received text of Aristotle should be αὐλητάς is
probably right. (See his *VS*, p. 58.)

(*b*) Most scholars since Cobet have held that 'the accuser' mentioned by Xenophon is
Polycrates, writing after Socrates's death (cf. p. 331 above), though Blass believed it was Meletus,
the actual prosecutor at his trial. (See Taylor, *VS*, 4f.) It is claimed that such a political complaint
could not have been brought forward at the trial owing to the amnesty declared by the democrats
at their restoration, for which see p. 382, n. 1, above and cf. Chroust, *S. M. & M.* 257.

(*c*) Chroust (*SM & M*, 58) quotes *Dissoi Logoi* 7 as evidence that objection to the lot was
only taken over by Socrates from the Sophists, but there is no reason why the writer should not
have got it from Socrates, even if his reasons for it are not Socratic. (See p. 319 above.)

No one need accuse Socrates of being anti-democratic, as we now understand democracy, simply because he objected to appointment by lot, for no democracy today, however extreme, would think of resorting to such a bizarre method.[1] Its use at Athens had at least in part a religious motive, being a way of leaving the decision to a god. But Socrates went further, and included popular election in his condemnation. Kings and rulers, he said (according to Xenophon, *Mem.* 3.9.10), are *not those who are chosen by the man in the street* (ὑπὸ τῶν τυχόντων) nor those on whom the lot falls nor those who owe their power to force or trickery, but those who know how to rule.[2] Xenophon describes his classification of the various forms of government thus (*Mem.* 4.6.12):

In his view both monarchy and tyranny were forms of rule, but differed one from the other. The rule of men with their consent and according to the laws of the state was monarchy, but rule over unwilling subjects, not according to law but at the whim of the ruler, was tyranny. A constitution in which the rulers were chosen from among those who fulfilled the requirements of the laws he called an aristocracy, when the qualification for office was property, a plutocracy, and when all the people were eligible, a democracy.

The suggestion in Euripides that Socrates favoured tyranny is monstrously unfair. For him the only tolerable form of government was the rule of law, regarded as a compact entered into voluntarily by all members of the state, whether high or low, and for that reason binding. From this obligation no individual could claim release on a plea of maladministration of the laws by those charged for the time being with giving effect to them, for the reason that such licence, if unchecked, would undermine the framework of law and order which guaranteed and protected the freedom and happiness of the whole body of citizens. The choice before the individual was either to obey the laws, or to get them changed by peaceful persuasion, or else to

---

[1] In speaking of Greek democracy, we are perhaps inclined to forget what a strange method of appointment the lot was. This is rightly emphasized by M. A. Levy in his *Pol. Power in the Anc. World* (p. 92), who calls it 'a method of appointing magistrates which was without precedent and has never since been seriously imitated'. Lesky (*HGL*, 498) more tersely calls it 'an obvious abuse'. On the nature and disadvantages of Athenian democracy see pp. 19f. above; for the use of the lot as its 'hallmark', references in Vlastos, 'Ισον. πολ. 3.

[2] Not 'those who know that they do not know how to rule'. Cf. p. 410, n. 1, above.

emigrate. This is made clear in the *Crito* and has been dealt with already (pp. 143, 146f.). It is not necessarily a democratic view, for both constitutional monarchy and aristocracy, as defined by Socrates, would fulfil his conditions, and he would probably have favoured the latter. Living under a democracy, his principles made him loyal to its laws, and his native Athens had penetrated too deeply into his bones to make the choice of emigration possible. How could Socrates, of all people, desert the most intellectually alive of all Greek cities where he could meet and argue with men of every shade of opinion, the magnet which attracted *sophistai* like Protagoras, Gorgias, Prodicus and Anaxagoras, the home of Euripides and Aristophanes, the place where he could gather around him a brilliant circle of younger men like Antisthenes and Plato? For preference, he never went outside its walls (*Phaedr.* 230c–d). That being so, he must obey the laws, a course not inconsistent with a profound disapproval of the way the city was governed in his latter days. 'No man can be safe', he says to the representative body of citizens which tried him, 'who genuinely opposes you or any other democracy and tries to prevent many wrongs and illegalities from occurring in the city. A true champion of justice must keep to himself and avoid politics or he will not last long.'[1]

The truth is that, although Socrates might call himself the only true statesman (and one can see what he means), he was not interested in politics as ordinarily understood. He lived and spoke according to certain principles, which brought him into conflict, now with the dictatorial Thirty and again with the restored democracy, and set him apart from all political ambitions. We cannot therefore judge of his political ideas until we have made an examination of his whole philosophy of life, into which they had to be fitted as consequential. It included the conviction that not only wealth but power, reputation and honour were as nothing compared to the well-being of one's soul, that the unexamined life was not worth living because goodness, or the right state of the soul, depended on knowledge, especially self-knowledge, and that to suffer any injury, even death, was better than to commit one, because wrongdoing harmed the soul.

[1] Plato, *Apol.* 31e–32a. 'Democracy' (Athenian variety) for πλῆθος, as Tredennick translates it, seems a fair rendering.

If ever it was true that the teaching of a philosopher is not to be separated from the whole man, it is true of Socrates, but so far I have tried to convey a sense of personal acquaintance with him before proceeding to more strictly philosophical topics. One may like or dislike him, but at least it is difficult to disagree with the general verdict of his time as he himself summed it up: 'This reputation which I have—it may be true or it may be false, but at any rate the view is held that Socrates is different from the general run of mankind.' This uniqueness above all was what struck his young friends: 'no other man is like him, living or dead; that's the amazing thing'.[1]

ADDITIONAL NOTE: SOME OPINIONS ON SOCRATES'S POLITICAL VIEWS

In 1939 two American scholars, A. D. Winspear and T. Silverberg, published a study of Socrates purporting to apply to him the genetic method which has had considerable success with Plato and Aristotle. They decided that he came from a humble background, as the son of a skilled artisan, and in his younger days was characterized by a rugged honesty, an acceptance of poverty, and a close connexion with the democratic movement, coupled with a devotion to natural science and a materialistic and sceptical outlook. His democratic activity brought him into contact with intellectual and political leaders and so led to a marked improvement in his material and social position. After a transitional period he was won over to the conservatives, surrendered his independence for the flattering approval of the nobility and threw in his lot with a wealthy and aristocratic set which included Alcibiades, Crito, the family of Aristides, Plato (whose 'loathing for democracy' is apparent) and his relatives, and the wealthy manufacturer Cephalus. The accusations concerning Plato's uncle Critias were all too true, and the apologias of Plato and Xenophon worthless: starting as a vigorous democrat, he became a bloodthirsty tyrant under the influence of none other than Socrates himself. The religion of Socrates accorded with his politics, for 'the new gods whom he was accused of introducing were the mystic divinities of the Pythagorean sects—the militant protective deities of international conservatism' (p. 76). (Taylor is brought into the witness box here, although he traced Socrates's Pythagoreanism back to the *Clouds*, whereas in our authors' view Socrates was then in his healthy sceptical stage, and in the

---

[1] Plato, *Apol.* 34e and *Symp.* 221c.

Apology 'takes great pains to confuse the issue and to confound the recent suspicion with the earlier attack of Aristophanes', p. 77.) Socrates was now engaged in 'a conspiracy against the democratic constitution of Athens and an intellectual assault on the whole democratic way of life' (p. 84). Even his conduct at the trial of the generals is best interpreted not as a high-minded and courageous action, but 'a move in the incredibly complicated game that was being played by both sides in this hectic period' (p. 67). To make him out an idealist, above the contending factions, was a political ruse to which was directed 'the whole effort of the conservative faction'. As the tradition of idealist philosophy began to find expression, Socrates was caught up in it and 'shared the ascent of philosophy from earth to heaven' (a strange thing to say of the man who in the eyes of posterity 'primus philosophiam devocavit e caelo, et in urbibus collocavit et in domos etiam introduxit'; with Cicero at least, the 'conservative faction' failed in their efforts to get Socrates off the ground).

The character of Plato's *Apology* as an elaborate attempt to throw a veil of idealism over Socrates the political intriguer has evidently escaped Sir Karl Popper. He looks upon the *Apology* and *Crito* as Socrates's 'last will', and concludes from them that 'he showed that a man could die, not only for fate and fame and other grand things of this kind, but also for the freedom of critical thought, and for a self-respect which has nothing to do with self-importance or sentimentality' (*O.S.* 194). It was later that Plato betrayed him, 'just as his uncles had done'. He foisted Pythagorean exclusiveness on him, and in the *Republic* made his most successful attempt to implicate him in his own totalitarian ideas (195 f.). For Socrates was a lover of freedom, a democrat and a humanitarian, whereas the thesis of Popper's book is that 'Plato's political demands are purely totalitarian and anti-humanitarian' (88). He finds the Platonic theory of justice identical with the theory and practice of modern totalitarianism, but, far from being in this the heir of Socrates, Plato is guilty of one of the most heinous intellectual betrayals in history.

These two polar opposites may serve to indicate the twisting and turning to which the evidence can be subjected.[1] Nearest to the truth were surely the older generation of liberal thinkers, or as they have been called 'the Oxford school of neo-idealism', typified by A. E. Taylor and Ernest Barker.[2] Everyone may—perhaps must—be influenced by his own political and social preferences, but these at least were men who put scholarship before

---

[1] I would not be misunderstood as intending by this to put the two on the same level. Between the doctrinaire assertions of the American book and the learning and open-mindedness of Popper there can be no comparison.

[2] Havelock, *Lib. Temp.* 19.

apologetics. It may even have been an advantage that they were not caught up in the reaction against modern Fascism and other forms of totalitarianism. At any rate they cannot be accused of hostility to Socrates, and it was the evidence itself that caused Taylor to write of him (*Socr.* 150): 'It was out of the question that, with all his practical loyalty to the constitution, he should approve of the principle of democracy, the sovereignty of the multitude who have no knowledge of the good, and have never dreamed that such knowledge is a necessary qualification for the direction of their affairs.' And again (151, n. 1): 'His disillusionment as the temper of the Athenian democracy grew narrower and harder in the course of the great war would be all the bitterer that he had grown up in the great "fifty years" before the war, and presumably had hoped and expected very different things.' On p. 58, n. 1, he goes so far as to say that Alcibiades was speaking as a genuine Socratic when he told the Spartans that democracy was 'acknowledged folly' (Thuc. 6.89.5).

Barker's conclusion is simple (*Pol. Th. of P. & A.* 51): 'The anti-democratic trend of his teaching is obvious', and of Plato he says (p. 61): 'Belonging to a family of anti-democratic tendencies, he naturally became a member, somewhere about 407, of the circle which had gathered round Socrates. Here too democracy was out of favour . . . Politics was treated as an art: the proper conduct of political affairs was shown to depend on knowledge—a knowledge which neither the democratic assembly itself, nor the officials whom it appointed by the chance of the lot, could be said to possess.'

So far as Socrates had a political standpoint, and so far as it can be disentangled from the aberrations of his ancient admirers and enemies, it is in statements like these that we see him best.

XIV

PHILOSOPHICAL SIGNIFICANCE

(1) 'PHILOSOPHIA DE CAELO DEVOCATA'

For the Greeks themselves the name of Socrates formed a watershed in the history of their philosophy. The reason they give for this is that he turned men's eyes from the speculations about the nature of the physical world which had been characteristic of the Presocratic period, and concentrated attention on the problems of human life. In the most general terms, his message was that to investigate the origin and ultimate matter of the universe, the composition and motions of the heavenly bodies, the shape of the earth or the causes of natural growth and decay was of far less importance than to understand what it meant to be a human being and for what purpose one was in the world. This estimate of Socrates as a turning-point can be traced to Aristotle, though he does not perhaps give it such incontrovertible support as later writers supposed, and the exaggeratedly schematic view of Greek philosophy which it suggests was the work of the Hellenistic and Graeco-Roman periods. The chief testimonies in Aristotle are these:

(i) In the first chapter of *De partibus animalium* he is asserting the importance of recognizing the formal–final cause as well as the necessary or material. This had not been clear to earlier thinkers because they had no adequate conception of essence ('what it is to be' so-and-so) nor of how to define the real being of anything. Democritus had an inkling of it,[1] 'and in Socrates's time an advance was made as to the method, but the study of nature was given up (ἔληξε), and philosophers turned their attention to practical goodness and political science' (642a 28).

(ii) *Metaph.* 987b 1 ff. (and 1078b 17 which repeats it in slightly different words) assigns the change more definitely to Socrates. Aris-

---

[1] For Aristotle on definition before Socrates see vol. II, 483 f. (Democritus and the Pythagoreans: for the latter add *Metaph.* A 987a 20.)

417

totle is explaining Plato's theory of transcendent forms as having arisen out of the problem of how knowledge could be possible in a world which, as the Heracliteans seemed to have demonstrated, was in a perpetual state of flux. This theory he had encountered in his young days.

But when Socrates was busying himself with ethical questions to the complete neglect of nature as a whole, and was seeking in them for the universal and directing the mind for the first time to definitions, Plato, accepting his teaching, came to the conclusion that it applied to something other than the sensible world: the common definition, he reasoned, could not apply to any of the sensibles, since they were always changing.

It will be seen that in both these passages the switch from natural to ethical philosophy comes in by the way. The subject of both is what Aristotle consistently regarded as Socrates's chief contribution to scientific thought, namely his demand for definitions. The first does not even ascribe the switch to Socrates but to philosophers in his time, which is obviously correct. The second does not say that Socrates had never been interested in the study of external nature, but only that he had abandoned it by the time that Plato came into contact with him. Given that Plato was not only old enough to be interested in philosophy but had already been impressed by the difficulties of Heraclitean doctrine, this can hardly have been before his sixty-second year.

The tradition of Socrates as the philosopher who 'brought philosophy down from the skies' became widespread in the Hellenistic period, perhaps under the influence of the Stoic Panaetius,[1] and is familiar to us from Cicero. Its popularity has made it, whatever its historical basis, an important element in the history of thought. After speaking of Pythagoras Cicero says (*Tusc.* 5.4.10):

Ancient philosophy up to Socrates, who was taught by Archelaus the pupil of Anaxagoras, dealt with number and movement, and the source from which all things arise and to which they return; and these early thinkers inquired zealously into the magnitude, intervals and courses of the stars, and all celestial matters. But Socrates first called philosophy down from the sky,

[1] So Pohlenz thought (*Die Stoa* 1.194f., 2.10). Panaetius lived *c.* 185–109 B.C.

set it in the cities and even introduced it into homes, and compelled it to consider life and morals, good and evil.

And in the *Academica* (1.4.15):

Socrates I think—indeed it is universally agreed—was the first to divert philosophy from matters which nature herself has wrapped in obscurity, with which all philosophers before him had been concerned, and apply it to ordinary life, directing its inquiries to virtues and vices, and in general to good and evil. Celestial phenomena he regarded as beyond our comprehension, or at any rate, however well we might understand them, as irrelevant to the good life.

One may well wonder where the Sophists come in in all this. In the *Brutus* (8.30–1) Cicero acknowledges that they existed and that Socrates was acting in opposition to them. He introduces them mainly as rhetorical teachers (rhetoric being the subject of the *Brutus*), but sees the moral import of their teaching. As the power of expert oratory came to be recognized, he says, there arose a class of instructors in the art. This was the time when Gorgias, Protagoras, Prodicus, Hippias and many others rose to fame by claiming, arrogantly enough, to teach how speech could make the weaker cause the stronger.

Socrates opposed them [he goes on] and used to refute their instruction by his own subtle brand of argument. His fertile talk gave rise to a succession of accomplished thinkers, and it is claimed that then for the first time philosophy was discovered—not the philosophy of nature, which was older, but this which we are speaking of, whose subject is good and evil, and the life and manners of men.

If Socrates alone brought about the revolution which redirected men's thoughts from nature to human affairs, the whole first part of this volume has been written in vain. It is one of those clichés or over-simplifications of which written history is full. No doubt the assumption was that the Sophists did not deserve the name of philosophers. The great tradition running from Socrates through Plato to Aristotle already had the upper hand, and with the notable exception of the Epicureans, most schools, however diverse, liked to think of themselves as the heirs of Socratic thought. On the complex causes of the switch of interest from natural science to human affairs enough

Philosophical Significance

has already been said. More interesting now is the much disputed question whether it took place not only in the fifth century at large but in the mind of Socrates himself. Cicero does not deny it any more than Aristotle; indeed by linking Socrates with Archelaus and Anaxagoras he strongly suggests it, and there is much contemporary evidence in its support.

Much of what Cicero says could have been taken from Xenophon, whose contention is, briefly, that on the one hand Socrates was entirely guiltless of the charge of teaching 'what goes on in the heavens and beneath the earth', with all that that implied of atheism and impiety; but on the other hand this was not for want of knowledge: he was himself well versed in such sciences, but disparaged them as being of no practical use. In the first chapter of the *Memorabilia* (11 ff.) we are told that he 'never discussed' nature in general—the origin of the cosmos, or the laws governing celestial phenomena—as most philosophers did. Xenophon gives four reasons why he dismissed all this as folly:[1] (a) It is wrong to neglect the study of human affairs, which concern us much more nearly, so long as knowledge of them is so incomplete;[2] (b) no two scientists agree[3] even on fundamental questions such as whether the sum of things is one or infinitely many, whether everything moves or nothing moves, whether everything comes into existence and decays or nothing does; (c) natural science is of no practical use: studying the laws governing winds, waters and seasons does not give one power over these things; (d) not only are the secrets of the universe unfathomable, but to pry into them is displeasing to the gods.[4]

Xenophon lays great emphasis on the primarily utilitarian character

[1] (a)–(c) are in 1.1.12–15 (with (c) repeated at 4.7.5) and (d) in 4.7.6.
[2] Xenophon and Plato agree on Socrates's point of view here. Cf. *Phaedr.* 229e: 'I cannot yet, in the words of the Delphic precept, "know myself", and it seems to me ridiculous to be studying alien matters when still ignorant of this.'
[3] This of course was not original. Cf. Gorgias, p. 51 above.
[4] It was probably from Cicero rather than Xenophon that Milton took the Socratic sentiments which Adam utters in *P.L.* book 8, when he agrees with Raphael

> That not to know at large of things remote
> From use, obscure and subtle, but to know
> That which before us lies in daily life
> Is the prime wisdom; what is more is fume,
> Or emptiness, or fond impertinence,
> And renders us in things that most concern
> Unpractis'd, unprepared, and still to seek.

of Socrates's arguments. In general this was right. Socrates was an intensely practical person, and his equation of the good with what was useful or beneficial comes out as clearly in some of Plato's dialogues.[1] One may suspect, however, that having learned this, Xenophon sometimes made his own choice of examples according to his more commonplace ideas of what was truly beneficial, and that Socrates had other things in mind. Socrates, he says, advised studying geometry so far as it was necessary for measuring a plot of land to be bought or sold, or calculating the profit it would yield. Similarly astronomy should be learned in order to tell the time, the month and the year, in planning a journey, setting a watch and so on. Enough could be picked up from people like night hunters and pilots. 'But he strongly deprecated going so far as to study bodies revolving in different courses, planets and comets, or wearing oneself out in calculating their distances from the earth, their periods and the causes of them. He could see no use in it.' It is in this chapter too (*Mem.* 4.7.1–5) that he insists that Socrates knew what he was talking about. In the higher mathematics he was 'not inexperienced', and in the 'useless' parts of astronomy 'not uninstructed'.

All this accords sufficiently with the 'autobiographical' passage in Plato's *Phaedo* (96a ff.) to give good grounds for crediting the latter with some historical truth.[2] Socrates is there made to say that 'when he was young' he developed a passion for natural philosophy in the hope that it would explain the 'why' of things—why they are here, why they ever came into being, why they perish again. He studied the current theories of the origin of life, of physiology, psychology, astronomy and cosmology, but found them all unsatisfying and concluded that he had no aptitude for such subjects. His hopes were again raised by hearing that Anaxagoras had named 'mind' as the first cause, but dashed once more when he found that in its details Anaxagoras's

---

[1] See pp. 462 ff. below.

[2] It does not however accord with some of the more metaphysical parts of the *Republic*, where Socrates is made to express contempt for the application of mathematics and astronomy to practical ends, and to advocate using them as a means of directing the mind away from the physical world to that of the eternal Forms. See for instance the remarks about geometry at 526d–e, and their context. On a comprehensive view of all the evidence about Socrates, the only reasonable conclusion is that Plato is there reaching out beyond anything that the historical Socrates ever said. Kierkegaard drew attention to the contrast between Xenophon and Plato in this respect (*Irony*, 61 with n.).

system was just another set of physical theories like the rest. The distinctive character of mind as cause was simply ignored, and the explanations alleged were as material and mechanical as if intelligence had no part in them. Since Socrates remained convinced that a thing could only be explained in terms of its function, he gave up natural science after this and turned to entirely different methods of inquiry.

Plato uses this narrative for his own purposes, but it would be strange indeed if it had no basis in fact. To the inherent improbability may be added the congruence of the account with information from Xenophon, and with the equally reasonable supposition that the representation of Socrates in the *Clouds* is a farcical exaggeration of certain known trends of his thought rather than based on nothing at all. At the time of the *Clouds* Plato was a little boy, and may have slipped in the word 'young' about the Socrates of those days, so long before he knew him, even though he was a man of forty-six. Much more probably Aristophanes knew quite well that Socrates's enthusiasm for science had been on the wane for a long time: if he had ever embraced it, that was quite a sufficient handle for comedy,[1] once Aristophanes had decided to make Socrates the collective repository of most of his *bêtes noires*. The statement of Aristotle that the investigation of nature 'ceased' (ἔληξε) in the time of Socrates is an exaggeration. One has only to think of Diogenes of Apollonia, Archelaus (whose association with Socrates is probably historical; see vol. II, 239) and some of the Sophists themselves—Gorgias the pupil of Empedocles, and interested in his theory of pores and effluences, Alcidamas the author of a *Physicus*, Antiphon in the *Truth*, perhaps also Critias.[2] Democritus too was active until after the death of Socrates, though it is a moot point how much his work was known at Athens.

There is thus impressive evidence for a period in the life of Socrates

---

[1] This chronological point unnecessarily troubled Zeller, who is one of those who have seen not a shred of truth in the autobiographical passage of the *Phaedo*. E. Edelstein (*X. u. P. Bild*, 69–73) thought the historicity of the *Phaedo* guaranteed by its agreement with Xenophon.

[2] For Gorgias see Plato, *Meno* 76c; for Alcidamas, D.L. 8.56; for Antiphon, his frr. 23–32, DK; for Critias, Ar. *De an.* 405b5 (Empedoclean identification of the ψυχή with blood). Diels made this point in *SB Berlin* (1894), but he was probably wrong to build up Polus as a student of physics on the basis of Socrates's ironical σὺ γὰρ τούτων ἔμπειρος at *Gorg.* 465d (p. 357). Some of these, like Gorgias (who laughed at the physical theorists) and Critias, were no doubt mere dabblers; but the theories were certainly continuing to attract interest.

when he was intensely interested in natural science. It would take a lot to shake it, but some have seen it all overthrown—Aristophanes, Xenophon, and Plato himself in the *Phaedo*—by some pleas of Socrates in the *Apology*, a work which all sides in the dispute accept as historical. At 18b he denies that he is 'a wise man who theorizes about the heavens and has investigated everything beneath the earth, and makes the weaker argument the stronger', and at 23d he says these are the stock charges hurled at any philosopher whose accusers are at a loss for material. At 19c he adds,

You have seen it yourselves in the comedy of Aristophanes, someone called Socrates swinging around, declaring that he is treading the air and pouring out a great deal more nonsense about things of which I haven't the slightest understanding. I don't mean to disparage such knowledge . . . but the fact is that I take no interest in it. Moreover I can call most of you as witnesses to this, and I beg all who have ever listened to me talking (and there are a great many such) to inform each other by saying whether any of you have ever heard me discourse either much or little on these topics.

There is, then, the evidence that we have previously considered and there is this. It all happened some 2,400 years ago and our information is far from adequate. We cannot hope to know all that lies behind it. But it is reasonable to claim that these words of Socrates cannot annihilate all the rest. Assuming that they were actually used by him in his defence, we need not accuse him of 'lying for the sake of saving his skin'.[1] His study of the natural world may have ended forty years before, and was in any case an inquiry undertaken to satisfy himself. He never taught it publicly nor promulgated any theories of his own,[2] though no doubt he would eagerly debate the current theories with a few chosen friends. When he took to going

---

[1] The phrase about 'lying to save his skin' occurs in almost identical words in Hackforth (*CPA*, 148) and Popper (*OS*, 308). Popper finds that *Apol.* and *Phaedo* flatly contract each other and that only *Apol.* is to be believed. Hackforth also accepts *Apol.* as historical, and goes so far as to say (p. 147): 'It is not the least use to say that Socrates had dropped these pursuits when he found science unsatisfying . . . for the language which he uses rules out . . . the possibility that at any age whatever he engaged in scientific speculation or research.' Yet rather puzzlingly he can still suppose it 'quite likely that he started with the eager enthusiasm which Plato attributes to him in the famous autobiographical passage of the *Phaedo*' (pp. 152f.).

[2] The 'intellectual autobiography' of the *Phaedo* is a cento of current theories which even now can be assigned to their authors without difficulty. (See Burnet's notes *ad loc.*) There is no hint that Socrates made any original contribution.

round Athens accosting worthy citizens and questioning them, or talking to any bright young men whom he saw in the palaestra, it was because he had already recognized the futility of the scientists' speculations and the urgent need to know oneself, to find out 'what is pious, what impious; what fine, what ugly; what is just, what is unjust; what is prudence, madness, courage or cowardice; what is a state and what a statesman; what is meant by governing men, and what is a governor'.[1] If these were the questions that he had been pressing on the attention of all and sundry for the last thirty or forty years, can anyone say that his claim of indifference to natural science, made when he was on trial for his life, was falsified by an earlier period of study in it? In any case he had never taken it up for its own sake, or with the same questions in mind as the physical theorists themselves. His question was 'Why?' Why should there be a world like this, and why should we be in it? At first he thought this was what the scientists were asking too, and plunged into their discussions, until he discovered that they were only interested in the question *how* it all came about. Diogenes of Apollonia may have been an exception,[2] and it is noteworthy that in characterizing Socrates as a scientist it is first and foremost the air-theories of Diogenes which Aristophanes puts into his mouth. But Socrates may have already broken with natural science when Diogenes wrote, and while acknowledging his teleological tendency was not likely to be attracted back by a materialistic theory which embodied the directing power in one of the physical elements. Nevertheless, when he became unpopular with those in power, his earlier interest in the subject could be brought up against him like the youthful left-wing escapades of some respected American senator or philosopher today.

Socrates gave up science for ethics, the study of nature for the pursuit of practical principles. But, perhaps because of his early scientific studies, he insisted that ethics itself was a field of exact knowledge calling for the application of rigorous scientific method. For this method Aristotle believed that science would be for ever in

---

[1] Xen. *Mem.* 1.1.16. So also Aristotle, e.g. *EE* 1216b 4: Socrates used to investigate what is justice, what courage, and so with all the other parts of virtue, because he equated the virtues with knowledge.

[2] See vol. II, p. 362, n. 1.

his debt, while he deplored its exercise in a sphere to which he considered it inappropriate. In Aristotle's eyes (as Gigon has pointed out) Socrates plays a double role in the history of philosophy: he produced a method and a principle indispensable for the proper study and classification of natural phenomena, while at the same time his name marks the end of the scientific and the beginning of the ethical epoch in philosophy.[1] What this method was is the next thing that we have to inquire, only pausing first to note that here at last we have put our finger on the essential difference between Socrates and the Sophists. If the word *philosophy* is taken in its strict sense, as the search for knowledge, the old tradition was justified that he and he alone brought philosophy into human life. That is, he sought to make ethics and politics the subject of a scientific inquiry which should reveal universal laws or truths, in opposition to the scepticism and relativism that had turned all things into matters of opinion and left men's minds at the mercy of the persuader with the smoothest tongue. Even a Protagoras could not escape from this; a Gorgias or a Polus gloried in it.

(2) INDUCTION AND DEFINITION

As I have said,[2] for a thumbnail version of an earlier philosopher's contribution we can generally turn with confidence to Aristotle. Here are no dramatic masterpieces, to tantalize the historian of philosophy as much as they delight the lover of great literature. His bald notes may need elaboration, and possibly modification in the light of his known philosophical assumptions, but their terseness and lucidity make them excellent starting-points for our own study of one of his predecessors. The extent of Socrates's contribution to philosophy, as distinct from Plato's, was probably already a matter of debate in his own time, and his summing-up is this (*Metaph.* 1078b27): 'There are two things which may justly be credited to Socrates, inductive arguments and general definition.' The mention of definition connects the sentence with other passages, already quoted for their bearing on the

[1] See Gigon in *Mus. Helv.* 1959, 192. Compare also the interesting remarks of Deman, *Témoignage*, 78f.: 'Socrate s'est consacré à la recherche morale, mais il a apporté à cette recherche une préoccupation strictement scientifique', etc.

[2] P. 357 above. In the same section will be found what needs to be said about Aristotle's value as a source.

transition from natural to ethical philosophy (p. 417), whose main purport was the methodical advance initiated by Socrates in the comprehension of essence through definition. It is hardly fanciful to detect a note of disappointment in Aristotle's observation that the first man to grasp the importance of these indispensable aids to scientific thinking was the one who abandoned theoretical science for ethics, a subject in which, as he never tires of reminding us in his own ethical writings,[1] scientific accuracy neither can nor should be demanded.

Induction, Aristotle tells us (*Top.* 105a13), is the progress from the particular to the universal, and he illustrates it with an example of Socratic type: if the best navigator is the expert (in Aristotle's words 'the one with knowledge') and the best driver the expert, and so on, we infer that in general the expert (or knowledgeable) is in every occupation the best. Another example might be taken from Plato's *Gorgias* (474d ff.). Socrates gets Polus to agree that bodies are called beautiful (*kala*) because they are either useful or pleasure-giving, and then that the same is true of shapes, colours, sounds, *nomoi* and learning. From this the general conclusion is drawn that if anything is more beautiful than any other it must be either more useful or more pleasant or both. The mind is 'led on' (as the Greek word for induction, *epagōgē*, may signify),[2] from the observation of particular

---

[1] E.g. *EN* 1179b 1: οὐκ ἔστιν ἐν τοῖς πρακτοῖς τέλος τὸ θεωρῆσαι ἕκαστα καὶ γνῶναι, ἀλλὰ μᾶλλον τὸ πράττειν αὐτά. Not to have seen this was in his view a major error on the part of Socrates. Cf. pp. 452f. below.

[2] The word only becomes technical in Aristotle, and it is difficult to be sure what is the idea behind it. (Cf. however Plato, *Pol.* 278 a.) It often seems to be that suggested above (so Mure in note to O. Tr. of *An. Post.* 71a 8); e.g. at *Top.* 156a 4, ἐπάγοντα μὲν ἀπὸ τῶν καθ' ἕκαστον ἐπὶ τὸ καθόλου the implicit object of the verb is pretty clearly the interlocutor, and this personal reference is confirmed by the use of the passive at *An. Post.* 81b 2, ἀδύνατον δὲ τὰ καθόλου θεωρῆσαι μὴ δι' ἐπαγωγῆς . . . ἐπαχθῆναι δὲ μὴ ἔχοντας αἴσθησιν ἀδύνατον and 71a 21 ἅμα ἐπαγόμενος ἐγνώρισεν. Cicero seems to preserve this meaning when he defines it (in its translation 'inductio') as 'oratio quae rebus non dubiis captat assensionem eius quicum instituta est' (*De inv.* 1.31.51). On the other hand at *Top.* 108b 10, τῇ καθ' ἕκαστα ἐπὶ τῶν ὁμοίων ἐπαγωγῇ τὸ καθόλου ἀξιοῦμεν ἐπάγειν. οὐ γὰρ ῥᾴδιόν ἐστιν ἐπάγειν μὴ εἰδότας τὰ ὅμοια the verb seems to be used in a dual sense, of *bringing on* or adducing individual instances in order to *bring out*, or make apparent, the universal. The active in ἐπάγειν μὴ εἰδότας contrasts strongly with the passive with μὴ ἔχοντας at 81b 5. So also Cicero shortly after the passage just quoted has 'illud quod inducemus', not 'illum quem'. ἐπάγεσθαι (middle) is so used in the Hippocratic *De fractt.*, which may be slightly later in date than Aristotle. See the passages quoted by Taylor, *VS*, 73. On pp. 112f. he suggests that there may have been a different underlying metaphor. (For a full discussion of this question see Ross, *Analytics*, 481–3.)

instances to grasp a general characteristic shared by all the members of a class. It may be a class of people, things or events. Because the sun has risen with unfailing regularity for thousands of years, we infer not only that it will rise tomorrow but that we can predict the exact time of its rising in any given part of the world. An inductive conclusion may be falsified at any time by a new or newly discovered fact, unless it is made into a truism by refusal to give the name x to anything that has not all the qualities that we have decided to associate with x's. This we do not usually do. The black swans of Australia were not denied the name because hitherto the generalization 'All swans are white' had seemed a safe one. Yet without the constant use of this device of drawing inductions from a limited experience it would be impossible either for laymen to carry on their everyday lives or for scientists to pursue their researches. Since Socrates only employed a rudimentary form of it, with his eye on the good life rather than on logic or scientific method, its full discussion will be more appropriate in connexion with Aristotle. Yet it may be said that, though everyone uses it, with varying degrees of consciousness of what they are doing, logicians are as much concerned today as in the time of Aristotle with the problems that it raises and the obstinate fact that, indispensable as it is to thought and action, it appears to have no perfectly rational justification. Briefly, there are three possibilities:

(*a*) Complete enumeration. The general statement is only made with knowledge of every case falling under it. ('All boys in this school are in the age-group 12–18.') Here it does not seem that any inference has been drawn, but to make the general statement explicitly is a useful step towards drawing further conclusions and combining it with other similar information to make wider generalizations. It is only in these cases that induction can be reduced to valid syllogistic form as Aristotle wished to reduce it.

(*b*) Admission that the conclusion is only probable, and subject to review if a negative instance should be found. ('All schoolboys like holidays.')

(*c*) The claim that the human mind has a faculty of intuition enabling it to 'see' the universal after examination of a sufficient number of individual instances. Complete enumeration, except in certain very limited cases like the one cited above, is impossible at the individual level, but may be possible (or so at least it seemed to Aristotle) at the level of species. Consequently, in treating induction as a part of formal logic, Aristotle operates with species as units. He did however believe in intuition as justifying the initial inductive leap from particulars to the first, or lowest, universal, and in this he was assisted by the belief in specific forms as substantively existing essences, which was a legacy from Socrates through Plato. If specific form is something fixed in nature, it is reasonable to suppose that it may be detected and defined after only a partial examination of the particular instances which share it.

This is to anticipate. To return to Socrates, he was on the one hand at a much earlier, more tentative stage of thought, before logic had been codified and formalized at all, nor was its formalization his aim as it was Aristotle's; but on the other hand, because some form of inductive reasoning, more or less conscious, is a necessity of life, let alone of anything that can be called philosophy, it has been argued that Aristotle was wrong in attributing it in any special way to Socrates. On this it is sufficient to quote Ross:

It would, of course, be as untrue to say that Socrates invented inductive argument as, in Locke's phrase, to suppose that God has been 'so sparing to men to make them barely two-legged creatures, and left it to Aristotle to make them rational'. Professor Taylor can without difficulty produce instances of the use of ἐπάγεσθαι for inductive argument from the early Hippocratic writings. But surely anyone can recognize in Socrates, whether as depicted in the *Memorabilia* or as depicted in what are generally known as the 'Socratic' dialogues of Plato, a careful testing of general opinions by the examination of particular cases that is foreign to the previous schools of Greek philosophy, with which Aristotle is here contrasting Socrates. In this sense the ascription of inductive argument to him is thoroughly justified.

And again:

Aristotle cannot mean that Socrates was the first person who used inductive arguments or gave general definitions, but that he was the first who recognized the importance of them and systematically used the former to get the latter. The inductive arguments referred to are not scientific inductions but arguments from analogy such as we often find Socrates using in the *Memorabilia* and in Plato's 'Socratic' dialogues.[1]

[1] Ross, *Metaph.* 1.xliii and 2.422. The reference is to Taylor's *VS*, 72ff.

Aristotle's own way of describing Socratic arguments is somewhat similar, when he introduces them as a particular mode of persuasion in the *Rhetoric* (1393b4). The use of illustrative examples, he says, resembles induction, which is the starting-point of all reasoning.[1] One variety of it, which Aristotle calls 'the parallel' (παραβολή), is represented by the practice of Socrates, for instance the argument against filling government offices by lot on the ground that no one would use the lot to select athletes for a contest or a steersman from among a crew. The general lesson of these parallels, he adds, is that one ought in every case to choose the man who understands the job.

The nature of analogy, and its relation to induction, is a complex and much-discussed question. Perhaps the most satisfactory course is to refer analogy to the comparison of single cases and reserve induction, as Aristotle did, for the argument which leads from single cases to the universal.[2] Socrates employed both methods, but in the above passage Ross appears to be regarding analogy (as it is often regarded) as an earlier, looser and less systematic form of induction. To keep to induction (as credited by Aristotle to Socrates) for the present, its function is to establish, from a number of observed instances, a general characteristic of a whole class, e.g. of broad-leafed trees that they are deciduous. (The example is Aristotle's.) Although there must be thousands of broad-leafed trees which no one has ever seen, the zoologist draws this conclusion with confidence. Induction leads to definition because a definition consists of a collection of these general characteristics, selected with certain requirements in mind:[3]

(*a*) They must be essential to membership of the class, not accidental attributes of certain individuals within it. Many men have blue eyes, but this characteristic has no place in a definition of the species 'man'.

[1] Cf. *An. Post.* 100b 3, δῆλον δὴ ὅτι ἡμῖν τὰ πρῶτα ἐπαγωγῇ γνωρίζειν ἀναγκαῖον. This is because all knowledge originates in sensation, and it is induction that enables us to pass beyond the sensation of particulars to apprehension of the universals which provide the premises for syllogism. On *Rhet.* 1393b 4 see also p. 411, n. 3 (*a*) above.

[2] On the relation of induction to analogy see Lloyd, *P. & A.* 172–5 and Robinson, *P.'s Earlier D.* 207, and cf. p. 368, n. 1 above.

[3] These requirements are Aristotle's, based on his own development of Socratic thought including the concept of specific form (εἶδος).

(*b*) They must be collectively sufficient to mark off[1] the class of objects to be defined from all other classes of objects whatsoever. To call man a two-legged living creature is to name characteristics essential to the human race, but they do not constitute a definition, because they do not mark it off from the race of birds.[2] The sum of essential attributes forming the content of the definition was called, among other things, the form (*eidos*) of the class. The use of this word as a technical term of logic is post-Socratic, for there was no science of logic before Plato, and it was only Aristotle who systematized it and gave it anything like a technical vocabulary. But *eidos*, as we shall see, was one of the names used by Socrates for the essential nature that he was seeking to define. In popular use the word commonly designated outward appearance or shape, perhaps particularly of human physique, as being handsome or ugly, 'looking' powerful, weak and so forth. But in both literary and technical (especially medical) language it already meant the peculiar character or essential nature of anything, approximating sometimes to species or class. Thucydides says of the plague (2.50) that 'its *eidos* was beyond description', and in Herodotus the word approaches the meaning of class or species when he speaks (1.94.3) of 'dice, knucklebones, balls and all other *eidea* of playthings'. It is frequent in the medical writings, e.g. *Epidemics* 3.12 (III, 92 L.), 'Many other *eidea* of fevers were widespread, tertian, quartan, nightly, continuous . . .'[3] The use of it by Socrates led to momentous developments when it was taken over by Plato.

(3) RELEVANCE OF INDUCTION AND DEFINITION TO SOCRATES'S ETHICAL AIMS

The interest of Socrates in definitions is one of the best-attested facts about him. Apart from Aristotle, it is insisted on by both Xenophon

[1] This is the primary meaning of ὁρίζειν (ὁρίζεσθαι), the verb translated 'define' in Xenophon, Plato and Aristotle, namely to mark off the ὅροι or limits of a field or other territory from those of its neighbour.

[2] There is a story that Plato defined man as a featherless biped, whereupon Diogenes the Cynic produced a plucked chicken and said, 'There is Plato's man for you' (D.L. 6.40).

[3] Taylor's review of the uses of the word in *VS* may be conveniently studied in the summary of Gillespie (*CQ*, 1912, 179 f.), where it is followed by a criticism.

(who gives numerous examples besides the general statement, already quoted on p. 424, at *Mem.* 1.1.16) and Plato. But what was his motive? Again our authorities are unanimous, that it was not scientific but practical.[1] Aristotle's bare statement to this effect may be supplemented in particular from Plato. One feature in the thought and speech of his contemporaries seemed to Socrates particularly harmful. Whether in conversation, in political speeches or in the oratory of the law-courts, they made constant use of a great variety of general terms, especially terms descriptive of ethical ideas—justice, temperance, courage, *areté* and so forth. Yet at the same time it was being asserted by Sophists and others that such concepts had no basis in reality. They were not god-given virtues, but only 'by convention', varying from place to place and age to age. Serious thought about the laws of human behaviour had begun with a radical scepticism, which taught that it rested on no fixed principles but each decision must be made empirically and *ad hoc*, based on the expediency of the immediate situation (*kairos*). From this theoretical soil grew the pride of youthful rhetoric in its ability to sway men to or from any course of action by mastery of the persuasive use of words. In such an atmosphere it was not surprising that there was much confusion in the meanings attached to moral terms. Socrates noted this,[2] and disapproved of it. If these terms corresponded to any reality at all, he thought, then one meaning must be true and the others false. If on the other hand the Sophists were right, and their content was purely relative and shifting, it must be wrong to go on using the same words for different things and they ought to go out of use. He himself was convinced that

[1] That the first attempt at systematic inductive methods was made in the context of practical action adds interest to some remarks of the eighteenth-century Dutch mathematician s'Gravesande as paraphrased by E. Cassirer (*Ph. of E.* 61). On the inductive axiom that past experience is a guide to conclusions about the future he said: 'This is not strictly a logical, but a pragmatic axiom; its validity does not lie in the necessity of thought, but in that of action. For all action, all practical relationships with things, would be impossible, if we could not assume that the lessons of former experience will be valid in the future. Scientific prediction does not then involve the syllogistically necessary conclusions of formal logic; it is, nevertheless, a valid and indispensable conclusion by analogy. But we must and can be content with such a conclusion, for that must indeed be true whose denial would imply the negation of all man's empirical existence and all his social life.' On this Cassirer himself comments that 'things have taken a strange turn; the certainty of physics is no longer based on purely logical presuppositions but on a biological and sociological presupposition'.

[2] See the passages from Plato and Xenophon quoted on p. 165 above.

the first alternative was true, and that it was illegitimate and unhelpful for an orator to exhort the people to adopt a certain course of action as being the wisest or most just, or for advocates and jury to debate whether an individual had acted well or badly, justly or unjustly, unless those concerned were agreed upon what wisdom, justice and goodness *are*. If people are not agreed on that, but though using the same words mean different things by them, they will be talking at cross-purposes, and their discussions can make no progress either intellectually or—when ethical terms are in question—morally. Here Socrates was raising for the first time a fundamental question of philosophy, the question by what right we use general terms, including all nouns except proper names, and what is the factual content of such terms, and Aristotle was right to see that this was so. At the same time, as Aristotle also recognized, he did not see it as a logical or ontological question, but simply as an indispensable requirement for what to him was much more important: the discovery of the right way to live.[1]

In Socrates's opinion, then, if order is to be restored to thought on the rights and wrongs of human conduct, the first necessity is to decide what justice, goodness and other virtues are. According to his method, as described by Aristotle and illustrated in Xenophon and Plato (especially but not exclusively the earlier dialogues), the inquiry consists of two stages. The first is to collect instances to which both parties to a discussion agree that the name under consideration may be applied, e.g., if it is piety, to collect instances of agreed pious acts. Secondly, the collected instances are examined in order to discover some common quality in them by virtue of which they bear that name. If they do not share such a common quality, then he claimed it would be improper to go on applying the same word to them all. This common quality, or nexus of common qualities, is their nature, essence

---

[1] This may be what Aristotle had in mind when he said (*Metaph.* 1078b24) that Socrates sought for definitions because he wanted to syllogize, and a definition is the starting-point of a syllogism. Once again he has put it in his own language and seen it as a purely logical process, but Zeller (*Ph. d. Gr.* 129 with n. 2) has pointed to some cases where Socrates is shown using a definition as the basis for further demonstration; and this demonstration is always ethical, to prove that a certain line of conduct should or should not be followed. We must learn to distinguish good from bad, useful from harmful, in order to follow the one and avoid the other (διαλέγοντας κατὰ γένη τὰ μὲν ἀγαθὰ προαιρεῖσθαι τῶν δὲ κακῶν ἀπέχεσθαι Xen. *Mem.* 4.5.11, and cf. 4.1.5).

or 'form'[1] considered as pious. It will provide in fact, if it can be discovered, the definition of piety, abstracted from the accidental properties of time and circumstance which differentiate the individual cases falling under it. As a scientific method this is of course the necessary basis of any study like botany or zoology whose chief task is one of classification. Animals and plants are grouped in genera, species and sub-species according as they exhibit in common certain properties which are regarded by the trained investigator as structural and essential, though often very different from those which strike the eye of the casual observer. As such it was developed by Plato (compare his insistence on classifying according to the *natural* joints or divisions, κατ᾽ ἄρθρα ᾗ πέφυκεν, *Phaedr.* 265 e) and especially appreciated by Aristotle as the first systematic zoologist.

Socrates was not interested in botany or zoology but in his fellow men, and what he wanted to see classified and defined was their actions.

If anyone contradicted him on some point [says Xenophon] without being able to make himself clear, asserting without sufficient proof that so-and-so was wiser, more statesmanlike or braver, or anything of the same kind, he would lead the whole discussion back to the assumed definition.[2] 'You say your man is a better citizen than mine? Then let us consider what we mean by a good citizen.'

[1] That logic is not yet a science, but still feeling its way, is well shown by the variety of words and phrases used by Socrates in attempting to get his idea across, in contrast to the firm technical vocabulary of Aristotle. The *Meno* is a treasury of these. Socrates asks for the οὐσία (being, essence, 72b); the ἕν τι εἶδος (single form) which all the instances possess (72c and d); the ἕν κατὰ πάντων, διὰ πάντων, ἐπὶ πᾶσι (the one thing said of them all, running through them all, in them all, 73d, 74a, 75a); τὸ ἐπὶ πᾶσι ταὐτόν (what in them all is the same, 75a); ᾧ ταὐτόν εἰσιν ἅπασαι (that by which they are all the same, 72c); κατὰ ὅλου ἀρετῆς πέρι ὅτι ἐστί (of virtue in general, what it is, 77a); and frequently simply τί ποτ᾽ ἐστί (what it is). Cf. *Lysis* 222b and 223b, *Prot.* 361c, *Laches* 190d, *Charm.* 159a (where the definitions sought are respectively of a friend, of ἀρετή in general, of courage, and of σωφροσύνη).

[2] ἐπὶ τὴν ὑπόθεσιν, *Mem.* 4.6.13. Marchant (Loeb ed.) was surely right to translate the word by 'definition'. The man must be brought to see the underlying assumption of his loosely worded encomium, which is that wisdom, statesmanship and courage have a certain fixed nature and that the subject's behaviour is in accordance with that nature. Only if he can define his standard of reference will his praise have any significance. Similarly at *Euthyphro* 9d, τοῦτο ὑποθέμενος means 'on the definition that you have given' (i.e. of piety, that it is what is pleasing to the gods). Again in the *Meno*, when pressed to inquire whether virtue can be taught before they have decided what it is, Socrates reluctantly agrees on condition that they proceed ἐξ ὑποθέσεως, that is, on a hypothetical *definition*: if virtue is knowledge, then it will be teachable. This use of ὑπόθεσις in both Xenophon and Plato (cf. also *Phaedo* 100b ὑποθέμενος εἶναί τι καλὸν κτλ.) suggests strongly that it was genuinely Socratic, as Ross has pointed out (*Class. Ass. Proc.* 1933, 21).

Who is the good citizen in finance, in war, on an embassy, in debate before the Assembly? From such examples a conclusion could be drawn about good citizenship in general. The fault that he usually had to correct in his interlocutors is that when faced with a question of definition like 'What is courage?' or 'What is piety?' they saw no further than the first stage of the dual process. Some examples are:

Euthyphro, 62 d:

What I wanted you to tell me was not one or two of the numerous actions that are pious, but the actual form that we spoke of, which makes them all pious. You did say, didn't you, that impious acts were impious and pious acts pious by reason of a single form? Show me then what the form itself is, so that I can refer to it and use it as a standard, calling an action by you or anyone else pious if it resembles it but not otherwise.

Theaet. 146 e:

But the question, Theaetetus, was not what are the objects of science or how many sciences there are. My purpose in asking you was not to count them but to find out what knowledge itself is.

The same point is made in other dialogues (e.g. at *Laches* 191 c ff.), but the best exposition of the method is in the *Meno*. Without preamble this impetuous young man bursts out with the burning question of the day: 'Can virtue (*areté*) be taught, or how is it acquired?' How can I tell you that, replies Socrates, when I don't even know what it is[1] and have never met anyone who does? Meno is astonished. Has he not met Gorgias, and did not Gorgias know? Here Socrates exhibits a little of his notorious irony. It is Meno who interests him, and whom he wishes to draw out. So he says, 'I'm afraid I'm a forgetful person, and can't say just now what I thought at the time. Probably he did know, and you know his views, so remind me—or tell me yourself if you will. I expect you agree with him.' Meno does, 'so', says Socrates, 'we can leave him out of it, but tell me what *you* say virtue is'. The victim is now in the net, and proceeds to give a string of instances and types of virtue to his own satisfaction, but not to that

---

[1] In the *Protagoras* the question whether virtue can be taught is discussed at length, but there too Socrates returns at the end to what is for him the prior question of definition. They have got themselves into a muddle, he says, and what is needed is 'to make a determined attack on the question what virtue itself is: then we could return to the question whether or not it can be taught' (361 c).

of Socrates, who complains that he has been given a swarm of virtues when he only wanted the one thing, virtue. Taking up this metaphor, he gets Meno to agree that if asked what a bee is he would not list and describe different kinds of bee but mention the points in which they were all similar. Can he not do the same for virtue? Meno demurs: virtue does not seem to him to be on the same footing.[1] But under Socrates's guidance, and with specimen definitions of shape and colour to help him, he makes more than one attempt, only to have them shown up as defective by Socrates. This is done by citing counter-instances ('Virtue is the capacity to govern men': 'Then is it virtue in a slave to govern his master?' and so on), because naturally the same inductive process of adducing instances, which can lead to a sound definition, also shows up those that are faulty.[2] Young Meno is easy game, and can only collapse with the complaint that Socrates is a wizard who paralyses his mind and his tongue. But, although he

[1] See 72d, 73a, 74a–b.

[2] I hope it is not simple-minded to say this. Ross (*Class. Ass. Proc.* 1933, 20f.) says Socrates used inductive arguments in two ways: (*a*) to reach the definition of a virtue by agreement, examining cases in order to elicit the general principle common to them; (*b*) destructively, pointing out instances which conform to the proposed definition but are obviously wrong. Robinson (*P.'s Earlier D.* 48) even gives as one reason for his claim that there is no necessary connexion between *epagoge* and definition the fact that 'epagoge is a means to the destruction rather than the establishment of definitions'. But surely the method of arriving at a conclusion is also appropriate for testing it, amending it if necessary, and so getting nearer the truth. The conclusion 'All swans are white' was arrived at by induction, and induction showed it to be inadequate. The result is not destructive, but brings the naturalist nearer to the correct definition of a swan.

It can also be said (with Popper in his *Logic of Sc. Discovery*) that the process of falsifying a generalization is not inductive but deductive; i.e., if I understand the matter correctly, it is an argument of the form: 'The general assumption demands that all x's are y; but a, which is an x, is not y; therefore the assumption is false.' This way of putting it is linked to Popper's contention that in science all inferences are deductive: the scientist does not reason from observations to a general hypothesis (which of course can never be *proved* by observation), but first propounds a hypothesis and then tests it as far as possible by observation and experiment. (See also Hare, *Freedom and Reason*, 87f., 92, 109.) It would be rash to become involved at this point in the whole problem of the nature of induction, on which Popper has thrown so much light. But, after reading with some care what he says on the subject in *Conj. and Ref.* ch. 1, I still feel that the initial choice of one theory rather than another must be largely determined by prior observations, even taking into account his remarks about the selectiveness of our observations from early infancy and his claim that the observations which the theory sets out to explain themselves presuppose a framework of theories (p. 47). After all, 'unexpected and unexplained observations' do present themselves (p. 222), and we try to explain them by theory. As excuse for these presumptuous remarks I can only plead the extraordinary interest of Popper's views, which require a book, not a footnote, for their appraisal. To return to the safer ground of history, the process of scientific discovery as Aristotle saw it was from observations to general hypotheses, and in the use of *epagoge* he considered himself to be following Socrates.

himself is in need of the logical lesson that enumeration of instances is not the same as definition of a general concept, his vague feeling that virtue is not something to be defined like a biological species marks him as the pupil of Gorgias and reminds us that Socrates was not only teaching elementary logic but taking his stand on a much bigger question, the universality of value-judgments, in which he was opposed not only by the Sophists but afterwards by Aristotle, who recognized the scientific importance of his method while at the same times denying its applicability in this sphere.[1]

The *Meno* provides an example of the kind of questioning in which Socrates indulged, and which, with its 'numbing' effect that called forth such bitter complaint from Meno, made him so unpopular with all but his friends and sympathizers. We can now give more definite content to the picture of himself which he drew at his trial, going tirelessly round the city, in obedience as he said to the will of Apollo, and questioning one class of citizens after another—poets, politicians, craftsmen—in order to discover wherein lay their claim to wisdom and knowledge. He had one simple criterion. If a man knew anything, he could 'give an account (*logos*)' of it, and in his hands that maid-of-all-work among Greek words takes on the meaning 'definition' or something closely approaching it.[2] To the poets, then, he would put the question 'What is poetry?', to the politicians 'What do you understand by a *politeia*?' or 'You say you will establish a just order of society; now what exactly do you mean by justice?' And the poets would reply, 'Why, when I say poetry I mean the *Iliad* and the *Agamemnon*, and that little thing of my own that I recited at Olympia last month.' Then Socrates would set to work patiently and tirelessly as he did with Meno, pointing out that he had not asked for a list of poems but for a *logos* of the *ousia*—the essential nature—of poetry. What was the common property shared by Homer, Solon, Empedocles, the tragedians, down to the latest paean of Tinnychus that everyone was singing, which made people include them all under

---

[1] See pp. 253 f. above.

[2] Cf. *Laches* 190 c οὐκοῦν ὅ γε ἴσμεν, κἂν εἴποιμεν δήπου τί ἐστιν, Xen. *Mem.* 4.6.1 Σωκράτης γὰρ τοὺς μὲν εἰδότας τί ἕκαστον εἴη τῶν ὄντων ἐνόμιʒε καὶ τοῖς ἄλλοις ἂν ἐξηγεῖσθαι δύνασθαι. In Plato we find this sense of λόγος fairly well established, e.g. in ὁ τοῦ δικαίου λόγος or λόγος τῆς πολιτείας (*Rep.* 343 a, 497 c).

one head as poetry rather than calling them history or philosophy or anything else? And when any suggestion of the poets was refuted by the mention of another acknowledged poet who did not fit into their proposed definition, and they went away in a bad temper, Socrates could only sigh and conclude that they must indeed compose their poems in a divine frenzy, as mouthpieces of the god; for if they did it of themselves they would assuredly know what they were doing and could give a *logos* of it. With the craftsmen he was more fortunate. Ask a bronze-worker what he means by the *cire-perdue* method of casting, and he can give you a lucid and adequate answer. Their fault was a lack of modesty in failing to realize that they had not the competence to pronounce with equal ability on matters outside their province.

(4) THE NATURE OF SOCRATIC DEFINITION

The definitions sought by Socrates are sometimes criticized on the ground that they are 'persuasive definitions', a useful term which does not necessarily involve anachronism because it was first coined in the twentieth century.[1] In view of what has been written about this by others, what follows can be little more than a summing-up, and a fairly extensive use of quotation may be excusable. A persuasive definition is one in which the author, instead of simply seeking to clarify the usage of a word and prevent misunderstanding, has argued for that meaning of it of which he himself approves, and which, if adopted, will incline people towards the course of action which he thinks right. He takes a term expressive of value, like goodness, justice or beauty, to which people inevitably react favourably (it has 'emotive force'), and by defining it in a certain way enlists this favourable reaction to further his own moral or aesthetic preferences. 'Persuasive definitions alter the descriptive meaning of a word without disarming its emotive force; hence they are effective instruments of valuational reform.' 'The effect of saying that "the true definition of justice is $y\chi$" is to make people . . . apply the evaluative tone of the word "justice" to the thing described by the words $y\chi$.'[2]

[1] By C. L. Stevenson. See his article 'Persuasive Definitions' in *Mind*, 1938, or his book *Ethics and Language*.
[2] R. M. Gordon in *J. of Philos.* 1964, 436; R. Robinson, *Definitions*, 166.

Since Socrates's attempts to elicit definitions were concentrated on terms of value, it is very natural that he should fall under suspicion of acting in this way. 'The basic criticism, however', writes R. M. Gordon (*loc. cit.*), 'is not that Socrates surreptitiously *reforms* by offering definitions that are not morally neutral, but that he offers definitions that are not morally neutral.'

It would certainly be difficult to maintain a criticism that Socrates '*surreptitiously* reforms' (to transfer Mr Gordon's italics) by his definitions, whether or not they were morally neutral. It may be assumed at the outset that moral reform was his openly avowed object.[1] 'En cultivant la science il entendait promouvoir la vertu.'[2] But it does not follow that he was guilty of promulgating persuasive definitions. It may of course be true, as Stevenson wrote, that 'to choose a meaning [for justice] is to take sides in a social struggle', and that when theorists have sought to avoid the element of persuasion by defining their terms, 'ironically enough, these very definitions involved that same persuasion; and in a way that veiled and confused it, by making it appear to be purely intellectual analysis' (*loc. cit.* 344). It scarcely needs to be said that Socrates was unaware of the emotive theory of ethical language, although had it been explained to him he would have opposed it on the ground that to say '"this is right" means only "I approve of this"' was to play into the hands of sophistic relativism. Nor could it occur to him that in seeking to discover and define the good for man he might be guilty of the curiously named 'naturalistic fallacy' which, according to G. E. Moore, must inevitably be committed by any definition of 'good'.[3] In view of later advances in ethical theory, it may be claimed that the general question whether

---

[1] It hardly seems necessary to quote evidence, but one might mention that immediately after speaking of his continual search for definitions of moral terms (in *Mem.* 1.1.16, quoted on p. 424 above), Xenophon goes on to say that it was a knowledge of these and similar things which in his opinion would produce fine, liberal characters (καλούς κἀγαθούς), and those altogether ignorant of them were little better than slaves. In Plato's *Laches* (190b) he says that, because his two friends want their sons to acquire virtue and have their characters improved, therefore they must find out what virtue is. 'For how can we advise anyone how to acquire something when we have no idea what it is?'

[2] Deman, *Témoignage*, 80.

[3] See for instance *Theories of Ethics*, ed. Philippa Foot, p. 5. She adds that Moore never succeeded in explaining what he meant by a 'natural' property, and it was this difficulty which Stevenson claimed to be removing by his theory of emotive meaning.

an ethical term can be defined other than persuasively is no longer arguable, but, if intention is allowed to be relevant at all, one or two things may be added about Socrates. He was not a dogmatic moralist but an inquirer, who believed that an honest search after the truth about the principles governing human behaviour was most likely, simply because of the better understanding which it would ensure, to lead to an improvement in behaviour itself. It was the Sophists, not Socrates, who were the archpriests of persuasion, and it is to them that we must look for the clearest examples of persuasive definition. 'Justice is obedience to the established laws.' 'Justice is obedience to the dictates of nature, which are often contrary to the established laws.' 'Justice is the right of the stronger.' 'Justice is a device of the weak to frustrate the stronger.' Rhetorical assertions of this kind, thought Socrates, must be replaced by inductively based conclusions if we are to have any hope of finding out what justice or virtue is and living up to it. If the mind was at the mercy of bodily desires and pleasures (according to a Callicles the happiest state for a man to be in), it had little chance of making progress. 'Only the self-controlled can investigate the most important things, and *classifying them according to their kinds* both in discussion and in action choose the good and reject the bad.'[1] The mind must be fresh and keen only because the prerequisite of right action is to replace Sophistic persuasion by understanding of the facts. It would be difficult to improve on Barker's assessment of Socrates in this (*Pol. Thought of P. & A.* 47):

He differed from the Sophists in not attempting to teach new canons of conduct . . . He sought to elicit from the ordinary conduct of men a clear conception of the rules by which they already acted. He wished men to analyse carefully the duties of life, and to arrive at a clear conception of their meaning: he did not wish them to bring a new conception, acquired from some other source, and remodel life by its aid.

This is not inconsistent with the addition in the next paragraph :

But it was for no mere intellectual purpose that he craved for definitions: it was always for a moral end.

[1] Xen. *Mem.* 4.5.11. On this passage and the relation between knowledge and self-control or its opposite (ἀκρασία) see further pp. 456 f. below.

Barker cites the analogy of descriptive and prescriptive grammar. (It will be remembered that that of the Sophist Protagoras was prescriptive, pp. 219f., 221 above.) Prescriptive grammar is misguided, and grammar may be purely descriptive and yet help one to more correct usage: 'Get to know the rules by which you have all along been acting—unknowingly, and therefore imperfectly—and then you will write better Greek.' 'A man who had arrived at a general conception and expressed it in a definition had made explicit the rules on which he had hitherto been unconsciously and imperfectly acting; and his life would be the better for his acting by a known and explicit rule.'

To define something is to express one's understanding not only of what it is but equally, as has been noted (see (*b*), p. 430 above), of what it is not. It is a remedy for confusion, a 'sorting out of things according to their kinds'. So Xenophon, after the sentence just quoted (*Mem.* 4.5.12), says that Socrates derived the Greek word for discussion (διαλέγεσθαι) from a word meaning 'to collect apart',[1] because, properly understood, it was a procedure of joint deliberation among several people for the purpose of arriving at a definition. Underlying the procedure of Socrates is an assumption, or faith, never mentioned because not consciously recognized, that the kinds or classes to which particulars belong, the 'forms' which they possess, have a quasi-substantial nature and hence a stability which enables the essence of each to be grasped, described, and clearly distinguished from all other essences. It is hardly surprising if Socrates did not, in the first, pioneer attempt at such classification, solve at one leap the 'problem of universals' that has plagued philosophers from his day to our own, or arrive at the Wittgensteinian theory of 'family resemblances' which may at last have provided the right answer.[2] But two special circumstances may be mentioned, one common to

---

[1] διαλέγειν. The active is not otherwise in use, and Stenzel (*RE*, 862) notes the suggestion of paradox about the compound (contrast the common συλλέγειν) as a possibly Socratic touch. On this section in Xenophon and the important question of its independence of the *Phaedrus* and relation to that and other passages in Plato, see Stenzel, *RE*, 855–64. The difference between διαλέγειν here (corresponding to διαγιγνώσκειν at 4.1.5) and the διαίρεσις of a later stage of Plato's dialectic was explained by Zeller (*Ph. d. Gr.* 128, n. 4) before Stenzel (860f.). See also Diès, *Autour de P.* 228.

[2] See the claim of Bambrough in 'Universals and Family Resemblances', *Proc. Arist. Soc.* 1960–1; also L. Pompa in *PQ*, 1967.

most Greek thought and the other typically Socratic, as having helped to make his view what it was.

(i) It is probable that the notion of the *eidos* (meaning a natural kind) as something at least quasi-substantial already had a hold on Greek minds.[1] Cf. G. B. Kerferd in *CR*, 1968, 78:

Many of the less satisfactory uses of analogy in Greek thought seem to us to have a false ontological basis—a belief in the existence of natural kinds either at the phenomenal or at the transcendental level. When Plato in the first book of the *Republic* makes Socrates raise the question τοιοῦτος ἄρα ἐστὶν ἑκάτερος αὐτῶν οἶσπερ ἔοικεν; ['Is each such as that which he resembles?'] (349 d 10) he seems to be appealing to a widely held view that one similarity will be ontologically associated with others.

Such an inherited belief would be of great assistance to Socrates in forming his objective view of moral concepts in opposition to the Sophists, and is perhaps some slight evidence for believing that he came to it from an early study of natural science. It has also an important bearing on the Platonic 'Theory of Ideas', which in its hypostatization of forms, and their separation from particulars, may be seen rather as the culmination of a gradual process than as a radically new and revolutionary doctrine. Scholars dispute for instance whether the use of the phrase 'the *eidos* itself' at *Euthyphro* 6d implies the transcendent forms of the full Platonic theory. Probably not, but its use there in connexion with definition, as in the *Meno* and elsewhere, shows how the Socratic investigations constituted an important stage on the way towards complete hypostatization, the ground for which had already been prepared in the unphilosophical assumptions of Greek thought from which both took their rise.

[1] It is of interest that this use of the word is particularly well attested in medical contexts (as noted on p. 430 above), for the temptation to objectify diseases and their varieties has always been particularly strong for doctors, as Sir H. Cohen pointed out in *Philosophy*, 1952. 'Only in recent times', he wrote, 'has it been widely recognized that, however convenient may be a category of "diseases", they have no separate self-subsistence but are simply abstractions from experience.' Most of us still speak of influenza or malaria as a *thing*, yet we have never met a disease, only sick people; and no two of them repeat the same symptoms exactly. Cohen himself attributed the common mode of thought to a survival from the days when disease was explained as embodied in an evil spirit. 'Even when the spectral origin of the disease was forgotten, the idea of the disease as a clinical entity, a substantial essence with an independent existence, persisted.' The belief, as he remarked, can, by imposing an undue rigidity of treatment, be the reverse of beneficial to the patient. The same fallacy was pointed out much earlier by the French medical writer Cabanis, quoted by Grote, *Plato*, III, 524n.

(ii) More typical of Socrates himself was his teleological outlook, his conviction that to understand the nature of anything was to understand the function or purpose which it was intended to serve. A definition must state not only what we might regard as the essential attributes, but also, and primarily, the *ergon*, or work that the object in question has to perform. Relevant here is not so much the lesson of the natural world (though he was convinced that nature too was providentially designed, Xen. *Mem.* 1.4.4ff., 4.3.3ff.) as his favourite analogy from the crafts—the shoemakers, fullers and cooks, the builders and metal-workers that he so obstinately and tiresomely harped on to illustrate his points (*Gorg.* 491a, Xen. *Mem.* 1.2.37). It is Socratic when Plato in the *Cratylus* (389a–c) makes him say that if a man wants to make a shuttle he must look to the *eidos* of shuttles (the purpose of knowing the *eidos* is always a practical one), and this *eidos*, which he must understand and take as his model, is not simply the shape, or other observable properties, of another shuttle; it is determined by the part which a shuttle has to play in forwarding the work of the weaver. The proper definition of the *eidos* of shuttle does not state its 'form' in the ordinary sense (that it is a piece of wood carved in a certain shape and of certain dimensions), but describes how it is shaped and put together in the way best calculated to perform this task.[1]

(5) THE IGNORANCE OF SOCRATES

But did Socrates positively lay down these all-important definitions of moral virtues, or was his life a continually unsatisfied search for them? It is well known that those dialogues of Plato which have the best claim to be called Socratic tend to lead, ostensibly at least, to a negative conclusion. Possible definitions of the subject of inquiry—courage, temperance, friendship, knowledge, *areté*—are put forward, examined and rejected as faulty, with Socrates sometimes taking the blame for failure on himself. Even Xenophon, who in accordance both with his own temperament and his apologetic purpose shows us a much more positive Socrates, represents him far more often as con-

---

[1] That for Socrates everything, from a horse to a knife, has its own ἔργον and therefore its own ἀρετή or distinctive excellence, has been noted earlier (p. 90, n. 1).

sidering, or investigating (σκοπῶν), together with his friends, the nature of this or that virtue than positively stating what it is.[1] Although he turned others away from idleness and vice and implanted in them a desire for goodness, he never professed to teach but achieved his effect by example, manifesting his own goodness both in his actions and in 'the excellence of his conversation about virtue and human affairs in general' (*Mem.* 1.2.3, 18). Xenophon mentions a current criticism that Socrates exhorted men to goodness but was incompetent to show them the way to it, a criticism illustrated by the complaint in the Platonic dialogue *Clitophon* that Socrates continually preaches righteousness, like a god from his platform in a tragedy, but either does not know or declines to divulge the nature of this righteousness that he is always praising to the skies. To counter this criticism Xenophon simply refers, first, to his questioning and refutation of those who thought they knew everything, and secondly to his 'daily conversations' with his companions, as evidence that he did make men better (*ibid.* 1.4.1). To Euthydemus, indeed (*ibid.* 4.2.40), he did 'explain most simply and clearly what knowledge he considered most necessary and what practices were best'; but, Xenophon continues, his aim was not to make men cleverer, more efficient, or more skilled in speaking, but to implant *sophrosyné*.

Some other inquiries into the nature of this or that as recorded by Xenophon (e.g. of graphic art at *Mem.* 3.10 and of leisure at 3.9.9) have the tentative and exploratory character which we know from Plato, and we may fairly quote against him many passages in his own work, as well as other authorities, when, exceptionally and notably in *Mem.* 4, ch. 6, he claims to give a string of examples of Socratic definitions of such things as piety, justice, goodness, beauty and courage. They are not all in substance false to Socratic teaching,[2] but the stylized and neatly rounded arguments in which they are embodied certainly falsify the Socratic method.[3] Xenophon does not

---

[1] *Mem.* 1.1.16, 4.6.1 (σκοπῶν τί ἕκαστον εἴη τῶν ὄντων), 3.9.9 and elsewhere.

[2] E.g. the utilitarian conceptions of goodness and beauty as τὸ ὠφέλιμον and τὸ χρήσιμον, pp. 462f. below.

[3] Ritter (*Sokr.* 45f.) regarded these definitions, which he found 'extremely inept', as unintelligent borrowings from Plato. Anyone who has been subjected to a telephone call from a reporter and then read the result in print will suspect that he has an inkling of the way in which the neat little conversations were constructed.

actually mention Socrates's well-known confession of his own ignorance (Zeller, *Ph. d. Gr.* 118, n. 1), but he does show him disclaiming the part of a teacher, preferring to make his friends companions in investigation, and emphasizing the importance of self-knowledge and of not supposing that one knows what one does not (*ibid.* 3.9.6).[1] Aristotle gives us the general statement that 'it was the practice of Socrates to ask questions but not to give answers, for he confessed that he did not know' (*Soph. el.* 183b6–8), and Aeschines (p. 395 above) and Plato provide examples as from his own mouth. Most illuminating is that in the *Theaetetus*, where it is connected with the metaphor of midwifery.

I am so far like the midwife, that I cannot give birth to wisdom; and the common reproach is true, that though I question others, I can myself bring nothing to light because there is no wisdom in me. The reason is this: heaven constrains me to serve as a midwife, but has debarred me from giving birth. So of myself I have no sort of wisdom, nor has any discovery ever been born to me as the child of my soul. Those who frequent my company at first appear, some of them, quite unintelligent; but, as we go further with our discussions, all who are favoured by heaven make progress at a rate that seems surprising to others as well as to themselves, although it is clear that they have never learned anything from me; the many admirable truths they bring to birth have been discovered by themselves from within.[2]

The metaphor of intellectual conception and birth-pangs, as the result of *eros*, recurs in the *Symposium* (206c ff.) and the *Republic* (490b), where the lover of knowledge is said to 'have intercourse with' reality, to 'bring forth' intelligence and truth, and so to find release from 'travail'. Elsewhere the intercourse is of mind with mind, and Socrates claims that, like other midwives, he combines with his maieutic skill that of a matchmaker (*Theaet.* 151b) and even of a pander (Xen. *Symp.* 3.10). The close connexion of all this with his profession of ignorance, and its extension beyond Plato, leave no room for doubt that the whole complex is genuinely Socratic.[3]

[1] Cicero's claim (*Brutus* 85.292) to find Socratic irony in Xenophon as well as in Plato and Aeschines is not entirely unjustified. Cf. p. 337 above.

[2] *Theaet.* 150c–d, trans. Cornford. Many other examples of the profession of ignorance could of course be cited. Some references are collected by Deman, *Témoignage*, 64, to which it is worth adding *Charm.* 165b.

[3] The midwife figure itself occurs only in Plato, which made Dorothy Tarrant (*CQ*, 1938, 172) suspect that it might have been his invention, and Robinson (*PED*, 83) state dogmatically that he invented it 'long after Socrates' death'. Among others, however, Stenzel (*PMD*, 4) accepted

In plain terms, the maieutic method based on the professed barrenness of the midwife meant getting the patient, or pupil, to make a
general statement, usually, though not always, in the form of saying
'what x is' (and often, as in the case of Theaetetus and Meno, after
rejecting as inadequate a random enumeration of examples), and by
discussion showing that it is in some way defective. The pupil then
proposes another, which will improve on the previous one and so
bring him nearer the truth. Yet a third may be required, and even the
last to be suggested often breaks down and the dialogue ends with a
confession of failure, but at the same time on a note of hope. Thus
Socrates makes Theaetetus abandon successively the notions that
knowledge is (*a*) sensation, (*b*) true belief, (*c*) true belief plus explanation or account (*logos*). This exhausts the tale of Theaetetus's embryo
thoughts, but, says Socrates, if he conceives again his offspring will
be all the better for the scrutiny of these, and if he does not, he will be
a better man for the knowledge of his own ignorance.

This method could do much for a chosen pupil like Theaetetus,
if not necessarily in the production of new discoveries, at least as a
mental catharsis. Every one of Theaetetus's attempts to discover the
nature of knowledge proves to be a 'phantom' or 'wind-egg' (as
R. Robinson points out, *PED*, 84), and no doubt the merit of the
Socratic method lay rather in weeding out confused and ill-thought-out
ideas than in bringing new ones to light. Nevertheless mathematical
knowledge, in which young Theaetetus was already expert, was of the
a priori kind which does 'come out of oneself' and can be explicated
by the Socratic or an analogous method; and for Socrates and Plato
ethical truths had the same timeless and eternal value.[1] To those for
whom the method was unsuited, either youths whose minds 'have

---

it as historical, and there is no good reason to do otherwise. In the *Theaet*. Socrates develops the
figure by speaking of the 'miscarriage' of thoughts, and this recurs in the mouth of one of
Socrates's disciples in the *Clouds* of Aristophanes (*v*. 137; on this parallel however see Peipers,
Erkenntnistheorie, 714f.). Cf. p. 397, n. 1 above.

[1] See my Penguin edition of the *Prot*. and *Meno*, 109f. In the one clear instance of Socrates's
'drawing out of' a pupil, by question and answer, a correct positive conclusion, namely the
experiment on Meno's slave, the problem set is mathematical, and the inference is then drawn
that, if it can be solved in this way, so can the problem of defining ἀρετή. Unfortunately for the
maieutic method, this cannot be taken as a valid example of it as explained in the *Theaet*. since
Socrates himself (and Meno) did know the answer that he was trying to elicit. That was necessary
if Meno was to see the point of the experiment.

not conceived at all' or older men whose thoughts were already formed, it was only 'Socrates's usual affectation, shamming ignorance and doing anything rather than answer a question', 'his old game of never giving a positive answer himself, but taking up everyone else's answer and refuting it'. This is the *eironeia* which makes Thrasymachus so angry (*Rep.* 337a), and if we translate it 'irony' we water it down unduly. In the fifth century it was a term of abuse meaning plainly deceit or swindling, as in the *Wasps* (174) and the *Clouds* of Aristophanes, where it appears (at *v.* 449) in a list of villainous qualities along with imposture and all sorts of blackguardly conduct. In Plato's *Laws* (908e) it is used of the worst type of atheist who hypocritically pretends to religion. In Aristotle it is still a form of untruthfulness, and therefore blameable, but specialized into mock-modesty and regarded as preferable to boasting. He quotes Socrates as an example, and the softening down of the word may well have been an effect of the Socratic literature.[1] In Plato it retains its bad sense, in the mouth either of a bitter opponent like Thrasymachus or of one pretending to be angry at the way in which Socrates deceives everyone as to his real character (Alcibiades at *Symp.* 216e, 218d). It is not used for the gentle irony which he employs with his young friends when he puts himself on a level with them and says 'Come now, let's look into this, you and I, for I don't know any more about it than you do'.

The accusation of *eironeia* is also brought against Socrates (though the word is not used) in Xenophon. When he is threatened by the Thirty, Charicles objects to his conduct in 'asking questions when he knows the answers' (*Mem.* 1.2.36), and Hippias (*ibid.* 4.4.9) tells him that he is 'always mocking at others, questioning and refuting everybody but never willing to submit to examination or reveal his own opinion about anything'. It is true that Socrates preferred to ask questions of others, though occasionally in a Platonic dialogue he

---

[1] Arist. *EN* 1127b 22ff. On εἴρων and its derivatives see O. Ribbeck in *Rh. Mus.* 1876 and R. Stark, *Rh. Mus.* 1953, 79ff. Ribbeck describes it as 'ein derber, volkstümlicher Ausdruck, ja um es gerade herauszusagen, ein Schimpfwort'. In modern times 'Socratic irony' is sometimes taken in a much wider sense, in which it was the subject of Kierkegaard's book and of an attractive chapter by Friedländer (*Plato*, Eng. tr. 1, ch. 7). A more strictly scholarly account is in Zeller, *Ph. d. Gr.* 124–6. In Theophrastus (*Char.* 1) the εἴρων is still a man who will praise you to your face and attack you behind your back, and such characters are 'more to be avoided than vipers'.

offers his interlocutor the choice of roles.[1] But the accusation of *eironeia* in the full sense, involving deliberate deceit, can scarcely be maintained. We should not dismiss his profession of ignorance as altogether insincere. His mission was not to impart any body of positive doctrine, but to bring home to men their intellectual need, and then invite them to join with him in the search for truth by the dialectical method of question and answer. He claimed, for instance, that the knowledge necessary for the acquisition of virtue must comprise the discovery of the function of human life as such. Of any other teacher one would naturally expect that he would go on to expound what was this ultimate end or aim, but one may doubt whether it is to be found in the records of any teaching which can reasonably be attributed to Socrates. This, we may assume, was one of the chief reasons which made the more positive Plato feel it his duty not only to reproduce what Socrates said but also to go further and bring out what he thought were its implications. The essence of the Socratic method, the elenchus, is to convince the interlocutor that, whereas he thought he knew something, in fact he does not. Meno complained that its first effect was comparable to an electric shock: the mind went numb. This comparison with the electric sting-ray, said Socrates, would only be valid if the fish itself were in a state of numbness when it inflicts its shock; if he reduces others to doubt, it is only because he is in doubt himself, and this is precisely what Meno has heard from others (*Meno* 79e–80a). Not everyone, it seems, accused Socrates of the *eironeia* of asking questions when he knew the answers perfectly well. No doubt some irony (in the English sense) is present in his words to Meno. He knew that he saw more clearly than his companion what was needful. But he had no cut-and-dried system of knowledge to hand over, nor did he believe that knowledge handed over in this way, even if he possessed it to give, would do a man any good. In the controlled experiment on Meno's slave, undertaken to convince Meno of the value of being reduced to a confession of ignorance, Socrates demonstrates that, even when the teacher knows

---

[1] *Gorg.* 462b, *Prot.* 338c–d. The results are interesting, in the one case a speech for whose length Socrates very properly thinks an apology is due to Polus (465e), and in the other a brilliant parody of a Sophistic ἐπίδειξις whose solemn approval by such an authority as Hippias must have amused him.

the answer, it is sound educational method not to tell it to the pupil at once but to lead him to discover it step by step through the successive destruction of answers which are plausible but wrong.

Of the many attempts to sum up the aims and achievements of the Socratic conversations, this short one of Hackforth's is one of the best (*Philosophy*, 1933, p. 265):

Two points in particular should be noticed with regard to these conversations: first, that although the primary object is to convince the interlocutor of his own ignorance, yet, since the definitions suggested are always those shared by him with general opinion, or at least some large body of general opinion, the effect, or secondary object, is to show the unsatisfactoriness of commonly received ideas on matters of conduct; secondly, that since many of the definitions are the outcome of Socrates's own suggestions—in some cases actually formulated by him—and yet are found no less than those of his interlocutor to be untenable, Socrates has no ready-made system of ethics to impart. This is, of course, what we should expect from his disclaiming the office of a teacher; he is a fellow-searcher only. Yet it would be wrong to suppose that the results of such conversations are purely negative. For one thing, the discussion commonly reveals an element of truth in each definition;[1] for another, the interlocutor is helped by the lesson of intellectual honesty,[2] is shown an ideal of knowledge unattained, and a method whereby he may progressively attain, or at least approximate, thereto. Thirdly, the suggestion underlying the apparent failure of the discussions is that the whole problem of conduct can only be solved when viewed as a whole: the several 'virtues' cannot be defined nor understood nor possessed in isolation from one another, for they are all different applications of a single knowledge—the knowledge of good and evil.

---

[1] Versényi goes further (*Socr. Hum.* 118). The aporetic end of a dialogue, he says, 'does not mean that the dialogues contain nothing positive since, in the first place, there is hardly a dialogue that does not arrive at solutions to the problems discussed. These conclusions are negated at the end merely to prevent the student from uncritically accepting them instead of going through reflection that would make them his own.' This, I believe, goes too far. There is more truth in his continuation: 'In the second place, what is positive here is not to much something contained in the written word itself as something that takes place in the learner's soul, namely that he does in fact search for and acquire knowledge.' The question of positive content in Plato's early, 'Socratic' dialogues is also discussed by R. Dieterle in his Freiburg dissertation (1966), *Platons Laches u. Charmides: Unters. z. elenktisch-aporetisch. Struktur d. plat. Frühdialoge*. See the review by Easterling in *CR*, 1968.

[2] Since this article was written, some critics might cavil at the words 'intellectual honesty'. Fallacies are certainly committed in the Socratic dialogues of Plato, and it is a debated point how far either Plato or his master were unaware of them and how far Socrates may have used them deliberately in what he believed to be a good cause.

'In contrasting Socrates with the Sophists', wrote Ernest Barker (*Pol. Thought of P. & A.* 46), 'we must remember that in many respects he was one of them.' In many respects, yes, but in the words 'an ideal of knowledge unattained' Hackforth has put his finger on one of the vital differences between them. His identification with them by his contemporaries was indeed excusable. They held that knowledge (as opposed to shifting opinion) was impossible, for there were no stable and indisputable objects to be known. He demonstrated to everybody that what they called their knowledge was not knowledge at all. Superficially alike, the two statements were fundamentally different, for that of Socrates was based on an unshakeable conviction that knowledge *was* in principle attainable, but that, if there was to be any hope of attaining it, the debris of confused and misleading ideas which filled most men's minds must first be cleared away. Only then could the positive search for knowledge begin. Once his companion had understood the right way to the goal (the *method* in its Greek sense), he was ready to seek it with him, and philosophy was summed up for him in this idea of the 'common search',[1] a conception of the purpose of discussion directly contrary to the sophistic idea of it as a contest aiming at the overthrow of an opponent. Neither knew the truth yet, but if only the other could be persuaded of this, they might set out together with some hope of finding it, or at least approaching it more closely, for the man who has rid his mind of a false conception is already nearer the truth. To be a Socratic is not to follow any system of philosophical doctrine. It implies first and foremost an attitude of mind, an intellectual humility easily mistaken for arrogance, since the true Socratic is convinced of the ignorance not only of himself but of all mankind.

[1] Contrast, in the *Prot.*, Socrates's plea of σύν τε δύ' ἐρχομένω (348d) with Protagoras's reference to ἀγῶνες λόγων at 335a. Some of the many references in both Plato and Xenophon to his habit of κοινῇ ζητεῖν, συζητεῖν, κοινῇ βουλεύεσθαι etc. are collected by Zeller, *Ph. d. Gr.* 118, n. 3. See also the references to κοινὴ σκέψις at *Charm.* 158d, *Crito* 48d, and μετὰ σοῦ σκέψασθαι καὶ συζητῆσαι at *Meno* 80d, and on the agonistic character of sophistic debate p. 43 above.

(6) VIRTUE IS KNOWLEDGE

Three fundamental theses of Socrates are so closely related as to form scarcely separable parts of a single whole. They are: virtue is knowledge; its converse, that wrongdoing can only be due to ignorance and must therefore be considered involuntary; and 'care of the soul' as the primary condition of living well. As far as possible, something will be said about each in turn.

The Socratic paradox (as it is usually called) that virtue is knowledge bears directly on the characteristically fifth-century controversy over the method of acquiring it, whether by teaching or otherwise; and for this reason it has been necessary to say something about it already.[1] It puts Socrates squarely among his contemporaries, the great Sophists with whom he was crossing swords when Plato was unborn or an infant. We have also noted the wide sense of *areté* in earlier and current use (e.g. 'the *areté* of carpentry or any other craft', p. 252), which must have made the 'paradox' less paradoxical in his own time, and also makes it essential to remember that, if we use the English word 'virtue', it is only as a counter to stand for the Greek expression.[2]

Once again let us start from Aristotle, about whose general value as a source enough has been said already. In this case much of what he says can be traced back to the Platonic dialogues, but he has not on this account confused Socrates with Plato. That is plain from the undoubtedly genuine references, and is stated explicitly if we may take the following passage from the *Magna Moralia* (as we surely may) to represent Aristotle's opinion. In a brief historical survey the writer mentions first Pythagoras, then Socrates, then Plato, distinguishing the last two thus:[3]

[1] Pp. 257f., and for the question in general ch. x as a whole. Cf. also 25.

[2] The Greek habit of using 'knowledge' (ἐπιστήμη, ἐπίστασθαι and words of kindred meaning) to denote practical skill or trained ability, and of 'explaining character or behaviour in terms of knowledge', has often been remarked on. See Dodds, *Gks. & Irrat.* 16f., and cf. his *Gorgias*, 218; Snell, *Ausdrücke*, and *Philol.* 1948, 132. Adam on *Rep.* 382a notes the moral connotation of words like ἀμαθής, ἀπαίδευτος, ἀγνώμων, and remarks that 'the identification of ignorance and vice is in harmony with popular Greek psychology'.

[3] 1182a 20. In general I have been sparing of quotation from the *MM*, owing to the widespread view that it is a product of the Peripatos after Aristotle's death.

The effect of his [*sc.* Socrates's] making the virtues into branches of knowledge was to eliminate the irrational part of the soul, and with it emotion and moral character. So his treatment of virtue was in this respect mistaken. After him Plato, rightly enough, divided the soul into the rational and irrational parts and explained the appropriate virtues of each.

This is valuable information, comparable to what Aristotle tells us about the difference between the Socratic and Platonic treatment of universals, and justifies a belief that what he has taken from Plato as Socratic is genuinely so. It excludes the 'Socrates' of the *Republic* and many other dialogues, and is supported, as we shall see, by Xenophon. At the same time, in his concise and more advanced terminology Aristotle presents us with the 'virtue-is-knowledge' doctrine in its most uncompromising form, in order to point out its shortcomings and contrast it with his own. We may look at it in this form first, and afterwards consider whether its intellectual severity needs any mitigation if we are to get at the mind of Socrates himself.

Aristotle repeats several times that Socrates said or thought that 'the virtues are sciences' or a single virtue (courage) 'is a science'.[1] This he interpreted as an unqualified intellectualism, reached by analogy with pure science and with the practical arts. So *EE* 1216b2ff.:

Socrates believed that knowledge of virtue was the final aim, and he inquired what justice is, and what courage and every other kind of virtue. This was reasonable in view of his conviction that all the virtues were sciences, so that to know justice was at the same time to be just; for as soon as we have learned geometry and architecture we are architects and geometricians. For this reason he inquired what virtue is, but not how or from what it is acquired.

Aristotle comments that this is true of the theoretical sciences but not of the productive, in which knowledge is only a means to a further end, e.g. health in medicine, law and order in political science. Therefore to know what virtue is matters less than to know what conditions will produce it, 'for we do not want to know what courage or justice

---

[1] *EN* 1144b28 Σ. μὲν οὖν λόγους τὰς ἀρετὰς ᾠετο εἶναι· ἐπιστήμας γὰρ εἶναι πάσας; 1144b19, φρονήσεις ᾠετο εἶναι πάσας τὰς ἀρετάς; 1116b4, ὁ Σ. ᾠήθη ἐπιστήμην εἶναι τὴν ἀνδρείαν (also *EE* 1230a7). From the first passage, and *EE* 1246b33 καὶ ὀρθὸν τὸ Σωκρατικὸν ὅτι οὐδὲν ἰσχυρότερον φρονήσεως, ὅτι δὲ ἐπιστήμην ἔφη, οὐκ ὀρθῶς, Joël inferred (*E. & X. S.* 1.211) that Socrates called the virtues ἐπιστῆμαι but not λόγοι or φρονήσεις. Such a rigid terminology seems to be refuted by both Plato's and Aristotle's usage. For the former, see O'Brien, *Socr. Parad.* 79, n. 58, and for the latter p. 452, n. 3, below. Cf. also p. 501, n. 3.

is, but to *be* brave or just, just as we wish to be healthy rather than to know what health is'. This antithesis is one to make Socrates turn in his grave; 'for', he would protest, 'how can I know how virtue is acquired when I don't even know what it is?'[1] Aristotle on the other hand lays it down as his general policy for an ethical treatise (*EN* 1103 b 26): 'The present study does not aim at theoretical knowledge as others do, for the object of our inquiry is not to know what goodness is but to become good.' Even if one were to agree with Socrates that knowledge of the nature of courage or justice is a necessary precondition of becoming brave or just,[2] it would be difficult to concede that it is a sufficient one. Elsewhere (1144 b 18) Aristotle himself admits that Socrates was partly right: right in saying that reason[3] was a *sine qua non* of virtue, but wrong in identifying the two.

In Plato's *Protagoras*, as part of an argument for the unity of virtue, Socrates tries to maintain that courage, like any other virtue, is knowledge, because in any dangerous enterprise—diving in a confined space, cavalry engagements, light-armed combat—the trained expert will show more courage than the ignorant. Thus courage is knowledge of what is and what is not to be feared.[4] In an obvious reference to this passage, Aristotle asserted that its claim is the opposite of the truth.[5] Some may be cowards but face what appear to others to be dangers because they know them not to be dangers at all, e.g. in war there are many false alarms which the trained and experienced soldier can recognize as such; but in general those who face dangers owing to experience are not really brave. Those who are skilled at climbing masts, he says, are confident not because they know what is to be feared but because they know what aids are available to them in dangers. The example is similar to Socrates's of

---

[1] *Meno* 71 a, *Prot.* 360e–361a, *Laches* 190b.

[2] It is curious that Aristotle, in his irritation against Socrates, should go so far as to speak of knowing what goodness or health is and being good or healthy as alternatives, instead of saying only that Socrates's demand does not go far enough. In his own philosophy any practitioner must first have complete in his mind the εἶδος of what he wishes to produce—health if he is a doctor, a house if he is an architect or builder. Only then does he start to produce it. Thus the formal cause pre-exists in art as well as nature. See *Metaph.* 1032a 32–1032b 14.

[3] φρόνησις at 1144b 18, λόγος at b 29. In this book of the *EN* Aristotle has given his own technical sense to φρόνησις, but Socrates must have used these terms for what at other times he called knowledge. Cf. p. 451, n. 1, above. The cobbler who knows his trade is φρόνιμος at it (*Alc. I* 125 a).

[4] 349e–350a, 360d.   [5] *EE* 1230a6, and cf. *EN* 1116b4.

the divers, and he would hardly have considered it to invalidate his point. In fact however he was arguing at a different level, as he shows at a later stage (354a–b). Courage is not to be considered in isolation, because all virtue is one, to be summed up as the knowledge of what is ultimately good or evil. At this level death itself may not be an evil to be feared, if one knows that it may result in a greater amount of good, for instance the freedom of one's country. The paradoxical nature of the doctrine appears in a comparison with the superficially similar words of Pericles in the funeral oration (Thuc. 2.40.3): some are made bold by ignorance, he says, but the bravest are those who recognize most clearly what things are fearful and what enjoyable, and are not by this knowledge deterred from dangers. By this high but orthodox standard, men face physical dangers although they know them to be fearful; according to Socrates, they face them in the knowledge that what may happen to them is not an evil at all, if it is more beneficial than cowardice to the real self, the *psyche*.

Aristotle's chief objection to the doctrine is that which would occur to most people, namely that it makes no allowance for weakness of will, lack of self-control, 'incontinence', the effect of appetite or passion.[1] In book 7 of the *Ethics* (*EN* 1145b25) he makes it the starting-point of his own discussion of the right use of these terms, and once again begins with a reference to the *Protagoras*, where the question was raised (at 352b–c) whether knowledge, when it is present, can be 'hauled around like a slave by the passions'. 'Socrates', he continues, 'was totally opposed to this idea, on the ground that there is no such thing as incontinence: when a man acts contrary to what is best, he does not judge it to be so, but acts in ignorance.' So put, says Aristotle bluntly, the doctrine is in plain contradiction to experience; and most of us have to agree with Medea (as Euripides and Ovid depict her) that it is possible to see and approve the better course but follow the worse. Aristotle's own solution, cast in a form to deal most gently with the paradox, is reached through his more advanced technique of analysis. A crude dichotomy between knowledge and ignorance is not enough. Knowledge can be actual or

---

[1] ἀκρασία, usually translated 'incontinence', but more literally 'lack of mastery' over one's passions or lower nature; and πάθος, emotion, passion.

potential (i.e. acquired but not consciously present, as in sleep or drunkenness), universal or particular. After considerable discussion (not relevant here), he concludes that the wrongdoer may know the universal rule, but this is not the efficient cause of a particular action, which is motivated by particular knowledge (i.e. that this present action, in my individual circumstances, is or is not contrary to the rule and therefore wrong). It is this kind of knowledge which is overcome (banished from consciousness, rendered merely potential) by the temptation of pleasure, fear, etc.; but such immediate awareness of particulars is a matter of sense-perception only, and ought not, according to Aristotle's epistemology, to be called knowledge.[1] Thus by the application of Aristotelian distinctions of which Socrates never dreamed, something of his paradox can be saved: 'Because the last term (i.e. the particular)[2] is not a universal nor equally an object of knowledge with the universal, even what Socrates sought to establish seems to come about; for there is no incontinence when knowledge in the full sense is present, nor is it *that* knowledge which is "hauled about" by passion, but perceptual knowledge.' (1147b14.)

Plato contains many passages which support the interpretation of Socrates's dictum as over-intellectual and neglectful of moral weakness. When Aristotle says that in his view to understand the nature of justice was at the same time to be just, he was simply echoing the *Gorgias*, where this conclusion is drawn from an analogy with the practical arts: to 'learn justice' is to be just and will inevitably lead to just action (460b). In the *Laches* Socrates leads the search for a definition of courage, first to knowledge of what is or is not to be feared, and then to include the knowledge of all good and all evil things. This however would make courage identical with virtue as a whole, and Socrates ostensibly writes off the argument as a failure because they had begun by agreeing that it was only a part of it. In fact it has led to precisely what he believed to be the truth and endeavoured to demonstrate in the *Protagoras*. In the *Meno* (87cff.)

---

[1] Knowledge (ἐπιστήμη) must be demonstrable, and can only be of the universal. See *EN* 1139b18ff., 1140b30ff. (ἡ ἐπιστήμη περὶ τῶν καθόλου ἐστὶν ὑπόληψις ... μετὰ λόγου γὰρ ἡ ἐπιστήμη), and for a full account of its acquisition *An. Post.* 2, ch. 19.

[2] τὸ ἔσχατον has the double sense of the last (i.e. least inclusive) term of a syllogism (*An. Pr.* 25b33) and also the particular, which being ἄτομον (indivisible) comes last in the downward process of analysis from *summa genera*. (See Bonitz, index 289b39ff.)

he argues that virtue is knowledge on the ground that it must be held to be something good, i.e. always beneficial, never harmful, and all other so-called good things in life (health, wealth, and even a so-called virtue like courage if it is a thoughtless boldness, divorced from knowledge) may bring harm as well as good unless they are wisely and prudently used. Here again the argument is artfully contrived to stimulate thought by being led to ostensible breakdown. If virtue is knowledge, it can be taught, but a search for possible teachers (including the Sophists, who are somewhat lightly dismissed as a doubtful case) reveals none, so the deductive argument is wrecked on the shores of experience. A final suggestion is made, that 'right opinion', which comes to a man not by teaching but in some mysterious manner comparable to the gift of prophecy, may be as good a guide to action as knowledge, so long as it is present; its only fault is its fickleness. Once again the conclusion is that they do not yet know 'what virtue is in and by itself', and are therefore in no position to say how it is acquired.

Xenophon too bears out the intellectualism of Socratic ethics: 'Socrates said that justice and all the rest of virtue was knowledge' (*Mem.* 3.9.5),[1] and the same point is somewhat crudely developed in dialogue form at 4.6.6: no one who knows what he ought to do can think he ought not to do it, and no one acts otherwise than as he thinks he ought to act. In other places, however, Xenophon gives high praise not only to the continence of Socrates's own life but to his continual commendation, in his teaching, of the virtue of self-control—*enkrateia*, the opposite of that *akrasia*, or incontinence, which according to Aristotle was on his assumptions an impossibility.[2] This brings up the question whether the 'paradox' in fact represents such a one-sided view of morality as Aristotle made out. To Joël the solution was simple (*E. u. X. S.* 237): Aristotle, Plato's *Protagoras*, and Xenophon when he says Socrates believed virtue to be knowledge, are giving the genuine Socratic view; Xenophon when he makes Socrates preach self-control and condemn incontinence is giving his own. But it was scarcely as simple as that.

---

[1] Or 'skill acquired by learning', σοφία (pp. 27f. above). For its equation with knowledge cf. also *Mem.* 4.6.7 ὃ ἄρα ἐπίσταται ἕκαστος, τοῦτο καὶ σοφός ἐστιν, and Plato, *Prot.* 350d.

[2] See e.g. *Mem.* 1.5, 2.1, 4.5.

To start with Xenophon, his Socrates claims indeed that complete understanding of what is good will inevitably be reflected in action, but deplores *akrasia*, a yielding to the temptations of sensuality, greed or ambition, as the greatest obstacle to such understanding: 'Don't you agree that *akrasia* keeps men from wisdom (*sophia*) and drives them to its opposite? It prevents them from paying attention to, and properly learning, the things that are profitable by drawing them away to pleasures, and often so stuns their perception of good and evil[1] that they choose the worse instead of the better' (*Mem.* 4.5.6). This leads, later in the same conversation (4.5.11), to the assertion that the man of uncontrolled passions is as ignorant and stupid as a beast, because only the self-controlled are in a position 'to investigate the most important things, and classifying them according to their kinds, both in discussion and in action to choose the good and reject the bad'. Here the notions of moral self-control and the acquisition of knowledge are brought together in a way which involves no contradiction.[2] A teacher of mathematics would hardly be inconsistent in warning a weak-willed pupil that a life of drunkenness and debauchery is not conducive to success even in a purely intellectual pursuit. Some degree of moral discipline is a necessary prerequisite of all knowledge,[3] but most of all when what is sought is an understanding of relative values, in which a mind dulled and confused by unthinking indulgence in sensual pleasure will be especially at sea. It must also be remembered that Socrates's constant analogy for virtue was not theoretical science but art or craft (*techné*), mastery of which calls for both knowledge and practice. At *Mem.* 3.9. 1–3 Xenophon claims to give his answer to the question whether

[1] So Marchant (Loeb ed.) renders αἰσθανομένους ἐκπλήξασα, on the analogy of παύειν with participle. This gives a sense more obviously in keeping with the 'virtue is knowledge' doctrine, but I doubt if it can be paralleled. Simeterre (*Vertu-science*, 53, n. 72) more plausibly assumes it means that, *although* they perceive good and bad, yet, 'comme frappés d'égarement', they choose the bad, and he cites it as one of the rare passages that appear to contradict the 'virtue is knowledge' doctrine. But he adds that αἰσθάνεσθαι is not the same as knowing or possessing σοφία (3.9.5), and it is plain from the words προσέχειν τε τοῖς ὠφελοῦσι καὶ καταμανθάνειν αὐτὰ κωλύει that Xenophon has the doctrine in mind and intends no contradiction of it.

[2] On the 'inner connexion between διαιρεῖν and προαιρεῖσθαι' cf. the remarks of Stenzel in his *RE* article, 863f.

[3] As Aristotle agreed: intemperance distorts one's medical or grammatical knowledge (*EE* 1246b27).

courage is natural or can be learned. It remains on the level of Xeno-phon's comprehension—there is no progress towards the unification of virtue in a single knowledge of good and evil—but so far as it goes it agrees with *Protagoras* 350a (pp. 452f. above). Nature, says Socrates, plays a part, 'but courage is increased in every man's nature by learning and practice'. Soldiers will fight more bravely if they are using weapons and tactics in which they have been thoroughly trained rather than those with which they are unfamiliar. So too on a higher level in the *Gorgias* (509dff.), no one wishes to do wrong, but un-willingness is not enough; one needs a certain power, an art, and only by learning and practising this *techné* will he avoid wrongdoing. In the acquisition of *areté* Socrates did not deny a place to any of the three factors commonly recognized in the fifth century: natural gifts, learning, and practice.[1] Yet his view of the case was still original. Knowledge, in and by itself, of the nature of virtue was sufficient to make a man virtuous; but there was little chance of his learning the truth of it if he had not subjected his body to the negative discipline of resisting sensual indulgence and his mind to the practice of dialectic, the art of discriminating and defining.

Socrates's constant representation of *areté*, the art of good living, as the supreme art or craft, does then detract somewhat from Aristotle's criticism of him for treating it as if it were a theoretical science in which knowledge is the sole and final objective.[2] Although in the productive and practical arts the purpose is fulfilled in the product and not solely in the knowledge or skill itself, there is something in the argument that a skilled carpenter or weaver will inevitably turn out good work; to reduce his handiwork deliberately to the faulty level of a beginner's would be impossible for him. At the same time,

[1] For other examples in Xenophon see O'Brien, *Socr. Parad.* 146 n., and compare his whole note 27, from p. 144. On pp. 136–8 (n. 21) he discusses the qualifications to be made to the purely intellectualist interpretation of the definition of virtue as knowledge. When he speaks of Plato's doctrine that 'virtue is *not knowledge alone, but* knowledge (or right opinion) built on natural endowment and long training', one might well ask whether Plato believed that there was any other kind of knowledge. The selection and education of the guardians in the *Republic* suggest that he did not. Pp. 147f. state rather differently the way in which the virtues are 'not knowledge alone', bringing out more clearly one of the Platonic modifications of Socratic doctrine.

[2] Simeterre puts it well (*Vertu-science*, 71): 'Dans les techniques, et quelles qu'elles soient, on ne devient maître qu'après un long apprentissage, un sévère entraînement. On ne s'en dispense pas dans l'art difficile de la vertu.'

no one would claim that a simple analogy between this and moral action provides a complete, mature ethical theory. Socrates was the initiator of a revolution, and the first step in a philosophic revolution has two characteristics: it is so rooted in the traditions of its time that its full effects are only gradually realized,[1] and it is presented in a simple and absolute form, leaving to future thinkers the job of providing the necessary qualifications and provisos. The tradition in which Socrates was caught up was that of the Sophists, and his teaching would have been impossible without theirs, much of which he accepted. They based their lives on the conviction that *areté* could be taught, and he concluded that therefore it must be knowledge. Like them he upheld, as we shall see, the principle of utility and was impressed by what they said about the relativity of the good. Antiphon emphasized the need to be master of one's passions as a precondition of choosing the better and avoiding the worse, nor was his advocacy of 'enlightened self-interest' without its appeal for Socrates. Much of this has emerged in ch. x, and more will appear later.

As for the sublime simplicity of Socrates's dictum, that certainly owed much to his own remarkable character. As Joël epigrammatically expressed it, 'in the strength of his character lay the weakness of his philosophy'.[2] But it also reflects the pioneer character of his thought. His was the first attempt to apply philosophical method to ethics, and Aristotle showed perspicacity in giving generous recognition to the value of his achievement for the advance of logic, while deprecating its immediate and universal application to moral theory and practice. Socrates, it may be said, with his 'Virtue is knowledge', did for ethics what Parmenides did for ontology with the assertion that 'what is, is'. Both turned philosophy in an entirely new direction, and both left to their successors the task of refining a simple statement by examining and analysing the concepts underlying its terms, the use of which as single terms had hitherto concealed from consciousness a variety of meanings. Both stated as an absolute and universal truth something which needed to be said, which the advance of philosophy would never refute, but to which it would assign its due place as part of a

[1] See the quotation from T. S. Kuhn on p. 352 above.
[2] *E. u. X. S.* 1.256: 'Die Stärke des Charakters wird zur Schwäche der Philosophie.' See p. 258 above.

larger whole.[1] That is why it seemed worth mentioning Aristotle's refinements (pp. 451 ff. above), as an example of this process at work. 'Virtue is knowledge.' But what sort of knowledge? Actual, potential, universal, particular? And is knowledge the whole of virtue, or an essential integrating element in it?

If Socrates held virtue to be knowledge, whether or not he believed that either he or any man had acquired it, he must have had some conception of the object of that knowledge. Though a single object, it had two aspects. In one aspect it was knowledge of the end and aim of human life, which embraced and transcended all partial ends and individual arts such as those aiming at health, physical safety, wealth, political power and so on. These may or may not make for the best and happiest life, for they are all instrumental to further ends, and it depends how they are used. Secondly, the knowledge required is self-knowledge. We have seen that Socrates's conception of a definition is teleological (p. 442 above): to know the nature of anything is to know its function. If we could understand our own nature, therefore, we should know what is the right and natural goal of our life, and this is the knowledge which would give us the *areté* that we are seeking.

(7) ALL WRONGDOING IS INVOLUNTARY: SOCRATES A DETERMINIST?

If virtue is knowledge, and to know the good is to do it, wickedness is due to ignorance and therefore, strictly speaking, involuntary. This corollary made a deep impression on Plato, and in spite of his more advanced psychology he retained it as his own up to the end. If in his earlier works he attributes it to Socrates, he repeats it later in dialogues where Socrates is not even nominally the speaker. In the *Timaeus* the statement that 'no one is voluntarily wicked' is connected with a remarkable theory that all vices have their origin in somatic disorders,

---

[1] Joël is good on this, e.g. on p. 222 where he speaks of 'the general historical law that every new truth is at first accepted absolutely before its individuality and relativity are recognized'; and p. 249: 'Every beginning is one-sided, and Socrates marks the beginning of *Geistesphilosophie*.' One may however, while admitting the rationalistic bias of Socrates, differ from him over the extent to which Xenophon has distorted it. Simeterre's conclusion on this is sound (*Vertu-science*, 54): with his practical inclinations, he may have exaggerated the role of ἄσκησις and μελέτη, but if he has not maintained his master's thesis at every point, he has not failed to give us the essentials.

and in the *Laws* it is repeated on the more Socratic ground that no man will deliberately harm his most precious possession, which is his soul. In the *Protagoras* Socrates himself says: 'My own opinion is more or less this: no wise man believes that anyone sins willingly or willingly perpetrates any base or evil act; they know very well that every base or evil action is committed involuntarily.' In the *Meno*, an argument making a wickedly sophistical use of ambiguity is used to demonstrate that 'no one wishes evil', on the ground that 'to desire and obtain evil things' is a recipe for unhappiness, so that anyone who ostensibly wishes evil must be presumed to be ignorant that it is evil. The *Republic* asserts that, whether one considers pleasure, reputation or profit, the man who commends justice speaks the truth, while the man who disparages it (does not lie, but) speaks in ignorance. He must therefore be gently persuaded, for his error is not voluntary.[1]

Plato, then, maintained the paradox at all periods,[2] but Aristotle opposed it on the grounds that it makes men no longer masters of their own actions. 'It is irrational to suppose that a man who acts unjustly does not wish to be unjust or a man who acts dissolutely to be dissolute.' 'Wickedness *is* voluntary, or else we shall have to quarrel with what we have just said and deny that a man is the author and begetter of his actions.'[3] This criticism of the doctrine as deterministic is put most clearly in the *Magna Moralia*, and has been repeated in modern times. *MM* 1187a7 expresses it thus:

Socrates claimed that it is not in our power to be worthy or worthless men. If, he said, you were to ask anyone whether he would like to be just or unjust, no one would choose injustice, and it is the same with courage and cowardice and the other virtues. Evidently any who are vicious will not be vicious voluntarily. Neither, in consequence, will they be voluntarily virtuous.

Karl Joël was one who took this as a complete description of Socratic ethics, which he therefore regarded as primitively deterministic.

---

[1] *Tim.* 86d, *Laws* 731c and 860d, *Prot.* 345d, *Meno* 78a, *Rep.* 589c. Related are *Soph.* 228c, *Phileb.* 22b.

[2] Joël, as we have seen, rejected Xenophon's account on the grounds that it allowed for ἀκρασία, which on the Socratic paradox is impossible. But if we wish to pick on every apparent inconsistency, we can say equally that Plato himself denied that according to Socrates it is impossible to do wrong willingly. At *Crito* 49a he asks οὐδενὶ τρόπῳ φαμὲν ἑκόντας ἀδικητέον εἶναι; and what would be the point of asking this question if voluntary wrongdoing were impossible anyway?

[3] *EN* 1114a11, 1113b16.

Is No One Voluntarily Good?

All wrong action is involuntary. Whether we are good or bad does not depend on ourselves. No one wills unrighteousness, cowardice etc., but only righteousness etc. (*MM* 1187a). On this basis it would be nonsensical to exhort to virtue. The will as such cannot be improved, because it is entirely unfree, in bondage to the reason. (*E. u. X. S.* 266.)

That the beginning of psychology should be as primitive as the beginning of physical science (*ibid.* 227) is, as he says, natural enough; but what he is doing is to force this nascent psychology into the categories appropriate to a maturer stage. To say that if no one is voluntarily bad then no one is voluntarily good may seem an obvious inference, but it is nevertheless an inference drawn by Aristotle or his follower, not by Socrates.[1] Not for him the searching analysis, which we find in Aristotle, of the interrelated concepts of desire, wish, deliberation, choice, voluntary and involuntary, nor of the status of an act committed involuntarily but arising out of a condition brought on by voluntary action in the past. What Socrates did, as Aristotle frankly acknowledges, was to initiate the whole discussion out of which such analysis sprang. To Socrates the matter appeared thus. No man with full knowledge of his own and his fellows' nature, and of the consequences of his acts, would make a wrong choice of action. But what man has such knowledge? Neither himself nor anyone known to him. His awareness of this laid on him the obligation to make it clear to others, and having convinced them both of their ignorance and of the paramount need of knowledge, to persuade them to shun those ways of life which were an impediment to discovery and accept the help of his maieutic powers. As Joël himself goes on to say, he did not seek to prove (better, to discover) that virtue is good—that was a truism—but what virtue is. And he urged others to do the same. This *was* an exhortation to acquire virtue, in the only way in which Socrates thought it could be acquired.

NOTE. One of the best short expositions of the essence of Socraticism is Ritter's on pp. 54–7 of his *Sokrates*, where he states and answers four objections to the doctrine that virtue is knowledge. The fourth is that such intel-

---

[1] I think it is plain that the author of the *MM* has heard no more attributed to Socrates than that no one would choose to be unjust. The addition of the word σπουδαίους at line 7, and the conclusion ὥστε δῆλον ὅτι οὐδὲ σπουδαῖοι, are his own.

lectual determinism destroys the point of moral precept and the recognition of any strict or absolute duty. The gist of his answer is worth repeating to supplement the one above. True, he says, a man in possession of full knowledge would have no duty in the sense of a command laid on him by a higher authority which he must recognize, and it would be superfluous to demand moral action from him. Where there is natural necessity there is no duty. But in Socrates's (and Plato's) belief, imperfect and limited humanity is incapable of such complete insight. σοφία is for God, only φιλοσοφία for men.[1] Their search for wisdom is above all a search for self-knowledge. This cannot be taken for granted, but remains a duty, because the necessity of seeking knowledge is not always recognized, being in conflict with the urge towards pleasure and honour. It can only be maintained, in the face of many temptations, by an optimistic belief in its overriding value. Nevertheless the duty of self-examination may be felt so deeply that it sums up all duties in itself, and in content and importance does not fall below any of the fundamental moral demands that have ever been made or could be made.

(8) THE GOOD AND THE USEFUL

In *Republic* I (336c–d) Thrasymachus opens his attack by challenging Socrates to say what he means by justice or right conduct: 'And don't tell me that it is the necessary or the beneficial or the helpful or the profitable or the advantageous, but speak plainly and precisely, for if you give me such nonsensical answers I won't stand it.' Socrates was famous for this utilitarian approach to goodness and virtue.[2] At 339b he agrees that he believes justice to be something advantageous. In the *Hippias Major* he says: 'Let us postulate that whatever is useful is beautiful (or fine, *kalon*).'[3] In the *Gorgias* (474d) all things fine—bodies, colours, shapes, sounds, habits or pursuits—are so called either in view of their usefulness for some specific purpose or because they give pleasure. In the *Meno* (87d–e) he argues that, if *areté* is what makes

---

[1] Cf. *Apol.* 23a–b: Apollo revealed to Socrates the inadequacy of human wisdom and laid on him the task of bringing it home to others; Xen. *Mem.* 1.3.2: he prayed for no specific thing, because the gods know best what things are good.

[2] The terms used to connote utility include ὠφέλιμον, χρήσιμον, συμφέρον, λυσιτελοῦν. With the *Rep.* passage cf. *Clitophon* 409c.

[3] P. 388 above. The beauty competition in Xenophon's *Symp.* (described just before) is fought on the same arguments. The close connexion of καλόν with ἀγαθόν, and of both with usefulness for practical ends, has been remarked on already (pp. 170f.). A good example of their identification by Socrates in Xen. *Mem.* 3.8.5.

us good, it must be something advantageous or useful, since all good things are useful. Many things normally considered such—health,[1] strength, wealth—may in certain circumstances lead to harm. What we have to find is something always, unfailingly advantageous. Sometimes goodness is coupled with pleasure as well as usefulness, as in the *Protagoras* (358b): 'All actions aimed at this end, namely a pleasant and painless life, must be fine actions, that is, good and beneficial. If then the pleasant is the good . . .' The knowledge and wisdom necessary for a good life consist in acquiring an 'art of measurement' which will reveal the real, as opposed to the apparent, magnitude of pleasures. As with physical objects, they may deceive by appearing larger when close at hand, smaller when distant. If we are able to judge their actual measurements, we shall ensure not only a momentary, fleeting pleasure which may be followed by unhappiness, but the maximum of pleasure and minimum of pain throughout our lives. In the metric art, or hedonic calculus, lies salvation, since it 'cancels the effect of the immediate impression and by revealing the true state of affairs causes the soul to have peace and to abide in the truth, thus saving our life' (*Prot.* 356d–e).

The utilitarian conception of good is certainly Socratic. Xenophon makes him say, just before his identification of justice and the rest of virtue with knowledge (*Mem.* 3.9.4): 'All men, I believe, choose from the various courses open to them the one which they think will be most advantageous to them, and follow that.' An important consequence is that goodness is relative to a desired end. This is especially emphasized by Xenophon in two conversations, with Aristippus and Euthydemus.[2] Aristippus was a hedonist in the vulgar sense of indulging excessively in food, drink and sex, and had already been rebuked by Socrates for his unwisdom. He hopes to get his own back by asking Socrates if he knows of anything good, and then, when Socrates gives any of the usual answers and names some one thing commonly thought to be good, showing that in certain circumstances it can be bad. Socrates however counters by asking whether he is to name something good for a fever, or for ophthalmia, or for hunger or what, 'because if you are asking me whether I know of something good which is not the good *of*

---

[1] In Xenophon (*Mem.* 4.2.32) Socrates gives an example of circumstances in which the sick may have an advantage over the healthy.

[2] *Mem.* 3.8.1–7, 4.6.8–9.

anything, I neither know nor want to know'. Similarly with what is beautiful (*kalon*), Socrates knows plenty of beautiful things, all unlike one another. 'How can what is beautiful be unlike what is beautiful?' In the way that a beautiful (fine) wrestler is unlike a beautiful runner, a shield, beautiful for protection, differs from a javelin which is beautiful for its swift and powerful motion. The answer is the same for good and beautiful because what is good in relation to anything is beautiful in relation to the same thing. *Areté* is expressly mentioned as an example. The question whether in that case a dung-basket is beautiful leaves Socrates unperturbed. 'Of course, and a golden shield is ugly if the one is well made for its special work and the other badly.' Since everything has its own limited province of usefulness, everything may be said to be both good and bad, beautiful and ugly: what is good for hunger is often bad for fever, a build that is beautiful for wrestling is often ugly for running, 'for all things are good and beautiful in relation to the purposes for which they are well adapted'.

The conversation with Euthydemus follows the same lines. The good is nothing but the useful, and what is useful to one man may be hurtful to another. Beauty is similarly related to function. What is useful is beautiful in relation to that for which it is useful, and it is impossible to mention anything—body, utensil or whatever—which is beautiful for *all* purposes.

In these conversations Socrates is making exactly the same point that Protagoras makes in Plato's dialogue, that nothing is good or bad, beneficial or harmful, *in abstracto*, but only in relation to a particular object. (See pp. 166 f. above.) Similarly in the *Phaedrus* (p. 187, n. 3) he asks how anyone can call himself a doctor because he knows the effect of certain drugs and treatments, if he has no idea which of them is appropriate to a particular patient with a particular illness, at what stage they should be applied or for how long. Socrates did not scorn empiricism in the ordinary exigencies of life, he was as alive as any Sophist to the folly of imposing rigid rules indiscriminately, and one of the most indisputably Socratic tenets is that the goodness of anything lies in its fitness to perform its proper function. But once the importance of calculation is admitted, and hence the need for knowledge if pleasures are to be chosen with discrimination (and even a Callicles is forced to admit in the end that there are bad pleasures as well as good, because some are beneficial and others harmful, *Gorg.* 499b–d), Socrates is able to proceed, by apparently common-sense arguments, to stand common sense on its head. According to Xenophon (*Mem.* 4.8.6), when on trial for his life he could claim that no one had lived a better, or a pleasanter, more enjoyable life than he; for they live best who make the best effort to become as good as possible, and most pleasantly they who are most conscious that they are improving. Good (= useful or needful) things can obviously be arranged in a hierarchy: the right arms and equipment give soldiers the means to fight well; over and above this, the right strategy and tactics are needed if their fighting is to be effective; if this has brought victory, that only leaves further aims, and the means to them, undecided, for which a yet higher wisdom and knowledge are required. How is the former enemy to be treated, and how is the country to be so ordered that the fruits of victory are a peaceful, prosperous and happy life?[1] Every art—strategy, medicine, politics and the rest—has its own particular aim, to which particular means are relative. This is 'the good' for it—victory, or health, or power over one's fellows. But at the end of each there is always a further aim. Victory may turn sour on the victors, restored health may mean only the continuation of an unhappy life, political power may be frustrating. 'Men think of the practically useful as that helping them to get what they want, but it is more useful to know what is worth wanting.'[2] Thrasymachus and Clitophon were right to be annoyed when they asked in what consisted human excellence, righteousness or good conduct, and were put off with the answer that it was 'the useful'; for this was an answer without content. *What* is useful, *what* will further the ends of human life? The doctor as such, the general as such, know what they want to achieve—in the one case health, in the other victory—and this guides them in their choice of implements and means. But when it comes to the aim of human existence, the good life which the *areté* that we are seeking is to ensure, one cannot name any single, material thing. Any that could be mentioned might be misused, and

---

[1] This particular example is invented, not taken from a Socratic conversation; but it is essentially Socratic.

[2] Gouldner, *Enter Plato*, 182, which I quote to draw attention to his sensible remarks on this and the following page.

(as Versényi has pointed out, *Socr. Hum.* 76 f.) would in any case be a particular instance incapable of universality. What is wanted is 'that quality, characteristic mark, or formal structure that all good things, no matter how relative, particular and materially different, must share if they are to be good at all'.

Socrates agreed with the Sophists that different specific, or subordinate, activities had their different ends or 'goods', calling for different means to acquire them. On the other hand he deplored the extreme, individualistic relativism which said that whatever any man thought right was right for him. The ends, and so the means, were objectively determined, and the expert would attain them while the ignorant would not. Hence his insistence on 'leading the discussion back to the definition'. To decide who is the better citizen, one must inquire what is the function of a good citizen.[1] First he is considered in separate aspects: who is the good citizen in economic matters, in war, in debate and so forth? From these instances (as dozens of examples show) must be extracted the *eidos* common to them all, which would turn out to be knowledge—in this case knowledge of what a *polis* is and for what end it was constituted. Where Socrates went beyond the Sophists was in seeing the need for this formal definition. Yet he could never have satisfied a Thrasymachus, for seeing the need did not mean that he could fulfil it easily or quickly. Indeed he was only too well aware that the search was long and difficult, if not endless. It might take a lifetime, but it would be a lifetime well spent, for 'the unexamined life is not the life for a human being' (*Apol.* 38a). He laid no claim to the knowledge which was virtue, but only a certain insight into the right way to look for it. The clue lay in the close connexion between essence and function, between what a thing is and what it is *for*. One cannot know what a shuttle is without understanding the work of the weaver and what he is trying to make. To know what a cook or a doctor or a general is is to know his job, and leads to a knowledge of the particular *areté* which will enable him to perform it. If therefore we want to learn what is *areté* as such, the supreme or universal excellence which will enable us all, whatever our craft, profession or standing, to live the span of human life in the best possible way, we must first know ourselves, for

[1] This is Xenophon's example at *Mem.* 4.6.13 ff., quoted on pp. 433 f. above.

with that self-knowledge will come the knowledge of our chief end. Pursued to this extreme, the doctrine which started out as utilitarian and even selfish may end in such an apparently unpractical conclusion as that it is better to suffer wrong than to inflict it, and having done a wrong, better to be punished for it than to escape. For the real self, which is to be 'benefited', turns out to be the *psyche*, and this is only harmed by the commission of wrongful acts, and improved by chastisement.[1]

(9) SELF-KNOWLEDGE AND 'CARE OF THE SOUL'

One of Socrates's most insistent exhortations to his fellow-citizens was that they should look after—care for, tend—their souls (τῆς ψυχῆς ἐπιμελεῖσθαι). In the *Apology* he says (29d):

I will not cease from philosophy and from exhorting you, and declaring the truth to every one of you I meet, saying in the words I am accustomed to use: 'My good friend . . . are you not ashamed of caring for money and how to get as much of it as you can, and for honour and reputation, and not caring or taking thought for wisdom and truth and for your *psyche*, and how to make it as good as possible?'

And at 30a:

I go about doing nothing else but urging you, young and old alike, not to care for your bodies or for money sooner than, or as much as, for your *psyche*, and how to make it as good as you can.

The original word *psyche* avoids the overtones which the English translation 'soul' has acquired through centuries of use in a Christian context. As Socrates understood it, the effort that he demanded of his fellows was philosophic and intellectual rather than religious, though the *psyche* did not lack religious associations in and before his time. Burnet went so far as to say that 'not only had the word *psyche* never been used in this way, but the existence of what Socrates called by that name had never been realized'.[2] To make good this statement called for

---

[1] Plato, *Gorg.* 469b, 509c, 477a. Such doctrine was not to be produced on every occasion, nor in answer to every kind of question. In judging conversations like that with Aristippus, it is important not to forget what Grote pointed out (*Plato*, III, 538): 'The real Socrates, since he talked incessantly and with everyone, must have known how to diversify his conversation and adapt it to each listener.'

[2] 'Socratic Doctrine of the Soul', *Ess. & Add.* 140. The above translations from the *Apology* are his.

an inquiry into the history of the word which he proceeded to make, as others have also done. By the fifth century it had certainly acquired remarkably complex associations. There was still the Homeric conception of it as the breath-soul which was a worthless thing without the body and had no connexion with thought or emotion. There was the primitive ghost-*psyche* which could be summoned back to prophesy and to help or take vengeance on the living. There was the *psyche* of the mystery-religions, akin to the divine and capable of a blessed life after death if the necessary rites or practices had been observed, with the addition, among the Pythagoreans, of the pursuit of *philosophia*. *Psyche* could mean courage, and 'of a good *psyche*' (εὔψυχος) brave, or it could mean bare life, so that 'to love one's *psyche*' was to cling to life in a cowardly way,[1] and swooning was a temporary loss of *psyche* (λιποψυχία). Both in the Orphic and in the Ionian-scientific tradition this life-substance was a portion of the surrounding air or *aither* enclosed in a body, and would fly off to rejoin it at death. This, though material, was the divine element and seems to have been associated with the power of thought,[2] as the *psyche* also is in Sophocles when Creon says that only power reveals the *psyche*, thought and mind of a man (*Ant.* 175–7). Here it verges on character, and it is used in moral contexts also. Pindar speaks of 'keeping one's *psyche* from unrighteousness',[3] and Sophocles of 'a well-disposed *psyche* with righteous thoughts'.[4] The law of homicide demanded forfeiture of 'the

---

[1] In the very speech in which he exhorts the Athenians to 'care for their *psyche*' in an entirely different sense, Socrates can also use φιλοψυχία in this sense of a clinging to mere life (*Apol.* 37c). ἔμψυχος is of course a common word for living or animate.

[2] Although in Eur. *Hel.* 1014 the subject is νοῦς, and in *Suppl.* 533 πνεῦμα, both seem identical with the ψυχαί of the Potidaea epitaph. See Guthrie, *Gks. & Gods*, 262f., and cf. the phrase ὅσ' ἔστ' ἔμψυχα καὶ γνώμην ἔχει at *Medea*, 230. At fr. 839.9ff. the aetherial part is nameless.

[3] *Ol.* 2.70. This might be said to be in an Orphic setting, since the passage deals with transmigration and the blessedness awaiting those who have lived three righteous lives in succession.

[4] Fr. 97 N. Since this is a little inconvenient for Burnet's argument, he can only say that it 'goes rather beyond its [the *psyche*'s] ordinary range' (p. 154), and he is similarly impelled to play down the significance of Soph. *Phil.* 55 and 1013 (p. 156). It must be said, however, that *psyche* is sometimes used as a synonym for a person, even redundantly or periphrastically, as when Electra, clasping the urn which she supposes to contain the ashes of Orestes, calls it ψυχῆς 'Ορέστου λοιπόν—'all that is left of Orestes' (Soph. *El.* 1127). This should warn us not to give too much weight to the word in lines like ἀρκεῖν γὰρ οἶμαι... μίαν ψυχὴν τάδ' ἐκτίνουσαν ἣν εὔνους παρῇ or when Clytemnestra calls Orestes τῆς ἐμῆς ψυχῆς γεγώς—'my own offspring' (*ibid.* 775). Perhaps it has little more weight at *Ph.* 55, where 'to deceive the *psyche* of Philoctetes' means simply to deceive Philoctetes, though it is arguable that the periphrasis would hardly have been possible here if it had not been natural to associate the *psyche* with the mind.

psyche which did or planned the deed', combining the senses of life and the power of thought and deliberation.[1] When Aristophanes calls the school of Socrates 'a home of clever *psychai*', this may of course be a satirical allusion to his own use of the word (*Clouds*, 94).

These examples, many of them taken from Burnet's own collection, may make us hesitate to go the whole way with him in his belief that no one before Socrates had ever said 'that there is something in us which is capable of attaining wisdom, that this same thing is capable of attaining goodness and righteousness, and that it was called "soul" (ψυχή)'. More to the point is his observation (p. 158) that we do not dispose of Socrates's claim to originality by observing that his conception of the soul was reached by combining certain features of existing beliefs: 'the power of transfusing the apparently disparate is exactly what is meant by originality'. Nor does Burnet even mention what is perhaps the most distinctive feature of the Socratic doctrine, namely the description of the relationship of soul to body in terms of the craftsman analogy: soul is to body as the user to the used, the workman to his tool.

In brief, what Socrates thought about the human *psyche* was that it was the true self. The living man *is* the *psyche*, and the body (which for the Homeric heroes and those still brought up on Homer took such decided preference over it) is only the set of tools or instruments of which he makes use in order to live. A craftsman can only do good work if he is in command of his tools and can guide them as he wishes, an accomplishment which demands knowledge and practice. Similarly life can only be lived well if the *psyche* is in command of (ἄρχει) the body.[2] It meant purely and simply the intelligence,[3] which in a properly

---

[1] ἡ δράσασα καὶ βουλεύσασα ψυχή, Antiphon Tetr. Γ. α. 7. This is quoted by Burnet (154f.), who passes somewhat lightly over the evident power of the *psyche* to initiate and plan an action.

[2] Thus the later, Stoic epithet for the intelligence, τὸ ἡγεμονικόν, perpetuates the genuine Socratic idea. It is foreshadowed by the ἡγεμονοῦν of Plato, *Tim.* 41c. Cf. also the use of τὸ ἡγούμενον by Aristotle, *EN* 1113a6.

[3] Socrates's language is not completely consistent on this point. At *Alc. I* 133b he speaks of τοῦτον αὐτῆς τὸν τόπον ἐν ᾧ ἐγγίγνεται ἡ ψυχῆς ἀρετή, σοφία and immediately after of τῆς ψυχῆς ... τοῦτο περὶ οὗ τὸ εἰδέναι τε καὶ φρονεῖν ἐστιν. This language is construed by Jowett's editors (1, 601 n. 1) as expressing 'the view of reason as an innermost self *within* the human soul', a view which they call 'characteristic of the last phase of Plato's thought (*Philebus, Timaeus*)'. It is, I am sure, no more than a momentary concession to the common view of ψυχή as the seat of life. For Socrates throughout the dialogue, but especially when he describes the ψυχή as that which is to be cherished because its function is to govern the body, it is the mind, as indeed it is when he calls it that whose ἀρετή is σοφία, for a thing is rightly defined with

ordered life is in complete control of the senses and emotions. Its proper virtue is wisdom (σοφία) and thought (τὸ φρονεῖν), and to improve the *psyche* is to take thought for wisdom (φρόνησις) and truth (*Apol.* 29d, p. 467 above). This identification of the *psyche* with the self and the self with the reason might be said to have roots both in Ionian scientific thought and in Pythagoreanism, yet there was certainly novelty in Socrates's development of it,[1] apart from the fact that the ordinary Athenian, whom he particularly wished to persuade, was not in the habit of letting his life be ruled by either of these influences. The arguments leading to this conception of the soul have the familiar Socratic ring, and make clear its intimate connexion with his other fundamental conception, that of knowledge, and in particular self-knowledge, as the prerequisite of the good life. They are best set forth in the *First Alcibiades*, a dialogue which, whether or not Plato wrote it, was aptly described by Burnet as 'designed as a sort of introduction to Socratic philosophy for beginners'.[2]

Alcibiades, still under twenty, has ambitions to be a leader of men, both in politics and war. He ought then to have some understanding of such concepts as right and wrong, expedient and inexpedient. Socrates first gets him to contradict himself on these subjects, thus proving that he did not know their meaning although he thought he did. He next points out that it is not ignorance that matters, but ignorance that you are ignorant. Alcibiades does not know how to fly any more than he knows how to govern justly or for the good of the Athenians, but since he is aware of his ignorance he will not try, and no harm will be done.

reference to its ἀρετή. (In his analogy, the eye which wishes to see *itself* must look to the seat (τόπος) of its ἀρετή.) There is no contradiction between the view of the soul in the *Alc.* and that at *Apol.* 29d: to care for the ψυχή is to care for φρόνησις and ἀλήθεια.

[1] It may be that in some respects Democritus came close to the Socratic position, in spite of the inclusion of soul in his all-embracing materialism. Vlastos has claimed that he 'would advise men, exactly as did Socrates, to care for their souls' (*Philos. Rev.* 1945, 578ff.). Yet there are legitimate doubts about the genuineness of his ethical fragments, as well as about the relative dates of his writings and Socrates's dialectical activity, and I can add nothing to what I have said in vol. II, 489ff. On the constitution of the soul in Democritus, see the index *s.v.* 'atomists: soul'.

[2] *Ess. & Add.* 139. Cf. D. Tarrant in *CQ*, 1938, 167: 'an able exposition of the Socratic method of ἔλεγχος and induction. The personality of Socrates is . . . again drawn on familiar lines.' In antiquity the dialogue was universally accepted as Plato's, but its authorship has been doubted in modern times, especially by German critics, against whom it was stoutly defended by its Budé editor Croiset in 1920. More recently its authenticity has been upheld by A. Motte in *L'Ant. Class.* (1961). See also the appraisal by R. Weil in *L'Inf. Litt.* (1964), and the references given by the revisers of Jowett's *Dialogues of Plato*, vol. I, 601 n. 1.

Again (a favourite illustration), there is no harm in his knowing nothing of seamanship if he is content to be a passenger and leave the steering to the skilled helmsman, but there may be disaster if he thinks himself capable of taking over the helm.

Socrates next gets Alcibiades to agree that for success in life it is necessary to care for, or take pains over, oneself (ἐπιμελεῖσθαι ἑαυτοῦ), to improve and train oneself, and goes on to demonstrate that you cannot tend and improve a thing unless you know its nature. As always, he is trying to 'lead the discussion back to a definition' (p. 433 above). 'Knowing how' for Socrates must be preceded by 'knowing what', a lesson that the Sophists had failed to learn. First he draws a distinction between tending a thing itself and tending something that belongs to it. These are generally the subjects of different skills. To tend the foot is the job of the trainer (or doctor or chiropodist); to tend what belongs to the foot—i.e. shoes—belongs to the cobbler. Now such things as wealth and reputation are not ourselves but things belonging to us, and therefore to augment these externals—which many regard as a proper aim in life—is not to look after ourselves at all, and the art of tending ourselves is a different one. What is this art? Well, can anyone make a good shoe or mend one if he does not know what a shoe is and what it is intended to do? No. One must understand the nature and purpose of anything before one can make, mend or look after it properly. So in life, we cannot acquire an art of self-improvement unless we first understand what we ourselves are. Our first duty, therefore, is to obey the Delphic command, 'Know thyself', 'for once we know ourselves, we may learn how to care for ourselves, but otherwise we never shall'.[1]

How do we come by this knowledge of our real selves?[2] It is reached by means of a further distinction, between the user of anything and what he uses. Alcibiades is first made to admit that the two are always distinct: he and Socrates are people, conversing by means of *logoi*, and

[1] 128b–129a, 124a. Commendation of the Delphic precept occurs again in Plato at *Phaedrus*, 229e, and in Xenophon at *Mem.* 4.2.24 and 3.9.6, where not knowing oneself is equated with not knowing one's own ignorance, a folly which in the *Alcibiades* has already been exposed. Plut. *Adv. Col.* 1118c quotes Aristotle as saying that it was the starting-point of Socrates's inquiries into the nature of man. (ἀπορίας ταύτης there refers to the question τί ἄνθρωπός ἐστι, though this is not made clear by the passage as printed in the fragments of Aristotle by Rose (fr. 1) or Ross (*De phil.* fr. 1).) [2] τί ποτ' ἐσμὲν αὐτοί, 129b.

the *logoi* they use are different from themselves. A shoemaker is distinct from his knife and awl, a musician from his instrument. But we can go further. A shoemaker, we say, or any other craftsman, uses not only his tools but also his hands and eyes. We may generalize this and say that the body as a whole is something which a man uses to carry out his purposes, his legs to take him where he wants to go, and so on. And if we agree that such a statement is meaningful, we must agree that in speaking of a man we mean something different from his body—that, in fact, which makes use of the body as its instrument. There is nothing that this can be except the *psyche*, which uses and controls (ἄρχει) the body.[1] Therefore he who said 'know thyself' was in fact bidding us know our *psyche* (130e). Going back to the earlier distinction, to know the body is to know something that belongs to oneself, as a shoe to a foot, but not one's real self; and likewise to look after the body is not to look after one's real self. To know oneself is at once an intellectual and a moral insight, for it is to know that the *psyche*, not the body, is intended by nature or God (cf. 124c) to be the ruling element: to know oneself is to be self-controlled (*sophron*, 131b, and 133c). This may throw some further light on our earlier discussions of Socratic intellectualism (pp. 455 ff. above). It is at this point, too, that Socrates makes use of the argument to oppose the prevailing sexual standards: he himself may be correctly described as a lover of Alcibiades, because he loves his *psyche*; those who love his body love not Alcibiades, but only something belonging to him (p. 395 above).

All of this is familiar Socratic doctrine, the elements of which can be found repeated many times in the Socratic writings, but are so presented here as to bring out their interrelations in a single continuous argument. We are not surprised therefore when, after establishing that to know ourselves is to know the *psyche* and not the body, he goes on to say that if we want to know what the *psyche* is, we must look 'particularly at that part of it in which its virtue resides', and adds at once that this virtue of the *psyche* is wisdom (*sophia*). To know what something is is to know what it is *for*, and we have already discovered that

---

[1] It is difficult to understand what was in Jaeger's mind when he wrote (*Paideia*, II, 43) that 'in his [Socrates's] thought, there is no opposition between psychical and physical man'. The body is as extraneous to the man himself, his *psyche*, as the saw is to the carpenter.

this *ergon* or function of the soul is to rule, govern or control. That virtue is knowledge is true right through the scale of human occupations. The virtue of a shoemaker is knowledge, of what shoes are for and how to make them; the virtue of a doctor is knowledge, of the body and how to tend it. And the virtue of a complete man both as an individual and as a social being is knowledge of the moral and statesmanlike virtues—justice, courage and the rest—which all ambitious Athenian politicians carelessly claimed to understand, but of the nature of which it was Socrates's painful duty to point out that they (and himself no less) were so far ignorant.[1] Here we have the whole train of thought that lay behind the exhortation in the *Apology* to care for the *psyche* and for wisdom and truth, rather than for money or reputation, which it would have been inappropriate, or rather impossible, to unfold in a speech before the judges at his trial.

(10) RELIGIOUS BELIEFS OF SOCRATES: IS THE SOUL IMMORTAL?

The next point made in the *Alcibiades* comes rather unexpectedly to a modern reader, but is introduced by Socrates without preamble: 'Can we mention', he asks (133c), 'anything more divine about the soul than what is concerned with knowledge and thought? Then this aspect of it[2] resembles God, and it is by looking toward that and understanding all that is divine—God and wisdom—that a man will most fully know himself.' God, he goes on, reflects the nature of *psyche* more clearly and brightly than anything in our own souls, and we may therefore use him as a mirror for human nature too, if what we are looking for is the *areté* of the soul, and this is the best way to see and understand

[1] In describing the first serious attempt in history to define the meaning of the word 'good', I have not thought it helpful or fair to compare it directly with the ideas of the twentieth century A.D., as set forth in a book like R. M. Hare's *Language of Morals*. But one outstanding difference between the two may be noted. On p. 100 of that book Professor Hare speaks of certain words which he calls 'functional words', and the example he gives is a Socratic one: 'We do not know what a carpenter is until we know what a carpenter is supposed to do.' But the extrapolation from this kind of case to man in general is no longer allowed: '"man" in "good man" is not normally a functional word, and never so when moral commendation is being given' (p. 145). The point is elaborated in his essay reprinted in the Foot collection, pp. 78–82.

[2] τοῦτο αὐτῆς. As often, one envies the elusiveness which the omission of the noun makes possible for a Greek. It is by no means certain that 'part' is the best word to supply. τόπος at 133b is metaphorical, and carried over from the example of the eye. If pressed for a noun, the writer might well have suggested δύναμις.

ourselves.[1] With this passage in mind, Jowett's editors (1. 601 n. 1) say that in the *Alcibiades* 'the religious spirit is more positive than in Plato's earlier dialogues', and give this as a reason for supposing it a later and possibly spurious work. But the religious references in the *Apology* are equally positive, and the conception of a divine mind as a universal and purer counterpart of our own was common in the fifth century and is attributed to Socrates by Xenophon. In Plato's *Apology* Socrates says that it would be wrong to disobey God's commands through fear of death (28 e), and that, fond as he is of the Athenians, he will obey God rather than them (29 d), that God has sent him to the city for its good (30 d–e), and that the fortunes of the good are not neglected by the gods (41 d). He claims that it is 'not permitted (θεμιτόν)' for a better man to be harmed by a worse (30 d), and the forbidding agent is clearly not human but divine. Both *Apology* and *Euthyphro* mention his serious acceptance of the 'divine sign', which he regarded as a voice from God. How far one is justified in translating ὁ θεός simply as 'God' is a difficult question. At 29 d Socrates presumably has chiefly in mind Apollo and his oracle, and at 41 d he speaks of 'the gods' in the plural. Yet in some cases he seems to have advanced beyond the popular theology to the notion of a single divine power, for which 'God' is the least misleading modern equivalent. In any case it cannot be said that the religious language of the *Apology* is less 'positive' than that of the *Alcibiades*, and we certainly have no right to say that it is used in a different spirit.

Closest to the thought of the *Alcibiades* about God and the soul is the passage in Xenophon (*Mem.* 1.4.17) where Socrates says to Aristodemus: 'Just consider that your own mind within you controls your body as it will. So you must believe that the wisdom in the whole universe disposes all things according to its pleasure.' This supreme being appears at 4.3.13, in contrast to 'the other gods', as 'he who co-ordinates and holds together the whole cosmos', and a little further on

---

[1] The sentences about using God as a mirror are omitted from our manuscripts of the dialogue, but were read by Eusebius and other ancient authors. They are restored by Burnet in the Oxford text and in Jowett's translation, and are obviously necessary to complete the rather elaborate analogy with mirrors and the eye which Plato is drawing. Croiset's objection (Budé ed. 110 n. 1) that they only repeat what has gone before is misleading, nor is his claim convincing that their content has a Neoplatonic tinge.

in the same chapter the *psyche* of man is described as that which 'more than anything else that is human partakes of the divine'. The resemblance of the language here to that reported of Anaximenes, who compared the universal breath or air to the human soul, which is also air, and holds us together (vol. I, 131), reminds us how old is this connexion between human and universal soul. The intellectual character of the universal soul as divine *mind*, and its creative role, were emphasized in Socrates's own lifetime by Anaxagoras and Diogenes of Apollonia, and considering its possibilities for spiritualization it is not surprising that he should have taken over the belief and adapted it to his own teaching. At 1.4.8 he claims it is absurd that wisdom should 'by some lucky chance' reside in the tiny portions of matter which form our bodies, and yet 'all the huge and infinitely numerous bodies' in the universe should have achieved the regularity and order which they display without any thought at all.[1] His criticism of Anaxagoras was not that he made Mind the moving force behind the whole universe, but that having done so, he ignored it, and explained the cosmic phenomena by mechanical causes which seemed to have no relation whatsoever to intelligence.

The mentions of a god who is the supreme wisdom in the world, as our minds are in us, are associated with an insistence on his loving care for mankind. At 1.4.5 this being is 'he who created man from the beginning', and Socrates points out in detail how our own parts are designed to serve our ends, and at 4.3.10 how the lower animals too exist for the sake of man. God cares for men (as also in Plato's *Apology*, 41 d), takes thought for them, loves them, assists them, as well as being their creator.[2] All this excludes the supposition that Socrates merely shared the vague pantheism of contemporary intellectuals. He uses 'God' or 'the gods' indifferently, but with a bias towards the former, and we have seen mention of a supreme governor of the universe contrasted with lesser gods. In so far as he genuinely believed in the gods of popular polytheism (and Xenophon was emphatic in defending him against charges of neglecting their cult), he probably thought of them

---

[1] A similar argument is used in Plato's *Philebus* (29 b–30 b), a late dialogue which nevertheless has Socrates as its chief speaker. The idea behind it certainly goes back to the fifth century.
[2] See the phrases collected by Zeller, *Ph. d. Gr.* 178 n. 3.

as different manifestations of the one supreme spirit. This was the position of many thinking men, and an apparently indifferent use of 'the god', 'the gods' and 'the divine' (neuter) is characteristic of the age. 'If you make trial of the gods by serving them', says Xenophon's Socrates (*Mem.* 1.4.18), 'and see whether they will give you counsel in the things which are hidden from men, you will discover that the divine is such, and so great, that at one and the same time it sees and hears everything and is everywhere and takes care of everything.' The words 'in the things hidden from men' are a reminder that Socrates deprecated resort to oracles as a substitute for thought. In matters where the gods have given men the power to judge for themselves, they emphatically ought to take the trouble to learn what is necessary and make up their own minds: to trouble the gods about such things is contrary to true religion (ἀθέμιτα: see *Mem.* 1.1.9). To sum up, Socrates believed in a god who was the supreme Mind, responsible for the ordering of the universe and at the same time the creator of men. Men moreover had a special relation with him in that their own minds, which controlled their bodies as God controlled the physical movements of the universe, were, though less perfect than the mind of God, of the same nature, and worked on the same principles. In fact, if one looked only to the *areté* of the human soul and disregarded its shortcomings, the two were identical. Whether or not because of this relationship, God had a special regard for man, and had designed both man's own body and the rest of nature for his benefit.

These religious views are amply attested for Socrates, and they create a presumption that he believed the soul to persist after death in a manner more satisfying than the shadowy and witless existence of the Homeric dead; but in deference to many scholars who have thought him to be agnostic on this point, it must be looked at further. To call the soul, or mind, the divine part of man does not by itself imply personal, individual survival. The hope of the mystic was to lose his individuality by being caught up into the one all-pervading spirit, and this absorption was probably the expectation of all, mystics or natural philosophers, who believed in the airy (and ultimately aetherial) nature of the *psyche* and in the *aither* as a living and 'governing' element in the

universe. For believers in transmigration like the Orphics and Pythagoreans, individual survival, carrying with it rewards and punishments
for the kind of life lived on earth, was the fate only of those who were
still caught in the wheel and destined for reincarnation. The final goal
was again reabsorption.[1] In one form or another—through the
mysteries, the philosophers, and superstitions of a primitive antiquity—
this belief would be fairly widespread in the fifth century, and is probably behind Euripides's lines about the mind of the dead 'plunging
immortal into the immortal *aither*' (*Hel.* 1014ff.).

That is one reason for caution in using the reference in the *Alcibiades*
to the soul as divine as evidence that Socrates believed in personal
immortality. Another is the doubt expressed by some scholars concerning the date of the dialogue. Even if intended as 'an introduction to
Socratic philosophy' it might, if not written before the middle of the
fourth century, include in all innocence something that was not
Socratic. For the closest parallel to its statement of the divinity of the
human reason, put briefly and soberly with none of the language about
initiation, rebirth and so on which Plato adopted from the mystery-
religions, we have to look to Aristotle. In the tenth book of the *Ethics*
he argues that the best and highest form of human life would consist in
the uninterrupted exercise of the reason; 'but', he goes on (1177b27),
'it is not by virtue of our humanity that we can live this life, but in so
far as there is something of the divine in us'. A little later on, in
exact agreement with the *Alcibiades*, he says that nevertheless this divine
faculty of reason is above all others a man's true self (1178a7). If the
Alcibiades was written, as some think, about the time of Plato's death
and Aristotle's maturity, the addition might be very natural. It might
indeed be supposed (as Plato did suppose) that the soul's independence
of the body, and hence its immortality, were the natural consequence of
the sharp dualism of soul and body that is maintained in the main part
of the dialogue, the thoroughly Socratic argument that the body is not
the real man but only an instrument of which the man (that is, the
psyche) makes use. But we cannot yet say for certain that Socrates drew
that conclusion.

It is safer to turn first to the *Apology*, the most certainly Socratic of

---

[1] See vol. I, especially 480f. and 466 with n. 2.

all Plato's works.[1] There Socrates says in several places what he thinks about death. On no other subject is it truer to say that everyone has his own Socrates. Some read into these passages agnosticism, others religious faith in a future life. First of all the text must speak for itself. At 28e he says it would be shameful if, after facing death in battle at the command of the state, he should now through fear of death disobey the god's command to philosophize by examining himself and others.

To fear death is only an instance of thinking oneself wise when one is not; for it is to think one knows what one does not know. No one in fact knows whether death may not even be the greatest of all good things for man, yet men fear it as if they knew well that it was the greatest evil ... This perhaps is the point in which I am different from the rest of men, and if I could make any claim to be wiser than another, it is in this, that just as I have no full knowledge about the things in Hades, so also I am aware of my ignorance. This however I do know, that it is both evil and base to do wrong and disobey a better, be he god or man. Therefore I shall never fear nor run away from something which for all I know may be good, but rather from evils which I know to be evils.

After the death-sentence Socrates addresses a few words to those who had voted for his acquittal. First he tells them of the silence of his divine sign or voice (p. 403 above), which means that 'what has

---

[1] Concerning the historicity of the *Apol.* every shade of opinion has been held (see Ehnmark in *Eranos*, 1946, 106ff. for this, especially in its bearing on the question of immortality), but few have been found to deny its essential faithfulness to the Socratic philosophy. Admittedly a special case has been made of the third speech (38cff.), delivered after sentence has been passed, but even a sceptic like Wilamowitz agreed that in composing it 'Plato must have carefully avoided saying anything that Socrates himself could not have said' (Ehnmark, *loc. cit.* 108). There is really no good reason to separate this speech from the rest, and about the whole the most reasonable supposition is that Plato (who makes a point of mentioning his own presence at the trial: 34a, 38b), while doubtless polishing up and reducing to better order what Socrates actually said, has not falsified the facts or the spirit of his remarks. At the very most, he will have gone no further than Thucydides in reporting speeches in his history, some of which he had only heard at second hand. See p. 85 above. In Plato's case we must take into account that he was present himself and that the occasion was the final crisis in the life of the man whom he admired most in all the world. It is sufficient guarantee that he has given the substance of what Socrates said, and that, if anything has been added by way of vindicating Socrates's memory, it will be in keeping with his real character and views.

If it is still denied that we can know for certain whether Socrates himself used the opportunity of his trial to make such a complete *apologia pro vita sua*, we can only reply that it would have been an entirely reasonable thing for him to do, and that in any case the account of his life and beliefs which Plato gives us is true to the real man.

happened to me must be something good, and those of us who think death is an evil cannot be right'. He continues (40c):

Looking at it another way we may also feel a strong hope that it is good. Death is one of two things. Either the dead man is as if he no longer exists, and has no sensations at all; or else as men say it is a change and migration of the soul from here to another place. If we have no sensation, but death is like a sleep in which the sleeper has not even a dream, then it must be a wonderful boon; for if a man had to pick out the night in which he slept so soundly that he did not even dream, and setting beside it the other nights and days of his life, to compare them with that night and say how many better and pleasanter days and nights he had spent, I truly believe that not only an ordinary man but even the Great King himself would find them easy to count. If then that is death, I count it a gain, for in this way the whole of time will seem no more than a single night.

If on the other hand death is a sort of migration to another place, and the common tales are true that all the dead are there, what finer thing could there be than this? Would it not be a good journey that takes one to Hades, away from these self-styled judges here, to find the true judges who are said to dispense justice there—Minos, Rhadamanthys, Aeacus, Triptolemus and other demigods who were just in their own lives? Or what would not one of you give to meet Orpheus and Musaeus and Hesiod and Homer? I myself would have a wonderful time there, with Palamedes and Ajax son of Telamon and any other of the ancients who had met his death as the result of an unjust verdict, comparing my experiences with theirs. There would be some pleasure in that. Best of all, I could examine and interrogate the inhabitants of Hades as I do the people here, to find out which of them is wise, and which thinks he is though he is not. What would not a man give to question the leader of the great army at Troy, or Odysseus or Sisyphus or thousands more whom one might mention, both men and women? It would be an infinite happiness to consort and converse with them and examine them— and at any rate they don't put people to death for it there! For among the advantages which those in Hades have over us is the fact that they are immortal for the rest of time, if what we are told is true.

And you too, my friends, must face death with good hope, convinced of the truth of this one thing, that no evil can happen to a good man either in life or in death, nor are his fortunes neglected by the gods.

Then there is the final sentence of the whole *Apology*:

Now the time is up and we must go, I to death and you to life; but which of us is going to the better fate is known to none, except it be to God.

It is only by reading such passages as this at length that one can catch something of the flavour of the man, which was at least as much of an influence on his friends and posterity as any positive doctrine that he had to teach. Indeed, as these same passages show, with such a naturally undogmatic person it is not always easy to say what he did teach, and the majority who like and admire him tend to see in his language whatever they themselves believe. The agnostic greets him as a kindred spirit because he has said that to claim knowledge of what happens after death is to claim to know what one does not know: he states possible alternatives and leaves them open. The religious-minded is impressed by the fact that whenever he mentions death it is to say that it is something good. In this speech, it is true, he entertains the possibility that it may be either a new life, in which one will meet the great men of the past, or a dreamless sleep, and professes to see good in both. But one would not expect him to assert his innermost convictions in a public speech, in which indeed he treats the matter with a certain amount of humour, as when he imagines himself carrying on in the next world the inquisitorial activities which had made him so unpopular in this. One may feel with Taylor that 'it requires a singularly dull and tasteless reader not to see that his own sympathies are with the hope of a blessed immortality' (*VS*, 31). Hints of his own belief appear rather in statements like 'the fortunes of a good man are not neglected by the gods'. The man who believed that the souls of the righteous are in the hand of God, it may be said, is unlikely to have believed that death means utter extinction. The nature of death, he concludes, is unknown *except it be to God*; and that exception, one might argue, makes all the difference.

My own reading of the *Apology* inclines me to this second interpretation, but there is too much to be said on both sides for the question to be resolved on the basis of these passages alone. They must be taken with other considerations. It would be unusual, to put it no higher, for anyone with Socrates's views both about man as the supreme object of the care and solicitude of God, for whose sake the rest of creation exists (and for this one may cite both Plato's *Apology* and Xenophon as quoted on p. 475 above), and about the nature and importance of the human soul, to hold at the same time that physical death was the end and the soul perished with the body. A belief in the independence of the soul, and its indifference to the fate of the body, goes naturally with that sharp distinction between them which we find drawn not only in the *Alcibiades* but in the *Apology* and elsewhere in the more indubitably Socratic parts of Plato. Always for Socrates they were two different things, with the *psyche* (that is, the rational faculty) superior and the body only its sometimes refractory instrument. Hence the supreme importance of 'tendance of the *psyche*' (i.e. the training of the mind), and although Socrates saw this as issuing primarily in the living of a practically good life on earth, he most probably thought that just as it was of an altogether superior nature to the body, so also it outlived it.

Of course if one took the *Phaedo* as a mere continuation of the *Apology*, relating what Socrates said to his intimate friends on the day of his death with as much fidelity as the *Apology* employs in telling what he said before the five hundred judges at his trial, there would be no question about it; for there Socrates does maintain that the *psyche* not only is distinct from, and superior to, the body, but differs from it as the eternal from the temporal. It would, however, be here too a 'dull and tasteless reader' who did not sense the entirely different character of the two works, the intellectual modesty of the one and the human simplicity of its alternatives—either a dreamless sleep or a new life much like this one—and the elaborate combination in the other of mystical language about reincarnation with metaphysical argument about the soul's relation to the eternal Forms. As to this, I have already expressed the view (pp. 353 f. above) that if Socrates had not felt confident of personal immortality, it would have been impossible for Plato to have written an account of his last conversation and death, however imaginative in its details, of which the whole purpose was to instil such confidence. In marked contrast to the *Apology*, he tells us that he himself was not present, and he has felt free to support the simple, unproved faith of his friend with the kind of arguments that appealed to his more speculative nature. Even so, there are many touches of the well-remembered Socrates, not only in the perfect calm and steadfastness with which he goes to meet his death. Surely Socratic is the 'quiet laugh' with which he replies to Crito's request as to how they should bury him: 'Any way you please, provided you can catch me', with the explanation that the dead body which they will shortly see is something quite different from Socrates, the person now talking to them. The *Apology*, though innocent of any theories of reincarnation, speaks of death as a 'change of abode for the soul from here to another place' and 'like going to another country', and this language is exactly paralleled in the *Phaedo*.[1] In the *Phaedo* also Socrates repeats his hope of meeting among the dead with better men than those now living (63b). Even the Socratic profession of ignorance and posing of alternatives is not forgotten there (91b): 'If what I say is true, it is indeed well to believe it; but if there is nothing for a man when he has died, at least I shall be less troublesome to the company than if I were bemoaning my fate.' That however was before the final arguments, after which the Platonic Socrates takes over, and when he has described a possible course of events for the soul both in and out of the body, claims that even if one cannot be positive on such a matter, yet something like it must be true 'because the soul has been clearly shown to be (φαίνεται οὖσα) immortal' (114d). Plato thinks he has proved what Socrates only believed, the fact of the soul's immortality, but when it comes to the details of its fate he remembers again how the undogmatic Socrates, the knower of his own ignorance, used to speak. Something like his *mythos* must be true, 'for it is fitting, and it is worth taking a chance on believing that it is so—the risk is a good one —and one should repeat such things to oneself like a charm, which is why I have spun out the story at such length'. The reason, as always with Socrates, is practical: belief in the scheme of transmigration which he has outlined, with promotion to better lives for the good and *vice versa*, will encourage a man to think little of bodily pleasures, to pursue knowledge and 'deck the *psyche* with her proper adornments, self-control, justice, courage, freedom and truth' (114d–e).

The *Phaedo* is a dialogue inspired by Socrates, but in certain important ways going beyond him. To claim to separate the Socratic from the Platonic will seem to many presumptuous, but one can only follow

[1] Cf. *Apol.* 40c, μετοίκησις τῇ ψυχῇ τοῦ τόπου τοῦ ἐνθένδε εἰς ἄλλον τόπον with *Phaedo*, 117c, τὴν μετοίκησιν τὴν ἐνθένδε ἐκεῖσε, and 40e, εἰ δ' αὖ οἷον ἀποδημῆσαί ἐστιν ὁ θάνατος ἐνθένδε εἰς ἄλλον τόπον, with 61e, where Socrates speaks of himself as μέλλοντα ἐκεῖσε ἀποδημεῖν. (ἀποδημία also at 67b.) On the relations between the *Apol.* and *Phaedo* see also Ehnmark in *Eranos*, 1946.

one's own best judgment and leave the verdict to others. I have already given a character sketch of Socrates based on what seemed the most trustworthy evidence, and it is to this impression of his personality as a whole that we must turn for the answer to a question like this.[1] He seems to have been a man who, as Aristotle said, applied the whole of his remarkable intellectual powers to the solution of questions of practical conduct. In higher matters I would suggest that he was guided by a simple religious faith. Certain problems were in principle soluble by human effort. To trouble the gods with these was lazy and stupid. But there would always be truths beyond the scope of human explanation, and for these one must trust the word of the gods, whether given by oracles or through other channels.[2] There was no irony in the way he talked of his divine sign: he put himself unreservedly in the hands of what he sincerely believed to be an inspiration from heaven. He possessed the religious virtue of humility (which in others also has sometimes been taken for arrogance), and with it, despite his ceaseless questioning of everything in the human sphere, of unquestioning belief. There is nothing impossible or unprecedented in the union of a keen and penetrating insight in human affairs, and an unerring eye for humbug, with a simple religious piety. He cannot have laid such emphasis on the 'care' of the *psyche* as the real man, without believing that as it was both truly human and had some share in the divine nature, so also it was the lasting part of us, and that the treatment accorded it in this life would affect its nature and fortunes in the next (*Phaedo*, 63c). The difference between him and Plato is that whereas he was content to believe in immortality as the humbler and less theologically minded Christian does, as an article of simple faith, Plato felt the need to support it with arguments which might at least strengthen the fearful,

---

[1] It is obviously theoretically possible that parallels between *Apol.* and *Phaedo* are due to the Platonic character of the former rather than to Socratic elements in the latter. Only this feeling of personal acquaintance with an integral character, Socrates, enables one to reject such an—as I see it—incredible hypothesis.

[2] Xen. *Mem.* 1.1.6–9, especially 9: τοὺς δὲ μηδὲν τῶν τοιούτων οἰομένους εἶναι δαιμόνιον, ἀλλὰ πάντα τῆς ἀνθρωπίνης γνώμης δαιμονᾶν ἔφη. Hackforth put it well (*CPA*, 96): 'He was, I think, content and wisely content not to attempt an explicit reconciliation of reason with faith; not out of indifference, nor in a spirit of complacent, condescending toleration of traditional belief, but rather because he possessed that rare wisdom which knows that, while no bounds may properly be set to the activity of human reason—that the ἀνεξέταστος βίος is οὐ βιωτὸς ἀνθρώπῳ—yet ἡ ἀνθρωπίνη σοφία ὀλίγου τινὸς ἀξία ἐστὶ καὶ οὐδενός.'

if not convert the unbelieving. He sought to promote the immortality of the soul from religious belief to philosophical doctrine.

This however involves in the end an essential change of attitude. Once focus attention on the *psyche* to the extent necessary for a proof of its immortality, and one is inevitably, if insensibly, led to the attitude which Plato adopts in the *Phaedo*, of contempt for this life and a fixation on the other. Life becomes something that the philosopher will long to escape from, and while it lasts, he will regard it as practice, or training, for death; that is to say, as death is the release of soul from body, so he will hold the body in contempt (ὀλιγωρεῖν 68c), and keep the soul as pure from the taint of its senses and desires as is possible in this life.[1] One becomes immersed in Orphic and Pythagorean notions of the body as a tomb or prison for the soul, and this life as a kind of purgatory, from which the philosopher's eyes should be averted to gaze on the bliss of the world beyond. This attitude of Plato's I would venture to call essentially un-Socratic. One remark in Burnet's essay on the Socratic doctrine of the soul is profoundly true, but difficult to reconcile with his fixed idea that the *Phaedo* contains nothing but pure Socratic doctrine. 'It does not seem, then', he wrote, 'that this [belief in immortality] formed the ordinary theme of his discourse. What he did preach as the one thing needful for the soul was that it should strive after wisdom and goodness' (p. 159). These twin goals must be brought back to their Greek originals: *sophia*, the knowledge and skill essential for all good craftsmanship, from shoemaking to moral and political science; and *areté*, the excellence which meant being good *at* something, in this case living to the utmost of one's powers. Socrates saw his proper place not 'practising for death' in philosophic retirement (however Callicles might sneer), but thrashing out practical questions with the political and rhetorical teachers of Athens in her heyday, as well as instilling a proper sense of values into his younger friends in gymnasium or palaestra.

---

[1] See especially in the *Phaedo*, 61 b–c, 64a, 67c–e.

(II) THE LEGACY OF SOCRATES

Even systematic philosophers, whose ideas are perpetuated in voluminous writings, have been differently understood by their followers.
This was even more certain to happen with Socrates, who taught by
word of mouth and insisted that his only advantage over others was the
knowledge of his own ignorance. His service to philosophy was the
same as that which he claimed to have performed for the Athenian
people, namely to be a gadfly which provoked and stung them into
fresh activity. Much of his influence was due not to anything that he
said at all, but to the magnetic effect of his personality and the example
of his life and death, to the consistency and integrity with which he
followed his own conscience rather than adopting any belief or legal
enactment simply because it was accepted or enjoined, while un-
questioningly admitting the right of the state, to which he owed
parents, education, and lifelong protection, to deal with him as it
thought fit if he could not persuade it otherwise. Inevitably, therefore,
in the years following his death, the most diverse philosophers and
schools could claim to be following in his footsteps though some at
least of them may appear to us to be highly un-Socratic in their
conclusions. Here was an inspiring talker, of outstanding intellect and,
for his time at least, a unique power of logical discrimination, who was
prepared to devote all his time to an examination of human conduct,
in the conviction that life was not a meaningless chaos or the heartless
jest of an unfeeling higher power but had a definite direction and purpose. Nothing therefore was more important for himself or for others
than to ask themselves continually what was the good for man and
what the peculiarly human *areté* or excellence which would enable him
to attain that good. But it is essential to remember that, as we have seen
already, Socrates himself never claimed to have the answer to these
questions. He wished to counter those Sophists and others who saw
the best life as one of self-indulgence or tyrannical power, those whom
Plato's Callicles represents when he identifies the good with pleasure.
It must be true, for instance, to say that the orator who pleases the
demos may do them much harm, and that the one who aims at their

good may have to say some very unpalatable things; and though pleasure in itself may be *a* good thing, such statements as these would be impossible if pleasure and good were identical. How was he to show that such Sophists were wrong?

To a large extent he tried to do it by meeting them on their own ground. Granted that self-interest is paramount, and our object is to maximize our own enjoyment, success demands that it be enlightened self-interest. Unreflecting pursuit of the pleasure of the moment may lead to future misery. This is the thin end of the Socratic wedge. Everyone admitted it, but it follows that actions pleasant in themselves may lead to great harm, even if the meaning of harm is still restricted to what is painful. Hence pleasure cannot be itself the end of life. If we want a word to be the equivalent of 'good' (ἀγαθόν) and explain it, we must try another. Socrates himself suggested 'useful' or 'beneficial'. The good must be something which always benefits, never harms. Acts which in themselves give pleasure may now be referred to this as a higher standard. We may ask, still maintaining our attitude of pure self-interest, 'Will it be for my ultimate benefit to act thus?' Having got as far as this, it was easy for him to show that we cannot live the best life without knowledge or wisdom. We have seen how this is necessary to acquire the 'art of measurement' whereby we can calculate the course of action which will in the long term give us the maximum of pleasure and the minimum of pain. In the *Protagoras*, where to the dismay of some of his admirers he apparently champions the cause of pleasure as the good, he gets Protagoras first to agree that the pleasure on which we base our calculations must be in the future as well as the present, and finally to include under 'pleasure' everything that in other dialogues (e.g. *Meno*) he describes as 'beneficial'. All this is carefully excluded when in the *Gorgias* he argues *against* the equivalence of pleasure with the good. 'Pleasures' in the *Protagoras* include most of what in modern speech comes under the heading of 'values', with at least as much emphasis on spiritual values as on any others.

So it turned out that on a nominally hard-headed and even individualistically utilitarian basis one can, with Socrates for a guide, achieve at least as high and altruistic a code of morals as most people are ever likely to aspire to. It was not, as we know, the sum total of his teaching, which included the belief that the real self is the rational and moral *psyche*, and that therefore the true meaning of 'benefiting oneself' was benefiting one's *psyche*, which could only be harmed by a life of unpunished wrongdoing. I would add myself that in calculating the future benefit or harm likely to accrue from a course of action, he would include the treatment of the soul by the divine power in a future life. All this was an inspiration to his followers, but not a sufficient answer to moral sceptics, because it left open the question of what was in fact the ultimate end and purpose of human life. Advocacy of 'the beneficial' as the criterion of action leaves undecided the nature of the benefit which the doer hopes to receive. Socrates, the reverse of a hedonist by nature, had used the hedonistic argument, pressed to a logical conclusion, to turn the tables on the hedonists themselves, but this expedient had its limitations. It left open the question: 'Beneficial for what?' A man might still take even physical pleasure as his ultimate aim, provided he proceeded with just enough caution to ensure that the pleasures of the day did not interfere with those of the morrow. Or he might choose power. The attainment of this may well necessitate, as the biography of some dictators shows, a curtailment of pleasures in the ordinary sense, even a life of strict personal asceticism. The hedonic calculus provides no answer to this, and if Socrates says, 'But you are ignoring the effect on your *psyche* and what will happen to it after death', communication breaks down, as Plato showed in the *Gorgias*; for what he relies on is simply not believed by the adversary, nor is there any means of convincing him of what is to some extent an act of faith. (Cf. *Theaet.* 177a.)

In one way, then, the aim of Socrates's immediate followers and their schools was to give content to the 'good' which he had set them to seek but himself left undetermined. On the side of method, he bequeathed to them the negative virtues of elenchus or refutation, the dispeller of false pretensions to knowledge, and a sense of the supreme importance of agreeing upon the meaning of words, working towards definitions by means of dialectic or discussion. His insistence on definitions was noted by such widely different characters as Plato and Xenophon, and could lead, according to temperament, to a form of linguistic philosophy on the one hand and, on the other, to philosophic realism when Plato hypostatized the objects of definition and gave them independent existence.[1] Similarly his dialectical and elenctic skill could either be used constructively or lose itself in a somewhat barren eristic. In the eyes of Grote, Socrates himself was the supreme eristic,[2] and certainly his arguments, as they appear in Plato, were sometimes of a rather dubious nature; but at least his aim was not personal victory in a Sophistic contest, but the elucidation of the truth. Otherwise his life would have taken a different course, and he might have died a natural death.

As for the various answers which his pupils gave to the unanswered question of the good for man, one or two of these may be made the subject of a short concluding section before we turn, in the next volume, to the one who, whatever we may think of his faithfulness to their master's teaching, was one of the most universal thinkers of all time. The others, so far as our knowledge goes, seem to have seized on one aspect of Socrates and developed it at the expense of the rest. Plato, however much he may have built on to Socraticism in the way of positive doctrine, shows himself aware of its true spirit when his Socrates says that education does not mean handing over knowledge ready made, nor conferring on the mind a capacity that it did not have before, as sight might be given to a blind eye. The eye of the mind is not blind, but in most people it is looking the wrong way. To educate is to convert or turn it round so that it looks in the right direction (*Rep.* 518b–d).

[1] Perhaps the man who came nearest to the aims of Socrates in his search for the meanings of words was not a Greek at all, but a contemporary in a distant land who knew nothing of him. It was said of Confucius (*Analects*, 13.3) that when asked what he would do first if he were given charge of the administration of a country, he replied: 'It would certainly be to correct language' (World's Classics translation). His hearers were surprised, so he explained that if language is not correct, then what is said is not what is meant; if what is said is not what is meant, what ought to be done remains undone; if this remains undone, morals and arts deteriorate, justice goes astray, and the people stand about in helpless confusion. With this may be compared the words given to Socrates by Plato, *Phaedo*, 115e: 'You may be sure, my dear Cebes, that inaccurate language is not only in itself a mistake: it implants evil in men's souls' (trans. Bluck).

[2] See especially his *Plato*, III, 479, where he says that although the Megarians acquired the name of eristics, they 'cannot possibly have surpassed Socrates, and probably did not equal him, in the refutative elenchus... No one of these Megarics probably ever enunciated so sweeping a negative programme, or declared so emphatically his own inability to communicate positive instruction, as Socrates in the Platonic Apology. A person more thoroughly eristic than Socrates never lived.'

(12) THE IMMEDIATE FOLLOWERS OF SOCRATES

To know who were the closest followers or friends of Socrates, we can hardly do better than look at the list of those whom Plato is careful to mention by name in the *Phaedo* (59b) as present with him in his last hours in the prison, or whose absence Plato felt must be accounted for. Phaedo the narrator was said to be a native of Elis.[1] The Athenians present included Apollodorus, Critobulus and his father Crito, Hermogenes, Epigenes, Aeschines, Antisthenes, Ctesippus and Menexenus. From other city-states there were Simmias, Cebes and Phaedondes from Thebes, Euclides and Terpsion from Megara. Aristippus and Cleombrotus were said to be absent in Aegina, and Plato himself was ill.[2] Simmias and Cebes, disciples of the Pythagorean Philolaus, of course play a large part in the *Phaedo*'s discussions of immortality, and Crito, Hermogenes, Ctesippus, Menexenus and Euclides appear also in other Platonic dialogues. Echecrates of Phlius, to whom Phaedo is telling the story, was also a pupil of Philolaus, which adds to the Pythagorean atmosphere of the dialogue.[3] All except Aeschines, Phaedo, Ctesippus and Cleombrotus occur in Xenophon as companions of Socrates. Of some, little or nothing is known. Aeschines we have already met as a writer of Socratic dialogues (p. 331), but the only companions of whom we know anything as philosophers are Antisthenes, Euclides and Aristippus, each of whom was the reputed founder of a school which maintained the particular aspect of Socraticism that

---

[1] Grote (*Plato*, III, 503 note *m*) opined that the historical circumstances of his capture and sale into slavery at Athens (D.L. 2.105) could only be explained on the assumption that 'Eleian' was a mistake for 'Melian'—a suggestion which Mary Renault used to dramatic effect in her novel *The Last of the Wine*. See however von Fritz in *RE*, xxxviii. Halbb. 1538 (also for everything known or conjectured about Phaedo).

[2] I had never paid much attention to this (though, as Burnet says *ad loc.*, 'many strange things have been written' about it) until an able colleague in a different subject said in a letter that Plato's conduct in deserting Socrates in his last hours, however unwell he might be, was to him unforgivable. In the context it is certainly a remarkable statement, and it might be interesting to speculate on why Plato inserted it. To judge him unfavourably on it would be manifestly unfair, since not only do we owe our knowledge of the circumstance solely to Plato himself but the whole of the *Phaedo*, to say nothing of other dialogues, reveals beyond doubt the reality and strength of his devotion to Socrates. His feelings may have been so intense that he could not bear the prospect of witnessing the actual death of 'the best, wisest and most righteous man that he knew'. He could have made his farewell earlier to an understanding Socrates. But since we have absolutely nothing to go on but his own four words, all such guesses at motivation are idle.

[3] For references see Bluck's *Phaedo*, 34 ff.

appealed to him. Of the opinions of these men themselves, Plato must have been well aware, but their successors can only have been active from the time of Aristotle onwards. It seems appropriate therefore to say something here about those who, like Plato, were personal friends of Socrates, and to leave a full discussion of their 'schools'—the Cynic, Cyrenaic and Megarian—to a later stage.

Each one seems to have taken a single feature of the conversations, or personal example, of Socrates, and carried it to extremes as representing for him the 'true' spirit of his teaching, while ignoring the rest as irrelevant. Antisthenes has already been considered.[1] For him what mattered about Socrates was that he was indifferent to worldly possessions and pleasures and proclaimed the supremacy of virtue. Following his example, Diogenes and the Cynics adopted an extreme asceticism and cult of poverty, with the ragged cloak,[2] staff and beggar's wallet as their badge together with a complete disregard of appearances and (perhaps a curious corollary of the cult of virtue) a deliberate flouting of accepted standards of decency in public behaviour. Not for them the occasional careful toilet in compliment to a friend and host, nor the pleasures of the *symposion* into which Socrates could throw himself with wholehearted enjoyment.

At the opposite extreme, at least on a superficial view, was *Aristippus*. Well might St Augustine marvel that these 'two noble philosophers, both of them in Athens and both Socratics, should find the meaning of life in such different, indeed irreconcilable goals' (*Civ. Dei*, 18.41). Aristippus, a native of Cyrene (whence the name of his followers, Cyrenaics), was said to have been brought to Athens by the fame of Socrates. He taught as a Sophist, the first of Socrates's pupils, it was said, to charge fees, and made sufficient reputation to be invited to the court of Dionysius[3] where he was said to have much enjoyed the luxurious life. An anecdote told by Diogenes Laertius (2.83) makes

---

[1] See especially pp. 304–11.

[2] This at least was Socratic. See p. 389 with n. 2 above. But Socrates wore it not from pride, but only because he had more important things than a new cloak to think about. His reported rebuke to Antisthenes (D.L. 2.36), who adjusted his cloak to show the rents, is true to character: 'I can see your vanity through your cloak.'

[3] No doubt the elder, as a scholiast on Lucian says (fr. 37 B Mannebach). See Grote (reference in next note).

him older than the Socratic Aeschines. Probably he was a little older than Plato, and Diodorus (15.76) speaks of him as still alive in 366. It may be assumed that he returned to Cyrene to end his days, where his daughter Arētē and grandson Aristippus (the 'mother-taught'), together with other Cyreneans, developed his hedonistic views and became known as the Cyrenaic school.[1]

Most of the evidence for his views is very late, and does not always distinguish clearly between Aristippus himself and later modifications by his followers, who after Epicurus were concerned to maintain certain differences from the rival conception of hedonism.[2] We also encounter him, however, in Xenophon and Aristotle, who are free from the possibility of such confusion, and with whom therefore we must start. In a passage of the *Metaphysics* Aristotle is arguing that not all forms of cause are to be looked for in every subject, e.g. in unchangeable things like the objects of mathematics there is no place for a cause of motion nor for goodness as a principle. He continues (996a29):

Therefore in mathematics nothing is proved by this kind of cause, nor is any demonstration made on the grounds that so-and-so is better or worse. Nothing of this kind is ever mentioned at all. For this reason certain Sophists, for instance Aristippus, disparaged mathematics because the other arts, even the vulgar ones like carpentry and cobbling, spoke always in terms of better or worse, whereas mathematics took no account of good and bad.[3]

According to Aristotle's Greek commentator, Aristippus went to the length of making this an argument for the non-existence of the objects

---

[1] For the above details about Aristippus see D.L. 65 f. etc. (frr. 1–8 Mannebach), and on his relations with Dionysius I, Grote's *Plato*, III, 549 note s. Mannebach (*A. et Cyr. Frr.* 89) would put the date of his death at c. 355. For Arētē and Aristippus Μητροδίδακτος D.L. 2.72 and 83, Aristocles (second century A.D.) *ap.* Eus. *P.E.* 14.18.

[2] C. J. Classen in *Hermes* 1958 aims at separating Aristippus from the Cyrenaics, but perhaps goes too far. It is difficult to maintain, on whatever grounds, that when D.L. describes the Cyrenaics at 2.86 as οἱ ἐπὶ τῆς ἀγωγῆς τῆς Ἀριστίππου μείναντες this *cannot* be interpreted as intended to mean that they kept to the teaching of Aristippus (p. 184). Mannebach (*A. et Cyr. Frr.* 86) says only that the word ἀγωγή signifies nothing more definite than 'vivendi quandam aut philosophandi rationem in universum'. Though Cyrenaicism as a whole is being reserved for later treatment, readers may like to have the following references to some of the literature on them and Aristippus. Texts are collected and commented on by E. Mannebach, *A. et Cyr. Frr.* (1961) and G. Giannantoni, *I Cirenaici* (1958). (My own references are to Mannebach's ed.) Otherwise one might select Grote's account in his *Plato*, III, 530–60, and Stenzel's article *Kyrenaiker* in the *RE*. (Natorp's on Aristippus is somewhat outdated.)

[3] These critics of mathematics occur again, unnamed, at 1078a33. The only other mention of Aristippus in Aristotle concerns his rebuke to Plato and has already been mentioned (p. 356, n. 2).

of mathematics, on the premise that 'everything that exists works for some good or fine end'.[1] He may well have claimed to find the germ of this curious ontological argument in Socrates, to judge from passages like Plato, *Rep.* 352 d ff.

We have already looked (pp. 463 f.) at conversations between Socrates and Aristippus in Xenophon in which Socrates avoided a trap by insisting on the relativity of 'good' to the particular end in view. On another occasion (*Mem.* 2.1) Socrates tried to pin Aristippus down to a choice of two types of life. There are those fit to govern others, who must have trained themselves to be courageous, enduring of hardships, physically fit and in full command of their appetites; and those lacking in these qualities, who are fit only to be subject to the rule of others, liable at any time to be robbed, enslaved or subjected to any other indignity or suffering. Aristippus replied that neither rule nor slavery appealed to him, but in his opinion there was a third, middle way: the road to happiness lay through freedom, which was certainly not the lot of a ruler or commander, with all the risks and hard work that it entailed. He wished only to pass through life as easily and pleasantly as possible, and thought that he could achieve this by not identifying himself with any particular state but being 'everywhere an alien (*xenos*)'.[2] It is in criticism of this predilection for the life of ease and pleasure that Socrates repeats the allegory of Prodicus about the choice of Heracles (pp. 277 f. above).

We need not yet go into the question (not always very meaningful) whether the companion of Socrates or his grandson of the same name should be regarded as the founder of the Cyrenaic school. Different views have been held, and one can hardly go beyond the judicious verdict of Mannebach (p. 88) that the grandson built the doctrine on foundations laid by his grandfather. (But see p. 494, n. 1 below.) So far as the sources allow us to differentiate between Aristippus and later

[1] Pseudo-Alex. *In Metaph.* 1078a31, fr. 154 A in M. εἰ γὰρ πᾶν, φησὶν ὁ 'Α., ὃν ἀγαθοῦ ἢ καλοῦ ἕνεκεν ἐργάζεται, τὰ δὲ μαθηματικὰ οὔτε καλοῦ οὔτε ἀγαθοῦ στοχάζεται, τὰ μαθηματικὰ ἄρα οὐκ εἰσιν.

[2] Aristippus is sometimes cited as the originator of the Cynic and Stoic κοσμοπολίτης. Perhaps the practical effect was much the same, but in form at least there is a difference between belonging everywhere and belonging nowhere, being πολίτης and being ξένο₅. Antisthenes, if not his followers, is actually said to have been opposed to Aristippus (as in most other things) in believing that the wise man ought to take part in government (Aug. *Civ. Dei*, 18.41, Aristippus fr. 231 M.).

modifications of his views, they supplement but do not contradict the information in Xenophon and Aristotle. Much is in the form of anecdote and repartee, including the kind of floating saying that is attributed to others also. They show that mixture of a kind of cockney wit with sheer boorish rudeness which also characterized Diogenes the Cynic. The one thing that some of Socrates's younger friends do not seem to have learned from him is urbanity, and if Aristippus really criticized an expression of Plato's because 'Socrates never spoke like that' (p. 356, n. 2 above), it was a case of pot and kettle if not of mote and beam. At the court of Dionysius he seems to have had the position of the licensed jester and parasite who in medieval times could speak to the king with an effrontery that would not be tolerated in an ordinary courtier. One example will suffice. When he asked for money Dionysius replied: 'But you said the wise man would never be in want.' 'Give me the money and then we will go into that.' Dionysius gave it, whereupon Aristippus replied, 'You see, I am not in want'.[1] He is generally represented as living a life of luxury and unrestrained pleasure, fond of rich food, drink, fine clothes, scents and women (frr. 72–83). As to ownership of wealth and possessions, he is said on the one hand to have asserted that, unlike shoes, one's property could never be too large for comfort (Stobaeus, fr. 67), and on the other to have advised his friends to limit their possessions to what they could save, with their own lives, from a shipwreck (fr. 9 A, B, D and E). No doubt he saw the advantage of enjoying the bounty of a tyrant rather than undergoing the toil of amassing one's own fortune and the responsibilities of looking after it. He was also said to have accepted the risks involved in such a course, and while he enjoyed wearing fine purple, to be willing to put up with rags if he had to (frr. 30–4). One pleasant story about him, told by a commentator on Horace, is reminiscent of Socrates's rebuke to Antisthenes (p. 490, n. 2 above). One day at the baths he took Diogenes's old cloak and left his own purple one behind. Diogenes followed him out without it, demanding the return of his own, whereat Aristippus chided him for caring so much about his reputation that he would rather go cold than put on a purple cloak (fr. 32c).

[1] D.L. 2.82, fr. 45 M. The story has more point in the Greek, where ἀπορεῖν means both to be in want and to be at a loss.

Diogenes Laertius (2.83–5) gives a long list of titles of writings by Aristippus, which lends some colour to Grote's suspicions of those who claim that he was a mere voluptuary, and that anything like a doctrine came from his grandson.[1] They may however have consisted largely of isolated apophthegms. That consideration apart, from the scattered late sources one may reasonably credit Aristippus the Socratic with the following views. Only practical principles of conduct should be studied, not mathematics (as we have seen) nor the physical world, for it was not knowable, nor, if it were, would the knowledge serve any useful purpose (fr. 145). Pleasure was the end at which the *psyche* should aim (frr. 156, 157, 161), and this hedonism was of the strictest sort. Pleasure was confined to bodily pleasure (frr. 181–3) and consequently to the pleasure of the moment: neither the anticipation of future nor the recollection of past pleasures could be called pleasure (frr. 207–9: in Mannebach's opinion Aelian in fr. 208 is beyond doubt preserving Aristippus's own words). Such pleasures of course are in any case mental rather than physical, but Aristippus had another reason, based on his theory that pleasure and pain were motions, the one smooth and the other rough, or, as it is also put, 'he showed that the *telos* (end or aim, i.e. in his case pleasure) is smooth motion spreading to the senses' (frr. 193 and following). These motions, though caused by and therefore contemporary with the bodily events, are communicated to the *psyche* (otherwise, presumably, we could not be conscious of them), and 'the motion of the *psyche* dies away with time' (fr. 209). It was in this glorification of bodily pleasures and insistence that pleasure consisted in motion that the followers of Aristippus were most at odds with the hedonism of Epicurus, who exalted the pleasures of the mind and the static or stable pleasures equated simply with absence of pain.

Like his teacher Socrates, Aristippus believed that a man should be

---

[1] Grote, *Plato*, III, 549 note *r*. The case for the younger Aristippus as founder of the school rests on a single statement of Aristocles (*ap.* Eus. *P.E.* 14.18, divided in M. between frr. 155, 163 and 201) that the elder said nothing clear about the τέλος but only that the substance of happiness lay potentially in pleasure. The younger σαφῶς ὡρίσατο τὸ τέλος εἶναι τὸ ἡδέως ζῆν, ἡδονὴν ἐντάττων τὴν κατὰ κίνησιν. This is not much to go on, especially as (*a*) Aristocles has just referred to the elder Aristippus as ὁ τὴν καλουμένην Κυρηναϊκὴν συστησάμενος αἵρεσιν, and (*b*) the doctrine that pleasure is a motion is one of the few that can with some confidence be ascribed to the elder. See Mannebach's note to fr. 193. Other late testimonies definitely refer to the Socratic Aristippus as founder of the school. See frr. 125, 126 A–C, 132 *et al.* On the existence and probable nature of Aristippus's writings see Mannebach on fr. 121, pp. 76ff.

master of himself, and never allow himself to be mastered, or overcome, by pleasures. But whereas to Socrates this seemed to entail of necessity the leading of a temperate life, the pupil drew no such conclusion. His view as reported (fr. 45, from Stobaeus) was that to be the master of pleasures meant not to refrain from them but to enjoy them without being at their mercy, just as to be master of a ship or a horse does not mean to make no use of it but to guide it where one will. For all his purple and his scents, he could claim that he had as much self-control as Diogenes, for just as, if a man had a body impervious to fire, he could safely commit himself to the flames of Etna, so the man with the proper attitude to pleasure could plunge into it without being burned or wasted (fr. 56).[1] Ancient writers loved to quote his retort on being reproached for his association with the famous courtesan Lais: 'I possess Lais, she does not possess me' (frr. 57 A–G). In conformity with this he enjoyed in full measure the pleasures that were at hand or easily procurable, but saw no reason to exert himself to gain pleasures the acquisition of which involved hard work or effort (frr. 54 A and B).

In spite of some modern opinion, it is scarcely rash to attribute also to Aristippus a sceptical theory of knowledge which agrees well with the ethic of immediate sensual pleasure to which, in his eyes, it must have been subordinate.[2] It is summed up in the sentence 'only of the

---

[1] One is reminded of the late J. L. Austin's comment on taking two portions of a favourite sweet of which there are only enough portions to allow one for each of the company: 'I am tempted to help myself to two segments and do so, thus succumbing to temptation . . . But do I lose control of myself? . . . Not a bit of it. We often succumb to temptation with calm and even with finesse.' This argument, from his Presidential Address to the Aristotelian Society (1956, pp. 24f.), is quoted and criticized by Gellner in *Words and Things* (Pelican ed. 1968), 242.

[2] To be strict, Eusebius attributed it to οἱ κατ' 'A. (or κατ' 'A. τὸν Κυρηναῖον) λέγοντες, and Aristocles to ἔνιοι τῶν ἐκ τῆς Κυρήνης (frr. 211 A and B, 212). Cicero and Sextus (frr. 213 A–C, 217) speak of the Cyrenaics, and D.L. (2.92) of 'those who maintained the ἀγωγή of Aristippus (*sc.* the Socratic) and were called Cyrenaics'. In another place (fr. 210) Aristocles refers a statement of similar meaning to the grandson, but on the difficulty of distinguishing the two from this source see p. 494, n. 1. Judging by what has been seen of them already, Eusebius and his source Aristocles, when they use the name Aristippus unqualified, are more likely to have meant the Socratic than the Μητροδίδακτος. Nevertheless what I have said above goes against the most recent scholarship. Mannebach (pp. 114–17) conjectures that the sceptical theory of knowledge was taught by the younger Aristippus, who however did not originate it but learned it from Pyrrho, an idea which, as he frankly notes, Pohlenz regarded as 'not within the bounds of probability'. The trouble is that supporters of the opposite view have relied heavily on a belief that certain passages in Plato are directed against Aristippus, a belief which, not being susceptible of proof, is not taken into account here. If certainty is impossible, at least the sceptical theory is in complete harmony with Aristippus's form of hedonism and was probably set forth in some of his fairly numerous writings.

feelings can we be certain'.[1] Sextus (*Math.* 7.190ff., fr. 217), after remarking that the Cyrenaic school, like the Platonic, appears to have had its origin in the teaching of Socrates, explains their view thus. We apprehend without possibility of error our own feelings, affections or sensations, but can know nothing of their causes. We can state incontrovertibly that we have a sensation of sweetness or whiteness but not that this sensation is produced by an object which is sweet or white. 'The affection which takes place in us reveals to us nothing more than itself.' Both he and Plutarch (*Adv. Col.* 1120b ff., fr. 218) adduce in this connexion the evidence of pathological states in which honey can produce a sensation of bitterness or an affected eye make everything appear tinged with red, and Sextus adds hallucinations. The affections or sensations are also described (by Cicero, see fr. 213 A) as 'interior motions' (or disturbances, *permotiones intimae*). The theory at once reminds us of Protagoras, and Eusebius (fr. 211 A) speaks of 'those who follow Aristippus in saying that only the feelings convey certainty, and again the followers of Metrodorus and Protagoras who say that one must trust nothing but the bodily sensations'. This does not suggest any great difference,[2] nor is it accurate, seeing that Protagoras applied the same canon to moral concepts like justice (pp. 171 ff. above). Cicero (*Ac. pr.* 2.46.142, fr. 213 A) tried to distinguish them in this way: 'The judgment of Protagoras is one thing, that that which appears to each man is true for him, and that of the Cyrenaics another, who think that nothing can be judged except the interior motions.' In so far as the tradition can be relied on, the difference amounts to this, that Aristippus and the Cyrenaics were epistemologically more sceptical than Protagoras (i.e. they thought that even less could be known), but ontologically less so, in that they would not go all the way with him in denying the existence of a reality outside ourselves. We simply could not say whether there was one or, if there was, what it was like. This slight modification of Protagoras's doctrine is very likely to have

---

[1] μόνα τὰ πάθη καταληπτά, frr. 211 A and B, 212, and in various paraphrases in the rest of frr. 211–18. πάθη is a wider word than αἰσθήσεις, including (and in some contexts confined to) the emotions, but ancient explanations of the doctrine show it to have rested primarily on sensation for its credibility.

[2] Though admittedly Eusebius later (14.19) quotes Aristocles as calling Metrodorus and Protagoras together τοὺς τὴν ἐναντίαν βαδίζοντας. Protagoras surely differed more from Metrodorus than from Aristippus.

been the work of a Socratic of the generation following Protagoras himself.[1]

Two further notes on Aristippus may be quoted from our late sources. The first (rather dubious perhaps) suggests that he had a Prodicean interest in differentiating between words of similar meaning or form.[2] The second (fr. 227) states that he called it ridiculous to pray and make requests to the divinity: doctors, he said, do not give food or drink to a sick man when he asks for it, but when it is good for him.

All this shows that, although ending up with such different conclusions, especially moral, Aristippus had listened to Socrates and remembered much of what he heard. In his scepticism he might claim that he was only carrying out the Socratic advice to be aware of his own ignorance. Like Socrates he eschewed political activity, though Socrates, far from being 'everywhere an alien', was heart and soul a citizen of Athens and loyal to her laws. Like Socrates too he was interested first and foremost in practical living and deprecated carrying mathematical and physical studies beyond the point at which they ceased to serve practical ends. Themistius was right in numbering him among 'the genuine band of Socrates' in so far as he kept to the study of good and evil and human happiness. (See fr. 143 in M.) Though his chosen goal was different, he echoed Socratic language in maintaining that the *psyche had* its goal or distinctive aim (τέλος τῆς ψυχῆς, fr. 156). With him also the teleological hypothesis applied not only to man but to all existing things, and he used the analogy of the humbler creative occupations to support it. His attitude to prayer went one stage further than Socrates, but is based on his teaching that since the

[1] I.e. Aristippus. Grote (*Plato*, III, 560) thought his doctrine substantially the same as the 'man the measure' of Protagoras, and indeed the difference is not great. Zeller (*Ph. d. Gr.* 350f.) granted that in asserting the subjectivity of all our impressions the two are identical, but saw a difference which I confess I do not find at all clear. The German runs: 'Ihre [*sc.* the Cyrenaics'] Ansicht unterscheidet sich von der seinigen nur dadurch, dass dieselben bestimmter auf die Empfindung unserer Zustände zurückführen, in dieser, nicht in der durch die aüsseren Sinne vermittelten Wahrnehmung, das ursprünglich Gegebene suchen.' He adds in a note that both Cicero and Eusebius (i.e. Aristocles) exaggerate the difference. But today the most favoured view is probably Mannebach's (p. 114) that it 'neither can be demonstrated nor is even probable' that the Cyrenaics were following in Protagoras's footsteps. Here again the argument has been confused by an understandable opposition to those who have tried to prove the contrary by reading Aristippus into Plato.

[2] Frr. 22 A and B. The example given is θάρσος and θράσος.

gods know what is good for us we ought not to pray for specific gifts (Xen. *Mem.* 1.3.2). As for his hedonism, which provides such a contrast both to Socrates's life and to the spirit of his teaching, we must always remember, first that Socrates did not himself answer his own question about the ultimate aim of human life and secondly that, as I have tried to show, what he did say lent itself certainly to a utilitarian, and even to a hedonistic, interpretation. Stenzel put it (*RE*, 2. Reihe, v. Halbb. 887) that the Cyrenaic doctrine of pleasure is not so much (as it had been called) a polar reversal of the Socratic ethic as a narrowing to the individual of a basic Socratic tenet. It might be more accurate to say that though both men had the individual in mind Aristippus left out much of what Socrates said about the nature of the *psyche* and the kind of conduct which would benefit it.

Finally, as justification for giving so much space to one who, it may be thought, exists only on the margin of philosophy, we have Plato. Plato never names Aristippus, and it would be dangerous to follow the older critics in using certain of his dialogues as evidence for Aristippus's views, on the assumption that he is necessarily the target of criticism. But the two were contemporaries and acquaintances, and when one thinks that in the *Theaetetus* Plato criticizes a sceptical theory of knowledge which certainly has affinities with the Cyrenaic, and that the *Philebus* is wholly devoted to discussion of the place of pleasure in the good life, raising such questions as whether pleasure is of the body or the soul, the status of pleasures of anticipation and memory, the relation of pleasure to movement and to the neutral state of absence of pain, it would be equally rash to exclude the possibility that he is replying to a fellow-pupil of Socrates who must have seemed to him to have gone wildly astray. The *Philebus* is universally, and with good reason, agreed to be one of Plato's latest dialogues, belonging to a period in which Socrates is made to hand over the whole conduct of a dialogue to another or else is absent altogether. Yet in the *Philebus* he is back again in the centre of the picture, directing the whole conversation. These are questions to consider when we come to Plato. But the possibility that he is sometimes attacking Aristippus must certainly not be denied *a priori* if we want to see his philosophy, as we should, as arising from the debates that raged in his own time, and in response to which he formulated his problems and produced his own answer to the Socratic question: What is the ultimate aim of human life?

Euclides of Megara (best called by the full Greek form of his name to avoid confusion with his more famous namesake), besides being mentioned by Plato as present during the last hours of Socrates, is made to narrate the conversation which forms the main part of the *Theaetetus*.[1] If a story of Gellius can be relied on (*Noct. Att.* 6.10), his acquaintance with Socrates went back to the Megarian Decree of 432, and the evidence of the *Theaetetus* shows him to have been still alive when Theaetetus was brought back from Corinth dying of wounds and dysentery. This must have been in 369 when Euclides was an old man of eighty or more.[2] After the death of Socrates, Plato and some of his other companions left Athens to stay for a while with Euclides at Megara,[3] and Megara, together with Thebes (or Boeotia) the home of Simmias and Cebes, is mentioned in *Crito* (53b) and *Phaedo* (99a) as a place in which Socrates himself could have found refuge had he chosen to evade the sentence of the Athenians. It is evident therefore that Euclides was an intimate member of the Socratic circle. As to his teaching we are even more at a disadvantage than with Aristippus. Plato never mentions him in a philosophical context, and Aristotle never assigns a doctrine to him by name, but speaks only of 'the Megarians', so that we have to rely solely on much later sources. The names of a number of his pupils are on record, as well as of later members of the school.[4] Among them was Eubulides, famous as the author of certain logical puzzles, including one which has troubled philosophers down to the present century: that, namely, which asks whether the man who says 'I am lying' is speaking the truth or not.

---

[1] More accurately, he orders a slave to read out the account of it which he had written earlier with the aid of notes made at the time, checked and supplemented by Socrates. Cf. pp. 343 f. above.

[2] He need not have been much older, since like other youths he could well have been attracted into the circle of Socrates at the age of 18 or little more. It has been disputed at which of two battles fought between Athens and Corinth in the manhood of Theaetetus he met his fate, that of 394 or that of 369, but the question was settled beyond reasonable doubt by Eva Sachs, in her monograph *De Theaeteto*, pp. 22ff. See also von Fritz in *RE*, 2.Reihe, x.Halbb. 1351f.

[3] D.L. (2.106 and 3.6) states this on the excellent authority of Hermodorus, a friend or pupil (ἑταῖρος) of Plato who wrote a book about him (Simpl. *Phys.* 247.33, 256.32). He added that Plato's age at the time was 28. On the question of the 'tyrants', fear of whom drove Plato and his friends to take this course, see Zeller, *Ph. d. Gr.* 402 n. 2.

[4] For these see e.g. Zeller, *Ph. d. Gr.* 246–8, and cf. p. 217 above.

His date is roughly indicated by the facts that he is said to have been a teacher of Demosthenes and to have made personal attacks on Aristotle.[1] 'The Megarians' as a school of thought are first mentioned in Aristotle, and may not have been recognized as such before his time.[2] It seems certain that they carried philosophy further than Euclides, especially in the development of logic, and it would therefore be unsafe to hold him responsible for a doctrine simply on the ground that it was called 'Megarian'. Six dialogues were ascribed to him (they are named in D.L. 2.108), but their genuineness was doubted by Panaetius the Stoic (*ibid.* 64).

Only one positive doctrine can be safely credited to Euclides, namely the unity of the good. The testimonies are:

(i) Cicero, *Ac. pr.* 2.42.129. Cicero begins somewhat oddly by saying that, 'as I have read', the *princeps* of the *Megaricorum nobilis disciplina* was Xenophanes, followed by Parmenides and Zeno. 'Then', he continues, 'came Euclides, a disciple of Socrates from Megara, after whom they were called Megarians. He said that that alone was good which was one, all alike, and always the same.'

(ii) D.L. 2.106: 'He declared that the good was one, though called by many names, sometimes wisdom, sometimes God, and again mind (*nous*) and so on. Things opposed to the good he rejected, saying that they did not exist.'

(iii) With these one may compare a passage from the history of philosophy of Aristocles quoted by Eusebius (*P.E.* 14.17), which speaks only of the Megarians without mentioning Euclides by name. He ranks them with those who condemned the senses and claimed that only reason was to be trusted. 'So said, in earlier times, Xenophanes, Parmenides, Zeno and Melissus, and later the followers of Stilpo and the Megarians. For this reason the last-named said that what is is one and anything else does not exist,[3] and that nothing comes into being or is destroyed or undergoes any movement whatever.'

---

[1] On the paradoxes of Eubulides see W. and M. Kneale, *Dev. of Logic*, 114 (and their index *s.v.* 'liar, the' for later attempts to solve it), and Grote, *Plato*, III, 482f. with note *o*. His attacks on Aristotle are mentioned by D.L. 2.108, and Aristocles *ap.* Eus. *P.E.* 15.2, and his connexion with Demosthenes by D.L. *ibid.* and [Plut.] *Vit. orat.* 845c.

[2] *Metaph.* 1046b29. Cf. the remarks of Taylor, *VS*, 19 n. 2.

[3] This is the sense whatever the exact reading, but the reading in Heinichen's (1842) and Gifford's (1903) editions, καὶ τὸ ἕτερον μὴ εἶναι, yields it much more naturally than καὶ τὸ μὴ ὂν ἕτερον εἶναι (Zeller, *Ph. d. Gr.* 261 n. 2), i.e. 'and the non-existent is something else'.

Euclides on the Unity of the Good

There was thus a tradition, represented by Cicero and Aristocles, which classified the Megarian as a continuation of the Eleatic school. Aristocles has assimilated it wholly to Parmenides by confining its basic dogma to the unity of being, without mention of the good. Nor does he so much as mention Socrates as an influence. Cicero and Diogenes, however, who profess to be speaking of Euclides in person, do bring in his association with Socrates, and the fact that for him the 'one being' was 'the good'. The tendency of older scholarship was to lay stress on the Eleatic element and assume that Euclides had been impressed by Parmenidean arguments before he met Socrates;[1] but the one doctrine which can be credited to him with certainty suggests that his approach was different from the Eleatic.[2] Both were agreed on the unity of what exists, and in this Euclides no doubt owed something to Parmenides; but the Eleatic was a doctrine of being, pure and simple, whereas Euclides, as a follower of Socrates, was concerned with the nature of the good. Assuming that the statement in Diogenes most fully represents his view (for it includes Cicero's version and also accounts for the doctrine of his followers that only one thing exists), what he said about the good was twofold: it is a unity though called by many names, and what is opposed to it—i.e. evil—has no existence. The first is a legitimate deduction from the teaching of Socrates that all virtue, or goodness, can be reduced to the one thing, wisdom or knowledge. Temperance, justice, courage, quickness of mind, memory, and a noble heart, no less than external advantages such as health, strength, physical beauty and wealth—all these (he says in the *Meno*) may be harmful as well as beneficial unless they are allied to, and guided by, knowledge and good sense. But it was agreed that the term 'goodness' ought only to be applied to that which always benefits, never harms, and this one unfailingly beneficial factor turns out to be wisdom.[3]

---

[1] E.g. Natorp, *RE*, VI, 1001; Zeller, *Ph. d. Gr.* 245 n. 3; Robin, *Greek Thought* (Eng. ed. of 1928), 162: 'That he was first attached to the principles of Eleaticism is certain.' If there is anything in the story that he was already consorting with Socrates in 432, this is unlikely.

[2] Cf. von Fritz in *RE*, Suppl. V, 707 ff., to whose discussion my own remarks are much indebted. He calls it the *Grunddogma*, and there is justice in Grote's remark (*Plato*, III, 475) that 'this one doctrine [*sc.* the identity of τὸ ἕν with τὸ ἀγαθόν] is all that we know about Euclides: what consequences he derived from it, or whether any, we do not know'.

[3] *Meno*, 87e ff. In using terms like knowledge, wisdom and good sense interchangeably, I am only following Socrates's example, who refers to goodness, almost in the same breath, as

Since Socrates was also a devout theist, who believed that God alone had full knowledge of what was good for man, Euclides could suppose that he was still carrying on the spirit of his master's teaching when he said that God too was but another name for the goodness which was knowledge.

In the *Republic* (505 b–c) Plato, through the mouth of Socrates, remarks on the absurdity of those who say that the good is knowledge, and when asked 'Knowledge of what?' can only reply 'Of the good'. This has been thought to be a criticism of Euclides,[1] though the fact that knowledge was for him one of the 'many names' applied to the good hardly justifies the inference. It is in fact a criticism that could with some justice be brought against Socrates himself, and it is followed very shortly by a repetition on Glaucon's part of the familiar complaint that Socrates always refuses to give a positive answer when asked whether goodness is knowledge or pleasure or anything else. After yet another protestation of his own ignorance, and the wrongfulness of talking as if one knows what one does not, he yields to pressure and undertakes to describe, not the good itself (that would be too ambitious), but something that he 'imagines to be the offspring of the good and to resemble it closely'. This turns out to be the sun, and we now have the famous disquisition on the degrees of knowledge, intelligibility and being under the images of the sun, divided line and cave, in the course of which 'the good' is described (at 509 b) as 'not identical with being (reality), but beyond and superior to it'. In other words, when the Platonic Socrates is persuaded or bullied into formulating a positive doctrine, we can be sure that we owe it to Plato himself, though he has sufficient recollection of the real Socrates, and sufficient

ἐπιστήμη, φρόνησις and νοῦς; and it will be noticed that the latter two are among the names which according to Euclides are given to the good. Thompson in his *Meno* says that φρόνησις is the mental faculty correlative to ἐπιστήμη, but it too could be used with a dependent genitive (φ. ἀγαθοῦ, *Rep.* 505 b and c), where the only possible English equivalent is 'knowledge'. Nevertheless I think there is a nuance of difference. The knowledge Socrates has in mind is not ἐπιστήμη as commonly used, to mean often no more than technical know-how. It is that 'knowledge of what is and is not to be feared' (*Prot.* 360 d) which sees pain or death as a lesser evil than dishonourable conduct, and this better deserves the name of insight or wisdom which φρόνησις also conveyed.

[1] E.g. by Zeller, *Ph. d. Gr.* 260 n. 1. Cf. Stenzel in *RE*, 2. Reihe, v. Halbb. 876f. Dümmler and others have thought of the ubiquitous Antisthenes. See Adam *ad loc.*: in his opinion the criticism applies, and was intended to apply, to Plato himself and other disciples of Socrates.

dramatic sense, to make him preface it with the warning that he can only offer an opinion, that unsubstantiated opinion is ugly and blind, and that he will probably make a fool of himself (506c–d).

The doctrine of Euclides, though we cannot reconstruct it fully, evidently resembled Plato's in so far as it elevated the good to the status of an eternal and unchanging metaphysical principle, but coming more deeply and immediately under Eleatic influence he equated it directly with the One Being of Parmenides and declared that it alone could be said to exist. The doctrine of a plurality of transcendently existing Forms was Plato's own. Even in the *Republic*, however, the good is made superior to the other Forms (objects of knowledge), which are said to owe to it in some unspecified way both their intelligibility and their existence (509b); and it appears from Aristotle that in his later years Plato equated it with unity ('the One'), to which he granted a higher grade of reality than to the Forms. The Forms themselves were now said, in Aristotle's terms, to have a 'material' as well as a formal component, owing their existence to the combination of the One with the great-and-small; that is, to the imposition of unity and limit on an indefinite continuum.[1] At this later stage the One is itself 'being' or 'existence' (οὐσία), whereas in the *Republic* the single Form of good was explicitly said to be 'not being but beyond being'. In view of this passage in the first book of Aristotle's *Metaphysics*, another in the last book (1091b13) which mentions no names is regularly referred to Plato by commentators. It runs: 'Of those who maintain the existence of the unchangeable substances, some identify absolute unity with absolute goodness, but thought that its substance lay chiefly in its unity.'[2] So far as our information from Cicero and Diogenes takes us, this could be a pretty accurate statement of the position of Euclides.[3] Both he and Plato thought deeply about the ontological difficulties bequeathed by Parmenides, and probably had many a friendly discussion about the nature of being and unity and their

[1] Ar. *Metaph.* 987b20. 'Material' is of course used in the Aristotelian sense, not in that of corporeality.
[2] Literally, they 'say the One itself is the Good itself, but thought that its substance was chiefly the one'.
[3] I do not think (though others may) that the use of the plural, τὰς ἀκινήτους οὐσίας, is an objection to this, especially since οἱ μέν indicates that Aristotle intended the phrase to embrace a wide class of which he is only mentioning a part.

relation to the good which had been the object of Socrates's unending search. No true pupil of Socrates could doubt that it existed, but to more metaphysical natures than his the doctrine of the unity of being created a serious problem.

Parmenides had said that besides the One Being nothing existed, Euclides that nothing existed besides the One Good or, to follow our sources more exactly, nothing *opposed* to it; that is, evil was non-existent. Von Fritz has pointed out (*RE*, Suppl. v, 716) that even this can be seen as a modification of Socratic teaching brought about by turning it (under Eleatic influence) into speculative theory. The corollary of 'virtue is knowledge' is that wickedness is error, for no one knowingly and willingly chooses to do wrong. This robs evil of any status as a positive power opposed to goodness and reduces it to mere intellectual inadequacy or absence of knowledge or, as von Fritz puts it, a 'logical nothing'. Unfortunately however we have no clue to the arguments by which Euclides arrived at his conclusion.

In saying that the good was one, and that what was opposed to the good did not exist, was Euclides maintaining a strict Parmenidean monism, only substituting 'good' for 'being' as the one thing that exists? In view of the scantiness of our information an answer to this question must be partly speculative, but is perhaps worth attempting. I have just hinted at the possibility that 'nothing *opposed* to the good' may not be the same as 'nothing *but* the good', which excludes a neutral class. Again, L. Robin may have been on the right lines in suggesting an analogy with the physical atomism of Leucippus and Democritus.[1] These thought that they were adhering to the Parmenidean canon of the unity of being by equating it with 'the solid' (or 'the full'), irrespective of the fact that this one being was represented by millions of tiny particles dispersed through space (which was 'non-being'). They were one in substance, and only 'the solid' existed. Similarly, in what Robin called a 'logical atomism', the one substance could be 'the good', single, homogeneous and unchanging, but could be dispersed through a plurality of particular things or living creatures as *their*

---

[1] *Gr. Thought*, 163. Since I do not find Robin's language altogether clear (particularly his use of the word 'essences'), I cannot claim to be reproducing his interpretation. I can only say that his comparison with atomism provided a starting-point for my own reconstruction, the conjectural nature of which must be admitted.

substance. To it they would owe their being, as the Forms did for Plato. In spite of differences caused by the interposition of the equally unchanging Forms between the Form of the Good and the changing particulars in the sensible world of becoming, the equation of existence with goodness (what is best is most fully real) would be a fundamental mark of resemblance between the ways in which these two men developed their common inheritance from Socrates.

In addition to his positive doctrine of the good as uniquely existent, two matters of philosophic method are recorded for Euclides by Diogenes (2.107).

(i) He attacked a proof by opposing its conclusions, not its premises. This has reminded scholars, not unreasonably, of the dialectical method of Zeno of Elea,[1] thus providing some further evidence of Eleatic influence on Euclides. The method, usually involving the *reductio ad absurdum* of an opponent's view, was apt to generate heat and be stigmatized as eristic, whence perhaps the anecdote (D.L. 2.30) that Socrates, observing his fondness for eristic arguments, once said to him, 'You will be able to get on with Sophists, Euclides, but not with men'.

(ii) He rejected the argument from parallel cases. The component cases, he said, must be either similar or dissimilar. If they are similar, it is better to deal with the original case itself rather than what resembles it; if dissimilar, the comparison is irrelevant.[2] Here Euclides dares to criticize the use of analogy to which Socrates himself was so much addicted. In interpreting him, we must bear in mind that the word (ὅμοιος) translated 'similar' was ambiguous in Greek, wavering in meaning between similarity and complete identity.[3] If the subject of the argument and the other objects chosen to illustrate it are only instances of the same thing, it is better to draw conclusions from the subject itself than from the others; if the identity is incomplete, the

---

[1] E.g. Natorp, *RE*, VI, 1002; Robin, *Gr. Thought*, 163. For von Fritz, on the other hand, it corresponded to the usual practice of Socrates (*RE*, Suppl. V, 717), in amusing contrast to Robin, in whose eyes it showed that Euclides had 'abandoned the inductive dialectic of Socrates'. (It looks as if Robin is running this argument and the next together, in the reverse order to D.L.'s, as parts of a single compound argument. I doubt if this is right.)

[2] εἰ μὲν ἐξ ὁμοίων, περὶ αὐτὰ δεῖν μᾶλλον ἢ οἷς ὅμοιά ἐστιν ἀναστρέφεσθαι· εἰ δ' ἐξ ἀνομοίων παρέλκειν τὴν παράθεσιν.

[3] See vol. I, 230 and 305, and cf. the phrase τὸ αὐτὸ καὶ ὅμοιον in Arist. *GC*, 323 b 11.

comparison introduces an irrelevant factor which may be misleading. Gomperz gives as an example that Euclides would not have deduced the necessity of expert knowledge in statesmanship from analogies with pilots, farmers or doctors, in which partial resemblances go with important differences, but solely from consideration of the facts of political life.[1]

The foregoing account has shown, I hope, that even from the scanty evidence at our disposal we can form some idea of what Euclides took from Socrates and how he modified or developed it; and also of certain resemblances and differences between his version of Socraticism and that of his friend and contemporary Plato. Like Plato he wished to give a theoretical or metaphysical backing to the mainly practical and ethical teaching of Socrates about the good; and both men were convinced that in any such theory the Eleatic doctrine of being had to be taken into account.[2] But whereas Plato accommodated it to a place in a grandiose metaphysical scheme in which the Pythagoreans and Heraclitus also played a part, as well as Socrates and the genius of its author himself, Euclides seems to have clung more closely to both the methods and the results of Parmenides and Zeno. He was even further removed than Plato from the empirical world, and moved in a world of dialectical abstractions and dilemmas depending on the uncompromising use of an 'either–or' dichotomy. There are hints of this in what we are told of the man himself, and it certainly applied to his followers, whose achievements were mainly in the field of logic. Working by means of paradoxes and puzzles, or logical traps, they earned for themselves the name of eristics, but the advances that they made were real and important.

As with Antisthenes and Aristippus, scholars have claimed to detect veiled criticisms of Euclides in a number of dialogues of Plato. (They include the *Euthydemus*, *Republic*, *Parmenides*, *Theaetetus* and *Sophist*.) However, since for every scholar who makes this claim there is another

---

[1] Gomperz, *Gr. Th.* II, 188 f. Von Fritz (*loc. cit.*) thought it more likely that the criticism was aimed at Platonic myths and similes than at the analogical arguments of Socrates. He mentions the ambiguity of the word λόγος (which can include μῦθος), but says nothing about παραβολή, which Aristotle used to denote precisely the Socratic argument from analogy. (See p. 429 above.)

[2] For Plato, see index to vol. II, *s.v.* 'Plato: debt to Parmenides'.

to deny it, it will be best to continue the policy adopted for Aristippus, and deny ourselves the use of Plato as an aid to the reconstruction of his thought. Enough has been said, however, to show the close connexions, both personal and philosophical, between the two, and this should add interest, when the time comes, to our study of Plato himself.

BIBLIOGRAPHY

The following list contains full particulars of books or articles mentioned (often with shortened titles) in the text or notes. In addition, a few titles have been included which may be useful for reference although there has not been occasion to mention them in the course of the work, but the list makes no pretensions to completeness. More extensive bibliographies relating to the Sophists will be found in Untersteiner's *The Sophists* and in the separate fascicules of his *I Sofisti*. The concluding section of Kerferd's 'Recent Work on Presocratic Philosophy' (*Am. Philos. Q.* 1965) is also useful. For Socrates, there are the bibliographies in Magalhães-Vilhena's two books and Gigon's commentaries on Xenophon's *Memorabilia*, books I and II, and the useful survey of the state of scholarship by Cornelia de Vogel in *Phronesis*, 1955.

Collections of source-material have in this volume been included in the general bibliography under the names of their editors.

The Greek commentators on Aristotle are referred to in the text by page and line in the appropriate volume of the Berlin Academy's edition (*Commentaria in Aristotelem Graeca*, various dates).

ADAM, A. M. 'Socrates, "quantum mutatus ab illo"', *CQ*, 1918, 121–39.

ADAM, J. (ed.). *Platonis Apologia Socratis*. Cambridge, 1910.

ADAM, J. *Platonis Protagoras, with introduction, notes & appendices*. Cambridge, 1921.

ADAM, J. *The Republic of Plato, edited with critical notes, commentary & appendices*. 2 vols., Cambridge, 1926–9. (2nd ed. with introduction by D. A. Rees, 1963.)

ALTWEGG, G. *De Antifonte Sophista I: de libro περὶ ὁμονοίας scripto*. Basel, 1908.

AMANDRY, P. *La mantique apollinienne à Delphes: essai sur le fonctionnement de l'oracle*. Paris, 1950.

AMUNDSEN, L. 'Fragment of a Philosophical Text, P. Osl. Inv. 1039', *Symbolae Osloenses*, 1966, 5–20.

ANDERSON, W. D. 'The Importance of the Damonian Theory in Plato's Thought', *TAPA*, 1955, 88–102.

ANDERSON, W. D. *Ethos & Education in Greek Music*. Cambridge, Mass., 1966.

ANSCOMBE, G. E. M. and GEACH, P. T. *Three Philosophers*. Ithaca, N.Y. and Oxford, 1961.

ARNIM, H. VON. *Xenophons Memorabilien und Apologie des Sokrates*. Copenhagen, 1923 (Royal Danish Academy of Science, Philos.-Hist. section, no. 8.1).

AULITZKY. 'Korax', *RE*, XI (1922), 1379–81.

AYER, A. J. *Philosophical Essays*. London, 1954.

BACON, F. *Philosophical Works*, ed. J. Spedding, R. L. Ellis and D. D. Heath, 5 vols., London, 1875–9.

BAILEY, C. *The Greek Atomists and Epicurus*. Oxford, 1928.

BAITER, J. G. and SAUPPE, H. (eds.). *Oratores Attici*. 2 vols., Zurich, 1839–50.

Bibliography

BAKER, W. W. 'An apologetic for Xenophon's *Memorabilia*', *CJ*, XII (1916–17), 293–309.

BALDRY, H. C. *The Unity of Mankind in Greek Thought*. Cambridge, 1965.

BAMBROUGH, J. R. 'Universals and Family Resemblances', *Proceedings of the Aristotelian Society*, 1960–1, 208–22.

BAMBROUGH, J. R. (ed.). *Plato, Popper and Politics*. Cambridge (Heffer), 1967.

BARKER, E. *Greek Political Theory: Plato and his Predecessors*. 2nd ed., Cambridge, 1925.

BARKER, E. (ed.). *Social Contract: Essays by Locke, Hume and Rousseau*. London (World's Classics), 1947 (and later reprints).

BARKER, E. *Political Thought of Plato and Aristotle*. New York and London, 1959.

BARNES, H. *An Existentialist Ethics*. New York, 1967.

BAYNES, H. G. 'On the Psychological Origins of Divine Kingship', *Folklore*, 1936, 74–104.

BAYONAS, A. 'L'art politique d'après Protagoras', *Revue Philosophique*, 1967, 43–58.

BERNAYS, J. *Gesammelte Abhandlungen*, herausgegeben von H. Usener. Berlin, 1885.

BIEBER, M. 'Maske', *RE*, XXVIII. Halbb. (1930), 2070–120.

BIGNONE, E. *Studi sul pensiero antico*. Naples, 1938.

BINDER, G. and LIESENBORGHS, L. 'Eine Zuweisung der Sentenz οὐκ ἔστιν ἀντιλέγειν an Prodikos von Keos', *Museum Helveticum*, 1966, 37–43.

BJÖRNBO. 'Hippias', *RE*, VIII (1913), 1706–11.

BLAKE, R. *Disraeli*. London, 1966.

BLASS, F. *Die attische Beredsamkeit*. 2nd ed., 3 vols., Leipzig, 1887–98.

BLASS, F. *De Antiphonte sophista Iamblichi auctore*. Kiel, 1899.

BLUCK, R. S. *Plato's Meno, edited with Introduction and Commentary*. Cambridge, 1961.

BORTHWICK, E. K. Review of Anderson's *Ethos and Education in Greek Music*, *CR*, 1968, 200–3.

BRÖCKER, W. 'Gorgias contra Parmenides', *Hermes*, 1958, 425–40.

BRÖCKER, W. *Die Geschichte der Philosophie vor Sokrates*. Frankfurt am Main, 1965.

BRZOSKA, J. 'Alkidamas', *RE*, I (1894), 1533–9.

BURKE, J. T. A. 'A Classical Aspect of Hogarth's Theory of Art', *Journal of the Warburg and Courtauld Institutes*, 1943, 151–3.

BURKERT, W. *Weisheit und Wissenschaft: Studien zu Pythagoras, Philolaos und Platon*. Nürnberg, 1962.

BURKERT, W. Review of Untersteiner's *I Sofisti*, *GGA*, 1964, 141–4.

BURNET, J. *Plato's Phaedo, edited with introduction and notes*. Oxford, 1911.

BURNET, J. *Greek Philosophy: Part I, Thales to Plato* (all published). London, 1924.

BURNET, J. *Plato's Euthyphro, Apology of Socrates and Crito, edited with notes*. Oxford, 1924.

Bibliography

BURNET, J. *Essays and Addresses.* London, 1929.

BURNET, J. *Early Greek Philosophy.* 4th ed., London, 1930.

BURY, J. B. *A History of Greece to the Death of Alexander the Great.* London, 1900. (3rd ed. by R. Meiggs, 1951.)

BURY, R. G. *The Symposium of Plato edited with introduction, critical notes and commentary.* Cambridge (Heffer), 1909.

BURY, R. G. *Sextus Empiricus, with an English translation.* 3 vols., London, Cambridge (Mass.) and New York (Loeb ed.), 1933–6.

CAIZZI, F. 'Antistene', *Studi Urbinati*, 1964, 25–76.

CAIZZI, F. D. *Antisthenis Fragmenta.* Milan, 1966.

CALDER, W. M., III. 'Socrates at Amphipolis', *Phronesis*, 1961, 83–5.

CALOGERO, G. *Studi sull'Eleatismo.* Rome, 1932.

CALOGERO, G. 'Gorgias and the Socratic Principle *Nemo sua sponte peccat*', *JHS*, 1957 (1), 12–17.

CAMPBELL, A. H. 'Obligation and Obedience to Law', *Proceedings of the British Academy*, 1965, 337–55.

CAMPBELL, L. *The Theaetetus of Plato, with a revised text and English notes.* Oxford, 1883.

CAPIZZI, A. *Protagora: le testimonianze e i frammenti, edizione riveduta e ampliata con uno studio su la vita, le opere, il pensiero e la fortuna.* Florence, 1955.

CASSIRER, E. *The Philosophy of the Enlightenment*, transl. F. C. A. Koelln and J. P. Pettegrove. Princeton Univ. Press, 1951. (Beacon Press repr. 1962.)

CATAUDELLA, Q. 'Intorno a Prodico di Ceo', in *Studi di antichità classica offerti . . . a E. Ciaceri.* Genoa, 1940.

CATAUDELLA, Q. 'Chi è l'Anonimo di Giamblico?', *REG*, 1950, 74–106.

CHERNISS, H. *Aristotle's Criticism of Presocratic Philosophy.* Baltimore, 1935 (reprinted New York, 1964).

CHIAPPELLI, A. 'Per la storia della Sofistica greca', *Archiv für Geschichte der Philosophie*, 1890, 1–21.

CHROUST, A. H. *Socrates, Man and Myth.* London, 1957.

CLASSEN, C. J. 'Aristippos', *Hermes*, 1958, 182–92.

CLASSEN, C. J. 'The Study of Language among Socrates' Contemporaries', *Proceedings of the African Classical Associations*, 1959, 33–49.

CLASSEN, C. J. 'Bemerkungen zu zwei griechischen Philosophie-historikern', *Philologus*, 1965, 175–81.

CLOCHÉ, P. 'L'Affaire des Arginusines', *Revue Historique*, 1919, 5–68.

COHEN, SIR H. 'The Status of Brain in the Concept of Mind', *Philosophy*, 1952, 259–72.

COLE, A. T., JR. 'The *Anonymus Iamblichi* and its Place in Greek Political Theory', *HSCP*, 1961, 127–63.

COLE, A. T., JR. 'The Apology of Protagoras', *Yale Classical Studies*, 1966, 101–18.

COOK, R. M. 'Amasis and the Greeks in Egypt', *JHS*, 1957, 226–37.

COPE, E. M. *The Rhetoric of Aristotle with a Commentary*, revised and edited by J. E. Sandys. 3 vols., Cambridge, 1877.

Bibliography

COPE, E. M. *An Introduction to Aristotle's Rhetoric.* London, 1867.

CORNFORD, F. M. *The Origin of Attic Comedy.* Cambridge, 1914.

CORNFORD, F. M. *Before and After Socrates.* Cambridge, 1932 (and later reprints).

CORNFORD, F. M. *Plato's Theory of Knowledge.* London, 1935 (and later reprints).

CORNFORD, F. M. *The Republic of Plato, translated with introduction and notes.* Oxford, 1941 (and later reprints).

COULTER, J. A. 'The Relation of the *Apology of Socrates* to Gorgias's *Defense of Palamedes* and Plato's critique of Gorgianic rhetoric', *HSCP*, 1964, 269–303.

CROISET, A. 'Les nouveaux fragments d'Antiphon', *Revue des études grecques*, 1917, 1–19.

CROSS, R. C. and WOOZLEY, A. D. *Plato's Republic, a Philosophical Commentary.* London, 1964.

CROSSMAN, R. H. S. *Plato Today.* 2nd ed., London, 1959.

CUFFLEY, V. 'The Classical Greek Concept of Slavery', *JHI*, 1966, 323–42.

D'ADDIO, M. *L'idea del contratto sociale dai Sofisti alla Riforma.* Milan, 1954.

DAVISON, J. A. 'Protagoras, Democritus and Anaxagoras', *CQ*, 1953, 33–45.

DECHARME, P. *La critique des traditions religieuses chez les grecs.* Paris, 1904.

DEMAN, T. *Le témoignage d'Aristote sur Socrate.* Paris, 1942.

DES PLACES, E. Review of Heinimann's *Nomos und Physis*, *L'Antiquité Classique*, 1965, 673 f.

DEVEREUX, G. *From Anxiety to Method in the Social Sciences.* The Hague and Paris, 1967.

DEVEREUX, G. 'Greek Pseudo-homosexuality and the Greek Miracle', *Symbolae Osloenses*, 1967, 69–92.

DEVLIN, LORD. 'The Enforcement of Morals', *Proceedings of the British Academy*, 1959, 129–51.

DEVLIN, LORD. *The Enforcement of Morals.* London, 1965. (Oxford p.backs, 1968.)

DIEHL, E. 'Kritias', *RE*, XI (1922), 1901–12.

DIEHL, E. (ed.). *Anthologia Lyrica Graeca*, 2 vols., Leipzig, 1925.

DIEHL, E. 'Moschion', *RE*, XXXI. Halbb. (1933), 345–7.

DIELS, H. *Doxographi Graeci.* Berlin, 1879.

DIELS, H. 'Gorgias und Empedokles', *Sitzungsberichte der preussischen Akademie* (*SB Berlin*), 1884, 343–68.

DIELS, H. and KRANZ, W. *Die Fragmente der Vorsokratiker* (Greek and German). 10th ed., 3 vols., Berlin, 1960–1.

DIÈS, A. *Autour de Platon: I. Les voisinages: Socrate. II. Les dialogues—esquisses doctrinales.* Paris, 1927.

DITTENBERGER, W. *Sylloge Inscriptionum Graecarum.* 3rd ed., 4 vols., Leipzig, 1915–21.

DITTMAR, H. *Aischines von Sphettos: Studien zur Literaturgeschichte der Sokratiker.* Berlin, 1912.

DOBSON, J. F. *The Greek Orators.* London, 1919.

DODDS, E. R. *Euripides, Bacchae, edited with an introduction and commentary.* Oxford, 1944.

Bibliography

DODDS, E. R. *The Greeks and the Irrational.* California Univ. Press, 1951.

DODDS, E. R. *Plato, Gorgias, a Revised Text with Introduction and Commentary.* Oxford, 1959.

DOVER, K. J. 'Eros and Nomos', *BICS*, 1964, 31–42.

DOVER, K. J. *Aristophanes: Clouds, edited with introduction and commentary.* Oxford, 1968.

DRACHMANN, A. B. *Atheism in Pagan Antiquity.* London, 1922 (transl. from Danish).

DREXLER, H. 'Gedanken über den Sokrates der platonischen Apologie', *Emerita*, 1961, 177–201.

DUDLEY, D. R. *A History of Cynicism.* London, 1938.

DÜMMLER, F. *Akademika: Beiträge zur Litteraturgeschichte der sokratischen Schulen.* Giessen, 1889.

DUPRÉEL, E. *La légende socratique et les sources de Platon.* Brussels, 1922.

DUPRÉEL, E. *Les Sophistes.* Neuchâtel, 1948.

EASTERLING, H. J. Review of R. Dieterle's *Platons Laches und Charmides* (Freiburg diss., privately printed, 1966), *CR*, 1968, 236 f.

EDELSTEIN, E. *Xenophontisches und platonisches Bild des Sokrates.* Berlin, 1935.

EDELSTEIN, L. *The Idea of Progress in Classical Antiquity.* Baltimore, 1967.

EHNMARK, E. 'Socrates and the Immortality of the Soul', *Eranos*, 1946, 105–22.

EHRENBERG, V. *Die Rechtsidee im frühen Griechentum.* Leipzig, 1921.

EHRENBERG, V. 'Isonomia', *RE*, Suppl. VII (1940), 293–9.

EHRENBERG, V. 'The Foundation of Thurii', *AJP*, 1948, 149–70.

EHRENBERG, V. *Sophocles and Pericles.* Oxford, 1954.

EHRENBERG, V. *Society and Civilisation in Greece and Rome.* Cambridge, Mass. (Harvard Univ. Press), 1964.

Entretiens sur l'antiquité classique (*Fondation Hardt*), vol. 8, *Grecs et Barbares.* Vandœvres–Genève, 1962.

ERASMUS, S. 'Richterzahl und Stimmenverhältnisse im Sokratesprozess', *Gymnasium*, 1964, 40–2.

ERBSE, H. 'Sokrates im Schatten der aristophanischen Wolken', *Hermes*, 1954, 385–420.

FEHLING, D. 'Zwei Untersuchungen zur griechischen Sprachphilosophie: I. Protagoras und die ὀρθοέπεια, II. φύσις und θέσις', *Rheinisches Museum*, 1965, 212–30.

FERGUSON, A. S. 'The Impiety of Socrates', *CQ*, 1913, 157–75.

FERGUSON, J. 'On the Date of Socrates's Conversion', *Eranos*, 1964, 70–3.

FESTUGIÈRE, A. J. *Epicurus and his Gods*, transl. C. W. Chilton. Oxford (Blackwell), 1955.

FIELD, G. C. 'Aristotle's Account of the Historical Origin of the Theory of Ideas', *CQ*, 1923, 113–24.

FIELD, G. C. 'Socrates and Plato in the Post-Aristotelian Tradition', *CQ*, 1924, 127–36.

FIELD, G. C. *Plato and his Contemporaries.* London, 1930.

Bibliography

FIELD, G. C. 'Plato's *Republic* and its Use in Education', *Journal of Education*, 1945, 161–2.

FINLEY, M. I. (ed.). *Slavery in Classical Antiquity: views and controversies*. Cambridge (Heffer), 1960.

FITE, W. *The Platonic Legend*. New York, 1934.

FOOT, P. (ed.). *Theories of Ethics*. Oxford, 1967.

FRANKENA, W. K. 'The Naturalistic Fallacy', *Mind*, 1939, 464–77 (reprinted in Foot, *q.v.*).

FRAZER, J. G. *Pausanias's Description of Greece, translated with a commentary*. 6 vols., London, 1913.

FREEMAN, K. *The Pre-Socratic Philosophers: a companion to Diels*, Fragmente der Vorsokratiker. Oxford (Blackwell), 1946.

FRIEDLÄNDER, P. *Plato*, transl. H. Meyerhoff, vol. I, *An Introduction*, London, 1958, vol. II, *The Dialogues, First Period*, 1964 [actually 1965].

FRITZ, K. VON. 'Zur antisthenischen Erkenntnistheorie und Logik', *Hermes*, 1927, 453–84.

FRITZ, K. VON. 'Megariker', *RE*, Suppl. V (1931), 707–24.

FRITZ, K. VON. 'Theaitetos (2)', *RE*, 2. Reihe, X. Halbb. (1934), 1351–72.

FRITZ, K. VON. 'Antisthenes und Sokrates in Xenophons *Symposion*', *Rheinisches Museum*, 1935, 19–45.

FRITZ, K. VON. 'Phaidon (3)', *RE*, XXXVIII. Halbb. (1938), 1538–42.

FRITZ, K. VON. 'Protagoras', *RE*, XLV. Halbb. (1957), 907–21.

FRITZ, K. VON. 'Xeniades', *RE*, 2. Reihe, XVIII. Halbb. (1967), 1438–40.

GANTAR, K. 'Amicus Sibi I', *Živa Antika*, 1966, 135–75.

GAY, P. *The Enlightenment: an interpretation (the rise of modern paganism)*. London, 1967.

GELLNER, E. *Words and Things*. London, 1959 (reprinted by Penguin Books, Harmondsworth, 1968).

GELZER, T. 'Aristophanes und sein Sokrates', *Museum Helveticum*, 1956, 65–93.

GIANNANTONI, G. *I Cirenaici: raccolta delle fonte antiche. Traduzione e studio introduttivo*. Florence, 1958.

GIANNANTONI, G. 'La pritania di Socrate nel 406 a. C.', *Rivista critica di storia della filosofia*, 1962, 3–25.

GIERKE, O. *Natural Law and the Theory of Society, 1500–1800*, transl. with introduction by E. Barker. Cambridge, 1934.

GIGANTE, M. *Nomos Basileus*. Naples, 1956.

GIGON, O. *Sokrates, sein Bild in Dichtung und Geschichte*. Bern, 1947.

GIGON, O. *Kommentar zum ersten Buch von Xenophons Memorabilien*. Basel, 1953. Ditto, *zum zweiten Buch*, 1956.

GIGON, O. Review of Magalhães-Vilhena, *Le problème de Socrate*, *Gnomon*, 1955, 259–66.

GIGON, O. 'Die sokratische "Doxographie" bei Aristoteles', *Museum Helveticum*, 1959, 174–212.

GILLESPIE, C. M. 'The Use of εἶδος and ἰδέα in Hippocrates', *CQ*, 1912, 179–203.

GILLESPIE, C. M. 'The Logic of Antisthenes', *Archiv für Geschichte der Philosophie*, 1913, 479–500 and 1914, 17–38.

GLADIGOW, B. 'Zum Makarismos des Weisen', *Hermes*, 1967, 404–33.

GOMME, A. W. *A Historical Commentary on Thucydides*. 3 vols., Oxford, 1945–56.

GOMPERZ, H. *Sophistik und Rhetorik*. Leipzig and Berlin, 1912.

GOMPERZ, T. *Greek Thinkers: A History of Ancient Philosophy*. 4 vols., London, 1901–12. (Vol. I transl. L. Magnus, vols. II–IV by C. G. Berry.) Re-issued in paperback, London, 1964.

GORDON, R. M. 'Socratic Definitions and Moral Neutrality', *Journal of Philosophy*, 1964, 433–50.

GOULDNER, A. W. *Enter Plato*. London, 1967.

GRAHAM, H. G. 'The Classics in the Soviet Union', *Classical World*, LIV (1960–1), 205–13.

GRANT, SIR A. *The Ethics of Aristotle, Illustrated with Essays and Notes*. 4th ed., 2 vols., London, 1885.

GREENE, W. C. *Moira: Fate, Good and Evil in Greek Thought*. Harvard Univ. Press, 1944. Repr. New York and Evanston, 1963.

GREENLEAF, W. H. *Order, Empiricism and Politics: two traditions of English thought, 1500–1700*. Oxford (for Univ. of Hull), 1964.

GROTE, G. *Plato and the other Companions of Sokrates*. 3rd ed. 3 vols., London, 1875.

GROTE, G. *A History of Greece from the Earliest Period to the Close of the Generation Contemporary with Alexander the Great*. 10 vols., 6th ed., vol. 7, London, 1888.

GRUBE, G. M. A. *Plato's Thought*. London, 1935 (and later reprints).

GUNDERT, H. 'Platon und das Daimonion des Sokrates', *Gymnasium*, 1954, 513–31.

GUTHRIE, W. K. C. 'Notes on some passages in the second book of Aristotle's *Physics*', CQ, 1946, 70–6.

GUTHRIE, W. K. C. *The Greeks and their Gods*. London, 1950 (and later reprints).

GUTHRIE, W. K. C. *Orpheus and Greek Religion*. Corrected ed., London, 1952.

GUTHRIE, W. K. C. *Plato, Protagoras and Meno*, translated with introduction, summaries, etc. Harmondsworth (Penguin Books), 1956 (and later reprints.)

GUTHRIE, W. K. C. *In the Beginning: some Greek views on the origins of life and the early state of man*. London, 1957.

HACKFORTH, R. *The Composition of Plato's Apology*. Cambridge, 1933.

HACKFORTH, R. 'Socrates', *Philosophy*, 1933, 259–72.

HACKFORTH, R. *Plato's Phaedrus, translated with introduction and commentary*. Cambridge, 1952.

HAMILTON, E. and CAIRNS, H. (ed.). *The Collected Dialogues of Plato including the Letters*. New York, 1961.

HAMILTON, W. *The Symposium by Plato, a new translation*. Harmondsworth (Penguin Books), 1951 (and later reprints).

HARDT FOUNDATION. *See Entretiens* . . .

HARE, R. M. *The Language of Morals*. Oxford, 1952 (and later reprints).

Bibliography

HARE, R. M. *Freedom and Reason*. Oxford, 1963 (and later reprints).

HARRISON, A. R. W. *The Laws of Athens: Family and Property*. Oxford, 1968.

HARRISON, E. L. 'Was Gorgias a Sophist?', *Phoenix*, 1964, 183–92.

HARRISON, E. L. 'Plato's Manipulation of Thrasymachus', *Phoenix*, 1967, 27–39.

HART, H. L. A. *Law, Liberty and Morality*. Oxford, 1963.

HAVELOCK, E. A. 'The Evidence for the Teaching of Socrates', *TAPA*, 1934, 282–95.

HAVELOCK, E. A. *The Liberal Temper in Greek Politics*. London, 1957.

HEATH, T. L. *A History of Greek Mathematics*. 2 vols., Oxford, 1921.

HEINIMANN, F. *Nomos und Physis: Herkunft und Bedeutung einer Antithese im griechischen Denken des 5. Jahrhunderts*. Basel, 1945 (reprinted 1965).

HIRZEL, R. *Der Dialog*. 2 vols., Leipzig, 1895.

HIRZEL, R. Ἄγραφος νόμος. *Abhandlungen der sächsischen Akademie der Wissenschaften, Ph.-hist. Klasse*, 1903, no. 1.

HOBBES, T. *Leviathan*, ed. R. Waller. Cambridge, 1904.

HOGARTH, W. *The Analysis of Beauty*, ed. J. T. A. Burke. Oxford, 1955.

HOLLAND, R. F. 'On Making Sense of a Philosophical Fragment', *CQ*, 1956, 215–20.

HOURANI, G. F. 'Thrasymachus' Definition of Justice in Plato's *Republic*', *Phronesis*, 1962, 110–20.

HUG, A. 'Symposion-Literatur', *RE*, VIII. Halbb. (1931), 1273–82.

HUME, D. *Essays and Treatises*. Edinburgh, 1825.

HUME, D. *Of the Original Contract*. In *Social Contract*, ed. Barker, *q.v.*

JACOBY, F. *Diagoras ὁ ἄθεος*. Berlin, 1960. (*Abhandlungen der Berliner Akademie der Wissenschaften, Ph.-hist. Kl.*, 1959, no. 3.)

JAEGER, W. *Paideia: the Ideals of Greek Culture*, transl. G. Highet. 3 vols., Oxford, 1939–45 (vol. 1, 2nd ed.).

JAEGER, W. *The Theology of the Early Greek Philosophers*. Oxford, 1947.

JAEGER, W. *Aristotle: Fundamentals of the History of his Development*, transl. R. Robinson. 2nd ed., Oxford, 1948 (and later reprints).

JANELL, W. 'Die Echtheit und Abfassungszeit des Theages', *Hermes*, 1901, 427–39.

JOAD, C. E. M. 'Plato Defended', *Journal of Education*, 1945, 163–5.

JOËL, K. *Der echte und der Xenophontische Sokrates*. Berlin, 1893.

JOËL, K. *Geschichte der antiken Philosophie*. 1. Band, Tübingen, 1921.

JOHN, H. 'Das musikerziehende Wirken Pythagoras' und Damons', *Das Altertum*, 1962, 67–72.

JONES, W. H. S. *Hippocrates, with an English Translation*. Vols. I, II and IV, London and New York (Loeb ed.), 1923–31.

JOSEPH, H. W. B. *Essays in Ancient and Modern Philosophy*. Oxford, 1935.

JOWETT, B. *The Dialogues of Plato translated into English with Analyses and Introductions*. 4th ed., 4 vols., Oxford, 1953.

KAERST, J. 'Die Entstehung der Vertragstheorie im Altertum', *Zeitschrift für Politik*, 1909, 505–38.

Bibliography

KAHN, C. H. *Anaximander and the Origins of Greek Cosmogony*. New York, 1960.

KAHN, C. H. 'The Greek Verb "to be" and the Concept of Being', *Foundations of Language*, 1966, 245–65.

KAHRSTEDT, U. 'Meletos (3)', *RE*, XXIX. Halbb. (1931), 503 f.

KAIBEL, G. 'Aristophanes, der Komiker', *RE*, II (1896), 971–94.

KELSEN, H. 'Platonic Justice', *International Journal of Ethics*, XLVIII (1937–8), 367–400.

KELSEN, H. 'Platonic Love', *American Imago*, 3 (1944), 3–109.

KENNEDY, G. *The Art of Persuasion*. London, 1963.

KERFERD, G. B. 'The Doctrine of Thrasymachus in Plato's *Republic*', *Durham Univ. Journal*, 1947, 19–27.

KERFERD, G. B. 'The First Greek Sophists', *CR*, 1950, 8–10.

KERFERD, G. B. 'Protagoras's Doctrine of Justice and Virtue in the *Protagoras* of Plato', *JHS*, 1953, 42–5.

KERFERD, G. B. 'The Relativism of Prodicus', *Bulletin of the John Rylands Library*, XXXVII (1954–5), 249–56.

KERFERD, G. B. 'Gorgias on Nature or that which is not', *Phronesis*, 1955, 3–25.

KERFERD, G. B. 'The Moral and Political Doctrines of Antiphon the Sophist', *PCPS*, n.s. IV (1956–7), 26–32.

KERFERD, G. B. 'Thrasymachus and Justice: a Reply', *Phronesis*, 1964, 12–16.

KERFERD, G. B. Review of Lloyd's *Polarity and Analogy*, *CR*, 1968, 77–9.

KERN, O. (ed.). *Orphicorum Fragmenta*. Berlin, 1922.

KIERKEGAARD, S. *The Concept of Irony, with constant reference to Socrates*. Transl. with introduction and notes by L. M. Capel, London, 1966.

KIRK, G. S. and RAVEN, J. E. *The Presocratic Philosophers*. Cambridge, 1957. (Selected texts with introduction and commentary.)

KNEALE, W. and M. *The Development of Logic*. Oxford, 1962.

KNIGHT, A. H. J. *Some Aspects of the Life and Work of Nietzsche, and particularly of his connexion with Greek literature and thought*. Cambridge, 1933.

KOCK, T. *Comicorum Atticorum Fragmenta*. 3 vols., Leipzig, 1880–8.

KÖRTE, A. 'Sophron', *RE*, 2. Reihe, v. Halbb. (1927), 1100–4.

KROLL, W. 'Rhetorik', *RE*, Suppl. VII (1940), 1039–1138.

KUHN, T. S. *The Copernican Revolution*. Cambridge, Mass., 1957.

LAGERBORG, R. *Platonische Liebe*. Leipzig, 1926.

LASLETT, P. *See* LOCKE, J.

LASSERRE, F. Plutarque *De la musique* (text, translation and commentary, with a study of musical education in Greece). Lausanne, 1954.

LEE, H. D. P. *Plato, the Republic: a new translation*. Harmondsworth (Penguin Classics), 1955.

LEISEGANG, H. 'Platon (1) Der Philosoph', *RE*, XL. Halbb. (1941), 2342–537.

LESKY, A. *A History of Greek Literature*. 2nd ed., transl. J. Willis and C. de Heer, London, 1966.

LEVI, A. 'Le teorie metafisiche logiche e gnoseologiche di Antistene', *Revue de l'histoire de la philosophie*, 1930, 227–49.

Bibliography

LEVI, A. 'The Ethical and Social Thought of Protagoras', *Mind*, 1940, 284–302.

LEVI, A. 'Studies on Protagoras. The Man-measure Principle: its meaning and applications', *Philosophy*, 1940, 147–67.

LEVI, A. 'Ippia di Elide e la corrente naturalistica della Sofistica', *Sophia*, 1942, 441–50.

LEVINSON, R. B. *In Defense of Plato*. Cambridge, Mass., 1953.

LEVY, A. W. 'Socrates in the Nineteenth Century', *JHI*, 1956, 89–108.

LEVY, M. A. *Political Power in the Ancient World*, transl. Jane Costello. London, 1965.

LEYDEN, W. VON. 'Aristotle and the Concept of Law', *Philosophy*, 1957, 1–19.

LITTRÉ, É. *Œuvres Complètes d'Hippocrate. Traduction nouvelle, avec le texte grec en regard . . . accompagné d'une introduction, de commentaires médicaux, etc.* Paris, 1839–61.

LLOYD, G. E. R. 'Who is Attacked in *On Ancient Medicine?*', *Phronesis*, 1963, 108–26.

LLOYD, G. E. R. *Polarity and Analogy: two types of argumentation in early Greek thought*. Cambridge, 1966.

LLOYD, G. E. R. 'The Role of Medical and Biological Analogies in Aristotle's Ethics', *Phronesis*, 1968, 68–83.

LLOYD-JONES, H. 'Zeus in Aeschylus', *JHS*, 1956, 55–67.

LOCKE, J. *Second Treatise on Civil Government*. In *Social Contract*, ed. Barker, q.v.

LOCKE, J. *Two Treatises of Government*. Edited by P. Laslett, Cambridge, 1960.

LOENEN, D. *Protagoras and the Greek Community*. Amsterdam, 1940.

LONGRIGG, J. 'Philosophy and Medicine: some early reactions', *HSCP*, 1963, 147–75.

LORENZ, K. and MITTELSTRASS, J. 'On Rational Philosophy of Language: the Programme in Plato's *Cratylus* Reconsidered', *Mind*, 1967, 1–20.

LURIA, S. 'Antiphon der Sophist', *Eos*, 1963, 63–7.

MAAS, P. 'Kinesias', *RE*, XXI. Halbb. (1921), 479–81.

MAASS, E. 'Untersuchungen zur Geschichte der griechischen Prosa: I. Über die erhaltenen Reden des Gorgias', *Hermes*, 1887, 566–81.

MAGALHÃES-VILHENA, V. DE. (i) *Le problème de Socrate: le Socrate historique et le Socrate de Platon*. (ii) *Socrate et la légende platonicienne*. Paris, 1952.

MAGUIRE, J. P. 'Plato's Theory of Natural Law', *Yale Classical Studies*, 1947, 151–78.

MAIER, H. *Die Syllogistik des Aristoteles*. Tübingen, I. Teil, 1896, II. Teil, 1900.

MAIER, H. *Sokrates, sein Werk und seine geschichtliche Stellung*. Tübingen, 1913.

MANNEBACH, E. (ed.) *Aristippi et Cyrenaicorum Fragmenta*. Leiden, 1961.

MARCHANT, E. C. *Xenophon, Memorabilia and Oeconomicus, with an English translation*. London and Cambridge, Mass. (Loeb ed.), 1959.

MAYER, H. *Prodikos von Keos und die Anfänge der Synonymik bei den Griechen*. Paderborn, 1913.

MEINEKE, A. *Comicorum Graecorum Fragmenta*. 5 vols., Berlin, 1839–57.

MENZEL, A. (1) 'Protagoras als Gesetzgeber von Thurioi', (2) 'Die Sozialphilosophischen Lehren des Protagoras'. Both now in his *Hellenika* (*Gesammelte kleine Schriften*), Baden-bei-Wien, 1938, pp. 66–82 and 83–107.

MERLAN, P. 'Alexander the Great or Antiphon the Sophist?', *CP*, 1950, 161–6.

MERRY, W. W. *Aristophanes: The Clouds, with introduction and notes.* Oxford, 1916.

MEWALDT, J. *Kulturkampf der Sofisten.* Tübingen, 1928.

MEYER, T. *Platons Apologie.* Stuttgart, 1962.

MOMIGLIANO, A. 'Prodico di Ceo e le dottrine del linguaggio da Democrito ai Cinici', *Atti della Accademia delle Scienze di Torino, Classe di Scienze morali, storiche e filologiche*, LXV (1929–30), 95–107.

MOMIGLIANO, A. 'Sul pensiero di Antifonte il sofista', *Rivista di filologia classica*, 1930, 129–40.

MONDOLFO, R. *Problemi del pensiero antico.* Bologna, 1936.

MONDOLFO. *See also* ZELLER-MONDOLFO.

MOORE, G. E. *Principia Ethica.* Cambridge, 1903.

MORRISON, J. S. 'The Place of Protagoras in Athenian Public Life', *CQ*, 1941, 1–16.

MORRISON, J. S. 'An Introductory Chapter in the History of Greek Education', *Durham Univ. Journal*, 1949, 55–63.

MORRISON, J. S. 'The Origins of Plato's Philosopher-Statesman', *CQ*, 1958, 198–218.

MORRISON, J. S. 'Antiphon', *PCPS*, 1961, 49–58.

MORRISON, J. S. 'The *Truth* of Antiphon', *Phronesis*, 1963, 35–49.

MOSER, S. and KUSTAS, G. L. 'A Comment on the "Relativism" of Protagoras', *Phoenix*, 1966, 111–15.

MOTTE, A. 'Pour l'authenticité du "Premier Alcibiade" ', *L'Antiquité Classique*, 1961, 5–32.

MÜLLER, C. W. 'Protagoras über die Götter', *Hermes*, 1967, 140–59.

MÜLLER, E. *Sokrates in der Volksversammlung.* Zittau, 1894.

MURRAY, G. *Aristophanes: a Study.* Oxford, 1933.

MURRAY, G. *Greek Studies.* Oxford, 1946.

NATORP, P. 'Alexamenos', *RE*, I (1894), 1375.

NATORP, P. 'Eukleides aus Megara', *RE*, VI (1909), 1000–3.

NAUCK, A. (ed.). *Tragicorum Graecorum Fragmenta.* 2nd ed., Leipzig, 1889.

NESTLE, W. *Euripides, der Dichter der griechischen Aufklärung.* Stuttgart, 1901.

NESTLE, W. 'Untersuchungen über die philosophischen Quellen des Euripides', *Philologus*, Supplementband VIII, 1899–1901, 557–665.

NESTLE, W. 'Kritias', *Neue Jahrbücher für das klassische Altertum*, 1903, 81–107 and 178–99 (reprinted in his *Griechische Studien*, Stuttgart, 1948, 403–29).

NESTLE, W. 'Die Schrift des Gorgias "Über die Natur oder über das Nichtseiende"', *Hermes*, 1922, 551–62.

NESTLE, W. *Platon: Protagoras.* 7. Auflage, Leipzig and Berlin, 1931.

NESTLE, W. 'Die Horen des Prodikos', *Hermes*, 1936, 151–7 (reprinted in *Griechische Studien*, Stuttgart, 1948, 403–29).

NESTLE, W. 'Xenophon und die Sophistik', *Philologus*, 1939, 31–40 (reprinted in *Griechische Studien*, Stuttgart, 1948, 430–50).

NESTLE, W. *Vom Mythos zum Logos*. 2nd ed., Stuttgart, 1941.

NEUMANN, H. 'On the Madness of Plato's Apollodorus', *TAPA*, 1965, 283–9.

NEURATH, O. and LAUWERYS, P. 'Plato's *Republic* and German Education', *Journal of Education*, 1945, 47–59.

NEWMAN, W. L. *The Politics of Aristotle, with an introduction, two prefatory essays and notes critical and explanatory*. 4 vols., Oxford, 1887–1902.

NORTH, H. *Sophrosyne: self-knowledge and self-restraint in Greek literature*. New York, 1966.

NOTT, K. 'German Influence on Modern French Thought', *The Listener*, 13 Jan. 1955.

O'BRIEN, D. 'The Relation of Anaxagoras and Empedocles', *JHS*, 1968, 93–113.

O'BRIEN, M. J. *The Socratic Paradoxes and the Greek Mind*. Chapel Hill (Univ. of N. Carolina Press), 1967.

Oxyrhynchus Papyri, ed. B. P. Grenfell, A. S. Hunt *et al.* 1898– (in progress).

PAGE, D. L. 'Pindar: P. Oxy. 2450, fr. 1', *PCPS*, 1962, 49–51.

PARKE, H. W. 'Chaerephon's Inquiry about Socrates', *CP*, 1961, 249f.

PEARSON, A. C. 'Atheism (Greek and Roman)', *Encyclopaedia of Religion and Ethics*, ed. Hastings. Vol. 2, Edinburgh, 1909, 184f.

PEIPERS, D. *Untersuchungen über das System Platos. Erster Theil: Die Erkenntnistheorie Platos*. Leipzig, 1874.

PFLEIDERER, E. *Sokrates, Plato und ihre Schüler*. Tübingen, 1896.

PHILLIPSON, C. *The Trial of Socrates (with chapters on his life, teaching, and personality)*. London, 1928.

PLÖBST. 'Lysias', *RE*, XXVI. Halbb. (1927), 2533–43.

POHLENZ, M. 'Anonymus περὶ νόμων', *Nachrichten der königlichen Gesellschaft der Wissenschaften*, Göttingen (Ph.-hist. Klasse), 1924, 19–37 (reprinted in his *Kleine Schriften*, vol. II, 314–32).

POHLENZ, M. 'Nomos', *Philologus*, 1948, 135–42 (reprinted in his *Kleine Schriften*, ed. H. Dörrie, Hildesheim, 2 vols., 1965, vol. II, 333–40).

POHLENZ, M. 'Nomos und Physis', *Hermes*, 1953, 418–38 (reprinted in his *Kleine Schriften*, vol. II, 341–60).

POHLENZ, M. *Die Stoa: Geschichte einer geistigen Bewegung*. 2 vols., Göttingen, 3rd ed., 1964.

POMPA, L. 'Family Resemblance', *Philosophical Quarterly*, 1967, 63–9.

POPPER, Sir K. R. *The Logic of Scientific Discovery* (transl. from German). London, 1959.

POPPER, Sir K. R. *Conjectures and Refutations*. 2nd ed., London, 1965.

POPPER, Sir K. R. *The Open Society and its Enemies*, vol. 1, The Spell of Plato, 5th ed., London, 1966.

RADERMACHER, L. *Artium Scriptores: Reste der voraristotelischen Rhetorik*. Vienna, 1951 (*Sitzungsberichte der Österreichischen Akademie*, 227, 3).

Bibliography

REICH, H. *Der Mimus*, vol. 1, parts 1 and 2. Berlin, 1903.

RENSI, G. *Figure di filosofi*. Naples, 1938.

REYNEN, H. 'Philosophie und Knabenliebe', *Hermes*, 1967, 308–16.

RIBBECK, O. 'Über den Begriff des εἴρων', *Rheinisches Museum*, 1876, 381–400.

RICHTER, G. M. A. *Portraits of the Greeks*. London, 1965.

RIST, J. M. 'Plotinus and the Daimonion of Socrates', *Phoenix*, 1963, 13–24.

RITTER, C. *Sokrates*. Tübingen, 1931.

ROBIN, L. 'Sur une hypothèse récente relative à Socrate', *REG*, 1916, 129–65.

ROBIN, L. *Greek Thought and the Origins of the Scientific Spirit*, transl. from *La Pensée Grecque* by M. R. Dobie. London, 1928. (A third ed. of the French was published by P.-M. Schuhl in 1963.)

ROBINSON, R. *Definitions*. Oxford, 1950.

ROBINSON, R. *Plato's Earlier Dialectic*. 2nd ed., Oxford, 1953.

ROGERS, B. B. *The Clouds of Aristophanes. The Greek text revised with a translation into corresponding metres, introduction and commentary*. London, 1916.

ROSENMAYER, T. G. 'The Family of Critias', *AJP*, 1949, 404–10.

ROSS, W. D. *Aristotle's Metaphysics, a revised text with introduction and commentary*. 2 vols., Oxford, 1924.

ROSS, W. D. 'The Problem of Socrates', *Classical Association Proceedings*, 1933, 7–24.

ROSS, W. D. *Aristotle's Prior and Posterior Analytics, a revised text with introduction and commentary*. Oxford, 1949.

ROUSSEAU, J.-J. *Social Contract and Discourses*. London (Everyman ed.), 1913 (reprinted 1966).

ROUSSEAU, J.-J. *The Social Contract*, transl. G. Hopkins. In *Social Contract*, ed. Barker, *q.v.*

RUSSELL, Lord. *Autobiography*, vol. II, London, 1968.

SACHS, E. *De Theaeteto Atheniensi Mathematico*. Berlin Diss. 1914.

SALOMON, M. 'Der Begriff des Naturrechts bei den Sophisten', *Zeitschrift der Savigny-Stiftung für Rechtsgeschichte, Römische Abteilung*, 1911, 129–67.

SCHLAIFER, R. 'Greek Theories of Slavery', *HSCP*, 1936, 165–204 (reprinted in Finley, *Slavery*, *q.v.*).

SCHMID, WILHELM and STÄHLIN, O. *Geschichte der griechischen Literatur*. 1. Teil, Die Classische Periode, 3. Band, 1. Hälfte. Munich, 1940.

SCHMID, WOLFGANG. 'Das Sokratesbild der Wolken', *Philologus*, 1948, 209–28.

SHOREY, P. *What Plato Said*. Chicago, 1933.

SCHULTZ, W. 'Herakles am Scheidewege', *Philologus*, 1909, 489–99.

SCHWEITZER, A. *The Quest of the Historical Jesus*. 3rd ed., London, 1954.

SELTMAN, C. T. *Approach to Greek Art*. London, 1948.

SHOREY, P. 'Φύσις, μελέτη, ἐπιστήμη', *TAPA*, 1909, 185–201.

SICKING, C. M. J. 'Gorgias und die Philosophen', *Mnemosyne*, 1964, 225–47.

SIDGWICK, H. 'The Sophists', *Journal of Philology*, 1872, 288–307, and 1873, 66–80.

SIMETERRE, R. *La théorie socratique de la vertu-science*. Paris, 1938.

SINCLAIR, A. T. *A History of Greek Political Thought*. London, 1951.

Bibliography

SKEMP, J. B. *Plato's Statesman: a translation of the Politicus of Plato with introductory essays and footnotes.* London, 1952.

SNELL, B. *Die Ausdrücke für den Begriff des Wissens.* Berlin, 1924 (*Philol. Untersuchungen*, 29).

SNELL, B. 'Das früheste Zeugnis über Sokrates', *Philologus*, 1948, 125–34.

SNELL, B. *The Discovery of the Mind: the Greek Origins of European Thought.* Oxford (Blackwell), 1953.

SOLMSEN, F. Review of Heinimann's *Nomos und Physis* in *AJP*, 1951, 191–5.

STARK, R. 'Sokratisches in den Vögeln des Aristophanes', *Rheinisches Museum*, 1953, 77–89.

STEGEMANN, W. 'Teisias', *RE*, 2. Reihe, IX. Halbb. (1934), 139–49.

STENZEL, J. 'Antiphon', *RE*, Suppl. IV (1924), 33–43.

STENZEL, J. 'Kyrenaiker', *RE*, XXIII. Halbb. (1924), 137–50.

STENZEL, J. 'Logik', *RE*, XXV. Halbb. (1926), 991–1011.

STENZEL, J. 'Sokrates (Philosoph)', *RE*, 2. Reihe, V. Halbb. (1927), 811–90.

STENZEL, J. *Plato's Method of Dialectic*, translated and edited by D. J. Allan. Oxford, 1940.

STEVENSON, C. L. 'Persuasive Definitions', *Mind*, 1938, 331–50.

STEVENSON, C. L. *Ethics and Language.* New Haven (Yale Univ. Press), 1945.

STRAUSS, J. 'The Liberalism of Classical Political Philosophy', *Review of Metaphysics*, 1959, 390–439.

STRYCKER, E. DE. 'Les témoignages historiques sur Socrate', *Mélanges Grégoire*, II (= *Annuaire de l'Institut de Philologie et d'Histoire orientales et slaves*, 1950), 199–230.

TARRANT, D. *The Hippias Major Attributed to Plato, with introductory essay and commentary.* Cambridge, 1928.

TARRANT, D. 'The Pseudo-Platonic Socrates', *CQ*, 1938, 167–73.

TARRANT, D. 'The Touch of Socrates', *CQ*, 1958, 95–8.

TATE, J. (*a*) 'The Greek for Atheism', *CR*, 1936, 3–5. (*b*) 'More Greek for Atheism', *CR*, 1937, 3–6.

TATE, J. Review of W. K. C. Guthrie, *The Greek Philosophers from Thales to Aristotle*, *CR*, 1951, 156f.

TAYLOR, A. E. *Varia Socratica.* First series, Oxford (Parker), 1911.

TAYLOR, A. E. *Plato, the Man and his Work.* London, 1926 (p.back reprint, 1960).

TAYLOR, A. E. *A Commentary on Plato's Timaeus.* Oxford, 1928.

TAYLOR, A. E. *Socrates.* London, 1932.

THEILER, W. 'Νόμος ὁ πάντων βασιλεύς', *Museum Helveticum*, 1965, 69–80.

THOMSON, G. *The Oresteia of Aeschylus, edited with introduction, translation and commentary in which is included the work of the late W. G. Headlam.* 2 vols., Cambridge, 1938.

THOMPSON, E. S. *The Meno of Plato, edited with introduction, notes and excursuses.* London, 1901 (reprinted 1937).

THORSON, T. L. (ed.). *Plato, Totalitarian or Democrat?* Englewood Cliffs. N.J., 1963.

TREDENNICK, H. Translations of Plato's *Apology, Crito* and *Phaedo*. Harmondsworth (Penguin Books), 1954.

TREU, M. 'Xenophon', *RE*, 2. Reihe, XVIII. Halbb. (1967), 1567–982.

TREVELYAN, H. *The Popular Background to Goethe's Hellenism*. London, 1934.

TURNER, E. G. 'Athenians learn to write: Plato, *Protagoras* 326d', *BICS*, 1965, 67–9.

'UEBERWEG–PRAECHTER.' Ueberweg, F. *Grundriss der Geschichte der Philosophie*, ed. K. Praechter. 13th ed., Basel, 1953 (photographic reprint of 12th ed., 1923).

UNTERSTEINER, M. *The Sophists*, transl. K. Freeman. London, 1957.

UNTERSTEINER, M. *I Sofisti, testimonianze e frammenti*, Florence. Fasc. I, *Protagora e Seniade*, 2nd ed., 1961. Fasc. II, *Gorgia, Licofrone e Prodico*, 2nd ed., 1961. Fasc. III, *Trasimaco, Ippia, Anon. Iamblichi,* Δισσοὶ λόγοι, *Anon.* π. νόμων, *Anon.* π. μουσικῆς, 1954. Fasc. IV (with A. Battegazzore), *Antifonte, Crizia*, 1962.

VERSÉNYI, L. 'Protagoras's Man-measure Fragment', *AJP*, 1962, 178–84.

VERSÉNYI, L. *Socratic Humanism*. New Haven, Conn., and London (Yale Univ. Press), 1963.

VLASTOS, G. 'Ethics and Physics in Democritus', *Philosophical Review*, 1945, 578–92, and 1946, 53–64.

VLASTOS, G. *Plato's Protagoras: B. Jowett's translation extensively revised by Martin Ostwald, edited with an introduction by Gregory Vlastos*. New York, 1956.

VLASTOS, G. ''Ισονομία πολιτική', *Isonomia, Studien zur Gleichheits-vorstellung im griechischen Denken, herausgegeben von J. Mau und E. G. Schmidt*. Berlin, 1964, 1–35.

VOGEL, C. J. DE. *Greek Philosophy. A collection of texts, selected and supplied with some notes and explanations*. Vol. I, *Thales to Plato*, Leiden, 1950.

VOGEL, C. J. DE. 'Une nouvelle interprétation du problème socratique', *Mnemosyne*, 1951, 30–9.

VOGEL, C. J. DE. 'The Present State of the Socratic Problem', *Phronesis*, 1955, 26–35.

VOGT, J. *Sklaverei und Humanität: Studien zur antiken Sklaverei und ihrer Erforschung*. Wiesbaden, 1965.

VOLKMANN, H. Review of Gigante's *Nomos Basileus, Gnomon*, 1958, 474f.

WEBSTER, T. B. L. *From Mycenae to Homer*. London, 1958.

WEHRLI, F. *Die Schule des Aristoteles: Texte und Kommentar* (Basel), Heft X: Hieronymos von Rhodos, Kritolaos, Rückblick, Register, addenda, 1959; Heft VII: Herakleides Pontikos, 1953; Heft II: Aristoxenos, 1945.

WEIL, R. 'La place du Premier Alcibiade dans l'œuvre de Platon', *L'Information Littéraire*, 1964, 75–84.

WENDLAND, P. Review of H. Gomperz's *Sophistik und Rhetorik, GGA*, 1913, 53–9.

WILAMOWITZ-MOELLENDORFF, U. VON. *Analecta Euripidea*. Berlin, 1875.

WILAMOWITZ-MOELLENDORFF, U. VON. *Aristoteles und Athen*. 2 vols., Berlin, 1893.

WILAMOWITZ-MOELLENDORFF, U. VON. *Platon*. 2 vols., Berlin, 1920.

WILAMOWITZ-MOELLENDORFF, U. VON. 'Lesefrüchte', *Hermes*, 1927, 276–98.

Bibliography

WILAMOWITZ-MOELLENDORFF, U. VON. *Der Glaube der Hellenen.* 2 vols., Berlin, 1931–2.

WILCOX, S. 'The Scope of Early Rhetorical Instruction', *HSCP*, 1942, 121–55.

WINSPEAR, A. D. and SILVERBERG, T. *Who was Socrates?* New York (Cordon Co.), 1939.

WOODBURY, L. 'The Date and Atheism of Diagoras of Melos', *Phoenix*, 1965, 178–211.

ZELLER, E. *Die Philosophie der Griechen*, 2. Teil, 1. Abteilung, *Sokrates und die Sokratiker: Plato und die alte Akademie.* 5. Auflage, Leipzig, 1922 (repr. 1963).

'ZELLER–MONDOLFO.' La filosofia dei Greci nel suo sviluppo storico. Florence, various dates from 1932. (Zeller's work translated and enlarged by R. Mondolfo.)

'ZELLER–NESTLE.' E. Zeller, *Die Philosophie der Griechen*, 1. Teil, 1. Hälfte (7th ed., 1923) and 2. Hälfte (6th ed., 1920), edited by W. Nestle (Leipzig).

ZEPPI, S. 'L'etica di Prodico', *Rivista critica di storia della filosofia*, 1956, 265–72.

ZEPPI, S. 'La posizione storica di Antiphon', *Rivista di storia della filosofia*, 1958, 357–71.

ZEPPI, S. *Protagora e la filosofia del suo tempo.* Florence, 1961.

ZIEGLER, K. 'Xenarchos', *RE*, 2. Reihe, XVIII. Halbb. (1967), 1422.

INDEXES

I. INDEX OF PASSAGES QUOTED
OR REFERRED TO

524

Index of passages quoted or referred to

535

GENERAL INDEX

Bold figures denote a main or more important entry. The entries for modern scholars are often selective, and as a rule no entry is made where the text has no more than a reference

Adimantus, 94 n. 3, 99, 103

Aeschines of Sphettus, 30, 327, 331, 395, 489

Aeschylus, 28, 49, 50, 121, 158 n. 3

Agathon, 273, 401

agnosticism, 23, 234 f.

agriculture, as origin of law and civilization, 61 f., 239

aidōs, 66

air, divinity of, 232, 233, 247, 364, 468

aither, divinity of, 232, 233, 247, 364, 468, 476

akrasia, 455, 456

Alcibiades, 237, 274, 301, 308, 348, 381; relations with Socrates, 300, 383 n. 1, 395, 414, 470 ff.

Alcidamas, 48 n. 1, 157, 220, 274, 311–13; on slavery, 24, 159 f.

Alcmaeon, 31, 195

Alexamenos of Teos, 332 n. 2

Ameipsias, 360

analogy, 429; use of in natural philosophy, 368 n. 1

ananké, 100

Anaxagoras, 18, 30, 154 n. 4, 203, 226, 232, 248, 421, 475

Anaximander, 14, 136 n. 2, 194

Anaximenes, 194

Andron, 102

animals, as models of human behaviour, 104, 114 n. 4, 368

'Anonymus Iamblichi', 71 ff., 253 n. 1, 256, 280; authorship and date, 314 f.

Antigone, 22, 120, 127

Antimoerus, 37

Antiphon, 52, 122 n. 4, 125 n. 1, 128 n. 3, 143, 145, 208, 285–94; upholds *physis* against *nomos*, 22, 100, 107–13, 119, 130, 146, 203, 291; on birth and race, 24, 152 f., 156, 161; *On Truth*, 107 ff., 291; equates justice with conformity to law, 108, 111, 138; *On Concord*, 150 n. 1, 286 ff.; as mental therapist, 168, 290 f.; on education, 168; how far a sceptic, 202 f.; on language, 202–4; study of nature, 203; on God and providence,

230, 231, 245, 288; on *sophrosyne*, 259; identity of, 285 f., 292–4; date, 286 with n. 2; on time, 292

Antisthenes, 117, 165, 182 n. 2, 274, 304–11, 489; on impossibility of contradiction, 209 ff.; on definition, 210 f.; retort to Plato, 214; monotheism of, 247–9; date and setting, 304 ff.; relation to Socrates, 305 ff., 395; to Cynics, 306 f., 307 n. 1; pupil of Gorgias, 306; character, 307, 341; doctrine of virtue, 308; anti-egalitarian, 308; reply to Parmenides, 309; as Homeric critic, 309 f.; attacked Plato, 310; theories of his influence, 310 f., 323, 347; works, 311; in Xenophon, 341

Anytus, 38 n. 1, 39; attacks Sophists, 36, 37, 251; as accuser of Socrates, 381 ff.

Aphrodite, 229, 230

Apollo (*see also* Delphic oracle), as legislator, 17, 77, 135

Apollodorus, 344, 489

Archelaus (philosopher), 58 with n. 1, 116, 165, 418, 422

Archelaus of Macedon, 294, 309 n. 1

Archytas, 151

Areopagus, 78

areté, how acquired, 25, 250 ff., 317 f. ('Double Arguments'); political, 64 ff.; according to Protagoras, 65 ff., to Aristotle, 68, to 'Anon. Iamblichi', 71; as practical skill, 66 n. 1, 252, 450; as fitness for function, 90 n. 1, 252 f.; aristocratic associations, 250 ff.; utililarian conception of, 462 f. *See also* Socrates

Arginusae, affair of, 143 n. 1, 379 f.

Aristippus 1, 277, 356 n. 2, 463, 467 n. 1, 489, 490–8

Aristippus 2 (grandson of 1), 491, 492, 495 n. 2

Aristogeiton, speech against, 75 ff., 138, 145

Aristophanes, 49, 158, 361–77; on function of poets, 29 f.; on sophists, 33; critic of the new morality, 100, 114

Aristotle, 355–9, 424, 425 ff., 432 n. 1; relation to Sophistic, 53 f.; on acquiring virtue, 68; his classification of laws, 123 f.,

536

INDEX OF SELECTED GREEK WORDS

Greek words tranliterated in the text will be found in the general index